COLLABORATIVE DECISION MAKING: PERSPECTIVES AND CHALLENGES

Frontiers in Artificial Intelligence and Applications

FAIA covers all aspects of theoretical and applied artificial intelligence research in the form of monographs, doctoral dissertations, textbooks, handbooks and proceedings volumes. The FAIA series contains several sub-series, including "Information Modelling and Knowledge Bases" and "Knowledge-Based Intelligent Engineering Systems". It also includes the biennial ECAI, the European Conference on Artificial Intelligence, proceedings volumes, and other ECCAI – the European Coordinating Committee on Artificial Intelligence – sponsored publications. An editorial panel of internationally well-known scholars is appointed to provide a high quality selection.

Series Editors:
J. Breuker, R. Dieng-Kuntz, N. Guarino, J.N. Kok, J. Liu, R. López de Mántaras,
R. Mizoguchi, M. Musen, S.K. Pal and N. Zhong

Volume 176

Recently published in this series

ISSN 0922-6389

Collaborative Decision Making: Perspectives and Challenges

Edited by

Pascale Zaraté
Université de Toulouse, INPT-ENSIACET-IRIT, France

Jean Pierre Belaud
Université de Toulouse, INPT-ENSIACET-LGC, France

Guy Camilleri
Université de Toulouse, UPS-IRIT, France

and

Franck Ravat
Université de Toulouse, UT1-IRIT, France

Press

Amsterdam • Berlin • Oxford • Tokyo • Washington, DC

ISBN 978-1-58603-881-6

Publisher
IOS Press
Nieuwe Hemweg 6B
1013 BG Amsterdam
Netherlands
fax: +31 20 687 0019
e-mail: order@iospress.nl

Distributor in the UK and Ireland
Gazelle Books Services Ltd.
White Cross Mills
Hightown
Lancaster LA1 4XS
United Kingdom
fax: +44 1524 63232
e-mail: sales@gazellebooks.co.uk

Distributor in the USA and Canada
IOS Press, Inc.
4502 Rachael Manor Drive
Fairfax, VA 22032
USA
fax: +1 703 323 3668
e-mail: iosbooks@iospress.com

LEGAL NOTICE

The publisher is not responsible for the use which might be made of the following information.

PRINTED IN THE NETHERLANDS

Collaborative Decision Making: Perspectives and Challenges
P. Zaraté et al. (Eds.)
IOS Press, 2008

v

Preface

The Collaborative Decision Making Conference (CDM08) is a joined event. This conference has for objective to join two working groups on Decision Support Systems: the IFIP TC8/Working Group 8.3 and the Euro Working Group on Decision Support Systems.

The first IFIP TC8/Working Group 8.3 conference was organised in 1982 in Vienna (Austria). Since this year the IFIP conferences present the latest innovations and achievements of academic communities on Decision Support Systems (DSS). These advances include theory systems, computer aided methods, algorithms, techniques, and applications related to supporting decision making.

The development of approaches for applying information systems technology to increase the effectiveness of decision-making in situations where the computer system can support and enhance human judgements in the performance of tasks that have elements which cannot be specified in advance.

To improve ways of synthesizing and applying relevant work from resource disciplines to practical implementation of systems that enhance decision support capability. The resource disciplines include: information technology, artificial intelligence, cognitive psychology, decision theory, organisational theory, operations research and modelling.

The EWG on DSS was created in Madeira (Portugal) following the Euro Summer Institute on DSS, in May 1989. Researchers involved in this group meet each year in different countries through a workshop. Researches in this group come from Operational Research area but also from Decision Theory, Multicriteria Decision Making methodologies, Fuzzy sets and modelling tools.

Based on the introduction of Information and Communication Technologies in organisations, the decisional process is evolving from a mono actor to a multi actor situation in which cooperation is a way to make the decision.

For 2008, the objective was to create a synergy between the two groups around a specific focus: Collaborative Decision Making. Papers submitted to the conference have for main objectives to support Collaborative Decision Making but with several kinds of tools or models. 69 papers have been submitted coming from 24 countries. 34 full papers have been selected organised in 8 themes constituting the part I of this book. 9 short papers have been accepted as short papers organised in 3 themes constituting the part II. Nevertheless, a variety of topics are also presented through several papers coming reinforce the vivacity of researches conducted in Decision Support Systems.

The contributions are organised as follows:

Part I: Full Papers
Models for Collaborative Decision Making
Collaborative Decision Making for Supply Chain
Collaborative Decision Making for Medical Applications
Collaboration tools for Group Decision Making
Tools for Collaborative Decision Making
Collaborative Decision Making in ERP
Knowledge management for Collaborative Decision Making
Collaborative Decision Making Applications

Part II: Short Papers
Tools for Collaborative Decision Making
Collaborative Decision Making: Cases studies
Organisational Collaborative Decision Making

Hoping that joined projects could emerge from groups' members during and after the conference and hoping that new challenges could arise during the conference concerning Decision Support Systems researches. It is then our responsibility to maintain this domain an attractive and interesting investigating area. For the future, new conferences will be organised for both groups: the IFIP TC8/WG8.3 and the EWGDSS, hoping that this event, CDM08 2008, will stay the meeting point.

As editors of this book, it is our duty to conclude by expressing our gratitude to all contributors to these proceedings, to the members of the steering and program committees who helped us selecting the papers, making this conference as interesting as possible and preparing these proceedings.

Pascale Zaraté, CDM08 Chairperson
Jean Pierre Belaud, CDM08 Organisational Committee member
Guy Camilleri, CDM08 Organisational Committee member
Franck Ravat, CDM08 Organisational Committee member

Contents

Organisational Collaborative Decision Making

Part I
Full Papers

Models for Collaborative Decision Making

Collaborative Decision Making: Perspectives and Challenges
P. Zaraté et al. (Eds.)
IOS Press, 2008

A Cooperative Approach for Job Shop Scheduling under Uncertainties

C. BRIAND[a,1], S. OURARI[b] and B. BOUZOUIAI[b]
[a] Université de Toulouse, LAAS CNRS, France
[b] CDTA, Alger, Algérie

Abstract. This paper focuses on job shop scheduling problems in a cooperative environment. Unlike classical deterministic approaches, we assume that jobs are not known in advance but occur randomly during the production process, as orders appear. Therefore, the production schedule is adapted in a reactive manner all along the production process. These schedule adaptations are made according to a cooperative approach, that is the major originality of this paper. Each resource manages its own local schedule and the global schedule is obtained by point-to-point negotiations between the various machines. We also suppose that local schedules are flexible since several alternative job sequences are allowed on each machine. This flexibility is the key feature that allows each resource, on the one hand, to negotiate with the others and, on the other hand, to react to unexpected events. The cooperative approach aims at ensuring the coherence between the local schedules while keeping a given level of flexibility on each resource.

Keywords. cooperative scheduling, flexibility, robustness, dominance.

Introduction

Many research efforts in scheduling assume a static deterministic environment within which the schedule is executed. However, considering any real enterprise environment, the probability for a pre-computed predictive schedule to be executed as planed is quite weak. Many parameters related to a scheduling problem are in fact subject to fluctuations. The disruptions may arise from a number of possible sources [3][7][13]: job release dates and job due dates may change, new jobs may need to be taken into account, operation processing times can vary, machine can breakdown, etc.

One way to take theses disruptions into account, while keeping the schedule performance under control, consists to use a two-level resolution scheme: an off-line scheduling level builds up a predictive schedule, then a on-line scheduling level adapts the predictive schedule all along the production process, taking disruptions into account. Notions of flexibility and robustness are defined in order to characterize a scheduling system able to resist to some parameter variations. The flexibility refers to the fact that some schedule decisions are kept free during the off-line phase in order to be able to face unforeseen disturbances during the on-line phase [12]. Robustness is closely linked to flexibility; actually, flexibility is often injected into a deterministic solution in order to make it robust with regard to some kinds of uncertainty sources.

---

[1] Corresponding Author: C. Briand, Université de Toulouse, LAAS CNRS, 7 Avenue du Colonel Roche, 31077 Toulouse, Email: briand@laas.fr

The literature connected to scheduling with uncertainties is growing. A classification of the scheduling methods is proposed in [7], [17] and [13]. Some methods generate a predictive schedule which is reactively repaired (i.e. some local adaptations are made inside the schedule) for taking unexpected events into account, aiming at minimizing the perturbation made inside the original schedule [21]. Others approaches, referred to as proactive, construct predictive schedules on the basis of a statistical knowledge of the uncertainties, aiming at determining a schedule having a good average performance [16][22][23]. Some other approaches use both proactive and reactive methods since all unexpected events cannot be taken into account inside the proactive phase. In this class of approaches, a temporal flexibility [13][16] or a sequential flexibility [2][5][11] is often inserted into an initial deterministic solution in order to protect it against unforeseen events. Indeed, a solution which is sequentially or temporally flexible characterizes a set of solutions that can be used in the on line phase by moving from an obsolete solution to another one, while minimizing the performance loss. Among such approaches, one can distinguish approaches based on the notion of operation groups [2][3][11] which allow the permutation of certain contiguous tasks on a resource. Another kind of approach is proposed in [5] for the one machine problem, where the characterization of a flexible family of solutions is based on the use of a dominance theorem. This approach is used in this paper.

Basically, in the on-line as well as in the off-line phases, scheduling is usually considered as a global decision problem since the scheduling decisions deal with the organization of all the resources [6]. However, in many application domains (supply chain management, industrial projects, timetabling …), resources are often distributed among a set of actors which get their own decisional autonomy. Consequently, a global scheduling approach seems unrealistic since each actor cannot control its own organization. In this case, a cooperative approach is better suited: scheduling decisions have to be negotiated between the actors intending to converge towards a compromise that satisfies both local and global performances. Such approaches are proposed in [8][18][19] [20].

The paper is organised as follows: at first, some notions, useful for the comprehension of the proposed approach, are described in Section 1. Section 2 presents the assumptions that have been made for defining the cooperative scheduling problem. Section 3 introduces the global coherence notion as well as the various cooperation functions. Section 4 focuses on the negotiation process that concerns pair of actors, this negotiation process being more formalized in Section 5.

1. A Robust Approach for the Single Machine Scheduling Problem

A single machine problem consists of a set V of n jobs to be scheduled on a single disjunctive resource. The processing time p_j, the release date r_j and due date d_j of each job j are known. The interval $[r_j \ d_j]$ defines the execution window of each job j. A job sequence is referred to as feasible if all the jobs of V are completed early, i.e. if Eqs (1) is satisfied. Regarding the feasibility objective, this problem is NP-hard [15].

$$\forall \, i \in V, \quad s_i \geq r_i \quad et \quad f_i = s_i + p_i \leq d_i \tag{1}$$

Considering the one machine scheduling problem with execution windows, a dominance theorem is stated in the early eighties by Erschler et al. [9]. The theorem uses the notions of top and pyramid which are defined on the basis of the job execution intervals $[r_i \ d_i]$. Let us remind to the reader that a condition of dominance enables the reduction of the solution search space: only the non-dominated solutions are kept. We notice that for a one machine problem, a sequence S_2 is dominated by another sequence S_1 if the feasibility of S_2 implies that S_1 is feasible. Before presenting the theorem, the notions of a top and a pyramid need to be defined.

Definition 1. A job $t \in V$ is called a top if there does not exist any other job $i \in V$ such that $r_i > r_t \wedge d_i < d_t$

The tops are indexed according to the ascending order of their release dates or, in case of equality, according to the ascending order of their due dates.

Definition 2. Given a top t_α, a pyramid P_α related to t_α is the set of jobs $i \in V$ such that $r_i < r_{t_\alpha} \wedge d_i > d_{t_\alpha}$

Considering Definition 2, it can be noticed that a non-top job may belong to several pyramids. The functions $u(j)$ and $v(j)$ indicate the index of the first pyramid to which the job j belongs and the index of the last job to which the job j belongs, respectively. Erschler et al. give the proof of the following theorem, further referred to as pyramidal theorem, in [9].

Theorem 1: *A dominant set of sequences can be constituted by the sequences such that:*
- the tops are ordered according to the ascending order of their index;
- only the jobs belonging to the first pyramid can be located before the first top and they are ordered according to the ascending order of their release dates (in an arbitrary order in case of equality);
- only the jobs belonging to the last pyramid can be located after the last top and they are ordered according to the ascending order of their due dates (in an arbitrary order in case of equality);
- only the jobs belonging to the pyramids P_k or P_{k+1} can be located between two successive tops t_k and t_{k+1} so that:
* • the jobs belonging only to P_k but not to P_{k+1} are sequenced immediately after t_k according to the ascending order of their due dates (in an arbitrary order in case of equality),*
* • then the jobs belonging both to P_k and P_{k+1} are sequenced in an arbitrary order,*
* • and lastly are sequenced the jobs belonging only to P_{k+1} but not to P_k in the ascending order of their release dates (in an arbitrary order in case of equality).*

The previous theorem enables to characterise a set of dominant sequences. Let us note that this set of dominant sequences is independent of the numerical values of the processing times p_j as well as the explicit values of r_i and d_i. Only the total relative order of the release and due dates is considered. In [10] and [4], it is shown that this set is also dominant with regards to the optimisation of the regular criteria T_{max} , the maximum tardiness, and L_{max}, the maximum lateness.

In [5], it is also shown how, given a problem V and its corresponding set of dominant sequences S^V, determined in accordance with the pyramid theorem; it is possible to associate to each job i a lateness interval $[L_i^{min}, L_i^{max}]$ where L_i^{min} and L_i^{max} respectively represent the best and the worst lateness of job i among all sequences of S^V.

The computation of the lateness intervals can be performed in polynomial time by determining for each job j the most unfavorable and the most favorable sequences, i.e. the sequences implying the smallest and greatest delays for the job amongst all sequences in S^V respectively. Figure 1 depicts the structure of these sequences for any job j. The notations A, B and σ represent job sub-sequences as illustrated in Figure 1, and t_k is the kth top.

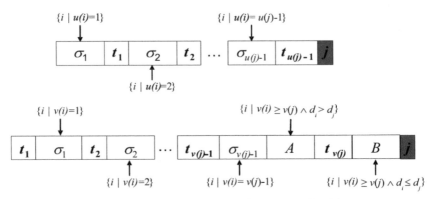

Figure 1. Most favorable and unfavorable sequences for a job j

Given L_i^{min} and L_i^{max} , the optimal lateness L^{max} is bounded as follows:

$$Max_{i \in V}\left(L_i^{min}\right) \le L_{max} \le Max_{i \in V}\left(L_i^{max}\right) \qquad (2)$$

According to Eq. (2), it is possible to determine whether a dominant set of sequences is acceptable, relatively to its worst performance. On the other hand, it is shown in [5] and [14] how to eliminate from the dominant set some "worst sequences" in order to enhance the worst performance.

Let us also remark that the L_i^{min} and L_i^{max} values allow to deduce the values of the best and worst starting time s_i^{min} and s_i^{max} of each job i, according to Eq. (3).

$$s_i^{min} = L_i^{min} + d_i - p_i \text{ and } s_i^{max} = L_i^{max} + d_i - p_i \qquad (3)$$

2. Cooperative Framework

The Job Shop Scheduling problem is considered as follows. T jobs have to be processed on $M = \{M_1, \dots M_m\}$ machines. Jobs consist of a sequence of operations to be carried out on the machines according to a given routing. Each machine can process only one operation at a time. The jth operation of a job i is referred to as o_{ij}. Its duration id denoted $p_{i,j}$. The commonly considered objective is to minimize the makespan which corresponds to the total duration of the schedule. The job shop scheduling problem is NP-hard [15]. It is possible to decompose it into m interdependent one machine sub-problems, where each operation is characterized by its execution interval $[r_{ij}, d_{ij}]$. For each sub-problem, the objective consists to minimize the maximum lateness. We highlight that the sub-problems are interdependent because the optimal sequence determined on a given machine must be consistent (according to the routing constraints) with the other optimal sequences established for the other resources [1].

As stated above, we suppose that each resource is associated with a decision center (DC) which manages its own local schedule, exchanging information and products with other DCs. We also assume that each DC gets its own decisional flexibility. In our case, this flexibility corresponds to the number of dominant sequences that can be characterized by the pyramidal theorem.

The DCs are crossed by products flows. Considering a particular DC_i, we can distinguish, according to the routing constraints, its upstream centers and its downstream centers. An upstream center is the supplier of the downstream center, which can be viewed in its turn as its customer.

In this work, we assume that each DC cooperates with its upstream and downstream DCs using point-to-point communication. The cooperation aims at bringing the actors to collectively define (by negotiation) the delivery date of the products, while giving each actor enough flexibility for reacting to disturbances.

We now consider a negotiation process carried out between two DCs. If we focus on decision center DC_i which must perform a set of operations V_i, this DC has to negotiate for each operation $o_{u,v} \in V_i$:

- with the upstream DC which performs $o_{u,v-1}$, in order to define a temporal interval $[\ r_{uv}^{min}\ \ r_{uv}^{max}\ ]$ (further referred to as $[r_{uv}]$) corresponding to the availability interval of $o_{u,v-1}$.
- with the downstream DC which performs $o_{u,v+1}$, in order to define a temporal interval $[\ d_{uv}^{min}\ \ d_{uv}^{max}\ ]$ (further referred to as $[d_{uv}]$) corresponding to the delivery interval of $o_{u,v}$.

We note that interval $[r_{uv}]$ for the machine performing o_{uv} corresponds to interval $[d_{u,v-1}]$ for the machine performing $o_{u,v-1}$. Also, $[d_{uv}] = [r_{u,v+1}]$.

We also highlight that setting product delivery intervals between two DCs (instead of a fixed delivery date) gives more flexibility to each DC for managing its own local organization. We assume that the $[r_{uv}]$ and $[d_{uv}]$ negotiations give rise to contracts between DCs. This contract corresponds to a supplier-customer mutual commitment: the upstream DC commits to delivery its product in a given temporal interval, while the downstream DC commits to start the execution of the next operation on this product in the same interval.

3. Local and Global Consistency and Cooperation Functions

Under the previously defined assumptions, each DC has to build up a local schedule that must be consistent with the availability and delivery windows $[r_{uv}]$ and $[d_{uv}]$. Using the approach described in Section 1, each local schedule is flexible, and each operation is characterized by a best and a worst starting date [$s_{uv}^{\min} s_{uv}^{\max}$] (referred to as [s_{uv}]). The local consistency of [s_{uv}] with the negotiated intervals [r_{uv}] and [d_{uv}] can be expressed by the following inequalities:

$$r_{uv}^{\min} \leq s_{uv}^{\min} \leq r_{uv}^{\max} \text{ and } d_{uv}^{\min} \leq s_{uv}^{\max} + p_{uv} \leq d_{uv}^{\max} \tag{3}$$

The above conditions (2) impose, on the one hand, that a DC never plans to start the execution of an operation of a job before it becomes available (i.e. $r_{uv}^{\min} \leq s_{uv}^{\min}$) and, on the other hand that, in the worst case, the job must be delivered on time (i.e. $s_{uv}^{\max} + p_{uv} \leq d_{uv}^{\max}$). The others two inequalities avoid a over-autonomy state, in which a DC would ask an upstream DC to achieve a job earlier than necessary (i.e. $r_{uv}^{\max} < s_{uv}^{\min}$), and the situation where a job would be achieved, in the worst case, earlier than necessary (i.e. $s_{uv}^{\max} + p_{uv} < d_{uv}^{\min}$).

As in [18], we consider that the underlying functions of a cooperation process are the negotiation, the coordination and the renegotiation. A negotiation process is initiated when a DC asks for the first time its upstream or downstream DCs to perform an operation on a new job to be taken into account in the shop. This operation corresponds to the next or to the preceding operation to be performed on the job, according to its routing. Negotiation aims at finding the intervals [r_{uv}] or [d_{uv}] for operation o_{uv}. Let us remark that new job arrival corresponds to the occurrence of a new order. We suppose that a delivery interval is associated to the order (this interval being eventually reduced to a point). The aim of the negotiation is to define the intervals [r_{uv}] and [d_{uv}] of the new operation, trying to respect the local consistency constraints (see Eq. (3)) for the already existing operations.

During the negotiation related to the insertion of a new operation, it can be suitable to renegotiate some already existing intervals [r_{ij}] and [d_{ij}] so as to improve the completion time of the new operation. This renegotiation situation also occurs when a disturbance makes an interval [s_{ij}] inconsistent (with regards to Eq (3)) with the current values of [r_{ij}] and [d_{ij}]. The goal of the renegotiation process is to recover the local consistency.

Negotiation and renegotiation are carried out by exchanging interval requests between pairs of DCs. An initiator DC issues an interval proposal [r_{uv}] or [d_{uv}] to another either upstream or downstream DC. The latter can either accept the proposal or refuse it by issuing a counterproposal.

Since local schedules are evolving over time, it is necessary that DCs coordinate themselves so that the organization remains globally feasible (i.e. Eq. (4) must be satisfied). This coordination corresponds to the asynchronous exchange of the values of the availability and delivery intervals of the operations. When Condition (4) is violated, a re-schedule has to be performed on the DC which detects the violation. Moreover, if the change of a best or worst start date is inconsistent with Condition (3) then a renegotiation is imposed between the concerned DCs.

$$s_{uv}^{\min} \geq f_{u,v-1}^{\min} = s_{u,v-1}^{\min} + p_{u,v-1} \text{ and } s_{uv}^{\max} \geq f_{u,v-1}^{\max} = s_{u,v-1}^{\max} + p_{u,v-1} \tag{4}$$

We point out that, during the various negotiations and renegotiations, issuing consistent proposals and counterproposals is not trivial. The following section focuses on this aspect.

4. Negotiation and Renegotiation

Considering a DC, the determination of a set of dominant sequences requires to define a total order among the r_{uv} and d_{uv} of all the jobs that the DC performs. Indeed, this order is required in order to apply the pyramidal theorem (see Section 1). Let us highlight that, while the negotiation process allows to determine the intervals $[r_{uv}]$ and $[d_{uv}]$, the values of r_{uv} and d_{uv} are not precisely fixed, hence there exists several possible total orders. Moreover, for each considered total order corresponds a specific dominant set of sequences, hence different values of $[s_{uv}^{\min} s_{uv}^{\max}]$. The determination on a DC of a pertinent total order between r_{uv} and d_{uv} requires to compare interval $[s_{uv}]$ with $[f_{u,v-1}]$ and $[f_{uv}]$ with $[s_{u,v-1}]$. These comparisons lead us to define an *inconsistency risk* notion.

We say that an inconsistency risk exists between two operations o_{ij} and $o_{i,j+1}$ if $s_{i,j+1}^{\min} < f_{ij}^{\max}$ is valid, i.e. the intervals $[f_{ij}]$ and $[s_{i,j+1}]$ overlap. Ideally, when the intervals $[f_{ij}]$ and $[s_{i,j+1}]$ do not overlap (see Figure 2), the inconsistency risk is null. Indeed, in this optimistic case, the worst completion value of o_{ij} is always consistent with the best earliest start date of $o_{i,j+1}$ whatever the execution sequences of the jobs will be on each DC. Nevertheless, in the general case, overlapping is allowed (see Figure 3). In this case there is a risk for the completion date of o_{ij} to be greater than the start date of $o_{i,j+1}$. Obviously, the larger the overlap interval, the greater the inconsistency risk.

Figure 2. Case of a null inconsistency risk

Figure 3. General case

The determination of a total order between release date and due dates must be guided by the aim of minimizing the inconsistency risk. However, this goal is not the only one to be considered. As discussed above, it is also necessary to maximize the DC's decisional flexibility so that the DC keeps its ability to face production disturbances or new job arrivals.

As a matter of fact, the decisional flexibility is linked to the number of dominant sequences characterized by each DC. An interesting property of the pyramidal theorem is that this number can be easily computed, using Eq. 5, without requiring any sequence enumeration. In this formula, n_q is the number of non-top jobs exactly belonging to q pyramids and N, the total number of pyramids.

$$\pi = \prod_{q=1}^{N} (q+1)^{n_q} \tag{5}$$

We can notice that π is maximal when there exist only one pyramid containing all the jobs. In this case π equals 2^{n-1}, where n is the number of jobs that the DC manages. Also we note that π decreases as pyramid number increases. In the worst case, all operations are tops, and $\pi = 1$.

Minimizing the inconsistency risk and maximizing the flexibility are two contradictory objectives. Indeed, the greater the number of dominant sequences, the wider the intervals $[s_{uv}]$, and subsequently, the greater the inconsistency risk. Conversely, to reduce the inconsistency risk, it is necessary to lose flexibility in order to tight the interval widths. Let us highlight that the above trade-off is also connected to the global system performance. Indeed, regarding a job shop scheduling problem with makespan minimization as global objective, the performance of the global schedule is much more effective as interval $[s_{uv}]$ decreases and flexibility decreases. Indeed, in every optimal schedule, any interval $[s_{uv}]$ is reduced to a point and the DC's flexibility is null.

5. A First Approach for Inter-DC Negotiation

In the previous section, we put in evidence the need of making a trade-off between inconsistency risk minimization and flexibility maximization. In the remainder of the paper, a first negotiation approach is sketched which enables to formalize a DC behaviour.

To simplify the problem, it is assumed that the pyramidal structure associated to each DC is such that each operation belongs to a single pyramid (i.e. $u(o_{ij})=v(o_{ij})$). Under this assumption, pyramids are referred to as independent. Therefore, a best completion time $f_P^{\min}$ and a worst completion time $f_P^{\max}$ can be associated to each pyramid P.

When a new operation o_{xy} has to be considered by a DC, it systematically receives a proposal from another upstream or downstream DC. If the proposal comes from an upstream center, a target interval of availability date $[r_{xy}]$ is proposed, in the other case, a target interval of delivery time $[d_{xy}]$ is proposed. Let us note that, independently from the proposal origin, it is always possible by propagation of the precedence constraints to determine a pair of target intervals $[r_{xy}][d_{xy}]$.

When receiving a negotiation proposal, a DC must at first, decides to which pyramid the new operation o_{xy} will be assigned: for instance, either to an already existing pyramid or to a new pyramid (of top o_{xy}) which will be inserted between two existing pyramids. The assignment of a new operation inside a pyramidal structure defines an optimization problem which is not addressed in this paper. Let us remark that this problem can be very complex when pyramid splitting is allowed. We also point out that the flexibility of the DC entirely depends on the solution of this problem since the flexibility is inversely proportional to the pyramid number.

Now, assuming that the new-task assignment has been decided (i.e. $o_{xy} \in P_\alpha$), a total order among the availability and due dates of the operations belonging to P_α must be defined. Indeed, this total order is required in order to determine the interval values $[s_{uv}]$ for each $o_{uv} \in P_\alpha$. This is also an optimisation problem where the objective is, at this time, to minimize the inconsistency risk.

In order to formalize this problem, a linear program is proposed below. Without loss of generality, we suppose that the n_α jobs of pyramid P_α are indexed according to the increasing order of $r_{ij}^{\min}$. For simplification, we also suppose that the order of the availability dates of the operations of P_α match the increasing order of $r_{ij}^{\min}$ (this assumption tends to favour the coherence between the $r_{ij}^{\min}$ and $s_{ij}^{\min}$ values). Since there is only one top in P_α, one consequence of this assumption is that the operation having the index n_α defines the top of P_α because this operation has the greatest availability date. Now it only remains to determine the order of the due dates and the intervals values $[s_{uv}]$ for each operation $o_{uv} \in P_\alpha$.

For this purpose, a linear program (LP) with integer variables is proposed below. The main decision variables are x_{ij}, $s_{ix}^{\min}$ and $s_{ix}^{\max}$. The decision variables x_{ij} are binary: $x_{ij}=1$ if the deadline of i is greater than the one of j, else $x_{ij}=0$. The values of these variables allow to deduce the total order of the due dates of the operations of P_α. Variables $s_{ix}^{\min}$ and $s_{ix}^{\max}$ are integers, and correspond respectively to the best and the worst start dates of o_{ix}. The parameters of the LP are the values of intervals $[r_{ix}]$ and $[d_{ix}]$, the processing time p_{ix} and the weights $w_{i(x-1)}$ and $w_{i(x+1)}$. The significance of these weights is further discussed in the paper.

$$\min L$$

$$x_{ij}+x_{ji} =1 \qquad\qquad \forall(i,j), i \neq j \qquad (6)$$

$$x_{ij}+x_{jk} - x_{ii} \leq 1 \qquad\qquad \forall(i,j,k) \qquad (7)$$

$$x_{ii} = 0 \qquad\qquad \forall i \qquad (8)$$

$$x_{in_\alpha} = 1 \qquad\qquad \forall i, i \neq n_\alpha \qquad (9)$$

$$s_{ix}^{\min} \geq s_{jy}^{\min} \geq f_{P_{\alpha-1}}^{\min} \qquad\qquad \forall(i,j), i > j \qquad (10)$$

$$s_{ix}^{\max} \geq \max(s_{jy}^{\min}, f_{P_{\alpha-1}}^{\max}) + \sum_{k=j}^{n_\alpha} x_{ki}\, p_{ki} + \sum_{k=1}^{n_\alpha} x_{ik}\, p_{ik} \qquad\qquad \forall(i,j), i \neq j \qquad (11)$$

$$L \geq w_{i(x-1)}(r_{ix}^{\max} - s_{ix}^{\min}) \qquad\qquad \forall i \qquad (12)$$

$$L \geq w_{i(x-1)}(s_{ix}^{\min} - r_{ix}^{\max}) \qquad\qquad \forall i \qquad (13)$$

$$L \geq w_{i(x+1)}(s_{ix}^{\max} + p_{ix} - d_{ix}^{\min}) \qquad\qquad \forall i \qquad (14)$$

$$L \geq w_{i(x+1)}(d_{ix}^{\min} - s_{ix}^{\max} - p_{ix}) \qquad\qquad \forall i \qquad (15)$$

Constraints (6)–(8) ensure that deadlines are totally ordered. Constraint (7) states that $(x_{ij} = 1) \land (x_{jk} = 1) \Rightarrow (x_{ik} = 1)$. Constraint (9) imposes to the operation associated to the job n_a to be the top (it gets the smallest due date). Constraint (10) ensures that the best and the worst start dates respect the increasing order of $r_{ij}^{\min}$. We also impose, according to the most favourable sequences (see figure 1), that these dates must be greater than the best completion date of the preceding pyramid P_{a-1}. Constraint (11) imposes that the worst completion date of each operation is determined according to the structure of the most unfavourable sequences (see figure 1). The expression $\sum_{k=j}^{n_a} x_{ki} p_k$ corresponds to the sum of the processing time of the jobs belonging to set A in the unfavourable sequence, while $\sum_{k=1}^{n_a} x_{ik} p_k$ corresponds to that of jobs belonging to set B.

The LP objective is the minimisation of the variable L which is determined according to constraints (12)-(15). This variable measures the greatest gap between $s_{ix}^{\min}$ and $r_{ix}^{\max}$ on the one hand, and $s_{ix}^{\max} + p_{ix}$ and $d_{ix}^{\min}$ on the other hand. In other words, we search to minimize the advance-delay of the operations according to contracted intervals $[r_{ix}]$ and $[d_{ix}]$. When $L = 0$, the inconsistency risk is obviously null, since the best start date of o_{uv} is equal to the worst delivery date of $o_{u,v-1}$ and the worst completion time of o_{uv} is equal to the best delivery date of $o_{u,v+1}$.

The weights $w_{i(x-1)}$ and $w_{i(x+1)}$ ponder, for each operation, the advance-delay according to the upstream/ downstream resource priority. The idea is to penalize more an advance-delay concerning an upstream/downstream resource having poor flexibility, and vice-versa.

The optimal solution of this LP allows the DC to know for all the managed operations, the values of their $s_{uv}^{\min}$ et $s_{uv}^{\max}$, and in particular, those of $s_{xy}^{\min}$ and $s_{xy}^{\max}$. On the basis of these values, negotiation/renegotiation proposals issued by the DC can be elaborated.

Conclusion

In this paper, the job shop scheduling problem under uncertainties is considered. At the opposite of the classical centralised scheduling techniques, a cooperative approach which gives each resource a decisional autonomy is proposed. The scheduling decisions result from point-to-point negotiations and renegotiations between resources. The cooperation process aims at characterizing a flexible family of solutions on each resource, this flexibility being used for facing production disruptions and new job arrivals. A negotiation/renegotiation process is started when a new operation is inserted, or when unexpected event occurs. It leads to adapt the interval structure associated to each resource. Basically, if the sequential flexibility is large, then the ability to absorb unexpected events is important, but the inconsistency risk becomes greater and the global performance gets weaker. Reversely, when the flexibility gets weaker, the global performance increases, however it is less reliable. Several cooperation bases have been laid down and a first formalization of the negotiation/renegotiation processes has been proposed. Our mid-term goal is to implement an automatic cooperative scheduling prototype in order to validate the cooperation approach and to improve it.

References

[1] J.Adams, E.BAlas & D.Zawack. The shifting bottleneck procedure for job shop scheduling. Management Science, vol.34, n°3, pages 391-401, 1988.

[2] A. Aloulou & M-C Portmann, Définition d'ordonnancements flexibles. Première application à un problème à une machine. GI'2001, Aix-en-Provence, 2001.

[3] Billaut J.C., Moukrim A., & Sanlaville E., Flexibilité et robustesse en ordonnancement. Hermes, Traité IC2, ISBN 2-7462-1028-2, 2005.

[4] C.Briand, M-J.Huguet, H.T.La & P.Lopez. Approche par contraintes pour l'ordonnancement robuste. Dans J-C.Billaut, A.Moukrim & E.Sanlaville, editeurs, Flexibilité et Robustesse en Ordonnancement, Traité IC2, ISBN 2-7462-1028-2, 2005, pp. 191-215.

[5] C. Briand, H. Trung La, & Jacques Erschler, A robust approach for the single machine scheduling problem. Journal of Scheduling, Special Issue on Project Scheduling under Uncertainty, Demeulemeester, E.L. and Herroelen W.S. (eds)., vol. 10, no. 3, pp 209-221, 2007.

[6] Chu C. & Proth J.M., L'ordonnancement et ses applications. Masson, Paris, France, 1996.

[7] Davenport A.J. & Beck J.C., A survey of techniques for scheduling with uncertainty. Disponible en ligne, 2000.

[8] Dudek G., Stadtler H., Negotiation-based collaborative planning between supply chain partners, European Journal of Operational Research, vol. 163, pp 668-687, 2004.

[9] J. Erschler, G. Fontan, C. Merce & F. Roubellat, A new dominance concept in scheduling n jobs on a single machine with ready times and due dates. Operations Research, vol.1, pp. 114–127, 1983.

[10] Erschler J., Fontan G. & Merce C., Un nouveau concept de dominance pour l'ordonnancement de travaux sur une machine. RAIRO Recherche Opérationnelle/Operations Research, Vol. 19, n°1, 1985.

[11] C.Esswein, A.Puret, J.Moreira & J.C. Billaut, An efficient methode for job shop scheduling with sequential flexibility. In ORP3, 2003, Germany

[12] GOThA, Flexibilité et robustesse en ordonnancement. Le bulletin de la ROADEF, 8 :10-12, 2002.

[13] Herrolelen W. &t Leus R., Robust and reactive project scheduling : A review and classification of procedures. International Journal of Production Research, Vol.42, No.8, 1599-1620, 2004.

[14] La H.T., Santamaria J.-L. & Briand C., Une aide à la décision pour l'ordonnancement robuste en contexte mono-ressource : un compromis flexibilité/performance. 6ème Congrès de la Société Française de Recherche Opérationnelle et d'Aide à la Décision (ROADEF'05), Tours (France), 14-16 Février 2005, pp 101-116

[15] Lenstra , J.K., Rinnooy Kan A.II.G & Brucker P., Complexity of machine scheduling problems. Annals of Discrete Mathematics 1, 343-362, 1977.

[16] Leon V.J., Wu S.D., & Store R.H., Robustness measures and robust scheduling for job shops. IIE Transactions, 26(5) : 32-43, 1994.

[17] Leus Roel, The generation of stable projects plans: complexity and exact algorithms. Thèse de doctorat, Department of Applied Economics, Katholieke Universiteit Leuven, Belgium, 2003.

[18] E. Monsarrat, C.Briand & P. Esquirol, Aide à la décision pour la coopération interentreprise. Journal Européen des Systèmes Automatisés, 39/2005.

[19] Portmann M.-C, Mouloua Z., A window time negotiation approach at the scheduling level inside supply chains, 3rd Multidisciplinary International Conference on Scheduling: Theory and Application, MISTA'07, Paris, 28-31 august, pp410-417, 2007.

[20] Quéré Y.L., Sevaux M., Tahon C. & Trenteseaux D., Reactive scheduling of complex system maintenance in a cooperative environment with communication time. IEEE Transaction on System, Man and Cybernetic- Part C: Applications and reviews, Vol 33, No.2, May 2003.

[21] Sabuncuoglu I., & de Bayiz M., Analysis of reactive scheduling problem in a job shop environement. European Journal of Operational Research, 126 (3) 567-586, 2000.

[22] Sevaux M. & Sörensen K., A genetic algorithm for robust schedules in a just-in-time environment. Rapport de recherche, University of valenciennes, LAMIH/SP-2003-1, 2002

[23] Wu S.D, Store R.H., & Chang P.C., One-machine rescheduling heuristics with efficiency and stability as criteria. Computer and Operations Research, 20, 1-14, 1993.

Collaborative Decision Making: Perspectives and Challenges
P. Zaraté et al. (Eds.)
IOS Press, 2008

Analysing the true Contribution of Decision Support Tools to Decision Making – Case Studies in Irish Organisations

Mary Daly*, Frédéric Adam* and Jean-Charles Pomerol**

Business Information Systems, University College Cork, Ireland.
**Laboratoire d'Informatique de Paris 6, Université Pierre et Marie Curie, Paris, France.*

Abstract: There is abundant evidence that the current business environment is pushing firms to invest increasing amounts of resources in sourcing state of the art IT capability. Some of this investment is directed towards developing the decision support capability of the firm and it is important to measure the extent to which this deployment of decision support is having a positive impact on the decision making of managers. Using existing theories, namely an adaptation of Humphreys' representation levels (Humphreys, 1989), to classify the type of support which managers can get from their decision support tools, we investigated the portfolio of decision related applications available to managers in 5 Irish firms. Our findings indicate that not all firms can achieve the development of decision support tools across all the categories of the framework. Managers need to be able to spell out the problems they are facing, but also need to be in a situation where they have clear incentives to make the efforts required in investigating high level problems, before firms can be observed to have a complete portfolio of decision support tools, not merely a collection of static reporting tools.

Keywords: DSS, representation levels, models, managerial decision making

1. Introduction

Since Ackoff's seminal and provocative paper [1], researchers have sought to propose concepts, systems and methodologies to achieve the goal of providing managers with information they need to make "proper" decisions under a variety of names, sometimes suggested by vendors of technology rather than the academic community. Throughout this time, it has remained true, however, that basic tools such as spreadsheets have formed the bulk of computer-based decision support [2].

Recently, new terms, such as Business Intelligence (BI), information cockpits or dashboards have been proposed [3, 4, 5] that leverage recent technologies – e.g., web technologies, relational databases, multi-dimensional modelling tools – to deliver the silver bullet solutions to managerial decision making difficulties. However, there is evidence (at least anecdotal) that the new tools will have a similar fate as previous instalments of decision support technologies with 40% of respondents to a recent study by the electronic forum *The Register* saying that the language used by vendors can often be ambiguous or confused, and a further 44% saying that vendors are creating an unhelpful mire of marketing speak around BI [6]. This is likely to be because, fundamentally, the problems raised by managerial decision making and the provision of information to support it – especially in situations involving high levels of uncertainty or equivocality [7, 8] – are of an intractable nature.

In this paper, we use Humphreys' framework of representation levels [9] and Adam and Pomerol's classification of decision support in terms of *Reporting*, *Scrutinising* and *Discovering* [10] to measure the extent of decision support provided by the portfolio of decision support tools of five Irish firms. After eliciting the specific problems inherent in supporting managerial decision making and presenting the two frameworks used in our study, we described the methods we followed and the 5 case studies on which our analysis is based. We then present our findings and conclusions with respect to maturity of the decision support capability of the firms we studied.

2. The Problem with Supporting Managerial Decision Making

Despite the claims of software vendors, there is some evidence that the problems inherent in proposing effective decision support are of such a nature that modern GUIs, interfaces and the myriads of tool kits available from software vendors to develop advanced dashboards with minimal programming expertise are unlikely to solve them conclusively. It is the enlightened selection, and accurate capture in the organisation's currently available data sources, of the critical indicators most useful to the business managers that are problematic. Evidently, these require collaboration between managers / users and IT specialists. This is an aged-old problem as far as Information Systems are concerned, which has been discussed in relation to Decision Support Systems, Executive Information Systems and generally any other type of systems that have been proposed for managerial support since the 1960's [1, 11, 12, 13, 14].

Despite years of research on how the work of managers can be supported by IT, developing computer systems that are ultimately adopted by top management has remained a complex and uncertain task. New technologies and new types of applications have come and gone, but information systems for executives raise specific problems, which have primarily to do with the nature of managerial work itself [15], as they are intended to tackle the needs of users whose most important role is "to create a vision of the future of the company and to lead the company towards it" [16; p. xi]. Lest these observations be dismissed as outdated, they are in fact as accurate today as they were when they were printed. Evidently, information systems can help with decision making and information dissemination, but managers also spend considerable in their role of "go-between", allocating work to subordinates and networking with internal and external peers [15, 17]. How computer systems can be used for these activities is largely unknown apart from the use of email and its derivatives,

3. Measuring the Extent of Decision Support Provided by Systems

It has been proposed that managers can leverage the data provided by their support systems for three types of inquiry [10]: (1) *reporting*, when managers ask questions that they understand well, (2) *scrutinising*, where managers ask questions which they understand in broad terms, but still find difficult to ask in specific terms, and (3) *discovering*, where managers are not sure what questions to ask, sometimes in the complete absence of model or even a specific problem to solve.

These 3 decision support activities are practical from a developer's viewpoint because they correspond to the level of knowledge that an analyst can gain *a priori* about an information need they are about to tackle. These three types of support can be matched against the level of understanding which managers have of the problems they face. Humphreys *et al.* [18] have usefully characterised this level of comprehension with their concept of *representation* levels. These five representation levels theorise on the evolution of managers' thinking as they learn about the reality that surrounds them, based on: (1) the degree of abstraction of the representation managers have of the problems to be tackled and (2) the degree of formalisation of the representations of the proposed solutions and the models to be built into information systems. The five representation levels can be illustrated with Humphreys and Berkeley's [18] description of the problem handling process, which is adapted in Table 1.

Table 1: Representations of Managers' Thinking at the different Cognitive Levels

Cognitive Level	Representations of Managerial thinking	Abstraction level
1	Representations are mainly cultural and psychological; managers are more or less aware of what problems may involve, but their expression is beyond language. Problems are shaped at this level but are beyond modeling and let alone decision support.	Maximum
2	Representations become explicit and problems can be broken into sub-problems, some of them formalised. The structuration of problems is still partial and managers refer to 'the marketing function' or 'the marketing process'. Data mining may be used to formalise ideas and test hypotheses. Pre-models may be designed but it is still hard for managers to discuss these with analysts.	
3	Decision makers are able to define the structure of the problems to be solved. They are able to put forward models for investigating alternatives solutions and to discuss these with analysts; these discussions can lead to small applications – eg OLAP tools.	
4	Decision makers perform sensitivity analysis with the models they have already defined so as to determine suitable input values; saved searches and views created using scrutinising tools can become increasingly formalised and move from level 3 to level 4.	
5	Managers decide upon the most suitable values and the representation of the problems is stable and fully operational. Report templates can be created, leading to regular or ad hoc reports available to managers with minimum effort or time.	Minimum

The process described by Humphreys [9] is a top down process whereby the structuration of the concepts investigated is refined from one level to the next over time. As noted by Lévine and Pomerol [19], levels 1 and 2 are generally considered as strategic levels of reflection handled by top executives (problem defining), whereas the remaining three levels correspond to more operational and tactical levels (problem solving). Although, all levels of management span the 5 levels, it is clear that lower levels of management are more likely to be given problems already well formulated to work on such that their thinking is mostly geared towards levels 3 to 5.

Level 1 in Table 1 is particularly important in that, at this early stage, the decision maker has total freedom to decide on a direction to follow. The only factors limiting the horizon of the decision maker are either psychological (unconscious) or cultural (*e.g.*: his or her educational background or experience). In the literature on human decision making, this initial step appears under the name "*setting the agenda*" [20] or "*problem setting*" [21]. This stage is also important because it conditions the outcome of the decision making process as avenues not considered at this stage are less likely to ever be considered. In addition, the natural progression across the levels of the framework is one that goes from 1 to 5, and rarely back to a previous stage unless a strong stimulus forces a change of mind about the situation.

This representation of managers' information needs is a simplification in that it separates what is essentially a continuous process into separate ones. However, from the point of view of the designer of management decision support systems, this framework has the great merit of clarifying what design avenues can be pursed to support managers in situations that are more akin to stage 1, stage, or any other stage.

Adam and Pomerol [10] argue that, if managers can name specific performance indicators and know how these must be represented, the situation corresponds to the fifth representation level in the Humphreys and Berkeley framework (especially if they are also able to calibrate performance level based on their own knowledge). This is essentially a reporting scenario where specific answers are given to specific questions. When, however, it is not exactly known how to measure or represent an indicator, this corresponds to levels 3 and 4 in the framework. This is more of a scrutinising situation where managers know they are on to something, but they are not sure how to formally monitor it. Finally, when managers are not sure what indicator should be monitored to measure emergent changes in the activities of their organisations, or changes to market responses, this is more akin to a level 2 situation, or a level 1 situation if managers are still at the problem finding stage [22]. The discussion between designers and managers is on-going, as different methods are experimented with to study how different indicators calculated in different ways based on different data sources respond. The development of the decision support capability of the firm thus becomes an iterative process where problems and their representations improve over time and where discovery turns into scrutiny and scrutiny turns into reporting over time.

This theoretical proposition, however, requires that the decision support capability of a firm ibes articulated around a complete portfolio of applications covering at least, levels 3, 4 and 5, if not all levels. Therefore, our study needs to ascertain that decision support tools provide a comprehensive help to decision makers in firms and that there is a natural progression from the higher towards the lower levels of abstraction.

4. Research Aims and Research Methods

In order to verify the validity of this presumption, we carried out a replicated case study of the extent of decision support provided in 5 Irish firms using the 5 cognitive levels and the 3 core types of support that decision support tools can provide, as described in Figure 1. To achieve high levels of insight into each firm's decision support capability, we enlisted the help of a number of candidates in the Executive MBA at University College Cork, so they would carry out the initial analysis and report on their findings in their own company. This formed part of their marking for the course and led to excellent work by most groups. In preparation for their field work, all MBA students were coached by one of the researchers in the application of the framework in Figure 1. Groups were formed and selected target organisations where the student worked (all as managers). The groups then presented their analysis to the researchers in extensive presentations and a detailed written report. These reports and presentations were used as research instruments for data collection and led to our analysis of the portfolio of decision support tools available to managers in each organisation. After the presentations, the researchers selected the most rigorously produced reports and focused their analysis on the 5 cases studies presented thereafter.

Figure 1: Matching Decision Support Tool contents to managerial needs (after Adam and Pomerol, 2007).

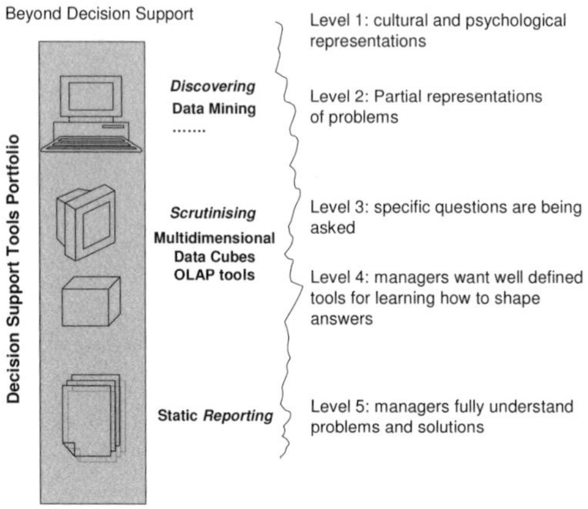

5. Presentation of cases and Discussion of Findings

5.1. The five case studies:

Table 2 below shows the key demographical data for the 5 companies in our sample. It indicates the spread of our observations across a range of industries, including manufacturing, services, food and a utility company. It also shows that the firms we studied cover a range of sizes from medium to very large. Our sample also covers three indigenous Irish firms and two multinational companies, where the Irish subsidiaries were studied. Finally, the five companies feature different domains of expertise, from engineering to health. Overall, this reflects our attempts to cover many different types of organisational settings and present a broad spectrum of observations.

Table 2: Summary of Company characteristics

	Company A	**Company B**	**Company C**	**Company D**	**Company E**
Activity	Private Healthcare Provision	Energy supply	Milk Products Manufacture	Medical Device Manufacture	Hi-Tech manufacturer
Turnover	€144 million	€1.1 Billion	€200 million	$4 Billion worldwide	€6 Billion worldwide
Profit	€3.9 million	€99 million	Not available	Not available	Not available
Employees	1,690	770	300	640 (Ireland)	1800 (Ire), 30,000 global
Ownership	Private Independent	State body	Irish co-operative	Private US multinational	Private US multinational

5.2. Decision Support Tools in 5 Companies

In the following sections, we present for each firm studied, a detailed and tabular account of the context of the firm, the challenges being faced by managers and the types of systems relied upon for decision support, classified according to the categories of the framework we adapted for this research, based on Humphreys and Berkeley's work [18]. In some case, the case data is factual and outlines specific applications used by managers in the case, whereas in some cases, it is aspirational in that little is known about how to design the support applications, although the agenda has been set [23].

5.2.1. Company A.

Company A is a private healthcare provider. The organisation has operations in five locations in Ireland. While individual patient admissions can be in the region of 60,000 per year, the primary source of revenue earned by the group is the private health insurers. Current government initiatives present a challenge for the organisation – the move towards co-located hospitals (mixing private and public facilities under the same roof) and the negotiation of new contracts for hospital consultants may mean substantial changes as to how healthcare is provided and funded in Ireland in the future.

Traditionally IT has been deployed in a standalone fashion, with each hospital implementing different IT systems. This created difficulties with preparing routine management and financial reports and in operational and strategic planning. Since 2006 a Business Intelligence Data Warehouse (BIDW) is being implemented. This consists of 11 data marts, spanning operational, clinical and administration aspects of the company. Considering the five cognitive levels and the three core types of support, the BIDW has provided decision support activity classified as outlined in table 3 below.

Table 3: Decision Support in company A.

Cognitive level	Decision Support Activity
Level 1. The challenge is to try to understand how patient care provision is changing due to medical and technology advances and government decisions and how these changes influence the revenue model	Providing better information for contract negotiation with health care purchases in *Discovery* mode should allow managers to run scenarios for the future and understand the impact of bottom line and operations.
Level 2. Optimising resource utilisation with improved financial performance	Resource utilisation modelling in areas such as outpatient's area, theatres and bed management. Utilising information derived at level 4 decision support activity, with trends and predictions for what changes are occurring within the health sector.
Level 3. Enabling benchmarking between hospital sites	Taking information derived at levels 4 and 5, and analysing performance across the hospitals
Level 4. Providing quantitative fact based data	Assessment of key business metrics in financial and clinical areas across all hospitals – bed occupancy by hospital, by consultant, theatre utilisation etc.
Level 5. The aim of the DW project is to provide access to operational and financial data to improve services delivered, and patient and financial outcomes.	Reporting activity is well developed. A Hospital Information System (HIS) enables the management of scheduled admissions, theatre scheduling and staff/consultant workload

Table 3 indicates the richness of company A from the point of view of the potential for a complete portfolio of decision support spanning all 5 levels of the framework. Whilst the BIDW project was clearly focused on providing robust and comprehensive visibility on operations, it has become the platform for the full spectrum of managerial decision support from reporting to scrutinising to discovering. Nevertheless, in table 3, we have presented the top two rows in grey to reflect that delivering support at these two difficult levels was still largely aspirational at the time of our study. Whilst level 3 is well covered by the implementation of the benchmarking concept, levels 1 and 2 still present specific design difficulties as managers seek to understand how they can use the data warehouse to face up to the challenges of the future. The lack of a model to capture the essence of decisions in these two domains remains a problem.

5.2.2. Company B.

Company B is a commercial State Body operating in the energy industry. The company is wholly owned by the Irish Government and consists of 2 main businesses – Gas transportation and Energy Supply. The residential gas market is the primary area of business. A new wholesale electricity market has come into operation in Ireland since November 2007. The effects of global warming and improved housing insulation standards will affect demand for energy in the future. Company B entered the retail electricity market in 2006, and currently holds 7% of the electricity market in Ireland. Company B is an interesting site from a decision support viewpoint, as outlined in table 4 below.

Table 4: Decision Support in company B.

Cognitive level	Decision Support Activity
Level 1. Considerations for the future direction and strategy for this company include: More competition in the residential gas market A single wholesale Electricity market, where company B is a new entrant The effect of global warming on energy demand The effect of better insulation standards employed in house construction	Trying to understand how the changes outlined will play out in the respective markets, and whether the company can be successful in the new operating environment. Accepting there will be significant change, consideration of the impact which these changes may have on current energy trading operations, and whether the current organisational structure and competencies are sufficient to deal with new opportunities and challenges.
Level 2. Considering the scenarios as presented at Level 1, what are the likely predictions? Company should expect to lose market share in the residential market where it currently holds 100 % share. Overall gas demand in this sector may decrease due to global warming, better insulation etc. How will the company operate in the electricity trading market	Regression analysis assesses the relationship between gas demand and degree days, price change and customer segmentation. The dataset represent 60% of the residential and small temperature sensitive Industrial and Commercial customers. The outputs are considered as a base case for 2012. The purpose is to discover what the operational environment may be like and the implications for the energy trading business, especially in terms of pricing.
Level 3. The decisions that must be made based on the projection of base Price (the price of electricity) are of such material value to the business that in-depth knowledge of the workings of the market is required. An informed view of where the SMP (System marginal price) will be for each half hour is a key strategic asset as well as an operational asset as it will help to determine what contracts should be entered into, as well as help to manage capacity on a day to day basis.	Portfolio modelling applications are used to support the identification/prioritisation of commercial activities – in relation to both gas and electricity. The organisation has invested in 2 market modelling applications to help in its forecasting of the SMP price. SMP price together with the business hedging strategy for the following 12 months determines what contracts are entered into and for what prices and quantities. Daily forecasts of SMP determine whether there is an opportunity to trade Irish power in the UK, or whether it would be more beneficial to purchase power in the UK, rather than face the exposure of balancing the portfolio of the SMP price.
Level 4. The organisation recognises the importance of analytics where optimisation and efficiency are key components to operating in a new energy trading environment	There are a number of systems in use which allow a level of scrutiny. Market-to-market reporting is used to predict the future benefit derived from entering into forward transactions enabling management to optimise purchase contracts, and allowing corrective action should the firm's hedging strategy require amendment. Daily trading and operations reporting facilitate the planning and prioritisation of the day's activities.
Level 5 Within the more traditional areas of business, decision support tools are in the realm of level 4 and 5, eg: the 'claims management' area.	Recent systems developments have replaced Excel spreadsheet reporting, and has enabled the capability of data analysis based on data warehouse technologies.

The first observation that can be made is that the engineering vocation of the firm has helped the creation of an "all-knowing" dashboard for reporting in real time on all security elements of the network. Flow, pressure, consumption etc. are monitored in real time. The reporting on maintenance and accidents is also very advanced.

On the commercial side, company B is extremely mature in its development of highly complex models for planning for consumption and justifying the price per cubic meter charged to the different categories of customers (which the Department of Finance must approve once a year and whenever price changes are requested). This has been largely based on spreadsheets of a highly complex nature, developed by specialists in econometrics and business modelling. Based on the generic scenarios, managers in the transportation department run simulations which are then used for price setting or also for justifying capital expenditure when network extensions are proposed. For some of the aspects of decision making at level 1, company C is still not able to define the models that may provide answers.

Altogether, this portfolio of applications adds up to a complex set of decision support covering the reporting and scrutinising side very comprehensively, and making a definitive contribution at the discovery level, if not in an organised fashion.

5.2.3. Company C.

Company C is a major international cheese manufacturer and also manufactures food ingredients and flavours, some of them on behalf of other companies. Headquartered in Cork, Ireland, it produces 25% of the total cheese manufactured in Ireland, and has been the largest manufacturer of cheese in Ireland for the last 20 years. Considering the five cognitive levels and the three core types of support, decision support activity can be classified as outlined in table 5 below.

Table 5: Decision Support in company C.

Cognitive level	Decision Support Activity
Level 1 The raw material of cheese is milk, ie 90% water. Company C do not know how to address the issue of yield and efficiency in this process.	There are no decision support tools in use.
Level 2 Dry hot summers mean poor milk yield and low milk quality which increases the cost of cheese. Company C don't understand the reasons for these variations.	There are no decision support tools in use.
Level 3 The production of cheese is difficult to perfect and reject production can be high. To understand the reasons for spoilage, analysis of the relationship between milk quality, cheese recipe used, production run and cheese storage is undertaken	There are no decision support tools in use, although "Best practice" rules could be establishes based on trends. Recipes and production methods for different milk quality at different times of year and optimal cheese storage temperatures to develop best flavour based on cheese quality would really help
Level 4 The production of cheese is a capital intensive activity, with fixed costs a significant percentage of the overall production cost. Controlling fixed costs and managing the milk throughput are critical.	Critical KPIs at scrutinising level are all produced manually based of various SCADA and forecasting systems. Excel spreadsheets are prepared and hand delivered to management in the form of weekly reports two working days after each weekend
Level 5 Company C produces cheese more efficiently than any of its competitors. Maintaining that efficiency is a core competency which drives a sustained competitive advantage. Relevant CSFs are based on a system of variances between budget and actual	Company C excel in dashboard technology to control and monitor all aspects of the production process. KPIs are reported upon in dashboard format and include: Milk cost per tonne of cheese, Direct wages cost per tonne of cheese, Direct energy cost per tonne of cheese.

Company C do not have any decision support systems to support upper level management decision making. All management reports are prepared in spreadsheets, with input from disparate transactional systems and SCADA type process control systems. Thus, company C shows a very different DSS foot print in comparison to companies A and B. In this site, the failure to support higher level decision activities is very evident and we could not identify any significant attempt to cover any decision need at levels 1, 2 or 3. This, however, was in sharp contrast with our findings at level 4 and 5, which clearly showed intense reporting and some limited scrutinising activities. A substantial body of mature DSS applications was developed over a number of years in the shape of dashboard type applications and a substantial body of manual preparation of data used for scrutinising operations was also undertaken, particularly on the factory floor.

Overall Company C shows the DSS profile of a less advanced organisation, where managers, for a variety of reasons, don't have the time or the incentive to seek to develop the models that could capture the essence of levels 1, 2 or 3 decisions.

5.2.4. Company D.

Company D is a medical device manufacturer, part of a US multinational. This company has seven manufacturing sites around the world, with a new facility currently being built in China. The Cork site is the largest manufacturing facility, accounting for approximately 40% of total production. For products in this market, gaining additional market share is largely dependant on price competiveness and there is, at this point, significant competition in the market where Company D is operating. Considering the five cognitive levels and the three core types of support, decision support activity in this site can be classified as outlined in table 6 below.

Table 6: Decision Support in company D.

Cognitive level	Decision Support Activity
Level 1. The Cork site is currently the largest accounting to 40% of total worldwide volume. The new facility in China will significantly change this balance and will imply increased competition between sites.	It is unclear how manufacturing will be allocated across sites in the future. There are no decision support tools in use.
Level 2. Competition is forcing the Cork plant to push for huge gains in productivity, space usage and operational efficiency.	There are no decision support tools in use.
Level 3. Competition both internally and externally is forcing the Cork site to consider its cost structure	There are no decision support tools in use.
Level 4. From the CSF's monitored at level 5, a core set of key performance indicators (KPI's) are produced and reviewed, with the frequency of review being determined both by the criticality of the operation and the availability of information.	Little drilldown capability is available to managers to facilitate *scrutinising*. The operation remains in reactive mode, but the systems capability to allow management to operate in a more proactive mode. A performance accountable culture could be achieved with improved reporting and dashboard capability.
Level 5. The Cork site has a number of critical success factors (CSF's) that if managed effectively can ensure the site is a success.	Current reporting systems monitor day-to-day operations and the ERP system provides some data. However manual systems generate most of the data in the weekly reports prepared by Finance - e.g., The "overall equipment effectiveness" dashboard allows drilldown in each machine's downtime but is not integrated with any other system

Although a large US multinational firm, Company D seems remarkably close to Company C in decision support terms, despite being having a totally different profile in general terms. This is more than likely due to our examination of a local manufacturing site, rather than the corporation overall. In other research, it has been observed that there was a tendency for a reduced scope of decision making at local level in highly integrated multinationals (particularly US multinationals). This pattern seem to be repeated in Company D where managers are very well equipped at level 5 and 4, where KPIs are clearly identified, but where decision making tools for scrutinising in general terms and for discovering are totally absent. This reflects the KPI-oriented culture of many MNCs where specific goals are handed down from headquarters to local sites for each functional area and converted into strict target by each manager. This culture means that the incentive and the time to develop specific DSSs at the higher levels of decision making are low because local managers have little autonomy of action.

5.2.5. Company E.

Company E is a world leader in products, services and solutions for information management and data storage. In recent years company E had expanded from developing hardware platforms that provide data storage to developing software and providing services to help companies of all sizes to keep their most essential digital information protected, secure and continuously available.

For the purposes of this study, the Global Services (GS) division was the focus. Global Services is Company E's customer support organisation, with almost 10,000 technical/field experts located in 35 locations globally and delivering "follow-the-sun" support in over 75 countries worldwide. An Oracle CRM and workflow system provides key operational data, including install base data, time tracking and parts usage recording. Business objects and Crystal reporting software is used for querying and reporting as required. Considering the five cognitive levels and the three core types of support, decision support activity can be classified as outlined in table 7 below.

Table 7: Decision Support in company E.

Cognitive level	Decision Support Activity
Level 1 No problem identified	No evidence found
Level 2 When increased resolution times are apparent, management can predict the potential impact on service levels based on the volume of service calls, the number of staff, and the introduction of new products and the quality of training delivered.	Each business unit has visibility of specific hardware products dashboards, with defective attributes flagged. This in turn allows GS to flag product issues to the engineering organisation, and to ensure further training where appropriate.
Level 3 Improving management ability to investigate the reasons for the outcomes at level 5, but where the cause and effect relationship is not as factual as at level 4	Scrutinising the performance of the business units and their ability to meet SLO's can highlight training needs – for newly released products for example. Management can then ask the training department to provide specific training across a wider audience.
Level 4 Improving management ability to investigate the reasons for the outcomes at level 5.	Tracking compliance of documented processes is essential as spikes in "Calls closed in 24 hrs" may indicate non compliance.
Level 5 Improving management ability at problem solving, and maintaining customer SLA agreements.	This is presented in Dashboard format with colour coding to indicate if SLA levels are not met. In the event of higher than expected incoming calls, More staff can be brought in if SLOs are not met.

Company E presents a profile that is similar to that of company D, as a part of a US MNC, with the difference that, in this case, our access in the case allowed us to study a global unit, rather than a local manufacturing unit. This results in a more complete landscape of applications, all the way up to level 2, where production problems and training needs can be anticipated before anyone has considered training to be a problem. This illustrate the natural progression of all decision problems up the levels of the framework over time, from the stage where managers cannot even express them properly, to the stage where they become part of the normal scrutiny activity of the firm, and, given time, fall into the general reporting area, based on well-defined models that capture the essence of the decision problem. Thus, the portfolio of decision support applications in companies in a state of permanent flux. Naturally, tracking this progression has a significant staff cost in terms of developers' and managers' time.

6. Conclusion

Table 8 below presents quick summary of our observations in terms of the levels of decision support we observed in the five companies. It indicates that the broad spectrum of firms we included in our sample is matched by a broad spectrum of findings with respect with the use of decision support applications.

Table 8: summary of levels observed in the 5 companies

	Company A	Company B	Company C	Company D	Company E
Level 1	X				
Level 2	X	X			X
Level 3	X	X			X
Level 4	X	X	X	X	X
Level 5	X	X	X	X	X

Prima facia, we observe that companies can be at a given level for different reasons, notably lack of expertise (company C) or lack of incentive (company D), which is quite different. Thus, the existence or absence of decision support at the scrutinising and discovery levels are about more than just the abilities of the managers and IS developers of the firm to properly model the issues facing them. Managers must also recognise the need to perform such activities and feel that the amount of autonomy that they have warrants the significant efforts required in conceptualising the problems. Otherwise, they may prefer to concentrate on the level 4 or 5 which allow them to manage the narrow indicators handed down to them by top management.

In firms where the context facing managers provides clear incentives to (1) attempt to formalise level 1 and level 2 problems and (2) to seek the help of developers in taking their decision support tools beyond simple end-user developed spreadsheets, organisations may display very complete portfolio of decision support applications spanning most levels (companies A, B and D). However, even in these firms, it will remain that, few organisations ever achieve a complete portfolio spanning the 5 levels on a permanent basis. In other words, reaching level 1 is not like reaching a threshold at which one is certain to remain. Quite the opposite, it is a matter of reaching a certain level of understanding of the problems facing the firm, at a particular point in time, where the environment is presenting a new, identifiable pattern of competition, regulation etc...until *Nature's* next move changes the state of play again and managers shift their focus on other, newer ideas, as they become aware of new challenges facing them. Yesterday's level 1 problems become level 2 or 3 problems, or drop off the agenda altogether. Tomorrow's level 1 problem, of course, will take time to crystallise.

7. Bibliography

[1]   Ackoff, R. L. (1967) Management MISinformation systems, *Management Science*, 14(4), pp. 147-156.
[2]   Fahy, M. and Murphy, C. (1996) From end user computing to management developed systems, in Dias Cuehlo et al. (Eds) Proceedings of the Fourth European Conference on Information Systems, Lisbon, Portugal, July 1996, 127-142.
[3]   Dover, C. (2004) How Dashboards Can Change Your Culture, *Strategic Finance*, 86(4), 43-48.
[4]   Gitlow, Howard (2005) Organizational Dashboards: Steering an Organization Towards its Mission, *Quality Engineering*, Vol. 17 Issue 3, pp 345-357.
[5]   Paine, K.D. (2004) Using dashboard metrics to track communication, *Strategic Communication Management*, Aug/Sep2004, Vol. 8 Issue 5, 30-33.
[6]   Vile, D. (2007) Vendors causing confusion on business intelligence - Is the marketing getting out of hand?, *The Register*, Business Intelligence Workshop, Published Monday 9th April 2007. Accessed on April 17th, 2007 from http://www.theregister.co.uk/2007/04/09/bi_ws_wk2/
[7]   Earl, M.J. and Hopwood, A.G. (1980) From management information to information management, In Lucas, Land, Lincoln and Supper (Eds) The Information Systems Environment, North-Holland, IFIP, 1980, 133-143.
[8]   Daft R. L. and Lengel R. H. (1986) Organisational information requirements media richness and structural design, Management Science, 32(5), 554-571.
[9]   Humphreys P. (1989) Intelligence in decision making - a process model in G. Doukidis, F. Land and E. Miller (Eds.) *Knowledge-based Management Systems*, Hellis Hovwood, Chichester.
[10] Adam, F. and Pomerol, J.C. (2007) Developing Practical Support Tools using Dashboards of Information, in Holsapple and Burstein, Handbook on Decision Support Systems, International Handbook on Information Systems series, Springer-Verlag (London), forthcoming.
[11] Keen, P.G. and Scott Morton, M.S. (1978), *Decision Support Systems: An Organisational Perspective*, Addison-Wesley, Reading, Mass.
[12] Rockart, J. and DeLong D. (1988), *Executive Support Systems: The Emergence of Top Management Computer Use*, Business One, Irwin: New York.
[13] Scott Morton, M. (1986) The state of the art of research in management information systems, in Rockart and Van Bullen (Eds) *The Rise of Management Computing*, Dow Jones Irwin, Homewood Illinois, pp 325-353 (Chapter 16).
[14] Watson, Hugh J. and Mark N. Frolick, (1993) Determining Information Requirements for an Executive Information System, *MIS Quarterly,* 17 (3), 255-269.
[15] Mintzberg, H. (1973) *The Nature of Managerial Work*, Harper and Row, New York.
[16] King W.R. (1985) Editor's comment: CEOs and their PCs., *MIS Quarterly*, 9, xi-xii.
[17] Kotter, J. (1984), What effective managers really do, *Harvard Business Review*, November/December, 156-167.
[18] Humphrey P. and Bekerley D., 1985, Handling uncertainty: levels of analysis of decision problems, in G. Wright (Ed.) *Behavioural Decision Making*, Plenum Press, London.
[19] Lévine P. and Pomerol J.-Ch., 1995 : The Role of the Decision Maker in DSSs and Representation levels, in Proceedings of the 29th Hawaï *International Conference on System Sciences*, 42-51.
[20] Simon H.A., 1997, *Administrative Behavior* (4th edition), The Free Press, NY.
[21] Checkland, P. (1981), *Systems Thinking - Systems Practice*, Wiley Publications, Chichester.
[22] Pounds, W. (1969) The process of problem finding, *Industrial Management Review*, 10(1), 1-19.
[23] Mintzberg, H. (1994) The Rise and Fall of Strategic Planning Reconceiving Roles for Planning, Plans, Planners, The Free Press, Glencoe.

Collaborative Decision Making: Perspectives and Challenges
P. Zaraté et al. (Eds.)
IOS Press, 2008

Context in the Collaborative Building of an Answer to a Question

Patrick BREZILLON[1]
LIP6, case 169, University Paris 6, France

Abstract. We describe how contextual graphs allow the analysis of oral corpus from person-to-person collaboration. The goal was to build a task model that would be closer to the effective task(s) than the prescribed task. Such a "contextualized prescribed task" is possible, thanks to a formalism allowing a uniform representation of elements of decision and of contexts. The collaborative process of answer building identified includes a phase of building of the shared context attached to the collaboration, shared context in which each participant introduces contextual elements from his/her individual context in order to build the answer with the other. Participants in the collaborative building process agree on the contextual elements in the shared context and organize, assemble and structure them in a proceduralized context to build the answer. The proceduralized-context building is an important key of the modeling of a collaborative decision making process.

Keywords. Contextual graphs, collaborative building of an answer, decision making, context

Introduction

How collaboration can improve document comprehension? Starting from the C/I comprehension model developed by Kintsch [8], Brézillon et al. [7] set up a series of several experiments aiming to test whether the ideas evoked during a prior collaborative situation can affect the comprehension processes and at which representation levels this may occur. The hypothesis was that collaboration affected directly the construction of the situation model. In order to test this hypothesis, Brézillon et al. [7] built an experimental design in two phases: 1) a collaboration phase, and 2) a comprehension phase (reading and questionnaire). In the comprehension phase, the authors run several experiments (with an eye-tracking technique) where participants of the experiments had to read a set of texts varying both semantically and from the lay-out. The general purpose was to correlate the verbal interactions occurring during the collaboration and the behavioral data (eye-movements and correct answers to questions) recorded during reading. In this paper, we focus on the modeling in the Contextual Graphs formalism of the collaborative verbal exchanges between two participants. The goal was to build an efficient task model that would be closer to the effective task(s) than the prescribed task. Such a "contextualized prescribed task" is possible, thanks to a formalism allowing a uniform representation of elements of decision and of contexts.

This study has two side-effects. There are, first, the need to make explicit the shared context for building the answer, and, second, the relative position of cooperation

---

[1] Corresponding Author: Patrick Brezillon, LIP6, case 169, University Paris 6, 104, ave. du Pdt Kennedy, 75016 Paris, France.

and collaboration between them. The shared context is the common background from which the two participants of the experiments will build collaboratively the answer. The building of this shared context is a step of the process that we study. Even if one of the participants knows the answer, s/he tries to build this shared context, and the answer building thus is enriched with the generation of an explanation for the other participant.

Our goal was to provide a representation of the different ways to build an answer according to the context of the question. Along this view, the context of the question is the shared context in which each participant introduces contextual elements from his/her individual context. In a collaborative decision making process, such a shared context must be built. The shared context contains contextual elements on which participants agree, eventually after a discussion and having provided an illustration. A subset of this shared context is then organized, assembled and structured to build the answer. The result of this answer building is a proceduralized context (Brézillon, 2005). In this paper, we put these results in the larger framework of collaborative decision making that discriminates a procedure and the different practices, the prescribed task and the effective task, the logic of functioning and the logic of use, etc. A practice is assimilated to a contextualization of a procedure.

Thus, our goal is to analyze how an answer is built, its basic contextual elements and the different ways to assemble these elements. The modeling of the answer building is made, thanks to a context-based formalism of representation called the contextual graphs [2].

Hereafter, the paper is organized in the following way. Sections 1 and 2 present the conceptual and experimental frameworks of our study. Section 3 sums up the main results, and Section 4 proposes a discussion from the lessons learned.

1. The Conceptual Framework

1.1. Introduction

Brézillon and Pomerol [5] defined context as "what constrains a focus without intervening in it explicitly". Thus, context is relative to a user's focus (e.g. the user, the task at hand or the interaction) and gives meaning to items related to the focus. The context guides the focus of attention, i.e. the subset of common ground that is relevant to the current task. For a given focus, context is the sum of three types of knowledge. There is the relevant part of the context related to the focus, and the irrelevant part. The former is called contextual knowledge and the latter is called external knowledge. **External knowledge** appears in different sources, such as the knowledge known by the participant but let implicit with respect to the current focus, the knowledge unknown to the participant (out of his competence), etc. **Contextual knowledge** obviously depends on the participant and on the decision at hand. Here, the focus acts as a discriminating factor between the external and contextual knowledge. However, the boundary between external and contextual knowledge is porous and evolves with the progress of the focus.

A sub-set of the contextual knowledge is proceduralized for addressing the current focus. We call it the **proceduralized context**. This is a part of the contextual knowledge is invoked, assembled, organized, structured and situated according to the given focus and is common to the various people involved in the answer building.

1.2. Contextual Graphs

A software was designed and implemented in this conceptual framework [2,3]. Contextual graphs are a context-based representation of a task realization. Contextual graphs are directed and acyclic, with exactly one input and one output, and a general structure of spindles. A path (from the input to the output of the graph) represents a practice (or a procedure), a type of task execution with the application of a selected method. There are as many paths as practices (i.e. as contexts). Note that if a contextual graph represents a problem solving, several solutions can be retained on different paths. For example, in the collaborative answer building to a question, the building can result from one participant alone, both of them or none of them. A contextual graph is an acyclic graph because user's tasks are generally in ordered sequences. For example, the repetition of the question often occurs at the beginning of the answer building, never during the process. A reason is that this is a way to memorize the question and retrieves all the (contextual) elements more or less related to the question.

Elements of a contextual graph are: actions, contextual elements, sub-graphs, activities and parallel action groupings.

- An **action** is the building block of contextual graphs. We call it an action but it would be better to consider it as an elementary task. An action can appear on several paths. This leads us to speak of instances of a given action, because an action which appears on several paths in a contextual graph is considered each time in a specific context.

- A **contextual element** is a couple of nodes, a contextual node and a recombination node; A contextual node has one input and N outputs (branches) corresponding to the N instantiations of the contextual element already encountered. The recombination node is [N, 1] and shows that even if we know the current instantiation of the contextual element, once the part of the practice on the branch between the contextual and recombination nodes corresponding to a given instantiation of the contextual element has been executed, it does not matter to know this instantiation because we do not need to differentiate a state of affairs any more with respect to this value. Then, the contextual element leaves the proceduralized context and (globally) is considered to go back to the contextual knowledge.

- A **sub-graph** is itself a contextual graph. This is a method to decompose a part of the task in different way according to the context and the different methods existing. In contextual graphs, sub-graphs are mainly used for obtaining different displays of the contextual graph on the graphical interface by some mechanisms of aggregation and expansion like in Sowa's conceptual graphs [12].

- An **activity** is a particular sub-graph (and thus also a contextual graph by itself) that is identified by participants because appearing in several contextual graphs. This recurring sub-structure is generally considered as a complex action. Our definition of activity is close from the definition of scheme given in cognitive ergonomics [9]. Each scheme organizes the activity around an object and can call other schemes to complete specific sub-goals.

- A **parallel action grouping** expresses the fact (and reduce the complexity of the representation) that several groups of actions must be accomplished but that the order in which action groups must be considered is not important, or

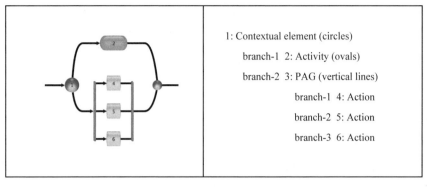

1: Contextual element (circles)

branch-1 2: Activity (ovals)

branch-2 3: PAG (vertical lines)

branch-1 4: Action

branch-2 5: Action

branch-3 6: Action

Figure 1. Elements of a contextual graph.

even could be done in parallel, but all actions must be accomplished before to continue. The parallel action grouping is for context what activities are for actions (i.e. complex actions). This item expresses a problem of representation at a lower granularity. For example, the activity "Make train empty of travelers" in the SART application [6] accounts for the damaged train and the helping train. There is no importance to empty first either the damaged train or the helping train or both in parallel. This operation is at a too low level with respect to the general task "Return back rapidly to a normal service" and would have otherwise to be detailed in three paths in parallel (helping train first, damage train first, both in parallel) leading to the same sequence of actions after.

A more complete presentation of this formalism and its implementation can be found in [2,3] and the software is freely available at http://www.cxg.fr. An example is given Figs 2 and 3 after in this paper. In the following, we use the syntax defined in Fig. 1 for all the figures representing a contextual graph.

1.3. Contextualized Task Model

Our goal is to develop an Intelligent Support Systems for helping users in their tasks and their contextualizing processes to reach their objective. Such systems need to have a knowledge base that is organized in a use-oriented way, not in a domain structure oriented way. The latter way corresponds to the procedures elaborated by the head of organizations, when the former way emerges from the practices developed by actors accomplishing their tasks in a given situation and in a given context. Bazire and Brézillon [1] discussed the different ingredients to consider in link with the context. As a consequence, an intelligent support system will use practices such as contextualization of procedures in an approach appearing as an extension of the case-based reasoning because the system will have past solutions, their contexts of validity, and the alternatives abandoned at the time of the building of the past solution (and their validity contexts). We use Contextual Graphs as a formalism for a uniform representation of elements of reasoning and of contexts in several applications (e.g. see [3]).

Leplat [9] pointed out the gap between the prescribed task and the effective task. Similar observations were made in other domains to differentiate procedures and practices [2], logic of functioning and logic of use [10], etc. Numerous examples were exhibited to illustrate this gap, some explanations were proposed to justify the gap, but no practical solution was proposed to fill this gap.

Brézillon [3] goes one step further the gap identification by showing that, first, the difference between the prescribed and effective tasks comes from the organization of the domain knowledge: The procedure relies on the natural structure of the domain knowledge. In the example of the diagnosis of a DVD reader, the domain knowledge (e.g. electrical part, mechanical part, video part, etc.) is organized in a parallel structure corresponding to the usual paradigm "divide and conquer". The practices have a use-oriented organization of the domain knowledge in the user's task, i.e. one first switch on the TV and the DVD reader (and thus power supply problems are fixed), second we introduce a DVD (and thus mechanical problems are consider), etc. The point to retain here is the need to prefer a practice model instead of the corresponding procedure.

Brézillon and Brézillon [4] came back on the fact that context is always relative to something called a focus [2] and went another step further by assimilating context to a set of contextual elements. First, this leads to make clearer the distinction between the focus and its context. In their example in the domain of road safety, a crossroad has a unique definition, when all the crossroads are specific and different each other. This is the metaphor of the situation dressing.

Second, their main point is to distinguish a contextual element (CE) and its possible instantiations. An instantiation is the value that can take the contextual element. For example, I have to invite friends for a diner (the focus). Among different CEs, I have the CE "restaurant". This CE has, in Paris, different instantiations like "French", "Japanese", "Italian", etc. When the focus will move toward "Go to the restaurant", the contextual element "restaurant" will be instantiated and included in the proceduralized context associated with the current focus (inviting friends for diner). The type of restaurant (the instantiation) will play a central role in the invitation.

Their third point concerns the interaction between CEs through their instantiations. For example, "Restaurant" = <Japanese> will imply that we expect to find chopsticks on the table instead of forks and knifes, no glasses but cups for tea, a different organization of the meal, etc. Thus, the instantiation of a CE may constrain the possible instantiations of other CEs. This can be expressed under the form of integrity rules.

Beyond the possibility of a relatively automatic organization of the domain knowledge (the proceduralized-context building), the fourth point deals with the possibility to establish rules for deducing the "expected behavior" of an actor in that specific situation (i.e. in the situation considered in the particular context). Such rules however do not help to solve all the problems, e.g. in the example of the restaurant, a vegetarian actors may eat in a Japanese restaurant as well as a French restaurant. It is important to point out here that this "expected behavior of actors" is a kind of prescribed task (or procedure) that is contextualized, but it does not represent practices that are obtained directly from effective behaviors of actors. This kind of "contextualized prescribed task" can be situated between the initial prescribed task and the effective tasks (the practice model).

2. Experimental Framework[2]

2.1. The Experimental Design

Eleven pairs of participants of the experiments were constituted. The participants were face to face, but did not see each other because they were separated by a screen. The experiment setup had two phases:

- Collaboration phase lasted during 1 min 30 s. Collaboration was induced by a general question: (e.g. "How does the oyster make pearls?").
- The reading/comprehension phase during which eye movements and answers to question were analyzed.

MP3 file corresponds to the verbal construction of the answer by the two participants for one question and 1 min 30 s is let for providing the answer. The eleven couples of participants had to address 16 questions. The 176 files were analyzed in two ways. We analyze the answer building for all the questions for each pair of participants. The goal was to establish a correlation inter-pairs in question management, and thus to have a relative weighting partner with respect to each question management. We also were looking for some particular roles in each pair between participants, such as a "master-slave" relationship between them, and also for comparing participants (background, level of interest in the experiment, previous relationships between participants of the experiments, etc.). This observation allows to understanding the type of roles that participants play in the experiment.

2.2. The Modeling of the Collaborative Building

For each question, we studied the answer building by all the pairs of participants. First, we look on the Web for the commonly accepted answer to the question in order to evaluate the quality of the answers provided by couples of participants. The quality of a given answer was estimated from:

- The "distance" to the consensual answer found on the Web,
- The answer granularity with respect to the question granularity (same level, too detailed or in too general terms).
- The education of the participants estimated in the other phases intervenes also here.

This is a delicate phase because one can give the right answer without knowing deep elements of the answer. For example, anybody knows the function of a refrigerator, but few know that this function relies on the 2nd principle of the Thermodynamics.

Second, we chose a sampling of few questions (with the 11 pairs of participants of the experiments). This preliminary study allowed us to identify four main building blocks in the answer-building process. The ordering of these building blocks however varies from one answer building to another one. Sometimes, a building block was not present in an answer building.

Third, we identified four types of collaborative building of the answer represented. These four paths are four sequences of the building blocks identified previously.

---

[2] This section is an abstracted presentation of the work presented in [7].

Table 1. Some data used in the modeling of the dialog model (see sections 3.1 and 3.3 for details)

MP3	7 (sparkling water)	9 (heredity diseases)	11 (drinking water)	15 (mineral water)
403	E2-b	E3-d	E4-d	E3-d
501	E3-a	E2-b	E2-b	E3-a
502	E1-e	E4-c	E4-d	E3-d
504	E3-e	E1-e	E1-f	E1-e
505	E1-f	E3-b	E3-e	E3-e
506	E2-b	E2-c	E2-b	E2-b
507	E3-e	E3-b	E3-b	E2-a
508	E1-e	E3-c	E1-g	E1-f
509	E2-b	E3-e	E2-e	E4-a
510	E3-e	E2-d	E1-e	E2-e
511	E1-g	E3-b	E1-e	E3-e
512	E2-e	E1-e	E2-b	E1-e
513	E1-f	E3-d	E1-f	E3-b

Fourth, it has been possible to specify more clearly the paths from the types of interaction inside each group and the quality of the answer (e.g. granularity). Finally, a contextual graph presents a synthesis of these first results.

Table 1 presents some of the data obtained from the analysis of the MP3 in order to establish our dialog model. See Sections 3.1 and 3.3 for the comments on this Table.

The whole analysis of the 176 MP3 files was then done. In a first time, the full transcription of the verbal exchange during the phase 1, for each participant, has been done from the MP3 files (transcription for partners working by pairs, answering at the sixteen questions). In a second time, the attended answers for each of the sixteen questions were set up. For example, for the question: "How does the oyster make pearls?" the answer expected is "A pearl arises from the introduction of a little artificial stone inserted into the oyster sexual gland. The oyster neutralizes the intrusive, the stone, surrounding it of the pearlier bag. Once closed, this pearlier bag secretes the pearlier material: the mother-of-pearl".

3. Results

From the initial subset of MP3 files, two models have been built, the *dialog model* and the *answer collaborative building model*. These models have been validated a posteriori on the whole set of MP3 files as mentioned in the previous section.

3.1. The Dialog Model

The *Dialog model* contained 4 phases:

E1. Reformulate the question

E2. Find an example

E3. Gather domain knowledge (collection)

E4. Build the answer from either characteristics or explanatory elements (integration).

Table 2. Different mean values for phases E1 to E4: frequencies into the collaboration (Col. 1), Range of occurrences (Col. 2), and Frequencies of occurrences (Col. 3)

	Collaboration	Range	Frequencies
E1	1	**1,27**	70
E2	10	**2,05**	58
E3	120	**1,98**	**133**
E4	71	**1,77**	**129**

For each pair of participants and for each question, the information was reported in a table (Table 1) allowing firstly to know in which order the 4 phases of the model dialog appeared, whether they appeared all four; and secondly, which of these phases is a collaboration phase. The participants reach the phase E4 only when they really built an answer, otherwise they collected the information without integrate them (phase E3). So, for each file, we have to identify in which order the phases appeared, to note which of these phases were collaboration phases and to report the information in a table. Results are presented into Table 2.

For example, column 1 indicates that collaboration used mostly phase E3 (i.e. gathering domain knowledge to constitute the shared context discussed previously) and unlike phase E1 (Reformulation of the question). Column 2 shows that phase 1 appeared mostly at the beginning of exchange and phase E2 (Find an example) at the end. Column 3 reveals that phases E3 and E4 (construction) are the most frequent phases carry out into the exchange. Furthermore, collaboration appeared the most often at the beginning of exchanges. See [7] for more details.

3.2. The Collaborative Building Model

The *contextual graph model* represented in Fig. 2 possesses 4 paths:

Path 1: Both partners do not know the answer.
Path 2: Both partners do not know the answer but each has elements of explanation.
Path 3: Co-building of the answer.
Path 4: One of the partners knows exactly the answer and provides it.

Path 1: No knowledge about the answer.
Both partners do not know the answer. They have no elements of the answer at all. However, they try to utter some rough ideas (example, a parallel with a known topic) in order to trigger a constructive reaction of the other.

Path 2: Elements of the answer.
Both partners do not know the answer but think to have elements for generating an explanation. Generally, a participant leads the interaction by proposing elements or asking questions to the other. Explanation generation is a kind of justification or validation to themselves of their general understanding of the question, without trying to build an answer.

Path 3: Two-ways knowledge.
Both partners have a partial view of the answer, know some of the elements of the answer and try to assemble them with the elements provide by the other. They have the

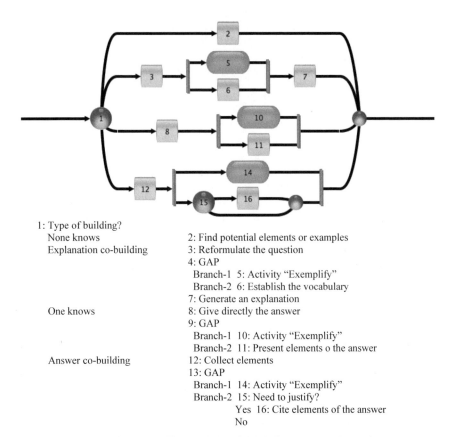

1: Type of building?
   None knows   2: Find potential elements or examples
   Explanation co-building   3: Reformulate the question
                                       4: GAP
                                         Branch-1 5: Activity "Exemplify"
                                         Branch-2 6: Establish the vocabulary
                                       7: Generate an explanation
   One knows   8: Give directly the answer
                                       9: GAP
                                         Branch-1 10: Activity "Exemplify"
                                         Branch-2 11: Present elements o the answer
   Answer co-building   12: Collect elements
                                       13: GAP
                                         Branch-1 14: Activity "Exemplify"
                                         Branch-2 15: Need to justify?
                                                      Yes 16: Cite elements of the answer
                                                      No

Figure 2. Contextual Graphs of the different collaborative building processes. Square boxes represents actions, circles, contextual elements and vertical lines, parallel action grouping.

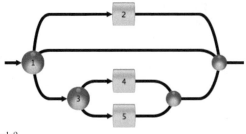

1: Type of example?
   Direct   2: Give the example
   no example
   indirect   3: Type of reference?
                          Personal   4: Give a counter-example
                          shared   5: Recall a stuff from the TV

Figure 3. Details of the activity "Exemplify" represented by ovals in Fig. 2. Square boxes represents actions, circles, contextual elements and vertical lines, parallel action grouping.

same position in the answer building, and there is not need for explanations between them or for external observer. This is a situation of maximal cooperation. However, without external validation, the quality of the answer is rather variable.

Path 4: One-way knowledge.

One of the partners knows exactly the answer, provides it immediately and spontaneously, and spends his/her time after to explain the other participant. Here the cooperation is unidirectional like the information flow.

Indeed, we can expect a relatively continuous spectrum between the path where one participant knows exactly (Path 4) and the situation where none of the participants knows (Path 1).

3.3. Typology of the Answers or Explanations

The typology aims to classify whether the answer has been given and the granularity of this answer. We thus distinguish (see Table 1):

- Answer required at the right granularity
- Answer required but at a superficial level
- Answer required but too detailed
- Partial answer
- Answer partially false
- False answer
- No answer.

In Table 1, the numbers represent the path in the contextual graph as defined in the previous section and the letters represent the typology of the answer. So, 3-b means Path 3: co-building of the answer, and b: answer required but at a too superficial level.

The distribution of the type of answers across the 4 main paths is discussed in [7]. Interestingly, results show that when partners collaborated by co-building the answer (Path 3), they gave mostly the correct answer either at superficial level (b) or partial answer (d). When either Path 2 (elements of answers) or Path 4 (One-Way) has been used, no difference in the type of answers emerges.

4. Discussion

Cooperation and collaboration are two ambiguous notions that have different meanings across domains, and sometimes from one author and another one. The difference between cooperation and collaboration seems related to the sharing of the participants' goal in the interaction. In cooperation (co-operation), each participant aims at the same goal and the task is divided in sub-tasks, each sub-tasks being under the responsibility of a participant. Thus, each participant intervenes in the shared goal through a part of the task. In collaboration, participants have different goals but interact in order to satisfy at least the goal of one of them, or one of his sub-goal. An example is the Head of a service and his secretary, often called a collaborator. The secretary takes in charge a part of the Head's task, but only as a support for the complex tasks of the Head.

However, we think that the difficulty to agree between cooperation and collaboration relationships is the lack of consideration for the dynamic dimension of relationships. Two participants may cooperate at one moment and collaborate at another moment. The shift comes from their background (their individual contexts) with respect to the current focus and their previous interaction (the shared context). If one participant can fix the current focus, then the other only agrees, and there is a minimal cooperation, i.e. collaboration for validating the answer. If none of the participants knows how to address the current focus, they try together, first, to bring (contextual) elements of an answer, and, second, to build the answer as a chunk of knowledge [11] or a proceduralized context, i.e. a kind of chunk of contextual knowledge [2]. This is a full cooperation.

Several lessons could be learned from these typologies by the DSS community:

- Repetition of the question occurs when the participants of the experiments wish to be sure to understand correctly the question, i.e. to be able to find some relationships between elements of the questions and contextual elements of their mental representation of the domain.

- An answer can be given at different levels of granularity. Thus, we observe correct answer at the right level as well as at a too low level of granularity (too many details) or too high level (rough description of the answer). For example, "gas" instead of "CO_2" for sparkling water. Participants of the experiments have a problem for finding the right granularity of their answer. One can know the answer but not the elements. As a consequence, participants may express an external and superficial position.

- Collaboration as a minimal expression of cooperation: one leads the interaction and the other only feeds in information (or only agrees), reinforces the statement of the other.

- When participants of the experiments gather contextual information, the goal is not to build immediately the answer because they want first to determine the granularity that their answer must have. Once, the level of granularity is identified, the selection of pieces of contextual knowledge to use in the proceduralized context is direct. When they can not identify the right level of granularity, they enter the process of an explanation generation.

- An explanation is given to: (1) justify a known answer, (2) progress in the co-construction of the answer by sharing elements and their interconnection; (3) when participants are not sure of the granularity of the answer (e.g. participants speak of 'gaz' instead of 'CO_2' for sparkling water). The explanation (given for an answer) is frequently less precise than an answer (generally at a macro-level), and is often for use between the participants.

Several groups were confused and explain instead of giving the answer (thus with additional details not necessary). The answer appears to be a kind of minimal explanation.

References

[1] Bazire, M. and Brézillon, P.: Understanding context before to use it. Modeling and Using Context (CONTEXT-05), A. Dey, B. Kokinov, D. Leake, R. Turner (Eds.), Springer Verlag, LNCS 3554, pp. 29-40 (2005).
[2] Brezillon, P.: "Task-realization models in Contextual Graphs." In: Modeling and Using Context (CONTEXT-05), A. Dey, B. Kokinov, D. Leake, R. Turner (Eds.), Springer Verlag, LNCS 3554, pp. 55-68 (2005).

[3] Brézillon, P.: Context Modeling: Task model and model of practices. In: Kokinov et al. (Eds.): Modeling and Using Context (CONTEXT-07), LNAI 4635, Springer Verlag, pp. 122-135 (2007).

[4] Brézillon, J. and Brézillon, P.: Context modeling: Context as a dressing of a focus. In: Modeling and Using Context (CONTEXT-07), LNAI 4635, Springer Verlag, pp. 136-149 (2007).

[5] Brézillon, P. and Pomerol, J.-Ch.: Contextual knowledge sharing and cooperation in intelligent assistant systems. *Le Travail Humain*, **62**(3), Paris: PUF, (1999) pp. 223-246.

[6] Brézillon, P., Cavalcanti, M., Naveiro, R. and Pomerol, J.-Ch.: SART: An intelligent assistant for subway control. Pesquisa Operacional, Brazilian Operations Research Society, **20**(2) (2000) 247-268.

[7] Brézillon, P., Drai-Zerbib, V., Baccino, T. and Therouanne, T.: Modeling collaborative construction of an answer by contextual graphs. Proceedings of IPMU, Paris, France, May 11-13 (2006).

[8] Kintsch, W.: Comprehension: a paradigm for cognition. Cambridge: Cambridge University Press (1998).

[9] Leplat, J. and Hoc, J.-M.: Tâche et activité dans l'analyse psychologique des situations. Cahiers de Psychologie Cognitive, **3** (1983) 49-63.

[10] Richard, 1983 Richard, J.F., Logique du fonctionnement et logique de l'utilisation. Rapport de Recherche INRIA no 202, 1983.

[11] Schank, R.C.: *Dynamic memory, a theory of learning in computers and people*, Cambridge University Press (1982).

[12] Sowa, J.F.: Knowledge Representation: Logical, Philosophical, and Computational Foundations. Brooks Cole Publishing Co., Pacific Grove, CA (2000).

Collaborative Decision Making: Perspectives and Challenges
P. Zaraté et al. (Eds.)
IOS Press, 2008

Some basic concepts for shared autonomy: a first report

Stéphane MERCIER, Catherine TESSIER

Onera-DCSD
2 avenue Edouard Belin BP 74025
31055 Toulouse Cedex 4 FRANCE

{stephane.mercier, catherine.tessier}@onera.fr

Abstract: In the context of supervisory control of one or several artificial agents by a human operator, the definition of the autonomy of an agent remains a major challenge. When the mission is critical and in a real-time environment, e.g. in the case of unmanned vehicles, errors are not permitted while performance must be as high as possible. Therefore, a trade-off must be found between manual control, usually ensuring good confidence in the system but putting a high workload on the operator, and full autonomy of the agents, often leading to less reliability in uncertain environments and lower performance. Having an operator in the decision loop does not always grant maximal performance and safety anyway, as human beings are fallible. Additionally, when an agent and a human decide and act simultaneously using the same resources, conflicts are likely to occur and coordination between entities is mandatory. We present the basic concepts of an approach aiming at dynamically adjusting the autonomy of an agent in a mission relatively to its operator, based on a formal modelling of mission ingredients.

Keywords: adaptive autonomy, human-robot interactions, authority sharing, multi-agent systems

Introduction

While there is no universal definition of autonomy, this concept can be seen as a relational notion between entities about an object [2, 5]: for instance, a subject X is autonomous with respect to the entity Z about the goal g. In a social context, entities like other agents or institutions may influence a given agent, thus affecting its decision-making freedom and its behaviour [4].

In the context of a physical agent agent evolving in the real world (i.e. an unmanned vehicle) under the control of a human operator, autonomy can be seen as the ability of an agent to minimize the need of human supervision and to act alone [20]: the primary focus is then rather the operational aspect of the autonomy than the social one. In this situation, pure autonomy is just a particular case of the agent – operator relationship, precisely consisting in not using this relationship.

However in practice, as automation within complex missions is not perfectly reliable and is usually not designed to reach the defined objectives alone, human supervision is still mandatory. Moreover, it seems that human intervention significantly improves performance over time compared to a neglected agent [10, 11].

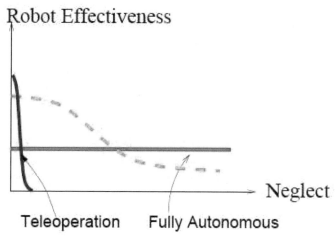

Figure1. Robot effectiveness and neglect time [10]

Adjustable autonomy

[22] first proposed a classification for operational autonomy, based on a ten-level scale. This model remains quite abstract, as it does take into account neither environment complexity nor the mission context. However, it provides an interesting insight into the interactions between an operator and an agent. This model has later been extended, using the same scale applied on a four stage cognitive information processing model (perception, analysis, decision-making and action) [18]. Based on the same principles, other scales for autonomy classification have also been proposed, e.g. [1].

Other approaches aim at evaluating an agent's autonomy in a given mission context, like MAP [12], ACL [6] or ALFUS [14]. The latter proposes to evaluate autonomy according to three aspects: mission complexity, environmental difficulty and human interface. However, this methodology aggregates many heterogeneous metrics and the meaning of the result is hard to evaluate. Moreover, qualitative steps are invoked, especially to set weights on the different tasks composing a mission and evaluate their importance. A similar limit exists with MAP and ACL, as they formally distinguish autonomy levels.

The idea that operational autonomy can be graduated leads to the concept of adjustable autonomy. The main principle is that machine and human abilities are complementary, and are likely to provide better performance when joined efficiently than when used separately [15]. A physical agent is thus capable of evolving at several predefined autonomy levels and switches levels according to the context. A level is defined by the complexity of the commands [8] or the ability to perform tasks without the need of operator's interventions [10]. The major limitation we can see in these approaches is the a priori definition of the levels, the static distribution of tasks among entities at each level, and the fact that the number of levels is necessarily limited. Interactions between the agent and the operator are thus restricted to a given set and are determined by autonomy levels, there is no possibility of fine dynamic task sharing.

To add more flexibility, [19] endow agents with learning capabilities based on Markov Decision Processes (MDP), allowing them to better manage the need for human intervention. Agents can define themselves their own autonomy levels, based on the user's provided intentions. However, this method does not seem directly applicable to critical systems, as the behaviour of learning agents facing unexpected situations is hard to validate. Moreover, it restricts the operator's interactions to the agent's needs.

Consequently the approach of [17] adds more human control on the agent: levels are not defined in a static way but come from a norm: permissions and restrictions describing the agent's behaviours are set by the operator. In order to do so, she/he has to create a complete set of rules, like « In case of medical emergency, consult the operator to choose landing location ». Some of the major issues associated with such an approach are the high number of rules to provide and then the risk of conflict between rules. The autonomy of the agent is anyway completely human-supervised and the agent has no possibility to adapt by itself.

Sliding autonomy [3] consists in determining whether a task should be executed by the agent alone or by the operator, using manual control; there is no direct reference to autonomy levels. Roles are not shared at the mission level, but are reconsidered for each action to realize. However, it seems there that the range of human-agent interactions is really restricted, as each task is performed either « completely autonomously » or « completely teleoperated ».

In contrast, collaborative control is an approach aiming at creating dialogs between the operator and the agent [9]: the agent sends requests to the human operator when problems occur, so that she/he can provide the needed support. This is again a restriction of all possible interactions: only dialog is used whatever the circumstances. In practice, almost all interactions are initiated by the agent's requests, and the operator acts almost exclusively as a support, she/he has not much initiative.

[21] have studied two authority sharing modes on a simulated space assembly task, SISA (System-Initiative Sliding Autonomy) where only the agent can request the operator's support, and MISA (Mixed-Initiative Sliding Autonomy), where the operator can also intervene anytime. The allocation between the agent and the operator is realized separately for each task, according to statistics to determine which entity will be the most efficient, which does not seem sufficient for a critical mission where errors are not tolerated. However, the sharing at the task level is an interesting idea, as it provides the most adaptive solution to the mission.

As shown by this literature review, it is often interesting to join human and machine abilities to carry out a mission, and adjustable autonomy seems a good principle. However, the fact that the human operator also is fallible is often neglected. While it is normal that the operator keeps the control of the agent, in most of the studies her/his input is not evaluated and accepted « as is » by the agent. Moreover, the simultaneous decisions and actions from an artificial agent and a human agent might create misunderstandings and lead to conflicts and dramatic situations [7].

1. Context of the study, hypotheses and objectives

We focus on the autonomy of artificial agents (e.g. unmanned vehicles, autopilots…) supervised by a human operator and achieving several goals for a given mission. Such agents evolve in a dynamic environment and face unexpected events. Consequently real-time reactions to these events in order to avoid dangerous situations and the loss of the agents themselves are compulsory. Additionally we consider systems where most of operational tasks can be associated with procedures, i.e. tasks must be executed in a precise order and respect strict constraints (as it is the case in aeronautics).

In an ideal context, the agents would be able to achieve their mission completely independently from the operator, a case that is hardly likely to occur in reality. This is however a necessary ability for the agents as communication breakdowns between the agents and the operator may occur during the mission. Beyond this extreme case, the agents may request the operator's help anytime for any task when an issue arises. However the operator her/himself is free to intervene at any stage of the mission in order to adjust the agents' behaviours according to her/his preferences, but also to correct their possible mistakes or improve their performance.

The focus is on obtaining the best possible performance for the global system resulting from the joint actions of the agents and of the human operator. The concept of performance is completely dependant on the mission type and therefore will not be addressed in this paper.

One of the main challenges is conflicts. The human operator's inputs may interfere with the agents' plans and break their consistency anytime, even if they are intended to improve the performance of a given task or correct an agent's mistake. But given the fact that an agent and the operator both have the possibility to directly execute actions, it is of first importance they remain coordinated so that they should not use the same resources at the same time for different purposes. For example, if the autopilot of a UAV and the operator simultaneously decide to move the vehicle in different directions, inconsistencies are very likely to appear in the flight of the vehicle and lead to an accident. Therefore conflicts must be detected and solved as soon as possible.

In order to detect conflicts, the intentions of all actors have to be clear or communicated to each other: mutual information is a key to avoid misunderstandings. While it is quite easy to access an agent's goals, it is much more difficult for an agent to know the operator's intentions. Regarding the operator, we consider her/him as a « black box », i.e. only her/his inputs in the system may provide information about her/his preferences and goals. Such inputs do not convey a direct meaning about the operator's goals, but this avoids making assumptions concerning the operator. However, as we focus on procedure-based systems, comparing the operator's inputs with known procedures brings some knowledge.

Finally our main objective can be summarized in the following question: why, when and how should an agent take initiative? When the environment has changed and the agent's plan needs to be updated? When the operator's inputs are inconsistent with the procedures (for instance with security constraints)? Or when they create conflicts with the system current goals?

2. Concepts and architecture

Mission decomposition and tasks

A mission consists in a set of high level goals the agents should reach. To do so, the agents will execute *tasks*, each task being supposed to provide an expected result while respecting some constraints (security, physical limits, authorizations, etc.). Each task that is executed uses and produces resources. A task can be decomposed into subtasks if necessary.

Planning and task allocation

Planning is one of the key tasks the agent should be able to execute. It lets the agent create structured lists of actions to perform, in order to achieve complex goals while satisfying the mission constraints. To do so, a model of the possible actions must be provided to coordinate them in a logical manner: for instance task B cannot be executed as long as task A is not completed, so the condition « done(task_A) » is a *precondition* (or: a *resource*) for task B.

As the agent has to react to unexpected events occurring during the mission, the plan of actions has to be continuously updated. This process is called replanning, and is a mandatory ability of the agent; in order to be useful, it also has to respect time constraints and be executed quickly.

Besides organizing the tasks that will be executed in a consistent manner, the planning process is also in charge of allocating them to the entities. For each individual task and depending on the current system situation, it assigns it either to one or several agents or to the operator. Among the considered criteria are global performance, safety, permissions and the operator's workload but also her /his situation awareness. Capacity models for each entity have to be provided in order to describe the nominal application conditions and a current estimation of the available resources for the tasks that each entity is likely to execute.

Situation Assessment

The situation assessment task [16] constantly analyzes the current state of the system; it compares the expected results of actions performed by the agents and the operator with the actual results and detects gaps that may appear. Moreover situation assessment estimates the possible future states of the system, according to the action plan and evolution models of the environment, of the system itself, and of all other relevant objects. This allows potentials conflicts to be detected.

A conflict represents a mismatch between a plan of actions and its execution. Unexpected events coming from the environment can make the plan outdated, this is a conflict with the environment. If the plan shows inconsistencies due to an input of the operator, this is a conflict between the agents and the operator.

A third objective of situation assessment is the recognition of procedures initiated by the operator. The only information about an operator's intentions is provided by her/his inputs into the system. However, if a pattern is recognized from these inputs and can be associated with one or several procedures known by the agents, this constitutes a valuable knowledge about the non-explicit goals of the operator and may contribute to anticipate her/his future actions.

Conflict solving

If conflicts that are likely to impact the mission are detected, they have to be solved. If several conflicts are detected simultaneously, they have to be prioritized according to the risk they involve.

The system is designed so that the agents adapt their behaviours thanks to the replanning process and task update. However, inconsistencies may appear as some goals or constraints may not be satisfied. Situation assessment points out the origin of the conflicts: unavailable resources, timeouts, contradictory goals, unsatisfied constraints... Therefore choices have to be made among the tasks and goals according to the involved risks and according to who (an agent or the operator) will be able to achieve them safely. This is one of the key points of authority sharing and adaptive autonomy: task reallocation for the best possible mission achievement, under the requirement that each agent and operator within the system is aware of this reallocation and of its outcome on the mission.

3. Basic concepts

In order to deal with shared authority and adaptive autonomy in an operational way, the basic concepts of a mission performed by physical agents and operators have to be considered. Indeed sharing authority among different entities and adapting autonomy dynamically during a mission will amount to reconsider task allocation and goal achievement, and to deal with the available resources within the system.

Context

A mission carried out by one or several unmanned vehicles monitored by one or several human operators.

System

The set of all vehicles and operators.

Agents

Let $\mathcal{A}$ be the set of all agents in the system. An agent $a \in \mathcal{A}$ is a vehicle or an operator. If the specificity of the operator is important, she/he will be referred to as a « human agent ».

Goals

Let $\mathcal{G}$ be the set of the mission goals. A goal is a state of the world the system tries to reach to fulfil its mission.

A goal is written: $g = <$ *goal, source* $>$, $g \in \mathcal{G}$
with *goal*: the goal itself;
and *source*: the origin of the goal (see definition below).

Constraints

Let $\mathcal{C}$ be the set of all the constraints. A constraint is a limit on the consumption of a resource, a state of the world to avoid or respect, etc.

A constraint is written: $c = <$ *constraint, flexibility, source* $>$, $c \in \mathcal{C}$
with *constraint*: the constraint itself;
flexibility: an information about the tolerance associated with the constraint;
and *source*: the origin of the constraint (see definition below).

Resources

Let $\mathcal{R}$ be the set of all possible resources. A resource represents a precondition for the execution of a task. Resources can be physical objects, energy, time, permissions, pieces of information, tasks, capacities, logical conditions... The set of all available resources for an agent at time t is written $\mathcal{R}_{avail}(t)$.

A resource is written:

$r = < resource, type, time - interval, source >, r \in \mathcal{R}$

with *resource*: the resource itself;

type: the characteristics of the resource (physical object or not, renewable or not, shareable, etc.);

time - interval $= [t_{start}, t_{end}]$: the time interval that defines the existence of the resource. The resource exists only between the times t_{start} and t_{end};

and *source*: the origin of the resource (see definition below).

Source

A source informs about the origin of a goal, a constraint or a resource.

A source is written: *source* $= < agent, task, t_{prod} >$

with *agent* the producing agent;

task the producing task;

and t_{prod} the production time.

Tasks

A task $\tau \in \mathcal{R}$ is a resource carrying out a function transforming resources to produce other resources, in order to reach a subset of goals $\mathcal{G}_\tau$ while satisfying a subset of constraints C_τ:

$\tau : \mathcal{P}(\mathcal{R}) \rightarrow \mathcal{P}(\mathcal{R})$ so that $\tau_{\mathcal{G}_\tau, C_\tau}(\mathcal{R}_\tau^{cons}) = \mathcal{R}_\tau^{prod}$

with $\mathcal{R}_\tau^{cons} \subseteq \mathcal{R}$ the resources used by τ;

$\mathcal{G}_\tau \subseteq \mathcal{G}$ the subset of goals the task τ aims to reach;

$C_\tau \subseteq C$ the subset of constraints τ must satisfy;

and $\mathcal{R}_\tau^{prod} \subseteq \mathcal{R}$ the resources produced by τ.

Planning

From high level goals and constraints, the planning task creates a structured list of tasks and subtasks, associates them with (sub)goals, (sub)constraints and resources and allocates them to agents. Based on task models, the resulting plan must be consistent (i.e. without any conflict) and is designed to satisfy the mission objectives. The plan encompasses all the tasks that will be executed by all the entities within the system (agents and human agents).

Situation assessment and the consequences of event

Let e be an event detected by an agent, either an event coming from the environment (or from the system itself, e.g. a failure) or an interaction initiated by the operator.

Let *conflict* be a gap between the plan and its (anticipated) execution detected by the situation assessment function:

conflict $= < object, t_{event}, t_{max} >$,

with *object* the violated constraint or the non-reached goal;

t_{event} the estimated occurrence time of the problem;

and t_{max} the maximal estimated deadline to react and solve the conflict.

When event e occurs, the situation assessment function estimates its consequences on all items within the system:

$$Conseq(e) = < \Delta \mathcal{G}_e, \Delta \mathcal{C}_e, \Delta \mathcal{R}_e, Conflicts_e >,$$

with $\Delta \mathcal{G}_e$ the affected goals of the mission;

$\Delta \mathcal{C}_e$ the affected constraints;

$\Delta \mathcal{R}_e$ the affected resources;

and $Conflicts_e$ the set of all conflicts generated by event e (it is of course possible that $Conflicts_e = \emptyset$). $Conflicts_e$ can be divided into

$< Conflicts_e^{\mathcal{G}}, Conflicts_e^{\mathcal{C}}, Conflicts_e^{\mathcal{R}} >$, respectively the conflicts about goals, constraints and resources.

When an event e generates a conflict, this conflict affects some goals, constraints and resources. As the sources of goals, constraints and resources are known, the conflict can be further identified as an intra-source conflict – e.g. a conflict between several contraints within an agent – or a inter-source conflict – e.g. a conflict involving an agent and the operator. The former case will trigger replanning whereas the latter is likely to involve a new sharing between the involved parties.

4. Future work and Conclusion

We have presented the general principles and some basic concepts for an approach of operational adaptive autonomy. Using situation assessment as a conflict detector within the system (agents + operator) or between the system and the environment, it is possible to identify the key elements of the conflicts so as to solve them in a relevant manner. This is indeed the very basis of dynamic shared authority or adaptive autonomy, i.e. reallocating tasks within the system so that conflicts should be solved safely with every entity being aware of what is being performed.

Task reallocation will take into account the current capacities of the agents and operators, the operators' desires, the constraints of the mission constraints, the priorities of the goals. Early conflict detection will allow agents to adapt their behaviours to the estimated operator's intentions as long as main constraints and objectives are respected, therefore improving the overall system performance. However, whether the operator intervenes or not, the agents are still expected to have the means to react "alone" to key issues.

Another aspect of adaptive autonomy is the fact that agents should be able to alleviate the operator's workload, e.g. relieving her/him of routine tasks and let her/him focus on key tasks of the mission. Again this is based on mutual situation monitoring and assessment and a better allocation of tasks and resources within the system when the context changes.

Current work focuses on a formal definition of mission execution, with the dynamic aspects of the basic concepts we have defined: goals, resources, constraints, tasks and on fine identification of what precisely is involved in task reallocation. At the same time experiments with several Emaxx UGVs (Unmanned Ground Vehicles) will be prepared at ISAE to assess our concepts for adaptive autonomy in real conditions. Reliability, overall performance and the operator's satisfaction will be among the observed criteria.

References

[1] J.M. Bradshaw, M. Sierhuis, A. Acquisti, R. Feltovich, R. Hoffman, R. Jeffers, D. Prescott, N. Suri, A. Uszok & R. Van Hoof. Adjustable autonomy and human-agent teamwork in practice : An interim report on space application. In *Agent Autonomy* [13], chapter 11.

[2] S. Brainov & H. Hexmoor. Quantifying Relative Autonomy in Multiagent Interaction. In *Agent Autonomy* [13], chapter 4.

[3] J. Brookshire, S. Singh, R. Simmons. Preliminary Results in Sliding Autonomy for Coordinated Teams. In *Proceedings of the AAAI'04 Spring Symposium*, Stanford, CA, 2004.

[4] C. Carabelea. and O. Boissier, Coordinating agents in organizations using social commitments, Electronic Notes in *Theoretical Computer Science* (Volume 150, Issue 3). Elsevier, 2006.

[5] C. Castelfranchi & R. Falcone. From Automaticity to Autonomy: the Frontier of Artificial Agents. In *Agent Autonomy* [13], chapter 6.

[6] B. T. Clough. Metrics, Schmetrics! How The Heck Do You Determine A UAV's Autonomy Anyway? In *Proceedings of the Performance Metrics for Intelligent Systems Workshop*, Gaithersburg, Marylan, 2002.

[7] F. Dehais, A. Goudou, C. Lesire, C. Tessier. Towards an anticipatory agent to help pilots. In *Proceedings of the AAAI 2005 Fall Symposium "From Reactive to Anticipatory Cognitive Embodied Systems"*, Arlington, Virginia, 2005.

[8] G. Dorais, P. Bonasso, D. Kortenkamp, B. Pell & D. Schreckenghost. Adjustable autonomy for human-centered autonomous systems. In *Proceedings of IJCAI'99. Workshop on Adjustable Autonomy Systems*, Stockholm, Sweden, 1999.

[9] T.W. Fong, Ch. Thorpe & Ch. Baur. Collaboration, dialogue and human-robot interaction. In *Proceedings of the 10th International Symposium on Robotics Research*, Lorne, Victoria, Australia, 2002.

[10] M. Goodrich, R. Olsen Jr., J. Crandall & T. Palmer. Experiments in Adjustable Autonomy. In *Proceedings of the IJCAI 01 Workshop on Autonomy, Delegation, and Control: Interacting with Autonomous Agents*. Seattle, WA, Menlo Park, CA: AAAI Press, 2001.

[11] M. Goodrich, T. McLain, J. Crandall, J. Anderson & J. Sun. Managing Autonomy in Robot Teams: Observations from four Experiments. In *Proceeding of the ACM/IEEE international conference on Human-robot interaction*, 2007.

[12] B. Hasslacher & M. W. Tilden. Living Machines. Los Alamos National Laboratory, 1995.

[13] H. Hexmoor, C. Castelfranchi & R. Falcone. *Agent autonomy*. Kluwer Academic Publishers, 2003.

[14] H. Huang, K. Pavek, B. Novak, J. Albus & E. Messin. A Framework For Autonomy Levels For Unmanned Systems (ALFUS). In *Proceedings of the AUVSI's Unmanned Systems North America 2005*, Baltimore, Maryland, June 2005.

[15] D. Kortenkamp, P. Bonasso, D. Ryan & D. Schreckenghost. Traded control with autonomous robots as mixed initiative interaction. In *AAAI-97 Spring Symposium on Mixed Initiative Interaction*, March 1997.

[16] C. Lesire, C. Tessier. A hybrid model for situation monitoring and conflict prediction in human supervised "autonomous" systems. In *Proceedings of the AAAI 2006 Spring Symposium "To Boldly Go Where No Human-Robot Team Has Gone Before"*. Stanford, California, 2006.

[17] K. Myers & D. Morley. Human directability of agents. In *K-CAP 2001, 1st International Conference on Knowledge Capture*, Victoria, Canada, 2001.

[18] R. Parasuraman, T.B. Sheridan, C.D. Wickens. A Model for Types and Levels of Human Interaction with Automation. *Systems, Man and Cybernetics, Part A, IEEE Transactions* on 30 (3), 286-297, 2000

[19] P. Scerri, D. Pynadath & M. Tambe. Adjustable Autonomy for the Real World. In *Agent Autonomy* [13], chapter 10.

[20] D. Schreckenghost, D. Ryan, C. Thronesbery, P. Bonasso & D. Poirot. Intelligent control of life support systems for space habitat. In *Proceedings of the AAAI-IAAI Conference*, July 1998.

[21] B. Sellner, F. Heger, L. Hiatt, R. Simmons & S. Singh. Coordinated Multi-Agent Teams and Sliding Autonomy for Large-Scale Assembly. In *Proceeding of the IEEE*, 94(7), 2006.

[22] T.B. Sheridan & W.L. Verplank. Human and Computer Control of Undersea Teleoperators. *Technical Report*, MIT Man-Machine Systems Laboratory,Ca.

Collaborative Decision Making: Perspectives and Challenges
P. Zaraté et al. (Eds.)
IOS Press, 2008

Negotiation Process for Multi-Agent DSS for Manufacturing System

Noria Taghezout[a], Pascale Zaraté[b]

A : Université d'Oran, taghezoutnour@yahoo.fr
B : Université de Toulouse, INPT-IRIT, zarate@irit.fr

Abstract. Agents and multi-agent systems constitute nowadays a very active field of research. This field is very multidisciplinary since it is sustained by Artificial Intelligence, Distributed Systems, Software Engineering, etc. In most agent applications, the autonomous components need to interact. They need to communicate in order to solve differences of opinion and conflicts of interest. They also need to work together or simply inform each other. It is however important to note that a lot of existing works do not take into account the agents' preferences. In addition, individual decisions in the multi-agent domain are rarely sufficient for producing optimal plans which satisfy all the goals. Therefore, agents need to cooperate to generate the best multi-agent plan through sharing tentative solutions, exchanging sub goals, or having other agents' goals to satisfy. In this paper, we propose a new negotiation mechanism independent of the domain properties in order to handle real-time goals. The mechanism is based on the well-known Contract net Protocol. Integrated Station of Production agents will be equipped with a sufficient behavior to carry out practical operations and simultaneously react to the complex problems caused by the dynamic scheduling in real situations. These agents express their preferences by using ELECTRE III method in order to solve differences. The approach is tested through simple scenarios.

Keywords. Multi agent System, Negotiation, Decision Support System (DSS), ISP (Integrated Station of Production), Dynamic scheduling, ELECTRE III.

Introduction

Software architectures contain many dynamically interacting components; each of them having their own thread of control, and engagement in complex, coordinated protocols. They typically have orders of magnitude which are more correctly and efficiently complex than those that simply compute a function of some input through a single thread of control.

As a consequence, a major research topic in computer science over the past two decades has been the development of tools and techniques for understand, modelling and implement systems for which interaction is essential.

Recently, agent technology has been considered as an important approach for developing industrial distributed systems. It has particularly been recognized as a promising paradigm for next generation manufacturing systems [1].

[2] develop a collaborative framework of a distributed agent-based intelligence system with a two-stage decision-making process for dynamic scheduling. Many features characterize the framework; more precisely, the two stages of the decision-

making process are the following: the fuzzy decision-making process and the compensatory negotiation process which are adequate for distributed participants to deal with imprecise and subjective information, to conduct practical operations.

In [3], the authors present a multi agent system that is an implementation of a distributed project management tool. Activities, resources, and important functions are represented as agents in a network. They present methods to schedule activities and resolve resource conflicts by message exchanging and negotiation among agents [3].

The work presented in [4] uses an architecture called PABADIS to model a distributed manufacturing system. Basic components in PABADIS are seen as agents and services; they work in cooperation and perform distributed tasks in a networked manufacturing plant.

In distributed intelligent manufacturing systems, agents can be applied and implemented in different ways; the most interesting points for our study are the following (see [1]):

Agents can be used to encapsulate manufacturing activities in a distributed environment by using a functional decomposition approach. Such functional agents include order processing, product design, production planning and scheduling and simulation.

Agents can be used to represent negotiation partners, either physical plants or virtual players; they also can be used to implement special services in multi agent systems like facilitators and mediators.

However, in the multi-agent domain individual decisions are rarely sufficient for producing optimal plans for satisfying all the goals. Therefore, agents need to cooperate to generate the best multi-agent plan through sharing tentative solutions, exchanging sub goals, or having other agents' goals to satisfy.

The potential for an increased role of Multi Agent System (MAS) for scheduling problems provides a very persuasive reason for our work. This approach can not only solve real time scheduling problems but it also offers the possibility to develop models for decision making processes by giving to the negotiation agents decision-making capacities in order to solve most of the conflict situations.

In order to achieve these goals, we propose a negotiation mechanism based on multi-agent system for complex manufacturing systems. The proposed approach uses a negotiation protocol where agents propose bids for requests. The bids may also include counter proposals and counter requests.

In order to implement Decision Making abilities, the Electre III methodology is chosen for the possibility given to decision makers to treat imprecise and subjective data [5]. The Contract Net Protocol is used because of its facility to implement negotiation protocols. Integrated Station of Production (ISP) agents are equipped with a sufficient behavior to carry out practical operations and simultaneously react to the complex problems caused by the dynamic scheduling in real situations. The unique property of this approach is that the problem resolution consists in two steps; the first one determines which behaviour is adopted by an agent if an unexpected event occurs, then during the second step the contract net protocol negotiation is opened among the agents to solve dynamic scheduling problem.

The paper is organized as follows: The DSS architecture and the main agents are described in Section 1; In Section 2, we present the negotiation protocol and its facilitating techniques; Section 3 is devoted to the integration of the multicriteria method ELECTRE III in the decision-making processes implemented in the internal structure of the negotiation agent; a scenario is described; Finally Section 4 concludes the paper.

1 Multi Agent Structure of Hybrid Piloting

Many algorithms are involved in distributed manufacturing control system. They are intended to enable a better understanding and consistent design of the new agents technology based paradigms; they also enabled to design and enhance the reasoning and decision-making capabilities to be introduced at agent level.

1.1 Agent – Based Scheduling In Manufacturing Systems

[4] identify two types of distributed manufacturing scheduling systems :
Those where scheduling is an incremental search process that can involve backtracking.
Systems in which an agent represents a single resource (e.g. a work cell, a machine, a tool, a fixture, a worker, etc.) and is responsible for scheduling this resource. This agent may negotiate with other agents how to carry out the overall scheduling.
At least we can mention some production systems where the scheduling is completely distributed and organized locally at a product level. Under this condition, a local and simplified scheduling is performed by such an agent to accomplish a limited set of tasks with some dedicated resources, along its production life cycle.

1.2 The Proposed Approach

Decision support system was designed to solve ill or non-structured decision problems [4], [6]. Problems where priorities, judgments, intuitions and experience of the decision maker are essential, where the sequence of operations such as solution searching, problem formalization and structuring is not beforehand known, when the criteria for the decision making are numerous and the resolution must be acquired at restricted or fixed time.
In the resolution of real time production management problems, each decision-making process of piloting is generally a multicriteria process [7]: the task assignment for example, is a decision-making process which results from a study on criteria of costs production, time of series change, convoying time, production quality, etc.
The multicriteria methodology exploitation allows integrating the set of these constraints, in particular by the fact that the assumptions, on which the latter are based, are closer to reality than optimization methods. In addition, the multicriteria approach facilitates the integration of human operator to DSS.
In real time production management, the DSS memorizes the current state-of the workshop. It knows constantly all possible decisions and the possible events involved. A detailed description of the workshop's state was given in our previous work [8]. We distinguish 3 contexts for the decision-making aid: (1) Decision-making aid in the context of an acceptable sequence; (2) Assistance for the admissibility covering; and (3) Negotiation support among different decision-making centres in a dynamic context.
The proposed DSS gives the decision centers the opportunity to make decisions in a dynamical context. A decision aid is then improved by a negotiation support. The

system suggests the selected decision in the set of planned solutions. As a conclusion, the proposed DSS in this approach addresses the situations described in levels 1 and 3.

The DSS architecture is composed of several modules. Each module has its own functionalities and objectives. The DSS architecture is described in Figure 1.

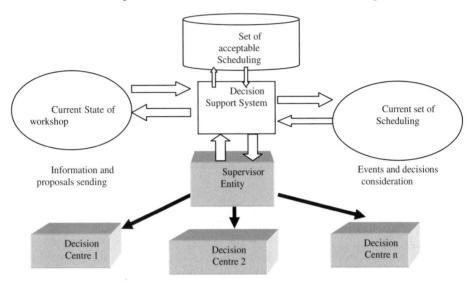

Figure 1. DSS Architecture

The analysis and reaction module is developed thanks to a multi-agent technology. The agent based system is decomposed into a supervisor agent and several ISP agents. Each ISP agent has the possibility to use resources. A detailed description is given in [7] and [8].

1.2.1 Supervisor Agent

The supervisor agent is composed by several modules.

Analysis and Reaction Module: This module performs a continuous analysis of messages which is accepted by the agent supervisor, across its communication interface. And, it activates the behaviours which correspond to them. It also updates the states of operations in the total agenda due to the messages sent by the ISP agents.

The Behaviours: In order to fulfil its task the entity supervisor has a set of behaviours implemented.

The First supervisor agent behaviour: is used to search the most satisfying resource for the production objectives and aims to seek the best agent of substitution for a reassignment operation (in the event of a local reassignment failure). Independently of the behaviours a global agenda must be found

The total agenda: This agenda allows the supervisor to represent and follow the evolution of all the tasks in the system. This agenda also allows reconstructing information of any local agenda in an ISP.

The communication interface: This module manages the messages in transit between the agent supervisor and all the other agents of the system.

The real time clock: It generates the time.

1.2.2 An ISP Agent

Each ISP agents are also composed by several modules and is described in figure 2.

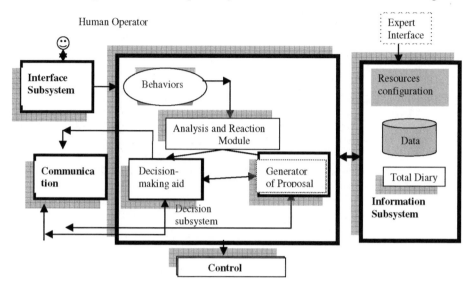

Figure 2. Architecture of the Negotiation Agent (ISP)

Analysis and Reaction Module: It constantly analyses the messages received by the ISP agent, across its communication interface, and activates the behaviours corresponding to the events received. So, the state of operations is updated.

The Behaviours: Three behaviours are implemented.

The First ISP agent behavior aims to manage the queue of the agent and select the next operation to be carried out. The Second ISP behavior corresponds to the allocation process and aims to search for the next best production agent to treat the following operation of the current work. The Third ISP behavior allows the search for a substitution machine among those that it controls (the best). This behavior is developed for reassigning operations which follow a failure.

The Local Agenda

The agenda, a form of representation of any ISP engagements obeys the following rules:

At each beginning of execution of an operation, the ISP agent registers in its agenda the beginning of this operation which it signals to the supervisor. At each end of an operation, the ISP agent registers in its agenda the end of this operation which it signals to the supervisor.

Interface Expert: allows to the human operator to consult and modify the ISP agent configuration, to know the present state of resources and follow the evolution of production activity.

The Communication Interface

This module allows the management of messages in transit between ISP agent and the other entities of the system.

The Real Time Clock

It generates the real time factor in the ISP agent.

Each negotiating agent gives to decision subsystems additional models such as:

The proposal generator constructs a proposal for a given task according to the initial parameters and the user's preference and interest. A proposal indicates a definite value for each negotiation attribute.

The decision making aid is applied when each agent evaluates the alternative solutions using a multi-criterion decision making technique. In our system, Electre III is used for this purpose. It considers all related attributes of the given task and gives a utility assessment to represent the satisfaction level of a proposal.

1.2.3 The Coordinator Agent

The coordinator agent, in our system, exchanges plan information with task agents to help them to coordinate their actions.

The coordinator agent provides two services to task agents:

It computes summary information for hierarchical plans submitted by the task agents, and,

It coordinates hierarchical plans using summary information.

This proposed architecture is described in Figure 3.

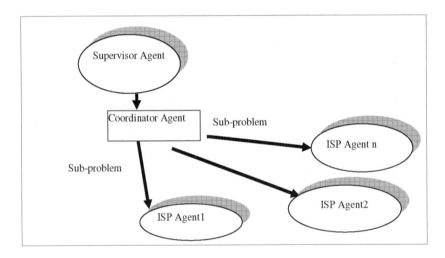

Figure 3. Architecture of the Coordinator Agent

The coordinator agent includes several types of functional modules such as: the task generation module, configuration module, a database and an interface. The generating task module is the core of this architecture; its role is to break up a complex problem into sub-problems. Through its participation, it offers a valuable assistance to the supervisory agent. It reduces its function of handling a problem which has occurred during the production. The coordinator agent analyzes the input events and assigns tasks to ISP agents in order to solve the events. The configuration module allows carrying out relevantly the distribution of sub-problem to the set of ISP entities taking into account all the data and parameters on the tasks (data resulted from the problem formulation phase).

The configuration module ensures the management of multiple negotiation steps and synchronizes the various obtained results. Finally the interface module manages the information exchanges between the agent coordinator and the other agents. The structure of this coordinator agent is described in the figure 4.

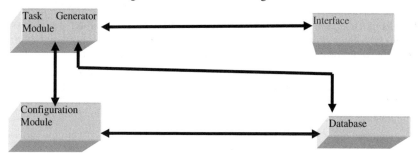

Figure 4. The coordinator agent structure

2 Decision Making Structure And Negotiation Protocol

The decision-making process is divided into two steps:

1. For the first step, ISP agents recognize the encountered problems, and start the local decision-making processes. In case of success, they adopt the adequate behaviors. The basic principle of resolution has been described in [8].

2. For the second step, ISP agents open negotiation after delays in the planned task execution or a conflicting situation causing a failure in the complex problem resolution.

The protocol is based on the classical contract Net approach. ISP agents express their initial preferences, priorities and data in the evaluation matrices. The decisional processes use the multicriterion assistance methodology, ELECTRE III. ISP agents could play several roles:

• An ISP agent, which meets the problem during its task execution, should make a decision in collaboration with other ISP agents; it is called the initiating ISP agent and is noted as IISP (Initiating Integrated Station Production).

• An ISP agent, which undergoes the delay consequences or disturbance in its task execution because of a conflict on the common resource or another unpredicted event, is called participating ISP agent and is noted as PISP (participating ISP).

The negotiation protocol is then organised as follows.

In multi-agent systems, negotiation is a key form of interaction that allows a group of agents to reach mutual agreement regarding their beliefs, goals, or plans [9]. It is the predominant tool for solving conflicts of interests. The area of negotiation is broad and is suitable for use in different scenarios [10]. [11] identifies three broad and fundamental topics, negotiation protocols, objects, and strategies, for research on negotiation.

Generally speaking, the outcome of a negotiation depends on many parameters-including the agent's preferences, their reservation limits, their attitude toward time and the strategies they used.

Although in most realistic situations it is not possible for agents to have complete information about each of these parameters for its opponent, it is not uncommon for agents to have partial information about some of them. The purpose of our study is not to allow the agent selecting the optimal strategy (see for example for this kind of situations [12]), but it helps to partially treat uncertainty.

2.1 Contract Net and Negotiation Policy

The contract Net protocol is a model for which only the manager emits propositions. The contractors only can make an offer but not counter-propositions. On the other hand, our proposition includes a process to consider the opinion of contractors, in order to find more quickly a common accepted solution [13] [14].

When a task (problem) comes to the negotiation agent coordinator, it is decomposed into subtasks (sub-problems). Subsequently, the coordinator invites potential ISP agents which possess the ability to solve the problem. Meanwhile, ISP agent analyzes the tasks and accordingly prepares bids.

2.2 Conversations

The negotiation protocol defines the interactions and rules between ISP agents in the negotiation process. The used protocol [15] is represented as a sequence diagram of the agent unified modeling language (AUML) as shown in Figure 5.

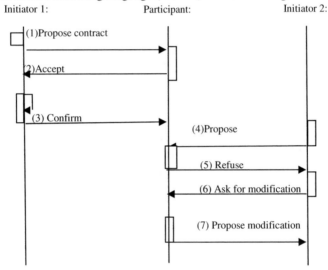

Figure 5. Common negotiation including conflict graph

3 Decision Aid Through ELECTRE III

Decision Making is a complex process due to several factors such as information incompleteness, imprecision, and subjectivity which are always present in real life situations at a lesser or greater degree [15]. The multicriteria methodology Electre III allows sorting out actions likely to solve a decision problem, on the basis of several alternatives on several criteria [5].

3.1 The negotiation model proposal

During the second stage of resource allocation, the IISP agent will open negotiation with PISP agent which is concerned with the result of ELECTRE III execution. This one must search the best resource. The framework of the negotiation model is depicted in Figure 6. It consists in various components such as:

The alternatives: This component gathers all resources classified from the best to the less good according to the sorting out performed by ELECTRE III. It corresponds to the multicriteria decision-making process application solving the problem of allocation of the best resource in case of breakdowns.

Criteria updating: Each agent is equipped with a module allowing at any time the calculation of the cost production function.

Selection function: Each negotiation agent possesses a selection function in order to evaluate the proposals and counter-proposals.

Each negotiation agent needs to consult the supervisor diary to know the state of execution of the activities of each agent ISP. Agents execute the method ELECTRE III before making their strategic and/or tactical decisions.

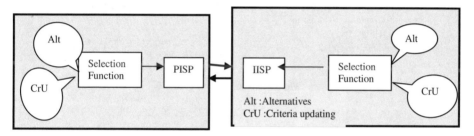

Figure 6. A general view of the negotiation agent strategy

3.2 List of selected criteria

The most relevant criteria in our study are given in Table1 (for more details about these criteria see [16]).

1. Code indicator	2. Entitled	3. Signification Axe	4. Min/Max
C1	Production cost	Cost	Min
C2	Time of a resource preparation of an operation	Delay	Min
C3	Potential Transfer Time	Delay	Min
C4	Next date of availability	Delay	Min
C5	Machine reliability indicator	Delay	Max
C6	Attrition rate	Quality	Max
C7	Characteristic tool	Quality	Max
C8	Level of specialization	Quality	Max

Table 1. List of selected criteria for assignment problems

A failure or a breakdown event is defined by the following items in Figure 7. and Figure 8.

```
{
    int r=0;
    DefaultListModel v3=new  DefaultListModel();    // Liste virtuelle
    v3.removeAllElements();
    String text=jList1.getSelectedValue().toString();
    for(int z=0;z<pfe.Cadre1.jdbTable5.getRowCount();z++)
    {
      if (pfe.Cadre1.jdbTable5.getValueAt(z, 3).equals(text))
      {
        ex Ba1 = new ex(false, n1); // Création d'objet : JProgressBar ; ex : classe
        d'exécution de JProgressBar
      Ba1.setBounds(new Rectangle(12, 9, 484, 28));    // Bordure de JProgressBar
        v3.addElement(pfe.Cadre1.jdbTable5.getValueAt(z, 0).toString());
        jdbTextArea1.append(" tâche 1 : Stop    :" +n1+"%"+ "\n"); //Affichage du
        pourcentage de la panne.
        tab[r][0]=T1;
        tab[r][1]=jLabel12.getText().toString();
        break;        }     }}
```

Figure 7. A breakdown event

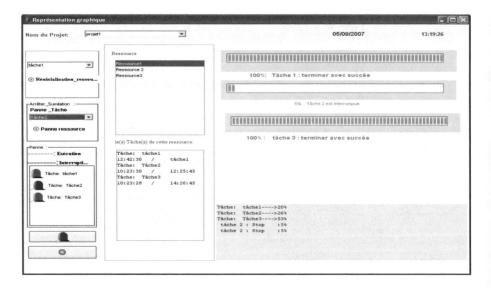

Figure 8. A breakdown event

In order to implement our protocol, Java is chosen as programming language because this programming language can maintain a high degree of openness and flexibility.

Scenario: Breakdown of a Resource

1. Resource n°1 controlled by agent 3 breaks down. The analysis and reaction module discerns this event and triggers off the associated behavior; if the process fails; ISP agent n°3 re-redirects the re-assignment request to the supervisor. This triggers off behavior named as the second behavior at the supervisor level.

2. The agent supervisor transmits the request towards other ISP agents (ISP 1, ISP 2) and treats the received answers to choose the best substitution machine.

3. The result will be announced to the chosen ISP agent as well as to the ISP agent applicant.

4. The ISP1 Agent answers favorably to the supervisor request (end of the first phase of the decision-making process).

5. The required resource is also programmed for the ISP4 agent according to the initial production planning, ISP3 and ISP4 agents are found in a conflicting situation.

6. The negotiation is then open: ISP3 agent becomes ISSP and ISP4 agent becomes PISP.

7. IISP agent activates the proposal generator, and formulates a new contract proposal. It sends the latter to PISP agent.

8. The agent formulates its contract, evaluates the received proposals simultaneously thanks to the set of preferences and priorities, initially contained in the evaluation matrix (the decision-making module presented in Figure 2 intervenes in the realization of this step). The proposal or counter-proposal evaluation is made by ELECTRE III.

4 Conclusions and Future Work

In this paper, we addressed an agent architecture-based model in order to present a multicriteria DSS which can be applied to solve some uncertainty problems in dynamic production system scheduling. The established negotiation contract thus deals with certain exceptions; it is based on the agent approach. The major advantage with this modeling paradigm consists in facilitating access to the executed tasks carried out by entities ISP. ELECTRE III is a tool that allows learning information about the opponent's preferences and their relative weights.

In our approach, we use the Contract Net Protocol for its advantage to be a dynamic and easy to implement algorithm.

One perspective of this work is to develop and extend the model for agents that could change their goals according for example new information that they receive. For these reasons, we aim developing an argumentation based strategy of negotiation; it will be more flexible than the contract net protocol but requires a greater reasoning mechanism incorporated in the agents for more details we will see [17]). The main effort will be then investigated in comparing the results.

The proposed architecture of the DSS is under development. One of our perspectives is to completely implement it, test it in a manufacturing industry in order to obtain feedback on the usability of the developed system.

References

[1] W. Shen, H.-J. Yoon, D.-H. Norrie : Applications of agent-based systems in intelligent manufacturing : An updated review, *Advanced engineering INFORMATICS* (2006), 415-431.

[2] Y.-M. Chen, S.-C. Wang : Framework of agent-based intelligence system with two stage decision making process for distributed dynamic scheduling, *Applied Soft Computing* (2005), 229-245.

[3] Y. Yan, T. Kuphal, J. Bode : Application of multi agent systems project management, *International Journal of Production economics 68* (2000), 185-197.

[4] J. Reaidy, P. Massote, D. Diep : Comparison of Negotiation protocols in dynamic agent-based manufacturing Systems, *International Journal of Production Economics* 99 (26) (2007), 117-130.

[5] B. Roy, D. Bouyssou, *Aide Multicritère d'Aide à la Décision,* Economica, Paris, 1993.

[6] A. Adla : A Cooperative Intelligent Decision Support System for Contingency Management, *Journal of Computer Science 2 (10), ISSN 1549-3636* (2006), 758-764.

[7] N. Taghezout : Expérimentation et Intégration de la méthode Electre I dans un système d'aide à la décision appliqué aux SAP, *SNIB'06, 5eme Séminaire National en informatique de Biskra, Vol.1* (2006), 196-206.

[8] N. Taghezout, P. Zaraté : A Multi agent Decision Support System For Real Time Scheduling, *The 4th International Workshop on Computer Supported Activity Coordination* (CSAC) Funchal, Madeira, Portugal, 12-13 June (2007), 55-65.

[9] Lin., Fu-ren : Integrating multi-agent negotiation to resolve constraints in fulfilling supply chain orders, *Electronic commerce research and applications journal* (2006), 313-322.

[10] J. Tian, H. Tianfield : Literature Review Upon Multi-agent Supply Chain Management, *Proceeding of the Fifth International Conference on machine Learning and Cybernetics*, Dalian (2006), 89-94.

[11] M. Beer, M. D'iverno, N. Jennings, C. Preist : Negotiation in Multi-Agent Systems, *Knowledge Engineering Review* 14(3) (1999), 285-289.

[12] S.F. Shaheen, M. Wooldridge, N. Jennings : Optimal Negotiation Strategies for Agents with Incomplete Information, The 8*th International Workshop on Intelligent Agents VIII* (2001), 377-392.

[13] M.-H. Verrons, *GeNCA : un modèle général de négociation de contrats entre agents*, Thesis Université des Sciences et Technologies de Lille, 2004.

[14] D. Randall, S. Reid : Negotiation as a Metaphor for Distributed Problem Solving in Communications, *Multiagent Systems, LNAI 2650* (2003), 51-97.

[15] N. Taghezout, A. Riad, A., K. Bouamrane : Negotiation Strategy For a Distributed Resolution of Real Time Production Management Problems, *ACIT*, 26-28 Nov 2007 LATTAKIA SYRIA (2007), 367-374.

[16] W. Shen : Distributed manufacturing scheduling using intelligent agents, *IEEE Intelligent Systems 17 (1)* (2002), 88-94.

[17] F. Kebair, F. Serin : Multiagent Approach for the Representation of Information in a Decision Support System, *AIMSA 2006, LNAI 4183* (2006), 99-107.

Collaborative Decision Making: Perspectives and Challenges
P. Zaraté et al. (Eds.)
IOS Press, 2008

Model Inspection in Dicodess

Matthias BUCHS and Pius HÄTTENSCHWILER

Departement of Informatics, University of Fribourg, Switzerland

Abstract. Dicodess is a model based distributed cooperative decision support system. It encapsulates the underlying model in a graphical user interface to shield users from the technical details of model configuration and optimization. However, a model usually evolves over time and therefore needs verification accordingly. Furthermore, users sometimes might want to have a better insight into the model to better understand a "strange" solution. Model views are a new concept for modeling language and domain independent model visualization. The focus is not on visualizing model input or model output but on the model's structure, the formalized knowledge. Modelers as well as domain experts are able to inspect a model visually in order to get a better understanding and to have a common base of discussion. The improvement of model understanding and communication among the people involved will lead to models of better quality. In this article we are proposing an integration of model views into Dicodess. This integration enables mutual benefit: Dicodess users get direct access to model visualization which through Dicodess' cooperative functionality can be done even in collaboration.

Keywords. optimization model visualization, distributed cooperative decision support, Dicodess

Introduction

Decision support systems (DSS) assist a user in making decisions in a potentially complex environment. Most of these systems shield the user from the technical details (models, documents, data etc.) that lie behind the user interface. In some cases however it would be very useful to know these details to get a better understanding of the system's behavior. In the concrete case of a model based DSS it would sometimes be helpful to know how something has been modeled. In this article we will present the integration of model inspection and visualization functionality into Dicodess, a model based DSS, and how the system's collaboration aids further enhance model understanding.

Section 1 introduces the concepts and principles of the Distributed Cooperative Decision Support System (Dicodess). Section 2 gives a short introduction into our concepts of model inspection. Finally, Section 3 details how the model inspection concepts could be integrated into Dicodess for collaborative model visualization in the context of decision support.

1. Dicodess

Dicodess is a framework for building model based distributed cooperative decision support systems. Section 1.1 presents the underlying principles that need to be understood when dealing with Dicodess. Section 1.2 will then discuss collaboration when using the software. The interested reader may get more information about Dicodess at [1,2].

1.1. Principles

Dicodess encapsulates the underlying mathematical model into a graphical user interface (GUI) which spares the user from the technical details of a modeling language. By doing manipulations in the GUI the user actually specifies and finally generates a complete decision support model. This process is called *structuring semi-structured problems*. Figure 1 shows the abstractions Dicodess uses to support the process.

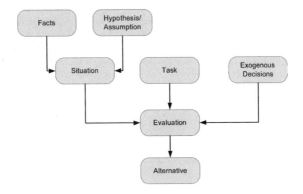

Figure 1. Abstraction of the decision process.

To structure a problem completely three things need to be specified: The situation (which is based on facts, but could also comprise hypotheses and assumptions), the task (which can be influenced by the problem statement) and exogenous decisions (which are dependent on external constraints like the decision maker's will or some law). Dicodess uses *distributed decision support objects* (DDSO) to represent among other things the elements described above. These pieces of knowledge are mostly independent, reusable and exchangeable. They can be managed (created, edited, exchanged, deleted, reused, combined etc.) separately by their respective object manager. Figure 2 shows a DSS user's object managers.

1.2. Collaboration

The object managers and their DDSOs assist the decision support process already very well. But one can reach even higher levels of efficiency when working in collaboration. With Dicodess it is possible to build dynamic groups of users working on the same decision problem. No configuration is needed. The users of the same group (federation) are discovered automatically. In these federations work can be split according to knowledge and responsibility. DDSOs can be exchanged thus sharing knowledge with others. People can work on separate objects in parallel or sequentially work on the same object. A

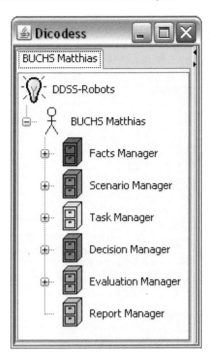

Figure 2. Dicodess' object managers.

flag mechanism informs a user about changes made by her or his colleagues. Communication is crucial in collaboration. Dicodess offers instant messaging with reference to a particular object. A chat and distributed voting service complete the communication aids for collaboration.

Figure 3 shows the user interface with more than one user online. Every user's objects (his or her working memory) appear in a separate tab. The white background of the selected tab indicates that the screenshot has been made on Matthias Buchs' (MB) system as the background of the local working memory is always some different color (cf. Figure 2). The small yellow/orange symbols on several of the nodes and the tab tell MB that Pius Hättenschwiler (PH) has created or modified one or several objects. This awareness is very important in a dynamic collaborative environment for users to know what has changed and what not. In the current example, PH has created a new scenario that specifies increased component prizes. MB could for instance copy this new scenario into his working memory and use it in his evaluation(s).

This was a very short introduction into the concepts and features of Dicodess. The next section will be about model visualization and inspection.

2. Model Inspection

This section provides the reader a short introduction into the field of optimization model inspection and visualization. Section 2.1 introduces the process of optimization modeling along with a problem that also applies to the context of DSS. Section 2.2 and 2.3 explain what model visualization is and how it helps to solve the aforementioned problem.

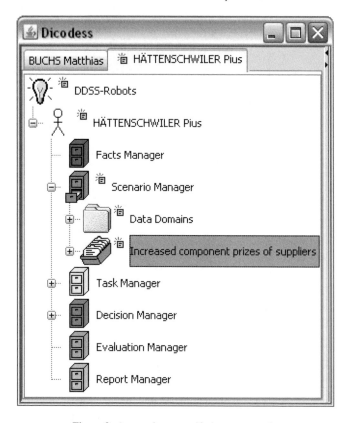

Figure 3. A second user specified a new scenario.

Finally, Section 2.4 and 2.5 introduce our concept for language independent optimization model visualization.

2.1. Optimization Modeling

Building optimization models is a creative task - some would even call it an art. As often in creative processes there is no single way how to achieve a goal. Nevertheless, there are some phases or stages that are frequently applied in one form or another:

Problem or business analysis: In this phase the problem or domain to be modeled is analyzed. The stakeholders in the project need to agree on a common view and goal.

Data collection or integration: The model's input data need to be collected, transformed (units etc.) and checked for consistency.

Model development: The actual formulation of the problem using a modeling language. Language, model type, granularity etc. need to be chosen.

Model validation or debugging: *"To err is human"*. Therefore, a model needs to be checked for errors. Its behavior should emulate reality with the requested precision.

Model deployment: Often a model is not used directly but through an encapsulating application such as a DSS (e.g. Dicodess). This application must be generated and further customized or built from scratch.

Model application, validation, and maintenance (refinements & extensions): When using (applying) optimization models for different use cases the user must validate the results and the model behavior in each use case. This leads to continuous model validation, refinement, extensions, and collections of model variants. Each model based knowledge base needs that kind of learning component in order to become really useful. Model inspection during this phase of the model life cycle is crucial.

The last phase "model application" often needs to reintroduce semantic information which mathematical modelers had abstracted from during the modeling process. This leads to specific use cases of so-called *semantic views of models*, which are particularly useful for end user to modeler communication. Developers of modern modeling languages like Paragon Decision Systems [3], ILOG [4] or Virtual Optima [5], to name just a few, provide powerful integrated development environments (IDE) that support a *modeler* in accomplishing the phases described above. But, as modelers are generally not familiar with the domain of the problem, communication with experts or knowledge bearers is crucial. Herein lays a problem:

2.1.1. Knowledge Transfer and Validation

It is difficult for an expert to verify if the domain has been modeled correctly. On the one hand, current modeling IDEs provide little visualizations of model structure and, on the other hand, domain experts are usually not used to read model code. As a consequence the latter have to analyze model output while varying model input and to try to determine (often guess) if the model's behavior is correct. Currently non-modelers are obliged to treat an optimization model as a black box.

2.2. Optimization Model Visualization

Research in psychology has shown that often diagrammatic representations are superior to sequential representations [6]. One reason is that our brain has a strong aptitude to identify patterns [7,8]. Besides cognition, experiments suggest that visual recall is better than verbal recall [9]. With the ever increasing power of desktop computers the use of electronic visual aids increased, and will continue to do so. In software engineering for instance, various kinds of visualizations play an important role. Although the unified modeling language UML [10] is certainly well-reputed, there are other, more specialized software visualizations [11] to create visual representations of software systems based on their structure [12], size [13], history [14] or behavior [15]. Even though mathematical modeling is somewhat akin to software engineering, visualizations do not play the same role. Surprisingly, the efforts in optimization model visualization concentrate almost entirely on visualization of model input and model output, keeping the model itself a black box. Those visualization concepts range from general [16,17] to very domain specific approaches. However, visualizations in software engineering often represent *software structure* and are *not only targeted to technically skilled people (programmers etc.) but to other stakeholders in a project (e.g. system owners, domain experts, etc.) as well.* After all, a system owner would probably want to know how the business processes are implemented. Therefore, the following question is certainly justified: "Why are visualizations of optimization model structure so scarce?". We do not have a satisfactory answer to that question. A first tentative explanation could be that there are much less people involved in optimization modeling than in software engineering. Therefore, motivation to invest in sophisticated visualization concepts and their implementation is certainly smaller. Second, most of the people involved in the development and maintenance of an optimization model are modelers. As the latter are more mathematically and technically skilled people they tend as a group to favor formulas and code. This fact does not mean that modelers would not profit from visual aids but merely that the demand is rather small. These and certainly other reasons caused visualizations in optimization modeling to be not as sophisticated and varied as in software engineering. This leads us to the definition of our understanding of optimization model visualization:

Definition 1 *Optimization model visualization comprises all graphic representations of model input, model output and model structure that can be used to inspect, understand and communicate the knowledge represented by an optimization model.*

Clearly, optimization model visualization uses concepts from information visualization as well as from knowledge visualization as it contains "*...computer supported, interactive, visual representations of abstract data to amplify cognition*" [18] and uses "*...visual representations to improve the creation and transfer of knowledge between at least two people*" [19]. It is explicitly broader than currently understood by many people as they mean visualization of model input and especially model output when talking about model visualization. The following section introduces possible applications of optimization model visualization.

2.3. Knowledge Transfer Among Several People

Optimization model visualization as defined in the previous section can be used to fight the information overflow and can therefore be applied in many cases. In the context of this article we want to mention the abstract use case where at least two parties are involved. Here, visualizations are used to transfer knowledge. One or several users (often modelers) prepare visualizations for one or several other users (modelers and/or non-modelers). Such visual representations might be used for documentation purposes or for validation of an optimization model by one or several domain experts. This helps to tackle the problem of knowledge transfer and model validation as described in Section 2.1.1.

2.4. Metamodel

Mathematical modeling languages developed considerably over time. Each language offers slightly or even substantially different syntax and concepts compared to its competitors. Thus, we propose a *metamodel* abstracting from those differences. It contains only constructs that are essential for the purpose of model visualization and inspection. Figure 4 shows the metamodel in a UML notation. It is by no means intended to be complete but fulfills well its purpose.

In a nutshell, a mathematical model consists of a (ordered) list of interdependent elements. Elements can have a collection of attributes, which are basically name/value pairs providing additional information about the element like name, type etc[1]. As the world of mathematical models is often multidimensional, elements can be indexed by a (ordered) list of dimensions. Finally, elements can contain other elements to reflect

---

[1]Note that our element attributes should not be confused with the attribute elements Arthur M. Geoffrion introduced in his concept of structured modeling [20].

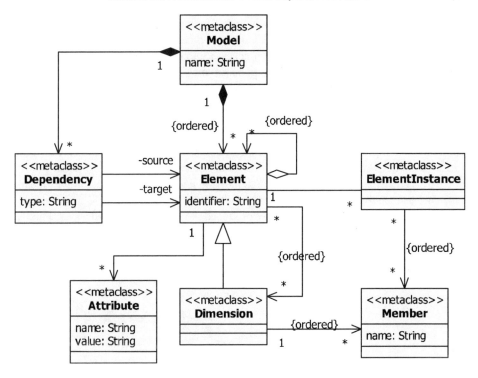

Figure 4. A metamodel of mathematical models for model inspection.

the hierarchical structure of many modeling languages. To apply our visualization concepts to a model implemented in a particular modeling language one needs to map the language's components or features to the constructs in the metamodel.

2.5. Model Views

Model views are built upon the metamodel previously defined to be independent of the concrete modeling language a model is implemented with. Therefore, the main parts to consider are elements, their attributes and dependencies. As an optimization model will possibly contain a considerable amount of elements and dependencies, we need to be able to make a selection of potentially interesting components to fight the information overflow. Depending on the question being investigated, the filtered elements should also be sorted according to one or multiple criteria. Finally, the resulting dependencies and elements should be arranged (laid out) in a way most suitable to the structure at hand. Thus, the basic components of a model view are *a dependency filter, an element filter, a sort and a layout.*

Currently we distinguish three different kinds of views based on the components introduced above with increasing complexity: *structural views*, showing the static structure extracted from the model's syntax, *instance views*, showing element and dependency instances from the instantiated or even optimized model, and *advanced views*, further processing the filtered elements and dependencies before layout, thus increasing the expressiveness of the view.

Building a model means abstracting from contextual details not necessary for the generalized problem representation. As a consequence, semantic information about the domain gets lost. It is possible and often necessary to (re-)introduce semantic information in model views. Model elements can be grouped together to emphasize a connection. Furthermore, one can assign each element an individual icon, thus visualizing its meaning. Finally, elements can be tagged with additional information. This facilitates the explanation of an element, but can also be used for element filtering.

Figure 5 shows an example of an advanced view applied to an academic model of a company which produces robots. This *information flow view* extracted the product flow from the model which in the source consists of several hundred lines of code. Subsequently, each element has been assigned an individual icon visually expressing its meaning. One can easily see that the company uses components to assemble robots. These components are partly bought and partly produced in-house by some processes. Finally, the mounted robots can be stocked.

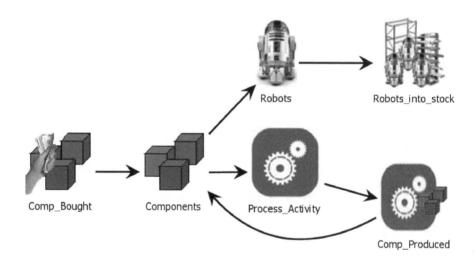

Figure 5. Product flow of robots production with added icons.

It is important to note that the view presented above has been *generated* based on the model (via the metamodel abstraction) and *not created* with some graphics tool. Reality and the idea or image one has of reality do not need to be the same. Additionally, what somebody models also does not necessarily need to coincide with the idea he or she has (e.g. what he or she actually wanted to do). As a consequence, a model can sometimes be far away from reality. The generation of the model views eliminates this source of error as no intermediate processing through persons is necessary. Obviously, model analysis becomes faster and more accurate.

This very small introduction showed a glimpse of the power and usefulness of our model inspection concept. Presenting all the concrete model views of each kind would certainly be beyond the scope of this article. A more detailed description can be found at [21]. Let us now turn the focus to integrating these concepts into Dicodess. The next section will present our proposition how model views can be used in Dicodess to do model inspection in collaboration.

3. Model Inspection in Dicodess

In this section we will introduce the integration of the model visualization concept (cf. Section 2) into Dicodess. This combines the strengths of both worlds. The DSS users are finally able to inspect the encapsulated model, and thanks to Dicodess' collaboration facilities this model inspecting can be done together with other people. As a motivation for the reader and for a better understanding we will start with an example decision support scenario. The Decision Support Systems research group at University of Fribourg (Switzerland) has built a Dicodess based DSS for the Swiss government. The application supports decision making in case of a crisis in the Swiss food supply chain. As Dicodess is a model based DSS, the "business logic" or "domain knowledge" needed to be formalized in a mathematical model. From the government side there is a designated person working regularly with the DSS. Additionally, a group of domain experts joins a couple of times per year to work on scenarios using the system in collaboration. Consider now the following cases:

The person in charge of the application changes the job or retires. The successor is new in the field and therefore needs to learn among other things about the food supply chain. As the model contains that knowledge in a formalized manner, it would be natural and logical to use it for learning. Unfortunately, the chances that such a person has skills in mathematical programming are little. And even if he or she had, the complexity of such a real world model is considerable. The Dicodess instance on the other hand shows only a very limited and highly specialized part of the model. Its structure cannot be visualized through the system. What would be needed is a mechanism to extract the relevant structure (i.e. the right parts with the right granularity) from the model. Until now this was impossible. Consequently, the person needed to study texts (description, specifications...) and hand drawn diagrams. This is not satisfying because of additional sources of errors and misunderstandings and the extra overhead (not to talk about keeping these documents synchronized with the model after maintenance).

In the second case the experts need to evaluate a brand new scenario with the DSS because of a changed situation or political reasons[2]. It might be that the anticipated impacts are quite dramatic and different from things that have been investigated in the past and that the model does not behave as expected. In such a situation it can be that the experts are able to find an explanation and therefore will confirm the solution. But it is also possible that a until then unknown bug has been discovered. During that verification process the experts need to find out if some particular rules and relations have been modeled correctly. As in the first case, there is no way the experts can do that by themselves. A modeler needs to search in the model to answer their questions. This situation is again not satisfying as the modeler presents a bottleneck and the indirection via modelers introduces additional sources of errors.

The examples show two situations where users of a Dicodess based DSS need to have a closer look at the encapsulated model: (1) *documentation* or *knowledge transfer* and (2) *verification* or *validation*. This section describes how our ongoing research

---

[2]Examples of such scenarios are pandemiae, natural disasters caused by global warming etc.

project for optimization model inspection provides facilities to solve the aforementioned problems in Dicodess. It is important to note that Dicodess and the model visualization concepts (and their prototype implementation) are completely independent subjects. Until now, neither depended on the other. In the sequel of this article we will call the implementation of the model visualization concepts *model inspector*. Dicodess actually encapsulates a collection of model parts together with many data sets that can be combined and configured in the graphical user interface (GUI) to a concrete model instance representing a specific use case, which is then optimized. This means that a concrete model configuration only exists within Dicodess. Technically adept people would be capable of exporting specific model instances of chosen model variants out of Dicodess. These could subsequently be loaded into the standalone version of the model inspector for inspection. Of course there are drawbacks to that:

- The average user cannot do this
- The process is tedious
- Collaboration between users (modelers, experts etc.) is not supported directly

A specific use case containing a specific model configuration is represented in Dicodess by an evaluation object (see Figure 1). It is therefore natural to initiate model inspection based on this kind of DDSO. By choosing the `Inspect Model` command from the context menu of a selected evaluation the model inspector is started and the user can investigate the preloaded underlying model using the concepts and functionality briefly introduced in Section 2. This clearly eliminates the first two drawbacks: Any single user has easy access to specific model configurations from within Dicodess. But of course a user might want to reuse model visualizations previously defined to continue investigations where he or she left off. And the third drawback, collaboration, is not dealt with so far. However, because of the complexity of real world decision problems and the joining of different domains, model inspection wins greatly when performed in collaboration where each expert contributes some knowledge of his or her particular area. Doing collaboration in Dicodess means creating, specifying, editing and exchanging objects. Each kind of object is used for a particular purpose. Therefore, we introduce a new type of DDSO for model visualizations. The obvious choice is to define a *Model View DDSO* as a storage and transport vehicle for model views. Each type of object is managed by its own manager (cf. Figure 2). Consequently, we also introduce a *model view manager*. The model inspector has a software abstraction making it independent of the way how model views are stored. The software simply serializes and deserializes model views without caring where they go to or come from. The storage model of the standalone version is file based whereas the one of the Dicodess integration is Model View DDSO based. This will become the main interface between the model inspector and Dicodess. In doing so we get the object specific functionality from Dicodess: Creating, copying, exchanging, deleting. Through the built-in awareness other users get informed as soon as a model view has been created or changed by any user within the federation. Object specific messages can be sent when more information exchange is needed. Figure 6 summarizes the object flow between Dicodess and the Model Inspector. Note that through the software abstractions `ModelEngine` and `ViewStore` the model inspector does not need to know what particular modeling system is used and how the model views are stored. This greatly simplifies the integration of the two systems. Similar combinations are thinkable with other systems as well.

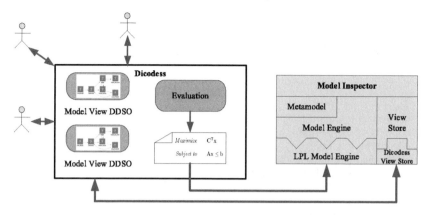

Figure 6. The object flow between Dicodess and the Model Inspector

In creating the new manager with its objects in Dicodess and integrating these with the model inspector we achieved our goals: Even average users with no technical skills can inspect concrete model configurations from Dicodess. Furthermore, Dicodess' collaboration facilities enable users to share their insights, mutually benefiting from the knowledge of each individual. Thus, not only the previously mentioned drawbacks are dealt with, but the two tasks from the introducing example, documentation and validation, are supported as well.

4. Conclusion

Dicodess provides a unique way to support the process of structuring semi-structured problems in collaboration. The concept of DDSOs and their respective managers enables both sharing and reusing pieces of information for decision problem specification in a user friendly way. Thereby the user never needs to see any mathematical model code. This very strength becomes a problem when doing model verification or when questions concerning a "strange" solution arise. The new concept of model views has the potential to increase the understanding of an optimization model. Not only can a single user see graphically presented many aspects of a model but multiple users (modelers, experts, decision makers etc.) get also a common base of discussion. The integration of model inspection functionality into Dicodess combines the strengths of both worlds. On the one hand it is possible for users of a model inspector to work in collaboration (as long as they work with a common model base driving Dicodess, of course). On the other hand it is possible for Dicodess users to inspect any given model configuration within the system without having to do cumbersome hacks.

References

[1] A. Gachet. *Building Model-Driven Decision Support Systems With Dicodess.* vdf Hochschulverlag AG, 2004.

[2] A. Gachet. Dicodess - A Software for Developing Distributed Cooperative DSS. http://dicodess.sourceforge.net, 2008. [Online; accessed 16-March-2008].

[3] Paragon Decision Technologies. AIMMS. http://www.aimms.com, 2008. [Online; accessed 16-March-2008].

[4] ILOG. ILOG. http://www.ilog.com/products/optimization, 2008. [Online; accessed 16-March-2008].

[5] T. Hürlimann. Virtual Optima's LPL. http://www.virtual-optima.com/en/index.html, 2008. [Online; accessed 16-March-2008].

[6] J. Larkin and H. Simon. Why a Diagram is (Sometimes) Worth Ten Thousand Words. *Cognitive Science*, 11:65–99, 1987.

[7] G. A. Miller. The magical number seven, plus or minus two: Some limits on our capacity for processing information. *Psychological Review*, 63:81–97, 1956.

[8] K. Koffka. *The Principles of Gestalt Psychology.* Harcourt Brace, New York, 1935.

[9] S. M. Kosslyn. *Images and Mind.* Harvard University Press, Cambridge, MA, 1980.

[10] D. Pilone and N. Pitman. *UML 2.0 in a Nutshell.* O'Reilly, 2005.

[11] J. T. Stasko, J. B. Domingue, M. H. Brown, and B. A. Price. *Software Visualization.* MIT Press, 1998.

[12] C. Best, M.-A. Storey, and J. Michaud. Designing a Component-Based Framework for Visualization in Software Engineering and Knowledge Engineering. In *Fourteenth International Conference on Software Engineering and Knowledge Engineering*, pages 323–326, 2002.

[13] M. Lanza. CodeCrawler - polymetric views in action. In *19th International Conference on Automated Software Engineering*, pages 394–395, 2004.

[14] F. L. Lopez, G. Robles, and B. J. M. Gonzalez. Applying social network analysis to the information in CVS repositories. In *International Workshop on Mining Software Repositories (MSR 2004)*, pages 101–105, 2004.

[15] A. Kuhn and O. Greevy. Exploiting the Analogy Between Traces and Signal Processing. In *IEEE International Conference on Software Maintenance (ICSM 2006)*, 2006.

[16] Wolfram Research. Mathematica. http://www.wolfram.com, 2008. [Online; accessed 16-March-2008].

[17] MathWorks. MatLab. http://www.mathworks.com, 2008. [Online; accessed 16-March-2008].

[18] S. K. Card, J. D. Mackinlay, and B. Shneiderman. *Readings in Information Visualization; Using Vision to think.* Morgan Kaufman, Los Altos, CA, 1999.

[19] M. Eppler and R. Burkhard. Knowledge Visualization. http://www.knowledgemedia.org/modules/pub/view.php/knowledgemedia-67, 2004. [Online; accessed 16-March-2008].

[20] A. M. Geoffrion. Introduction to Structured Modeling. *Journal of Management Science*, 33:547–588, 1987.

[21] M. Buchs and P. Hättenschwiler. Model Views: Towards Optimization Model Visualization. *Submitted for publication*, 2008.

Collaborative Decision Making
for Supply Chain

Collaborative Decision Making: Perspectives and Challenges
P. Zaraté et al. (Eds.)
IOS Press, 2008

Cooperation Support in a Dyadic Supply Chain

François GALASSO [a,1], Caroline THIERRY [b]
[a] *Université de Toulouse, LAAS-CNRS, 7 avenue du Colonel Roche, Toulouse, France*
[b] *Université de Toulouse, IRIT, 5 allées Antonio Machado, Toulouse, France*

Abstract: To improve the supply chains performance, taking into account the customer demand in the tactical planning process is essential. It is more and more difficult for the customers to insure a certain level of demand over a medium term period. Then it is necessary to develop methods and decision support systems to reconcile the order and book processes. In this context, this paper aims at introducing a collaboration support tool and methodology dedicated to a dyadic supply chain. This approach aims at evaluating in term of risks different demand management strategies within the supply chain using a simulation dedicated tool. The evaluation process is based on an exploitation of decision theory and game theory concepts and methods.

Keywords: supply chain, simulation, collaboration, decision theory, risk

Introduction

Implementation of cooperative processes for supply chain management is a central concern for practitioners and researchers. In aeronautics, this cooperative processes are characterised by a set of point-to-point relationship (customer/supplier) with a partial information sharing [1]. Moreover, due to a big difference among the supply chain actors in terms of maturity it is more or less difficult to implement collaborative processes for the different companies. In particular, SMEs have a partial vision of the supply chain and a lack of efficient tools in order to analyse the uncertain information transmitted from the customers and thus to be able to take advantage of this information in a cooperative way [2]. The good comprehension of the demand is a key parameter for the efficiency of the internal processes and the upstream supply chain [3]. Thus it is important to provide the suppliers with methods and systems for a better understanding of the demand and a better integration in the supply chain planning processes. In this paper, we aim at providing to the aeronautics suppliers a decision support to take advantage of the information provided by the customers in a cooperative perspective even if this information is uncertain. Thus, we propose a risk evaluation approach which is based on a simulation of planning process of the point-to-point supply chain relationship. More precisely we are concerned with the impact of the demand management processes in the planning process. After an introduction of the studied system and the addressed problematics (§2) we propose a state of art (§3) on collaboration in supply chain management and Supply Chain Risk Management. Then

---

[1] Corresponding Author: François GALASSO, LAAS-CNRS, 7 avenue du Colonel ROCHE, 31077 TOULOUSE Cedex 4, France; E-mail: galasso@univ-tlse2.fr

we describe the simulation approach proposed in order to evaluate the risks linked to the choice of the demand management and transmission strategies (§4). At last, we illustrate the proposed methodology on a case study (§5).

1. System under Study and Problematics

In this paper we are concerned with a dyadic supply chain with a supplier (SME) and a customer. In the context of this study (cf. Figure 1.), the customer transmit a demand plan to the supplier. During the customer planning process a frozen horizon is considered (within this frozen horizon no decision can be revised). Firm demands are transmitted to the supplier within this frozen horizon. *Firm demands* are related to the period closed to the present time. They are defined on a given time horizon, called firm horizon (*FH*). After this horizon, decisions can be revised within a given interval. This interval is part of the cooperation partnership between the supplier and the customer. We call "forecast" or "flexible" demands the couple (forecast value, flexibility level) which is transmitted to the supplier. The flexibility level is expressed in term of percentage of variation around the forecast value. The minimum and maximum values of the flexibility interval will be called "flexibility bounds" here after. These flexible demands are defined on a given time horizon, called flexible horizon (*LH*) which is part of the cooperation process between the customer and the supplier. Firm and flexible orders are transmitted to the supplier with a given periodicity.

Figure 1. Study positioning

Moreover, in this paper, concerning the planning process at a given moment, the supplier is supposed to use a given optimisation procedure using an ad hoc model via an Advanced Planning System, which is not the object of this study. The APS compute determinist data thus the supplier has to pre-compute the flexible demands transmitted by the customer as a couple (value, flexibility level). Different types of behaviours can be envisaged according to the degree of knowledge of the supplier on his customer's behaviour (for example, trend to overestimation or to underestimation).

2. State of Art

Supply chain management emphasises the necessity to establish collaborative interactions that rationalize or integrate the forecasting and management of demand, reconcile the order and book processes, and mitigate risks. This awareness of both academics and practitioners alike is linked, in particular, to the Bullwhip effect whose influence has been clearly shown and studied [4], [5]. Recently, many organizations have emerged to encourage trading partners to establish collaborative interactions (that rationalize or integrate their demand forecasting/management, and reconcile the order-book processes) and to provide standards (that could support collaboration processes): RosettaNet [6], Voluntary Inter-industry Commerce Standards Association [7], ODETTE [8], etc. On the other hand, McCarthy and Golicic [9] consider that the process of collaboration brought by the CPFR (Collaborative Planning, Forecasting and Replenishment) model is too detailed. They suggest instead that the companies should make regular meetings to discuss the forecast with the other supply chain partners and that they develop shared forecast. So there is a need to evaluate these standards.

In the same way, many recent research papers are devoted to cooperation in the context of supply chain management. Under the heading of cooperation, authors list several aspects. One of these aspects on which we focus in this paper is cooperation through information sharing. Using Huang *et al.* literature review [10], we can distinguish different classes of information which have a role in the information sharing literature: (1) product information, (2) process information, (3) lead time, (4) cost, (5) quality information, (6) resource information, (7) order and inventory information, (8) Planning (forecast) information. Another aspect of cooperation concerns the extension of the information sharing to collaborative forecasting and planning systems [11], [12]. In this paper, we will focus on planning information sharing (forecast) [13], [5]. We focus particularly on the risk evaluation of the cooperative planning process within a dyadic supply chain. Supply chain Risk Management (SCRM) is the "management of external risks and supply chain risks through a co-ordinated approach between the supply chain partners in order to reduce supply chain vulnerability as a whole" [14]. Up to now there is still a "lack of industrial experience and academic research for supply chain risk management" identified by Ziegenbein and Nienhaus [15], even if, since 2004, there is an increasing number of publications in this field. More specifically, the question of the risk management related to the use of Advanced Planning Systems has to be studied [16]. Nevertheless, little attention has been paid to risk evaluation of new collaborative processes [17], [18], [19]. This is also true when planning processes under uncertainty are concerned [20] even if the problem of the management tactical planning with an APS has been introduced by Rota *et al.* [21] and the problem of robustness has been studied by Génin *et al.* [22].

3. Decision and Collaboration Support Under Uncertainty

In order to provide a collaborative decision support to both actors in the dyadic supply chain, we present an approach for risk evaluation of the choice of:
- the planning strategies (demand management) by the supplier
- the demand transmission strategies (size of the firm horizon) by the customer.

This risk evaluation process (§4.1) uses a simulation tool which embeds a model for the behaviour of both actors of the considered supply chain (§4.2).

3.1. Risk Evaluation Approach Using Simulation

Within a dyadic supply chain, both actors have to determine their behaviours (internal strategies) to design a common cooperative strategy. The main problem of the *supplier* is to choose a strategy concerning the demand management in order to take into account the demand transmitted by the customer within its planning process. Regarding the *customer* demand management process, an important decisional lever is the length of the firm and flexible horizon. Through this lever, the customer adapts the visibility of the supplier on the demand. Thus, the supplier has more or less time to react and adapt its production process. For each actor of the dyadic supply chain, the different potential strategies are evaluated and compared for several scenarios of demand. At the supplier level, the definition of a cost model (a cost being associated to each parameter of the model) enables the calculation of *the global gain* obtained by the use of each strategy regarding each scenario. This gain can be considered as representative, at an aggregated level, of the combination of all indicators. The values issued from the global gain indicator enable the manager responsible of the planning process to evaluate the risks associated to the strategies that he envisaged. At the customer level, the performance indicator used is the *cost of backorders*. However, the best policy can be different depending on the considered scenario of demand evolution. Thus, it is necessary to compare each strategy considering the whole set of scenarios. In such a context, such a comparison is possible using a decision criterion in order to aggregate the indicators obtained for each scenario. In the frame of the problem under study, it is hardly possible to associate probabilities to the occurrence of each scenario. Thus, the evaluation can be done through the use of several decision criteria (which may lead to different results) based on the gain obtained after the simulation of each scenario: Laplace's criterion (average), Wald's criterion (pessimistic evaluation), Hurwicz's criterion (weighted sum of pessimistic and optimistic evaluation), Savage's criterion (minimising the maximum regret), etc. The results given by the different criteria can be gathered into a risk diagram on which the manager in charge of the planning process can base its decision making [23]. A general diagram is, presented and detailed in Figure 2.

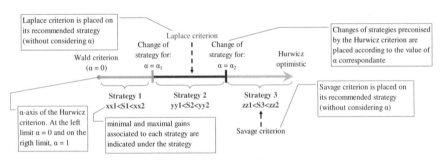

Figure 2. General risk diagram

In this diagram, the demand management strategies are positioned regarding the risk propension of the decision maker: these strategies are thus positioned on an axis corresponding to the values of α between 0 and 1 and noted α-axis. The evolution of the value of this criterion as a function of α for each strategy is represented on a curve following the formula of the Hurwicz criterion: $H_S(\alpha) = (1-\alpha) \, m_S + \alpha \, M_S$ (with m_S the minimal gain and M_S the maximal gain obtained applying the strategy S). From this curve, the values of α_i indicating a change in the proposed strategy can be determined. Then, the strategies are specified on the diagram. For each strategy, the associated minimal and maximal gains are given. Furthermore, if the represented strategies are proposed by other criteria (Laplace or Savage), these criteria are attached to the relevant strategy (without considering the value of α). Moreover, in order to engage a cooperative process, it is necessary to consider the objectives of both actor of the supply chain. To perform this multi-actor decision making process, we propose a game theory based approach. A first step consists in the determination of the propension to risk by the decision maker (using the risk evaluation approach presented here before). Then we simulate a two actors' game in order to obtain a Nash equilibrium if such an equilibrium exists (in game theory, the Nash equilibrium is a solution in which no player has anything to gain by changing only his or her own strategy unilaterally).

3.2. Behaviour Model Within the Simulation Tool

In order to model the dynamic behaviour of both actors we define:
- The behaviour models of the customer enabling the calculation of firm demand and forecasts transmitted to the supplier,
- The behaviour models of the supplier embedding:
  o The management process of the demand
  o The planning process

The simulation of these behaviours relies on a fixed step time advance. This period corresponds to the replanning period.

3.2.1. Model of the customer's behaviour

The evolution of the customer demand is simulated by a model enabling a macroscopic point of view of the customer's behaviour. This model permits the calculation of the customer demand at each simulation step. The flexible demand transmitted to the supplier is established taking into account a trend and a discrepancy around this trend. The consolidation process of the demand calculates the firm demand according to the flexible demand established at the previous planning step. During the foremost simulation step, the demand is initialised by the calculation of a flexible demand from the trend and the discrepancy over the whole planning horizon and then, the consolidation process is rolled-on over the firm horizon.

In the example depicted by Figure 3, the trend is linear and grows-up at a 5 produced units per period rate.

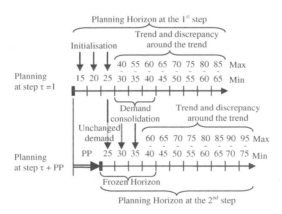

Figure 3. Customer's behaviour model

The discrepancy is, in a simplified way, of +/- 5 units at each period. The modelled scenario is the one in which the customer overestimates the flexible demand. The firm demand is therefore calculated as equal to the lower bound of the transmitted flexible demand at the previous simulation step.

The customer demand is noted $D_{p,t}^{\tau}$. The discrepancy is modelled by an interval limited by the following bounds:

- $\underline{D}_{p,t}^{\tau}$, is the lower bound of the tolerated discrepancy over the flexible demand,
- $\overline{D}_{p,t}^{\tau}$, is the upper bound.

The demand expressed at each period are always within the interval defined by $\left[\underline{D}_{p,t}^{\tau},\overline{D}_{p,t}^{\tau}\right]$ at each end-item p, period t and planning step τ. They are modelled as the following (1).

$$\begin{cases} D_{p,t}^{\tau}, & \forall p, \forall t \in FH^{\tau} \\ D_{p,t}^{\tau} \in \left[\underline{D}_{p,t}^{\tau},\overline{D}_{p,t}^{\tau}\right] & \forall p, \forall t \in LH^{\tau} \end{cases} \tag{1}$$

The evolution of the demand between two successive steps is formalised by the following relations:

$$D_{p,t}^{\tau} = D_{p,t}^{\tau-PP} \quad \forall p \ \forall t \in \left\{FH^{\tau-PP} \cap FH^{\tau}\right\} \tag{2}$$

$$D_{p,t}^{\tau} \in \left[\underline{D}_{p,t}^{\tau-PP},\overline{D}_{p,t}^{\tau-PP}\right] \forall p \ \forall t \in \left\{LH^{\tau-PP} \cap FH^{\tau}\right\} \tag{3}$$

$$\left[\underline{D}_{p,t}^{\tau},\overline{D}_{p,t}^{\tau}\right] = \left[\underline{D}_{p,t}^{\tau-PP},\overline{D}_{p,t}^{\tau-PP}\right] \forall p \ \forall t \in \left\{LH^{\tau-PP} \cap LH^{\tau}\right\} \tag{4}$$

Eq. (2) shows that the firm demands are not modified between two successive planning steps. New firm demands (as they result from the consolidation process) remain consistent with their previous "flexible" values (Eq. 3). The flexible bounds do not change between two planning steps (Eq. 4).

3.2.2. Model of the supplier's behaviour

The *management of the supplier's demand* process enables the definition of the demand that will be taken into account in the supplier's planning process in its deterministic form. This management process depends on the uncertainty associated to the customer's demand. Thus, regarding the considered horizon (i.e. firm or flexible), the supplier will satisfy either $\hat{D}_{p,t}^{\tau} = D_{p,t}^{\tau}$ over the firm horizon or $\hat{D}_{p,t}^{\tau} = f(\underline{D}_{p,t}^{\tau},\overline{D}_{p,t}^{\tau})$ over the flexible horizon in which $\hat{D}_{p,t}^{\tau}$ is the deterministic demand on which the planning process is based. The definition of a value $\hat{D}_{p,t}^{\tau}$ is made through the use of the demand management strategy f.

The planning behaviour is modelled as a planning problem using a mixed integer linear planning model (similar to those used in Advanced Planning Systems (APS)). Such a model is detailed in [3]. This model aims at maximising the gain calculated at each planning step while conserving a certain commonality and possess the following characteristics: multi-product, multi-components, bills of materials management, possibility to adjust internal capacity through the use of extra-hours, change the workforce from one to two or three-shifts-work and subcontracting a part of the load. This model uses the deterministic demand in order to generate plans over the whole planning horizon regarding the internal and subcontracted production as well as the purchases for each supplier. Each decision variable has its own dynamics and can be subject to a specific anticipation delay (and thus a specific frozen horizon) before the application of such decisions.

4. Illustrative example

In this section, the collaborative decision making process detailed in section 3 is applied to an academic example. The example considers the case of a single final product representative of the aggregation at the tactical level of a family of end-items.

4.1. Parameters for the supplier

The temporal features of the production system introduce different frozen horizons according to the considered decision. The internal production delays are low compare to the subcontracted production delays. Regarding the capacity adjustments, the use of extra-hours requires lesser anticipation than subcontracting. The recourse to the subcontractor induces higher over costs than using extra-hours. We consider two rank 2 suppliers (supplier's suppliers) S1 and S2. S1 requires more anticipation than S2 but is less expensive. Thus, it is interesting to notice that the supplier has the ability to choose among its suppliers in order to balance the need for a reactive supplier (i.e. choosing the supplier 2) and minimising the purchasing cost as the first supplier is less expensive.

4.2. Design of experiments

In order to facilitate the organisation of its supplier, the customer transmits two possible trends for his demand. The first trend (T1) reflects a strong punctual increase of the demand with the acceptation of orders beyond the standard production capacity. The second trend (T2) corresponds to a moderate increase as viewed by the customer. The punctual increase, expected for periods 20 to 25 is much lower than the previous one.

Moreover, the demand is characterised by a flexibility of +/- 20% required for each trend. At each period, the minimum, maximum and average values of the demand are given and compared to the cumulated capacity levels.

Figure 4 (respectively Figure 5) shows the first trend (respectively the second trend) corresponding forecasts.

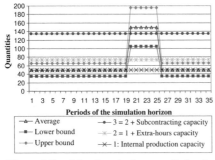

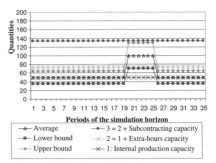

Figure 4. Trend 1 and production capacity levels   **Figure 5.** Trend 2 and production capacity levels

According to its height, the peak will have more or less influence on the planning process and may require different uses of production capacities (internal or subcontracted) while taking into account the production delays [3]. In order to simulate several collaborative behavioural aspects, two behaviours of the customer are studied:

- the behaviour of overestimation (resp. underestimation) of the demand noted "Min" (resp. "Max"). In that case, the customer will finally order the lower (resp. the upper) bound of the flexible demand.
- the length of the firm horizon transmitted by the customer to the supplier. This provides the supplier with more or less visibility.

As the planning process proceeds, the understanding of the trend on the supplier side improves. The authors assume here that the supply chain has been defined so that the length of the horizon on which is given the customer's demand enables the supplier to use all his decisional levers (i.e. use of extra-hours, subcontracting and use of both suppliers). This length encompass the 4 periods necessary for the use of the subcontractor plus the four periods necessary to the use of the supplier 1 at rank 2 plus the 2 periods of the planning periodicity that is 12 periods.

Over the flexible horizon, the demand is known under its flexible form. The percentage of flexibility is + and – 20 % of the average values.

In order to manage the uncertainty on the flexible demand, the supplier uses two planning strategies, S1 and S2, in its demand management process:

- S1: choose the maximum of the flexible demand
- S2: choose the minimum of the flexible demand

These strategies are evaluated against different scenarios for the behaviour of the customer. This evaluation is done running simulations that are designed as a combination of:

- a trend of the evolution of the demand (T1 or T2),
- a type behaviour for the customer (overestimation denoted "Min" or under-estimation denoted « Max » of the demand),
- a planning strategy of the supplier (concerning the choice of the maximal flexible demand denoted S1 or the choice of the minimal denoted S2).
- the visibility: length of the firm horizon transmitted by the customer.

The cost parameters and temporal parameters remain constant for each simulation.

4.3. Supplier risk evaluation

The gains obtained during the simulations with the use of the strategy S1 (i.e. the supplier integrates the maximum values of the demand) and S2 (i.e. the supplier integrates the maximum values of the demand) are presented in Table 3. In this table, the best and the worst obtained for each behaviour of the supplier are shown in bold and are: 476 378 and 235 470 for the first strategy and of 403 344 and 264 853 for the second one.

Table 3. Results obtained for FH = 4 and LH = 8

	Trend 1		Trend 2	
	Scenario « Min »	Scenario « Max »	Scenario « Min »	Scenario « Max »
S1	245 201	**476 378**	**235 470**	444 191
S2	291 798	**403 344**	**264 853**	383 765

According to these results, we aim to establish the risk diagram for a firm horizon length of 4 periods. To do so, it is necessary to calculate from which value of the realism coefficient α of the Hurwicz criterion a change of strategy is "recommended" (cf. Figure 6).

In order to visualise this specific point, we draw the line of equation:

- $H_{S1} = (1-\alpha) \times 235\ 470 + \alpha \times 476\ 378$ for S1 and
- $H_{S2} = (1-\alpha) \times 264\ 853 + \alpha \times 403\ 344$ for S2.

It is now possible to establish the risk diagram (Figure 7). Firstly the α-axis symbolising the risk propension of the decision maker is drawn highlighting the value of the parameter α indicating a change of strategy (here for α = 0,29). Then, both strategies S1 and S2 are placed on the axis. Finally, the other criteria (Laplace and Savage) are placed in the diagram over the strategy that they recommend.

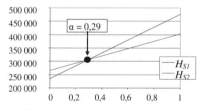

Figure 6. Point of change of strategy

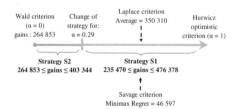

Figure 7. Risk diagram for FH=4 and LH=8

We can notice on this diagram that when pessimistic point of view is adopted (α tends to 0) the planning strategy using the minimal demand (S2) is recommended. The weighted Hurwicz criterion proposes a change in the strategy applied for an optimism degree of 0.29 (values comprised between 0 and 1). This value means that the strategy S2 may be envisaged by the supplier even if other criteria such as Laplace or Savage recommend the choice of the strategy S1. S1 is also recommended by the Hurwicz criteria for values over α = 0.29. Thus, the supplier will have an interest in requiring other information (i.e. information from the customer or upon the global market evolution) in order to determine if he should be pessimistic or not. These results furnish further meanings to a simple simulation giving raw gains according to several scenarios. Indeed, in a first approach, it could be obvious that the higher the demand is, the higher the gains are. Nevertheless, disruptions may call into question the occurrence of a scenario leading to such gains and the raw results remains uncertain. Therefore, through the risk diagram, we afford not solely information regarding an interesting strategy to be applied but also an indication about the relevance of this choice.

4.4. Collaborative risk evaluation

In a collaborative perspective, the customer may assume a consolidation of its demand over a longer horizon if an indication can be given that this will improve the availability of the final products and reduce the backorders. In return, the supplier wish to maximise the gains obtained through the application of its demand management strategies. In fact, we looked for a solution in which none of these two players has anything to gain by changing his or her own strategy unilaterally: a Nash equilibrium is searched among the different strategies used by the customer and the supplier. So, we reiterate the previous design of experiments according to 3 different firm horizon length (6, 8 and 10) to which are added the corresponding flexible horizon length (6, 4 and 2) in order to keep a constant planning horizon length of 12 periods. These different lengths constitute the demand transmission strategies of the customer. For each set of simulations we obtain the gains and the cost of backorders. The actors are considered to be pessimistic (application of the Wald criterion). Thus, in order to compare the different scenarios, we extract for each strategy of the supplier (i.e. S1 and S2) and each potential visibility given by the customer, the worst gain and the most important backorder cost. The results are given in Table 4.

Table 4. Comparative results for each couple of strategy and visibility

Visibility	Supplier Strategy S1	S2
4	(235 470 , 14 260)	(264 853 , 96 040)
6	(256 284 , 13 620)	(264 853 , 52 140)
8	(262 128 , 12 300)	(264 853 , 30 700)
10	(264 557 , 12 300)	(264 853 , 19 940)

Then, the two players can evaluate the results in Table 4 according to their own performance criterion. In the case of the customer, the 3 first customer strategies are dominated by the fourth one as it generates lowest levels of backorders whatever the strategy that the supplier could use. Thus, one solution is obtained for a visibility of 10 periods for the firm horizon as depicted by Table 5.

Table 5. Comparative results for each couple of strategy and visibility

Visibility / Supplier Strategy	S1	S2
10	(264 557 , 12 300)	(264 853 , 19 940)

On its side, the supplier searches for the solution generating the highest gains. These gains are obtained using the strategy S2 whatever could be the customer strategy as given in Table 4. Table 6 shows the final result without the dominated solutions for both the supplier and the customer.

Table 6. Elimination of the dominated solutions for the customer and the supplier

Visibility / Supplier Strategy		S2
10		(264 853 , 19 940)

Thus, the Nash equilibrium is obtained for the couple (S2 , 10). This example illustrates the interest of integrating a cooperative approach in order to define a common strategy based on a couple of local strategies.

5. CONCLUSION

This article proposes a decision support framework for a collaborative management of the demand in a dyadic supply chain. A simulation tool has been defined in order to evaluate and compare gains and backorder levels obtained according to several behaviours of a supplier and a customer. In this customer-supplier relationship, the uncertainty inherent to the demand has an impact on the performance of the chain. In that way, both the customer and the supplier has an interest in collaborating through the definition of planning strategies. These strategies aim at improving production conditions at the supplier level while reducing backorder costs for the customer. A decision support methodology for the collaborative planning process is given firstly, through the use of a risk diagram based on decision theory criteria. This diagram gives more information than a simple evaluation of the plans established by the supplier according to the demand given by the customer. Indeed, it stresses which strategy can be privileged according to the decision maker's degree of optimism. Moreover, the customer role in the planning process for this dyadic supply chain is studied through the use of its decisional lever concerning the visibility he gives to its supplier. A game is led in order to find a Nash equilibrium. In this win-win situation, a couple of demand management strategies both for the customer and the supplier has been identified.

There are many perspectives to this work. Thanks to our generic model of the planning process, wider numerical experiments will be facilitated. Furthermore, an extension to linear or networked supply chains could be investigated. Thus, we may obtain a set of strategies that can be used at each rank of the chain while improving its global performance.

References

[1]   J. François, F. Galasso, Un cadre générique d'analyse des relations dans la chaîne logistique interentreprises. *Proceedings from the 6th Congrès international de génie industriel,* Besançon, France, (2005).

[2]   F. Galasso, C. Mercé, B. Grabot, Decision support for supply chain planning under uncertainty. *Proceedings from the 12th IFAC International Symposium Information Control Problems in Manufacturing (INCOM),* St Etienne, France, **3** (2006), 233-238.

[3]   E. Bartezzaghi, R. Verganti, Managing demand uncertainty through order overplanning. *International Journal of Production Economics,* **40** (1995), 107-120.

[4]   H.L. Lee, P. Padmanabhan, S. Whang, Information Distortion in a Supply Chain: The Bullwhip Effect, *Management Science,* **43** (1997), 546-558.

[5]   T. Moyaux, *Design, simulation and analysis of collaborative strategies in multi-agent systems: The case of supply chain management,* PhD thesis, Université Laval, Ville de Québec, Canada (2004).

[6]   Rosetta, http://www.rosettanet.org, visited January 17, 2008 (2007).

[7]   Vics, http://www.vics.org/committees/cpfr/, visited January 17, 2008 (2007).

[8]   Odette, http://www.odette.org, visited January 17, 2008 (2007).

[9]   T. McCarthy, S. Golicic, Implementing collaborative forecasting to improve supply chain performance, *International Journal of Physical Distribution & Logistics Management,* **32**(6) (2002), 431-454.

[10]   G.Q. Huang, J.S.K. Lau, K.L. Mak, The impacts of sharing production information on supply chain dynamics: a review of the literature. *International Journal of Production Research,* **41**(7) (2003), 1483-1517.

[11]   G. Dudek H. Stadtler, Negotiation-based collaborative planning between supply chains partners, *European Journal of Operational Research,* **163**(3) (2005), 668-687.

[12]   S. Shirodkar K. Kempf, Supply Chain Collaboration Through shared Capacity Models, *Interfaces,* **36**(5) (2006), 420-432.

[13]   L. Lapide, New developments in business forecasting, *Journal of Business Forecasting Methods & Systems,* **20** (2001), 11-13.

[14]   M. Christopher, Understanding Supply Chain Risk: A Self-Assessment Workbook. Cranfield University, School of Management, http://www.som.cranfield.ac.uk/som/research/centres /lscm/risk2002.asp, visited January 17, 2008. (2003).

[15]   A. Ziegenbein, J. Nienhaus, Coping with supply chain risks on strategic, tactical and operational level. *Proceedings of the Global Project and Manufacturing Management Symposium.* Richard Harvey, Joana Geraldi, and Gerald Adlbrecht (Eds.), Siegen, (2004), 165-180.

[16]   B. Ritchie, C. Brindley, *Risk characteristics of the supply chain – a contingency framework.* Brindley, C. (Ed.). Supply chain risk. Cornwall: MPG Books Ltd, (2004).

[17]   J. Småros, *Information sharing and collaborative forecasting in retail supply chains,* PhD thesis, Helsinki University of Technology, Laboratory of Industrial Management, (2005).

[18]   C. Brindley, (Ed.), *Supply chain risk.* MPG Books Ltd., (2004).

[19]   C.S. Tang, Perspectives in supply chain risk management, *International Journal of Production Economics,* **103** (2006), 451-488.

[20]   J. Mula, R. Poler, J.P. García-Sabater, F.C. Lario, Models for production planning under uncertainty: A review, *International Journal of Production Economics,* **103**(1) (2006), 271-285.

[21]   K. Rota, C. Thierry, G. Bel, Supply chain management: a supplier perspective. *Production Planning and Control,* **13**(4) (2002), 370-380.

[22]   P. Génin, A. Thomas, S. Lamouri, How to manage robust tactical planning with an APS (Advanced Planning Systems). *Journal of Intelligent Manufacturing,* **18** (2007), 209-221.

[23]   J. Mahmoudi, Simulation et gestion des risques en planification distribuée de chaînes logistiques. Thèse de Doctorat, Sup'aero, France (2006).

87

On the Development of Extended Communication Driven DSS within Dynamic Manufacturing Networks

Sébastien Kicin[a], Dr. Christoph Gringmuth[a], Jukka Hemilä[b]

[a] CAS Software AG, Innovation & Business Development, Karlsruhe, Germany
Email: sebastien.kicin@cas.de; Christoph.Gringmuth@cas.de
[b] VTT Technical Research centre of Finnland, Helsinki
Email: Jukka.Hemila@vtt.fi

Abstract. The slow progress to date regarding inter-organizational collaborative decision management within manufacturing supply chains is due to a lack of common understanding of this concept, and the difficulty of integrating external requirements of customers and suppliers into opaque internal decision control. In this paper, we focus on the production management of dynamic manufacturing networks that is characterized by non-centralized decision making. We set out to clarify internal decision collaboration concepts based on research and technology led on collaborative work and enterprise modeling techniques, and discuss how IT can support and improve business and managerial decision-making within supply chains. This paper begins with examining the Communication Driven Decision Support System (DSS) concept and its integration within a supply chain point of view. A framework for inter-organizational decision support is then discussed and linked to the traditional Decision Support Systems and the overall Information Management solutions. We conclude that the effectiveness of supply chain collaboration relies upon two factors: the level to which it integrates internal and external decisions at strategic, tactical and operational levels, and the level to which the efforts are aligned to the supply chain settings in terms of the geographical dispersion, the demand pattern, and the product characteristics.

1. Research Context

This paper is supported by the R&D project ESKALE ("Trans-European Sustainable Knowledge-Based Manufacturing for Small and Medium Sized Enterprises in Traditional Industries") that is developing a supply-chain oriented production management framework for manufacturing SMEs. This framework aims to support decision management while reinforcing customer and supplier orientation. It will act as an integrative environment to interface and interconnect different units of the manufacturing SMEs and related existing operative systems (PPS, CAM, CAD, etc.). An innovative prototype called Manufacturing Information Portal (MIP) will demonstrate this approach. ESKALE is a trans-national research project funded by the Finnish Funding Agency for Technology and Innovation (Tekes, FI) and the Forschungszentrum Karlsruhe (PTKA, DE). The project consists of 1) four end-user SMEs: Hubstock Oy (FI), Ovitor Oy (FI), Gleistein Ropes (DE) and Bischoff International AG (DE), 2) one software provider: CAS software AG (DE) and 3) two research institutes: Technical Research Centre of Finland (VTT, FI) and Bremen Institute for Production and Logistics (BIBA, DE).

2. Introduction

Successful objectives are generally achieved through decisions that: 1) are based on clear data; 2) Manage expectation; 3) Capitalize on the creativity, skills and resources available and 4) Build and maintain relationships. A good decision-making process can help minimize fall-out from even a bad decision, and fosters collective ownership for learning and moving on. A bad decision-making process may lead to sabotage of even a good decision [1].

A supply chain is comprised of many value-adding nodes, each of which receives many inputs and combines them in various ways in order to deliver numerous unique outputs for multiple consuming nodes. If each node in the value network makes decisions in isolation, the potential grows for the total value in one or more supply chain is much less than it could be. Each node could eliminate activities that do not add value to its own transformation process and try to provide the highest possible margin, subject to maximizing and maintaining the total value proposition for a supply chain. This ensures long-term profitability, assuming a minimum level of parity in bargaining position among partners and in advantage among competitors. But eliminating non-value adding activity in the supply chain through better decisions necessitates some high level of collaboration with other organizations in the supply chain. How far this collaboration can extend, how effective it will be, and the financial impact (for each company and for a supply chain) are mainly determined by industry structure, access to information and technological advances.

The Collaborative Decision Making (CDM) concept is usually well known for addressing real time collaboration issues in the Air Traffic Management area (e.g., airline operators, traffic flow managers and air traffic controllers). Little work has been done for applying CDM concepts to manufacturing internal decision management and even less to manufacturing supply chains. CDM in manufacturing supply chain needs not only information sharing and common awareness between actors, but also coherent and flexible collaborative procedures and clear identification of internal decision centres. (Location where information is assembled and decisions are made). We consider therefore the following overall requirements for the framework for inter-organisational group decision experimentation:

- A generic model that ensures the internal coherence of collaborative decision procedures and identifies decision centers to anticipate collective failures,
- An approach that allows "one-to-many" interactions of manufacturing enterprises ensuring adequate customers' and suppliers' decision involvement and awareness while respecting confidentiality and protecting know-how.

3. Current situation of manufacturing supply chains

We analyzed the situation of the ESKALE end-users and led interviews with other manufacturing companies and consulting companies. Our main findings are:

- Today co-operations are still often built up hierarchically, because smaller enterprises are only involved as subcontractors of large-scale enterprises. Collaboration issues can then be solved by OEM (Original Equipment Manufacturer) by forcing on coordination and centralized solutions for their network members. But this increases investment efforts for companies involved in several supply chains, thus restricting business opportunities to a very few number of supply chains.

- Supply-chain systems are good at automating operative tasks, but they still are not good at assisting these users in making strategic and tactical decisions. Collaboration in the supply chain is mainly going through the sales and procurement/purchase units of the manufacturing companies, where: 1) Many "wrong", "diffuse" or "out-to-date" decision information are a) forwarded to the partner or b) collected from the partners (e.g. production planning, product drawings); 2) Many of basic supply chain decisions are made with no, bad, or rudimentary, information on the real impact of the decision.

Bringing production/resources planning and product development relevant data into the sales and procurement/purchase units of the supply chain to support collaborative decision-making is a key challenge. These units require a finer level of information than available today. New methods and tools are needed that present the information in a useful way during the decision-making process, and not afterwards.

4. The Emerging Communication Driven DSS

Through the recent network technology breakthrough, the Decision Support Systems (DSS) concept also expanded to the area of Communication Driven DSS - also known as Group Decision Support Systems (GDSS) - that includes communication, collaboration and network technologies. A Communication Driven DSS is a hybrid DSS that emphasizes both the use of communications and decision models and intended to facilitate the solution of problems by decision-makers working together as a group [2]. This type of DSS currently directly benefits from the Computer Supported Cooperative Work (CSCW) approach and the related groupware technology that may be used to communicate, cooperate, coordinate, solve problems, compete, or negotiate [3]. While groupware refers to real computer-based systems, means the notion CSCW the study of tools and techniques of groupware as well as their psychological, social and organizational effects. CSCW is a generic term which combines the understanding of the way people work in groups with the enabling technologies of computer networking, and associated hardware, software, services and techniques [4]. Groupware supports any king of communication means (emails, phones, etc.), scheduling, document sharing and collaborative writing systems, tasks and other group organisational activities. As groupware tools tend to make informal knowledge explicit, practitioners of collaborative decision management have been quick to adopt advances in groupware tools.

Communication Driven DSS can be categorized according to the time/location matrix using the distinction between same time (synchronous) and different times (asynchronous), and between same place (face-to-face) and different places (distributed) [5]:

- Synchronous Communication Driven DSS applications support people collaborating in real time over distance. This is the case of same time/different places, where people can share a computer workspace in which the work of the entire group is presented to each team member with continuous real-time update. This means creating a "virtual" space, where a participant may join the meeting from his own workstation and work with the others in the same manner as in a real meeting room.

- Asynchronous Communication Driven DSS tools are located on a network to which all members have access through their individual workstations. Members of the group can work on different schedules and join the virtual space at a time at their own choosing, either being located in offices in different cities or co-located.

Communication Driven DSS tools usually cover the following solutions:

- Email is the most common Communication Driven DSS application. Even relatively basic email systems today usually include features for forwarding messages, creating mailing groups, and attaching files. Other features have been more recently explored like automatic sorting and messages processing.

- Newsgroups and mailing lists technologies are very similar in spirit to email systems except that they are intended for messages among large groups of people. In practice the main difference between newsgroups and mailing lists is that newsgroups only show messages to a user as an "on-demand" service, while mailing lists deliver messages as soon as they become available.

- Workflow systems allow documents to be routed through organizations through a relatively-fixed process. Workflow systems may provide features such as routing, development of forms, and support for differing roles and privileges. As organisations grow and their internal operation becomes increasingly complex there is need to manage the information flows.

- Hypertext is a system for linking text documents to each other, with the Web being an obvious example. Whenever multiple people author and link documents, the system becomes group work, constantly evolving and responding to others' work.

- Group calendars allow scheduling, project management, and coordination among many people, and may provide support for scheduling equipment as well. This also helps to locate people.

- Collaborative writing systems are document management facilities that may offer both real-time support and non-realtime support. Word processors may provide asynchronous support by showing authorship, by allowing users to track changes and make annotations to documents and by helping to plan and coordinate the authoring process. Synchronous support allows authors to see each other's changes as they make them, and usually needs to provide an additional communication channel to the authors as they work.

5. Build a Flexible Framework for Transparent Decision Management

Manufacturing decision structures are usually based on ad hoc decision structure and tacit knowledge. Many research works emphasized individual decision-making behaviour but individual decision-making is just one of several contexts of DSSs. DSSs have been used to support five decision-making contexts: individual, group, organizational, inter-organizational, and societal [6]. Our work is focusing simultaneously on the organizational and inter-organizational dimensions and on the way to integrate these different collaboration levels. Our framework is aiming at achieving decision transparency and proper enterprise-wide communication driven DSS implementation. We will consider the collaboration between decision teams as well as the collaboration between supply chain actors.

Whether a decision group is dealing with supplying, stock management, procurement, planning, human resources management, or technical resources management, it is important to take into account the customer's and suppliers point of view and to consider the common interest of the supply chain. Enterprise should not assume that they know what's important to the customers. They should ask them, pay attention to and measure call center complaints, find out when the customers need the products and track stock-outs to trace sales lost due to product unavailability.

6. Modeling Enterprise-wide Decision Management

An enterprise-wide DSS is linked to a large data warehouse and serves many managers within one company. It should be an interactive system in a networked environment that helps a targeted group of managers makes decisions. Essentially, various contexts are collections of decision-making activities in different manners and/or using different processing techniques. In complex decision-making contexts, the decision-making process is not a simple sequence of information-processing activities any more, but rather a network of activities, a collection of sequences that intersect at many points. The participants might be at different levels, performing different/relevant tasks. Coherence between medium-term level decisions (e.g. production planning) and short-term level decisions (e.g. production scheduling) is of primary importance as it allows reduction of cycle times and thus the increase of the performance of the workshops. Indeed, in workshops, manufacturing a product requires the coordination of various resources such as machines, operators, transport means, etc. This justifies the need for consistency between decisions of different levels.

6.1. GRAI Approach

We identified one enterprise modelling approach to build a representation of enterprise-wide decision management. The GRAI model is a reference through which various elements of real manufacturing world can be identified. The macro conceptual model is used to express one's perception and ideas on the manufacturing system which is decomposed as a set of 3 sub-systems [7]:

- The physical sub-system (people, facilities, materials, techniques) which transform components into finished products.
- The decision sub-system which controls the physical sub-system.
- The information sub-system which links the physical and decision sub-systems.

Particularly within the decision subsystem one finds a hierarchical decision structure composed of decision centres that is used for modelling the decisional structure of the enterprise. Decision centres are connected by a decision frame (objectives, variables, constraints and criteria for decision making.

The GRAI grid concept lies in the fact that any management decision that needs to be taken will always be made with reference to a horizon of time. Managers typically define strategic, tactical, operational and real-time management levels. These levels implicitly involve a hierarchy of decision functions structured as according to decision horizons (periods). The GRAI grid model further classifies functions of management distinguishing three functions: Product management; Resource management; and coordination / planning. As an outcome of this approach, GRAI's goal is to give a generic description of manufacturing system focusing the system's control (production management, in broad sense). The manufacturing system control is treated, at the beginning, from a global point of view and later as a hierarchy of decision centres structured according to time horizons.

Horizon/Period	1. Manage Products	2. co -ordinate plan	3. Manage Resources
Strategic			
Tactical			
Operational			
Real -time			

Figure 1 - Management function vs. Decision horizon [8]

The relationship between decision centres is shown on a matrix, which links the hierarchical position of a decision to the relevant function. The matrix (GRAI grid) links to a GRAI net, which indicates the decision, information and activities carried out at a decision centre [7]. The coordination criterion is temporal. Therefore, a couple of temporal characteristics define each decision level (strategic, tactical and operational):

- Horizon. The time interval over which the decision remains unchanged,
- Period. The time interval after which decisions are reconsidered.

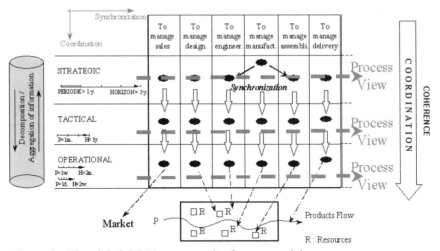

Figure 2 - The global GRAI conceptual reference model

The main idea behind the GRAI grid & nets is to allow modelling globally a decision system. The use of these tools besides the GRAI approach gives an interesting opportunity to managers and analysts: to study a given production system, to analyse it, to identify some improvements axes, and finally to build a new running of that system.

The main objective of our approach is to help manufacturing companies and particularly SMEs to implement a relevant Communication Driven DSS at their premises. This DSS will be used specifically for their production management system. A serious constraint regarding the applicability of the project results is that the specification, implementation and deployment of the solution should be easy and quick. Therefore, the idea is to define a set of generic GRAI grids and nets. These models should represent the case of the most common companies. We will identify first various typologies of companies and their structure. Once these typologies are accepted, we will identify the corresponding GRAI grid and nets. This will provide the library of "generic models" of the production management of manufacturing firms.

6.2. Specific GRAI grid

Each enterprise has its own characteristics, needs and requirements. The set-up of an Enterprise-wide DSS in a given firm cannot be done without any knowledge of its running. Therefore, we want to be able to use an enterprise-oriented GRAI grid for a given enterprise (belonging to a given typology identified earlier). This Grid will be first focused on production management system of the studied enterprises.

- *Supplying, Stock management and Procurement*: These functions manage products inside an enterprise. We consider specifically the supplying function for the long-term decisions. Obviously decisions made by this function will have direct influences on the logistics of bought components and raw materials. Once these components and raw materials inside the firm, managers should manage them inside the stocks. Decisions made here are therefore related to stock management problems. Allowing technical and human resources to work is possible when the procurement function synchronise the distribution of components and needed raw materials to them. This is the final function of this global function. We consider that the components and raw materials are ready for treatments.

- *Planning*: Decisions made in this function are related to the synchronisation of products and resources. Generally these decisions are divided into three levels: global production planning (Master Production Scheduling), detailed production planning (Material Requirements Planning) and finally operations scheduling. These are the main decisions one should identify in a given firm for the production planning.

- *Technical and Human resources management*: In order to be ready to treat components, raw materials and provide them an added value, enterprises should manage their human and technical resources. Decisions regarding the human resources are: 1) training and hiring for long-term, 2) planning and definition of working teams and 3) allocation of resources to short-term tasks.

7. The extended Enterprise-wide Communication Driven DSS

7.1. Concept

While the Inter-Organizational DSS refers to DSS services provided through the web to company's customers or suppliers [2] (e.g. product configurator), we understand our extended Communication Driven DSS as an enterprise-wide (intra) DSS stressing "one-to-many" strategic and tactical interaction with customers and suppliers to support internal decision making. This environment involves supply chain stakeholders into internal decision making as well as to inform them about decisions. Little work has been done on the GRAI model on the sales (i.e. customer) side and supplier management side. We explored an extension to these areas while targeting a prototype implementation based on existing enabling technologies. Figure 3 illustrates our approach based on two companies A and B that are members of supply chain "1". At operational management and shop floor levels as well as between both levels, existing decision flows within and between companies are already well structured. Indeed, current enabling business applications (e.g. Enterprise Resource Planning systems) usually provide an integrated view of the operational information across the functions within a company with the potential to build gateway to other companies. But this provides the required transparency of only transactional relevant information to supply chain partners and not on strategic and tactical planning. At these last levels, inter-organizational decision flows are not well formalized and hampered by:

- processes and communication disruptions
- low level of internal information integration and aggregation
- missing rules for information transactions and need for partner specific rules
- important management reluctance due to confidentiality and protecting know-how

This leads to severe losses of time, information and effort efficiency:

Velocity: very time-consuming product development phase, long-term production planning agreement (down and upstream) and production resources preparation

- *Quality:* non conforming products, product return, high quality control cost
- *Synchronization*: Non-consistent and not up-to-date production and resources planning, undesirable logistic delivery effects (bullwhip effect) and lack of production reactivity.

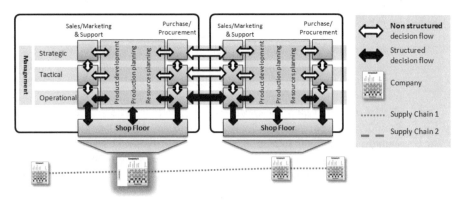

Figure 3 - ESKALE decision flows model in non hierarchical networks

In our approach, sales and purchase/procurement units are not only integrating suppliers/buyers information but also using internal sources to gather supplier/customer relevant information. These units are therefore turned toward the company itself and simultaneously to the outside. The buyer's purchase unit should be seen both as the complement to the seller's sales units and to the buyer's sales units. Synergies between both units could be created instead of antagonisms. Decision will be thus smoothly and quickly taken both through the company itself but also through the supply chain, from one node to another. Each member of the supply chain is making decision in a decentralized manner but involving its direct customers and suppliers and forwarding real-time decision information. This favor participation of manufacturing enterprises in several production networks at the same time. This approach is reflected as well through the business applications that are usually used by both units namely CRM and SRM solutions. Based on this framework, we will develop a prototype that will be an adaptation of existing CRM and SRM solutions and then build pilot implementations at end-users sites demonstrating the success of the approach.

7.2. Customer Relationship Management (CRM)

CRM stands for Customer Relationship Management which is a strategy used to learn more about customers' needs and behaviours in order to develop stronger relationships with them. The idea of CRM is that it helps businesses use technology and human resources to gain insight into the behaviour of customers and the value of those customers. The process can effectively: 1) provide better customer service; 2) make call centres more efficient; 3) cross sell products more effectively; 4) help sales staff close deals faster; 5) simplify marketing and sales processes; 6) discover new customers and 7) increase customer revenues.

CRM is usually considered as part of the marketing, sales and service. Analytical CRM provides analysis of customer and lead behaviour to aid product and service decision making (e.g. pricing, new product development etc.) and allow for management decisions, e.g. financial forecasting and customer profitability analysis. We will use this approach into our overall enterprise-wide decision making system and directly integrate this technology within our overall prototype platform. Access to customer data will be promoted as far as possible through the whole enterprise decision making structure in order to increase customer orientation while leading decisions. The situation of customer should sometimes be taken into account as a whole in order to really understand the context and make the right decision. If the sales, marketing and service department are usually leading communication with customers, the results of these activities should be taken into account in many other units.

7.3. Supplier Relationship Management (SRM)

SRM systems are usually focusing on following activities.
1. Collaborative product design, integrating procurement issues starting at the product design by involving suppliers through a collaborative development platform
2. Sourcing targeting at identifying potential suppliers and mapping them according to prices, capacity, delivery delay and product quality. Then, the best suppliers could be requested to compete for selection.
3. Reverse auctions for the selection of the supplier by allowing to submit three types of request to suppliers: 1) A Request for Quotation (RFQ) to invite suppliers into a bidding process; 2) A Request for Information (RFI) to collect written information about the suppliers capabilities and 3) A Request for Proposal (RFP) inviting suppliers to submit a proposal on a specific commodity or service.
4. The negotiation process involving very sensitive steps like overall situation understanding, argumentation exchange, packaging of potential trades and reaching a final agreement.

7.4. Precustomization and customizability

Precustomization and customizability are two attributes of *DSSs*. For example, if a system provides access to predefined datasets, it is precustomized; if a system allows its users to modify those datasets or create new datasets, it is customizable.

Each enterprise and each relationship has its own characteristics, needs and requirements. The set-up of our solution into a company cannot be done without any knowledge of its overall typology, its specific running and the specificity of each collaborations. The solution we are targeting will be therefore:

- *Pre-customized*: the system will provide predefined enterprise datasets to allow quick deployment;
- *Customizable*: in the system ramp-up phase, the solution will allow easy and quick modification of those datasets according to the company profile. Following to this ramp-up phase, it will also help business information re-engineering at end-user sites by a clearer and regular visualization of the current information exchange architecture
- *Personalised*: the system will allow for easy and quick adaption of the relationships model according to each specific partnership.

8. Technical architecture

The targeted enterprise-wide DSS architecture will include following components:

- *Personalised Information* to filter the information to meet the individual's work style and content preferences. The personalisation features of the desktop are important to assist the user in his daily decision work. Personalisation capabilities range from the look of the desktop to what is displayed where, to filtering and profiling capabilities. Profiling is the capability to continuously update ones profile based on current interest so that relevant information for decision making can be retrieved on an on-going basis. Different pre-defined personalisation according to the employee's decision profiles will be provided.
- *Communication and Collaboration* - forum for decision making interactions among employees. Groupware functionality permitting calendaring, document contributions, process management, work scheduling, chat etc. enable group decision participants to cooperate within their specific decision centres.
- *Document and Content Management* components to create centralized repositories, or libraries, containing all of the unstructured data they generate. Powerful search and retrieval tools make this information easily available for use and decision collaboration across the entire enterprise. Versioning and security profiles ensure lifecycle document integrity.
- *Groupware Calendar* provides an easy-to-use view of organisations decision events, activities, and scheduling.
- *Work organisation and optimisation* covers the following elements: 1) *Processes* - We will see the interaction between decision centres managed in a portal environment through the interaction of different decision workflow at different entry and exit points. The portal will enabled the companies to easily specify and manage decision processes, such as supplier selection or new

employee's introduction; 2) *Publish and Distribute* - support content creation, authorisation, inclusion and distribution. The challenge is not in providing the decision information but rather in approving what is made available to the portal through workflow processes; 3) *Presentation* - integration of information to feed the individual's desktop and 4) *Search* - facility to provide access to information items. The taxonomy structure provides the basis for sifting through information. Simple keyword searches are not enough. Sophisticated capabilities are continuously being developed these will eliminate upwards of 80% of the user effort to filter out unwanted material.

- *Customer relationship* will focus on CRM features to 1) support operational, tactical and strategic communication for collaborative decision making with customers and 2) lead analysis of customers' behaviour and needs.
- *Supplier relationship* will focus on SRM features to 1) support operational, tactical and strategic communication for collaborative decision making with suppliers and 2) lead analysis of suppliers' activities and service quality.

9. Distributing Data-Driven and Model-Driven DSS results

One key issue is also that our solution provides access to other DSS that are necessary for decision making (Data-Driven, Model-Driven and Knowledge-Driven DSS). Our platform, while focusing on organizational issues, will constitute a gateway to the necessary DSS resources. Indeed, data integration across different manufacturing company boundaries is still a major issue. Many systems are already implemented into manufacturing SMEs (CAD, CAP, PPS etc.) independently across the company and accordingly to the main target groups (mainly following organizational structure) without clear information contents demarcations or interoperability. Large manufacturers already set individual solutions but this happen via difficult and expensive gateways or servers. Indeed, only for few very critical operational information flows (eg. those related to product specification and workflow), data transfer solutions are usually already available. In the same time, a whole raft of manufacturing companies (mainly big ones) separately invested in business systems such ERP to automate the financial operations and aspects of the business, such as orders, sales and basic procurement activities. Nevertheless, all these approaches are still far away from a fully achieved transparency of the company allowing for successful decision making. Information are not effectively consolidated and communicated for use in the rest of the company, mainly due to breach in communication systems and lack of expertise in this area (particularly for SMEs). Specific data are available at very specific places, through specific island solutions, and cannot offer global information access to employees according to their individual decision needs. We will develop a holistic approach to map the different systems according to their functionalities and build an integrative system. To this aim, we will consider the decision centers identified through the GRAI model and their associated DSS and IMS. This system will complement existing operational flow, while aggregating all necessary data and disseminating them across the company according to individual decision making needs and access rights.

10. Conclusion

This paper presented our first findings and the approaches that we are following to address collaborative decision management within manufacturing networks. There are two major aspects in the development of a high quality decision management within non-hierarchical manufacturing networks: 1) clear enterprise-wide decision management structure and 2) involvement of customers and suppliers into decision processes. These two aspects are overlapped and interact. The customer orientation involves CRM technologies; the supplier orientation involves SRM technologies.

Our enterprise modelling approach will allow building an integrative enterprise-wide platform connected to other DSS and Information Management solutions. Defining manufacturing typology and related enterprise models ready for precustomization, mapping other IT solutions within the models and defining customisation rules will be the key research issues.

However, while dealing with enterprise networks, we should keep in mind that one of the most important barriers to collaboration is trust. Mutual trust is a condition sine qua non for any decision management partnership, but with widely divergent and geographically separated parties special efforts may be needed to achieve it. While selecting suppliers with a solid reputation will provide the basis, building up trust will heavily depend on openness and good communication. With regard to the customer: a customer partnership strategy based on a step-by-step win-win approach will allow a gradual build-up of trust through interaction leading to tangible results.

References

[1]   Collaborative Decision-Making: A Tool for Effective Leadership OD Network Annual Conference 2004 - Karp Consulting Group, Inc. & Lara Weitzman Organization Development & Dynamics
[2]   D. J. Power, Decision Support Systems - Concepts and Resources for Managers - Greenwood Publishing, 2000, ISBN: 1-56720-497-X
[3]   Glossary of terms pertaining to Collaborative Environments, Retrieved 1 December 2007, from EU Commision   web   site: http://ec.europa.eu/information_society/activities/atwork/collaboration_at_work/glossary/index_en.htm
[4]   Wilson, P. (1991). Computer Supported Cooperative Work: An Introduction. Kluwer Academic Pub.
[5]   R. Bakker-Dhaliwal, M.A. Bell, P. Marcotte, and S. Morin, Decision support systems (DSS): information technology in a changing world - Philippines. Retrieved 20 November, 2007, from IRRI web site: http://www.irri.org/publications/irrn/pdfs/vol26no2/irrn262mini1.pdf
[6]   Qian Chen, TEAMDEC: A GROUP DECISION SUPPORT SYSTEM. Thesis submitted to the Faculty of the Virginia Polytechnic Institute and State University, 1998
[7]   Manufacturing Management. Retrieved 4 December, 2007, from Advanced Manufacturing Research Centre   (AMRC)   web   site   of   the   University   of   Sheffield: http://www.amrc.co.uk/research/index.php?page_id=18
[8]   Bernus P., Uppington G. "A Co-ordination of management activities - mapping organizational structure to the decision structure". In Coordination Technology for Collaborative Application - Organizations, Processes, and Agents, W.Conen and G.Neumann (Eds), LNCS 1364, Springer Verlag, Berlin pp25-38, 1998

Collaborative Decision Making: Perspectives and Challenges
P. Zaraté et al. (Eds.)
IOS Press, 2008

99

ECLIPS
Extended Collaborative integrated LIfe cycle Planning System

A. PEYRAUD[a], E. JACQUET-LAGREZE[b], G. MERKURYEVA[c],
S. TIMMERMANS[d], C. VERLHAC[e], V. DE VULPILLIERES[f]

[a] *Aurelie.Peyraud@eurodecision.com,* [b] *Eric.Jacquet-Lagreze@eurodecision.com,*
[c] *gm@itl.rtu.lv,*
[d] *Sara.Timmermans@mobius.be,* [e] *Celine.Verlhac@eurodecision.com,*
[f] *Veronique.deVulpillieres@eurodecision.com*

Abstract. ECLIPS is a European research project, partially funded by the European Commission in the context of its Research Framework Programme 6. Six partners participate in this research project: MÖBIUS (Belgium), EURODECISION (France), LoQutus (Belgium), the Technical University of RIGA (Latvia), Huntsman Advanced Materials (Germany), PLIVA-Lachema Diagnostika (Czech Republic). For more information about ECLIPS we recommend to visit the project web site www.eclipsproject.com. The overall goal of this project is to extend supply chain expertise to recent evolutions: globalisation, products diversification, and shortening of products life cycles. We consider that any life cycle can be divided into three phases: introduction, maturity and end-of-life. Three main issues are considered: Improve the statistical prediction of the demand at the beginning and at the end of a product life. Increase the profit during maturity phase by making cyclic the production at all levels of the process. From a pure mathematical point of view, Multi-Echelon Cyclic Planning induces an additional cost. However, simplification of production management and increase of the manufacturing efficiency should counterbalance this cost. More generally, to improve the whole life cycle management of products in supply chain, including switches between the three phases.

Keywords. mixed integer linear problem, large-scale problem, cyclical scheduling, supply chain management, forecast, Genetic Algorithm

1. Ambition of the ECLIPS project

In order to address the current supply chain challenges, MÖBIUS, a consulting company specializing in Supply Chain and Business Process Management, has launched the ECLIPS research project with 5 other partners. The total **ECLIPS consortium** is composed of the following members:

MÖBIUS (Fr, Be, UK)	Project coordinator
Riga Technical University (Lv)	Academic partner, specialized in artificial intelligence
Eurodécision (Fr)	Optimization experts
LoQutus (Be)	Expert in information systems and data integration

Pliva-Lachema Diagnostika (Cz)   Industrial   partner   /
pharmaceuticals

Huntsman Advanced Materials (De) Industrial partner / chemicals

ECLIPS stands for "**Extended Collaborative integrated Lifecycle Planning System**". This 3 years research project was launched in the second quarter of 2006. It is supported by the European Commission within the **Sixth EU Framework Programme** for Research and Technological Development.

The objective of the ECLIPS project is to **provide breakthrough solutions** for the current challenges to the industry. Companies are facing ever more **complex supply chains**, increased portfolio diversification and **shortening product lifecycles**. ECLIPS explores and develops solutions, in terms of **concept and software**, in order to take up the challenges of global Supply Chain optimisation.

ECLIPS defined **3 key research topics** for the different stages in a general product lifecycle:

- Introduction and end-of-life: Improved statistical forecasting,
- Maturity phase: Multi-echelon cyclic planning,
- Lifecycle integration: Automated switching in Supply Chain management.

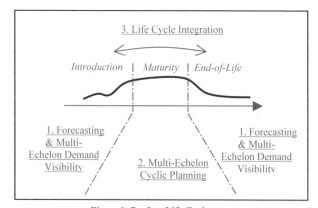

Figure 1. Product Life Cycle

For the **introduction** and the **end-of-life** product phase, ECLIPS has set up, by using artificial intelligence techniques, the methodology to create a library of introduction and end-of-life product profiles. From this database, a profile will be allocated to newly introduced or dying products. The forecast will automatically adapt itself to changes in the actual sales for the new or dying items.

In the **maturity** phase, ECLIPS will set up an integrated synchronization of the multiple steps in the Supply Chain through a multi-echelon cyclic planning technique. The synchronization will avoid intermediary stocks between each process and as such reduce the average stock within the global Supply Chain. The used technique is mixed integer linear programming.

Moreover, ECLIPS will automate the **switching** from one technique to another throughout the lifecycle. This issue is unexplored, even from an academic perspective. This research is aimed at tackling the continuous shortening of the product life cycle.

We developed a software component which can be bolted onto existing ERP and APS packages and that will give access to a number of expert functions for those systems. A software component has been developed for each key topic of research.

2. Research and development

2.1. Product Introduction / End of life: Forecasting

In the past, the issue of product introduction and end-of-life was less important. However, the shortening of product life cycles, due to the growing requirements of product diversification and customisation, makes this issue ever more important.

Nowadays, many companies are struggling to control the process of effective product introduction and end-of-life. This control includes an efficient management of demand forecasting, but the traditional forecasting techniques (such as time series) are not adapted for the following reasons:

- Concerning the introduction of the product, the company is facing the lack of historical data or a lack of market knowledge,
- Concerning the product end-of-life, the company is likely to delay the decision to stop the sales and production of that product. The marketing department prefers to keep the product on the market as long as possible, in case a customer would still be interested.

Companies therefore need to manually calculate a demand forecast for new and end-of-life product. This means:

- Biased and often over optimistic forecasting when it is carried out through an aggressive sales plan,
- Static forecasting which does not reflect or adapt to the incoming sales information.

This static approach is not only a source of unused stock but also of unmatched demand.

The current forecasting techniques and manual forecasting have not had satisfying results. Therefore, we need to explore new techniques in order to respond to the management issues of new and end-of-life products.

Against the background of these challenges, ECLIPS has developed a technique of making forecasts for new and dying products with the explicit functionality that these forecasts will adapt themselves as new actual demand information becomes available.

The scheme in below presents the general methodology and the flows of the data in the forecasting algorithms developed by ECLIPS:

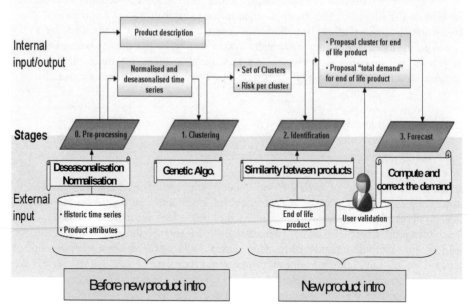

Figure 2. Forecasting algorithm

Forecasting of products demand in the in/outtroduction phase is as a process divided into three main stages:

- **Clustering**: Using cluster analysis for summarising the data about in/outtroduction phases of different products. Clustering will create automatically a number of groups of alike or related product in/outtroduction profiles (set of clusters). A genetic algorithm has been used to determine the clusters. In the case of outtroductions, the clustering stage will create a set of clusters and the obsolescence risk linked to each cluster. Where so far we were dependent on rules of thumb for the risk assessment with respect to the probability that the next periods of demand would fall below a given critical threshold, it is now possible to determine this probability with far more accuracy. The defining of order fulfillment strategies like MTO and MTS can strongly benefit from this.
- **Identification**: Identification finds the closed historical product introductions based on weighted quantitative and qualitative criteria. It proposes a number of "nearest" clusters and initial demand for the product
- **Forecasting**: Forecasting product demand level according to its cluster by translating it in absolute demand and possibility to correct and update that forecast when new demand becomes available. As the new product's behavior deviates from the supposed cluster, traditional forecasting methodology can take over. In the case of outtroduction phase, the user will have the ability to select a threshold level for which the probability will be stated that the demand will drop below it.

A real life application of the three aforementioned stages requires the **pre-processing** of the data. In the general scheme of the research, the stage of data pre-processing will be regarded as the zero stage. Pre-processing is the task that will transform the data on historic product or product family in/outtroductions into a set of databases that is suited for the consequent stages of the ECLIPS forecasting methodology. Pre processing consists in aggregating, selecting, cleaning (which includes among others deseasonalisation) and normalising the data.

Below, we present an example of clustering results. The following graph represents a view of all historic products introductions:

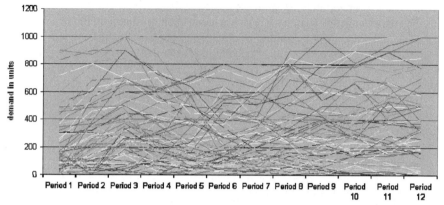

Figure 3. Overview of all historical product Introductions

The graphs below present the different introduction profiles (or clusters) obtained:

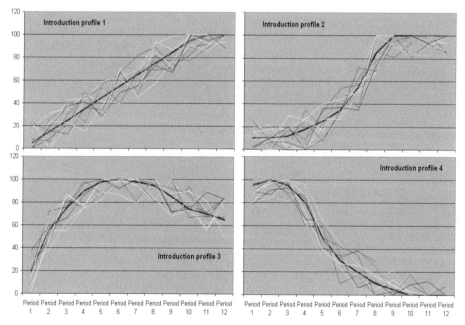

Figure 4. Introduction profiles

One of the identified clusters is ascribed to a new product using similarity measures of the product to products in the clusters. The user can validate or change the proposed profiles. The relative values of the profile allow the forecasting calculation in absolute values by using the forecasting of the demand level.

2.2. Maturity Phase: Multi-Echelon Cyclic Planning

ECLIPS has investigated the integrated synchronisation of the multiple stages of the supply chain through multi–echelon cyclic planning. In the industries using batch processes, a cyclic plan does also bring the opportunity to determine and hold an optimal sequence for producing multiple products.

The diagram below presents a multi–echelon cyclic planning in the pharmaceutical industry. The network is composed of 3 sites (3 echelons). A process which has a 4 week cycle is planned at each site. The solid blue segments represent the beginning of a process and the hatched segments represent the end of a process after a certain lead time.

The lead time is 2 weeks for the highest echelon and 1 week for the lower echelons. We can note that the echelons are synchronized. Indeed, the stock of one upstream echelon is directly consumed by the following echelon.

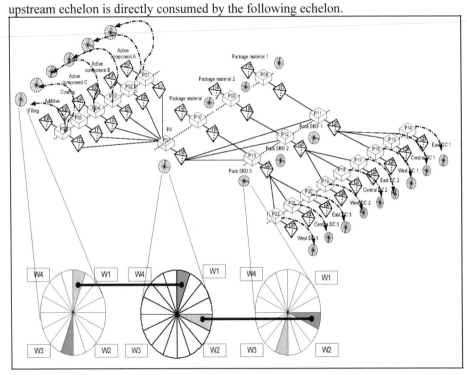

Figure 5. Example of multi-echelon cyclic planning

Synchronisation can avoid intermediate stocks between each process and thus decrease the average stock of global Supply Chain. In a classic diagram, these processes would be independent and the stock wouldn't be optimised.

The illustration above is a simple example of three synchronised cycles of three different process but the cycles can be different for each process and the obtained results are linked to the optimisation of the total global costs instead of optimizing each echelon independently.

ECLIPS constraints are applied to the frequency of production but not to the quantity. These frequencies are optimised for the global supply chain. Today, a Mixed

Integer Linear Programming is used to solve this problem. This year, we will extend our research by using the RSM (Response Surface Methodology).

2.2.1. Conceptual model

The underlying idea of Multi-Echelon Cyclic Planning is to use **cyclic schedules for mid term planning** and coordination **at multiple echelons** in the supply chain.

An optimization model has been developed that aims mainly at finding the optimal cycles of production in a generic supply chain network by minimizing the setup, production and holding costs while taking into account constraints such as production and storage capacity limitations. The model determines also when the production should be switched on and gives as an output the optimal production and stock level for each period of the planning horizon.

The generality of the model allows considering any type of multi-echelon network. The generality is obtained by representing the network through stages. A stage corresponds to a process part and a stockpoint. A process can be production, transportation or any possible handling of physical goods that requires time and resources.

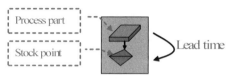

Figure 6. A stage consists of a process part and a stockpoint

A whole network can then be modeled as follows:

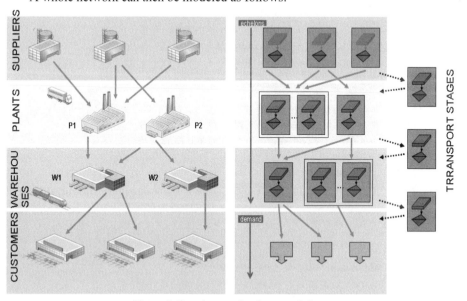

Figure 7. Generic network - Conceptual views

The model calculates the optimal cycle of production at every stage.

2.2.2. Mixed Integer Linear Program : assumptions and model

The assumptions that have been considered so far are presented below. The conceptual developments that are started in 2007 will relax these assumptions.

- Lead times of processes are constant
- Process capacities are finite
- Independent demand at the end stages and at the intermediate stages
- Fixed set-up and ordering cost
- Linear inventory holding cost
- Multiple products
- No backlogging allowed
- Lead-time is defined on the process part of a stage; Zero lead-time between stages
- Infinite production / consumption rate
- Multi-echelon cyclic planning policy
- Demand is known (deterministic) but not necessarily constant

Here follows a brief presentation of the model (MILP).
The mathematical model requires the following data:
- Network description
- BOM (Bill of material)
- Demand
- Capacities (min/max for production and storage)
- Costs

The model aims at determining different types of variables:
- Production quantity for each stage and time step
- Storage level for each stage, product and time step
- Status of the process (switched on/off) for each time step
- Cycle for each stage

The constraints taken into account are:
- Demand constraint for each customer, product and time step
- Production capacity constraints by stage and time step
- Storage capacity constraints by product, stage and time step
- Cyclic constraints
- Shared capacity constraints (if existing on storage and production for group of stages)

The objective is to minimize the production costs, the setup costs and the holding costs.

2.3. Lifecycle integration: Automated Switching

The idea is to develop automated switching:
- in the forecasting domain: when to switch to and from product introduction / termination techniques based on artificial intelligence.
- in the planning domain: when to switch towards and away from multi-echelon cyclic planning

For switching in forecasting we will focus on measuring forecast accuracy. The technique that gives the better prediction is preferable. The following graph illustrates that traditional forecasting techniques perform better as the demand pattern becomes more stable towards the maturity phase.

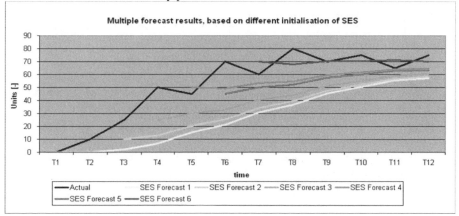

Figure 8. SES forecast performance according to algorithm initiation

For switching in planning we first need to explain the concept of a "best practice":

- the fact that the policy is cyclic is an extra constraint on the planning, as such it is theoretically not the most optimal policy
- in general we believe the efficiency of a planning policy is inversely related to its complexity, more simple policies perform better, we believe cyclic planning policy to be simple and intuitive, everything in life goes in cycles, this explains why we perceive a cyclic planning as something natural

The combination of these two implies that the best policy in theory is not necessarily the best policy in practice. We call the best policy in practice a "best practice". We believe multi-echelon cyclic planning to be a "best practice". Indeed, in practice, it is more efficient and simpler. This is illustrated in the following diagram:

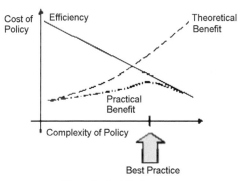

Figure 9. Best Pratice

Moreover, multi–echelon cyclic planning involves considerable benefits. Schmidt E., Dada M., Ward J., Adams D. in *Using cyclic planning to manage capacity at ALCOA* (Interfaces, 31(3): 16-27, 2001) present the case of the company **Aluminium Corporation of America** (ALCOA) which has implemented cyclic planning at a bottleneck operation to improve capacity management. It implies the following direct improvements:

- WIP inventory has decreased 60 %.
- Over 8 months output increased by 20%.
- Backlog of customer orders decreased by 93% (from 500000 pounds = about five months of production to only 36000 pounds = about 10 days of production).
- The realized capacity increased from 70% to 85%.
- The production rate increased by +/-20%.

We switch to and from cyclic planning in controlling the additional theoretical cost of the multi-echelon cyclic plan. The calculation of this cost is the following:

$$ACCS = \frac{(Cyclic - Noncyclic\ Solution\ Cost)}{Noncyclic\ Solution\ Cost}$$

The research results show that this theoretical cost is impacted by 2 main parameters:

- Coefficient of demand variation (CODVAR);
- Capacity utilization (CAP);

The graph below represents the additional theoretical cost of the multi-echelon cyclic plan according to the above parameters:

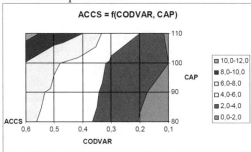

Figure 10. Additional theoretical cost of a multi-echelon cyclic plan

We strongly believe that an ACCS of 10% will be reached by using a more efficient policy in practice. It will allow us to use a cyclic planning for very variable products in limited capacity environment.

3. Software Development: Add-Ons / Services

3.1. Software presentation

The ECLIPS solution is composed of the following major functionalities:

- Communication capabilities (supports both internal as external communication)
- Forecasting
- Switching
- Planning
- Simulation capabilities (in progress)
- Operational capabilities

Each of these functionalities can be situated in one of the 3 major layers – Integration Layer, Business Layer and GUI Layer – of the ECLIPS solution.

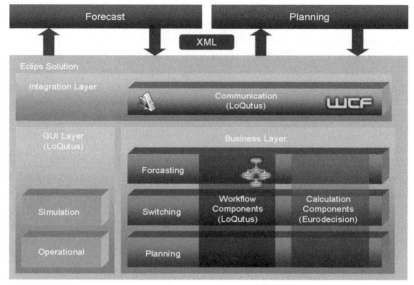

Figure 11. ECLIPS Software

3.2. Advantages of the software developed by ECLIPS

The table below compares the functionalities of the existing ERP/APS softwares with those developed by ECLIPS by presenting the advantages that the ECLIPS project gives:

Current ERP/SC software	ECLIPS	Advantages
Manual and static forecasts for New Product Introduction / End of Product Life	New Quantitative Techniques from the domain of artificial intelligence: - Clustering - Libraries of similar profiles	- Better forecasting for new products - Better stock depletion of old products - The right product in the right place at the right time - Closing the gap between marketing and stock/production operations
Single echelon management of multiple locally integrated planning blocks	Coordination through multi echelon cyclic planning: - Linear Programming with constraint - Response Surface Methodology	- Elimination of Bullwhip Effect - Significant reduction of the cyclic Stock - More effective Capacity Utilisation - Collaboration through the Supply Chain without extensive sharing of information
Ad hoc management of transitions in the product lifecycle	Integrated Lifecycle Management: - Measuring forecast accuracy - Measuring of the additional theoretical cost of cyclic planning	- Smoother transition between life cycle phases - Better forecasting and planning throughout the product lifecycle - Cost simulation of alternative forecasting and planning policies

3.3. Proof of concept

Huntsman Advanced Materials offers an ideal environment to test the tool developed by ECLIPS, in particular for the multi echelon cyclic planning system. Indeed, the environment of this company is very complex and consists of up to 4 echelons that are planned independently…if we don't take the transportation process between each site into account. It is a global environment, with long distances between each site and large volumes in production and transportation.

Pliva-Lachema Diagnostika (PLD) environment can't be more different. PLD is an SME active in the production of clinical tests. Its principal market is Eastern Europe and Russia. All purchase, production and distribution operations are made on the same site at Brno in Czech Republic.

The fact that we can test our concepts in such different environments allows us to make strong conclusions in the potential of ECLIPS for the companies in different sectors.

4. Way forward

The Simulation component is currently developed and will be integrated in the software. The "best practice" assumptions will be validated through simulation.

By the end of the 2nd year of the ECLIPS project, the extended research on maturity and switching components will be finished; the implementation and testing of the updated components will be done in the 3rd year.

We also plan to operate the software in real life during the 3rd year. The tool will be installed at the site of the industrial partners Pliva-Lachema Diagnostika and Huntsman Advanced Materials.

References

[1] Ph. Vallin (1999) "La logistique: modèles et méthodes de pilotage des flux", 4ème édition, Economica
[2] Ph. Vallin (1999) "Détermination d'une période économique robuste dans le cadre du modèle de Wilson", RAIRO Recherche Opérationnelle 33, 1, 47-67
[3] H. Wagner and T.M. Whitin (1958) "Dynamic Version of the Economic Lotsize Model", Management Science 5 89–9
[4] A Bayesian Model to Forecast New Product Performance in Domestic and International Markets - R.Neelamegham P.Chintagunta - Marketing Science, 1999
[5] Forecasting and Inventory Management of Short Life-Cycle Products - AA Kurawarwala, H Matsuo - Operations Research, 1996
[6] An exploratory investigation of new product forecasting practices - KB Kahn - Journal of Product Innovation Management, 2002

Collaborative Decision Making: Perspectives and Challenges
P. Zaraté et al. (Eds.)
IOS Press, 2008

Ethical Issues in Global Supply Chain Management

Andrew M McCosh

Alvah Chapman Eminent Scholar in Management and Ethics
Florida International University, Miami

Abstract. The paper addresses the general nature of a supply chain as a human artifact with potential for greatness and for failure like any other. The exact nature of the possible failures and successes are discussed, and the ethical issues identified. The hazards of adversarial supply chain management, especially the more vicious forms of it, are identified. Intra-chain brutality is rarely as profitable as mutual supportiveness if we think, as the world's first international lawyer said we should, prudently and well into the future. The paper concludes with one drastic example of what happens when we do not.

Keywords. Ethics, Supply Chain Management. Globalisation, Competitiveness

Introduction

[1] defined competition in the first dictionary over two centuries ago. He said competition was endeavoring to gain what another endeavored to gain at the same time. On that basis, the parties might share the benefit, or one might succeed completely, to the other's acute loss. This is still the situation. [2] has suggested that competition has changed a bit since the great dictionarist was active. Now, says [2], competition is not really between companies, it is between supply chains. Perhaps there is no real difference. The old style fully integrated corporation was a supply chain all on its own. The new style supply chain, brought into being by (inter alia) the current fashion for focus on core businesses, is a collation of specialized firms which do, between them, the same job as the old ones did, only faster. In any event there is competition, and it is carried on at a fierce pace. My task in this paper is to consider whether there are any ethical issues in this situation. If there are, we have to consider what can be done to deal with them.

[3] defines a supply chain as a set of three or more companies linked together by flows of products, finance, services, and information in an ideally seamless web. He admits, however (P48), that there are very few of these seamless webs in operation. There aren't enough managers available who have the skills to make the seamless web work right. We appear, then, to have a seamless web with holes in it. To some extent, therefore, there must be a repair crew attached to at least some of the supply chains to repair damaged links as may be necessary. We might speculate that the supply chains with fractured links would display inconsistencies and occasional failures in performance, however industriously the repair crews bend to their tasks. We do not actually need to speculate. [4] have studied these events, and have concluded that the effect of these deficiencies has been very considerable. Using the event study

methodology which is standard in finance research, they show that "supply chain glitches" cause the share values of the companies in which the glitches happen to drop by nearly a fifth during the year in which the glitch is announced. Interestingly, the share price drop comes in three stages. Half of the drop precedes the announcement of the glitch, so the share market was aware that something was adrift. A third takes place on the announcement day, and the remaining sixth takes place slowly over the next six months.

I have begun with this negative story for a reason. There has been a great flood of enthusiastic hype about the value of supply chains, the benefits that can arise from their use, and the advantages which accrue from managing them skillfully. I do not doubt that many supply chains are highly beneficial to the participating firms, and may also be of value to final customers of the chain. [5] provide some evidence to this effect. [6] also gave a recent instance of the benefits in his account of how a Hong Kong retailer worked with [1]'s inventory system. I merely note that a supply chain is a humanly constructed artifact in which all the important non-standard transactions are performed by people, not by EDI. The supply chain managers are, I assume, doing their best. They are doing their best under serious pressure, notably time pressure, but also performance or quality pressure.

When any human system is being designed, and when a pressure point is identified at the design stage, the designer may well try to come to a judgment on how the pressure point is going to be handled. As a general rule, though, the designer will not be able to enforce his judgment. The standing culture of the enterprise will be brought into operation, instantly and automatically, when a critical event takes place. Douglas [7] identified Theory X businesses and Theory Y businesses over forty years ago. Theory X states that workers are an idle lot and the only way to get action is to threaten them with various dire consequences. Theory Y says that workers are really good people who would like to contribute to the welfare of the firm, given half a chance, and if they are encouraged and supported they will come through and support the business in its hour of need.

If the company experiencing a glitch is a theory X company, the whip will come out, usually metaphorically. If it is a theory Y company, the workers will rally round and fix the problem, in the sure and certain knowledge that they will be reasonably rewarded for their endeavours. When we have a supply chain, however, the situation can get complicated. If one of the companies is a theory X company, and thinks the other company (which works on theory Y) caused the glitch, we have a major problem in the making. The behaviours of the two sets of managers involved at the point of dispute will be in acute conflict, at least on the first few occasions when a dispute arises. The problem may be made worse if the supply chain members are situated in different countries, each of which has different expectations concerning how a business, and a business partner, should behave.

Let me illustrate with the tale of a supply chain, concerned with the entire process of supply of a luxury good. There were five companies in the chain, and slightly more than that number of countries.

Activity	Selling Price To next chain Member	Location
Extraction	100	Cote d'Ivoire
Refinement	250	South Africa
Production	550	Belgium

| Distribution | 700 | UK |
| Consumption | 1000 | USA,UK,France,Holland,etc |

The approximate final selling price of one thousand was achieved by the retail enterprises in various locations, notably New York, London, Paris, and the other standard luxury goods selling locations. This price chain was stable for ten years. A sudden lurch in the confidence of the customer group who buy this product took place. Despite an effort to ignore the market decline, the situation was not tenable. The final price had to give. After a period, the situation (more or less) restabilised as shown below. The restabilisation was a ferocious process, involving violent arguments, threats of legal action, actual legal actions, and (it is rumoured) at least one murder.

Activity	Selling Price To next chain Member	Location	New Selling Price to next Chain Member	Percent Drop
Extraction	100	Cote d'Ivoire	15	85
Refinement	250	South Africa	125	50
Production	550	Belgium	425	23
Distribution	700	UK	575	18
Consumption	1000	Luxury Spots	750	25

Nobody in this supply chain could be expected to view the change with enthusiasm. The London location suffered the smallest revenue decline, and managed to hold on to its unit revenue margin, but even 18% is rather painful. The retailers were suffering serious business declines on other luxury product lines, and were moderately stoical about the loss. It had happened before, and it would happen again. The high-tech production operation in Belgium was able to hold on to its unit revenue margin as well, because of a virtual monopoly on the relevant production skills. As so often happens, the entities which suffered the most were the earliest in the supply chain. South Africa dropped from a margin per unit of 150 to 110. Cote d'Ivoire dropped a disastrous 85% to 15 per unit.

Financially, it is clear that the demand drop requires some kind of change in the transfer price sequence used in this global supply chain. Entrepreneurially, none of the parties wants to take any of the loss if they could avoid it. Morally, if we want the supply chain to continue to exist, using force on the others will not work. If you choose to act brutally against one of the other units of the global supply chain, they will obey you, and they will respect you. But only until they can get behind you with a sharp dagger. In the example, the companies (and countries) early in the supply chain have formed a new alliance with a production company in a middle eastern country, and the chain described in the example has ceased to operate.

We have a choice. When you are trying to create a new enterprise, you always have a host of choices to make, including the general attitude and culture that you will adopt. The ruling coalition has that option. While operating within or close to the law, the coalition, which may only have one member, can decide to adopt any one of a wide range of possible corporate cultures. At one extreme we have the "corporation" that built the pyramids. Any slave who became too exhausted to keep hauling on the rope that dragged the sledge that carried the stone that Pharaoh wanted was simply beheaded. There are no enterprises operating at that extreme nowadays. We do have quite a number of third world companies which make very severe demands on their workforces, including children. Many of these companies make subassemblies of products which are to be exported to first world countries, and some at least of the ultimate buyers might be horrified to learn of the conditions under which the products, and especially the sub-assemblies, are made. A recent triumph of the Ashoka fellowship scheme has been to persuade major Brazilian companies to "police" their own supply chains, all the way back to the children in the woods who prepare charcoal for smelting iron. This has resulted in the children going to school and working in alternate weeks. This has been a success story, but there are too many others we have yet to rectify.

The opposite choice is exemplified by the paternalistic companies. The owner-managers of these try to ensure the welfare of their workers. The Rowntree organisation, a candy maker in the UK, was one example. The Cadbury organisation, run by another Quaker family, was another. Aaron Feuerstein, owner of Malden Mills in Lawrence, Massachusetts, who kept on all the workers after a catastrophic fire, and was rewarded by their dedication to the task of bringing the company back to full operation, was another. They can be criticized for being paternalistic, if you feel so inclined, but it was a much better way to operate than the opposite extreme.

Most of us do not want to operate at either of these extremes, certainly not the Pharoahonic one. We want to behave decently, but we want to be prosperous as well. We are quite happy for the workers to be prosperous, within reason. We are quite happy for our suppliers to be prosperous. Unfortunately, the world is not always organised in a fashion which enables everyone to achieve this goal. We have to do a balancing act. We probably do not want to be unethical. At the same time, we do not want to be so ethical that we put ourselves out of business. How can we get this balance right?

In the next section, I offer a discussion of a few of the concepts of ethics, as they have been developed over the last three millennia. After that I shall deal with a number of the conflicts that can arise in a Global Supply Chain, and suggest some mottoes to bear in mind. A supply chain that is run by the lead company in the manner in which Pharoah's executive team built the pyramids will not last. A supply chain that is not managed at all is unlikely to last either. I hope to convince you that skilful management, parsimonious finance, and consistently ethical interpersonal relations will provide the best possible result. You may say you knew that already. In that case, there are quite a few other people who could usefully be taught what it means.

1. Ethical Thinking Precedes Ethical Management Action

The first job to be done in carrying out an ethical analysis of a proposed management action is to specify, as precisely as possible, what the current proposal amounts to. Exactly what do we have in mind? The second step is to draw up a list of the people, or groups of people, who will be affected for good or ill by our current proposal. Thirdly, we have to draw up a list of the consequences for each of these people or groups. Some of these consequences will be very beneficial, potentially long-term, very exciting, and totally positive. Others will be horrible and instantaneous. You should not try to go beyond the groups reasonably close to the proposed change. Perhaps twenty people or groups would be enough. This list of the people affected, for good or ill, is an essential preparation for ethical thinking. Then, we bring to bear the thinking of some of the world's greatest minds on how the situation should be handled. I have time here to consider only four of them.

First, listen to Hugo Grotius, the world's first international lawyer. He invented the idea that a law might apply to more than one kingdom. A philosopher whose practical clout in 1625 meant he was consulted by every important king in Europe. Another of his inventions was the "prudent man", a creature still revered in legal circles, but elusive in modern business. "When choosing an action" said Grotius " think what a prudent man, who looks well into the future, would do in this situation".

Then let us hear from Immanuel Kant. Perhaps the greatest intellect who has ever lived. His older contemporary, Isaac Newton, certainly thought he was. His 1780 rule for how we should treat each other was known as the categorical imperative. The one rule we should never disobey. "Always treat people, including yourself, as an end in him or herself, never only as a means to an end". We may not, in other words, regard people as disposable machine tools, to be discarded when they seem to have grown blunt.

The third authority is Aristotle. The brains behind Alexander the Great's 350BC invasions of most of the known world, including India, Aristotle was the creator of the doctrine of the mean. Virtues are the mean point between two vices. For instance, using modern terminology, he said that "cost-effectiveness is the virtue that lies between the vices of prodigality and meanness". The ability to get that judgment right is acquired the same way all the other moral abilities are learned, by habit and practice. Aristotle was emphatic that you cannot achieve morality by listening to teaching or by reading; you have to practice it.

My fourth and last source is also the most ancient. [8] died about 370BC. He was the most up-beat philosopher I have found anywhere, a direct follower and interpreter of Confucius. His ideas were contained in a book which has been read by every Chinese who has sought a role in government for the last thousand years. "As a leader, be benevolent, and be inspiring. Your people will be loyal to you if YOU are considerate towards them". Another of his dicta was "people are naturally good. But they can learn how to be evil if they are taught how".

The aggregation of these ancient "sound-bites" could be written in the following terms:

> Long-term prudence
> Treat people with respect
> Don't waste resources, especially human resources
> Manage inclusively and considerately to build loyalty.

When we bring these ideas together with the more conventional criteria for judging a new management concept, we will find that we cannot really add up the various assessments and obtain a meaningful total. An ethical assessment can be obtained, as we will show below. A financial and business assessment can be obtained, using DCF and Gap analysis and various other tools. However you cannot add an ethical score of "appalling" to a financial net present value of "plus three billions" and get a total. You have a strategic objective, you have a financial objective, and you have an ethical objective. You cannot add them together. They are different in kind. Let us examine the business and financial issues first, and the ethical ones after that.

2. The Business and Financial Issues

One of the reasons why supply chain management, especially global SCM, became a subject for discussion was the financial imperative. A current fashion among institutional shareholders is to pester managers to focus on their core business. Non-core businesses have been and continue to be systematically sold off. In some instances, core elements of the business were sold off as well, in the belief that a small, specialized, sub-contractor may be able to do part of the job better than a department of the big firm could. "Better" in this context might mean faster, higher quality, or at lower cost, among other possibilities. When this is done, the big firm has a supply chain, and if it does not manage that chain, it is liable to be worse off than it was before. Supply chain management is therefore an inevitable result of corporate focus. SCM, however, does not always mean smaller capability. [9] note that having a substantial amount of flexible capacity in times of uncertainty may be an absolute necessity, not a luxury.

Additional reasons for the creation of global supply chains have been listed by [10]. Transport and communications technologies have improved beyond recognition. Protective tariffs have been removed, to a considerable extent. This has enabled desirable products from advanced countries to displace more primitive editions of the same item made in less developed nations. This is not all good news, as we will note below, but it has certainly facilitated the growth of globalised supply chains. Another reason for GSCM listed by Hill is the development of "super-countries". ASEAN, EU, and NAFTA are all facilitating the internationalization of products and services.

A benefit arising from sourcing a product from a relatively poor country is discussed in [11]. When a plant is relocated from a rich country to a poor country, the transfer makes a small contribution towards international equality. The laid-off employees of the company in the rich country are, at least for a time, less well off than they were and the GNP of the rich country dips a little. The newly hired employees of the same company in the poorer country now have a job, or perhaps have a better job than before. The GNP of the poorer country goes up, slightly. These changes are individually minute, but when a lot of these relocations happen, the total can get significant. Some of these moves are made with great reluctance. Stride-rite, an American shoemaker, was very proud of its US-based production facilities, but it was eventually forced by competition to move many of them to China [12]. Their US workers cost $1300 a month, while the Chinese (who worked a fifty hour week) cost $150.

It is very important to note that the plant relocations mentioned above are far from being panaceas. They will only benefit the company if the workforce in the new country is at least reasonably productive. [12] reports that the "Maquiladora" plants in northern Mexico had a substantial cost advantage compared to plants on the other side of the border. A wage ratio of $1.64 to $16.17, or roughly ten, was mentioned. [13], however, reports that the productivity ratio in some border plants was about the same, but in the opposite direction. I should make it clear that they were studying different plants, and that Finn was reporting on Mexican plants which were relatively new.

Two additional points of concern from a business viewpoint might be mentioned. [14] warns against developing close friendships along a supply chain. If we do not watch out, she argues, such friendships could cause our negotiators to be weak, and could damage our return on investment. My personal experience from running a business was different. Having a friendship with some of our suppliers meant they would do things for us that they would not do for other customers. When it came to renewal time, we fought like cats for two days. Friendship was restored for the next 363 days. This issue needs to be considered, but could go either way.

Secondly, [15] notes that extensive disputes take place all along the supply chain. He mentions the advertising spends, for instance, in which local dealers want the large firm to help place newspaper ads in their territories, while the manufacturer would rather spend on national TV campaigns to support the product. These disputes all add to the friction in GSCM, though they can usually be resolved eventually.

The coupling and decoupling of a supply chain, whether caused by disputes or otherwise, are important issues, but they are hardly new. I attended part of a course taught by [16] in which this problem was an important component, and in which various simulation modeling methods, notably Monte Carlo, could be deployed to understand the issues. His Industrial Dynamics book remains a valuable contribution to the problem.

There are two very specifically <u>financial</u> issues which affect the ways in which supply chains are managed and promoted as the best way forward. The first of these is a negative influence on the operation of the supply chain approach. Stock options are now a major element in the remuneration of managers of businesses. A stock option is specific to a company. It is affected, indirectly, by the success of the supply chain(s) to which the company belongs. But it is really only calculated on the basis of the performance of the company. If Christopher is right and true competition now takes place between supply chains rather than companies, we have a potentially dysfunctional reward system. [15] has shown how two companies can, quite rationally, produce a suboptimal result by this means. In his example, the manufacturer sells product to the retailer at the price which sets marginal cost equal to marginal revenue. The retailer sells at the price which sets his MC=MR as well. However, Munson shows that it is a matter of pure luck if the selling price thus obtained will produce the optimal level of revenue for the entire channel (the two companies acting together). Managers of the two businesses each of them anxious to optimize his stock option values, will be motivated to set the channel return at a level below that which could easily be achieved.

The second purely financial issue which affects supply chains is the campaign for shareholder values. Major institutional investors are constantly pushing for managers to act to improve shareholder wealth, and exerting pressure on supply chain members to "do more with less" is one route towards this goal. It is a matter of concern that these institutional investors are, by their nature, biased away from considering the damage they may be doing. The institutions leading the charge for shareholder value are Calpers, Nycers, and TIAA-Cref. These are pension funds for public employees. They can afford to be indifferent if a few thousand private sector workers are fired. Their pensioners and future pensioners are not going to be affected. There is a systemic bias present.

3. Ethical Specifics in Global Supply chain Management

Let us now consider the operations of a supply chain and the ethical issues which arise in managing it. I am confident that the ethical issues which will affect a supply network will be more complicated still, and I specifically exclude consideration of this topic. A supply chain is not necessarily linear, but I shall assume that any given member of the chain will convey products, services, information, or money in the same direction consistently. I will discuss power issues, employment issues, trust issues, organization issues, and conclude with an ethical summary.

Product Flow.	A >>>>>>>>>> B	>>>>>>>>>>> C
Product		
Rectification Flow	A <<<<<<<<<< B	<<<<<<<<<<< C
Finance Flow	A <<<<<<<<<< B	<<<<<<<<<<<< C

(Operational)

Finance Flow　　　　A <<<<<<<<<< B >>>>>>>>>>>> C

(Investment)

Company B is the dominant force in the supply chain shown. It is the main source of investment funding for the other members. Company A is a source of product, which is further processed by B and then shipped to C for distribution. If a product is defective, it will be shipped back to B, and if need be to A, to be rectified. C collects the sales revenues, keeps some of them, and transmits the rest to B, which forwards a portion to A.

4. Power Issues

This simple supply chain can be managed in a Theory X manner or in a Theory Y manner. Some writers have suggested that Walmart is a clear Theory X supply chain manager [15] did not use the term Theory X, but his description matched it closely). I believe that Ford Motor is another, using its market power to force suppliers to adopt Ford's own edition of EDI, then forcing the suppliers to the suppliers to adopt Ford's edition of EDI as well. This edition of EDI is not, I have been told, used by any other supply chains, so a company seeking to serve another major company as well as Ford would have to obtain and maintain a second EDI edition. Perhaps some chain-dominating companies may regard the stress caused their suppliers by this as a disciplinary advantage. At the same time, it should be understood that the use of EDI in general is very widespread among supply chains, and enables considerable efficiencies to be achieved. Branded EDI, however, is a different matter. It imposes serious switching costs on all the chain members. This feature would obviously affect the main company, B, as well as the rest of the chain, but they can rely on their size to evade this switch cost problem.

The four ethical writers we looked at earlier might be consulted to see whether the Theory X approach to GSCM is sound. Ethically speaking, [8] said that we should be benevolent and inspiring; our people will be loyal if we are considerate to them. It does not seem that the Theory X approach to management fits this image. "Benevolence" and "consideration" do not seem to figure in this scheme. What about Aristotle, then? Cost-effectiveness is the virtue that lies between the vices of prodigality and meanness. There is no evidence, among Theory X supply chain managers, of intentional profligacy. The concept of "lean and mean management" remains a feature of modern business, having started life as a joke in one of Mr Macnamara's speeches. One manager in a supply chain, who worked for the dominant firm, described his job as "keeping our suppliers one inch from bankruptcy. This approach seems unlikely to generate goodwill. The suppliers cannot be expected to exert themselves beyond the minimum if that is the attitude of the chain leader. The cost of that hostility cannot be small.

5. Employment Issues

Clearly, cost cutting was one of the reasons for setting up the supply chain in my example, as well as in many other groupings. Reducing the numbers employed is an important element in cost cutting. Nobody owes me (or you either) a job for life.

However, there are ethical and unethical ways of going about the downsizing task. The less ethical way is an abrupt shutdown of a facility without notice and accompanied only by the legal minimum cash compensation. This action is quite typical of a Theory X business. Caterpillar has never recovered from the local loss of reputation it incurred in the UK from its abrupt closure of a factory, very soon after having received a massive government grant to open it. The government minister who felt he had been treated unethically is still, fifteen years later, making speeches about the incident, to keep the company's reputation as low as possible.

Recall the maxim of Immanuel Kant [17]. Always treat people as an end in themselves, never just as a means to an end. He explained that we can always trade value for value, but people do not have value. People have dignity instead, which is not a tradeable good. [18] explains that people are respected because of this dignity, which he explains as their potentiality to do good, to appreciate beauty, and so on. You cannot ethically dispose of a person without taking steps to contribute towards sustaining that potentiality.

A Theory Y company is just as keen on cost reduction, we may assume. However, they go about it in a different manner. They seek to remove people by redeployment, by voluntary release supported by a payout, by providing outplacement counseling and consultancy, and perhaps by providing an office and a phone to assist people in their job search. A reputation for being a good employer in bad times is likely to give the firm more applications, by better people, when business picks up again. A Theory X manager might grunt scornfully in answer to that claim. He might allege that any firm wasting its cash on all these extraneous items to help laid-off workers would not still be in business by the time the economy revived. Theory X people tend to say things like that. There is almost no evidence of it, however.

The problem of ethics in employment has a long history. There is a under-specification in the original paper by Ricardo in which the vitally important doctrine of comparative advantage was first described. In one of his examples, he showed that if ten workers in England could produce a bolt of cloth, but nine workers in Portugal could do that, and if twelve workers in England could produce a barrel of wine, while eight workers in Portugal could do that, then trade should happen. Even though Portugal beat England on both topics, they could both benefit by specialization. Twenty Englishmen could make two bolts of cloth, in which England had a comparative advantage, and sixteen Portuguese could make two barrels of wine, and then they could do a swop. However, there were 22 workers in England under the old regime and 20 now, and there were seventeen workers in Portugal, and sixteen now. The benefit from trade will only hold up if there is something else for the three spare workers to do. Economists tend to dismiss this argument by saying there was bound to be something for them to do. Try telling that tale to some of the very poor countries at the start of many supply chains. Ricardo made a sound argument for trade among reasonably prosperous countries, as his choice of England and Portugal illustrates. It does not apply, without significant alterations, however, if there are virtually no alternative employments in one of the countries engaging in the trading arrangement. A version of this argument has been reported in [19].

6. Matters of Trust

In the example I gave earlier, the brunt of the downshift was borne by the weakest businesses, those at the start of the supply chain. This result is very common. The businesses at the two ends of each supply chain are often the smallest in the chain, and therefore the easiest ones to "beat up on". Some chains have small companies only at one end, as, for instance, the Walmart supply chain, in which the small companies are at the start. Automotive chains tend to have relatively small companies at both ends. It does not really matter where you are in the chain if you are small. You are vulnerable if the big firm(s) makes to decision to get nasty. This may, however, still be preferable to not being in the chain at all.

Consider the case of a manufacturer who operates through a dealer network. any shoe makers work this way, for instance. What is the ethical view if they suddenly decide to distribute via their own factory outlets in addition? et us assume that the dealer and the outlet are both in the same city, but are not very close to one another. Rotius would ask whether we have thought this through in a prudent manner. What, he might ask, do we expect our dealer to do in reaction to our move? He might start selling other people's shoes in addition to ours. He might switch completely to another manufacturer. He might take us to court if he has a contract, and we have missed out some tiny step in the dissolution process. He might just yell and scream, but not actually do anything. Depending on his power in the local market, we might have cause to fear his reaction or we might feel we could alienate him with impunity. In any case, a reaction is highly probable. [8] makes the same point. We are certainly not being benevolent or inspiring towards our dealer. He will not be loyal to us, given that we are being seriously inconsiderate towards him.

In his introductory ethics text, Norman [20] cites Bradley as the philosopher who has put the greatest emphasis on trust as an ethical concept. Trust, he observed, is universal. It is simply not possible to operate in any human society without trusting someone, indeed without trusting many people. In a speech, I heard Robert Macnamara (President of Ford, Defense Secretary of the USA, President of the World Bank, in turn) say "……you have to have trust in your partners, and you have to be reasonable, and you have to trust your partners to be reasonable, otherwise it will be all talk and no achievement". [21], in a paper that looks to the future of supply chains, emphasize three foreseen critical features: a commitment to long-term trust of other chain members; integrated logistics; and honest data sharing.

Unfortunately, there is some evidence that these features are not as available as we might have hoped. Contracts are written by industrious lawyers who seem to be paid by the word. These contracts cover every conceivable contingency, but mysteriously fail to consider the disputes that actually take place. This keeps the lawyers in work, but it does nothing for inter-company trust.

Leakage of private information is another area where trust can be damaged. In certain negotiations, information may be conveyed on a private basis. In certain industries, it is common for this private information to be shared among members of a supply chain, including members who are competitors of the firm which gave the information. There are circumstances in which the action of sharing these data could give rise to a civil law suit. In virtually all cases, the action would be unethical. Kant would take no more than a second to condemn the leakage, as a most blatant failure to treat the company which initially provided the information with respect. It is a matter of simple duty, he would add, to behave in a trustworthy manner. [22], a very important ethical philosopher, observed that the ability of a society to continue to exist depends on a collective will to preserve order and concord in that society. To achieve that concord, it is utterly essential to perform on promises and on contracts. The contract or promise to keep information secret is exactly the kind of promise that must be kept, if the society is to avoid disintegration.

It is not all bad news, though. Three recent papers show that trust is gaining ground as a major element in several important supply chain systems. BP is a huge company in the oil industry, third largest on earth. [23] has fairly recently done a study of the ten largest oil companies, and published very complete results. Alone of the oil majors, BP has announced that it believes ethics will be "the main new fulcrum of competition among the top ten oil companies". A commentator described this company statement as "courageous", but reading some of his commentary it becomes clear that he really meant "crazy". The company has stuck by its policy in various recent publicity material, however. Secondly, a paper by [24] discusses the relationship between an auto parts maker and their dealers. This is a relationship built totally on trust, with minimal documentation. The dealers know they will be supported, so they work very hard for this supplier. Sales growth of 78% has been their mutual reward. Third, a paper by Waddock discusses corporate responsibility audits. These voluntary investigations, following a pattern designed by a team of which she is a member, have brought out numerous opportunities for improving the companies' performance, sometimes by increasing the level of trust, and sometimes by behaving a little more civilized manner to personnel. Interestingly, some of the largest benefits have been straightforward business process improvements, which the corporate responsibility people spotted on their way round the firm.

7. Conclusions

[22] has observed that there is no such thing as moral knowledge. Moral beliefs come from sentiment. They do not arise from reason. It may be that we will conclude that certain aspects of the Enron situation were illegal, and we may use reason to determine whether they were or were not. But to decide whether they were moral is a matter of sentiment. When we say something is virtuous, we do so out of sentiment. It feels right. When we say something is vicious, we do so again out of sentiment. It was a wrong action. Further, we are inclining ourselves and others to take some action in response. If it was a good feeling, the action we take in response may simply be to applaud. If it was a bad feeling, we may decide to punish.

The contribution of the ethical philosophers is to explain to us exactly why we feel the way we do about certain actions that have been taken, or that are proposed. When we are designing a supply chain, we have to identify the people or groups who will be affected by its creation. I suggested a maximum of twenty groups, to avoid overwhelming ourselves. We have to consider how each of these people or groups is going to be affected by the proposal, and to assess the extent of the impact on each group the planned actions will have. How is each group going to react? If a given group is likely to react negatively, is that going to be fatal to the proposal? If they are powerless, and likely to react negatively, can we do something to alleviate the damage we are doing to them, in advance if possible? If they are powerful, and likely to react negatively, what can be done in advance that would be prudent and effective. The proposed course of action should not, in general, be regarded as sacrosanct. When you do an ethical appraisal as well as a financial one you are likely to find that you have to change the plan.

You are much less likely to wind up in big trouble if you carry out an ethical appraisal instead of just a financial one. One of the last century's best brains belonged to Robert Ashby. He was nominated for a Nobel Prize, but died before the committee could consider his case. He proved that if you have a real system which has N dimensions to it, you can only control that real system properly if you have a control system which also has N dimensions to it. If you try to control a real system which has N dimensions by using a control system with N-1 dimensions it will only work part of the time. If our real system is a supply chain, and we want it to continue in operation for a lengthy period, with satisfaction all round, then we have to use Ashby's law. We have to consider, formally, all the dimensions of success that are of interest. If we want the system to be financially profitable, then we need a system to control that dimension. If we want the system to be ethical, then we need a system to control that dimension. Our measurements and plans have to reflect the complexity of the real system. For a Global Supply Chain, that means a global, ongoing, continuous process for checking that the chain is behaving ethically, in addition to the system for checking that the chain is operating on a profitable basis.

Let us conclude with one more story. [25] have reported that there are definite and measurable negative consequences from operating a supply chain in a hostile, Theory X mode. Their paper reports on accidents and complaints surrounding the Firestone P235 tires used on many Ford SUVs. A detailed statistical study seems to show that defective tires were produced in abnormally large numbers during two specific time periods at a plant in Decatur, Illinois. The first period occurred when the Firestone management unilaterally changed the plant from 8 to 12 hour shifts, to 24-hour working, to alternated day/night shift work, and also imposed a pay cut. The second period was when the strike ended, and replacement workers hired by Firestone during the strike were working alongside the returning workers who had been on strike. Tires produced in Decatur at other times were much less error prone. Tires produced at other plants were much less error prone. Krueger and Mas estimate that the fraught atmosphere of Decatur during these two periods may have led to forty fatalities more than would otherwise have occurred. The Wall Street Journal commented that the study "strongly suggests that squeezing workers, even in an age of weakened unions, can be bad management, especially when employers abruptly change the rules". Brute force, they observe, can backfire, and the consequences can be severe. The company's market capitalization has dropped by ten billion dollars. Forty people may have died. As an advocate for Theory Y and for ethical management procedures, I rest my case.

References

[1] J.L. Johnson, T. Sakano, J.A. Cote, N. Onzo: The exercise of interfirm power and its repercussions in US-Japanese channel relationships, *Journal of Marketing* Vol 57 Issue 4 (1993), 1-10.
[2] M. L. Christopher, *Logistics and Supply Chain Management*, London, Pitman, 1992.
[3] J.T. Mentzer, (ed) *Supply Chain Management*, London, Sage Publications, 2001.
[4] V.R. Singhal, K.B. Hendricks: How Supply Chain Glitches Torpedo Shareholder Value, *Supply Chain Management Review* Jan-Feb (2002), 18-24.
[5] R.M. Monczka, R.J. Trent: Global Sourcing: A development approach, *International Journal of Purchasing and Materials Management* Vol 27 issue 2 (1991), 2-8.
[6] Cheung, Ki-Ling: A Risk-Return Framework for Inventory Management, *Supply Chain Management Review* Jan-Feb (2002), 50-55.

[7] McGregor, Douglas, *The Human Side of Enterprise*, New York, McGraw Hill, 1960.

[8] Mencius, (translation by DC Lau), Penguin 1970.

[9] D. Simchi-Levi, L. Snyder, M. Watson: Strategies for Uncertain Times, *Supply Chain Management Review* Jan-Feb (2002), 11-14.

[10] C.W.L. Hill, *International Business:- Competing in the Global Market Place*, Chicago, Richard D Irwin, 1997.

[11] A.M. McCosh, *Financial Ethics*, Boston USA, Kluwer Academic Publishers, 1999.

[12] D.C. Korten, *When Corporations Rule the World*, Kumarian Press, New York 1995.

[13] D.R. Finn, *Just Trading:- On the Ethics and Economics of International Trade*, Washington DC, Churches' Center for Theology and Public Policy, 1996.

[14] A.M. Porter: Supply alliances pose new ethical threats, *Purchasing* May 20 (1999).

[15] C.L. Munson: The Use and Abuse of Power in Supply Chains, *Business Horizons* Jan-Feb (1999).

[16] J. Forrester, *Industrial Dynamics*, MIT Press, 1958.

[17] R.J. Sullivan, *An Introduction to Kant's Ethics*, Cambridge University Press, 1994.

[18] B. Brody, *Life and Death Decision Making*, Oxford, Oxford University Press, 1988.

[19] H.E. Daly, J.B. Cobb, *For the Common Good:- Redirecting the Economy toward the Community, the Environment, and a Sustainable Future*, 2nd ed, Boston, Beacon Press, 1994.

[20] R. Norman, *The Moral Philosophers:- An Introduction to Ethics*, Oxford University Press, 1983.

[21] D. Hume D, *Enquiry Concerning the Principles of Morals*, 1751.

[22] B.J. LaLonde, J.M. Masters: Emerging logistics strategies – blueprints for the next century, *International Journal of Physical Distribution and Logistics Management* Vol 24 issue 7 (1994), 35-47.

[23] PIRA energy group report: Common financial strategies found among top ten oil and gas firms, *Oil and Gas Journal* April 20 (1998).

[24] N. Kumar, L.K. Scheer, J.E.M. Steenkamp: The effects of supplier fairness on vulnerable resellers, *Journal of Marketing Research*, Vol 32, Feb (1995), 54-65.

[25] A.B. Krueger, A. Mas, *Strikes, Scabs and Tread Separations:- Labor Strife and the production of Defective Bridgestone/Firestone Tires*, Working Paper 461, Industrial Relations Section, Princeton University, Princeton NJ, 65pp, 2002.

Collaborative Decision Making
for Medical Applications

Collaborative Decision Making: Perspectives and Challenges
P. Zaraté et al. (Eds.)
IOS Press, 2008

An Integrated Framework for Comprehensive Collaborative Emergency Management

Fonny SUJANTO[a], Andrzej CEGLOWSKI[a], Frada BURSTEIN[a1],
Leonid CHURILOV[b]
[a] *Monash University, Australia*
[b] *University of Melbourne, Australia*

Abstract. Effective decision making plays a paramount role for successful emergency management (EM). Decisions should include collaborating inputs and feedback from a wide range of relevant emergency stakeholders such as emergency agencies, government, experts and communities. Although this kind of collaborative decision making is ideal, the process can be lengthy and complex. While there has been substantial research in EM, there is a lack of integrated frameworks to structure these contributions. Without an integrated framework, the decision making process can be inefficient and suggestions of the stakeholders may be neglected or excluded inadvertently. This paper presents the "Integrated Framework for Comprehensive Collaborative Emergency Management" (IFCCEM). IFCCEM aims to provide a collaborative mechanism so that all agencies as well as communities can contribute in the decision making. IFCCEM is based on the 'All Hazards Approach' and can be used by all agencies. The developed framework is illustrated with an application for collaborative decision making.

Keywords: disaster, emergency management, disaster management, integrated framework

Introduction

In emergency management (EM) there have been policy shifts from 'single agencies' to 'partnerships'; from 'science driven' to 'multi-disciplinary' approach and from 'planning *for* communities' to 'planning *with* communities' (Salter as cited in [1]). Major EM organisations such as Emergency Management Australia (EMA) and Federal Emergency Management Agency (FEMA) have stressed the importance of active collaboration in EM that bonds all participants for a mutual goal. This indicates the need for a collaborative decision making process. Emergency service organisations and academic researchers have conducted a wide range of research on EM systems. A number of models have been proposed [2, 3, 4, 5]. However, there is no conceptual framework to integrate this cumulative knowledge into a comprehensive structure for collaborative decision making.

---

1 Corresponding author: Centre for Organisational and Social Informatics, Monash University, Melbourne, PO Box 197, Caulfield East, 3145, Victoria, Australia; Frada.Burstein@infotech.monash.edu.au

The objectives of the paper are to identify a set of desirable properties that an "Integrated Framework for Comprehensive Collaborative Emergency Management" (IFCCEM) should possess to provide a comprehensive and integrated view of EM and to support collaborative decision making processes. These objectives are achieved through the design science research principles (e.g. [6]) that guide the process of building new artefacts and explains how and why a proposed design initiative has potential for the desired change.

The rest of this paper is organized as follows. In Section 2, we review the existing research on EM. Section 3 provides a set of desirable properties for an integrated framework in EM. These properties are developed by identifying and incorporating the properties of existing EM models. Section 4 proposes a framework called the "Integrated Framework for Comprehensive Collaborative Emergency Management" (IFCCEM). Section 5 provides illustrations on the usage of IFCCEM for decision support. The paper is concluded with a summary and future direction for this research.

1. Cumulative Research in Emergency Management

According to the Federal Emergency Management Agency - FEMA, EM can be defined as follows "organized analysis, planning, decision-making, and assignment of available resources to mitigate, prepare for, respond to, and recover from the effects of all hazards" [7]. Rising population, environmental degradation, settlements in high-risk areas, social pressures, technological failures and terrorism mean that EM will remain a long-term global focus [8; 9, 10]. Despite EM's significance, a literature review reveals that there is no standardised definition of its concepts. For instance, there is no standard definition of a "disaster" [11, 12]; "vulnerability" [13, 14, 15] and "preparedness" [16]. People commonly use the terms such as a *tragedy, crisis, major incident, catastrophe*, and *emergency* interchangeably with a *disaster*. In the last decades researchers have attempted to distinguish disaster from other terms. Green and Parker, [as cited in 17] distinguished between a 'major incident' and a 'disaster'. A major incident is a harmful event with little or no warning and which requires special mobilization and organization of the public services whereas in a disaster it is the public who are the major actors. Auf Der Heide [18] distinguished 'disaster' from 'routine emergency' through their different characteristics. Quarantelli argued that 'disaster' is different from 'catastrophe'[19]. Emergency Management Australia (EMA) provides unambiguous definitions of emergency and disaster [20]. *Emergency* is defined as "an event, *actual or imminent*, which endangers or threatens to endanger life, property or the environment, and which requires a significant and coordinated response". *Disaster* is described as "a *serious disruption* to community life which threatens or causes death or injury in that community and damage to property which is beyond the day-to-day capacity of the prescribed statutory authorities and which requires special mobilization and organization of resources other than those normally available to those authorities." Shaluf et al argued that 'disaster' and 'crisis' are different events in which the crisis is more comprehensive than the disaster [12]. In this paper, the terms 'emergency management' and 'disaster management' are used interchangeably to include the diverse range of types of events and to make the proposed framework applicable to all major types of hazard situations.

Emergency Management Australia (EMA) produced four concepts that should be applied in the EM arrangements: (1) *All Agencies (or Integrated) Approach* where all agencies participated in any disaster or emergency perform together as an active partnership; (2) *All Hazard Approach* whereby there should be a set of management arrangements capable of encompassing all hazards; (3) *Comprehensive Approach* that consists of prevention, preparedness, response and recovery (PPRR) strategies; and (4) *Prepared Community* where community is informed of local hazards and recommended protective measures and actively participated in community-based voluntary organizations. The importance of the "All Hazard Approach" is also highlighted by Canada's Manitoba Health [21].

NFPA provided a set of criteria for disaster or EM programs and the key elements of the programs by releasing the NFPA 1600 standard. The elements are *laws and authorities; hazard identification, risk assessment, and impact Analysis; hazard mitigation; resource management; mutual aid; planning; direction, control, and coordination; communications and warning; operations and procedures; logistics and facilities; training; exercises, evaluations, and corrective actions; crisis communication and public information; and finance and administration* [22].

Quarantelli presented ten criteria for good disaster management [19]. Peterson and Perry [23] provided a detailed review on disaster management exercises. Perry and Lindell [24] presented guidelines for the emergency planning process. Turoff et al [25] provided the Design of a Dynamic Emergency Response Management Information System (DERMIS). McEntire and Myers [16] discussed the steps to prepare a community for disaster including: establishing EM ordinances; assessing hazards, vulnerability and risks; creating an emergency operations plan; developing a warning system; identifying and acquiring resources; instituting mutual aid agreements; and training; exercising and educating the public.

While these contributions provide the basis for the proposed integrated framework for the effectiveness of EM, the absence of a conceptual framework into which data are placed and transformed into meaningful information hamper the analysis and evaluation of disasters and cause impediment in the prevention and mitigation of future events [26]. Furthermore, without a structural framework, beginners in EM need extra time and effort to search and analyse different sources of literature in order to get a comprehensive picture of EM systems. Crondstedt [1] argued that 'PPRR' is obsolete and recommended the 'risk management' to be the focus of EM. On the other hand, McEntire, Fuller, Johnston and Weber [27] compared five disaster paradigms namely: (1) 'comprehensive emergency management'; (2) 'disaster-resistant community'; (3) 'disaster-resilient community'; (4) 'sustainable development and sustainable hazards mitigation' and (5) 'comprehensive vulnerability management' and concluded that the first four paradigms are insufficient in addressing the triggering agents, functional areas, actors, variables and disciplines as compared to the 'comprehensive vulnerability'.

2. Analysis of desirable properties of the Integrated Framework for Comprehensive Collaborative Emergency Management (IFCCEM)

The aim of the IFCCEM approach is to preserve strengths of existing models and to utilise the efforts invested in their development [28]. To identify *a set of desirable properties* for the framework, we focussed on ten existing emergency management models, which taken together encompass the essential parts of EM: Traditional [29], Expand-contract [29], Disaster crunch [2], Disaster release [2], HOTRIP [4], Onion model of crisis management [3], System failure cultural readjustment model (SFCRM)

[5]. Ibrahim-Razi's model [30], Emergency risk management (ERM) [31], Integrated disaster management (DM) [21]. Other existing models were also reviewed and considered as inputs into the IFCCEM, but these inputs were not identifiable enough to be listed separately. The useful properties of these models were identified and assembled so that the integrated framework IFCCEM could be built based on these properties. The task of evaluating the properties of existing models was subjective and it is not possible to have an accurate and complete review of the existing models.

The proposed properties may be used as a starting point for discussion and research, rather than considered a final product. The desirable properties of IFCCEM were derived based on existing models that appear in multiple models as listed below.

1. The proposed framework should have a clear objective **(Purpose)**.
2. It should be applicable for all types of hazards as recommended by Canada Manitoba, EMA and FEMA **(All hazards approach).**
3. It should provide a coordinated mechanism so that all agencies involved in an emergency situation can work together as also suggested by EMA **(All agencies (integrated) approach).**
4. It should cover all phases of disaster: prevention, preparedness, response and recovery as suggested by EMA and FEMA **(Comprehensive)**.
5. The activities in the framework should be organised in a structural manner **(Systematic).**
6. The framework should be a cyclical and continuous process **(Cycle)**.
7. It should be flexible for expansion to meet a complex situation requirement. On the other hand, the model is also can be downsized for a simpler situation **(Flexible)**.
8. This framework should recognise the importance of identifying various sources of elements including internal, external, direct and indirect for a thorough analysis and evaluation **(Internal and external factors)**.
9. It should provide a means to identify the cause and effect relationship of EM elements **(Cause-effect)**.
10. The framework should be unambiguous and clear. Users from all backgrounds should able to comprehend the framework. This means no prerequisite knowledge is required to understand the model **(Transparent)**.
11. It should be practicable in a real emergency or disaster situation **(Practicable)**.
12. The elements of this framework can occur simultaneously and their relationship is non-linear **(Dynamic- non-linearity relationship)**.
13. The elements of the framework should be continuously evaluated and communicated for further improvement **(Dynamic - feedback, investigation, reporting and improvement)**.
14. The framework should be able to assist the users to think and analyse the emergency situations in a better way **(Working tool)**.
15. The users can easily maintain the framework **(Manageable)**.
16. The target of users covers all different types of emergency stakeholders. For instance, governments, first responders, volunteers and people **(Generic)**.

From the decision support perspective the above properties are desirable because they represent the characteristics an integrated framework should have in order to facilitate the collaborative decision making process. Note also that depending on the purpose of the design activities, these properties can be further classified into meaningful categories. For IFCCEM, five selected categories are Purpose; User-friendliness; Wide Content Coverage; Easy to Customise and Maintain; and Features and Tools (Figure 1).

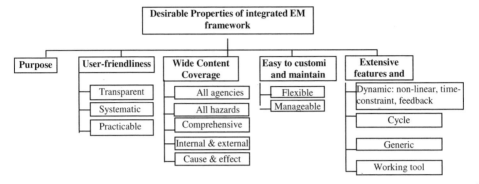

Figure 1: Desirable properties of ICCEM

As emergency management is dynamic and continuously evolving, both the categories and properties themselves will be subject to further expansion and modification.

3. Developing Integrated Framework for Comprehensive Collaborative Emergency Management (IFCCEM)

This section presents an overview of IFCCEM that meets the set of desirable properties introduced in Section 3. Manitoba Health's *Integrated Disaster Management Model* that was discussed in Section 2 is used as a skeleton to build IFCCEM. The cumulative knowledge and research are incorporated to develop the IFCCEM. The IFCCEM identifies the links between their complementary views of EM and incorporates them into a structural mechanism. The framework is comprehensive and illustrates the principles of such integration.

The cumulative knowledge and research are synthesized in IFCCEM. IFCCEM identifies the links between various views described in existing emergency management models as well as Industry Standards and best practices including United Nations, EMA, FEMA, ADPC, ADRC and NFPA 1600. We reconciled the recent approaches described in research journals and reports together with emergency case studies. Extensive analysis of knowledge from emergency experts has been undertaken to come up with the list of desirable properties of IFCCEM. As a result we believe the framework brings together complementary views and incorporates them into a comprehensive structure. Due to the paper size limitation, we cannot describe every single element of it. We will only briefly discuss the six main components (A to F) of IFCCEM and some of their sub-components (Figure 2).

A. Strategic Policy and Program – The EM process starts with setting out strategic policy and programs that regulate and manage all elements of EM. The development of the policy and programs should involve active participation from various types of emergency stakeholders. This is to ensure they have shared understanding and are committed to protect their society from the risks of disasters. The key purpose of policy and program is to ensure the risk of disaster is eliminated or reduced at the lowest possible level.

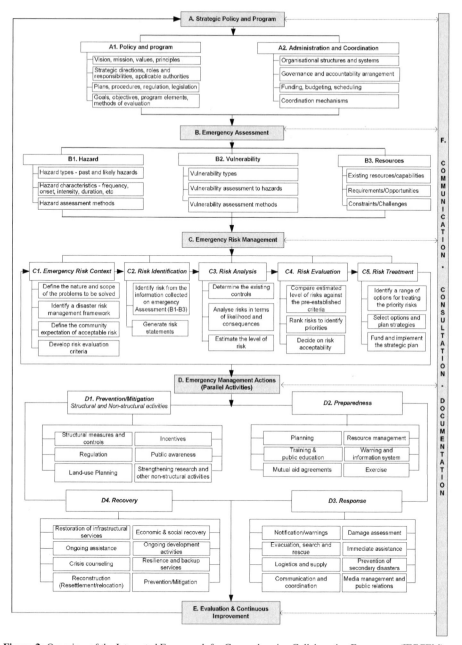

Figure 2: Overview of the Integrated Framework for Comprehensive Collaborative Emergency (IFCCEM)

B. Emergency Assessment – It consists of assessing and collecting reliable and comprehensive information on the three causal factors of an event: hazard, vulnerability and resources that are essential for disaster risk management tasks.

- *B1. Hazard* **assessment** involves collecting information about past and likely hazards that threaten the safety of the community and convert them into meaningful information. Hazard can be categorized into three main types based on its origin: natural, human-made and hybrid hazards. A wide range of potential hazard types and their characteristics should be identified and assessed in this task. Existing models such as *HOTRIP*, *SFCRM and* Ibrahim-Razi's model of technological man-made disaster precondition phase can be used to assess the possibility of reoccurrence of the human-made hazards.

- ***B2. Vulnerability assessment*** includes assessing the vulnerability of people and environment to the hazards which has been mapped in the previous step and determining elements at risk. The concept of the disaster crunch model is applied in the task whereby the root causes of vulnerability should be investigated and identified. Physical, social, cultural and economic aspects of the society should be included in the assessment.

- ***B3. Resources assessment*** encompasses assessing the adequacy of existing resources in coping with the effects of potential hazards. Resources assessment is very important as it identifies weaknesses of current resources and indicates areas that required further improvement. It also highlights the high-priority communities that should receive more attention (i.e. Resources < Hazard + Vulnerability). The information of the resource assessment will be further analysed in the disaster risk management and the shortcomings in this area will be addressed in the resource management activity (which is a sub-element of preparedness).

C. Emergency Risk Management

The emergency risk management model of EMA (discussed in Section 2) is incorporated in the framework. Emergency risk management is comprised of the following five main activities [31]:

- ***C1. Establish the context of risk management***: This activity involves defining the disaster risk management framework, the scope of the issues, the stakeholders, community's expectation of acceptable risk and criteria for risk evaluation.

- ***C2. Identify risks:*** The information collected from hazard, vulnerability and resource assessment is used to identify the risks that threaten the community.

- ***C3. Analyse risks:*** The identified risks are analysed in terms of likelihood and consequences to estimate the level of risk. The disaster risk analysis may include the use of sophisticated computing techniques that integrate hazard phenomena with the elements at risk and their associated vulnerabilities. Thousands of scenarios are developed through a computer simulation process to determine total risk (Total risk = Hazard*Elements at Risk*Vulnerability) [32].

- ***C4 Evaluate risks:*** In this activity, the estimated level of risks is evaluated and compared against the pre-established risk evaluation criteria defined in the previous activity. The risks are then ranked to identify the priorities and the decision whether or not the risks are acceptable.

- ***C5. Treat risks:*** If the risks are not acceptable, they have to be treated. A range of options for treating the priority risks should be identified. Once the options are evaluated, the implementation strategies and financing plan should be developed to ensure the effectiveness and efficiency of disaster management actions to treat the risks

D. Emergency Management Action

Emergency management action consists of prevention/mitigation, preparedness, response and recovery resulting from the decisions made in the disaster risk management process. These activities can be carried out simultaneously.

- ***D1. Prevention/mitigation*** consists of structural and non-structural activities aimed at eliminating or reducing the impact of disasters. While structural activities focus on engineering construction and physical measures, non-structural activities include economic, management and societal measures [33]

- ***D2. Preparedness*** aims to generate well-prepared communities and coordinated emergency operations. It involves activities such as planning; mutual aid agreement; resource management; public education; and exercise [21, 24].

- ***D3. Response*** is sum total of actions taken in anticipation of, during and immediately after a disaster to ensure its effects are minimized [31, 7]. Disaster response tests the effectiveness of the preparedness strategies and the mitigation measures. The weaknesses and issues arising from actual emergency responses have to be documented through the feedback channel.

- ***D4. Recovery*** aims at not only restoring the conditions of the incapacitated communities back to normal but also at improving the existing controls and measures. The recovery activities aftermath disasters overlap with the response and move towards prevention/mitigation actions [31, 7].

E. Evaluation and Continuous Improvement

Issues and challenges in EM may never end as EM is dynamic in nature. The weaknesses in the EM operations were revealed when it occurred. The integrated EM should identify all potential hazards situations and capable of managing all sorts of hazards. The effectiveness of each EM element should be regularly evaluated using the appropriate measurements. There should be a balance of continuous improvements in all areas of EM.

F. Communication, Consultation and Documentation

Feedback received throughout the entire EM process should be communicated, consulted and documented for evaluation and continuous improvement. The benefits of the documentation include exploiting improvement opportunities, retaining the knowledge and providing an audit trail [31]. Communication strategies should be established to ensure accurate information.

IFCCEM satisfies its aims as specified in the Introduction and encapsulates all properties as shown in Figure 1. Emergency management stakeholders, including the beginners, should be able to understand the framework. The ways the proposed framework can be used as a tool for collaborative decision support are discussed in next section.

4. Application of IFCCEM for Collaborative Decision Making

Generally the decision making process in EM is carried out in an uncertain, complex, dynamic and time-constrained environment. It may involve decisions related to the need to resolve current problems or potential future events or to improve the systems.

Regardless of the types of decisions being made, the decision making process should involve active participation of all emergency stakeholders. The ultimate aim is to provide the decision maker with the needed information to set the right strategies and choose optimum courses of action.

According to Nelson [33], the responsibilities for EM can be accorded to three main groups of emergency stakeholders: (1) scientists and engineers; (2) public officials and (3) citizens. The scientists and engineers are responsible for hazard assessment, hazard prediction, risk reduction, early warning development and communication systems. Public officials such as emergency services and government institutions are in charge of risk assessment, planning and code enforcement, early warning or notification, response and communication.

Citizens are responsible of understanding of hazards on their communities and their potential effects as well as early warning and communication systems that have been implemented and explained by their public officials. These main groups of stakeholders can be further classified into more categories. However, for the purpose of a simple illustration (Figure 3), we only use these three groups of stakeholders and some selected elements of IFCCEM. In times of an emergency event, for instance, IFCCEM can be used as a collaborative decision making tool prior to deciding on emergency management actions (Figure 3). The inputs and feedback from relevant stakeholders are collaborated so that the disaster risks are more accurately identified, analyzed and evaluated and emergency responses can be carried out effectively.

Another advantage of IFCCEM is that elements of the framework can be expanded for more detailed analysis to support decision making. To illustrate the framework, the 'hazard' component is used as an example. Figure 4 depicts how 'hazard' can be expanded to hazard types (natural, human-made and hybrid, for instance), hazard characteristics, hazard assessment methods and so forth.

The organization can select the hazard classification according to their needs. Natural hazards may be classified as (a) geological hazards such as earthquake, tsunami, volcano, landslide, etc (b) meteorological hazards including flood, drought, fire, famine, etc and (c) biological hazards such as emerging diseases and animal or insect infestation. [22].

Human-caused hazards may be caused deliberately or accidentally. Intentional actions include terrorism, strike, criminal activity, wars and sabotage of essential services. Examples of accidental or error-caused events are building collapse, utility failure, water pollution, transportation accident and explosions. Errors can, in turn, be distinguished into latent and active errors [34,35].

While latent errors are caused by technical and organizational actions and decisions that have delayed consequences, active errors are caused by human behaviour, with immediate effects. Active errors can be further distinguished into *skill-based, rule-based* and *knowledge-based errors* [34, 35, 36, 37]. *Skill-based errors* occur when there is a break in the routine while attention is diverted. While *rule-based errors* occur when the wrong rule is chosen due to the misperception of the situation or the misapplication of rule, *knowledge-based errors* occur when an individual is unable to apply existing knowledge to a novel situation. Once the potential hazards have been identified, their characteristics should be assessed including their frequency, scale, duration, destructive potential and etc.

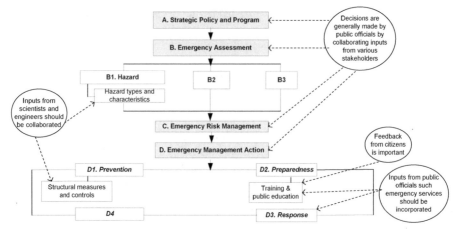

Figure 3: A snapshot of IFCCEM (Figure 2) to illustrate its usage in collaborative decision support

The methods of hazard assessment include (1) *data collection* from existing assessments, scientific data, hazard maps; socio-economic or agricultural surveys; (2) *deterministic approach* by analysing historical hazard data using mathematical models; (3) *probabilistic approach* by assessing hazard in terms of probability; and (4) *output method* by presenting hazard assessment through hazard mapping [38].

Breaking down the elements of IFCCEM into sub components provides more opportunities to identify which specific stakeholders are responsible for each component (see Figure 4).

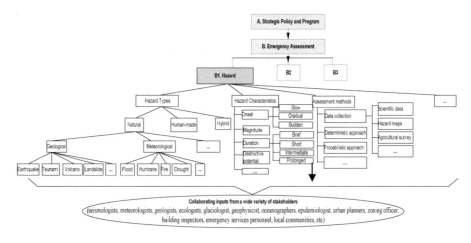

Examples of Hazard Assessment							
Hazard	Onset	Duration	Potential effects	Injuries and death	Public health consequences	Site Parameter	Possible risk controls
Earthquake	Sudden	Brief	Building collapse, disruption to utility, heavy dust, frequent fires and chemical spills	Many	Loss of utilities – hygiene, sanitation and many homeless	Intensity of ground shaking; Peak ground acceleration (%)	Hazard mapping, earthquake warning, building codes, insurance, etc

Figure 4: An Illustration on the use of IFCCEM as a working tool for decision support

Hence, it facilitates more elaboration of the inspiration and suggestions from a wider range of stakeholders for collaborative decision making. Comprehensive information can help decision makers to choose and implement the best course of EM actions.

5. Conclusion

The advantage of a collaborative approach to managing emergency or disaster situations has been increasingly recognised [39, 38, 7, 1]. Although the amount of research in EM is tremendous, there is a lack of a conceptual framework to structure the development cumulative knowledge. The aim of this paper was to develop an integrated framework 'IFCCEM' that has the desirable properties and also integrates multiple views of EM for collaborative decision making. Instead of mirroring the entire process of EM in detail, this framework simplifies the process into a systematic structure accessible by any user. It consists of the six key steps (cf. Figure 2): (1) defining strategic policy and program; (2) assessing causal factors of emergency/disaster for risk management (i.e. hazard, vulnerability and resources); (3) managing disaster risks and select the best course of actions; (4) implementing EM actions (i.e. Prevention, Preparedness, Response, Recovery); (5) evaluating the course of actions for further improvement; (6) communicating, consulting and documenting the whole process of decision making. The application of the developed framework for collaborative decision making illustrated the feasibility and potential benefits of IFCCEM. As a subject for our future research, the IFCCEM is being used as a foundation for building an ontology for EM to represent and populate the problem domain description.

References

[1] Crondstedt, M. (2002). "Prevention, preparedness, response, recovery – an outdated concept?" Australian Journal of Emergency Management 17(2): 10-13.

[2] Blaikie, P., T. Cannon, I. Davies, et al. (1994). At risk-vulnerability and disasters. Harper Collins.

[3] Mitroff, I. I. and T. C. Pauchant (1989). "Do (some) organizations cause their own crises? The cultural profiles of crisis-prone vs. crisis-prepared organizations." Industrial Crisis Quarterly 3 4(3): 269-283.

[4] Shrivastava, P., I. Mitroff, D. Miller, et al. (1988). "Understanding industrial crises." Journal of Management Studies 25(4): 283-303.

[5] Toft, B. and S. Reynolds (1994). Learning from Disasters. Oxford.

[6] Hevner, A. R., March, S. T., Park, J. and Ram, S. (2004) Design science in information systems research. MIS Quarterly, 28:1, pp.75-105.

[7] Federal Emergency Management Agency (2006). "Principles of Emergency Management: Independent Study." Retrieved 3 November, 2007, from http://training.fema.gov.au.

[8] Petak, W. J. (1985). "Emergency management: a challenge for public administration." Public Administration Review Special Issue: 3-6.

[9] Quarantelli, E. L. (1997a). "Future disaster trends: implications for programs and policies." from www.udel.edu/DRC/preliminary/256.pdf.

[10] de Guzman, E. M. (2003). Towards total disaster risk management approach. Asian Conference on Disaster Reduction.

[11] Koenig, K. L., N. Dinerman and A. E. Kuehl (1996). "Disaster nomenclature - a functional impact approach: the PICE system." Academic Emergency Medicine 3(7): 723-727.

[12] Shaluf, I. M., F. Ahmadun and A. M. Said (2003a). "A review of disaster and crisis." Disaster Prevention and Management: An International Journal 12(1): 24-32.

[13] Kasperson, J.X. and R.E. Kasperson (2001). International workshop on vulnerability and global environmental change: a workshop summary. Sweden, Stockholm Environment Institute (SEI).

[14] Guimarães, R. J. R. (2007). "Searching for the vulnerable: a review of the concepts and assessments of vulnerability related to poverty." The European Journal of Development Research 19(2): 234-250.

[15] Schoon, M. (2005). A short historical overview of the concepts of resilience, vulnerability and adaptation. Workshop in Political Theory and Political Analysis, Indiana University.

[16] McEntire, D. A. and A. Myers (2004). "Preparing communities for disasters: issues and processes for government readiness." Disaster Prevention and Management: An International Journal 13(2): 140-152.

[17] Parker, D. and J. Haudmer (1992). Hazard management and emergency planning: perspectives on Britain. London, James and James Science Publishers.

[18] Auf der Heide, E. (1989) Disaster response: principles of preparation and coordination. St. Louis, C.V. Mosby Company.

[19] Quarantelli, E. L. (1997b). "Ten criteria for evaluating the management of community disasters." Disasters 21(1): 39-56.

[20] Emergency Management Australia (1998). Australian Emergency Manual — Australian Emergency Management Glossary. Emergency Management Australia, Canberra: Commonwealth of Australia

[21] Manitoba Health (2002). "Disaster management model for the health sector: guideline for program development." Retrieved 7 May, 2004, from http://www.gov.mb.ca/health/odm/model.pdf.

[22] National Fire Protection Association (2007). "NFPA 1600: standard on disaster/emergency Management and business continuity programs, 2007 Edition." Retrieved 11 November, 2007, from http://www.nfpa.org/PDF/nfpa1600.pdf.

[23] Peterson, D. M. and R. W. Perry (1999). "The impacts of disaster exercises on participants." Disaster Prevention and Management: An International Journal 8(4): 241-255.

[24] Perry, RW. and MK. Lindell (2003). "Preparedness for emergency response: guidelines for the emergency planning process." Disasters 27(4): 336-350.

[25] Turoff, M., M. Chumer, B. Van de Walle, et al. (2004). "The design of a dynamic emergency response management information system (DERMIS)." Journal of Information Technology Theory and Application 5(4): 1-36.

[26] Sundnes, K. O. and M. L. Birnbaum (2003). Health disaster management guidelines for evaluation and research in the Utstein style. United States, Prehospital and Disaster Medicine.

[27] McEntire, D. A., C. Fuller, C. W. Johnston, et al. (2002). "A comparison of disaster paradigms: the search for a holistic policy guide." Public Administration Review 62(3): 267-281.

[28] Neiger, D. (2005). Value-focused process engineering with event-driven process chains: a systems perspective . PhD Thesis. Melbourne, Australia, Monash University.

[29] Atmanand (2003). "Insurance and disaster management: the Indian context." Disaster Prevention and Management: An International Journal 12(4): 286-304.

[30] Shaluf, I. M., F. Ahmadun and S. Mustapha (2003b). "Technological disaster's criteria and models." Disaster Prevention and Management: An International Journal 12(4): 305-311.

[31] Emergency Management Australia (2000). Emergency risk management applications guide. Emergency Management Australia, Canberra: Commonwealth of Australia

[32] Schneider, J., M. Hayne and A. Dwyer (2003). Natural hazard risk models: decision-support tools for disaster Management. EMA Australian Disaster Conference, Canberra.

[32] United Nations Development Programme (1992). An overview of disaster management (2nd Ed). NY.

[33] Nelson, A. S. (2004). "Assessing hazards and risk." Retrieved 12 November, 2007, from www.tulane.edu/~sanelson/geol204/hazardousgeolproc.pdf

[34] Battles, J. B. (2001). "Disaster prevention: lessons learned from Titanic." Baylor University Medical Center Proceedings 14: 150-153.

[35] Williams, P. M. (2001). "Techniques for root cause analysis." Baylor University Medical Center Proceedings 14: 154-157.

[36] Leape, L. (1994). "Error in medicine." JAMA(272): 1851-1857.

[37] Reason, J. (1990). Human error. Cambridge, Cambridge University Press.

[38] Emergency Management Australia (2005). "EMA publications." Retrieved 11 November, 2007, from http://www.ema.gov.au.

[38] Krovvidi, A. (1999). Disaster mitigation through risk management. Workshop on Natural Disaster Reduction: Policy Issues & Strategies.

[39] Asian Disaster Preparedness Center (ADPC) (2007). ADPC website. Retrieved 11 November, 2007, from http://www.adpc.net/v2007/.

Collaborative Decision Making: Perspectives and Challenges
P. Zaraté et al. (Eds.)
IOS Press, 2008

The Decision-Making Journey of a Family Carer: Information and Social Needs in a Cultural Context

Lemai NGUYEN[a], Graeme SHANKS[b], Frank VETERE[b] and Steve HOWARD[b]

[a]*School of Information Systems, Deakin University, Victoria, Australia 3010*
E-mail: lemai@deakin.edu.au
[b]*Department of Information Systems, The University of Melbourne,*
Victoria, Australia 3010

Abstract. While the important role of family as carer has been increasingly recognised in healthcare service provision, particularly for patients with acute or chronic illnesses, the carer's information and social needs have not been well understood and adequately supported. In order to provide continuous and home-based care for the patient, and to make informed decisions about the care, a family carer needs sufficient access to medical information in general, the patient's health information specifically, and supportive care services. Two key challenges are the carer's lack of medical knowledge and the many carers with non-English speaking and different cultural backgrounds. The informational and social needs of family carers are not yet well understood. This paper analyses the web-log of a husband-carer who provided support for his wife, who at the time of care was a lung cancer patient. It examines the decision-making journey of the carer and identifies the key issues faced in terms of informational and social practices surrounding care provision.

Keywords. Health information systems, decision-making, information needs, social networking, culture, carer

Introduction

Health information systems exist to support the needs of various stakeholders including hospital administrators and management, clinicians including doctors and nurses, and patients and their families and carers. These systems include hospital administration systems, electronic health records, computer-aided diagnostic systems, imaging informatics, pharmaceutical systems and patient health education systems [2,7,4,13]. However the level of system and information integration and dissemination is low [13]. Furthermore, although health service delivery is being transformed by information and communication technologies, there are fundamental issues that remain unsolved about the communication and interaction of different stakeholder groups.

The traditional focus of health information systems has been on the provision of comprehensive, timely and accurate information and medical knowledge to doctors, nurses, administration staff, hospital management, and other healthcare organisations. More recently, the availability and growth of Internet-based medical information has led to the provision of information services to the patient, their families and carers [5].

In addition, social networking systems have enabled peer help and peer support systems to develop and flourish.

In this paper we explore the decision-making journey of a husband-carer who provided support and care for his wife, who at the time of care was a lung cancer patient. We do this by analyzing his blog (web-log) that was written over a six month period.

We firstly discuss the patient and family carer community group and their need for supportive care. This is followed by a description of the research method and data analysis approach used. We then present an analysis of the data in the blog, examine the decision-making journey of the husband-carer and identify a number of issues that emerge in terms of information and social needs within a particular cultural context. The paper concludes with a discussion of the requirements for future health information systems that meet the needs of the carer, and suggestions for future research.

1. The Patient and Family Carer Community and Supportive Care

Although health information systems are used by a number of stakeholder groups, in this paper we focus on the patient, family and carer stakeholder community. Communities of practice [17] differ in important ways that are important to the design and use of health information systems. Three characteristics of communities of practice are particularly important, their values, modes of action and orientation towards technology [14,8].

Values – These are the principles that guide and orient the activity of communities of practice. Technology must contribute to these values in order to be perceived as useful by community participants. Clearly care-givers' values centre on the concept of "care" [10]. The values of community support groups or families of chronic suffers are elements such as wellness or happiness. This contrasts with management values of organisational efficiency, effectiveness and flexibility.

Modes of Action – Activities of patient families and support networks may be spontaneous, creative, improvised or playful. This contrasts with managerial practice which emphasises deliberative forms of action such as planning [8,15].

Orientation Toward Technology – Chat rooms that bring together support communities, web-sites that provide information about diseases and treatments and SMS messages that simply engender intimacy between family members are examples of relevant technologies. This contrasts with the managerial community that views information technology in instrumental terms.

All stakeholders – the patients, their carers, the clinicians and the medical administrators – share the common goal for the patient's rapid and long-lasting recovery. However their respective Values, Modes-of-Action, and Orientation-Toward-Technology are often different. This difference is accentuated when we examine the stakeholder roles through a supportive care perspective.

Supportive care helps the patient and their carers to cope with cancer. It helps a patient maximise the benefits of treatment, and to live as well as possible with the effects of the illness (National Institute for Clinical Experience NICE, 2004). Supportive care deals with information provision (e.g. physiology of illness, treatment options, management strategies, etc.), access to specialist services (e.g. psychiatric, palliative care providers, spiritual guidance) and social support (e.g. community care, peer-support, family support). Supportive care is not restricted to a particular stage of a disease. It can occur throughout the illness trajectory – from diagnosis, to treatment, and then to cure, continuing illness or bereavement [12].

Even though supportive care can be provided by all stakeholders, and is the "responsibility of all health and social care professionals" ([12], p. 20), the supportive care provided by family and friends is more likely to extend through many stages of the illness. Furthermore, a family carer is often the conduit through which supportive care resources, such as specialist help and information, are accessed on behalf of the patient.

With respect to our study, focusing in the decision-making journey of a family carer, we ask three research questions:

1. What are information needs of the family carer providing supportive care?
2. What are the social needs of the family carer?
3. What are the cultural influences on the information and social needs of the family carer?

2. Research Approach – An Interpretive Study

This study uses a qualitative, interpretive analysis [16] of a blog created by a Vietnamese man, Tran (pseudonym), who was the primary carer for his wife Le (pseudonym). The interpretative case study approach studies in-depth a single phenomenon in its native context and allows the researchers to gain an in-depth understanding of the nature and complexity of the processes that take place [3]. Interpretive case study has been used widely in Information Systems (see for example [16]) as well as Healthcare research (for example see [6]). The case study approach was adopted in this research to examine the decision-making journey, including the information and social needs of Tran.

Le was diagnosed of lung cancer when she was 28 years old, immediately after giving birth to her second child early in 2005. Le was treated at a public hospital in Hanoi, later in a private clinic in Singapore, and then back to Hanoi at two other hospitals. As a consequence of chemotherapy, her immune system was too weak to help her fight against a chest infection. She died in August 2005 in Hanoi. The nature of this disease and the patient's family circumstance (two young children including an infant) put the patient, her family and particularly her primary carer (husband) through an intensive and emotional decision-making journey.

The data used in this case study is secondary data. The primary source was an online diary published on a Web site, i.e. a blog. The diary, which started from 25/03/2005 and ended on 25/08/2005 and contained over 42 thousands words, was written by Tran, a 34 year old software engineer, during these five months of his wife's intensive treatment. The diary was a live story – a series of events, which happened as he and his wife were going through their fight against her lung cancer. The diary was referred to by the husband as 'a sad fairly tale' as it had a sad ending which was not known to the writer-carer, the patient, nor the Web reader. It was real and live, and revealing and insightful to the researchers. It also strengthened the urgency and importance of the findings from this study to practice and research.

From the early days of the diagnosis, Tran knew very little about cancer. In order to provide care for his wife, and most of all, to save her life, he gradually learned about this life threatening illness. It was a long on-going learning process as the illness developed and as he and his wife went through different stages of care planning and treatment course. At first, he believed in Vietnamese traditional medicine and learned about it. Later he learned more and more about Western contemporary medical knowledge and technologies used in cancer treatment. As he learned a lot about medical advancements and technologies in cancer treatment, and went through a range of different emotions, from hopeless to hopeful, denying to accepting the truth, he felt a strong need to write down and share his experience with others. The diary documents their experience, step by step, at times day by day, about how they went through the treatment course, their physical and emotional reactions to it, and their learning and decision-making. The diary is a rich source of personal experiences, observations and reflections. In the diary, Tran also made reflective (and comparative) notes about treatments and working cultures at different places. The diary and the story of the couple were featured on television, various Vietnamese web-sites and newspapers. The web-site, in which his diary was published, attracted approximately four thousand web messages left by visitors, and by late 2007 there are over three millions page viewers. The messages and stories gave support and encouragement to Tran and his wife, and shared with them personal experiences in fighting with cancer. The web site (and its associated forum) became a rich source of information and support for other Vietnamese cancer patients and their families in Vietnam and overseas. The diary, visitors' stories and messages, which Tran referred to in his diary, were selected and used as an additional source of data for this study. The text is written in Vietnamese. Some English medical terminology is used occasionally. Images (medical CT scans and his family photos) published on the web sites were also collected to assist the researchers in their analysis of the text.

Qualitative data was analysed using the meaning condensation technique [9]. The researchers used a cyclical process of summarizing long passages of text from the diary into brief statements with condensed meaning. These statements were then coded and classified into categories, which were further explored for themes and theme relationships that emerged. This inductive process allowed new concepts (themes and their relationships) to emerge and be internally validated.

3. Decision-Making Journey of the Family Carer

The supportive care role that Tran played involved a complex decision-making journey over a six month period. We report the findings of our study in terms of the information needs, social needs and cultural influences experienced by Tran.

3.1. Information Needs of the Family Carer

The information needs of Tran centre around 'care' for the wellness and happiness of the patient and can be understood through three on-going activities: Information Searching, Information Interpretation and Information Sharing.

3.1.1. Information Searching

As a husband carer, Tran has a patient with one strong, clear goal in care provision: to save her life. In order to achieve this goal, he continuously searches for information. As often perceived by many other patients and their families, a 'cancer diagnosis' is a shocking one. As a non-medical professional, Tran knew little about this illness. His information search journey started early and continuously developed during the whole process of care planning and provision. There are three primary types of information that Tran needed, collected and used: (i) patient-specific facts (through direct observations), (ii) patient-specific health records, and (iii) illness-specific information.

Patient-specific facts. Tran recorded events which occurred at home and his observations of stages of his wife's illness as well as her response to treatment, for example pain, fainting, feeding, sleeping, having illusion, feeling tiredness, changes in emotions, etc... Many of these facts raised new questions or lead to new actions. For example *"her heartbeat was getting slower, she was tired and felt asleep. She woke up, had a cup of milk, took medicine and still seemed tired and sleepy. Is this a result of Fentanyl?"*. Later, when he found out that she did not feel well he decided to take out Fentanyl transdermal patches. His recording of facts and observations, although very rich in detail, was rather intuitively selective. Although he learned to measure his wife's heart beats and observe her response to treatment, his selection of observation details was not conducted in a structured way as a nurse would do in the hospital, for example periodically taking temperature or blood pressure.

Patient-specific health records. Tran accompanied his wife to different clinicians and specialists at multiple departments for respiratory care, imaging, oncology, chemotherapy, neurology, psychology, and nutrition at various hospitals in Hanoi as well as in Singapore. He received and monitored all diagnoses and monitoring reports, blood testing results, and X-Ray and CT images.

Illness-specific information. Tran gathered information about the illness that his wife suffered: lung cancer and cancer in general, different treatment methods, success rates, side effects, and experience by other patients and their families. He used multiple information sources including health Web sites, reader's messages and emails on his personal Web site, hospital information leaflets, personal contacts with doctors in the field, family and circle of friends, and previous patients. He commented about the lack of information about cancer and cancer treatment in Vietnamese on the Internet.

Tran's information search process was fragmented, improvised and situated, in contrast to a systematic and rational medical information collection process. Two factors led to this. First, Tran was not a medical professional. He did not know in advance what information he would need and what would be available. He had to use different intuitive cues and multiple accessible sources (direct observations, medical reports, leaflets, web sites, information exchange with doctors and friends etc) to build up his fragmented knowledge about the situation and directions for further information search. His care provision was often interrupted by a new development with the illness or his wife's response to treatment. For example, at the beginning, Tran was searching for information about traditional Vietnamese treatment herbs. When he found out that his wife did not feel better, he took her to the hospital for an X-ray. They were shocked to see that one lung did not appear in the image. He decided to adopt a contemporary treatment approach. This led him to search for information about chemotherapy and look for a good doctor in Singapore.

Second, as the husband of the patient, Tran had very rich contextual information including patient-specific facts, patient-specific health records provided by different doctors and specialists, and illness-specific information. The details of how his wife felt and hoped before each session, how she responded to the treatment including pains, emotions, meals, illusions, hope and fear were important to the husband as her happiness and wellbeing were the foci of his care. These details would be important in care planning, provision and evaluation but would be very costly and time consuming for the medical practitioner to collect, especially when on-going home-based care is preferable. In addition, as the patient moved between different hospitals and doctors, their health records may not be easily accessible. The different types of information require different approaches to collect and record. Without professional training, Tran recorded and attempted to integrate these multiple sources of information on his blog.

3.1.2. Information Interpretation

Tran's information interpretation was also part of an on-going learning process. As he collected multiple types of information, Tran continuously interpreted and related the information to make sense of his wife's situation. For example, Tran related his observations of his wife's health state, an operation to place a tube within her esophageus due to the metastasis of lung cancer cells, the doctor's explanation, and the CT images taken in Singapore before and during the operation to make sense of the situation. He placed the images in chronological sequence on the window sill against the sunlight in their hotel room and related each of them to his observations of his wife's health state, events which occurred, and the doctor's explanations. Some medical practitioners may assume that their short consultation sessions are sufficient for patients and families. Tran spent enormous time integrating and interpreting the information he received from multiple sources and his direct observations.

Without professional training in medicine, Tran's information interpretation evolved during the whole care process, starting from a very simple explanation to more and more complex ones. He used simple concepts and metaphorical thinking to understand the medical terms and treatment options. For example, in his 'unfair battle with the century illness' Tran referred to oriental traditional herbs (for example pawpaw, artemisinin powder, escozul) as 'skilled ground soldiers' which could not match with the fast growth and fierce attack of the 'enemy tanks' (cancer cells) and referred to chemotherapy as an air force which would be strong enough to kill the tanks. After this reasoning exercise, Tran felt more confident with selecting the chemotherapy option that he discarded earlier on.

Tran also needed to confirm his understanding of the situation with a doctor. He felt better and more confident when doctors confirmed his understanding of his wife's situation. Sometimes, a need to confirm his interpretation initiated a request to see a doctor. For example, one night in Singapore, both Tran and his father-in-law were very concerned that his wife was developing illusions during a chemotherapy treatment cycle. Tran tried to relate events that occurred one night when his wife was unwell. She had been taking Stilnox everyday since she had fallen down and had a brain CT scan, three weeks earlier. That night Tran called a doctor to their place. He and his father-in-law felt some relief when the doctor confirmed the accumulated side effect of Stilnox: "After our exchange of information, the doctor agreed (with my guess) that it was only a side effect of Stilnox. And three of us were relieved to wait for a new day". They decided not to use this drug any more.

The above and many other examples show his strong need to understand and evaluate medical diagnosis, treatment options, procedures, and evaluation reports. By better understanding the situation, Tran felt empowered and in control when providing care for his wife.

3.1.3. Information Sharing

Tran reflected upon his information and experiences and shared his stories with others. Although he admitted that he had never written a diary previously in his life, this time, he felt a strong need to share information. Tran wrote in his diary: *"Now as fate has placed my family in front of a dreadful challenge, I feel a strong motivation to write down our experiences, in the hope of bringing something to you, a reader of my diary"*. Through his web site, he met many new friends and was happy to be able to offer useful information: *"We were able to assist some people at least with information"*. While providing care for his wife in Singapore, Tran often shared his learning about new technologies and medical processes (CT, PET imaging, how an operation was performed, how doctors communicated) or how to read a blood indicator, and the effects and side effects of drugs with readers of his diary. Tran often expressed his willingness to share his learning with Vietnamese doctors. As he learned about how cancer could be diagnosed and how chemotherapy works, he was eager to be able to collaborate with doctors in Singapore and Vietnam to develop a cost effective treatment scheme for Vietnamese patients.

Information sharing not only helped others, but as a social networking activity had a positive effect on Tran's coping with emotions and stress. We will elaborate on this in the section below.

3.2. Social Needs of the Family Carer

Tran shared his information and experiences and received tremendous support from his immediate family, extended family, colleagues and friends, healthcare practitioners and organizations, and a wider community of Vietnamese Web users in Vietnam as well overseas. Tran and his wife received different forms of support including emotional, financial, expertise, experience and availability.

Tran's family was the nucleus of on-going care. Looking after two young children, including an infant and a pre-school child, while providing care for his wife at the fourth stage of lung cancer was extremely difficult. Tran and his wife received tremendous emotional support from their extended family who were always available to help. Grandparents took care of grandchildren for the husband to care for his wife and travel with her to Singapore. Tran often consulted his aunt, who was a medical doctor, to receive explanations of medical terms and his wife's medical records. It is very important to note that while the doctors suggested and carried out the treatment (actions) based on their professional knowledge and training decision making skills, Tran and his family consulted, 'negotiated' with the doctors and made many decisions, for example: *"…the whole family 'voted' that my wife should stop after the fifth cycle of chemotherapy. I also considered opinions by doctors including those in Vietnam as well as in Singapore"*. Examples of other decisions include: which hospital(s) would be most appropriate? Would a friends' recommendation of a private doctor in Singapore be a good one? Where should Tran's wife continue subsequent chemotherapy cycles? And when should he take his wife to the hospital during her last days? The family relationship and situation provided trust and a context and for many care decisions.

His friends also provided emotional, expertise and experience support. He searched for explanations and aggressively collected information about contemporary cancer treatment approaches through personal contacts with medical practitioners, a family relative and a friend respectively. At one stage, Tran wanted to provide treatment for his wife while hiding the truth about the fourth stage cancer diagnosis to protect her from shock and keep her well-being. He discussed possible chemotherapy options with his friend who was a doctor. It was his friend who tried to convince him not to do so without her consent and suggested that they go to Singapore. Later, he also contacted previous patients who received chemotherapy from the doctor recommended to him by his friend. His close contact and frequent conversations with various family friends, work friends and web friends about medicines, treatment options, effects and side effects, and the nature of the illness are repeated many times throughout his diary. Tran's feelings about being able to explain and interpret information and his eagerness to share information after each event indicates that he felt empowered and in control – a source of energy that helped him in proving on-going care and coping with his own tiredness and distress.

Supportive care came in various forms: availability (being there with the husband and wife or their children), emotion (to understand and share emotions with them), expertise (in their medical knowledge), experience (in coping with the illness, pains, and treatment methods), and finance (to fund their trip to Singapore and hospital fees). In this paper, we stress emotional support. The journey that Tran took to search for ways to care for his wife and save her over the eight months since the diagnosis and the sad ending was very emotional. Emotions played an important role in Tran's care for his wife. For example, initially Tran was searching for information about oriental traditional herbs in cancer treatments, and preparing and giving oriental medicines to his wife. He and his family were very hopeful. Later, he was very concerned that her health was getting worse, not better. He decided to take her to the hospital for an X-ray. They were deeply shocked to find out that one of his wife's lungs did not appear on the X-ray, and neither his wife nor he could say a word. Neither could his father-in-law when looking at the X-ray. Later, he built hope again when he found a possible explanation that the lung could still be there and chemotherapy was necessary. Every page of his diary was about emotions, a wide range of emotions: happy, hopeful, building hope, fearful, worried, concerned, frightened... Each event and piece of information was strongly associated with emotions. Some advice from a Singaporean doctor: "*where there is still life, there is still HOPE*" was their motto during the eight months in their '*unfair fight*' to guide him through even the darkest hours.

3.3. Cultural Influences on the Information and Social Needs of the Family Carer

Two important cultural factors observed in this story are a strong connection to Confucian virtues and a belief in oriental medicine. According to Vietnamese Confucianism, three virtue-relationships for men include King and Subjects, Father and Son, and Husband and Wife. The three virtue-relationships for women include Following Father, Following Husband, and Following Son. Tran and his father-in-law were influential within their family network, and played an important role in considering and planning care and treatment options. Tran provided his wife with strong protection, selfless devotion, endless love and care. He hid the total truth about the illness and revealed only part of it: "*carcinoma instead of cancer*" and "*tumours or benign tumours instead of malignant or metastasis*". He filtered information and stories by other patients and their families and shared with her only stories with positive endings. His wife was comfortable and absolutely trusted him that he would do his best for her. This cultural perception about the care-giver's role and the decision-making responsibility of the husband was well accepted and supported by their various communities: their family and extended family, circle of friends and hospitals in Vietnam and Singapore. There was a shared understanding between the husband, father-in-law and other doctors, nurses, medical practitioners, web and face-to-face friends about the husband's role and responsibilities in decision-making.

The second cultural factor observed in the diary was the husband's belief in traditional Vietnamese cancer treatment methods as complementary to 'proper' (or Western) cancer treatments. At the beginning, Tran learned about and applied various traditional medicines to treat his wife. Later, during the chemotherapy course, he travelled to villages and searched for people who practiced Vietnamese oriental medicine. He sought an oriental explanation of what cancer was and what caused it. Tran searched for different information about cancer treatments and applied a combination of both contemporary cancer treatment and Vietnamese traditional methods. Using both contemporary and traditional cancer treatment methods has become a popular approach that Vietnamese cancer patients and their families.

4. Discussion

The planning and delivery of care for patients with chronic illness is an ongoing process that is rich in informational and social activity, and involves many stakeholders. We have explored the decision-making journey of a family carer, specifically the husband of a wife with terminal lung cancer, through his informational and social practices and needs.

We have argued that the information needs and practices of the family carer are best understood as an iterative process of information search, information interpretation and information sharing. Three types of information emerged from the study: patient-specific facts (through direct observations); patient-specific health records; and illness-specific information. The carer's lack of medical knowledge and his rich contextual knowledge about his wife's situation led to an information search process that was fragmented, improvised and situated, rather than systematic and rational. Tran spent enormous time integrating and interpreting the information he received, using simple concepts and metaphorical thinking to understand the medical terms and treatment options. He shared the information and his understanding with other patients, carers and doctors to help cope with emotions and stress. Our findings refined and extended previous work in understanding the information needs of patients [1] and their family carers [11].

Tran's needs were not confined to information however. Social needs are best understood as relating to various forms of support (both given and received), including emotional, financial, wishing to learn from the experience of others, and the availability of social others during the ongoing process. Social network technologies hold great promise in responding to such needs, creating online communities of practice that include the patient's immediate and extended family, friendship networks, other patients and their families, the wider community of 'web friends' and the professional care giver community at large. However, social network sites are generally limited in the support they provide for information rich tasks.

Finally, we highlighted the cultural influences that infuse both information and social acts. We show a relationship between the family care decisions and cultural background. In Vietnamese families, the strong family relationships, informed and influenced by Confucianism and traditional belief systems, still play a very important role.

Further work is required to extend our understanding. Firstly, whilst informational needs and acts have been intensively explored over the last 50 or so years, when conducted within a health context the frame of reference is invariably care giving as 'work' conducted by medically trained 'workers' in clinical 'work settings'. Our understanding of social needs and acts has a rather more recent history, and informal carers have been a topic of interest for technologists in the past few years only. We have much learn from our sister disciplines, especially Computer Supported Cooperative Work, though even here the orientation to 'work' is not always a helpful lens through which to view the intensely social, emotional and spiritual nature of care giving. How might we rethink the nature of care giving, so that it amounts to more than informational work? Secondly, we understand very little about the interrelationships between informational and social acts. How might informational and social needs and practices be fashioned so as to be mutually supportive, and appropriately configured across the various stakeholder communities? Thirdly, the bridge between understanding needs and designing supportive systems is as ever non-trivial, but this is especially so in design contexts that involve multiple communities of practice with different values, practices and needs for technology who are engaged in the collective effort of care provision. How might systems be constructed that blend the best elements of information technologies (databases, powerful and flexible search algorithms) and social technologies (social network sites, blogs), so as to support a practice that is at once informationally rich, and yet socially embedded?

References

[1]   Adams, A. and A. Blandford (2005). Digital libraries' support for the user's. *Information Journey.* IEEE and ACM Joint conference of digital libraries ACM/IEEE JCDL 2005.
[2]   Ayres, D., J. Soar and M. Conrick (2006). Health Information Systems. *Health Informatics: Tranforming Healthcare with Technology*. M. Conrick, Thomson, Social Science Press. Chapter 14: 197-211.
[3]   Benbasat, I., D.K. Goldstein and M. Mead (1987). "The Case Research Strategy in Studies of Information Systems." *MIS Quarterly* **11**(3): 368-386.
[4]   Bental, D., A. Cawsey, J. Pearson and R. Jones (2000). *Adapting Web-Based Information to the Needs of Patients with Cancer*. The proceedings of International Conference on Adaptive Hypermedia and Web-based systems, Trento, Italy.
[5]   Gerber, B.S. and A.R. Eiser (2001). "The Patient-Physician Relationship in the Internet Age: Future Prospects and the Research Agenda." *Journal of Medical Internet Research* **3**(2): e15.
[6]   Graham, M. and A. Nevil (2007). *HBS108 Health Information and Data*, Pearson Education Australia.
[7]   Hovenga, E., M. Kidd and B. Cesnik (1996). *Health Informatics: An Overview*. Churchill Livingstone, Australia.
[8]   Howard, S., F. Vetere, M. Gibbs, J. Kjeldskov, S. Pedell and K. Mecoles (2004). *Mediating Intimacy: digital kisses and cut and paste hugs*. Proceedings of the BCSHCI2004, Leeds.
[9]   Kvale, S. (1996). *Interviews: an introduction to qualitative research interviewing*. Thousand Oaks, Calif., Sage Publications.
[10]   Nelson, S. and S. Gordon (2006). *The Complexities of Care: Nursing Reconsidered*. Ithica, Cornell University Press.
[11]   Nguyen, L. and G. Shanks (2007). *Families as carers – Information needs in a cultural context*. Proceedings of 18th Australasian Conference on Information Systems, Toowoomba, Australia.
[12]   National Institute for Clinical Excellence, N. I. f. C. E. (2004). Guidance on Cancer Services – Improving Supportive and Palliative Care for Adults with Cancer. The Manual. London, United Kingdom, National Health Service.
[13]   Soar, J. (2004). *Improving health and public safety through knowledge management*. Thailand International Conference on Knowledge Management, Bangkok, Thailand.
[14]   Susman, G.I., B.L. Gray, J. Perry and C.E. Blair (2003). "Recognition and reconciliation of differences in interpretation of misalignments when collaborative technologies are introduced into new product development teams." *Journal of Engineering Technology Management* **20**: 141-159.

[15] Vetere, F., M. Gibbs, J. Kjeldskov, S. Howard, F. Mueller and S. Pedell (2005). *Mediating Intimacy: Designing Technologies to Support Strong-Tie Relationships*. Proceedings of the ACM CHI 2005, Portland, Oregon, USA.

[16] Walsham, G. (1995). "Interpretive case studies in IS research: Nature and method." *European Journal of Information Systems* (4): pp. 74-81.

[17] Wenger, E. (1998). *Communities of Practice: Learning, Meaning, and Identity*, Cambridge University Press.

Collaborative Decision Making: Perspectives and Challenges
P. Zaraté et al. (Eds.)
IOS Press, 2008

Promoting collaboration in a computer-supported medical learning environment

Elisa BOFF[a,d], Cecília FLORES[b], Ana RESPÍCIO[c] and Rosa VICARI[d]

[a] Departamento de Informática/Universidade de Caxias do Sul, Brasil, eboff@ucs.br
[b] Departamento Saúde Coletiva/Universidade Federal de Ciências da Saúde de Porto Alegre, Brasil, dflores@fffcmpa.edu.br
[c] Departamento de Informática and Centro de Investigação Operacional/Universidade de Lisboa, Portugal, respicio@di.fc.ul.pt
[d] Instituto de Informática/Universidade Federal do Rio Grande do Sul, Brasil, rosa@inf.ufrgs.br

Abstract. This paper addresses collaborative learning in the medical domain. In particular, it focuses on the evaluation of a component specially devised to promote collaborative learning using AMPLIA. AMPLIA is an intelligent multi-agent environment to support diagnostic reasoning and the modeling of diagnostic hypotheses in domains with complex, and uncertain knowledge, such as the medical domain. Recently, AMPLIA has been extended with a new component providing support in workgroup formation. Workgroups are proposed based on individual aspects of the students, such as learning style, performance, affective state, personality traits, and also on group aspects, such as acceptance and social skills. The paper also presents and discusses the results of an experiment evaluating the performance of workgroups composed according to suggestions provided by the system.

Keywords. collaborative learning, group processes, medical education, problem-based learning.

Introduction

The advent of computer usage as well as the constant development of the capacities of new technologies has brought a new vision regarding the possibilities in using computer support for learning and training. Medical education is not an exception and during the last decade several systems for support learning of medicine have been proposed. These approaches are mainly concerned with collaborative learning, problem-based learning and computer based simulations [1].

According to [2], within less than one student generation, communication and information technology (C&IT) will be repositioned as an integral component of the medical knowledge domain. *Although C&IT has affected learning in all the domains, medical education has some unique aspects, not least that the learning takes place during clinical care, and it offers opportunities to test methods of learning not used in other contexts.*

Clinical reasoning is the way an expert resolves a clinical case – from a possible diagnostic hypothesis, the professionals look for evidence that confirm or reject their hypothesis. This type of reasoning is named top-down, because it starts from the diagnosis to find evidence; this way, the evidence justifies the diagnosis. The student, however, does the opposite; he/she looks for a diagnosis that justifies the evidence, because he/she does not have a diagnostic hypothesis. His/her reasoning is bottom-up, starting from evidence to reach a diagnosis.

The AMPLIA system, an intelligent multi-agent environment, was designed to support the medical students' clinical reasoning. For this purpose, AMPLIA has a Bayesian Network editor which can be considered an intelligent e-collaborative technological tool. Recently, the system editor has been extended to provide the creation of virtual workgroups to solve tasks in a collaborative way.

Advances in Intelligent Tutoring Systems (ITS) have proposed the use of architectures based on agent's society [3] [4] [5]. The group dynamic has also been addressed by much research and in different areas. The multi-agent approach is considered suitable to model the group formation and coordination problem. In addition, it has shown a very adequate potential in the development of teaching systems, due to the fact that the nature of teaching-learning problems is more easily solved in a collaborative way.

In a real classroom, students form workgroups considering mainly the affinity between them. Sometimes, workgroups are composed taking into account geographical proximity (especially for Distance Learning), but these groups do not always present a good performance in learning activities. Here, the system analyses the several students and proposes heterogeneous and small groups considering individual and social aspects, such as learning style, personality traits, acceptance and sociability.

This paper presents and discusses probabilistic networks to model the aspects of individuals, and to promote collaboration between individuals. The following section summarizes some concepts related with collaborative learning. An overview of software specially developed to support learning in the medical domain is presented in section 3. Section 4 describes the group model integrated in AMPLIA. Section 5 presents and discusses an experiment assessing the quality of the collaborative component. Finally, the paper ends with conclusions and future perspectives.

1. Collaborative learning

In the learning and teaching arena, cooperation can be seen as a special type of collaboration. *Collaboration* is a philosophy of interaction and personal lifestyle where individuals are responsible for their actions, which include learning and taking into account the abilities and contributions of their peers [6]. Collaborative learning is a method of teaching and learning in which students explore a significant question or create a meaningful project. A group of students discussing a lecture or students from different schools working together over the Internet on a shared assignment are both examples of collaborative learning. However, *cooperative* learning is a specific kind of *collaborative* learning. In cooperative learning, students work together in small groups on a structured activity. They are individually accountable for their work, and the work of the group as a whole is also assessed. Cooperative groups work face-to-face and learn to work as a team.

Collaborative learning environments (CLE) are systems specially developed to support the participation, collaboration, and cooperation of users sharing a common goal. In a CLE, the learner has to be active in order to manipulate objects, to integrate new concepts, to build models and to collaborate with each other. Additionally, the learner must be reflective and critical.

Learning environments should provide students with a sense of safety and challenge, the groups should be small enough to allow plenty of contribution and the group tasks should be clearly defined. Although several authors use the cooperative learning concept as defined by Piaget [23], our perspective follows the definition of [7]. Thus, collaboration here is seen as a joint work to achieve common goal, without the division of tasks and responsibilities.

Collaborative learning systems design should take into account social factors [8] [9]. Vassileva and Cao et al. concluded about the importance of considering sociological aspects of collaboration to discover and describe existing relationships among people, existing organizational structures, and incentives for collaborative action. Hence, learning environments may be able to detect and solve conflicts, provide help for task performing and motivate learning and collaboration. In addition, Vassileva discusses strategies and techniques to motivate collaboration between students. Cheng [10] proposes a motivation strategy for user participation, based on persuasion theories of social psychology. In [9], the goal is to find how people develop attitudes of liking or disliking other people when they interact in a CSCW environment, while in a collaborative-competitive situation. More precisely, the research investigates how they change their attitudes towards others and how the design of the environment influences the emergent social fabric of the group.

Prada [11] developed a model that supports the dynamics of a group of synthetic agents, inspired by theories of group dynamics developed in human social psychological sciences. Based on these theories, they considered different types of interactions that may occur in the group.

In a CLE, the learner has to be active, manipulate objects, integrate new concepts, build models to explain things, and collaborate with other people.

2. Computer-supported learning in medicine

Besides AMPLIA, we can highlight another learning environment or medical software that can be used in education. In Table 1 we selected several environments related to AMPLIA and we summarized their main features. Such ITS had been chosen because they are similar to AMPLIA in their application and student's model.

A Bayesian network-based appraisal model was used in Conati's work to deduce a student's emotional state based on his/her actions [12]. The probabilistic approach is also used in the COMET System [13], a collaborative intelligent tutoring system for medical problem-based learning. The system uses BN to model individual student knowledge and activity, as well as that of the group (users connected in the system). It incorporates a multi-modal interface that integrates text and graphics so as to provide a communication channel between the students and the system, as well as among students in the group. COMET gives tutoring hints to avoid students being lost.

Medicus is a tutorial system that does not include collaboration aspects. It supports a single user interacting with the system and uses BN to model knowledge [14].

Table 1. Intelligent tutoring systems (ITS) comparison

Systems	Objectives	Interaction tools	Tutoring	Student's model	Strategies
AMPLIA	Diagnostic hypothesis construction	Chat Bayesian Network Collaborative editor	Socio-affective tutor to motivate collaboration and to join student in groups	Knowledge; Self confidence; Cognitive state; Take into account social and affective information to model individual and groups	From hints and quizzes to problems and discussions
COMET [13]	Problem solving; Collaborative learning	Chat Bayesian networks Medical images	It has an artificial tutor to help student learning	Individual and groups Knowledge and Activities	From hints to collaborative discussion
I-Help [9]	Personal Multi-agent Assistant (offer help to students)	Forums On-line materials Chat	Personal assistant based on probabilistic reasoning	Student profile	Agents negotiation to find the suitable hint
Prime Climb [12]	Educational game to help students learn number factorization	Clicking on interface	Pedagogical agent that provides tailored help, both unsolicited and on demand	Bayesian network to infer students' emotion	Emotional state leads to agent action choice
Bio World [15]	Problem solving	Text Frames Multimedia	Constructing hypothesis	Knowledge Self confidence	Contextual help
Medicus [14]	Problem solving	Bayesian networks	Constructing his model	Knowledge	Help suggestions
Promedas [16]	Diagnostic decision support	Bayesian networks	Entering findings	Knowledge	Explanations

Most of the above environments use knowledge-based models, like the AMPLIA system. Moreover, the strategies used consider the interaction between the user and the system. However, group interactions or group models were ignored. This functionality is observed in the AMPLIA model and it distinguishes our system from the similar environments shown in Table 1.

AMPLIA innovates by including a student model considering cognitive, social, and affective states [17]. This model allows the evaluation of individual student profiles and, afterwards, the proposal of the creation of work groups. We envisage applying the system to promote the collaboration, through the web, of several students solving a clinical case together. Additionally, AMPLIA takes into account self-confidence insofar as each group announces the confidence level regarding the proposed solution. Hence, driven by this confidence level, the tutor adjusts an adequate strategy to guide students. Therefore, AMPLIA's features contribute to improve CLE design.

3. Group model

3.1. AMPLIA's Collaborative Editor

The first version of AMPLIA's editor allowed only one student to work with the system at a time [18]. Therefore, it wasn't collaborative. According to learning theories in medicine based on problem-based learning [19], the editor was extended to allow several students to operate it simultaneously in a collaborative fashion. Thus, besides the online editing support (see Figure 1), the system was provided with a group model designed through the Social Agent, whose main goal was to motivate collaboration and improve group activity. The collaborative editor is part of the AMPLIA Learner Agent. As depicted in Figure 1, BN editing is possible in the system through buttons available in the toolbars. There are menu options to insert nodes, arcs and probabilities.

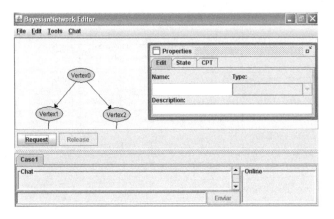

Figure 1 – The Collaborative Bayesian Net Editor

Figure 1 shows part of the BN that is under development by a group of students. In the smaller window, on the right, we can see the Node's Properties Editor, where the CPT (*Conditional Probability Table*) associated with variables (nodes) can be updated. At the bottom of the screen we can find collaborative editing options, including online users' listing and a chat tool.

3.2. The Social Agent

The Social Agent is based on social psychology ideas (to support social aspects) and affective states. The main goal of the Social Agent is to create students' workgroups to solve tasks collaboratively [17] in the AMPLIA system. Interaction is stimulated by recommending the students to join workgroups in order to provide and receive help from other students. The Social Agent's knowledge is implemented with BN. In the AMPLIA, each user builds their own BN for a specific pathology using the collaborative graphic editor. During this task, the Social Agent recommends other students that may participate in the BNs development.

The student feature set is based on the social and collaborative theories. The information collected to define a suitable recommendation includes: Social Profile, Acceptance Degree, Affective State (Emotion for Self and for Outcome), Learning

Style, Personality Traits, Credibility and Student Action Outcome (Performance). The Social Profile and the Acceptance Degree were detailed in [17]. The socio-affective agent selects the action that maximizes this value when deciding how to act. The influence between nodes is shown in Figure 2. This network is made up of a decision node (rectangle), a utility node (diamond) and uncertainty nodes (oval).

The model of [12], based on the OCC Model [20] is used to infer emotion. The affective states can be considered as an emotional manifestation at a specific time. Conati modeled a BN to infer emotions and consider the students' personality, goals, and interaction patterns to reach emotions [21] [12], thus obtaining values for the states of *Personality Traits* and *Affective State* nodes. The states of *Credibility* and *Student Action Outcome* nodes are informed by other AMPLIA agents.

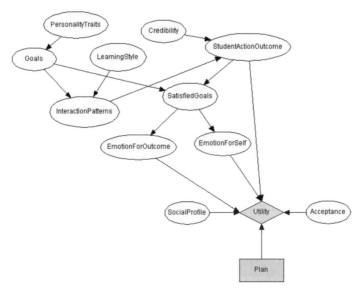

Figure 2 – Decision network of the student model

The *Student Action Outcome* node represents a possible classification for the student's BN model, which may take the values: *Unfeasible*; *Incorrect*; *Incomplete*; *Feasible* and *Complete*. Finally, the decision node *Plan* is responsible for recommendation, which is the suitable group for a student. Such plans are selected from a function of utility (node *Utility*). The *Plan* node states are *recommend* and *do not recommend* a student to join a workgroup. The *Utility* node selects the student that maximizes the *recommend* value.

3.3. Strategies for group proposal

The Social Agent uses different strategies to suggest a particular student to a workgroup. Students can join different groups whereas each group can work with different study cases, knowing that within medicine the teaching approach relies mostly on problem-based learning.

Participation in a group depends on the approval of the student by the members of the group. When the student is invited to join the group, he/she may also accept or decline the offer. When the student refuses to participate in a workgroup, the system may inquire him/her about the reason of the declination by presenting him/her with the following alternatives: (*i.*) I do not have interest in this subject; (*ii.*) I am temporarily unavailable; and, (*iii.*) I do not have interest in interacting with this group. The actions of the users are stored in the student model. This model is employed when the Social Agent looks for students to join a workgroup. The groups are dynamically formed, based on the task being carried out. The students can participate in several groups simultaneously, according to their interest. Each group must contain at least one student with the leadership role.

When a student acts actively in the learning environment, interacting and making contributions to the development of the BNs, the Social Agent records this information and verifies if he was not the one to collaborate actively in the network construction - which can be reinforced when the student had his work modified several times.

The Social Agent also tries to create groups with democratic profiles or sharing roles, where all team members are able to lead the team. This occurs when the responsibility for the operation of the team is shared – role-sharing – leading to shared accountability and competencies. The leader should focus on the process and keep the team functioning within a problem solving process.

When students overtly share the leadership or facilitator role, they are more attentive to team maintenance issues when they reassume a certain role, as they can get to know the team leader's responsibilities [19].

Some strategies can be useful to improve learning in groups, such as: working at giving good feedback, getting silent members involved, confronting problems, varying the leadership style as needed, working at increasing self-disclosure, summarizing and reviewing one's learning from group experiences (analyzing the data to discover why the group was more effective or less so and providing final feedback to members on their contribution) and celebrating the group's accomplishments.

The groups must also be formed by students with different levels of performance. Considering we have six people including students with performance categorized as excellent, average and regular, it is better to join two classmates of each level.

4. Experiments and Results

We conducted an experiment with AMPLIA involving a class of 17 undergraduate medicine students. All students were in the first term of their graduation and, therefore, they had not known each other for long. This experiment intended to assess the performance of the groups either spontaneously composed or proposed by AMPLIA, as well as the quality of group suggestions. Additionally, the students were inquired about their preferences regarding the type of learning (individual against collaborative).

The experiment was conducted in two steps, in each of which the class was organized in 6 groups of students. In the first step, students composed their own groups spontaneously. In the second one, the students were rearranged in groups suggested by the Social Agent.

First of all, the AMPLIA environment was presented to students to clarify the use of BN in the construction of diagnostic hypotheses. It is important to highlight that the class did not know BN concepts. The students organized themselves in 6 groups and they built a BN to prove a diagnostic hypothesis for the same subject. Then, the 6 groups were rearranged according to the suggestion of the Social Agent and each group solved a new diagnostic problem (equal for all the groups). At the end, the students answered two questionnaires. One of them assessed the use of AMPLIA as pedagogical resource. The other one aimed at analyzing the performance of the groups composed by the Social Agent.

As we expected, 82% of students preferred working with groups elected by them. However, 18% favored the groups composed by the system. On the other hand, 100% of students said that they liked the groups suggested by the Social Agent and that they would work again with that group formation.

When asked about the group performance (Figure 3), 58% of students pointed out that both groups (spontaneously composed and system proposed) had a similar performance. Only a single student affirmed that the group proposed by the system was *much better*, while 36% considered that the spontaneously formed group performed better (*much better* and *slightly better*).

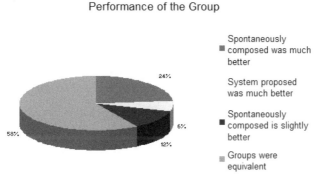

Figure 3 – Group Performance

The students approved the collaborative way of working. Only 6% of students commented that the group dynamic does not improve learning, while 59% of them affirmed that working in groups can improve learning and 35% of them corroborated that workgroups definitely improve learning.

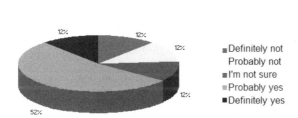

Figure 4 – Helpfulness of group suggestion

Regarding the collaboration between colleagues, the students showed that most of them approved the group dynamic as an alternative to individual learning. In fact, 94% students declared that learning is improved when they work in small groups. The same percentage also affirmed learning was easier during the group activity, while only 6%

felt ashamed during group interaction and considered that being within a group does not help the learning function.

Finally, when asked about the quality of the system's group suggestion (Figure 4), 52% of students affirmed that *probably* the system suggestion can help the choice between available groups, while 12% of them corroborated that the system suggestion *definitely* helps their choice, meaning that 64% found the suggestions helpful. Only 24% thought that the group suggestion did not help them.

To summarize, students preferred to work in a collaborative way. All the students involved in this experiment stated that they would work again with the group proposed by the system. This reveals that, although most of the students preferred to work with people they already had affinities with, the system is able to produce a satisfactory distribution of students among groups. Concerning the groups' performance, the majority declared that both groups were equivalent. The system produced suggestions that helped people choosing groups. In addition, it should be mentioned that system proposed groups obtained better solutions to the problem. We cannot conclude this out performance was due to a better quality of the groups, as happened in the second step, when the students present experience in solving the diagnostics.

5. Conclusions and future perspectives

AMPLIA is an ITS designed to support medical students' clinical reasoning. The AMPLIA environment contributes to the CLEs research area because it takes into consideration cognitive, affective and social states in the student's model. We aim at reducing the teachers' involvement, giving more autonomy to students. The tutor recommendation mechanism explores the social dimension through the analysis of emotional states and social behavior of the users. In this direction, we aim to contribute to the design of learning environments centered on students' features and collaborative learning.

Boff [22] discusses previous experiments with AMPLIA. The AMPLIA's pedagogical impact was evaluated, in 2005, by an experiment assessing how AMPLIA can help students, from the point of view of teachers, and from the point of view of students. The authors of this study also concluded that students are mainly concerned with learning to produce correct diagnoses, and with being confident in their diagnoses. In 2006, the pedagogical methodology used by AMPLIA and its potential use in Medical Education were evaluated through a major experiment involving 62 people: teachers, graduate and undergraduate students. Here, a new collaborative feature of the system is assessed.

By now, the system considers the profiles of the students, analyses them, and proposes group formations, using the Social Agent. Afterwards, each group is assigned to a given diagnosis problem and builds the corresponding diagnosis network. The group is given space and time to discuss their options and the solution is built through collaboration of the group members. The tutor evaluates the final group solution.

This work is a starting point to indicate that the social agent reasoning can be used to make up groups with good performance. The results are rather promising as the majority of students, though preferring to work in groups of people they previously knew, confirmed that groups proposed by the system performed similarly or better. Besides, all students would work again with the AMPLIA proposed group, meaning that group proposals were adequate. So, we can conclude that the Social Agent's model converges towards to students' expectation and reality. In the future, we will conduct experiments to assess the performance of different groups suggested by the Social Agent and also analyze negative results that can be an interesting contribution to the research community.

AMPLIA is continuously being extended. In the near future, the system will be available for use on a Local Area Network (LAN), and, a Web version is envisaged.

Acknowledgements

This research has been partially supported by POCTI/ISFL/152 and CAPES/GRICES.

References

[1]   Le Beux, P. and Fieshi, M. (2007) Virtual biomedical universities and e-learning, International Journal of Medical Informatics 76, 331-335.
[2]   Ward, J.P., Gordon, J. Field, M.J. and Lehmann, H.P. (2001) Communication and information technology in medical education, Lancet 357, 792-796.
[3]   Giraffa L. M., Viccari R. M. and Self, J. (1998) Multi-Agent based pedagogical games. Proceedings of ITS, 4.
[4]   Mathoff, J. and Van Hoe, R. (1994) Apeall: A multi-agent approach to interactive learning environments. In: European Workshop On Modeling Autonomous Agents Maamaw, 6, Berlin.
[5]   Norman, T. J. and Jennings, N. R. (2002) Constructing a virtual training laboratory using intelligent agents. International Journal of Continuing Engineering Education and Lifelong Learning 12, 201-213.
[6]   Panitz, T. (1997). Collaborative versus cooperative learning: A comparison of two concepts which will help us understand the underlying nature of interactive learning. Retrieved on 2008 from http://home.capecod.net/~tpanitz/tedsarticles/coopdefinition.htm.
[7]   Dillenbourg, P., Baker, M., Blaye, A. and O'Malley, C. (1995) The evolution of research on collaborative learning. In: P. Reimann & H. Spada (Eds). Learning in humans and machines. Towards an interdisciplinary learning science, 189-211. London: Pergamon.
[8]   Vassileva, J. (2001) Multi-agent architectures for distributed learning environments. In: AIED, 12, 1060-1069.
[9]   Cao, Y., Sharifi, G., Upadrashta, Y. and Vassileva, J. (2003) Interpersonal Relationships in Group Interaction in CSCW Environments, Proceedings of the User Modelling UM03 Workshop on Assessing and Adapting to User Attitudes and Affect, Johnstown.
[10] Cheng R. and Vassileva, J. (2005) User Motivation and Persuasion Strategy for Peer-to-peer Communities. Proceedings of HICSS'2005 (Mini-track on Online Communities in the Digital Economy/Emerging Technologies), Hawaii.
[11] Prada, R. and Paiva, A. (2005). Believable Groups of Synthetic Characters. Proceedings of AAMAS'05.
[12] Conati, C. (2002) Probabilistic assessment of user's emotions in educational games. Journal of Applied Artificial Intelligence 16(7-8) 555–575.
[13] Suebnukarn, S. and Haddawy, P. (2003) A collaborative intelligent tutoring system for medical problem-based learning. In Proc. International Conference on Intelligent User Interfaces, 14-21.
[14] Folckers, J., Möbus, C., Schroder, O. and Thole. H.J. (1996) An intelligent problem solving environment for designing explanation models and for diagnostic reasoning in probabilistic domains. In: Frasson, C., Gauthier, G., and Lesgold, A. (eds.) Procs. of the Third Int. Conf. Intelligent tutoring systems. Berlin: Springer (LNCS 1086) 353–62.
[15] Lajoie, S. P. and Greer, J. E. (1995) Establishing an argumentation environment to foster scientific reasoning with Bio-World. In: Jonassen, D. and McCalla, G. (eds.) Proceedings of the International Conference on Computers in Education, Singapore, 89-96
[16] Wiegerinck, W., Kappen, H., ter Braak, E., ter Burg, W., Nijman, M. and Neijt, J. (1999) Approximate inference for medical diagnosis, Pattern Recognition Letters, 20 1231-1239.
[17] Boff, E., Flores, C., Silva, M. and Vicari, R. (2007) A Collaborative Bayesian Net Editor to Medical Learning Environments. Artificial Intelligence and Applications (AIA 2007). Innsbruck, Austria.
[18] Vicari, R., Flores, C. Silvestre, A., Seixas, L., Ladeira, M. and Coelho, H. (2003) A multi-agent intelligent environment for medical knowledge, Artificial Intelligence in Medicine 27, 335–366.

[19] Peterson, M. (1997) Skills to Enhance Problem-based Learning. Med. Educ. Online [serial online] 1997; 2,3. From: URL http://www.med-ed-online/

[20] Ortony, A., Clore, G. L. and Collins, A. (1988) The cognitive structure of emotions, Cambridge University Press.

[21] Zhou X. and Conati, C. (2003) Inferring User Goals from Personality and Behavior in a Causal Model of User Affect, Procs. of IUI 2003, International Conference on Intelligent User Interfaces, Miami, FL, U.S.A, 211-218.

[22] Boff, E. and Flores, C. (2008) Agent-based tutoring systems by cognitive and affective modeling, in Jaques, P., Vicari, R. and Verdin, R. (Eds.), Idea Group, Inc (to appear).

[23] Piaget, J., (1995) Explanation in sociology. In: J. Piaget, Sociological studies, New York: Routledge.

Collaboration Tools
for Group Decision Making

Collaborative Decision Making: Perspectives and Challenges
P. Zaraté et al. (Eds.)
IOS Press, 2008

A Binomial Model of Group Probability Judgments

Daniel E. O'LEARY

Marshall School of Business, University of Southern California,
Los Angeles, CA 90089-0441

Abstract. Research in psychology has found that subjects regularly exhibit a conjunction fallacy in probability judgment. Additional research has led to the finding of other fallacies in probability judgment, including disjunction and conditional fallacies. Such analyses of judgments are critical because of the substantial amount of probability judgment done in business and organizational settings. However, previous research has been conducted in the environment of a single decision maker. Since business and other organizational environments also employ groups, it is important to determine the impact of groups on such cognitive fallacies. This paper finds that groups substantially mitigate the impact of probability judgment fallacies among the sample of subjects investigated. A statistical analysis, based on a binomial distribution, suggests that groups investigated here did not use consensus. Instead, if any one member of the group has correct knowledge about the probability relationships, then the group uses that knowledge and does not exhibit fallacy in probability judgment. These results suggest that at least for this setting, groups have a willingness to collaborate and share and use knowledge from the group.

Keywords. Group Judgments, Knowledge set, Consensus Judgment, Probability Reasoning, Reasoning Fallacies

1. Introduction

There has been substantial research in psychology regarding probability judgment fallacies. The classic work of Tversky and Kahneman [1983] found that, in contradiction to probability theory, on average, individuals rank the intersection of two events as more likely than one or both of the two events. This is in violation of probability axioms, and thus is referred to as the so-called "conjunction fallacy" (and in general as probability judgment fallacies). Although there has been substantial research about individual judgments, (e.g., [11]), there has been limited research exploring such judgment issues in the context of groups.

Research in the ability to process probability information is critical since most organizational decision-making occurs under conditions of uncertainty. However, much organizational decision-making is performed in the context of groups. Thus, the concern is not only with individuals, but also with groups. As a result, one purpose of this paper is to investigate the existence of probability judgment fallacies in group decisions.

In order to analyze that issue, this research generates and tests a model designed to predict the probability that group judgment will be correct. A binomial model [1] is used to test to alternative views of the ways that groups make decisions, including consensus and the notion that if any one member is correct, then the group will be correct. Finding a model of the group process is critical to the development of computational models to simulate mirror worlds or reality [5] or models of groups.

1.1. Probability Models in Business

Probability judgments are essential in business. A number of industries deal with probabilities directly, such as gaming industries and the insurance industry. Within any given industry there are also a number of direct opportunities for probability measurement. For example, research and development, pensions, guarantees, warranties all require probability judgment. The direct importance of probability judgment has been stressed by a number of researchers in those disciplines. Although there is an extensive literature on using decision analysis (e.g., Schum [1987]), in many situations, business does not involve formal models for generating the probabilities of such events. There may not be sufficient time or there may not be sufficient problem understanding to develop a formal model. Accordingly, intuitive judgment often is the method used to assess uncertainty. Thus, there is concern with the existence of possible errors in probability judgment.

An important aspect of business decision-making is that those probability judgments are not made only by individuals. Typically, groups, directly or indirectly, make those judgments in pursuit of a common goal (e.g., Simon [1957]). Thus, a critical issue in the analysis of the business and organization decisions is the impact of groups on probability assessments.

1.2. Computational Models of Organizations

Increasing emphasis is being placed on computational models of organizations. For example, Gelernter [1992] examined the development of "mirror worlds." Such software models of organizations can be used to support decision-making and to study the design of organizations. Mirror worlds and other computation models of organizations, are based on "understanding" various organizational processes. Since the results in the paper are studied using binomial models, the research presented here could be used to facilitate the development of such computational models to predict and study decision making. Further, the results provide insight into "how" groups make decisions.

1.3. Findings

I find that the use of groups of size three has a substantial impact on mitigating the existence of probability judgment fallacies in those situations where groups provide a single solution to a decision problem. Groups develop fewer fallacies and function as much more expert than individuals. Since much of organization decision-making is a group activity, this suggests that the use of groups can reduce some of the potential problems associated with probability judgment fallacies. These results also suggest that it can be critical for organizations to use group decision-making in certain situations.

I also find that a binomial model can be used to describe that group decision-making. The binomial model is used to investigate two different solution approaches:

if any one member of the group has correct knowledge about the particular pair of probabilities then the group will not have probability judgment fallacies about that pair, and in contrast, consensus. The research finds that the first approach cannot be rejected, using statistical analysis. These results suggest, that at least for this setting, group members are willing to collaborate and share knowledge.

2. Selected Prior Research

The problem addressed in this paper brings together group research and probability judgment research. This section (1) differentiates between individual and group behavior; (2) summarizes the notion of "knowledge set;" and (3) summarizes some aspects of previous research on individual's probability judgment.

2.1. Group Behavior

Group decisions often differ from individual decisions. Throughout the group literature there is the notion of "group behavior" or group decisions (e.g., Simon [1957]), as compared to individual decisions. These terms are used since, as noted by Weick [1969, p. 32], "People in aggregates behave differently than do people in isolation." (A general review of the literature is summarized in Davis [1992].)

   This paper is concerned with a particular kind of group behavior. In particular, the concern is with those groups that must provide a common solution to a decision problem. For example, insurance companies must issue a policy at a single rate; audits require that the audit team present a single financial statement opinion; firms must either invest or not invest. This is different than other group environments where multiple decisions or recommendations can result from the group.

2.2. Knowledge Sets and Consensus in Group Settings

The notion of knowledge sets (knowledge bases) argues that individuals have a knowledge base, developed from past experience, education, etc. (e.g., Simon [1981] and Lenat and Guha [1989]). That knowledge guides their solution generating processes. Subjects carry their knowledge from situation to situation. As the knowledge changes, the knowledge set changes. Thus, if the subjects have had training in probability theory, then it would be expected that training would become part of their knowledge set. The knowledge sets of the group and the individuals in the group are closely related. According to the knowledge set view, if one member knows something then the entire group will have access to that knowledge.

   In general, it is assumed that the knowledge set of the group is limited to the union of the knowledge sets of the group members. For discussion purposes, assume that the knowledge of individual i can be written as $KS(i) = (k(i,1), ..., k(i,m))$, where $k(i,j)$ is some subset of knowledge, for individual i. For a group of individuals a and b, the group knowledge set would be $KSg(a,b) = (k(a,1), ..., k(a,m), k(b,1), ..., k(b,m))$. If the group is making judgments about probability then only one member may need to understand probability in order for the group to generate a correct solution.

   The notion of knowledge sets has received much application in artificial intelligence (e.g., Simon [1981] and Lenat and Guha [1989]). In addition, it is not unusual for the developers of computer systems (e.g., decision support systems and expert systems) to assume that that the use of a computer program will increase the knowledge set of the user. Effectively, those developers assume that the augmented human and computer system can function with a knowledge set limited only by the union of the two knowledge sets.

An alternative approach to group decision-making is that of consensus (e.g., Black [1958]). If groups use consensus then "majority votes" is used to generate the solution. Consensus generally generates a better solution than individual decision-making. However, when structured as a binomial distribution it can be shown that there is a nonzero probability that the majority will vote for the wrong solution.

The knowledge set approach assumes that there will be sharing of knowledge for the common good and that the appropriate knowledge will be recognized and used. In contrast, the consensus approach, sees group decision making as a much more political process, where those with inappropriate knowledge may dominate.

2.2.1. Recognizing Knowledge and Incentives for Using the Knowledge and Feedback

There are multiple mechanisms by which a group can recognize the appropriate knowledge. For example, a member of the group can declare that they "know" how to solve the problem or that they have "seen" this kind of problem before.

However, just because the group has and recognizes the knowledge does not mean that they will use the knowledge. In general, there need to be the appropriate incentives in place for the members of the group to let the correct knowledge "bubble-up" for group use. One set of such incentives is that the payoff for using the knowledge is greater than not using it.

In some settings, information about knowledge and its implementation is provided to groups or individuals. This paper does not employ feedback or account for feedback. It investigates the use of knowledge in a single setting over time, without any feedback as to the quality of the knowledge employed by the group.

This is not unusual in many business settings. For example, a group is often brought together to construct a proposal, and that proposal is either accepted or not accepted. In either case, the decision is made on a single constructed document.

2.3. Probability Judgment Research

There has been substantial research into individual probability judgment (e.g., Smedslund [1990] for a literature review). The literature shows that individuals make errors when performing probability judgments. For example, Tversky and Kahneman [1983] provided multiple sets of experimental evidence that people assess the probability of the intersection of two events to be greater than the probability of at least one of the events. This is in contradiction to probability theory and is called the conjunction fallacy. In particular, Tversky and Kahneman [1983] used the "Predicting Wimbledon" case. Given a brief scenario, subjects were asked to rank the probability of four different sets of events: (a) XXX will win the match (b) XXX will lose the first set (c) XXX will lose the first set but win the match (d) XXX will win the first set but lose the match. It was found that subjects, on average, assigned a greater probability to c than to b. Thus, there was a conjunction fallacy in the average of the subjects' probability judgments.

There are some explanations that have been proposed for the existence of such probability judgment fallacies. For example, in some cases the temporal sequence of events, referred to here as "temporal differences," does not match the sequence of causation (Einhorn and Hogarth [1986]). Disease (cause) results in a positive test result (effect), yet it is by the test that we determine the existence of the disease. In those situations, causation and temporal order reversal can confuse probability judgment.

However, the phenomenon of violation of probability axioms has been quite persistent in a variety of research contexts. In particular, it has led Tversky [1994] to develop an alternative to probability in order to model individual probability judgment.

2.4. Groups and Probability Judgment Research

Unfortunately, it appears that there has been limited research involving the impact of groups on probability judgment research. This paper is designed to mitigate that gap in the literature.

3. Hypotheses

The hypotheses of individual and group performance are based on the discussions of groups differing from individuals, the notion of knowledge sets for individuals and groups, and the probability judgment research discussed in the previous section. Individual subjects are compared to groups of subjects, and two different types of group decision making (knowledge sets and consensus) are compared.

3.1. Probability Theory and Research Hypotheses

Probability theory provides a number of relationships between different sets of events. Let $Pr(A)$ be the probability of A. Let there be two events, A and B, where neither probability is zero. Let the union of two events be denoted "$\vee$" and the intersection of two events be denoted "$\wedge$." If subjects (either groups or individuals) use probability judgments consistent with probability theory, then we would have the following:

Conjunction Hypothesis: Subjects will estimate $Pr(A \wedge B) < Pr(A)$ and $Pr(A \wedge B) < Pr(B)$.

Disjunction Hypothesis: Subjects will estimate $Pr(A \vee B) > Pr(A)$ and $Pr(A \vee B) > Pr(B)$.

Conjunction/Disjunction Hypothesis: Subjects will estimate $Pr(A \wedge B) < Pr(A \vee B)$.

Conditional Hypothesis: Subjects will estimate $Pr(A|B) > Pr(A \wedge B)$

3.2. Comparing Group and Individual Judgments

This research investigates two different approaches to analyzing group judgment: knowledge sets and consensus. Each approach can be structured as a binomial distribution (see, e.g., Black [1958] for review of the consensus approach), $B(x;n,p) = C(n,x) \, p^x(1-p)^{(n-x)}$, where $C(n,x)$ is the number of ways that x successes can occur among n group members, p is the probability of a correct solution by an individual, (1-

p) is the probability of an incorrect solution ("violation"). Since the concern is with triads, n=3 throughout the paper.

The *knowledge set approach* assumes that if any one member has knowledge of the above hypothesized relationships then the group would be able to use that knowledge. Thus, assuming a knowledge set approach, if no members are successful (x=0) then the group would generate a solution in violation of the probability relationships. Given a binomial structure, group probability of violation (assuming a knowledge set approach) always is less than the individual probability of violation (some examples illustrating this point are presented later in the paper in table 3). As a result, assuming a knowledge set approach, leads to the notion that "three heads are better than one."

The *consensus approach* assumes that "majority votes" (two or three members in three member groups) (e.g., Black [1958]). Thus, if a majority violates any of the above hypotheses then the group would violate those same hypotheses using a binomial model. Using the binomial distribution, (1) the probability of an individual violation (with probability less than .5) will be greater than the probability of a group violation, when using consensus, and (2) the probability of an individual violation (with probability greater than or equal to .5) will be less than or equal to a group violation when using consensus.

Accordingly, in many group decision making situations described by either consensus or knowledge sets, groups will generate a better solution than the individual. As a result, we have the following hypothesis:

Group Hypothesis: Groups will exhibit fewer probability theory-based probability judgment fallacies than individuals.

Since both the knowledge set approach and the consensus approach can be formulated as a binomial model we can compare the probabilities that groups function using either knowledge set or consensus approaches. Since the knowledge set approach will result in the correct solution if any member has knowledge of the correct solution, the probability of a violation using the knowledge set approach is lower than the consensus approach. As a result, groups will more often get the "right" answer if they use a knowledge set approach. Thus, we have the following:

Knowledge Set versus Consensus Approach: Groups will use a knowledge set approach. (Groups will not use a consensus approach.) (*If one member knows then the group will use that knowledge.*)

3.3. MethodQuestionSubCases

Two different disguised companies were used as the basis for cases: Laser and Electra. In the first event A was "The company's bank renews a substantial line of credit" and event B was "The company losses a major customer." In the second, event A was "The system of internal controls is strong" and event B was "Initial testing reveals some errors."

For each case, sets to be ranked were preceded by a one-paragraph discussion. In case 1 subjects were told "You are in charge of the Laser audit. In the past year, the company has experienced some difficulties with the design of a new product line. Production problems have affected the quality of this line, which in turn, has resulted in slow sales. In addition, throughout the year, the company has been late in making its loan payments." In case 3, subjects were told, "You are planning a review of Electra's internal controls. Although the company has not emphasized a strong network of detailed control procedures, top management closely monitors the operations and overall management controls serve as an adequate substitute for detailed controls."

3.4. Groups

One of the most critical variables in groups is the number of group members, particularly in small groups (e.g., Simmel [1950] and Weick [1969]). The crucial transitions in group size are from one to two persons, from two to three, from three to four, from four to seven and from seven to nine (Weick [1969)]). In particular, Weick [1969, p. 38] refers to triads as the basic unit of analysis in organization theory. The triad is particularly important since it is the smallest group size that allows for alliance of two group members against one. Triads allow for cooperation, control and competition.

The groups were self-selected. The completion of the questionnaire contributed to the student's class grade. In the case of groups, the entire group got the same reward; the incentive could not be divided up.

3.5. Data Analysis

A critical part of the study was the data analysis, which took two different forms. The average rankings were analyzed as in Tversky and Kahneman [1983], for comparison purposes. Although average rankings were analyzed, the existence of violations in the different sets of group and individual could be easily camouflaged using averages. Accordingly, I focused directly on the *violations in the orderings*. Group and individual rankings were analyzed to determine the extent to which the two populations of groups and individuals developed rankings that had violations in them. A violation was defined as a ranking that was inconsistent with probability theory. For example, if $\Pr(A \wedge B)$ was ranked as more likely than $\Pr(A)$, then there was a violation. Each pair was analyzed separately. The focus on violations is new and thus required a different type of analysis than that associated with averages.

The analysis used the concept of violation to analyze both the average rankings, and individual and group rankings. A violation of probability theory in the average rankings is referred to as an "average violation." Violations in-group and individual rankings were analyzed using the notion of "violation rate," the total number of violations in a set of rankings, divided by the total number of subjects.

The relationship between individual and group violation rates was examined using a test of "difference in proportions" (e.g., [3, pp. 248-249]). This test is used to compare proportions from samples of different sizes, and results in a z - value that can be used to generate the probability that the violation rate of individuals and groups are significantly different. If the proportions are significantly different, then we can reject the hypothesis that the proportions are equal.

A comparison of the actual group violation rate to the expected group violation rate, under both an assumption of knowledge sets and consensus was tested using statistical analysis of a binomial model. First, the average individual violation rate associated with each probability pair (e.g., conjunction hypothesis, etc.) and case (either 1,2 or 3), was used as "p" in the binomial distribution for that analysis of that pair and case for the groups. Second, the theoretically correct probabilities were calculated from the binomial distribution, assuming both a knowledge set approach and a consensus approach. Third, this probability was used to generate the "theoretically" correct number of violations, under either the assumption of knowledge sets or consensus. Fourth, for each of consensus and knowledge sets, the theoretical (assuming the individual rate) was compared to the actual using a test of proportions (e.g., [3, pp. 248-249]), that was evaluated for each probability pair and case.

4. Findings

4.1. Groups versus Individuals

This section summarizes a comparison of the quality of the rankings of groups and individuals, comparing the results for each hypothesis. The average rankings are summarized in table 1 and the violation percentages are summarized in table 2. z-values, for the test of difference in proportions, between the violation rates of groups and individuals, are summarized in table 3.

Table 1. Average Ranking Value

Individuals (n=31)	Case 1	Case 2	Groups (n=12)	Case 1	Case 2
Pr(A)	3.41	3.70	Pr(A)	2.17	3.08
Pr(B)	1.93	2.00	Pr(B)	3.91	1.67
Pr(A ∧ B)	4.25	4.61	Pr(A ∧ B)	3.83	4.92
Pr(A ∨ B)	2.51	3.09	Pr(A ∨ B)	2.16	1.50
Pr(A|B)	4.42	5.19	Pr(A|B)	4.75	5.00

(1 is highest ranking.)

4.1.1. Comparing Groups and Individuals: Conjunction Hypothesis

The individual violation rate was statistically different than the group rate (tables 2 and 3), for the probability pairs Pr(A) : Pr(A∧B) and Pr(B) : Pr(A∧B), for three of the four individual measures, as compared to the groups. Thus, we reject the hypothesis that individuals and groups have the same violation proportions for those cases for both sets of individuals. Further, in all cases individual violation rate exceeded the group violation rate for both data sets.

4.1.2. Comparing Groups and Individuals: Disjunction Hypothesis

The individual subjects exhibited an average violation of the disjunction hypothesis in both cases (table 1). Groups had no average disjunction violation.

All four of the comparisons between each of the sets of individuals and groups for the probability pairs Pr(A):Pr(A∨B) and Pr(A):Pr(A∨B) are significantly different. Thus, we reject the hypothesis that individual and groups have the same violation proportions for all those cases. Further, in all cases individual violation rate exceeded the group violation rate.

4.1.3. Comparing Groups and Individuals: Disjunction/Conjunction Hypothesis

Neither the individuals nor the groups had an average violation of the disjunction/ conjunction hypothesis (table 1). Further, in all cases individual violation rate exceeded the group violation rate (table 2). However, both of the cases resulted in statistically significantly different violation rates between both sets of individuals and groups at the .01 level and the .05 level or better, respectively (table 3). Thus, for those cases, we reject the hypothesis that the two proportions are equal.

Table 2. Violation Percentage

	Individuals (n=31)		Groups (n=12)	
	Case 1	Case 2	Case 1	Case 2
a. $Pr(A) : Pr(A \wedge B)$	.45	.48	.00	.17
b. $Pr(B) : Pr(A \wedge B)$	.13	.16	.00	.00
c. $Pr(A) : Pr(A \vee B)$	.42	.45	.08	.08
d. $Pr(B) : Pr(A \vee B)$	.68	.77	.42	.42
e. $Pr(A \wedge B) : Pr(A \vee B)$	.39	.32	.00	.00
f. $Pr(A \wedge B) : Pr(A|B)$	.58	.68	.33	.58

Note: A violation occurs when rankings attributed to sets of events are inconsistent with probability theory.

Table 3. Comparing Groups to Individuals

-Values for Difference between Group and Individual Violation Rates

	Case 1	Case 2
a. $Pr(A) : Pr(A \wedge B)$	2.835***	1.908**
h $Pr(B) \cdot Pr(A \wedge B)$	1 307	1 480*
c. $Pr(A) : Pr(A \vee B)$	2.109**	2.272**
d. $Pr(B) : Pr(A \vee B)$	1.569*	2.244**
e. $Pr(A \wedge B) : Pr(A \vee B)$	2.538***	2.246**
f. $Pr(A \wedge B) : Pr(A|B)$	1.455*	0.580

Notes: Based on test of difference of proportions [3, pp. 249-250], * significantly different from each other at the .10 level or better, ** significantly different than each other at the .05 level or better, *** significantly better than each other at the .01 level or better.

4.1.4. Comparing Groups and Individuals: Conditional Hypothesis

Individuals had an average violation in both of the cases (table 1). One of the cases resulted in statistically significant differences between the groups and the other individuals. Thus, for those cases, we reject the hypothesis that the proportions are equal. Further, in all cases individual exceeded the group violation rate (table 2).

4.1.5. Comparing Groups and Individuals: Summary

Violation percentages were lower in all group categories compared to individuals. Ten pairs of group: individual violation rates (table 3) are statistically significantly different (< .10 level). This is strong evidence that groups make fewer and statistically significantly different portions of probability judgment errors than individuals.

4.2. Knowledge Sets versus Consensus

The research also compared the knowledge set hypothesis to the consensus hypothesis. In order to make this comparison, we need to compare what would happen if the average individual success rate were employed in a group setting, i.e., we need to translate the individual violation rates (table 2) into group violation rates (table 2) using the binomial under the assumption of both knowledge sets and consensus. First, each different individual probability of violation was gathered from table 2 and summarized as the first column in table 4. Second, the theoretical binomial probabilities, based on those individual probabilities of violation, were developed for both knowledge set and consensus approaches. Column (2) summarizes the probability that no members of a group are successful, i.e., the probability of a group violation under the knowledge set hypothesis. Column (4) summarizes the probability that a consensus judgment of two or three group members is not successful, i.e., group is in violation using consensus.

Table 4. Binomial Probabilities of Group Members with Knowledge of a Violation
(Column 1 is from table 2; 2. Column 4 = Column 2 + Column 3)

1	2	3	4
Individual Probability of Violation	Zero Members Successful (Knowledge Set)	One Member Successful (Consensus)	Two or Three Not Successful
0.06	0.0003	0.014	0.014
0.22	0.011	0.113	0.124
0.30	0.027	0.189	0.216
0.35	0.043	0.239	0.282
0.44	0.085	0.325	0.410
0.49	0.117	0.367	0.485
0.52	0.141	0.389	0.530
0.60	0.216	0.432	0.648
0.65	0.275	0.443	0.718
0.80	0.512	0.384	0.896
0.84	0.593	0.339	0.931

The results of the statistical significance of the comparison of the actual results in table 2 to those in table 4, for the *knowledge set hypothesis* are given in table 5A. None of the twelve cases is statistically significantly different. As a result, we cannot reject the hypothesis that the actual number of violations is the same as the theoretical amount as computed in the knowledge set approach. The results of the statistical significance of the comparison of actual violation rates to those in table 4, for the *consensus hypothesis* approach are given in table 5B. The results indicate that only three of the twelve case-probability relationship pairs are *not* statistically significantly different at the .10 level or better. Thus, for those three we cannot reject the hypothesis that the actual number of violations is the same as the theoretical amount as computed in the consensus approach. *It appears that consensus does not capture the results of the group process. Instead, these results strongly suggest that the knowledge set approach provides a better fit to the data than the consensus approach.*

Table 5. A and B: z-Scores for Test of Proportions

	A: Knowledge Set Approach		B: Consensus Approach	
	Case 1	Case 2	Case 1	Case 2
a. $Pr(A) : Pr(A \wedge B)$	0.06	0.307	0.411	2.399**
b. $Pr(B) : Pr(A \wedge B)$	0.573	0.364	1.704*	1.25
c. $Pr(A) : Pr(A \vee B)$	1.224	0.349	3.172***	1.664*
d. $Pr(B) : Pr(A \vee B)$	1.506	0.468	0.556	2.472**
e. $Pr(A \wedge B):Pr(A \vee B)$	0.726	1.032	1.984**	2.488**
f. $Pr(A \wedge B) : Pr(A|B)$	0.311	0.048	1.887*	1.986**

Notes: * significantly different from each other at the .10 level or better, ** significantly different than each other at the .05 level or better, *** significantly better than each other at the .01 level or better.

5. Contributions

This paper has a number of contributions. First, it demonstrates that in some situations groups appear to have better probability judgment than individuals. Second, this paper used a new methodology to evaluate the findings ("violations" associated with different rankings). Third, it provided evidence as to how probability judgment fallacies are mitigated, and how much better groups are likely to be compared to individuals. Fourth, a binomial model could be used to provide insight into group decisions.

References

[1]   Black, D., *The Theory of Committees and Elections*, Cambridge University Press, London, 1958.
[2]   Davis, J., "Some Compelling Intuitions about Group Consensus Decisions, Theoretical and Empirical Research, and Interpersonal Aggregation Phenomena: Selected Examples," *Organizational Behavior and Human Decision Processes*, Volume 52, (1992): 3-38.
[3]   Dixon, W. and Massey, F., *Introduction to Statistical Analysis*, McGraw-Hill, New York, 1969.
[4]   Einhorn, H. and Hogarth, R., "Judging Probable Cause," *Psych Bul*, Volume 99, No. 1, (1986): 3-19.
[5]   Gelernter, D., *Mirror Worlds*, Oxford University Press, New York, 1992.
[6]   Lenat, Douglas B. and R.V. Guha, *Building large knowledge-based systems: representation and inference in the Cyc project,* Reading, Mass.: Addison-Wesley, 1989.
[7]   Simmel, G., *The Sociology of Georg Simmel*, edited by K. Wolff, Free Press, New York, 1950.
[8]   Simon, H., *Administrative Behavior*, Second Edition, Free Press, New York, 1957.
[9]   Simon, H., *The Sciences of the Artificial*, Second Edition, MIT Press, Cambridge MA, 1981.
[10] Schum, D., *Evidence and Inference for Intelligence Analyst*, Univ. Press of Am, Lanham, MD, 1987.

[11] Smedslund, J., "A Critique of Tversky and Kahneman's Distinction Between Fallacy and Misunderstanding," *Scandinavian Journal of Psychology*, volume 31, (1990): 110-120.
[12] Tetlock, P.E., Peterson, R., McGuire, C., Chang, S., "Assessing Group Dynamics: A Test of the Groupthink Model," *Journal of Personality & Social Psychology*, September, 63, 3, (1992): 403-425.
[13] Tversky, A., "A New Approach to Subjective Probability," unpublished paper presented at the *Behavioral Decision Research In Management Conference*, May 22, 1994, MIT Sloan School
[14] Tversky, A. and Kahneman, D., "Extensional Versus Intuitive Reasoning: The Conjunction Fallacy in Probability Judgment," *Psychological Review*, Volume 90, No. 4, (October 1983): 293-315.
[15] Weick, K., *The Social Psychology of Organizing,* Addison-Wesley, Reading Massachusetts, 1969.

Information Technology Governance and Decision Support Systems

Rob MEREDITH

Centre for Decision Support and Enterprise Systems Research, Monash University
PO Box 197, Caulfield East, Victoria 3145, Australia
Rob.Meredith@infotech.monash.edu.au

Abstract. Information technology governance is the set of organizational structures that determine decision-making rights and responsibilities with regard to an organisation's information technology assets. Although an important sub-field of information technology, little research has been done on the issues relating to the governance of decision support systems. This paper argues that decision support systems are significantly different to other kinds of information technology, and that this means there is a need to consider issues specific to their governance. Orlikowski's [17] theory of the Structuration of Technology is used to highlight the fundamental differences between decision support systems and other kinds of information technology, and their respective relationships with organizational structures. Some preliminary recommendations and suggestions for further research into issues of decision support systems governance are made.

Keywords. IT governance, DSS, evolutionary development, structuration theory

Introduction

Weill & Ross [23] write that "IT governance is an issue whose time has come" (p.216). As a result of a renewed interest in corporate governance in general, as well as criticisms of information technology (IT) as a strategic tool [7], there is increasing pressure on the IT industry to demonstrate value to organisations, and to put in place organizational structures that can help to ensure that IT, as a corporate asset, is managed responsibly and effectively.

Most IT governance literature focuses on the governance of IT in general, giving little consideration to the characteristics of a given technology, rather focusing on political power structures in organisations and how this relates to particular governance decision structures [6]. In particular, attention has focused on whether the IT department or non-IT business units should dominate the determination of IT policy.

Decision support systems (DSS) are a significant aspect of today's IT industry. Although the current industry term for the concept is 'business intelligence' (BI) [5], DSS has a rich academic and industry history that stretches back to the 1970s. However, despite both corporate and IT governance receiving a significant amount of research attention, little has been written on governance issues for DSS specifically. The exception is a small body of literature on data warehousing governance (see [2, 21, 22], for example).

The purpose of this essay is to argue that DSS are different to other kinds of information systems in that they are 'chaotic' and 'subversive.' It will further argue that governance is, in large part, about control and enforcement. Given that approaches to controlling and managing chaotic and subversive processes or systems are significantly different to the control and management of predictable, stable processes or systems, it follows that approaches to DSS governance need to be different to the governance of other kinds of IT.

1. Decision Support Systems

1.1. Kinds of DSS

The term 'Decision Support System' is commonly attributed to Gorry & Scott Morton [11], who describe a framework of decision-support tools based on decision categories of "operational control," "management control," and "strategic planning" and a dichotomy of "programmed" versus "un-programmed" decision problems. Subsequently, various kinds of DSS have emerged providing varying levels of support [12, 14] ranging from the purely informational (i.e. passive support) to normative tools that recommend a course of action.

Industry practice has been dominated, at various times, by various kinds of DSS. In addition to spreadsheet-based DSS, systems such as Executive Information Systems (EIS), Group Support Systems (GSS), Negotiation Support Systems, Intelligent DSS, Knowledge Management-based DSS, and Data Warehouses have all been used to support managerial decision-making [5]. Current industry practice focuses on the use of data warehouses (see, for example, [15]) to provide the data infrastructure for so-called Business Intelligence (BI) systems. BI is the current term for what are functionally equivalent to the EIS of the 1980s and 1990s [5].

DSS therefore differ on a number of dimensions, including the technological approach adopted, the kind of support offered, the level of 'structuredness' of the decision supported, the level of management supported and the number of decision makers involved (one or many). They range from small, informal systems through to large-scale systems similar in nature to enterprise resource planning (ERP) systems. This is not to say that the size and scale of the DSS are positively correlated with their impact: some short-lived, small-scale DSS have had a profound impact (see [3], for a description of so-called "ephemeral" systems).

1.2. DSS as Chaotic Systems

Arguments that DSS are different to other kinds of information systems have been made since at least Gorry and Scott Morton [11]. This difference is particularly relevant when thinking about the development lifecycle for DSS. Traditional, engineering-based systems development processes such as the 'waterfall' model [18] do not cope well with the dynamic design requirements and usage patterns typical of DSS.

Keen [13] was the first to articulate the key factors that make development of decision support systems of any variety different to the development of other kinds of information systems. The primary reason for this difference is that any decision problem that benefits from the kind of analysis that a DSS can provide (specifically, semi- and un-structured decision problems) necessarily involves ambiguity and uncertainty. This makes the initiation and analysis phases in the waterfall model [18] difficult to complete. The kind of requirements specification that needs to occur in these phases comes from a detailed understanding of the task that the system is being designed to support. In a semi- or un-structured decision situation, it is this very understanding that the DSS is supposed to provide assistance with.

The result is that any DSS designed to assist with these kinds of decisions will be developed with an initially incomplete understanding of the users' requirements. The system itself "shapes" the users understanding of the decision problem, and therefore the users' information and support needs [13]. This in turn leads to novel, unanticipated uses of the system, and a need to evolve the functionality of the DSS.

Keen [13] conceptualized the development environment for any DSS using the framework depicted in Figure 1 below. In particular, he showed that interaction between the user and the system drives a need for evolutionary change as the system helps formulate the user's understanding of the decision problem, and the user utilizes the system in novel and unanticipated ways as a result.

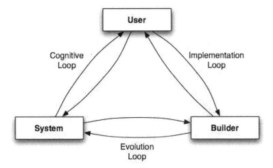

Figure 1. Keen's Adaptive Framework for DSS. Adapted from Figure 1 in [13].

This "cognitive loop" is the basis of the difference between transaction-processing systems and DSS, and Keen's [13] argument is that a need for evolutionary development and use necessarily holds true for any kind of DSS: if not, then the system cannot possibly provide meaningful 'support.' The evolutionary process itself – the act of changing the system through close interaction with the user as they use the system – as well as system use, provides insight to the decision problem.

Development of DSS must, therefore, be evolutionary. There have been various development methodologies proposed for DSS, and most incorporate this idea of evolutionary adaptation to user requirements to a varying degree. Sprague and Carlson [20], for example, describe four kinds of "flexibility" required of a DSS: flexibility for the user to solve the decision problem; flexibility to change the functionality of the DSS; flexibility to adapt a new DSS application; and flexibility to evolve the underlying technology. Similarly Arnott [3] described two different kinds of DSS adaptation: within- and between-application evolution.

The adaptation process can take place quite rapidly. Arnott [3] describes a DSS developed over a period of six weeks. The DSS evolved into four distinct systems used to investigate various aspects of the decision problem, including spreadsheet-based financial models and CAD-based architectural plans, shown in Figure 2. The development path was characterized by opportunism and unpredictability. DSS evolution is often dependent on factors outside of the control of the developers and the organisation, including the user's ability to understand the decision problem as well as technical and political disruptions [3].

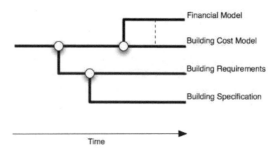

Figure 2. Evolution of a Building Project DSS. Adapted from Figure 4 in [3].

This unpredictability makes DSS a kind of 'chaotic' system in the sense that future properties and characteristics of the DSS design cannot be foreseen. This contrasts with the comparative stability and predictability of transaction-processing systems.

1.3. DSS as Subversive Systems

The way in which organizational structures are embedded in technology, or the way in which technology itself influences organizational structures frames how we understand the design and use of information systems [8, 17]. Orlikowski [17], drawing on Giddens' Structuration Theory [10], demonstrates that the influence between technology (as a tool and mediator of human agency) and organizational structure is bi-directional. Orlikowski's [17] "structurational model of technology" is depicted in Figure 3. Technology results from human actions such as design and development (arrow a), but also acts as a medium for human action (arrow b) through technology use. Institutional properties both influence what human actions are acceptable and/or possible with regards to technology (arrow c) and are shaped by technology (arrow d).

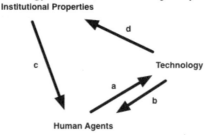

Figure 3. Orlikowski's Structurational Model of Technology [17].

Structuration theory is based on the three concepts of 'signification' (signs and language), 'legitimation' (norms and values, accepted was of doing things), and 'domination' (means of enforcing and controlling human action) [10]. Together, these three constitute organizational structures, and Orlikowski [17] argues that technology acts upon each of them in one of two ways: either through reinforcement or transformation. Generally, technology is intended to reinforce existing organizational structures, rather than transform them [17]. Arguably, even when the intent is to transform organizational structures, the intent of the technology is to embed and reinforce the new structure. Orlikowski [17] asserts (p.411): "[users] are generally unaware of their role in either reaffirming or disrupting an institutional status quo."

Further, when technology is used to transform rather than reinforce, it is usually in situations characterized by "high levels of stress, ambiguity and unstructured ... situations" [17] (p.412). In such situations, workarounds and other anticipated uses of the technology 'subvert' organizational structures.

Gorry and Scott Morton [11] differentiated between systems that are developed to support semi- or un-structured decisions (DSS) and systems designed to support structured decision problems ("structured decision systems", or SDS). While SDS support recurring, unambiguous decisions, DSS are designed in an unstructured (i.e. novel, ambiguous, and stressful) environment. The unanticipated uses of transformative technologies and consequent subversion of organizational structures described by Orlikowski [17] have a direct parallel in DSS use as described by Keen [13].

DSS are inherently subversive. While other kinds of technology can be transformative, their subversion of organizational structures is often unanticipated and unplanned. DSS are *intentionally* subversive since, by design, they directly influence decisions on organizational goals, policies, activities and direction.

2. IT Governance

Information technology (IT) governance outlines the "decision rights and accountability framework [that] encourage desirable behavior in the use of IT" [23] (p.8). It defines the principles, procedures, responsibilities and other normative aspects of managing an organisation and its resources [23].

As a subset of corporate governance, IT governance takes into account general corporate governance doctrines and strategies and applies them in the context of IT [23]. Much of the debate in the academic literature has, in the past, been concerned with power-structure issues, such as whether a given governance arrangement was centralized or decentralized, or a hybrid form of the two [6, 19, 21].

The power-structure view is a relatively narrow lens through which to view all of the issues related to IT governance. The work of Weill & Ross [23, 24] expands the scope of debate on IT governance to include a range of decision-types in addition to who specifically makes those decisions. These two issues – what decisions need to be made, and who should make them – are the basis of a matrix used to analyze the IT governance arrangements in a number of different organisations. Weill & Ross [23] define the following IT governance decisions:

- *IT Principles*. How IT should support the business.
- *IT Architecture*. Requirements for organizational standards and integration of systems.
- *IT Infrastructure Strategies*. Requirements for supportive services for IT applications.
- *Business Application Needs*. Requirements for information systems to support the business, whether developed internally or purchased.
- *IT Investment*. Selection and funding of IT initiatives.

They also outline the following archetypal arrangements for making these decisions:

- *Business Monarchy*. Centralized decision making by senior business managers/executives.

- *IT Monarchy.* Centralized decision making dominated by the CIO / IT department.
- *Feudal.* Decentralized decision making by business unit managers.
- *Federal.* A hybrid approach combining decision making by senior executives as well as business unit managers. This may or may not include the IT department.
- *IT Duopoly.* Decision making by the IT department and one other entity – either business unit management, or senior executives.
- *Anarchy.* Isolated, uncoordinated decision making by individuals or small groups.

Table 1, below, shows the most common governance structures found in [23]:

Table 1. Recommended IT Governance Arrangements from [23].

	IT Principles	IT Architecture	IT Infrastructure Strategies	Business Application Needs	IT Investment
Business Monarchy					██
IT Monarchy		██	██		
Feudal					
Federal				██	██
IT Duopoly	██			██	██
Anarchy					

Weill & Ross [23] point out that, in addition to the two issues described above, there is the further question of how governance decisions are to be implemented. Typical governance instruments include the use of formal policy statements, project management methodologies, documents outlining standards, advisory councils and committees, chargeback structures, appointment of business/IT relationship managers and service level agreements [23]. All of these instruments are means of controlling IT activities in an organisation. As with other management instruments, the typical intent is to increase managerial control, coordination and predictability.

As a subset of corporate governance, IT governance is used to ensure that an organisation's information systems are consistent with and embody organizational structures. Corporate governance principles and the strategic direction of the firm dictate IT governance principles, which in turn dictate the features, functionality, operation and use of individual information systems, as depicted in Figure 4.

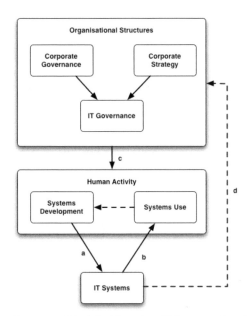

Figure 4. Flow of Corporate Governance Principles Through to IT Systems, adapted from Figure 3. Arrow labels have been maintained from Figure 3 for cross-reference. Dashed lines indicate a 'weaker' influence.

Based on Figure 3, Figure 4 decomposes Orlikowski's [17] "institutional properties" into corporate governance, strategy and IT governance, renaming them 'organizational structures.' It also decomposes Orlikowski's "human activity" into systems development and systems use. Corporate governance and strategy filter through IT governance and its corresponding governance instruments, which, through the activity of designing and developing the system (arrow c, then a), ensures that these structures are reflected in the deployed information system. In turn, this encourages a use of the system that is consistent with corporate organizational structures (arrow b).

An arrow has been introduced between systems use and development to reflect system redesign based on users' experiences. Both this, and d have been shown as dashed lines to indicate the relative weakness of the influence. In the case of the influence of use on development, modifications will typically be minor and more along the lines of maintenance rather than a full redesign. In the case of d, this influence is typically one of reinforcement, or, when transformative, it is often unintentional [17] and so not as direct or deliberate as the other influences.

3. IT Governance and DSS

The assumption behind Weill & Ross's [23] framework is that each intersection of governance decision and type of organizational culture represents a coherent, homogenous approach to IT governance within the domain of the relevant decision-maker's mandate. That is, in the case of a feudal information culture, each business unit determines the IT principles etc that apply to all IT within that business unit. Likewise where the mandate is enterprise-wide, all IT within the organisation will adhere to the same set of principles, architecture, and so on.

This assumption is present, not only in Weill & Ross [23], but also in the earlier IT governance literature. Although the IT governance debate acknowledged the possibility of different governance models for different parts of an organisation (at least under a decentralized or hybrid approach), the assumption is that governance arrangements will differ according to aspects of the organizational structure such as business units or the relative dominance of a central IT department. There is no recognition that approaches to governance may need to differ according to characteristics of the technology itself, in addition to characteristics of the organisation.

In section 1, it was argued that DSS are different in the way that they are developed and used compared to other kinds of IT. Whereas transaction-processing systems are developed to enforce and control one or more business processes, with the intent that the system will be as stable as possible, DSS are necessarily unstable and intentionally subversive.

The chaotic and subversive nature of DSS implies a different set of relationships between a DSS and organizational structures compared to other kinds of IT. There is an inherent tension between a governance structure predicated on control and predictability needed for transaction-processing systems, and the unpredictable development process that is necessarily a characteristic of DSS. Not only is control and predictability difficult to enforce with DSS, it is undesirable: "The label 'Support System' is only meaningful in situations where the 'final' system must emerge through an adaptive process of design and usage" [13] (p.15).

The chaotic nature of DSS development and use has two implications for the model in Figure 4. The first is that the influence between systems use and systems development is much stronger and more explicit than with other kinds of IT. It should be expected that as a DSS is being used, the user learns and experiments and that this will drive pressure for system change. IT and corporate governance instruments, put in place to manage and control systems development and use, can have a deleterious effect on this dynamic. One such case [4] describes a business intelligence project at a financial services company that failed, in large part, due to the project management methodology that was employed. The administrative overheads associated with the methodology "throttled" [4] (p.720) development on the business intelligence project to the point where the project was cancelled fourteen months after it began, with no DSS functionality actually delivered.

This leads to the second implication for the model in Figure 4. The link between organizational structures and DSS development and use should be less controlling (and more enabling) than for other kinds of IT. Although Weill & Ross acknowledge the need for an enabling aspect to IT governance [23] (pp.20-21), they don't see this occurring outside the normal IT governance structures in the organisation. While innovation is possible in such situations (Weill & Ross cite several examples), it is unreasonable to expect that this would typically work for the rapid, continuous and chaotic evolution required for DSS. DSS users and developers need the freedom and to be able to evolve the system as needs be, without having to continuously second guess or report to a 'stifling' [4] layer of bureaucracy. This devolution of power to small teams of DSS developers and users suggests that for DSS, an 'anarchic' decision-making structure would be more appropriate than the more structured approaches recommended by Weill & Ross [23]. This is supported by Arnott [4] where a subsequent, anarchic project was undertaken successfully at the same organisation.

The subversive nature of DSS also means a much more explicit and deliberate influence of the DSS on organizational structures. Because of the nature of decisions that DSS support, this often means that decision-makers are directly considering some aspect of organizational strategy or structure. By definition, a decision-making process is one where a commitment is formed to a particular course of action. In an organizational setting, this often means that a new course of action for the organisation is being committed to, thereby directly affecting organizational structures.

Figure 5 incorporates these changes to Figure 4 for DSS. Arrow c is now less deterministic, while the influences of systems use on development and the system on organizational structures are both significantly stronger.

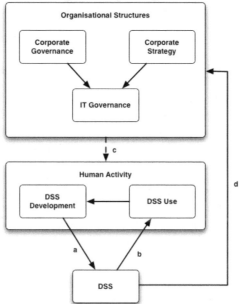

Figure 5. Structuration Theory Applied to DSS

3.1. Implications for the Governance of DSS

The chaotic and subversive nature of DSS implies that the necessary assumptions for the governance of DSS are different to those for the governance of other IT resources. Where the latter is intended to provide a capacity for control, predictability and conformance with corporate governance structures, the former can only be successful in an environment that encourages flexibility and experimentation.

There is a parallel between the idea of managing DSS development and use as a learning process [13], and managing creative processes in organisations, characterized as "idiosyncratic, unpredictable, random, [and] anarchic" [9] (p. 163). Such processes require very different managerial mindsets to other organizational processes [1, 9], and it is reasonable to assume that approaches to managing creative processes in organisations hold insight for managing DSS, and by extension, governing DSS.

Management of creative processes tends work better when not characterized by direct control and supervision [9]. There is also a need for freedom and encouragement to explore and experiment [1]. Excessive administration, surveillance, and a lack of autonomy tend to restrict such processes [16]. The same is true of DSS development and use: there is a need for flexibility to deviate from the governance structures put in place to manage and control other kinds of IT.

This is not, however, an argument for a completely free reign. Rather, it is an argument for an approach to the governance of DSS that places trust in the DSS team (including the users) to make development decisions within well-defined boundaries. Clearly, it is not desirable to arbitrarily violate IT management procedures in such a way as to negatively impact on the operation of other IT systems. Each deviation from accepted IT governance principles in the organisation should be made deliberately, in full awareness of the potential implications. The corollary of this is that the organisation must have clearly articulated IT governance structures already in place.

Weill & Ross [23] also acknowledge the need for some degree of creative IT experimentation in organisations (pp. 41-42), and argue that this kind of experimentation should be undertaken in an environment with explicit boundaries. The DSS team needs to be clear about what can or cannot be done. In other words, DSS development and use should operate in a kind of governance 'sandbox' where the team is free to experiment and adapt the system outside of normal governance structures.

DSS governance can therefore be characterized by the following points:

1. An organisation should have clear and explicit IT governance structures generally.
2. DSS should not be strictly bound by these structures.
3. There should be a clearly defined scope for DSS development and use, including budget and resources, goals and anticipated benefits.
4. This scope should not be overly constraining, and should be revised regularly.
5. There should be trust placed in the DSS team to develop the DSS as they see fit within the broad scope defined above.

4. Conclusion and Directions for Future Research

With a renewed focus on corporate governance in recent times as a result of legislative changes such as the Sarbanes-Oxley Act of 2002 in the US, and related legislation in other jurisdictions [23], as well as questions regarding the strategic benefit IT can deliver to organisations [7], IT governance is currently an important issue for the IT industry. IT governance helps to ensure that an important organizational resource is managed effectively, and that organizational structures are enforced through the systems that people use to do their work.

To date, however, little consideration has been given to the relationship between governance structures and the characteristics of the technology being governed. While extensive consideration has been given to the relationship between governance and organizational power structures, the same cannot be said of how principles inherent in a given technology (such as evolutionary development for DSS) integrates with various governance structures.

The motivation for IT governance in general is control and the enforcement of organizational structures. For most IT systems – especially transaction-processing systems – this is a reasonable aim. However, this is not the case for DSS.

Unlike other kinds of IT, DSS development and use is chaotic. DSS use subverts organizational structures. The typical assumptions behind the governance of IT in general are incompatible with these two characteristics.

DSS, therefore, may require a more flexible approach to governance: one that trusts DSS developers and users to use their judgment to assess the appropriateness of changes to the design and use of the system, rather than having to go through the bureaucratic procedures appropriate for other kinds of systems. This autonomy, though, should be used in light of clear boundaries and requirements: DSS governance should not be *carte blanche*.

The issues highlighted in this essay raise a number of interesting questions for future research:

- To what extent do different kinds of DSS require the kinds of governance recommendations in section 3.1? Do large-scale DSS such as business intelligence systems and data warehouses benefit from the same governance freedoms as smaller scale personal DSS?
- To what extent does the decision problem, or task, determine governance requirements for DSS?
- How much scope should be given, or conversely, how restricted should governance boundaries be for DSS development and use?
- What mechanisms are appropriate to encourage DSS evolution to maximize benefits to the organisation?
- How can conflicts between DSS governance and other organizational structures (including general IT governance) be resolved? How can other IT assets be protected from changes in, and resource demands by, DSS?
- What is the relationship between characteristics of a given technology and the assumptions that underpin its governance?

References

[1] T.M. Amabile, How to Kill Creativity, *Harvard Business Review* **76** (1998), 76-87.
[2] J. Ang and T.S.H. Teo, Management Issues in Data Warehousing: Insights from the Housing and Development Board, *Decision Support Systems* **29** (2000), 11-20.
[3] D. Arnott, Decision Support Systems Evolution: Framework, Case Study and Research Agenda, *European Journal of Information Systems* **13** (2004), 247-259.
[4] D. Arnott, Data Warehouse and Business Intelligence Governance: An Empirical Study, in: *Proceedings of the Creativity and Innovation in Decision Making and Decision Support: The 2006 IFIP WG8.3 International Conference on DSS*, Volume 2, F. Adam, P. Brezillon, S. Carlsson and P.C. Humphreys Editors, Decision Support Press, London, 2006, pp. 711-730.
[5] D. Arnott and G. Pervan, A Critical Analysis of Decision Support Systems Research, *Journal of Information Technology* **20** (2005), 67-87.
[6] C.V. Brown, Examining the Emergence of Hybrid IS Governance Solutions: Evidence From a Single Case Site, *Information Systems Research* **8** (1997), 69-94.
[7] N. Carr, IT Doesn't Matter, *Harvard Business Review* **81** (2003), 41-49.
[8] G. DeSanctis and M.S. Poole, Capturing the Complexity in Advanced technology Use: Adaptive Structuration Theory, *Organizational Science* **5** (1994), 121-147.
[9] M.T. Ewing, J. Napoli and D.C. West, Creative Personalities, Processes and Agency Philosophies: Implications for Global Advertisers, *Creativity Research Journal* **13** (2000-2001), 161-170.
[10] A. Giddens, *The Constitution of Society*, University of California Press, Berkeley, 1984.
[11] G.A. Gorry and M.S. Scott Morton, A Framework for Management Information System, *Sloan Management Review* **13** (1971), 55-70.
[12] M.T. Jelassi, K. Williams and C.S. Fidler, The Emerging Role of DSS: From Passive to Active, *Decision Support Systems* **3** (1987), 299-307.
[13] P.G.W. Keen, Adaptive Design for Decision Support Systems, *Data Base* **12** (1980), 15-25.
[14] P.G.W. Keen, Decision Support Systems: The Next Decade, *Decision Support Systems* **3** (1987), 253-265.

[15] R. Kimball, L. Reeves, M. Ross and W. Thornthwaite, *The Data Warehouse Lifecycle Toolkit*, Wiley, New York, 1998.

[16] M. Nagasundaram and R.P. Bostrom, The Structuring of Creative Processes Using GSS: A Framework for Research, *Journal of Management Information Systems* **11** (1994), 87-114.

[17] W.J. Orlikowski, The Duality of Technology: Rethinking the Concept of Technology in Organizations, *Organizational Science* **3** (1992), 398-427.

[18] W.W. Royce, Managing the Development of Large Software Systems, in: *Proceedings of the IEEE/WESCON Conference, August 1970*, The Institute of Electrical and Electronics Engineers, 1970, pp. 1-9.

[19] V. Sambamurthy and R.W. Zmud, Research Commentary: The Organising Logic for an Enterprise's IT Activities in the Digital Era - A Prognosis of Practice and a Call for Research, *Information Systems Research* **11** (2000), 105-114.

[20] R.H. Sprague and E.D. Carlson, *Building Effective Decision Support Systems*, Prentice Hall, Englewood Cliffs, New Jersey, USA, 1982.

[21] S. Suritpayapitaya, B.D. Janz and M. Gillenson, The Contribution of IT Governance Solutions to the Implementation of Data Warehouse Practice, *Journal of Database Management* **14** (2003), 52-69.

[22] H.J. Watson, C. Fuller and T. Ariyachandra, Data Warehouse Governance: Best Practices at Blue Cross and Blue Shield of North Carolina, *Decision Support Systems* **38** (2004), 435-450.

[23] P. Weill and J. Ross, *IT Governance: How Top Performers Manage IT Decision Rights for Superior Results*, Harvard Business School Press, Boston, USA, 2004.

[24] P. Weill and J. Ross, A Matrixed Approach to Designing IT Governance, *Sloan Management Review* **46** (2005), 25-34.

Collaborative Decision Making: Perspectives and Challenges
P. Zaraté et al. (Eds.)
IOS Press, 2008

How efficient networking can support collaborative decision making in enterprises

Ann-Victoire PINCE[1] & Patrick HUMPHREYS

London School of Economics and Political Science

Abstract: In today's global economy, and as a result of the complexity surrounding the working world, new ways of working are emerging. In particular, collaboration and networking gain increasing importance as they enable firms to face the new demands of a global economy. Within this context, it is necessary to understand how new ways of organising influence decision-making processes. This paper (i) explores the connection between networks and decision-making and (ii) tries to define how efficient networking can support reliable collaborative decision making .We argue that effective networking constitutes a fundamental support for decision-making. Our focus is on small and medium-sized companies where networking is particularly relevant because of their restricted means for action and resources. Our findings are based on seven semi-structured interviews, conducted within five French small and medium-sized companies. They confirm the allegation that enterprise decision-making is now embedded in network structures [3] and also offer a good basis for drawing guidelines, enabling effective networking and reliable decision-making.

Key words: Collaborative decision making, decision support, networks, small and medium-sized enterprises

Introduction

In today's global economy, and as a result of the complexity surrounding the working world, new ways of working are emerging. In particular, working patterns involving collaboration and networking gain increasing importance, as they enable firms facing new demands of a global economy [1]. Within this context, decision-making is no longer an individual or unitary process but rather, becomes increasingly collaborative [2]. Similarly, decisions are not shaped only according to the immediate environment anymore but are deeply influenced by the wider context in which organisations are embedded. The information available when a decision is made depends on the position of a company within a network. As information processing influences the decision-making processes, centrality is fundamental for decision-makers. Consequently, the impact of a network depends on the structures the organisation belongs to and on the information and influences reaching the organisation though it. Hosking & Morley support the idea that networking is a central activity in the decision making process and argue that it allows actors building up their own understanding and to mobilize

---

[1] London School of Economics and Political Science, Houghton Street, London WC2A 2AE, England UK,
E-mail: a.pince@lse.ac.uk; p.humphreys@lse.ac.uk

influence [3]. Contacts between professionals facilitate the assessment of possible threats and opportunities of new situations. Based on the information collected, decisions may be made, changes may be performed and difficulties may be anticipated.

The process of decision-making has traditionally been characterized, within the dominant *"rational choice"* paradigm as (i) a phase of information processing during which the decision maker identifies problems, specifies goals, search for alternatives and evaluates them, and (ii) a phase of selection of actions [4]. The limitations of this rational choice perspective have become evident in the context of provision of effective support for group and collaborative decision-making in organizations [5]. Awareness of these limitations has led to an *"attention based view of the context of collaborative decision making in enterprises"* [6], founded on Simon's claim that, in practice, collaborative decision processes, move through the stages of *Intelligence* (searching for the conditions that call for decisions), then *Design* (inventing, developing and analysing possible courses of action). Finally, the *Choice* phase focuses on *"selecting a particular course of action from those available"* according to what has been represented in a decision support model during the design phase.

According to the rational choice theory, making a choice terminates the decision-making process, but in organisational contexts, the decision process cannot terminate here, as the chosen future actions have only been prescribed, and, in the absence of continuing attention, may unfold not at all as expected by the decision maker. Hence, the focus now shifts to the implementation stage [7]. In collaborative decision making, all of these stages require participation and knowledge input from people with diverse positions within the enterprise, as none will have sufficient power or knowledge to process the decision on their own. Collectively they will need to gain access to a variety of contextual knowledge, and to decide what part, and how, this knowledge may need to be proceduralised. Brezillon & Zarate call this *"the proceduralised context"*, i.e., *"the part of their contextual knowledge that is invoked, structured and situated according to a given focus"* [8].

Simon cast organisational decision making within a problem-solving paradigm [9]: Participants in the decision making group engage in a collaborative process, operating within a proceduralised context, which spirals within the constraints of a decision spine [10] as the decision-making group sharpens the description of "the problem", progressively reducing participants freedom to consider how their options may be defined in developing structure and spiralling toward choice of the action to be prescribed to solve the problem.

However, Group Decision and Communication Support (GDACS), to be effective in support of innovative and creative decision making, communication activities within the interaction context need to focus on more than just developing the proceduralised context and spiralling down a decision spine. They also need to nurture the *"decision hedgehog"*, enriching the context which may be available for proceduralising whenever it is considered necessary to 'make a decision' within a spine [11], [12], [13].

Effective use of networks in this way during the process of collaborative decision making extends the interaction context that is available for gaining contextual knowledge beyond the individuals participating in the immediate collaborative decision making process, so that it is now permeable throughout the relevant networks and accessible through the narratives that flow within them. This provides a major enrichment of context, enabling more creative, innovative and effective decision making within the enterprise.

There are many forms of networks. In the frame of this study, the term network refers to social networks, in an informal form (e.g. friendship) or within formal structures such as associations of professionals. Most of the literature stresses the benefits of networks, highlighting their advantages in terms of innovation, knowledge and information sharing or process effectiveness. However, reaching an effective networking is extremely challenging due to socio-psychological elements such as the emergence of power conflicts or the difficulty to establish trust between members of a network. Janis illustrated that the socio-psychological factors involved strongly influence information processing activities within the collaborative decision-making process [14], [15]. Based on this observation, it is argued that networking activities should be facilitated and mediated in order to promote valuable information processing. A better understanding of networks' functioning, in terms of benefits, but also in terms of enablers and hinderers would then help enterprises to develop more effective networking patterns and hence, a more reliable decision-making processes. Thus, our current research aims to elaborate guidelines for good networking patterns, which would then improve decision-making processes.

This research should not be considered as providing prescriptions of how organisations should perform in a network. Rather, this study must be viewed as an exploration, providing an opportunity for a better understanding of networking processes among the range of firms approached and thus, as a guideline only.

1. The Changing Organisational Landscape: the Emergence of Networks

Within the organisational literature, there has been increasing recognition of the prevalence and importance of formal and informal inter-organisational relations as the solution to many problems exceeding the capacity of any single organisation [16]. Some authors, such as Newell *et al.*, attribute the emergence of these new ways of organising to (i) the globalisation of markets and (ii) the emergence of ICTs [17]. Other authors argue that in recent years, new working patterns emerged as the expression of the transition away from the 'modernity' – secured and controlled – towards a 'post-modernity' which is open, risk-filled and characterized by general insecurity [18]. In the post-modernity, boundaries tend to break down, increasing ambivalence, unclarity and contradictoriness; they also are the source of important disorientation. In this turbulent context, entering networks reduces uncertainty [19] and bring about a certain degree of orientation and belongingness [18]. Moreover, the increasing complexity associated with post-modernity renders current organisational issues too complex to be handled by one individual or one organisation only but require different competencies and different frames of references [20]. Although previous forms of organisations such as bureaucracy – characteristic of the modernity period – still exist, new ways of organising adapted to this new context, more fluid and dynamic than traditional structures, are emerging [3]; [21].

Central Issues Raised By Inter-Organisational Relations

Because networks are unusual forms of organising and are not governed by traditional hierarchical relationships, critical challenges have to be faced such as the development and maintenance of trust [22] or uncertainties and tensions between the processes of collaboration and competition between members.

Trust is central to the effective operation of networks, not only because trust eases cooperation [23] but also because a lack of trust between parties is one of the most important barriers to effective collaboration [24]. Trust is defined in various ways in the literature, though two issues seem central: first that trust is about dealing with risk and uncertainty, second that trust is about accepting vulnerability [16]. Whereas it is often assumed that trust is built through a process of continued interaction or communication [25], Newel & Swan suggest that this does not guarantee the development of trust especially when participants in the process are dissimilar. In such cases, increased communication merely helps to accentuate people's differences [16].

This question of similarity or diversity of members in a network is a core theme in the literature. Some authors stress the importance of heterogeneity in network membership. For instance, Casson & Della Giusta describe an entrepreneur as an information gatherer for whom diversity in networks is extremely useful, as they will learn little about what is new by exchanging with people who have similar backgrounds [26]. Similarly, Nahapiet & Goshal support heterogeneity [27]. They rely on the idea that significant progress in the creation of intellectual capital often occurs by bringing together knowledge from disparate sources. On the other hand, some argue in favour of homogeneity of members' characteristics [28], especially in facilitating communication within networks. Indeed, a common culture and a common language avoid misunderstandings that are caused when differences in basic values and beliefs lead to information being interpreted in an unintended way. A recent study by Moensted on strategic networking in small high-tech firms shows that alliance, confidence and trust become easier among firms and people with similar features [29]. The author states that while the complementarities will be positive in the initial stage, the heterogeneity may turn into a weakness and lack of trust in the process of collaboration. There is a paradox here as one of the main functions of networks is to provide complementarities, which themselves make it hard to create the type of trust which is necessary to "glue" relations for effective collaboration. Nooteboom claims that the real challenge lies in the right balance between stability and flexibility [30]. Some stability is needed to allow trust to develop, to create quality relationships and to facilitate exploration. However, this should not yield unnecessary rigidity and closeness in relationships that last too long and become too exclusive between partners.

This discussion echoes the disagreements among scholars about the strength of the ties required for an optimal network. The "strength" of a tie is a reflection of the combination of the amount of time, emotional intensity, intimacy, and reciprocal services that characterize that tie [31]. Granovetter suggests that an individual will have access to a greater amount and variety of resources, including information, when they are embedded within a network comprised mainly of 'weak' relations – a weak tie is defined as a distant and infrequent relationship [31]; [32]. On the opposite because strong relations also contained expressions of friendship, it can be argued that people are motivated to network in order to accrue the dual benefits of valuable information and advice and expressions of friendship, affection and possibly emotional support. Support for this argument is provided by Granovetter's 'embedded' perspective, which asserts that as 'social animals', people will engage in activities that allow them to simultaneously pursue economic and non-economic goals [33].

The last issue related to the process of networking that is important to discuss here is the coexistence of the opposite forces of competition and collaboration within networks. Easton argues that the degree to which competitors compete with each other depends on how intensely they interact with each other [34]. Easton also states that the degree of distance between competitors is of importance for the kind of relationship that emerges. Regarding collaboration, horizontal relationships between competitors, often characteristic of networks, have not been analyzed to the same extent as for vertical relationships. Cooperative relationships between vertical actors are easier to apprehend, as they are built on a distribution of activities and resources among actors in a supply chain. Conversely, horizontal relationships are more informal and invisible and are built mainly on informational and social exchanges [35]. Collaboration in business networks is expected to be easier than in vertical networks as relationships in business networks are generally built upon trust and mutuality [25]. Meanwhile, the literature reveals that collaboration may be a frustrating and painful process for the parties involved. Huxham & Vangen conclude that collaboration is a seriously resource-consuming activity and that it is only to be considered with parsimony [36].

Both processes of competition and collaboration occur in networks, and this generates tensions. On the one hand there is a demand for cooperation, as members of a network must create bonds in order to create long-term relationships. On the other hand, collaborative activities may be inhibited and the network effectiveness diminished by the co-presence of competitors. Bengtsson & Kock partly resolved this opposition by the concept of "coopetition" [35]. They propose that competitors can be involved in both cooperative and competitive relationships with each other and benefit from both. However, they also state that these two logics of interaction are so deeply in conflict with each other that they must be separated in a proper way in order to make a coopetitive relationship possible.

The extreme diversity of network structures and goals probably explains the lack of specific recommendations in the literature for an effective operation of networks. Although trust seems to be a constant requirement, it appears problematic to determine whether a network needs homogeneous or heterogeneous members, strong or weak ties between them and how to deal with the tension between competition and cooperation.

2. Research Methodology and Procedure

Given the objectives and the exploratory nature of the current study, a qualitative method was selected. Authors performed semi-structured in-depth interviews, conducted with companies' owners. Convenience sampling was employed. The sample was initially selected from a group of companies participating in a European project named InCaS – Intellectual Capital Statement for Europe (www.incas-europe.org). InCaS aims at strengthening the competitiveness and innovation potential of European small and medium-sized enterprises by activating their intellectual capital. During group discussions we conducted for the purpose of the InCaS project, networks repeatedly appeared to be a fundamental element for the firms' decision-making process. Five companies and seven participants constituted the sample, since some firms were owned by two individuals

Authors decided to focus on owners of companies only, as they are in charge of making and implementing major decisions. Moreover, they are expected to be the most concerned by the survival of their organisation and the most involved in networking activities. Moreover, to be part of the study, the organisation must legally be qualified as a small and medium-sized business. Such enterprises comprise, according to the European Commission, less than 249 employees and have a turnover not exceeding 50 millions of euros.

We were particularly interested in studying small firms because of their specific characteristic and difficulties in today's economy. Governments are now conscious of the importance of small and medium-sized businesses and of their contribution to the economic growth and employment as they represent 95% of enterprises and about 65% of employment. However, the OECD reports that despite their importance, small companies face difficulties in finding financial support, in developing good managerial abilities and a sufficient productivity [37]. Compared with larger companies, small firms also suffer from lack of time, resources and personnel [38] rendering them particularly reliant on networks and for which effective decision-making is a question of survival. As networks are becoming a commonly used practice among these firms, it is necessary to study and understand better their networking patterns and how to support better their efforts towards collaborative activities.

3. Findings and Discussion

A thematic analysis revealed the major perceived benefits of networking in the decision-making process. It also unfolded the main enablers and inhibitors for an effective network.

3.1. Benefits of Networking for Decisions Makers

First, it emerged from the results that networks have many forms. For instance, networks develop according to several geographical scales, from a local level to a global one. Our findings demonstrated that regional networks support small firms better than any other type of networks. Effectiveness of local networks is emphasised by Man who states that physical proximity is beneficial to collaboration in networks [39]. Proximity is expected to ease communication and to facilitate the transfer of knowledge and more particularly of critical knowledge to the specificities of the local environment. Ease of communication is enhanced by the fact that people in a region have similar cultural backgrounds and interests. Some authors even advocate that embeddedness in local networks of information is a major factor of competitiveness [40]. Moreover, regional networks are particularly effective in the process of partner selection as some phases can be omitted, as enterprises already know other businesses in their region [39]. Further, it can be argued that involvement in regional networks is an attempt to reduce uncertainty generated by the phenomenon of globalisation [18] and more particularly is an expression of the limitation of the use of ICTs. Findings showed that face-to-face interactions are favoured by small firms' owners in the process of building trust and reinforcing the strengths of the ties between local actors. By the quality of relationships and the amount of knowledge and information available, it appears here that regional networks constitute a major support for decision makers.

Second, it is important to stress the significance attributed by interviewees to community networks. The phenomenon can be related to the notion of "Old Boy Networks", which is frequently observed in the recruiting process [9] but has seldom been explored in the context of business networks. However, the results of this study suggest that elite networks are a central element supporting the development of small firms as they provide support and access to elitist spheres where important clients – unreachable by any other means – may be contacted. Ratcliff supports this argument by suggesting that elite connections may have considerable implications for developing business relations [41]. Our interviewees reported that their affiliation to elite networks allowed them to accessing first-hand information, such as market trends, that was other wise unavailable, yet crucial for the elaboration of strategies. Therefore elite networks play a central role in their decision-making processes.

Beyond their structures, we identified several perceived benefits of networks. All interviewees emphasised the necessity for networking. This requirement was not be limited to the early stage of a business. Networks were said to be crucial during the entire evolution of the company: to launch an activity, to survive and to exist. However, our interviewees' discourse on return on investment in networking was ambiguous. Their expression of the necessity to integrate networks and the large number of benefits that have been reported contradicted their perceived lack of return on investments. This may be due to what Man views as one of the most important difficulties of the network economy, which is to determine the true benefits of networking [39]. Both costs and benefits are difficult to measure and many are hidden.

In terms of benefits for the enterprise, the primary perceived advantage is access to information. Being in the right network and at the right position in it (exchange of information being dependant of the degree of contact between people) allows the individual to obtain early information and to be aware of new trends [28]. Moreover, having access to information at a regional level is crucial, as it facilitates the transfer of knowledge about the local market and local competitors. Issues of access to resources and information are often approached in the literature [42]; [39]. However, the importance of the concepts of visibility and credibility, which emerged in our data, are seldom cited in the literature. First, visibility is a fundamental benefit from networks for small firms because of their restricted budget. Networks tend to play a role of marketing agency, and facilitate the spreading of knowledge about companies involved in networks. Particularly, Powell claims that centrality in networks enhance visibility [24]. We argue that central connectedness shapes a firm's reputation and visibility, and this provides access to resources (e.g., attracts talented new employees). Second, our interviewees claimed that membership of particular networks improved the credibility of their companies. This result is supported by Koza & Levin who, through conducting a longitudinal case study of a professional service network in the public accounting industry, found that some member firms perceived belonging to an international network as a possible enhancement of their domestic prestige and credibility [43]. It served to attract clients that preferred an accounting firm that provides access to international resources, services, and expertise.

Visibility and credibility both relate to the notion of reputation. In a broad sense, the reputation of an actor is fundamentally a characteristic or an attribute ascribed to him by his partners [44]. In our study, it appeared that by their engagement in attractive networks, organisations become attractive partners themselves [45]. Moreover, it has been demonstrated that social status and reputation can be derived from membership in specific networks, particularly those in which such membership is relatively restricted [46]. The role of selection then becomes absolutely central. In terms of supporting collaborative decision-making, the reputation provided by the affiliation to visible and credible networks is important as it facilitate the integration to restricted circles where valuable piece of information may be gathered.

Further, our findings support the concept of the strength of the weak ties [32] as our results demonstrated that the owners of small enterprises use acquaintances in order to sustain their businesses and to find new clients. The concept originally emerged from a study of professional men seeking work in the Boston area in the 1970s, where

Granovetter found that weak ties (i.e., someone with whom you are acquainted but who travels in different social circles, such as a classmate from college) lead to jobs more readily than did strong ties among friends and family. Hence, acquaintances are valuable in finding employment because they provide non-redundant information that strong ties do not. Our findings suggest that having acquaintances facilitates finding new resources. Regarding collaborative decision making, our results confirmed Granovetter's later results on embeddedness, and indicate that the process is influenced mainly by strong-ties networks built up on trust, quality or resources and ease of communication, rather than by weak-ties [31].

3.2. Network Functioning: Facilitators and Inhibitors

Our findings revealed that power conflicts are perceived as major inhibitors of effective operation of networks. Despite the horizontal relationships expected in networks, power conflicts are not avoidable. Munro argues that, in networks, power operates through free-floating control and through the regulation of information flows [47]. As information is the major benefit that small firms get from networks, the expression of power in such networks thus deeply hinders the functioning of the structure and the potential support of networks in collaborative decision-making processes. On the other hand, acquisition of power in networks – through centralising the control of information flows on oneself as source or intermediary [48]; [49] – is difficult because potentially any point in the network can communicate directly with any other point.

Moreover, the tension that exists between competition and cooperation confused the small firms' owners. Uncertainty attached with the cooperation with potential competitors inhibits their participation within networks. This can be attributed to a lack of trust between parties and to a lack of face-to-face interactions [50]. Trust builds slowly, with time and through frequent contacts. After a few tests of each other's goodwill, it is expected that fear of competition would decrease while interest for cooperation would increase. This finding is supported by Malecki & Veldoheon who argue that although the cooperation that operates within networks first raises the possibility of competition among participating firms, experience shows to networks members that the complexity of the market is such especially small companies cannot operate in all markets and so, perception of threat for real competition is reduced [51]. Our findings emphasised the fundamental need to reduce competition anxiety in order to develop a "network philosophy", based on the idea that "who gives receives". The notion of exchange is central to an effective operation of networks.

In terms of facilitators of the networking process, our findings showed that selection of members is a good solution to support networks effectiveness. Jones *et al.* state that restricted access reduces coordination costs, and fewer partners increase interaction frequency, which can enhance both the actors' motivation and ability to coordinate smoothly [52]. Having fewer partners who interact more often reduces variance in expectations, skills, and goals that parties bring to exchanges, facilitating mutual adjustment. Moreover, the selection process assures current member of a network that new adherents have appropriate qualities and hence, selection supports the construction of competence trust [16].

The literature review provided in this report introduced the debate generated about the issue of diversity and similitude of members in networks. Casson & Della Giusta argued that diversity within networks is more favourable than similarity for small firms due to access to a wide range of information [26]. However, our findings show that small firms' decision-makers prefer joining networks comprised of homogeneous members. As supported by Moensted [29], our research found that trust become easier among firms and people with similar features. In particular, Newell & Swan's competence and companion trust are reinforced by common backgrounds [16].

It appears then that it is not the amount of information that companies can gather that interests small firms' decision-makers but rather the quality of the information and the optimal transfer of it. When favouring homogeneity, networks have to be careful to stay open. Too much closeness would limit potential new inputs and networks risk loosing their added value [30]. Moreover, long-term associations can lead to stagnation. When groups become too tightly knit and information passes only among few people, networks can become competency traps. Organizations may develop routines around relationships and rules that have worked in the past, but exclude new ideas [53]. Information that travels back and forth among the same participants can also lead to lock in, group think, and redundancy.

4. Practical Implications

Findings support the argument that, when functioning efficiently, networks support decision-making processes. However, it appears that some networks work better than others and hence that networks may not always provide an effective support for collaborative decision-making processes. In this section, we address some practical implications of what has been discovered and offer some elements for a better functioning and exploitation of networks.

While, in the following, we draw practical implications, we would like to stress at the outset that it is not possible to "manage" networks. Indeed, effective network management appears to be a difficult issue. The difficulties and frustrations attached with collaboration [36] and the fact that an estimated 60% of partnerships fail [54] support this argument. It seems sensible that, rather than trying to "manage" networks, we might try to find ways to enable them. However, it is important to keep in mind that networking patterns are diverse and complex [55] and that there is no single best way for networks to support collaborative decision making better in small firms. Researchers cannot predict the direction of development of a network, nor forecast the final effects of any network because of the large number of ways participants can act, react and interact [56]. Also, the current research is exploratory and is based on a very limited sample and hence, the reader should bear in mind that no general truth can be extracted from the following conclusions.

In our research, it first appeared crucial for networks to set up clear goals within a clear structure. Ambiguity should be avoided as much as possible. People should know why they are participating to the network and what their roles are. In order to clarify the situation conventions should be made explicit, potentially through a set of rules. Similarly, it is important that members identify the reasons why they are willing to join a network. Man argues that entering into an alliance or a network without a clear structure and strategy is one of the most important factors explaining network failure [39]. Successful networking requires being aware of the possibilities that different types of networks can offer and to choose the type of network that supports the goals the company has set out to achieve. Clarifying the goal of the network is the first essential step.

Second, it is more than necessary that a network keeps its dynamism, and more particularly, that members of a network do not act passively but provide an active and engaged participation. Engagement in the structure can be generated by facilitating the emergence of a common culture [57]. Note that a common culture does not exclude the emergence of sub-cultures attached to sub-groups within a network [58]. Furthermore, both our specific findings and the literature in general highlight the importance of selection [39] and the hypothesis that selection of members would enhance engagement in the structure, as it allows forming a homogeneous group of individual with smooth communication and mutual recognition.

Third, it is fundamental to increase interactions between members. Although Newell & Swan claim that interactions between heterogeneous members may stress their differences [16], it is expected that frequency and sustainability of relationships may help to build trust between homogeneous members [30]. One cannot install trust, but by facilitating interactions, one can create the conditions for trust to develop. The frequency of interactions and development of trust is also very important on the decision making side. Sutcliffe & Mcnamara argue that, when lacking knowledge about an exchange partner, decision makers will need a wider range of information upon which to assess possible consequences of their collaboration [2]. In contrast, in situations where decision makers know their partners, and have developed a trust-based relationship with them, they will require little new information and will have little need to conduct a wider information search. Consequently, information processing for collaborative decision making will be faster and more effective.

Fourth, networks require resources in order to function properly. This means that on the one hand, some financial support should be provided by members and on the other hand, that networks would benefit from a technological platform in addition to face-to-face interactions. For instance, a website or portal, with information, documents and possibilities for online discussions, would allow network members to sustain their interactions and to develop side relationships more easily.

Finally, the participants of this study conferred a place of importance to the fact of being central in a network. Being central in a network entails entering in power conflict and trying to control information flows [47]. That is why the researchers' belief on this point is that members of a network rather than seeking centrality should focus on the process of collaboration. The main principle of networking is the idea of exchanging and it this attitude should stay the main focus of networks for a better operation.

5. Concluding Remarks

Collaborative decision-making in enterprises is a complex process, which needs to be well understood and supported. Networks provide a valuable support on the information processing side. This study demonstrated the various benefits of networking within the decision-making process and in the perspective of enhancing such benefits, attempted to understand enablers and inhibitors of an effective networking. Based on the findings, guidelines for effective networking were drawn.

The research we have reported here is limited by its scope and its sample. However, its aim was to link the two domains of collaborative decision-making and network analysis and to explore this relationship. We have found strong and varied evidence for the kind of the deep support that networks can provide to decision makers and we consider that models could, and should, now be developed to enable this relationship to be profitable. In this respect, there is room for a lot more detailed research investigating the connection between networks and collaborative decision-making in a variety of contexts to try to define how, and to what extent, efficient networking can provide more reliable decisions.

References

[1] Kokkonen, P. & Tuohino, A. (2007). The challenge of networking: analysis of innovation potential in small and medium-sized tourism enterprises. *Entrepreneurship and innovation*, 8(1): 44–52.

[2] Sutcliffe, K.M. &Mcnamara, G. (2001). Controlling decision-making practice in organizations. *Organization Science*, 12(4): 484-501.

[3] Hoskings, D.M. & Morley, E. (1991). A social psychology of organizing: people, processes and contexts. New-York: Harvester.

[4] McGrew, A.G., &Wilson, M.J. (1982). *Decision making: Approaches and analysis*. Manchester: Manchester University Press.

[5] Cyert, R. M. and March, J.G. (1992) *A behavioral theory of the firm*, (2nd ed). Cambridge, MA: Blackwell Business

[6] Occasio, W., (1997) Towards an attention-based view of the firm, *Strategic Management Journal*, vol. 18, Summer Special Issue

[7] Humphreys, P. C. and Nappelbaum, E. (1997) Structure and communications in the process of organisational change. In P. Humphreys, S. Ayestaran, A. McCosh and B. Mayon-White (Eds.), *Decision support in organisational transformation*. London: Chapman and Hall.

[8] Brezillon, P. and Zarate, P. (2008) Group decision-making: a context-oriented view. *Journal of Decision Systems*, Vol. 13 (in press).

[9] Simon, C.J. & Warner, J.T. (1992). Matchmaker, matchmaker: the effect of old boy networks on job match quality, earnings, and tenure. *Journal of Labour Economics*, 10(3): 306-330.

[10] Humphreys, P. C. (2008a) Decision support systems and representation levels in the decision spine. In F. Adam and P. Humphreys (Eds) *Encyclopaedia of decision making and decision support technologies*. Hershey, PA, I.G.I Global, 2008

[11] Humphreys, P. C. and Jones, G. A. (2006) The evolution of group support systems to enable collaborative authoring of outcomes, *World Futures*, 62, 1-30

[12] Humphreys. P.C. and Jones, G.A. (2008) The Decision Hedgehog for Creative Decision Making. In: F. Burstein and C. Holsapple (Eds.) *Handbook of Decision Support Systems*. Berlin, Springer (in press)

[13] Humphreys, P.C., (2008b) The decision hedgehog: Group communication and decision support.In F. Adam and P. Humphreys (Eds) *Encyclopaedia of decision making and decision support technologies*. Hershey, PA, I.G.I Global, 2008

[14] Janis, I.L. (1972). *Victims of groupthink*. Boston: Houghton-Mifflin.

[15] Janis, I.L. and Mann, L, (1978) *Decision Making*. London: Macmillan.

[16] Newell, S. & Swan, J. (2000). Trust and inter-organizational networking. *Human Relations*, 53(10): 1287–1328.

[17] Newell, S., Scarbrough, H., Robertson, M. & Swan, J. (2002). *Managing knowledge work*. New-York: Palgrave.

[18] Beck, U. (2000). *The brave new world of work*. Malden, Mass: Politic Press.

[19] Uzzi, B. (1997). Social structure and competition in inter-firm networks: the paradox of embeddedness. *Administrative Science Quarterly*, 42: 35-67.

[20] Debackere, K. & Rappa, M. (1994). Technological communities and the diffusion of knowledge: a replication and validation. *R & D Management*, 24(4): 355–71.

[21] Kallinikos, J. (2001). *The age of flexibility: managing organizations and technology*. Lund: Academia Adacta.

[22] Ring, P.S. (1997). Processes facilitating reliance on trust in inter-organisational networks. In M. Ebers (Ed.), *The formation of inter-organisational networks*. Oxford: Oxford University Press.

[23] Putnam, R.D. (1993). The prosperous community: social capital and public life. *American Prospect*, 13: 35-42.

[24] Powell, W. (1996). Trust-based forms of governance. In R.M. Kramer and T.R. Tyler (Eds), *Trust in organisations: frontiers of theory and research*. London: Sage.

[25] Håkansson, H. & Johanson, J. (1988). Formal and informal cooperation strategies in industrial networks. In Contractor and Lorange (eds). Cooperative Strategies. *International Business*, 369-379.

[26] Casson, M. & Della-Giusta, M. (2007). Entrepreneurship and social capital: analysing the impact of social networks on entrepreneurial activity from a rational action perspective. *International Small Business Journal*, 25(3): 220–244.

[27] Nahapiet, J. & Ghoshal, S. (1998). Social capital, intellectual capital, and the organizational advantage. *The Academy of Management Review*, 23(2): 242-266.

[28] Cook, K. S. (1982). Network structures from an exchange perspective. In P. V. Marsden & N. Lin (Eds.), *Social structure and network analysis*. London: Sage.

[29] Moensted, M. (2007). Strategic networking in small high tech firms. *The International Entrepreneurship and Management Journal*, 3(1): 15-27.

[30] Nooteboom, B. (2004). *Inter-firm collaboration, learning and networks*. London: Routledge.

[31] Granovetter, M.S. (1985). Economic action and social structure: the problem of embeddedness. *American Journal of Sociology*, 91(3): 481-510.

[32] Granovetter, M.S. (1973). The strength of weak ties. *American Journal of Sociology*, 78: 1360-1380.

[33] Granovetter, M.S. (1992). Economic institutions as social constructions: a framework for analysis. *Acta Sociologica*, 35(1): 3-11.

[34] Easton, G. (1993). *Managers and competition*. Oxford: Blackwell.

[35] Bengtsson, M. & Kock, S. (2000). Coopetition in business networks - to cooperate and compete simultaneously. *Industrial Marketing Management*, 29(5): 411-426.

[36] Huxham, C. & Vangen, S. (2005). *Managing to collaborate: the theory and practice of collaborative advantage*, New York, NY: Routledge.

[37] OCDE (2005). SME and Entrepreneurship Outlook.

[38] Major, E.J. & Cordey-Hayes, M. (2000). Engaging the business support network to give SMEs the benefit of foresight. *Technovation*, 20(11): 589-602.

[39] Man, A.P. (2004). *The network economy: strategy, structure and management*. Cheltenham: Edward Elgar Publishing.

[40] Christensen, P.R., Eskelinen. H., Forsstrom. B., Lindmark, L. & Andvatne. E. (1990). *Firms in network: concepts, spatial impacts and policy implications*. Bergen: Institute of Industrial Economics.

[41] Ratcliff, R.E. (1980). Banks and corporate lending: an analysis of the impact of the internal structure of the capitalist class on the lending behaviour of banks. *American Sociological Review*, 45: 553-570.

[42] De la Mothe, J. & Link, A.N. (2002). *Networks, alliances, and partnerships in the innovation process*. Boston: Kluwer Academic.

[43] Koza, M.P. & Lewin, A.Y. (1999). The co-evolution of network alliances: a longitudinal analysis of an international professional service network. *Organization Science*, 10(5): 638-653.

[44] Raub, W. & Weesie, J. (1990). Reputation and Efficiency in Social Interactions: An Example of Network Effects. *The American Journal of Sociology*, 96(3): 626-654.

[45] Halinen, A. & Tornroos, J. (1998). The role of embeddedness in the evolution of business networks. *Scandinavian Journal of Management*, 14(3): 187-205.

[46] Burt, R.S. (1992). *Structural holes: The social structure of competition*. Cambridge, Mass: Harvard University Press.

[47] Munro, I. (2000). Non-disciplinary power and the network society. *Organization*, 7(4): 679–695.

[48] Vari, A, Vecsenyi, J., and Paprika, Z. (1986) Supporting problem structuring in high level decisions, in *New directions in research in decision making* (eds. B. Brehmer, H. Jungermann, P. Lourens and G. Sevon), North Holland, Amsterdam.

[49] Humphreys, P. C. (1998) Discourses underpinning decision support. In D. Berkeley, G. Widmeyer, P. Brezillon and V. Rajkovic (Eds.) *Context sensitive decision support systems*. London: Chapman & Hall

[50] Rocco, E. (1998). *Trust breaks down in electronic contexts but can be repaired by some initial face-to-face contact*, Conference on human factors in computing systems. New-York, NY: ACM Press.

[51] Malecki, E.J. & Veldhoen, M.E. (1993). Network activities, information and competitiveness in small firms. *Human Geography*, 75(3): 131-14.

[52] Jones, C. Hesterly, W.S. & Borgatti, S.P. (1997). A general theory of network governance: exchange conditions and social mechanisms. *The Academy of Management Review*, 22(4): 911-945.

[53] Levitt & March (1988). Organizational Learning. *Annual Review of Sociology*, 14: 319-340.

[54] Spekman, R.E., Isabella, L.A., & MacAvoy, T.C. (1999). *Alliance competence: Maximizing the value of your partnerships*. New York: Wiley.

[55] Ritter, T., Wilkinson, I.F., & Johnson, W.J. (2004). Firm's ability to manage in business networks: a review of concepts. *Industrial Management Marketing*, 33(3): 175-183.

[56] Håkansson & Ford (2002). How should companies interact in business networks? *Journal of Business Research*, 55(2): 133-139.

[57] Schein, E. (1992). *Organizational culture and leadership*. London: Jossey-Bass.

[58] Martin, J. (2002). Organizational culture: mapping the terrain. London: Sage.

Collaborative Decision Making: Perspectives and Challenges
P. Zaraté et al. (Eds.)
IOS Press, 2008

Visualising and Interpreting Group Behavior through Social Networks

Kwang Deok KIM[a], and Liaquat HOSSAIN[a]

[a]*School of Information Technologies, University of Sydney,*
1 Cleveland Street, Camperdown, NSW 2006, Australia

Abstract. In this study, we visualise and interpret the relationships between different types of social network (SN) structures (i.e., degree centrality, cut-points) and group behavior using political contribution dataset. We seek to identify whether investment behavior is network dependent using the political contribution dataset. By applying social networks analysis as a visualisation and interpretation technique, we find patterns of social network structures from the dataset, which explains the political contribution behavior (i.e., investment behavior) of political action committee (PAC). The following questions guide this study: Is there a correlation between SN structure and group behavior? Do we see patterns of different network structures for different types and categories of political contribution (i.e., support or oppose; level of contribution)? Is there a structural difference of networks between different types of support and oppose behavior? Do the group networks for support and oppose differ structurally on the basis of different types of political contribution patterns?

Keywords. Centralisation, Degree Centrality, Group behavior, Investment behavior, Social Networks, Visualisation

INTRODUCTION

Federal Election Commission (FEC) defines independent expenditures (IE) as an expenditure made by individuals, groups, or political committees that expressly advocate the election or defeat of a clearly identified federal candidate. These transactions are reported on various forms, such as FEC Form 3X or FEC Form 5 [16]. We use the IE dataset (in special, PAC data) and apply social networks analysis to visualise and interpret the structure and activities of political interest groups. In the wake of new restrictions on campaign finance, more political interest groups are drawn to IE as a means to involve themselves in politics and campaigns. Furthermore, IE are not subject to contribution limits. Under these unconstrained circumstances, it is possible to observe the political interest groups' investment behavioral traits to make expenditures on behalf of political candidates [7]. In this paper, we treat the political contribution dataset (i.e., PAC data) as one specific domain of group investment behavior. Furthermore, we suggest that the outcome of this study will help understand the application of social networks analysis for finding structures and relations in the context of group behavior. In this paper, we first present our social networks based model for studying cooperative and competitive behavior. Secondly, we advance four propositions for exploring the underlying relationships between the SN measures such as centrality, degree, cut-points and blocks and different types of group behavior such as cooperative and competitive behavior. Thirdly, we describe different SN based measures for studying group behavior. Fourth, we provide a background to our dataset and describe different SN techniques for visialisation and interpretation of dfferent types of group behavior using dataset. Lastly, we present our results and analyses for supporting our propositions. The outcome of our study suggest that different SN measures such as degree centrality, cut-points are useful measures for exploring group behavior from a large dataset. We therefore suggest that these SN based measures have significant impact on visualisation and interpretation of group behavior.

1. A Framework for Exploring Group Behavior

This section presents the framework for exploring the relationship between different measures of social networks and types of group behavior.

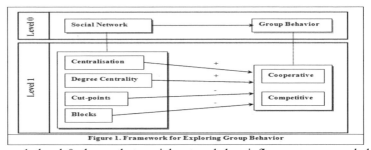

Figure 1. Framework for Exploring Group Behavior

In Figure 1, level 0 shows that social network has influence on group behavior. Networks can be used to understand group behavior as well. In exploring the implications of different types of social network that influence the group behavior, political contribution dataset was used [16]. Level 1 is driven from the level 0 and illustrates specific variables that describe four independent variables and two dependent variables. As Figure 1 depicts, the framework consists of two sets of variables. Four independent variables that describe the different types of social network: centralisation, degree centrality (i. e., key-player), cut points or stability and blocks or differentiation. Density and sub-groups are important to understand how the network behaves. Measures of centralisation help understand whether a graph is organised around its most central points. The points in the graph that are individually most central may not be especially informative. It is necessary, therefore, to investigate whether there is an identifiable structural centre of a graph. The structural centre of a graph is a single point or a cluster of points that, like the centre of a circle or a sphere, is the pivot of its organisation. A key player dominates the network tends to have network power [5,6]. There are some key actors that catalyse the group. In order to understand how the network works, it is important to figure out who the key actor (key-player) is. A cut-point is a pivotal point of articulation between the elements, but it is the weakest part of the graph as well. The more cut-points, the less stability. We are able to see how the stability of a network changes according to the change of cut-points. How large are the connected sub-groups? That is, are there a few big groups or a large number of small groups? Blocks which are divided by cut-points have strong connections among inner actors and can be seen as being the most effective systems of communications or exchange in a network [22]. However, the more blocks the more differentiations because a network should be separated to form a block. That is to say, we can see how the differentiations of a network changes according to the change of blocks. Two dependent variables that capture the group behavior--cooperative and competitive behavior on a group network is used in this study. People have tendencies to cooperate or compete in mixed-motive games and that these tendencies, or orientations, are stable. A number of researches have accumulated regarding various aspects of group behavior [11, 2]. Groups perceive their interests more competitively than individuals under the same functional conditions. In terms of political contributions, participants (i.e., payers who make contributions) can either cooperate or compete with another. In other words, payers can cooperate to *support* or compete to *oppose* a payee (i.e., a candidate who receives contributions). Below, we present our propositions which suggest relationships between measures of social networks and different types of group behavior.

Centralisation is the process by which the activities of an organisation, particularly those regarding decision-making, become concentrated within a particular location and/or group. In political science, this refers to the concentration of a government's power - both geographically and politically, into a centralised government. Many scholars acknowledge the importance of resources in organisational decision-making [3]. Financial resources have a direct relationship to the level of a group's political activity. The more money available to a group the more it spends on politics. That is, a campaign spending strategy with no contribution limits such as that provided by independent expenditures tends to give unequal influence to wealthy groups [7]. If PACs have greater influence on who serves in Congress and how members of congress view issues because they help finance campaigns, then individuals and groups with greater financial resources have the potential to make a bigger impact on policymaking than others [4]. Groups which can make large contributions are relatively few and limited. As the contributions increase, networks get centralised and become concentrated within a particular group. Carne et al. [7] argued that the most important factor driving participation in independent spending would be organisational goals. In particular, electoral-oriented groups are clearer when independent expenditures are made against particular candidates. They seek to change the composition of the legislation by support challengers who espouse their views because they typically do not anticipate that legislators can be swayed on the issues that are important to the group [20,12]. It means only specific groups which are unable to fulfill their own purposes make contributions to against. That is to say, only specific groups having clear reasons make contributions against candidates, which mean the networks for opposing will be denser than the networks for supporting.

- Proposition 1: *Degree of centralisation correlates to contributions.*

There are some key individuals that catalyse and organise the group. Also, a small number of informed individuals can lead the migration of larger numbers of individuals. Very few individuals (approximately 5 per cent) can guide the group. In particular, Couzin et al. [9] showed that the larger the group, the smaller the proportion of informed individuals required to lead it, which could be re-interpreted as the larger the group, the larger the proportion of a key player to dominant the group. In other words, a node having highest degree centrality (i.e., a key player or a leader) in a network will have more influence when the size of a network gets larger. In terms of group investment, such as political contributions, a node having highest degree centrality will be having the more influence as the amount of contributions increases.

- Proposition 2: *Level of contributions is dependent on a key player.*

Braungart [6] argued that power exists in all social relationships – it is universal and is described as a latent force. Bierstedt [5] observed that without power there is no organisation and without power there is no order. Emerson [13] offered a series of propositions concerning power relations as well. In general, power is defined as a property of social organisation rather than as a personal attribute; it rests in the dependency association between two or more persons or groups. That is to say, there is power ruling over group behavior networks. In his article "Power-Dependence Relations," Emerson identified a power relation may be either balanced or imbalanced. The imbalanced relationship is described as unstable since there will be certain cost in meeting the demands of the more powerful and changes in variables and so on. He argued about changes in the power relationship of balancing operations, and the first operation is withdrawal of the weaker which is quite related to the notion of cut-points. The notion of cut-points is explained in detail at Cut-points section. According to Degenne et al.'s [10] explanations about a cut-point, it is a node whose removal would increase the number of *strongly* connected components in the graph, which means the network would be reformed with components having strong relations to each other through getting rid of a cut-point. A cut-point is a pivotal point of articulation between the elements, but also it is a weakest part of the graph as well. The more the number of cut-points is in a network, the less the stability there is. That is to say, as the unbalanced (or unstable) network turns into the balanced one, the power of the network becomes stronger and more political contributions can be made from a well balanced power network through the balancing operation.

- Proposition 3: *Level of contributions is dependent on the stability of network.*

In his book "Society and Politics," Braungart [6] argued that greater differentiations leads to less coordination and a lower level of outputs. A differentiated group might have strong connections among inner members, but the outputs which the whole groups can produce may be poor in terms of group coordination. In other words, as the number of blocks having strong connections among inner members decreases, the more contributions could be made. More details about the notion of blocks are explained in the Methods section. Biersack et al [4] argued that the variations of support are larger than oppose groups. PACs are interested in specific policy outcomes and have developed a working relationship with members. They typically see the electoral process as a threat to the sets of relationships they have built up over the years. Thus, big electoral changes can represent a threat to a PAC's influence, and PACs may react to uncertainty by trying to protect threatened incumbents rather than carefully examining the issue positions of unknown challenger and open-seat candidates to determine who might better represent them. As he argued, PACs try to protect incumbents who they have a working relationship if they see the electoral process. The bottom line is that the resources are limited, which means they should make a decision whether they make contributions to support, oppose or both. Since these decisions are based on that prior learning, sudden changes in the electoral environment do not necessarily lead to significant changes in PAC behavior. Rather, PACs are expected to follow the same old rules, in spite of the different opportunities and risks that emerge in the current election cycle [4]. PACs are reluctant to change their behaviors and follow the same rules. In other words, they would rather make contributions to support candidates with whom they have maintained relationships. For them to make another contribution to oppose competitors (i.e., to protect their candidates), the sense of crisis which their supporting candidates might lose the election to challengers should be large enough. It draws a conclusion that relatively, a small number of PACs make contributions to oppose competitors compared to a number of PACs to support.

- Proposition 4: *Level of contributions is dependent on differentiations.*

2. Measures for Exploring Social Network Structures

In this paper, we will briefly explain about a set of centrality metrics.

2.1. Degree Centrality

The first natural and general measure of centrality based on degree. The degree of a point is firstly viewed as an index of its potential communications activity. Secondly, centrality is based on the frequency to which a point falls between pairs of other points on the shortest or geodesic paths connecting them. Degree is the total number of other points in its neighbourhood (strictly, its degree of connection). The degree of a point is a numerical measure of the size of its neighbourhood. In directed graph, the in-degree of a point is the total number of other points that have lines directed towards it; and its out-degree is the total number of other points to which it directs lines. Degree centrality is computed for every node i as a normalized sum of all edges connecting i to other nodes. Degree centrality operates on an assumption that highly connected actors in a network will be the ones wielding the most power. In directed graphs, it makes sense to distinguish between the in-centrality and the out-centrality of the various point. Network analysts have used centrality as a basic tool for identifying key individuals in a network since network studies began. It is an idea that has immediate appeal and as a consequence is used in a large number of substantive applications across many disciplines [15].

2.2. Cut points

A cut-point is one whose removal would increase the number of components by dividing the sub-graph into two or more separate sub-sets between which there are no connections. In the graph component (i) shown in Figure 2, for example, point B is a cut-point, as its removal would create the two disconnected components shown in sociogram (ii). Thus, cut-points are pivotal points of articulation between the elements that make up a component. These elements, together with their cut-points, are what Hage et al. described as *block*. The component in Figure 2, comprises the two blocks (A,B,C) and (B,D,E,F). The various cut-points in a graph will be members of a number of blocks with the cut-points being the points of overlap between the blocks. Hage et al. [22] have argued that blocks can be seen as being the most effective systems of communications or exchange in a network. Because they contain no cut-points, acts of communications and exchange among the members of a block are not dependent upon any one member. There are always alternative paths of communications between all the points in a block, and so the network that it forms is both flexible and unstratified.

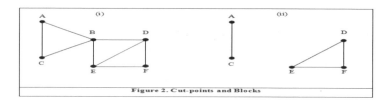

Figure 2. Cut-points and Blocks

2.3. Degree Centrality and Cut points

It can be seen from the above description that a large range of network measures are available for visualising and interpreting the structural properties of networks. The application of these measures for analysing the social structure is largely dependent on the characteristics of the dataset. In this study, we used two social network analysis measures (i. e., degree centrality and cut-points) among diverse analysis measures, such as degree centrality, closeness centrality, betweenness centrality and so on. In this regard, Freeman [19] suggest that a set of centrality measures (degree, closeness, and betweenness) have been adopted to approach the first question that a social network analyst asks when looking as a dataset, which is the key players in the network. The best way to overcome the drawbacks of single centrality is to take the combination of a set of centrality measure, which may produce contrary results for the same graph. It can be a case in which a node has a low degree centrality, with a high betweenness centrality. Freeman [19] demonstrated that betweenness centrality best "captures" the essence of important nodes in a graph, and generate the largest node variances, while degree centrality appear to produce the smallest node variances. At first, we decided to use both centrality measures, which is degree and betweenness centrality, to surmount the shortcoming of single centrality. However, we had to find alternative measures to substitute betweenness centrality due to the features of the political contribution data, which is quite porous and multi-cored [21]. During our exploratory phase of the dataset with regards to political contribution networks, we found that these are disconnected between sub-graphs which is connected within and therefore, can be defined as components of network. The notion of a component may be too strong to find all the meaningful weak-points, holes, and locally dense sub-parts of a larger graph, so we have chosen more flexible approach, that is cut-points. In this regard, betweenness centrality as *a cut-point* is the shortest path connecting two other nodes. A "between" actor could control the flow of information or exchange of resources, perhaps charging a fee or brokerage commission for transaction services rendered. On the basis of literature reviewed on measures of social networks, we decided to use degree centrality and cut-points measures for visualising and interpreting the group behavior from the political contribution data.

3. Data Collection and Analysis

In this study, we use data regarding political contributions (so called, coordination rule making data) that can be downloaded from FEC website provide information from disclosure reports filed by PACs, Party Committees, and individuals or groups during the period from January 2001 through December 2004.We used PACs related data from independent expenditures which is downloadable from FEC website. In order to visualise and generate diagnostic results with the political contribution dataset, we arranged the data by applying various sorting methods using Microsoft Excel software. Below, we highlight the steps that we used to deploy the data:

- Transactions not having the name of candidate and PAC have been discarded. If there was no specification about spending money to support or oppose a particular candidate, then it was also taken out.
- Although there may be more than two transactions between a same candidate and same PAC, we considered all same transactions into one. We also added all the amounts of contributions. For example, ENVIRONMENT2004 INC PAC spent money to oppose Bush, George W. more than ten times at different time intervals. We summed up all the transaction money. We have just regarded these transactions as one because we are interested in the amount of money instead of the number of transactions that occurred between a candidate and PAC.
- We adjusted for different names which were identical. For instance, George W. Bush and Bush, George W. is the same candidate. We had to find and unify all these kind of differences, which was time consuming.
- After sorting all transactions, we converted this file to text files and added some symbolic statements to make the data ready to be converted into VNA format [1].
- With the VNA file we have converted, we drew the sociogram (the network diagram or graph) through NETDRAW. We are able to have a following sociogram. In Figure 4, an up-triangle depicts a payer who makes political contributions to support or oppose a candidate. A circle represents a payee who receives contributions made by payer (i.e., a candidate).
- On NETDRAW we save the sociogram as UCINET data to calculate the centrality in terms of degree and number of cut-points.

Figure 3. An Example of VNA Format File

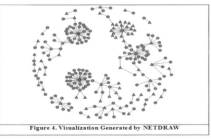

Figure 4. Visualization Generated by NETDRAW

The descriptive statistics above displays the mean value, standard deviation, network centralisation and so on. It describes how the centrality measures are distributed as a whole. Since we have explored the political contributions in the view of centrality and cut-points according to the different classifications of amounts of money (i.e., from $5k to $50k for supporting or opposing and so on), we have repeated the procedure of extracting, converting data, drawing sociograms with NETDRAW, and calculating values by UCINET.

DESCRIPTIVE STATISTICS			
	Degree	NrmDegree	Share
1 Mean	1.788	0.828	0.005
2 Std Dev	3.184	1.474	0.008
3 Sum	388.000	179.630	1.000
4 Variance	10.139	2.173	0.000
5 SSQ	2894.000	620.285	0.019
6 MCSSQ	2200.249	471.590	0.015
7 Euc Norm	53.796	24.906	0.139
8 Minimum	1.000	0.463	0.003
9 Maximum	28.000	12.963	0.072

Network Centralisation = 12.25%
Heterogeneity = 1.92%. Normalized = 1.47%
Actor-by-centrality matrix saved as dataset FreemanDegree

Figure 5. NETDRAW Degree Centrality Analysis Result

4. Network Effect on Group Behavior: Result and Discussions

Do we see patterns of different network structures for different types and categories of political contribution (i.e., competitive or cooperative; level of contribution)? We first categorised the political contribution data into four different parts ranging from $5,000 to $49,999 and from $50,000 to $499,999 and so on for exploring competitive and cooperative funding behavior towards a particular candidate. We applied two different measures—(i) degree centrality including network centralisation; and (ii) cut-points including blocks. Broadly speaking, although we used notions of degree and cut-points, we implicitly applied four different methods for our study such as: (i) degree centrality, (ii) network centralisation, (iii) cut-points and (iv) blocks. We found network centralisation measures useful for visualising whether the network is dense or sparse. It would be useful to express the degree of variability in the degrees of actors in observed network as a percentage of that in a star network of the same size. Furthermore, the Freeman network centralisation measures also suggest that centralisation measures express the degree of inequality or variance in the network as a percentage of that of a perfect star network of the same size.

- Proposition 1: *Degree of centralisation correlates to contributions*

We identified number of degrees for every nodes and percentage of network centralisation of categorised networks. We further calculated percentage of a node having highest degree centrality in the network, which means a node has biggest number of links among nodes. For example, if a network has total 1,000 links and node A has 100 links which is most high number of links among all nodes, then node A is a node has highest degree centrality (i.e., 10%). A list of percentage of network centralisation and a node has highest degree centrality in different categories for supporting and opposing is given in Table 1. We are therefore able to recognise that as the percentage of network centralisation increases the more the amount of money grows through Table 1. It means the network is becoming more centralised by hubs or leaders. This data reveals strong presence of leaders centralising the networks. In particular, we discover that same categories percentage of oppose is much bigger than support. In this regard, Carne et al [7] suggest that most interest groups are eager to contribute money to support rather than to oppose a candidate. Without special purposes they are reluctant to donate money to oppose a candidate, rather they are willing to support a candidate. They do not want to take risks. In the end, only a few groups (compared with whole groups) have particular purposes remaining and gathered together to oppose a candidate. Peculiarly when the amount of money becomes very huge this kind of phenomenon occurs often. Figure 6 below shows us the graph of network centralisation for opposing and supporting respectively.

Table 1. Percentage of Network Centralisation and a Node has Highest Degree Centrality				
	Network Centralisation		Highest degree centrality	
Categorised Contributions	Oppose (Competitive)	Support (Cooperative)	Oppose (Competitive)	Support (Cooperative)
1 $5,000 ~ 49,999	13.27%	12.25%	11.11%	7.20%
2 $50,000 ~ 499,999	26.29%	14.41%	16.40%	8.40%
3 $500,000 ~999,999	57.37%	36.68%	35.30%	25%
4 $1000000 ~	61.47%	32%	36.80%	21.40%

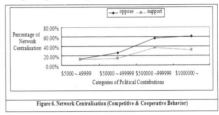

Figure 6. Network Centralisation (Competitive & Cooperative Behavior)

- Proposition 2: Level of contributions is dependent on a key player

As mentioned above, the first question social network analysts ask when looking at a dataset is who are the key players in the network. This is because key players or nodes in the network can reach and influence more people faster [19]. In political network, nodes with highest degree centrality can be ideal key actors to influence whole network. In particular, in order for us to see the relationship between the political network and a key player, we present Figure 7 which highlights the percentage of a node has highest degree centrality. This graph tends to follow the similar shape with the graph for network centralisation. We can see that as the percentage of highest degree centrality increases, the contributions increase. In other words, when the influence of a key player through a network increases the amount of contributions continues to grow.

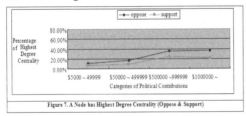

Figure 7. A Node has Highest Degree Centrality (Oppose & Support)

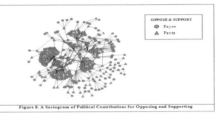

Figure 8. A Sociogram of Political Contributions for Opposing and Supporting

In Figure 8, we present a sociogram of political contribution data for opposing and supporting a candidate. Figure 9 shows us the combined result of network centralisation and a node has highest degree centrality for opposing and supporting respectively. Using this graph, we can argue that as contributions increase, the more the network has been centralised. The degree of centralised network has the key player or leader who has wider influence over the whole network regardless of opposing or supporting a candidate. We calculated the percentage of top ten from the political contribution dataset as well, and we were able to have the similar result (i.e., 89.3 per cent for supporting and 98.1 per cent for opposing). That is to say, the amount of contributions which upper ten groups made dominates most of independent expenditures. We are also able to see that the density of ten groups grasping the whole network for opposing is denser than supporting.

We calculated number of cut-points and blocks for every categorised network (see Table 2). We identified the percentage of network centralisation and highest degree centrality, we computed these two measures in similar way. In general, since notions of degree centrality and cut-points are contrary to each other, it could be complimentary to one another. The combination of different measures is the best way to overcome the drawbacks of single centrality. Besides, through calculating cut-points and blocks we are able to know which actors occupy a privileged position, indicating those who were in a position to liaise or be significant in the network [21] . We can see that as contributions increase, then number of cut-points and blocks decrease, which is the exact reverse to the percentage of network centralisation and highest degree centrality.

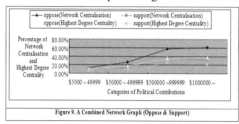

Figure 9. A Combined Network Graph (Oppose & Support)

Table 2. Number of Cut-points and Blocks

Categorized Contributions	Number of Cut-points		Number of Blocks	
	Oppose (Competitive)	Support (Cooperative)	Oppose (Competitive)	Support (Cooperative)
1 $5,000 ~ 49,999	8	37	36	183
2 $50,000 ~ 499,999	8	22	55	110
3 $500,000 ~999,999	4	5	17	28
4 $1000000 ~	2	5	19	21

- **Proposition 3:** *Level of contributions is dependent on the stability of network*

In Figure 10, we present a sociogram of political contribution data for supporting categorised from $5,000 to 49,999. A circle represents a payee (i.e., a candidate who receives contributions) and an up-triangle means a payer for the donations (i.e., a group which make contributions to support or oppose a candidate). Every node in blue (thick dark nodes in a black and white paper) indicates cut-points in this network. As we can see from Table 2 and Figure 11, the number of cut-points for supporting a candidate ($5,000 ~ 49,999) is 37. This sociogram shows the characteristics of political dataset as well, which is porous and multi-cored [20] . What we can tell through this graph is that there are a lot of differences. Although the line for supporting descends at a sharp angle, the line for opposing tilts gently. Regardless of categories for contributions, the gradient of opposing is very subtle and does not change as much as of supporting, which means groups for opposing a candidate have comparatively small key players but quite organized by a few cores have nothing to do with categories of contributions. Since a cut-point means a weak point of a network, the more cut-points a network has the less stability is. This unstable network has a tendency to decrease its unstable factors by getting rid of weaker which is cut-points in our study [13]. We are able to see Figure 10 follows proposition 3, that is, a network is getting stabilized and as the number of cut-points decreases, the amount of contributions increases.

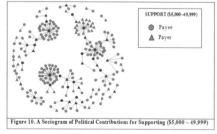

Figure 10. A Sociogram of Political Contributions for Supporting ($5,000 ~ 49,999)

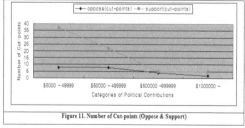

Figure 11. Number of Cut-points (Oppose & Support)

- **Proposition 4:** *Level of contributions is dependent on differentiations*

Blocks can be seen as being the most effective systems of communication or exchange in a network. Because they contain no cut-points, acts of communication and exchange among the members of a block are not dependent upon any one member.

There are always alternative paths of communication between all the points in a block, and so the network that it forms is both flexible [22]. As we can see in Figure 12, the number of blocks for supporting is far more than for opposing. This means a lot of groups for supporting are individually organised rather than being formed with key players systematically. The shape of curve for supporting decreases sharply on the contrary to the shape of curve for opposing which hardly changes. This result supports Carne et al.'s assertion [7] that most groups are eager to contribute money to support rather than to oppose a candidate. Because they do not want to take risks, a small number of groups have particular purposes remains and gathers together to oppose a candidate. In Figure 12, we are clearly able to see the pattern that the output (i.e., the amount of contributions) increases as the number of blocks decreases. Figure 13 depicts that a network is inclined to be stabilised through removing unstable factors, such as weak points and differentiations. We are able to see the tendency of a network, which is to decrease the uncertainty and increase the output. In terms of political contributions, the more stability a network has the more the amount of contributions made. Besides, we can also recognise the difference of variations between two types (i.e., support or oppose). With limited resources, PACs prefer making contributions to support rather than oppose a candidate because they tend to follow the prior learning and do not want any sudden changes in the electoral environment [4]. That is to say, the opposing network is well organised and centralised than supporting network. This is because PACs are reluctant not to make contributions to oppose a candidate unless they face the inevitable situations. As we can see from Figure 13, the gradient of supporting is steeper than the opposing.

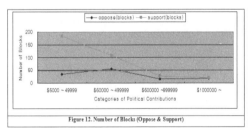

Figure 12. Number of Blocks (Oppose & Support)

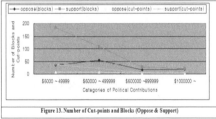

Figure 13. Number of Cut-points and Blocks (Oppose & Support)

5. Conclusion

In this study, we suggest that there is a correlation between social network structure and group behavior. We applied various measures, such as network centralisation, highest degree centrality, cut-points, and blocks, to study patterns of different network structures for different types and categories of political contribution dataset (i.e., competitive or cooperative behavior and different level of contributions). Based on the assumptions of centrality and cut-points measures, we compared different measures in diverse categories of political contributions to compete or cooperate with a candidate. We discovered and analysed centrality and cut-points of group networks change in different categories and types (i.e., competitive or cooperative) of contribution data. We also found that centrality tends to increase in direct competition to cut-points decreases as the level of political contributions increase, respectively. Focusing on different types of competitive and cooperative behavior, a structural difference of networks has been founded as well. Regardless of measures, groups have had a behavioral tendency when they donate money whether to compete or cooperate with a candidate. Because groups want to lessen any kinds of risks, they naturally tend to support a candidate rather than to oppose especially when the amount of contributions are comparatively small. However, as the contributions grow it is hard to find any major existence of differences. Additional tests with more diverse dataset of the explanation presented here need to be conducted. For example, the more political contributions, such as 2000 election cycle or another countries' contributions, the better firm results we can have. Cooper et al. [8] argued that the effect of future returns is strongest for firms that support a greater number of candidates which hold office in the same state that the firm is based. They mentioned about the connection between the future returns and geographical locations. Correlations existing between the information of candidates' offices and group behaviors remain an area of future work.

References

[1] Analytictech. (2006). "A brief guide to using NetDraw."   Retrieved December, 2006, from http://analytictech.com.
[2] Austin, W. G. and S. Worchel, Eds. (1979). The social psychology of intergroup relations. Belmont, CA, Wadsworth.
[3] Baumgartner, F. R. and B. L. Leech (1988). Basic Interests: The Importance of Groups in Politics and Political Science, Prineton, NJ: Princeton University Press.
[4] Biersack, R., P. S. Herrnson, et al. (1994). Risky Business? PAC Decisionmaking in Congressional Elections, M.E. Sharpe.
[5] Bierstedt, R. (1950). "An Analysis of Social Power." American Sociological Review 15(6): 730-738.
[6] Braungart, R. G. (1976). Society and Politics: Readings in Political Sociology, Prentice-Hall.
[7] Carne, M. A. and D. E. Apollonio (2003). Independent Expenditures and Interest Group Strategy. The Midwest Political Science Association Annual Meeting, Chicago, Illinois.
[8] Cooper, M. J., H. Gulen, et al. (2007). "Corporate Political Contributions and Stock Returns." Retrieved February, 2007, from http://ssrn.com/abstract=940790
[9] Couzin, I. D., J. Krause, et al. (2005). Effective leadership and decision-making in animal groups on the move. Nature. 433: 513-516.
[10] Degenne, A. and M. Forse (2004). Introducing Social Networks, SAGE.
[11] Doise, W. (1978). Groups and individuals: Explanations in social psychology, Cambridge Univ. Press.

[12] Eismeier, T. J. and P. H. Pollock (1988). Business, Money, and the Rise of Corporate PACs in Americal Elections, Westport, CT: Quorum Books.
[13] Emerson, R. M. (1962). "Power-Dependence Relations." American Sociological Review 27(1): 31-41.

[14] Engstrom, R. N. and C. Kenny (2002). "The Effects of Independent Expenditures in Senate Elections " Political Research Quarterly 55: 845-860.
[15] Everett, M. G. and S. P. Borgatti (1999). "The Centrality of Groups and Classes." Journal of Mathematical Sociology.
[16] FEC. (2006). "Data for Coordination Rulemaking."   Retrieved November, 2006, from http://www.fec.gov/press/coordruledata.shtml.
[17] Fleisher, R. (1993). "PAC Contributions and Congressional Voting on National Defense." Legislative Studies Quarterly 18(3): 391-409.
[18] Francia, P. L. (2001). "The Effects of The North American Free Trade Agreement on Corporate and Labor PAC Contributions." American Politics Research 29(1): 98-109.
[19] Freeman, L. C. (1978,1979). "Centrality in Social Networks Conceptual Clarification." Social Networks 1: 215-239.
[20] Gopoian, J. D. (1984). "What Makes PACs Tick? An Analysis of the Allocation Patterns of Economic Interest Groups." American Journal of Political Science 28(2): 258-81.
[21] Hage, P. (1979). "Graph Theory as a Structural Model in Cultural Anthropology." Annual Review Anthropology 8: 115-136.
[22] Hage, P. and F. Harary (1983). Structural models in Anthropology, Cambridge University Press.

Collaborative Decision Making: Perspectives and Challenges
P. Zaraté et al. (Eds.)
IOS Press, 2008

Supporting Team Members Evaluation in Software Project Environments

Sergio F. OCHOA[a], Osvaldo OSORIO[a], José A. PINO[a]

[a]Department of Computer Science, University of Chile, Santiago, Chile
{sochoa, oosorio, jpino}@dcc.uchile.cl

Abstract. Companies are increasingly encouraging employees to work cooperatively, to coordinate their activities in order to reduce costs, increase production, and improve services or just to augment the robustness of the organization. This is particularly relevant in the software industry where the available time frames are quite tight. However, many software companies do not formally evaluate their team performance because the available methods are complex, expensive, slow to deliver the results or error-prone. In case of software companies that evaluate team performance, they have also to deal with team members feeling about the fairness of such evaluations. This paper presents a method intended to evaluate the software team and their members' performance in a simple and fast manner, involving also a low application cost. The method, called Team Evaluation Method (TEM), is supported by a software tool, which reduces the application effort. The proposal has been used to evaluate software development teams, and the obtained results are satisfactory.

Keywords: Team members' evaluation method, software team performance, evaluation of cooperative behavior, work group, diagnose IT tool.

Introduction

The globalization and rapid changes being experienced by organizations today require employees with new capabilities. Team work and multidisciplinary work are requirements to face the challenges of competitiveness and efficiency imposed by the market. If an organization is not able to rapidly and appropriately react, then it is a candidate to die.

Currently, any component playing a relevant role within the organization should be subject to careful analysis. Clients, suppliers, processes occurring within and outside the organization, and the human assets must be evaluated to find out how they can provide additional value to the system. Nevertheless, human assets, or rather, their capabilities, are significant for the performance of the organization as a whole. Particularly, team work is one of the key capabilities that employees should have. This team work could be loosely or tightly coupled [15], and it is mainly focused on coordinating the team members' activities in order to reduce costs, increase production, and improve services or just to augment the robustness of the organization.

Team members performance evaluation is the main tool used by several organizations to diagnose how well the group is working [1, 2]. This tool also allows team members to dissuade inappropriate behaviors and incite the good ones. The process of using this tool allows the detection of strengths and weaknesses as well, thus giving the organization the opportunity to plan the early encouragement of behaviors considered positive and the discouragement of negative behaviors [1].

The team members' performance evaluation is particularly critical in areas like software development, in which the development teams need to be highly coordinated since the available time to develop the products is usually quite tight [19]. The problems with team members' behavior directly influence the project outcomes. Thus, the performance of the members should be evaluated periodically, and the persons should feel comfortable with such evaluations. Moreover, evaluations must provide enough feedback to help people self-improve. Since this monitoring process should be frequently applied, the evaluation method has to be simple, fast and with low application cost.

Many software companies do not formally evaluate their teams' performance because the current existing methods are complex, expensive, slow to deliver the results or error-prone [14]. In case of those organizations which evaluate team performance, they must also deal with team members' feeling about the fairness of such evaluations [5]. Handling these issues, this paper presents a team member evaluation method, called TEM (Team Evaluation Method). TEM is a simple and fast evaluation method involving a low application cost. The method is supported by a software tool, which eases its applicability. Both, the tool and the evaluation method were used to evaluate software development teams. The obtained results show the proposal not only is useful to diagnose the team behavior, but it also helps the team members to identify and correct undesired attitudes.

Next section presents the application scenario of the proposed evaluation method. Section 2 discusses the related work. Section 3 describes the Team Evaluation Method. Section 4 presents the developed tool to support this process. Section 5 shows and discusses the experimental results. Finally, Section 6 presents the conclusions.

1. Application Scenario

Software development is a collaborative, highly dynamic and stressing activity. *"Organisations need to measure the performance of their software development process, in order to control, manage and improve it continuously. Current measurement approaches lack adequate metrics"* [7].

Software project team members play one or more roles (analyst, designer, programmer, project manager, etc). Each role is critical and it has particular duties and rights that allow the team to carry out the development process following a project plan. Problems with a role are directly translated to problems in the project. Typically these problems are the cause for delays in product delivery, poor quality of the final product, or an increment of the project risk.

The given development time is usually too short; thus, team members need to work collaboratively and highly coordinated [19]. Early detection of problems is mandatory. Otherwise, the costs of solving the problems increase, and consequently, they may have a major impact on the project budget. Therefore, the team members' evaluation process should be carried out frequently.

Moreover, team members should feel the evaluation is fair enough in order to avoid generating conflicts inside the group. The project success depends on the capability to keep the collaboration capability and the positive interdependence among team members. Therefore, the evaluation should be fair for all of them. In addition, the evaluation does not have to be invasive and has to provide enough feedback to help team members to improve themselves.

If the evaluation method is to be applied periodically, then the application effort should be low to avoid affecting the project budget. Furthermore, the feedback provided by the method has to be rich enough to: (a) identify undesired attitudes within the group, (b) help the involved persons to improve, (c) help managers to embed the lessons learned in the organizational software process. Next section briefly discusses previous work addressing this problem.

2. Related Work

Software process measurement has been a research discipline for over 20 years, but there is a large gap between research and industry [7]. Briand et al. analyzed many software metrics and point out that few metrics have successfully survived the initial definition phase and are used in industry [6].

On the other hand, most available measurement approaches for software process evaluation are oriented to improve the software process focused on the technical issues, such as risks management, requirements elicitation or changes management. Some of the most well-known methods are: Goal Question Metric [9], Statistical Process Control [12], Business Process Performance Measurement [8] and Capability Maturity Model Integration [20]. None of these methods measure the collaborative work and the team members' performance. Moreover, they are complex, expensive, slow to deliver the results or error-prone [7, 14]. Thus, they are unsuitable to solve the stated problem.

The applicable methods for team members' performance evaluation come from other disciplines such as management or psychology [16, 17, 18]. Although they are accurate enough, most of them are complex and involve an important effort of manual processing. This processing makes these measurement methods slow, expensive and error-prone [14].

Several researchers have identified important benefits from using IT-supported measurement processes [1, 13, 14]. Some of these benefits are: low cost, reduced elapsed time, and low error rate. However, Lowry et al. point out the benefit of using IT support for evaluating individual and group performance depends on group size and social presence [11]. Sherestha & Chalidabhongse also support the use of technology to support evaluation processes [14]. They also mention the limitations of the current evaluation processes. Next section describes a new method considering this previous work.

3. The Team Evaluation Method

TEM is a method applicable to small development teams (4-7 persons). In case of larger teams, the method can be used by grouping the persons by role or by development units. Our experience indicates it is possible to use TEM with both agile and traditional development processes. However, the development team to be evaluated has to meet the following requirements [3, 4]: (1) the whole team should be responsible for the final result (not just a few group members), (2) roles must be specified, (3) hierarchies within the team should not be strong or restrictive, (4) most tasks to be performed are suitable for group collaboration rather than individual work, (5) communication and coordination among group members is needed to perform the tasks, and (6) there is trust among team members concerning their teammates' shared goals and work.

TEM includes two kinds of periodical evaluations to diagnose the group work: internal and external evaluations. Internal evaluations (IE) reflect the vision of the team members about their own performance and external evaluations (EE) represent the stakeholders' point of view (i.e. clients, suppliers and company managers). Both are independent and they involve three phases (Fig. 1): questionnaire definition, evaluation and feedback. A software tool supports these phases.

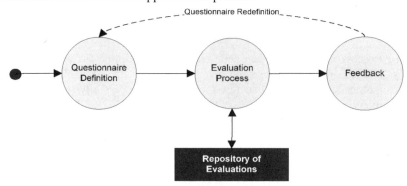

Figure 1. TEM Process

Questionnaire definition phase. The tool to be used in the evaluation should be defined during this phase. The tool should be appropriate to evaluate group work, short and clear. The team can create a new questionnaire for each project or reuse a previous one. Usually this last option is the most convenient, inexpensive and easy to adopt.

Evaluation phase. The evaluation phase allows evaluators to respond the questionnaire and store the results in the repository. As part of this process, the evaluators are able to retrieve all their previous evaluations from the repository. Therefore, they can support the new evaluations based on their previous ones and the evolution they have observed in the meantime.

Feedback phase. The evaluators (peers for IE and stakeholders for EE) now meet with the evaluated persons (a team member for IE or the whole team for EE) to deliver their feedback. This phase has differences for IE and EE, thus they will be explained in detail in sections 3.1 and 3.2.

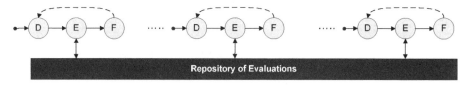

Figure 2. TEM used during a software project development

Internal evaluations are typically applied more often than external evaluations. If we consider these evaluations (just internal or external ones) in the project timeline, we have a set of evaluations modeled in Fig. 2. In every evaluation process, the evaluators revise the weaknesses identified in the previous processes as a way to monitor the team member/group evolution.

3.1. Internal Evaluations

The internal evaluations are mainly required to early detect inappropriate behaviors in team members and provide an early feedback intended to correct them. These evaluations usually help to enhance the group cohesion and self-regulation. The internal evaluations involve a co-evaluation and a self-evaluation (Figure 3). Both use the same measurement tool: a questionnaire.

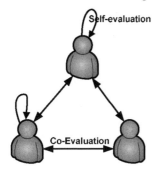

Figure 3. Internal Evaluation Process

In the co-evaluation, each team member evaluates each other, no matter the hierarchies, if there is any. On the other hand, each member evaluates his/her own work in the self-evaluation. The questionnaire used in these evaluations (Table 1) considers two types of responses: open (free text) and typed (Always, Regularly, Sometimes, Infrequently, Never). The questionnaire presented on Table 1 is an example. It was obtained as result of evaluating software development teams in real scenarios during the last 5 years, and it was also the one used during the experimentation process.

The format of the responses must be simple and clear (typed responses), and also allow team members to provide enough feedback to help partners to improve their anomalous behaviors (free text responses). Each issue in the questionnaire should be easy to understand and respond. Ambiguities usually jeopardize the usefulness of this type of tools.

Table 1. Questionnaire for Co/Self-Evaluation

Statement	Response Type
1. The evaluated person considers the project as a team work, offering support for the project tasks.	Typed
2. The evaluated person is able to ask for help when having problems.	Typed
3. The evaluated person completes the assigned tasks in a good way, making clear the work done and trying to generate as much value as possible during each workday.	Typed
4. The evaluated person shows dedication and creativity to achieve project success.	Typed
5. The evaluated person shows interest to investigate new solutions and to acquire new skills to be able to complete the assigned tasks.	Typed
6. The evaluated person is open to interact with other persons, easing team work.	Typed
7. The evaluated person looks for a trusting relationship with the client/user through a continuous interaction (intending to clarify requirements, make changes, contribute to make clear the project progress and validate the work done).	Typed
8. The evaluated person is able to accept mistakes made and is open to receive criticism.	Typed
9. The evaluated person is objective and accepts changes when needed.	Typed
10. The evaluated person prevents knowledge fragmentation within the team, by sharing information and offering timely support.	Typed
11. Describe the evaluated person's strengths.	Free Text
12. Describe the evaluated person's weaknesses.	Free Text

The questionnaire contains twelve evaluation items. Our experience indicates the questionnaire should be short and clear if we expect voluntary persons evaluate all items. The first five items of the questionnaire are oriented to evaluate the team members' capabilities for personal work. The following five items are intended to evaluate the capabilities for collaborative work, and the remaining two ones try to provide additional feedback to help team members to improve their collaborative behavior.

The internal evaluations are anonymous and usually accessible just for the team leader and the corresponding evaluated team member. The evaluations are anonymous since the probability of being honest increases if the evaluator is not identifiable. In addition, we reduce the probability of conflict between evaluators and the evaluated person.

During the evaluation phase, each member uses the TEM software tool in order to complete the self- and co-evaluation. Then, the software generates an evaluation report including the self-evaluation and the peers' evaluations for each team member during feedback. This phase consists of a meeting where each team member (or the team leader) has the opportunity to say something about the evaluation made by his/her mates. When the evaluation discussion ends, the team leader presents a general evaluation of the team, highlighting the major strengths and weaknesses.

3.2. External Evaluations

External evaluations are based on the opinions stakeholders and other non-team members have on the development team. Relevant external evaluators may be clients, users, managers, and other teams (Fig. 4). Not all external evaluator types must necessarily participate in a specific evaluation. Thus, e.g., other development teams may not be relevant for a certain evaluation. Preferably, external evaluators should be those people having a direct relationship with the team and therefore, they are able to provide an objective assessment of it.

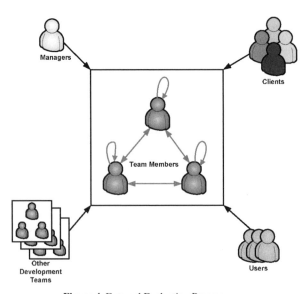

Figure 4. External Evaluation Process

These evaluations provide a diagnosis on anomalous situations within the group [1, 10]: Leniency, Harshness, Halo Effect, Similarity, Central Tendency, First Impression and Recency Effect. The external evaluations are not as frequent as the internal ones. External evaluations are done infrequently because they provide a general perspective about weaknesses and strengths of the team and these features usually do not change in a couple of weeks. However, it is important to consider that every time an external evaluation is done, an internal one should be done as well. This is because in the feedback process there is an important relationship between these two evaluation types, which can be used by team members to improve the individual and group behaviors.

Likewise internal evaluations, the tool used for external evaluation can be created for each project or reused (and adjusted) from a previous one. It also has the same length and simplicity constraints. Then, the evaluation process is carried out in a similar way to the internal evaluations. However, the feedback process is a bit different. The team meets individually with every evaluator. Before the actual meeting, each team member receives the evaluation report, which includes the self- and co-evaluations, and the external evaluation (considering all the evaluators). It adheres to the feedback recommendations given by London [1, 13]. Then, each team member analyzes the data in order to try to understand the evaluator's perspective and also the relationship between his/her behavior and the team evaluation. Next, the team meets with each evaluator in a typical feedback meeting. Finally, there is a team meeting to try to assimilate the feedback and decide any required change.

4. The Supporting Tool

The TEM tool is a web application supporting the setup and TEM process for a Project (Fig. 5). One setup is required by each software project and it includes the definition of the development teams, users of the systems and the stakeholders. The system can manage multiple projects and multiple development teams for each Project. The functionality directly related with TEM includes: (a) specification of evaluation metrics, (b) incorporation of assessments, (c) gathering of the results, (d) data analysis, (e) reports generation, (f) reports retrieval.

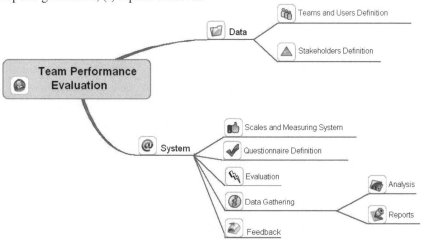

Figure 5. Functionalities of the TEM supporting tool

The application was developed using a Content Management System called Joomla! Fig. 6 shows the tool main user interface. The functionality provided by this tool is grouped in three categories: (1) Users and External Tools, used for setup and management of the tool, (2) Teams, used mainly for evaluations setup, and (3) Evaluations, used to support the TEM model.

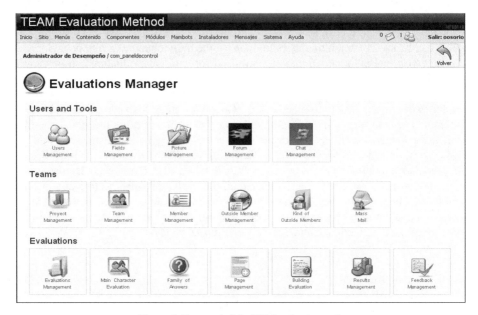

Figure 6. Front-end of the TEM evaluation tool

The functionality and the usability of this software were evaluated with ten real users and two experts in Human-Computer Interaction. The tool used in the assessment was a questionnaire based on Nielsen's usability evaluation items [21]. A score between 1 and 7 was assigned to each item. The tool got an average evaluation score of 6.0, and items scored between 5.7 and 6.5. These numbers show the tool is useful in terms of the functionality it provides and the effort required accessing these services.

5. Obtained Results

The tool was assessed in two academic and one professional development scenarios (Table 2). The academic scenario involves 10th semester courses in computer science at the University of Chile. These courses ask students to develop real software projects during 12 weeks for an external client. A project is assigned to a team of 5-7 students. In the case of the professional development scenario (case 3), the elapsed time for the project was 16 weeks. A traditional software process was used for the first and the third case. By contrast, the second case used an agile development methodology.

Table 2. Cases applying TEM and the supporting tool

Case 1	Case 2	Case 3
Course *CC61A: Software Project*. It involved 3 teams composed of 5-6 members, plus a couple of clients (external evaluators).	Course *CC62V: Agile Development Workshop*. It involved 2 teams, composed of 6 - 7 members, plus a couple of clients (external evaluators).	Software Company X. It involved one team composed of 5 developers; there were 2 clients and 2 users (external evaluators).

Two internal evaluations and one external evaluation were performed for each case and development team. A total of 406 assessments were gathered by the tool. A relevant evaluation item was the measurement of the times for submission of peers' assessments. The tool includes an agent which notifies evaluators when a submission is due. Before, when no notifications existed, late evaluation submissions averaged 31%. By contrast, using the notifications agent, late submissions ranged between 0 and 19%. Finally, it is important to mention that no evaluations were in the "undelivered" category.

TEM was applied twice to each team. The internal evaluations score increased between 10-30% for every team between the first and second applications. In addition, the external evaluations indicate most of the stakeholders have observed an improvement of the team behavior after the first internal evaluation. The feedback provided by evaluators was rich and informative for the team members. It could be showing that TEM can be useful not only to evaluate team members' performance, but to help the team members to improve their individual and collective behavior.

6. Conclusions

Software companies require software process performance measurement systems in order to reach higher levels in the Capability Maturity scale [20] and gain long term competitive advantages. However there is a lack of adequate metrics to measure and improve the performance of the software development team [7]. The work reported in this paper improves software performance measurement with a stakeholder's approach that fosters balanced and goal-oriented metrics.

The method and its supporting tool not only evaluated team members' performance, but also provided useful information to the team members to adjust their behavior according to the goals set by the group itself and other relevant people. Furthermore, repeated use of the process let people to review their progress.

The cases showed both team members and stakeholders had positive opinions on the advantages of the approach and system over no evaluation at all or naive evaluation methods previously known to them. The method effectiveness, low cost and iterative nature were the most highly valued features.

Formal experiments are planned. They should provide further data on the advantages and disadvantages of the method. We are particularly interested in studying the trade-off between time invested on evaluations and value obtained with the evaluations.

Acknowledgement

This work was partially supported by Fondecyt (Chile), grants N°: 11060467 and 1080352.

References

[1].   London, M. (2003). Job Feedback: Giving, Seeking and Using Feedback for Performance Improvement (2 ed.), New Jersey, Lawrence Erlbaum.
[2].   North, A. (2004), Introduction to Performance Appraisal. URL: http://www.performance-appraisal.com/intro.htm.
[3].   Belbin, M. (2003). Nobody is perfect, but a team can be. URL: http://www.belbin.com
[4].   Flores, F., Solomon R. (2003), Building Trust: In Business, Politics, Relationships and Life, New York: Oxford University Press.
[5]   Villena, A. (2008) An Empirical Model to Teach Agile Software Process. MSc Thesis. Univ. of Chile.
[6]   Briand, L., Morasca, S., Basili, V. (2002) An Operational Process for Goal-Driven Definition of Measures. IEEE Transactions on Software Engineering, 28 (12), 1106 – 1125.
[7]   List, B., Bruckner, R., Kapaun, J. (2005) Holistic Software Process Performance Measurement from the Stakeholders' Perspective. Proc. of BPMPM'05, Copenhagen, Denmark, IEEE CS Press.
[8]   Kueng, P., Wettstein, T., List, B. (2001) A Holistic Process Performance Analysis through a Process Data Warehouse. American Conf. on Inf. Systems (AMCIS 2001), Boston, USA.
[9]   Basili, V., Rombach, H. (1988) The TAME Project: Towards Improvement-Oriented Software Environments. IEEE Trans. on Software Engineering 14 (6), 758-773.
[10]. P. Lencioni (2003). The Five Dysfunctions of a Team: A Leadership Fable. San Francisco, Jossey-Bass.
[11]. P. Lowry, T. Roberts, N. Romano., P. Cheney, and R. Hightower (2006), The Impact of Group Size and Social Presence on Small-Group Communication: Does Computer-Mediated Communication Make a Difference?, Small Group Research 37: 631-661.
[12]. Florac, W., Carlton, A. (1999). Measuring the Software Process: Statistical Process Control for Software Process Improvement, Addison-Wesley.
[13]. M. London, (1995). Self and interpersonal insight: How people learn about themselves and others in organizations. New York: Oxford University Press.
[14]. S. Sherestha, J. Chalidabhongse, (2007). Improving Employee Performance Appraisal Method through Web-Based Appraisal Support System: System Development from the Study on Thai Companies, IEICE Trans. on Information and Systems, E90-D(10), 1621-1629.
[15]. Pinelle, D., Gutwin, C. (2005) A Groupware Design Framework for Loosely Coupled Workgroups. European Conference on Computer-Supported Cooperative Work, 119-139.
[16]. DiMicco, J.M., Pandolfo, A. and Bender, W. (2004). Influencing Group Participation with a Shared Display, Conf. on Computer Supported Cooperative Work (Chicago, IL).
[17]. Hackman, J.R. (2002). Group influences on individuals in organizations, in Dunnette, M.D. and Hough, L.M. eds. Handbook of Industrial and Organizational Psychology.
[18]. Mandryk, R.L., Inkpen, K. (2004). Physiological Indicators for the Evaluation of Co-located Collaborative Play. Computer Supported Cooperative Work (CSCW). Chicago, IL.
[19]. Ochoa, S., Pino, J., Guerrero, L., Collazos, C. (2006). SSP: A Simple Software Process for Small-Size Software Development Projects. Proc. of IWASE'06, Santiago, Chile. SSBM 219. pp. 94-107.
[20]. SEI. (2002). Capability Maturity Model Integration, vers. 1.1. Software Engineering Institute. CMU.
[21]. Nielsen, J. (1993). Usability Engineering. Academic Press, London.

Collaborative Decision Making: Perspectives and Challenges
P. Zaraté et al. (Eds.)
IOS Press, 2008

Consensus Building in Collaborative Decision Making

Gloria PHILLIPS-WREN [a,1], Eugene HAHN [b] and Guisseppi FORGIONNE [c]

[a]*The Sellinger School of Business and Management, Loyola College in Maryland,
Baltimore, MD 21210*
[b]*Salisbury University, Salisbury, MD 21801*
[c]*University of Maryland Baltimore County, Baltimore, MD 21250*

Abstract. Developing consensus is crucial to effective collaborative decision making and is particularly difficult in cases involving disruptive technologies, a new technology that unexpectedly displaces an established technology. Collaborative decision making often involves multiple criteria. Multicriteria decision making (MCDM) techniques, such as the analytical hierarchy process (AHP) and multiattribute utility theory (MUAT), rely on the accurate assignment of weights to the multiple measures of performance. Consensus weighting within MCDM can be difficult to achieve because of differences of opinion among experts and the presence of intangible, and often conflicting, measures of performance. The method presented in this paper can be used to develop a consensus weighting scheme within MCDM. This paper presents a statistically-based method for consensus building and illustrates its use in the evaluation of a capital project involving the purchase of mammography equipment as disruptive technology in healthcare management. An AHP architecture is proposed to evaluate the best decision from the proposed

Keywords. collaboration, multicriteria decision making, analytic hierarchy process, consensus

Introduction

Cancer is the second leading cause of death in the United States after heart disease ([1]). Improvements in diagnosis, treatment or continuing care of cancer can make large differences in an individual's quality of life and survival from this disease. As innovations in technology become available, medical providers are faced with evaluating both the potential improvements in care for their patient load and the business rationale surrounding new capital projects. Many such capital projects are extremely expensive, leading to regional specialization in health-care delivery. Medical facilities must weigh factors such as patient care, availability of similar resources at nearby facilities, cost, expected usage patterns, future projections, and disruptive technologies in making the decision to undertake a capital expenditure. Such decisions are particularly difficult with large differences in expert opinion in the case of disruptive technologies, defined by Christensen [2] as a new technology that unexpectedly displaces an established technology.

---

[1] Corresponding author: The Sellinger School of Business and Management, Information Systems and Operations Management, 4501 N. Charles Street, Baltimore, MD 21210; E-mail: gwren@loyola.edu

A disruptive technology was recently examined by Pisano et al. [3] in a study of 49,500 women and their mammography screenings. In the Pisano et al. study, film and digital mammography had similar screening accuracy (NCI [4]) as had been found in past studies, including those from the U.S. Food and Drug Administration. Although the standard of care for the past 35 years has been film mammography, the study showed that digital mammography was significantly better in screening women who had very dense breasts and in women under age 50 (NCI, [4]). Alternatively, the study showed no improvement for women over age 50 or those without very dense breasts. There was no difference in false positives, machine type, race, or breast cancer risk. Although a direct relationship between digital mammography and reduction in breast cancer deaths cannot be definitely established, death rates from breast cancer have been declining since 1990 and are believed to be the result of earlier detection and improved treatment (NCI, [4]). The implication is that the use of digital mammography may lead to earlier detection of breast cancer in some women within the identified group, and that earlier detection will lead to improvement in health.

The primary differences between film and digital mammography are in the medium for storage and transmission. Both use X-rays to produce an image, although digital mammography uses approximately three-quarters the radiation dosage. Standard film mammography, while diagnostically accurate in many cases, is analog and limited by the film itself since it cannot be significantly altered, for example, for contrast. Digital mammography takes an electronic image of the breast that can be stored or transmitted electronically. In addition, software such as intelligent decision support technologies can potentially assist radiologists in interpreting screening results. These benefits can potentially reduce the number of false positives with a concomitant increase in quality of life for some people. Cost effectiveness may be improved with digital mammography due to differences in the storage mediums.

There are higher costs with digital mammography compared to film. Radiologists who interpret digital mammography must undergo additional training (NCI, [4]). Digital systems are expensive, costing approximately 1.5 to 4 times more than film systems (NCI, [4]).

The National Cancer Institute (2007) estimates that only 8% of breast imaging units currently use digital mammography. Differences in quality of life due to reduction in false positives, cost effectiveness, and effect of reader studies have not been determined. Thus, decision makers in medical facilities face many uncertainties and differences in expert opinion about the benefits and costs of digital mammography as a capital project. Decision makers must weigh many factors when deciding whether to replace film mammography systems with digital mammography equipment. To make this decision, they require collaboration and consensus building among experts who may have large differences in opinion about the multiple factors.

The purpose of this paper is to develop a collaboration model and apply it to the mammography screening decision faced by one Maryland hospital. The paper is organized into the following sections. First, there is a review of multiple criteria decision making and consensus building literature. The review is used to develop the proposed collaboration model. Next, an application is presented and analyzed. Finally, the paper presents conclusions and discusses the implications for MCDM and collaborative decision making.

1. Multiple Criteria Decision Making

When a decision problem involves multiple, often conflicting and intangible, measures of performance, multiple criteria decision making (MCDM) is a popular formulation and solution methodology. While there are many MCDM techniques, each requires the assignment of weights to the multiple performance measures.

In the absence of any contrary information, the weights for the multiple measures are often assumed to be equal. Yet, equal weights are not always accurate. In such circumstances, the weights can be assigned subjectively by the decision maker, perhaps with the aid of a Likert scale or other psychometric scaling tool, objectively through an empirical probability distribution, or through a decision analysis that guides the decision maker toward an accurate judgment.

Guided assistance can be an effective tool in the weighting assessment. Forgionne [5], for example, utilized decision and game theory to assist decision makers in assessing probabilities for uncontrollable inputs in a decision situation. These guided subjective assessments then were compared to the known actual event probabilities, and the comparison revealed that the guided subjective estimates were statistically equivalent to the actual likelihoods.

Such a guided weighting approach may be particularly useful in collaborative decision making (CDM), where different collaborators may have alternative views regarding the criteria. In such cases, it will be necessary to determine a consensus weighting scheme to resolve potential conflicts among collaborators. A consensus scheme may also alter the decision making process.

In this situation, the determination of the weights becomes important. However, assignment of weights is still an open research issue. In this paper, we examine the performance implications of three different methods of weight elicitation and the concomitant outcomes on the decision process.

2. Collaborative Judgment Elicitation and Combination

In this section, we describe our methods for eliciting judgments as well as expert-specific weights. We then describe our mathematical framework for combining these judgments to form a consensus weighting scheme for MCDM.

2.1. Mixture Distributions

Given that experts typically experience uncertainty in decision making, it is desirable to represent expert beliefs through probability distributions. One family of probability distributions that permits a wide variety of beliefs to be represented is the finite mixture distribution ([6]; [7]).

The finite mixture distribution takes the form:

$$g(y \mid \Psi) = \sum_{i=1}^{I} w_i f_i(y \mid \psi_i) \qquad (1)$$

where f and g are densities, i indexes the I components of the mixture, ψ_i is the set of parameters for expert i, $\mathbf{\Psi}$ is the collection of parameters over all experts, and w_i is the weight for expert i. While distributions as in (1) are known as finite mixture distributions in the statistical literature, they have also been termed linear opinion pools in the literature on aggregation of expert opinion because of the direct additive combination of expert information.

The general family of mixture distributions, both including scale as well as finite mixtures, provide a flexible framework to represent expert belief regarding probabilistic phenomena (e.g., [8]; [9]; [10]). This flexibility can come at a cost of greater complexity than would be associated with the use of marginal distributions ([11]). This tradeoff is especially true for scale mixture distributions. By contrast finite mixture distributions can be elicited as a series of marginal distributions, which then can be weighted as components of the finite mixture. This approach in effect decomposes a more complex distribution into a linear combination of elements, reducing the burden on the experts.

The determination of the weights becomes important, but the manner in which these are to be assigned is still an open issue. The choice of equal weights (e.g., Hendry and Clements, [12]) is perhaps a natural one, particularly in the context of forming a comparative baseline against other weighting systems. Hall and Mitchell [13] review additional weighting systems which are derived based on mathematical criteria, including weights derived via Bayesian model averaging as well as the Kullback-Leibler information criterion. A comparative perspective was taken by Woodward et al [14] who examined the use of maximum likelihood approaches to minimum distance approaches in the estimation of the weights in a finite normal mixture based on sample data. They found that the former approach was better when components were normal while the latter was better under departures from normality.

Mixture distributions are utilized with some regularity in forecasting contexts, where it is of interest to combine information from various sources (e.g., [15]; [13]) as this has been shown to be beneficial with regard to predictive accuracy ([16]). However, it appears to also be another open question as the extent to which they can be utilized to improve the outcomes from group-based multiple criteria decision making.

2.2. Elicitation Methods

We considered the following three methods for obtaining expert-specific weights. The first is equal weighting of all experts whereby $w_i = 1/n$. In the second method, experts self-rated their expertise, and these self-ratings were transformed into weights. Specifically, experts rated themselves on a scale of 1 to 5 where 5 represented the highest level of experience. If the self-rating of expert i is s_i, then $w_i = s_i /\Sigma\, s_i$. In the third method which was based on the objective criterion of years of experience with the years of experience for a given expert being e_i, we formed $w_i = e_i /\Sigma\, e_i$. Hence, the methods comprise the gamut of assuming *à priori* equivalency, weight proportional to subjectively-assessed expertise, and weights proportional to an objective assessment of experience. Other weighting methods are possible such as asking experts to rate themselves as well as all other experts in a round robin, and we will explore these in future research.

3. Application to Healthcare Decision Making

A privately-run, comprehensive, public hospital in Baltimore, Maryland, received expert advice from various sources about the purchase of digital mammography equipment. Although digital mammography is a disruptive technology and opinions about its efficacy and costs vary widely, hospital managers determined that they would quantify the decision problem using traditional metrics and attempt to build consensus through a collaborative decision making approach. We compared the approach utilized by the hospital with other methods suggested by our research. The results are presented in the following discussion.

The metric utilized to make a decision on a capital project in the hospital is primarily the Net Present Value (NPV) with a general hurdle value greater than zero. The NPV is used in capital budgeting to provide the present value in current dollars of a series of future cash flows with a given rate of return. It is calculated by taking an income stream (in our case a five year projection) and finding the current value of the income stream. In general, higher NPV is desirable, although capital projects may be attractive as long as the NPV is greater than zero.

The factors considered by the hospital for this capital project are growth from new cases, gross charges on new case growth, increment of new technology over legacy, reimbursement on growth in new cases, reimbursement on existing cases, film savings from Picture Archiving and Communication Systems (PACS), and Operating Expenses (depreciation and variable costs). Factors such as potential increases in productivity, decrease in retakes, and patient satisfaction were not considered. The cash flow calculation was completed for a five-year time horizon. Expert opinion differed greatly on volume growth from new cases, the primary determinant of IRR in this case. Cost of the units, estimated films savings from PACS and operating expenses were better known. Although experts wanted to include potential losses in screenings if digital mammography became a standard of care not available at the hospital, no acceptable measure was agreed upon. The mean baseline estimates for the Baltimore region representing consensus from the experts were Film savings from PACS of $20,280 per year with no change over the five year time horizon, and Operating Expenses of $507,468 with a 1% straight line increase per year. Differences between expert opinions are shown in Table 1. It should be noted that different geographic regions will have different values for the variables. For example, growth from new cases depends on the competitive environment such as competing hospitals or health care facilities, patient's perceptions of quality, and physician recommendations as this technology progresses. Other regions of Maryland in which the Baltimore Health System operates, such as the greater Washington, D.C. area, have quite different environments.

Table 1. Expert opinion on growth from new cases together with a subjective assessment of expertise by the expert and an objective assessment of expertise by the hospital (Scale: 1= low confidence and 5=high confidence).

Expert	min	most likely	max	Subjective assessment	Objective assessment
1	0%	5%	10%	1	5
2	5%	10%	12%	4	3
3	10%	11%	20%	3	3

The usual method of arriving at a collaborative decision in the hospital is to calculate three different proforma statements representing low, mean and high estimates. That is, the hospital generates one statement with all variables at the lowest estimated value, one with all at the mean, and one with all variables at their highest estimated values. The probability that any one of the iterations will actually occur is zero.

Effective and efficient business strategy development is crucial to achieve a competitive advantage in the marketplace. In the healthcare market, the challenges are complex and dynamic for business management. One way to assist the evaluation process is by applying computer simulation that uses an econometric model delivered to support decision making ([17]). The variability in the values of variables can be expressed with a probability density function. Each expert contributed a minimum, maximum and most likely value which we represented with a triangular distribution as shown in Figure 1. To arrive at a collaborative decision, these distributions were combined using the information in Table 1 and the three weighting methods discussed previously. The resulting mixture distributions are shown in Figure 2 with their statistics in Table 2.

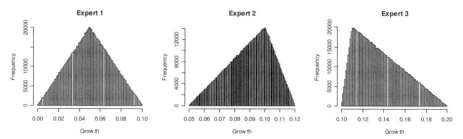

Figure 1. Individual distributions: Expert opinion on growth from new cases.

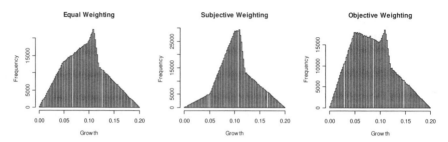

Figure 2. Mixture distributions by weighting method: Expert opinion on growth.

Table 2. Mixture distribution summary statistics (1 million iterations)

Weighting Method	Mean	S.D.	2.5 Percentile	97.5 Percentile
- Equal	9.22%	4.04%	1.93%	17.4%
- Objective	10.25%	3.48%	3.16%	17.5%
- Subjective	8.46%a	4.10%	1.66%	17.1%

Most of the variability among the mixture distributions revolves around the mean and the 2.5 percentile, while the upper tail of the distributions is fairly consistent. All of the mixtures have more dispersion than any of the individual distributions as can be deduced from the graphs. To determine the effect of the mixtures on decision variables, the mixtures were implemented in the healthcare model. Two output values are shown: (a) The distribution of cash flow in year 1 in Figure 3 with the range in all cases from 300 to 600 thousand dollars; and, (b) the Net Present Value (NPV) for years 0-5 in Table 3. The NPV gives the value of the capital investment over years 0-5 in current day dollars at a rate of 4%. As can be seen in Figure 3, the Cash Flow in Year 1 reflects the mixture distributions in general shape. The NPV exhibits more variability with different mixture distributions, particularly in the mean. The results suggest that the mixture distribution used in the analysis may affect decision making. Although this paper does not address the question of which decision is best, it does suggest that consensus building around expert opinion is needed to accurately represent the mixture distribution.

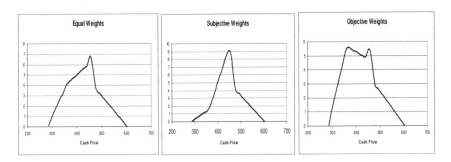

Figure 3.   Effect of mixture distributions on Cash Flow in Year 1 (100,000 iterations).

Table 3. Summary statistics NPV years 0-5 from mixture distributions (100,000 iterations).

Weighting Method	NPV Mean	NPV S.D.	5.0 Percentile	95.0 Percentile
- Equal	$ 1,988	$ 191,342	- $ 296,915	$ 332,915
- Objective	- $ 14,242	$ 190,541	- $ 310,827	$ 314,619
- Subjective	$ 23,691	$ 187,826	- $ 270,160	$ 346,670

In order to determine the "best" decision, i.e. whether to invest in digital mammography equipment, from the three ways to develop consensus, an analytic hierarchy process (AHP) evaluation methodology can be employed. The AHP is a multi-criteria method that can incorporate both qualitative and quantitative criteria into a single metric ([18]). We have implemented the AHP previously to compare decision support systems and to determine their effect on the process of, and outcome from, decision making ([19]). We propose that the architecture shown in Figure 4 and based on our previous research can be used to determine the best decision arising from different consensus methods.

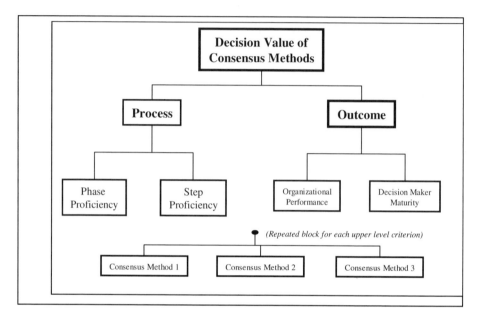

Figure 4. Proposed AHP architecture to evaluate consensus methods.

4. Summary

Developing a consensus is crucial to effective collaborative decision making. This consensus is especially important in critical decision making tasks, such as healthcare decision making. This paper has presented a statistically-based method for consensus building and illustrated its use in the evaluation of mammography equipment as a capital project in healthcare management.

The method is applicable beyond the illustration presented here. Multicriteria decision making (MCDM) techniques, such as the analytical hierarchy process (AHP) and multiattribute utility theory (MUAT), rely on the accurate assignment of weights to the multiple measures of performance. Consensus weighting within MCDM can be difficult to achieve because of differences of opinion among experts and the presence of intangible, and often conflicting, measures of performance. The method presented in this paper can be used to develop a consensus weighting scheme within MCDM. For example, eigenvalue calculations within AHP can be modified to incorporate the consensus weighting methodology and then delivered effectively through available AHP software, such as Expert Choice.

The potential MCDM suggests the following research question and hypotheses for future investigation:

> Research Question: Can the proposed consensus weighting scheme result in more decision value than alternative schemes, such as equal weighting?
>
> Null Hypothesis: The consensus weighting scheme results in no more decision value than alternative schemes.
>
> Alternative Hypothesis: The consensus weighting scheme results in more decision value than alternative schemes.

These questions can be answered in the future by experimenting with the data from the illustrative healthcare application presented here and/or through additional studies.

Acknowledgements

The authors would like to thank the Baltimore Health System and our graduate students for their assistance with insight into healthcare decision making.

References

[1] CDC.Center for Disease Control. Accessed on September 25, 2007, from http://www.cdc.gov/cancer/az/.
[2] Christensen, C. *The Innovator's Dilemma: When New Technologies Cause Great Firms to Fail.* Harvard Business School Press, Boston, MA, 1997.
[3] Pisano, E., Gatsonis, C., Hendrick, E., Yaffe, M., Baum, J., Acharyya, S., Conant, E., Fajardo, L., Bassett, L., D'Orsi, C., Jong, R., and Rebner, M. Diagnostic Performance of Digital versus Film Mammography for Breast Cancer Screening - The Results of the American College of Radiology Imaging Network (ACRIN) Digital Mammographic Imaging Screening Trial (DMIST). *New England Journal of Medicine*, published online September 15, 2005 and in print on October 27, 2005.
[4] NCI. National Cancer Institute. Accessed on September 23, 2007, from http://www.cancer.gov/cancertopics/factsheet/DMISTQandA.
[5] Forgionne, G.A. Parameter estimation by management judgment: An experiment. *Review of Business and Economic Research* (Spring), 1974.
[6] Titterington, D.M., Smith, A.F.M. and Makov, U.E. *Statistical Analysis of Finite Mixture Distributions.* Wiley, Chichester, 1985.
[7] McLachlan, G.J. and Basford, K.E. *Mixture Models: Inference and Applications to Clustering.* Marcel Dekker, New York, NY, 1988.
[8] Dalal, S. R. and Hall, W. J. Approximating priors by mixtures of natural conjugate priors. *Journal of the Royal Statistical Society, Series* B, 45, 278–286, 1983.
[9] Diaconis, P. and Ylvisaker, D. Quantifying prior opinion. In *Bayesian Statistics 2* (eds) J. M. Bernardo, M. H. DeGroot, D. V. Lindley and A. F. M. Smith, Amsterdam: North-Holland, 133–156, 1985.
[10] Genest, C. and Zidek, J. Combining probability distributions: A critique and an annotated bibliography. *Statistical Science*, 1, 114–135, 1986.
[11] Hahn, E.D. Re-examining informative prior elicitation through the lens of Markov chain Monte Carlo methods. *Journal of the Royal Statistical Society, Series A*, 169(1), 37–48, 2006.

[12] Hendry, D.F. and Clements, M.P. Pooling of forecasts, *Econometrics Journal*, 7(1), 1-31 , 2004.

[13] Hall, S. and Mitchell, J. Combining density forecasts. *International Journal of Forecasting*, 23, 1–13, 2007.

[14] Woodward, A., Parr, W., Schucany, W. and Lindsey, H. A Comparison of Minimum Distance and Maximum Likelihood Estimation of a Mixture Proportion. *Journal of the American Statistical Association*, 79, 590-598, 1984.

[15] Hand, D.J. Good practice in retail credit scorecard assessment. *The Journal of the Operational Research Society*, 56(9), 1109-1117, 2005.

[16] Stock, J. and Watson, M. Combination forecasts of output growth in a seven-country data set. *Journal of Forecasting*, 23, 405–430, 2004.

[17] Ha, L. and Forgionne, G. Econometric simulation for e-business strategy evaluation. *International Journal of E-Business Research*, 2(2), 38 – 53, 2006.

[18] Saaty T.L. A scaling method for priorities in hierarchical structures. *Journal of Mathematical Psychology*, 234-281, 1977.

[19] Phillips-Wren G., Hahn E., Forgionne G. A multiple criteria framework for the evaluation of decision support systems. *Omega*, 32(4), 323-332, 2004.

Tools for Collaborative Decision Making

Collaborative Decision Making: Perspectives and Challenges
P. Zaraté et al. (Eds.)
IOS Press, 2008

Data Quality Tags and Decision-making: Improving the Design and Validity of Experimental Studies

Rosanne PRICE[a,1], Graeme SHANKS[a]

[a]Dept. of Information Systems, The University of Melbourne, Victoria, Australia 3010

Abstract. Providing decision-makers with information about the quality of the data they are using has been empirically shown to impact both decision outcomes and the decision-making process. However, little attention has been paid to the usability and relevance of the data quality tags and the experimental materials used in studies to date. In this paper, we highlight the potential impact of these issues on experimental validity and propose the use of interaction design techniques to address this problem. We describe current work that applies these techniques, including contextual inquiry and participatory design, to improve the design and validity of planned data quality tagging experiments. The benefits of this approach are illustrated by showing how the outcomes of a series of contextual inquiry interviews have influenced the design of the experimental materials. We argue that interaction design techniques should be used more widely for experimental design.

Keywords. experimental design, interaction design, data quality tags, data quality, decision support systems

Introduction

Data quality problems are widespread in practice and can impact the effectiveness of decision-makers. Support for decision-making[2] has focused on both the data used and the nature of the decision-making processes. Issues related to ensuring good quality data (data quality [3] definition, assessment, improvement, and management) [1,2,3,4,5,6,7] and decision-making strategies [8,9] have received considerable attention. In contrast, there has been relatively little consideration of a complementary approach based on providing decision-makers with information about the actual quality of available data [10,11,12]. Such metadata, called data quality (DQ) tags, allow decision-makers to consider the relative quality of different types of data. It is unlikely that all the data used to make a decision is of a uniform quality, especially given the multiple and/or external sources common in organizational data collections. In this context, the use of DQ tags could potentially impact both how a decision is made (the decision process) and what decision is made (the decision outcome). For example, the

---

[1] Corresponding Author: Rosanne Price, Dept. of Information Systems, University of Melbourne, Victoria, Australia 3010; E-mail: Rosanne.price@infotech.monash.edu.au (or gshanks@unimelb.edu.au for Graeme Shanks).

[2] The focus here is on multi-criteria decision-making on-line using structured data.

[3] The term data quality is used synonymously with information quality in this paper, to mean the quality of either stored data or received information (i.e. as presented to users).

use of DQ tags could impact the decision-making efficiency (e.g. if decision-makers take time to consider data quality), the resultant decision (e.g. if criteria that would otherwise be considered are disregarded because of their low quality ratings), or the decision-maker's confidence in that decision. Since the use of DQ tags is associated with significant overheads with respect to tag creation, storage, and maintenance; the adoption of DQ tagging as a business practice would need to be justified by a clear demonstration of its efficacy. Thus research into the effects of DQ tagging on decision-making constitutes a necessary pre-requisite step to any proposed implementation of DQ tags.

In designing experiments to study the effects of DQ tagging on decision-making, the researcher must necessarily make decisions regarding the design of the DQ tags to be used in the experiments. Since the use of DQ tags is not a common part of current business practice, there are—in general—no typical real-world precedents or widely-understood conventions available to guide the researcher in designing or the user in understanding tag semantics and representation. The novelty of this experimental component complicates the experimental design in that the specific choices made in designing the tags may impact the observed experimental results. To illustrate, we consider the typical research questions addressed in previous DQ tagging experiments [10,11,12]: 'when (under what circumstances) are DQ tags used?' and 'how does the use of DQ tags affect decision outcomes?' Either of these questions could be affected by the tag design. For example, an ambiguous tag design resulting in varying interpretation of tag semantics by different participants could lead to random error that impacts the reliability of the experiment. An additional consideration in the experimental design is the degree to which the contrived paper or software artefact used in the experiment for decision-making is representative of actual decision-making environments in practice. This has obvious implications for the generalizability of the study.

It is our assertion that a rigorously designed DQ tagging experiment requires explicit consideration of usability issues such as understandability and relevance when designing the DQ tags and the paper or software decision-making artefact to be used in the experiment. In fact, this paper and our current work is motivated by the observation that such considerations have received relatively little attention in DQ tagging research to date. A further assertion—and the focus of this paper—is that one way to address such issues is by consultation with users during the design process. Thus we are currently using interaction design techniques to plan quantitative DQ tagging experiments. This approach evolved in response to questions that arose while designing DQ tags for the planned experiments. Specific questions related to which aspects of data quality and which possible DQ tag representations were the most understandable and relevant to users. In addressing these questions explicitly, the goal is to improve the design and validity of the planned DQ tagging experiments.

The rest of the paper is structured as follows. Previous work in DQ tagging is described in Section 1, including a discussion of the limitations therein that motivated our plans for DQ tagging experiments. In Section 2, we consider research issues relevant to the design of such experiments and how they can be addressed using interaction design techniques. The resulting exploratory study in interactive experimental design and the results achieved to date are described in Section 3. Finally we conclude with a discussion of the implications of the current work in the broader context of designing empirical experiments.

1. Previous Work in Data Quality Tagging

Laboratory experiments have been used [10,11,12] to examine how decision outcomes are affected by the use of DQ tags, but have limitations with respect to the data sample size, tags, and/or experimental interface used. Only small paper-based data sets of fewer than eight alternatives (i.e. records) were used in [10] and [11]. This is in marked contrast to the large data sets characterizing on-line decision-making, with obvious implications for the generalizability of the experimental results to on-line decision-making. Furthermore, these experiments did not fully control participants' decision-making strategy (e.g. participants had to calculate the rating for each alternative in order to use the weighted additive strategy; alternatives were not presented in an order corresponding to a given strategy). In fact, a post-test revealed that "most subjects used a combination of strategies" [11, p183]. Consequently, observed decision outcomes that were attributed solely to the use of tags could actually have depended (partly or completely) on the strategy or strategies used—as was shown by Shanks and Tansley in [12]. This study addressed both concerns of scale and of strategy by using an on-line interface with 100 alternatives and a built-in decision-strategy, with separate interfaces for different decision-making strategies.

None of the DQ tagging experiments reported to date have considered the semantics (i.e. underlying meaning), derivation (method used to calculate tag values), or alternative types (based on different data quality criteria) of tags (see also [13]). For example, the only guide to the meaning of the quality tag used is its label (reliability in [10,11] and accuracy in [12]), without any further explanation (except that accuracy is given as a synonym for reliability for readers but not for experimental participants in [10,11]). Only one type of tag of unspecified meaning and derivation is considered. In fact, a DQ tag could potentially be based on a number of different DQ criteria discussed in the literature (for a discussion of the use of different types of metadata in decision-making, see [13,14]; for surveys of DQ frameworks, see [3,15]). For example in [13], Price and Shanks discuss the definition of DQ tags based on data correspondence (to the real-world) versus conformance (to defined integrity rules). in [12, p4], Shanks and Tansley allude to the importance of tag design issues such as representation: "The way the data quality tags are represented can affect decision behaviour and should be designed to promote effective decision-making." They further acknowledge that "the determination and representation of data quality tags is a complex issue beyond the scope of the present study" [12, p4]. The potential impact of tag design on experimental validity (is the tag representation understandable?) and generalizability (are the tag semantics meaningful, relevant, and useful for decision-making in practice?) are directly related to questions of usability.

The experimental interface of previous DQ tagging experiments, including tag design, was apparently determined with limited user (i.e. potential experimental participants and/or decision-makers) consultation. The only explicit test of usability discussed in previous DQ tagging work were pilot tests of the experiment in [11]. Thus usability concerns were addressed in the artificial context of the experiment itself rather than in the context of actual decision-making practice. The resultant feedback from pilot tests is thus likely to relate more to the internal coherence of the experiment rather than the relevance and understandability of the materials in reference to actual decision-making practice. For example, most of the experiments use an interval scale to represent data quality values. However, this representation may not be the most relevant or meaningful one for decision-makers assessing data quality in practice.

Furthermore, such a scale may give a misleading or unrealistic (and thus less believable) impression of the precision of the data quality measurement.

We illustrate further using the example discussed in the Introduction, i.e. the experimental use of DQ tags whose meaning is not explicitly defined. Although not explicitly explained in the experimental materials, the meaning of the DQ tags may be considered clear by individual subjects in the pilot test because they have their own internal interpretations. However, there might not be agreement between the interpretations of different subjects or between their interpretations and that of the researcher—this was not evaluated in the pilot test since it was conducted only with reference to the experiment rather than to decision-making or data quality in practice. In fact, the difficulties that users have in articulating their knowledge or concerns out of context—as, for example, in a pilot study—are described in [16, p307] and [17, p241-243]. Interaction design techniques [16,17,18,19] have been used to address this problem in the context of designing IT systems and products; however, to our knowledge, these techniques have not been applied to experimental design.

Finally, an open issue raised in [11] that has not yet been addressed in the literature is the question of how decision-making processes are affected by DQ tags. Previous work has focussed on whether the use of tags change decision outcomes such as the actual decision made (e.g. the apartment(s) selected from rental property listings), the decision-maker's confidence that the decision is correct, and the consensus between different decision-makers. The effect of DQ tags on the decision-making process has not been directly examined, except in a limited way with respect to the time taken to make a decision (i.e. a fixed time allowed as an independent variable in [11] and elapsed time measured as a dependent variable in [12]).

In the next section, we introduce the empirical study planned in response to the above-mentioned limitations of DQ tagging research to date, discuss experimental design issues related to tag design and usability, and propose the use of techniques to improve experimental design for the planned study.

2. Designing Materials for Data Quality Tagging Experiments

Our initial decision to conduct additional research in DQ tagging was motivated by two primary considerations:
1. the need to explicitly consider and specify DQ tag semantics and derivation and;
2. the need for direct examination of cognitive decision-making processes to explain observed effects (or lack thereof) of DQ tags on decision outcomes.

To this end, an empirical study was designed to examine the effects of DQ tags in the context of on-line, multi-criteria, and data-intensive decision-making. An example of such a decision is the selection of a set of rental properties to visit based on characteristics such as the rental price, location, and number of bedrooms from an on-line database of available rental properties. This domain is selected for the planned empirical study in order to be consistent with most previous DQ tagging research (e.g., [10,11,12]. The first phase of the empirical study involves experiments examining the effects of DQ tags on decision outcomes, using DQ tags with explicitly specified semantics and derivation based on a semiotic[4] information quality framework proposed

---

[4] Semiotics refers to the philosophical theory of communication using signs.

by Price and Shanks in [3]. This is to be followed by a laboratory-based cognitive process tracing study in order to understand and explain the observed impact of DQ tag use on decision-making processes.

In contrast to other paper-based DQ tagging studies (e.g. [10,11]), the computer-based study of Shanks and Tansley [12] is directly relevant to the design of the planned empirical study—both with respect to methodology (a similar methodology is used for the first experimental phase of the study) and experimental materials. As in [12], we adopt a relational database-type interface and use Microsoft Access software for development – both well-understood and widely used. Issues of scale and decision-making strategy (each potentially affecting the impact of DQ tagging) are similarly addressed through the use of two separate on-line interfaces, each with 100 alternatives and a different built-in decision-strategy. Additive and Elimination-by-attribute strategies are selected based on their contrasting properties (i.e. compensatory and alternative-based versus noncompensatory and attribute-based respectively, see [13, p79] for further explanation).

Central to the planned DQ tagging experiments – and distinguishing them from previous work in the field – is the emphasis on tag design. Issues that must be considered in defining tags include the tag's meaning (i.e. semantics), representation, granularity, level of consolidation, and derivation. Clearly, the range of issues implies consideration of a potentially unmanageable number of possible tag designs. However, since the creation, storage, and maintenance of tags incurs additional costs that offset potential benefits; it is desirable restrict the scope to those choices that are likely to be the most practical in terms of simplicity[5], cost, and use. In the following two sub-sections, we discuss DQ tag design issues related to cost and usability concerns respectively.

2.1. Cost-based Concerns

Although DQ tags might be useful for decision-makers, their derivation, storage and subsequent use incur expensive overheads and raise serious cost-based concerns. Three design issues relevant to cost in DQ tagging are tag meaning, granularity, and level of consolidation. We consider each of these issues in detail and suggest cost-effective solutions (i.e. design choices).

The issue of tag meaning (i.e. semantics) relates to the specific underlying data quality characteristic whose value is represented by the DQ tag. Different types of DQ tags can be defined based on the data quality categories and criteria in the semiotic information quality framework proposed by Price and Shanks in [3]. The three categories are data conformance to rules, correspondence to represented real-world entities, and use (i.e. as described by an activity or task, its organizational or geographic context, and user characteristics). The first two categories are relatively objective in nature, whereas the third category is necessarily subjective since it is based on context-specific information consumer views (see [2] for a detailed discussion). Objective quality measures can be provided for a given data set since they are inherently based on that data set. In contrast, subjective quality measures are context dependant (e.g. varying based on the individual stakeholder or task) and therefore must be associated with additional contextual information. Thus, it can be argued that

---

[5] Simplicity has implications for cost (usually cheaper) and use (usually more understandable and easier to use).

limiting tags to objective quality aspects will reduce overhead (e.g. as additional storage and maintenance is required for contextual information). This means that tags based on the objective view of data quality (i.e. rule conformance and real-world correspondence) are more practical than those based on the subjective view of data quality (i.e. context-specific use).

Data granularity can be specified at different levels of granularity (i.e. schema, relation, column, row, field within the relational model) with the obvious trade-off that overheads and information value increase at finer tagging granularities. In the context of relational or table-based data models, column-level tagging is a natural compromise in the context of multi-criteria decision-making, since the underlying cognitive processes involve evaluation of alternatives (i.e. records) in terms of relevant criteria (i.e. attributes or columns). Column-level DQ tagging is the coarsest degree of granularity still likely to have impact on decision-making without incurring the excessive and/or escalating costs of record-based or field-based tagging in large and/or expanding data sets.

The level of consolidation used in defining a DQ tag is closely related to the question of granularity. For example, consider two alternative designs possible for tagging a given column based on data conformance to rules (i.e. the degree to which column values obey the data integrity rules applicable to that column). One possibility is to have separate tags for each data integrity rule relevant to that column. Alternatively, a single composite tag could be used that combines information across the set of data integrity rules relevant to that column. Although the first design is more informative, the latter simplifies use and reduces storage overheads. A single composite tag for rule conformance is thus the preferred choice given the previously stated objectives of restricting scope to limit potential cost and complexity.

2.2. Usability Concerns

The previous section describes the decisions made regarding tag design during the initial design phase of the DQ tagging empirical study; however, additional questions were raised in the process of developing the actual materials and procedures to be used in the DQ tagging experiments. These questions forced us to re-visit the design issues of DQ tag meaning and representation and to explicitly consider usability issues in designing DQ tags and the decision-making interface for the planned experiments. In this section, we first describe the questions and then propose the use of interaction design techniques to address these questions.

The first question raised was related to the types of DQ tags (with respect to tag semantics or meaning) that should be used. The initial proposal included two different types of tags based on the data's conformance to rules and correspondence to real world respectively. However, the results of our subsequent work developing an instrument to measure consumer-based (i.e. subjective) data quality [20] suggest that users do not think of quality in terms of rule conformance and have difficulty understanding this concept. These results thus led us to question whether the planned use of DQ tags based on rule conformance would be cost-effective. If users were unlikely to understand or use such tags, then why expend limited resources on their derivation? Furthermore, our experience in conducting the empirical field work required to develop the instrument highlighted the difficulty of finding sufficient numbers of participants to satisfy the recommendations for the statistical technique used (i.e. factor analysis in that case, which requires a large number of participants for statistical significance). Similar concerns in the current study emphasized the importance of carefully selecting the types of tags to be tested to ensure that they are likely to be understandable to users, useful for decision-making, and practical to implement. Thus, if there was an inexpensive way to determine in advance the types of DQ tags most likely to be useful for decision-making, we could potentially reduce the number of participants required for the experiments.

The second question raised was with respect to the specific DQ tag representation and decision-making interface to use in DQ tagging experiments. We reasoned that the best design of experimental materials was one that was understandable to decision-makers and compatible with decision-making processes in practice. In contrast, an "ineffective" design could potentially negatively impact the experimental validity of DQ tagging experiments and increase the chance that experimental observations were a result of inappropriate experimental materials rather than manipulation of independent variables. These considerations added further motivation to find an inexpensive way to canvas user opinions on the design of the planned DQ tagging experiments.

These questions led us to consider the possibility of applying interaction design techniques to the design of DQ tagging experiments. Because such techniques are typically heuristic in nature and involve only a small number of participants, they are relatively inexpensive to conduct. Interaction design techniques range from techniques intended to solicit user feedback on design requirements or prototypes to others that involve the users as equal partners in design, but have in common an emphasis on the importance of user consultation in design. The potential benefits of interaction design techniques are especially relevant to the design of DQ tags, since their novelty (with respect to common business practice) means that their design cannot generally be guided by precedent.

By defining a set of sub-goals based on the issues discussed above, it is possible to identify the most relevant interaction design technique(s) for each. Four sub-goals are defined as a pre-requisite to designing the DQ tagging experiments:

1. to understand decision-making in practice;
2. to find effective DQ tag semantics;
3. to find effective DQ tag representations, and;
4. to query the effectiveness of the proposed decision-making interface based on Shanks and Tansley's study [12] in the context of the planned DQ tagging experiments.

In the current context, considerations of tag and interface design *effectiveness* are specifically with respect to their understandability to the user and relevance to (including compatibility with) common business practice. After consideration of a number of different interaction design techniques, we concluded that the two techniques most relevant to these goals were contextual inquiry and participatory design workshops.

Contextual inquiry is the interrogatory component of contextual design, a customer-centred design approach described in [19]. Contextual inquiry is based on the premise that the most effective way to identify and understand user requirements is in the actual work context. This technique involves on-site interviews of users, while they perform their work tasks in their actual work environment. Thus, contextual inquiry is well suited to addressing the goal of understanding decision-making in practice - an important prerequisite to the design of DQ tagging experiments.

In contrast, participatory design techniques [16,18,21] involve users as equal partners in design using paper-based prototyping and are particularly suitable for custom-built systems for a small group of people [18, p215]. This technique typically involves a workshop consisting of four successive stages:

1. participant introductions;
2. background tutorials, e.g. demonstrating the domain(s) of interest;
3. a collaborative design session using a set of system components (fixed or modifiable) and use scenarios pre-defined by developers and users respectively, and;
4. a final walkthrough of the resultant design and design decisions.

Participatory design workshops can be applied to the design of the DQ tagging experiments, including both DQ tags and the decision-making interface. However, since the use of DQ tags in decision-making is novel; further questions arose as to how they should be introduced to workshop participants during the tutorial training session. Presenting a single tag design could bias the subsequent design process; however, introducing too many design options could be confusing. In the same way, the novelty of DQ tag use in practice could complicate efforts to define realistic use scenarios. As a result, we decided to modify the initial contextual inquiry sessions with an exploratory segment that could provide guidance in creating workshop materials (i.e. pre-defined system components and use scenarios, initial tutorials).

In the modified contextual inquiry, an exploratory segment is added after the standard contextual inquiry session. This ordering ensures that the exploratory segment will not bias the initial demonstration of current decision-making practice. Users are first asked to reflect on possible ways to improve the demonstrated decision-making task using DQ tags and then asked to review a proposed experimental design. By asking users about DQ tags and experimental design in their actual work context rather than an artificially introduced context, we expect that users would find it easier to articulate their concerns and opinions, as discussed earlier in Section 1. Furthermore, soliciting user opinions in a variety of actual decision-making contexts (as compared to the workshop or empirical study) may offer additional insights.

In the next section, we describe our planned interaction design approach in more detail, review the current status of this work, and discuss preliminary results that confirm the value of this approach.

3. Using Interaction Design for DQ Tagging Experiments

We first discuss the modified contextual inquiry sessions. In the context of a single role such as that of decision-maker, recommendations are for six to ten interviews across a variety of work contexts [19, p76]. Potential subjects must regularly use an on-line system and data collection (e.g. database, data warehouse, spreadsheet) to make a multi-criteria based and data-intensive decision. They must be able to demonstrate that process on-site. Since prior DQ tagging research has found that decision-makers with professional experience are more likely to use tags [11], we further restrict interviewees to those with professional experience.

In the standard part of the interview, users are first asked to give an overview of the decision they will demonstrate and the data and software used to make the decision. As they demonstrate the decision-making process, we interrupt as necessary to ask for explanations of what they are doing and why, for demonstrations of problems experienced and how they are solved, and for on-going confirmation of our interpretations based on observation and enquiry. In addition to the standard questions asked in contextual inquiry, we additionally ask them what strategies they are using to make the decision, e.g. attribute (decision criterion) or record (decision alternative) based strategies.

In the exploratory segment, we first ask them what changes might be made to improve their decision-making process. In particular, we ask whether and what types of additional data quality information might help them make the decision, and how it might be of help (e.g. in making a better decision, in confidence in the decision made). These questions give feedback on the types of DQ tags (i.e. tag semantics or meaning) that they believe would be useful in their specific work context. We then ask them how they would like such information displayed—asking them for suggestions and showing them possible alternatives. This question relates to the representation of DQ tags (with respect to tag name, value, and explanation) that is most effective given their work context. The interviewees are then shown the decision-making interface used in the computer-based DQ tagging study by Shanks and Tansley [12] (see Figure 1), as this software interface is potentially suitable for re-use in the planned computer-based DQ tagging study. Interviewees are asked to give feedback on the understandability and usability of the interface. Finally, they are asked to review their answers to previous questions on DQ tag design in the context of the experimental interface and rental property application domain.

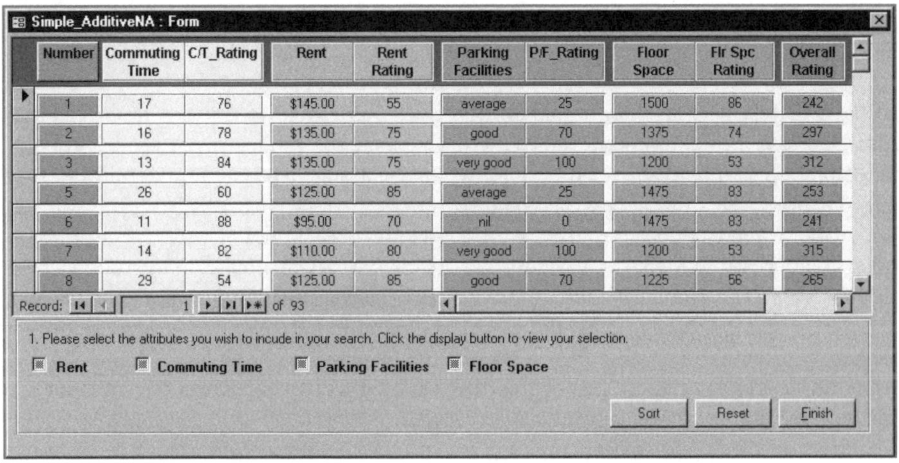

Figure 1. Proposed Interface for Additive Decision Strategy based on Shanks and Tansley [12]

Results from the contextual interviews will be used to guide the design of materials for subsequent participatory design workshops. Sessions of 4-6 participants will be repeated until saturation (i.e. evidence of repetition in feedback). As in the interviews, participants must be decision-makers with professional experience. Additionally, they must have at least some minimal experience with the domain used in the workshop (i.e. property selection) prior to their participation. In line with [12], the workshop usage scenarios are based on selecting a set of rental properties to visit from a relational database using an interface with built-in decision strategy. Tutorials on the use of DQ tags to make such a decision will be given for different decision strategies. Participants will then be asked to collaboratively design the interface for such a decision and to explain their choices. The results of this exercise will be used to guide the design of the planned DQ tagging experiments and cognitive process tracing study.

The contextual inquiry interviews are currently in progress, with five completed to date. These interviews involve a diverse set of organizational roles (of the interviewee), decision-making tasks, decision-making domains, and type of on-line decision-making software used. Preliminary results suggest that, in general, there is considerable consensus in user preferences even across a variety of decision-making contexts. Although there has been some variation in the preferred representation of DQ tag values depending on the specific application domain, there has been consistent agreement with respect to issues of DQ tag semantics (i.e. relevant DQ tag types) and proposed experimental design despite the range of work contexts examined thus far. To illustrate, we discuss in detail the feedback on DQ tags and experimental design in the planned experimental context of rental property selection.

Every decision-maker interviewed to date has agreed on the type of DQ tag they considered the most relevant to rental property selection. Of the three categories of data quality discussed in Section 2.1 (i.e. data conformance to rules, correspondence to the real-world, usefulness for task), interviewees felt that potential renters would be most interested in the degree of real-world correspondence. There was unanimous agreement that the value of this tag (for the rental property domain) was best represented by a value range indicated symbolically, whereas most previous DQ tagging experiments have used a single numerical figure to represent DQ.

Each interviewee independently raised the same issue with respect to the understandability of the proposed decision-making interface for rental property selection. In common with other DQ tagging studies to date, this interface included numerical ratings that show the relative desirability of properties with respect to criteria that have different types (i.e. domains) of values (e.g. price in dollars, floor space in square meters). For example, a relatively high rental price for a given rental property (i.e. compared to that of other properties) would be associated with a lower desirability rating for price. This rating can then be directly compared to the ratings with respect to floor space, whereas otherwise users would have to compare dollar values (for price) to square meters (for floor space). However, decision-makers found these ratings very confusing and felt that they should be omitted. They preferred to make their own judgements of desirability. Thus, the use of contextual interviews has helped identify a problem with explicitly rating the characteristics of decision alternatives—a technique commonly used in previous DQ tagging research, with consequent implications for the degree of validity of previously published results.

Based on these preliminary findings, the planned experimental interface in future DQ tagging work would be modified to omit numerical ratings (i.e. of criteria values), to include a DQ tag based on real-world correspondence, and to represent DQ tag values symbolically using ranges in order to improve the understandability and relevance of the experimental design. Thus, indications of the benefits of using interaction design techniques to guide design of DQ tagging experiments are already evident.

4. Conclusion

This paper highlights the importance of usability and relevance considerations in the design of materials for DQ tagging experiments and proposes a novel means of addressing such concerns using interaction design techniques. Such techniques have particular relevance for the design of DQ tags given their novelty in the context of actual business practice and the consequent lack of real-world precedents for tag design. The use of contextual enquiry anchors the design of experimental materials in the work setting of decision-makers and helps understand decision-making in practice. The use of participatory design involves decision-makers as partners in the design of experimental materials. Preliminary results show that the experimental design has benefited considerably from the contextual inquiry interviews. We argue that the use of interaction design techniques has improved the usability and relevance of our experimental materials and thus provides better support for experimental validity. Although the specific focus of this paper is on design of DQ tagging experiments, we believe that the principles involved and the proposed approach have wider applicability to research in decision support systems and to experimental design in general.

Acknowledgements

An Australian Research Council discovery grant was used to fund this project.

References

[1]   BALLOU, D.P., and PAZER, H.L, "Modeling data and process quality multi-input multi-output information systems", *Management Science*, 31:2, 1985, 150-162
[2]   PRICE, R., and SHANKS, G. "A Semiotic Information Quality Framework", *Proceedings of the IFIP International Conference on Decision Support Systems (DSS2004)*, Prato, Italy, 2004, 658-672
[3]   PRICE, R. and SHANKS, G., "A Semiotic Information Quality Framework: Development and Comparative Analysis", *Journal of Information Technology*, 20:2, 2005, 88-102
[4]   SHANKS, G., and DARKE, P., "Understanding Metadata and Data Quality in a Data Warehouse", *Australian Computer Journal*, 30:4, 1998, 122-128
[5]   STRONG, D.M., LEE, Y.W., and WANG, R.Y., "Data Quality in Context", *Communications of the ACM*, 40:5, 1997, 103-110
[6]   WANG, R. Y. and STRONG, D. M. "Beyond accuracy: What data quality means to data consumers", *J. Management Information Systems*. 12:4, 1996, 5-34
[7]   WAND, Y. and WANG, R., "Anchoring Data Quality Dimensions in Ontological Foundations", *Communications of the ACM*, 39:11, 1996, 86-95
[8]   PAYNE, J.W., "Task Complexity and Contigent Processing in Decision Making: An Information Search and Protocol Analysis", *Organisational Behaviour and Human Performance*, 16, 1976, 366-387
[9]   PAYNE, J.W., BETTMAN, J.R., and JOHNSON, E.J., *The Adaptive Decision Maker*, Cambridge, Cambridge University Press, 1993
[10] CHENGULAR-SMITH, I.N., BALLOU, D., and PAZER, H.L., "The Impact of Data Quality Information on Decision Making: An Exploratory Analysis", *IEEE Transactions on Knowledge and Data Engineering*, 11:6, 1999
[11] FISHER, C., CHENGULAR-SMITH, I.N, and BALLOU, D., "The Impact of Experience and Time on the Use of Data Quality Information in Decision Making", *Information Systems Research*, 14:2, 2003, 170-188
[12] SHANKS, G. and TANSLEY, E., "Data Quality Tagging and Decision Outcomes: An Experimental Study", *Proc. IFIP Working Group 8.3 Conference on Decision Making and Decision Support in the Internet Age*, Cork, July, 2002, 399-410
[13] PRICE, R. and SHANKS, G., "Data Quality and Decision-making", in F. Burstein and C. Holsapple (eds.) *Handbook on Decision Support Systems*, Berlin/Heidelberg, Springer Verlag, 2008, 65-82
[14] EVEN, A., SHANKARANARAYANAN, G., and WATTS, S., "Enhancing Decision Making with Process Metadata: Theoretical Framework, Research Tool, and Exploratory Examination", *Proc. of the 39th Hawaii International Conference on System Sciences (HICSS2006)*, Hawaii, 2006, 1-10
[15] EPPLER, M.J., "The Concept of Information Quality: An Interdisciplinary Evaluation of Recent Information Quality Frameworks", *Studies in Communication Sciences*, 1, 2001, 167-182
[16] PREECE, J., ROGERS, Y., and SHARP, H., *Interaction Design: Beyond Human-Computer Interaction*, New York, John Wiley and Sons, Inc., 2002

[17] HOLTZBLATT, K. and JONES, S., "Conducting and Analyzing a Contextual Interview (Excerpt)", *Readings in Human-Computer Interaction: Towards the Year 2000*, San Francisco, Morgan Kaufmann Publishers, Inc., 2000, 241-253

[18] BENYON, D., TURNER, P., and TURNER, S., *Designing Interactive Systems*, Harlow, Addison-Wesley, 2005

[19] BEYER, H. and HOLTZBLATT, K., *Contextual Design: Defining Customer-Centered Systems*, San Francisco, Morgan Kaufmann Publishers, Inc., 1998

[20] PRICE, R., NEIGER, D and SHANKS, G. *Developing a Measurement Instrument for Subjective Aspects of Information Quality*, Communications of the Association for Information Systems (CAIS), 22, Article 3, 2008, 49-74

[21] GAFFNEY, G., "http://www.ideal-group.org/usability/Participatory_Design.htm", accessed 31/07/2007, 1-3

Collaborative Decision Making: Perspectives and Challenges
P. Zaraté et al. (Eds.)
IOS Press, 2008

Provision of External Data for DSS, BI, and DW by Syndicate Data Suppliers

Mattias STRAND[a] and Sven A. CARLSSON[b]

[a]*School of Humanities and Informatics, University of Skövde, Sweden*
E-mail: mattias.strand@his.se
[b]*Informatics and Institute of Economic Research, School of Economics and*
Management, Lund University, Lund, Sweden
E-mail: sven.carlsson@ics.lu.se

Abstract. In order to improve business performance and competitiveness it is important for firms to use data from their external environment. More and more attention is directed towards data originating external to the organization, i.e., external data. A firm can either collect this data or cooperate with an external data provider. We address the latter case and focus syndicate data suppliers (SDSs). They are the most common sources when incorporating external data into business intelligence, DSS, and DW solutions. SDSs are specialized in collecting, compiling, refining, and selling data. We provide a detailed description regarding the business idea of syndicate data suppliers and how they conduct their business, as well as a description of the industry of syndicate data suppliers. As such, the paper increases the understanding for external data incorporation and the possibility for firms to cooperate with syndicate data suppliers.

Keywords. Syndicate data suppliers, data warehousing, external data, DSS, BI

1. Introduction

The external environment is a significant contingency for organizations. The criticality of external data has been stressed for a long time [1]. Today, when organizations have to "sense-and-response"-operate faster and better than competitors the use of external data is a critical organizational issue [2]. In the last years the importance of 'competing on analytics' has been stressed. It is considered as one of few ways for organizations to compete. Said Davenport, "Organizations are competing on analytics not just because they can—business today is awash in data and data crunchers—but also because they should. At a time when firms in many industries offer similar products and use comparable technologies, business processes are among the last remaining points of differentiation" [3]. External data is an important part of competing on analytics. Hence, it has become increasingly important for firms to monitor the competitive forces affecting their business and competitiveness [4,5]. As a consequence, more and more attention has been directed towards data originating external to the own organizations, i.e., *external data* [2]. We see also an increased interest in the literature and many scholars stress the benefits of using external data. The following quotations illustrate the perceived benefits of incorporating external data:

- Oglesby claims that "Companies who use external data systems have a strategic advantage over those who don't, and the scope of that advantage is growing as we move deeper into the information age" [6, p. 3],
- Stedman states that "external data helps us understand our business in the context of the greater world" [7, p. 2], and
- Inmon argues that "the comparison of internal and external data allows management to see the forest for the trees" [8, p. 272].

External data is used in strategic, managerial and operational business and decision processes. In alignment, a majority of companies incorporate their external data from organizations specialized in collecting, compiling, refining, and selling data [9,10]. Kimball [11] refers to these specialized and commercial data suppliers as *syndicate data suppliers* (SDSs).

The research area of external data incorporation is currently expanding and different aspects of external data incorporation are addressed. In acquiring external data, a firm can either collect its external data or cooperate with an external data provider. We address the latter case and focus on syndicate data suppliers (SDSs). As noted above, most organizations acquire their external data from SDSs. The supplier side of the supplier-consumer constellation of external data provisions is only fragmentarily covered in the literature. Therefore, we intend to provide a description of SDSs' business environment, the industry they are competing in, and their core business process. The motive for describing the supplier side is two-folded. Firstly, it fills a gap in the current DSS, BI, and DW literature and it contributes in making current research regarding external data incorporation more complete. Secondly, in describing the SDSs, organizations may increase their ordering and informed buying capabilities and find better ways to cooperate with SDSs.

The material creating the foundation for this work originates from five interview studies, as well as two extensive literature reviews. The interview studies covered: data warehouse (DW) consultants (two studies), consumer organizations (two studies), and one study towards SDSs. The studies were originally conducted within the scope of establishing a state of practice description regarding external data incorporation into data warehouses. The total number of interviews comprised 34 different respondents, all representing unique companies. The distribution of the respondents was: 12 DW consultants, 13 consumer organizations (banking, automotive, media, groceries, petroleum, and medical), and 9 SDSs. The interviews lasted on an average for 75 minutes and the transcripts ranged from 1370 to 7334 words (4214 words on average). Here, it is important to state that although the SDSs were, naturally, able to give the most detailed information regarding their industry, the two other groups of respondents contributed with details and aspects not mentioned by the SDSs. Although the relevant literature is sparse, a thorough literature review was done.

The remainder of the paper is organized as follows. The next section presents different ways for firms to acquire external data. This is followed by two sections presenting: 1) the business idea of SDSs, and 2) the industry of SDSs. The final section presents conclusions and recommendations for further research.

2. Enhancing DSS, BI, and DW Through External Data

The literature accounts for two main directions related to the concept external data. Firstly, external data may concern data crossing organizational boundaries, i.e. the data is acquired from outside the organization's boundary [e.g. 11]. Secondly, external data may also refer to any data stored or maintained outside a particular database of interest, i.e. the data is external to the database but internal from an organizational point of view [e.g. 12]. Since this work focuses on data which is exchanged between organizations, the direction accounted for by e.g. Kimball [11] was adopted. In defining such data, the definition suggested by Devlin [13] was adopted. According to Devlin external data is: "Business data (and its associated metadata) originating from one business that may be used as part of either the operational or the informational processes of another business" [13, p. 135].

External data may be acquired from different types of suppliers (or sources). Strand et al. [9, p. 2466] account for the most comprehensive categorization of different suppliers. According to them, external data may be acquired from the following suppliers (or sources):

- Syndicate data suppliers
- Statistical institutes
- Industry organizations
- County councils and municipalities
- The Internet
- Business partners
- Bi-product data suppliers.

The different types of suppliers are briefly described. *Syndicate data suppliers* are organizations with the very core business model of collecting, compiling, refining, and selling data to other organizations. Since they are the main focus of this paper, they will be extensively described below. Different types of governmental *statistical institutes* are delivering statistics concerning e.g. the labor market, trade, population, and welfare. Some of the data delivered from statistical institutes may be acquired for free based on legislative rights, but occasionally these institutes take a commission for processing the data and for consulting. *Industry organizations* are also delivering data. Naturally, this data is specific and therefore often only interesting for a particular industry or even a subsection of an industry. Often, these industry organizations deliver industry averages concerning, e.g., performance and sales, for comparisons with internal measures. *County councils and municipalities* may also deliver data. The data they deliver is similar to what governmental statistical institutes deliver, but narrower in its scope due to their geographic boundaries. The *Internet* is considered a fairly unexplored source of data. Scholars have describe different applications for acquiring and sharing external data from web pages [14,15]. For example, the following applications are found: product pricing via competitors' web pages, preparation of a marketing campaign based on weather forecasts, and personnel planning based on promoted events advertised on the Internet. A problem is that the data quality of the data acquired from the Internet is questionable and therefore many organizations hesitate in applying Internet data as a base-line for decision making [16]. *Business partners* are also possible external data sources. Normally when data is exchanged, the organizations are cooperating and the data may therefore be very specific. Therefore, this specific type of data supplier should not be considered as an "open" supplier for everyone else to buy from. Instead, business partner is a very specific type of external data supplier. In addition, although the data is external according to the definition introduced above, it may be value-chain internal, making it even more difficult to, from a business perspective, consider it as an external data supplier. Finally, Strand et al. [9] account for *bi-product data suppliers*. These organizations are generating large amounts of data as a result of their core businesses. This data may be interesting for other organizations to procure. Strand et al. [9] present an example adopted from Asbrand [17], describing how the National Data Corporation/Health Information Services (NDC/HIS) in Phoenix, U.S., sells its medical data to, e.g., advertising agencies and stock analysts.

3. The Business Model of Syndicate Data Suppliers

As said above, the SDSs are organizations specialized in collecting, compiling, refining, and selling data to other organizations. To further detail the description of the SDSs and to make the description of their business model more vivid, it is important to illustrate the ways in which the SDSs conduct their business. Broadly, the SDSs sell data for two different types of applications.

First, the SDSs sell data via on-line services. To exemplify: *A customer wants to by a cellular phone at a local store. To make sure that the customer is likely to pay the monthly bills from the network provider, the salesperson checks the customer's credit-ability, by sending his/her civic registration number to an online-service catered for by a SDS. Based on the result of the request (absence or existence of registered payment complaints), the salesperson is allowed or not to proceed the business transaction.* This category of syndicate data is normally related to business functions at an operative level and may be characterized as small and singular information units regarding a particular organization or person. The data may concern, e.g., postal addresses, delayed payments, or annual incomes. The coverage of the data is very narrow and since it is distributed via the Internet, the data format is more or less standardized. Since the data is needed when a certain situation arise, it is normally acquired on-demand, although the service per se often is based upon a contract with a SDS.

Second, the SDSs sell their data in batches and distribute the data via different distribution technologies, for example, FTP-nodes, web hotels, CD-ROMs, and e-mail attachments, to customers for database integration. To exemplify: *Company A experiences problems in establishing reasonable credit payment times for their customers. Therefore, they procure credit ratings (CR) of organizations from a SDS. Due to the volume of the customer stock, it is not considered feasible to state an online request for every customer. Instead, Company A decides to subscribe to the data on a monthly basis and integrate it internally. The credit rating is ranging from 1 to 5, in which 5 indicates a customer with a superior credibility, whereas 1 is a serious warning flag. These values are derived values created in a data enrichment process by the SDS. By combing the CR with the internal credit time, standardized to 4 weeks, Company A may automatically recalculate the credit time for each customer. The automatic recalculation updates the credit time attribute as follows: CR 1 = 4–4 weeks; CR 2 = 4–3 weeks; CR 3 = 4–2 weeks; CR 4 = 4–1 week; and CR 5 = 4±0 week.* This category of data is normally the category of syndicate data associated with tactic and strategic decision-making. Such batch data is also rather complex and comprises large data sets which may involve hundreds of attributes and millions of rows of data.

Of these two categories of applications, the latter one is the one growing most. During the last decade, most SDSs have expanded the number of products/services related to batch deliveries. There are several reasons for this growth pattern, including decreased costs for data storage and the increased use of the Internet as a high-capacity data delivery channel. However, the respondent said that the most important reason is simply an increased competition, forcing the SDSs to develop their businesses and expand the services they deliver. The competition is mostly industry-internal, but other types of organizations have started to sell data. For example, governmental agencies are traditionally, from a SDS point of view, one of the most common sources for raw data. However, nowadays these agencies have also started to sell data, since it has become a way of letting data handling and management carry its own costs. The strong competition naturally influences the pricing of the online data and most suppliers claimed that the pricing of the data they sell is under a strong price pressure. For example, one SDS-respondent claimed that: *"the competition is very strong [...] and the price for the raw data is fast approaching the marginal cost"*.

Based on the interviews, it seems likely that batches or services with a specific focus on integrated solutions will increase in the future, since it has turned out to become one of the few application areas still expanding and where there will be market-shares to acquire. To exemplify, one SDS-respondent claimed: *"We notice an increased demand for data deliveries that are not in the shape of traditional online services, but are integrated toward different types of solutions, such as DWs, and I would like to say that these data integrating solutions is an area that is constantly growing and will continue to grow"*. In order to deal with the increasing competition, the suppliers strive towards finding novel ways of sharpening their competitive edge. Some examples that emerged during the interviews can be used to illustrate this. First, in general the SDSs collaborate with their customers in more formalized ways. Some of the SDSs claimed to take a much more active role in the actual integration of the batch data and the customers' internal data management. One initiative concerned a *customer master dimension* in a DW. The SDS stored the dimension in its internal systems and refreshed the data periodically. The dimension was then mirrored towards the customer's star-schemas and analysis tools. Consequently, besides eventual security issues, the customer was not concerned with the normal problems related to the data integration. Second, the SDSs sell data to each other, in order to acquire more complete data sets or in order to acquire data that would complement the data they already maintain and sell. Third, the SDSs adapt to new technological innovations in order to facilitate data acquisition, transformation, and distribution. For example, XML is granted a lot of interest by a majority of the suppliers and is considered as the next major trend within the industry, due to its abilities to facilitate automatic data extraction, refinement, and distribution. One respondent (SDSs interview study) stated that: *"XML in combination with the Internet is, for us that have been writing communication protocols, like a dream come true. It is a complete dream"*. Also the customers stressed the importance of XML, although they strongly indicated that the SDSs are the beneficiaries of XML. Said one interviewee (banking interview study): *"They [the SDSs] will most certainly take advantage of the cost reductions that XML may contribute with, but I would be very surprised if that is reflected on the invoice the send us"*. The results of the interview study towards the SDSs indicate that there is still much work remaining for the SDSs, until they may take full advantage of XML. Furthermore, in conjunction with XML, the SDSs also expressed an interest in web services. A shift to the standards of XML allows the SDSs to make the interface of the servers available via different types of web services. In relation to XML and web services it is also worth mentioning that the SDSs expressed a large interest in UDDI.[1] By registering in UDDI the SDSs could expose themselves, their industrial belongings, as well as, their product portfolios.

In conjunction with the fact that the SDSs claimed to see a minor shift in their business model, from solely online data delivery, into a mixture of services and products, online, as well as, in batches, another interesting phenomenon arose. Some of the SDSs claimed the pricing of the batch data to be very difficult and something that may require novel ways of cooperating with the customers. In contrast to online data, which is rather straightforward to price, batch data is a much more complex to price—the discussions in Shapiro and Varian [18] shows the problems in pricing complex digitalized services. The sales contracts of batch data may be negotiated several times with respect to its content, in which the customer may decrease the data amounts required as a means for lowering the costs. At the same time, the SDSs have to conduct costly efforts in selecting the appropriate data from their internal sources and compile it according to the customers' demands. If solely applying a pricing procedure based on data amounts, the supplier would have to conduct a lot of knowledge-requiring work in selecting only the appropriate data, but only getting paid for relatively small amounts of delivered data. To exemplify, one of the respondents in the SDS interview study provided the following statement to emphasize the pricing dilemma of batch data: "*Not long ago, we hade a customer that requested a XML-file with every company in City A, that is a joint-stock company and has a profit that exceeds 10 percentage of the turnover. This type of request is common, but we often negotiate the price individually for each customer. In this case, we calculated the price of the data set based on the number of data rows. In the price, we also distributed the costs for selecting, sorting, and compiling the data per row. The customer found the price to high and since the price was based on number of rows, she also added a selection on companies with at least 40 employees. Thereby, the number of rows were drastically reduced and consequently, also the price. However, for us it became problematic, since it meant more work for us but less money in compensation. How do you make it obvious for the customers that they are paying for information as well as exformation?*"

4. The Industry of Syndicate Data Suppliers

To further describe the industry of SDSs, besides the description of the business environment introduced above, a starting point could be to categorize the SDSs. In making such a categorization, several different perspectives may be applied. First, the SDSs may be categorized according to the coverage of the data they sell. From this perspective, we have identified two main categories: 1) SDSs selling economical data, and 2) SDSs selling demographic data. Since most suppliers are capable of delivering both types of data, this categorization does not contribute to any larger extent in distinguishing the SDSs.

Secondly, the SDSs may also be categorized according to the products/services they sell. The analysis of the material reveals that the suppliers sell three broad types of

---

[1] UDDI (Universal Description, Discovery and Integration) is a platform-independent, XML-based registry for businesses worldwide to list themselves on the Internet. It is an open industry initiative enabling businesses to publish service listings and discover each other and define how the services or software applications interact over the Internet.

products/services. The most elementary and common type of products/services encompasses rather straightforward data on a detailed level, covering individual persons or organizations, e.g. address information, payment complaints, incomes, and credit ratings. The next, and somewhat more advanced type, encompasses models for different types of valuations or estimations, e.g. credit ratings, scoring models, and prospect identification. This type of data requires more advanced transformations and refinements of the "raw" data. In the third type, the data suppliers sell data from the two previous mentioned types combined with tailor-made services. The third type represents the most advanced products/services and is often the most costly for the customers. Still, most SDSs are capable of delivering all three types of products/services. Therefore, it becomes a rather indecisive way of categorizing the SDSs.

Third, the SDSs may be categorized according to their role or position within the SDS industry. Studying the details of the industry reveals two subtypes of SDSs. First of all, some SDSs are acting in a monopoly situation, commissioned by a governmental authority. Normally, these *monopoly SDSs* have a specific responsibility to maintain and provide certain data contents or services, considered as nationally important. Acting in a monopoly situation may be very beneficial, but a monopoly may also restrict the SDS. Since they are under a commission, they may also be regulated with respect to which data they are allowed to store and sell. In addition, since they are under a commission, new products or services must be approved and therefore, they might not be able to respond to novel customer needs as fast as other SDSs.

The other subtype is SDSs retailing other SDSs' data or services. The *retailing SDSs* sell their own data and services, as well as other SDSs' data and services, allowing customers to combine different data and services from different suppliers. This makes the industry rather complex, since two suppliers may be cooperating and competing at the same time, even with rather similar products or services. Still, this is the most straightforward way of categorizing the SDSs.

5. The Core Business Process of Syndicate Data Suppliers

The analysis shows that the core business process of the SDSs comprises the following three activities: 1) *acquire data from data sources*, 2) *integrate, refine, and enrich data*, and 3) *sell and deliver data*. Below, each process activity is described.

5.1. Acquire Data from Data Sources

SDSs acquire their raw data from a variety of different sources. The three main suppliers of data are: 1) governmental agencies, 2) other SDSs, 3) and bi-product data suppliers. In addition, SDSs also buy data from consumer organizations, but this is quite rarely. The data is acquired via the Internet from, e.g., FTP-nodes and Web-hotels. In addition, if necessary, the SDSs also acquire the data from their suppliers on DVD/CD-ROMs or as e-mail attachments. E-mail attachments are only a complementary data distribution technology, due to the limited capabilities of sending large data sets.

5.2. Integrate, Refine, and Enrich Data

The acquired data is integrated into the SDSs' internal databases. The databases may vary from simple relational databases to complex data warehouse systems storing terabytes of data. Integrating, refining and enriching the data is the both the hard work and the value creation work for the SDSs. Since they have the data as their major corporate asset, a high quality data is a business cornerstone for the SDSs, or as one respondent (SDS study) expressed it: *"Without high quality data, you may equally well go and apply for liquidation, so tough is the competition. High quality data is not a sales argument, it is rather a lifeline"*. The results of the empirical studies also illustrate that the customers nowadays has become more data quality sensitive and demand high data quality. Therefore, the data quality refinements conducted by the SDSs will further increase in extent. Currently, the SDSs conduct manual, as well as, automatic data quality verifications. The manual data quality verifications may be to phone private persons and asking them for the spelling of their first- and surnames (names is one of the most difficult data elements to verify, due to the wide variety of spellings). Since this is very time-consuming, and thereby costly, these types of data quality verifications are conducted on a random sample basis. The automatic controls may range from, e.g., verifying check-sums of the data records, to verifications of the spelling of city names and probability tests of monthly incomes. To be more precise, a city indicated as either Neu York or New Yorc is automatically translated into New York. However, as much of the data that the SDSs compile and refine is acquired from governmental agencies, with loads of manual input, spelling errors are rather common and may be more troublesome to correct than the above examples. As a consequence, the SDSs have started to apply more and more advanced linear, as well as non-linear techniques, for verifying the quality of the data they sell.

The empirical studies also suggest that the consumers of syndicate data and even private persons have become more aware of the importance of correct data, and therefore, the SDSs have also notice an increased interaction with their customers For example, the SDSs are contacted by customers pointing out the existence of errors in the data. A few SDSs also indicated that they procure external support from data quality verifiers to control the quality of the data. In addition, most respondents pinpointed the importance of refining and adding a value to the data they sell. Therefore, the SDSs constantly strive towards developing new services, based upon different refinements, which may contribute to increased customer value. The material also revealed two common approaches for developing these services. First, the SDSs identify new data or combinations of data that have not previously been exploited, but which may contribute to consumer value. Based upon this new data, they develop services which they try to sell to their customer. Second, the SDSs receive requests from consumer organizations for data or services which they currently are not delivering. Based upon these requests, they try to develop services and extend them with further beneficial features or data in order to enhance the services offered to the user organizations.

5.3. Selling and Delivering Data

Most SDSs had internal resources for identifying prospects and selling data or services. However, a few SDSs also outsourced these initiatives to organizations specialized in marketing and sales. The study indicates that the SDSs also collaborate with hardware and software vendors for identifying prospects and establish business relations. Analyzing the collaboration with hardware vendors, two different collaborations can be identified. First, the SDSs and the hardware vendors collaborate in development projects, in which the SDSs are taking an active part and populate the customers' solutions with combinations of internal and external data. Second, many hardware vendors have informal collaborations with SDSs, suggesting a specific SDS for their customer organization. With respect to the software vendors, a few SDS respondents indicated that they cooperate, or plan to cooperate, with software vendors on formalized certificates. The underlying idea was that the SDSs and the software vendors agree upon different formats, structures, and representations of the data, meaning that a consumer organization following a certain certificate does not have to transform the external data being incorporated into the internal systems. The sales argument was that the customer could drastically reduce the resources spent on data transformations. Furthermore, a majority of the SDSs applied a traditional approach of data delivery, i.e. the SDSs distribute the data to the user organizations via the data distribution technologies noted above. Normally, the customers are responsible for the integration of the external data into their internal systems. However, in order to decrease the data distribution and data transformation problems of the customer organizations, some of the SDSs have decided to use another approach. Instead of delivering the data to their customers, they acquire the customers' internal data and integrate it with the data they sell. Thereafter, they deliver the enhanced internal data back to the customers. Finally, and as indicated previously, some SDSs sell their data via retailing SDSs.

6. Conclusions

In order to conclude the description of the SDSs, a number of key characteristics of the SDSs are worth mentioning. The SDSs are:

- *Working in a highly competitive environment*: they are exposed to a strong competition, both within the industry and from other actors in the domain. All respondents claimed that they are under a strong competition (of course the SDS in a monopoly situation had a diverging opinion) and that the competition does not only come from other SDSs, but also from the governmental agencies, selling their data directly to the consumers.
- *Densely interrelated*: they are collaborating with a lot of different actors, including e.g. other SDSs, outsourced sales and marketing companies, and DW consultants. The collaboration also seems to increase, since the SDSs constantly strive towards finding novel ways of increasing their sales amounts. This is utmost important for them, since the pricing of the data caters for low margins to make profit on.
- *Highly data quality aware*: data quality is a prerequisite for being able to survive on the market and therefore the SDSs spend a lot of resources verifying the quality of the data they acquire and sell. The manual data quality controls are very costly, but most SDSs stated that it is a cost that must be taken, for being able to assure the consumers a high data quality.
- *Working under strong legislations*: the SDSs are under a strong pressure from different regulatory boards. State laws and regulations must be followed and they hinder the SDSs from, for example, acquire certain data or combining certain data into novel services. Thereby, it becomes hard for the SDSs to de-

velop novel services. It forces them to compete with other means, such as support offered, data quality, and project collaborations.

- *Data refinement- and data enrichment driven*: in order to survive and sustain their competitive edges, the suppliers are spending a lot of resources on refining and enriching the raw data. To illustrate, a respondent in the SDS-study said: "*we do not want do be considered as only a bucket of raw data, we want to be considered as a contributory business partner that enriches the customers internal data with our own indexes, calculations, and ratings*".

7. External Data Provision: Quo Vadis?

Firms are increasingly relying on external data for 'competing on analytics'. Firms can acquire external data from syndicate data suppliers (SDSs). In this paper we have looked at SDSs by describing the business environment of SDSs, the industry of SDSs, and the core business process of SDSs. As noted, the knowledge of SDSs is very limited and fragmented. Although, our study is a step in increasing our knowledge about SDSs, further research addressing different issues is needed.

In this paper, we have addressed the supplier side of the supplier-consumer constellation. Future research could address the consumer side as well as the supplier-consumer relationship. The former could address technical, organizational, and motivational issues related to the incorporation of acquired data from SDSs as well as studying the impact of the use of external data on competing on analytics. Such studies can use different theories, for example, the absorptive capacity as a dynamic capability theory [20]. Absorptive capacity is a firm's ability to "…recognize the value of new, external information, assimilate it, and apply it to commercial ends" [20]. The supplier-consumer relationship can, for example, be studied from a network perspective [19].

Changes in businesses and business environments will affect organizations' requirements for external data and will lead to new business challenges for SDSs. For example, Carlsson and El Sawy [2] suggest that organizations and decision-makers in turbulent and high-velocity environments are able to manage at least five tensions. The tensions are [2]:

- The tension between the need for quick decisions and the need for analytical decision processes.
- The tension around empowering middle managers and management teams at various organizational levels in the midst of powerful and impatient top executives.
- The tension around the managerial need for action and the need for the safest execution of decisions that may be bold and risky.
- The tension between programmed quick action learning loops and the increased requirement for emergence and improvisation.
- The tension around expending effort to eliminate the digital divide with other organizations versus finding expedient ways to communicate through heterogeneous digital infrastructures.

The successful management of the tensions requires new ways for managing data and new approaches to competing on analytics. For SDSs it means new challenges in terms of delivering data faster, to new constellations, for example, eco-systems [21] instead of single organizations, and with enhanced data refinement, etc.

There exist firms offering services that, in part, compete with traditional SDSs offerings. For example, Zoomerang (zoomerang.com) offers a web-based application service that can be used by firms to create custom web-based surveys (acquire external data). Via a web-based menu-driven system, the firm can create a survey and customize it in different ways. The created survey can be sent to customers using the firm's e-mail list or to a sample provided by Zoomerang. It can also be placed as a link on a website. It is also possible to manage the survey, for example, by controlling the status and inviting new customers. Based on the responses received, Zoomerang calculates the result and presents it using tables and graphs.

References

[1] S.M. McKinnon & W.J. Bruns, *The Information Mosaic*. Harvard Business School Press, Boston, 1992.
[2] S.A. Carlsson, & O.A. El Sawy, Managing the five tensions of IT-enabled decision support in turbulent and high velocity environments, *Information Systems and e-Business Management* forthcoming (2008).
[3] T.H. Davenport, Competing on analytics, *Harvard Business Review* **84**(1) (2006), 98-107.
[4] D. Arnott & G. Pervan, Eight key issues for the decision support systems discipline, *Decision Support Systems* **44**(3) (2008), 657-672.
[5] T.H. Davenport & J.G. Harris, *Competing on Analytics: The New Science of Winning*. Harvard Business School Press, Boston, 2007.
[6] W.E. Oglesby, Using external data sources and warehouses to enhance your direct marketing effort. *DM Review* **December** (1999), available at: http://www.dmreview.com/editorial/dmreview/print_action. cfm?EdID=1743 [Accessed March 13, 2003].
[7] C. Stedman, Scaling the warehouse wall, *Computerworld* (1998), available at: http://www. computerworld.com [Accessed March 13, 2003].
[8] W.H. Inmon, *Building the Data Warehouse*. Second ed. John Wiley & Sons, New York, 1996.
[9] M. Strand, B. Wangler & M. Olsson, Incorporating external data into data warehouses: Characterizing and categorizing suppliers and types of external data, in *Proceedings of the Ninth Americas Conference on Information Systems* (pp. 2460-2468), Tampa, FL (2003).
[10] M. Strand, B. Wangler & C.-F. Lauren, Acquiring and integrating external data into data warehouses: Are you familiar with the most common process?, in I. Isabel Seruca, J. Filipe, S. Hammoudi, & J. Cordeiro (Eds.) *Proceedings of the 6th International Conference on Enterprise Information Systems (ICEIS'2004) – Vol 1* (pp. 508-513), Porto: INSTICC – Institute for Systems and Technologies of Information, Control and Communication (2004).
[11] R. Kimball, *The Data Warehouse Toolkit*. John Wiley & Sons, New York, 1996.
[12] T. Morzy & R. Wrembel, Modeling a multiversion data warehouse: A formal approach, in O. Camp, J. Filipe, S. Hammoudi, & M. Piattini (Eds.) *Proceedings of the 5th International Conference on Enterprise Information Systems (ICEIS) – Part 1* (pp. 120-127), Setubal: Escola Superior de Tecnologia do Insituto Politécnico de Setubal (2003).
[13] B. Devlin, *Data Warehouse: From Architecture to Implementation*. Addison Wesley Longman, Harlow, 1997.
[14] N. Stolba & B. List, Extending the data warehouse with company external data from competitors' websites: A case study in the banking sector, in *Proceedings of Data Warehousing 2004 (DW 2004)*, Physica Verlag, 2004.
[15] Y. Zhu & A.P. Buchmann, Evaluating and selecting web sources as external information resources of a data warehouse, in T.W. Ling, U. Dayal, E. Bertino, W.K. Ng, & A. Goh (Eds.), *Proceedings of The Third International Conference on Web Information Systems Engineering* (pp. 149-161), IEEE Computer Society Los Alamitos (2002).
[16] R.D. Hackathorn, *Web Farming for the DW – Exploiting Business Intelligence and Knowledge Management*. Morgan Kaufmann Publishers, San Francisco, 1999.
[17] D. Asbrand, Making money from data, *Datamation*, 1998, available at: http://datamation.earthweb.com [Accessed June 21 2003].
[18] C. Shapiro & H.R. Varian, *Information Rules: A Strategic Guide to the Network Economy*. Harvard Business School Press, Boston, 1999.

[19] H. Håkansson (Ed.), *International Marketing and Purchasing of Industrial Goods: An Interaction Approach*. John Wiley & Sons, Chichester, 1982.

[20] S.A. Zahra & G. George (2002). Absorptive capacity: a review, reconceptualization, and extension, *Academy of Management Review*, **27**(2) (2002), 185-203.

[21] M. Iansiti & R. Levien, The Keystone Advantage: What the New Dynamics of Business Ecosystems Mean for Strategy, Innovation, and Sustainability. Harvard Business School Press, Boston, 2004.

Visually-Driven Decision Making Using Handheld Devices

Gustavo Zurita[a], Pedro Antunes[b], Nelson Baloian[c], Felipe Baytelman[a],
Antonio Farias[a]

[a] Universidad de Chile, MCIS Department, Business School, Chile
[b] University of Lisboa, Faculty of Sciences, Portugal
[c] Universidad de Chile, Computer Science Department, Chile

Abstract. This paper discusses group decision making from a visual-interactive perspective. The novelty of our approach is that its major focus is on developing a collection of visual-interactive elements for group decision-making. Our research departs from a collection of representative meeting scenarios to identify common decision-making elements and behavior similarities; and to elaborate a collection of feature sets realizing those common elements and behavior into visual-interactive artifacts. The paper also describes a handled application demonstrating the proposed feature sets. This application has been extensively used to support a wide range of meetings. An important contribution of this work is that the principle behind its approach to decision-making relies almost exclusively on gestures over visual elements.

Keywords: Decision-Making Elements. Group Support Systems. Handheld Devices.

1. Introduction

Research on collaborative decision-making (CDM) is widespread and has addressed the interrelationships between decision sciences, organizational sciences, cognitive sciences, small groups research, computer supported collaborative work and information technology. Considering such a wide range, it is understandable that the interplay between CDM and the user-interface seems in general relatively unimportant. Of course, in some specific contexts it has emerged as a central problem. For instance, Decision Support / Geographical Information Systems naturally emphasize the role of the user-interface [1]. Tradeoff analysis in multiple criteria decision making also gives significant importance to the problem [2]. Other CDM areas where interest in the user-interface has emerged include information landscapes [3], strategic visualization [4], and studies on group awareness [5]. Finally, another research context emphasizing the importance of the user-interface concerns decision support using mobile technology such as Personal Digital Assistants (PDA) and mobile phones, mostly because of the different display constraints and interaction modes, pervasiveness, serendipity and wireless access [6].

One area where the interplay between CDM and the user-interface is unexplored concerns meeting support. For instance, Fjermestad and Hiltz [7] analyzed most significant research prior from 1982 to 1998 and found no experiments specifically addressing the user-interface.

Since the area is mostly unexplored, the major purpose of this paper is answering two questions: What relationships may be found between the most common meeting scenarios and CDM tasks and processes? What subsequent relationships may be found between CDM and the most commonly supported visual-interactive artifacts? These questions are addressed in a concrete setting considering the use of handheld devices (more specifically PDA) in meetings.

From this inquiry we obtained a generic and coherent collection of visual-interactive artifacts capable to support the rich requirements posed by decision making using handheld devices. These visual-interactive artifacts were implemented in an application, designated NOMAD, which has been used with success in various meetings, mostly in the educational field. The contribution of this research to CDM research consists in: a) Based on a task-process taxonomy and a collection of meeting scenarios, we identify and characterize a set of decision-making elements recurrent in meetings. b) Departing from the above elements, we define a collection of visual-interactive feature sets expressing behavior similarities, i.e. the similar ways people construct and interact with decision-making elements. And c) we present an implementation of the proposed visual-interactive feature sets.

The remaining sections of this paper are organized in the following way: in section one we start by identifying several user-interfaces requirements related with CDM; then, in section two we present the collection of meeting scenarios that have framed our research on technology support to meetings; the section three is dedicated to characterize the decision-making elements found most relevant in the adopted scenarios; the section four characterizes the common functionality associated to the decision-making elements; section five provides more details about the NOMAD application and presents results from its use in several meetings; finally, in section six we discuss the outcomes of this research.

1. Requirements

Gray and Mandiwalla [8] reviewed the current state-of-the-art in CDM and identified the following important requirements:

Multiple group tasks. Groups develop different ways to accomplish their tasks, depending on the specific participation, context, location, problems and adopted approaches. For instance, opportunistic decisions may emerge in any time and place, and with a variable number of participants. More thorough decisions however may be result from the interaction with previous and subsequent decision processes. A meeting may be set up to resolve a problem, share information, define an action plan, brainstorm, or even to accomplish all this at the same time. This requirement stresses the importance of flexibility in information management.

Group dynamics. Often people come and go from collaborative decision-making processes, according to availability and required skills and contributions. This group dynamics has significant implications to information management, in order to avoid delays, digressions and information losses. The arrival of newcomers and latecomers should be as seamless as possible. And departures should not represent any disruptions to the remaining group. This requires seamlessly managing the group dynamics.

Visual tools for decision-making. Visual tools contribute to decision making by making information more perceptible, natural and simpler to manipulate.

Simple human-computer interfaces. Simpler human-computer interfaces contribute to free decision makers from the cognitive effort handling routine low-level activities, such as interacting with keys, menus and widgets, so they can concentrate on the task at hand.

Various interaction modes with technology. Collaboration may involve the participation of people with various degrees of proficiency with technology and these people should not feel inhibited to participate and contribute to the process outcomes. The availability of multiple interaction modes with technology, adapted to the types of users, their proficiency and roles assumed during the decision process, is fundamental to the CDM process.

Researchers noted there is an increase in the role of concepts maps, images, and other visual-interactive artefacts as mediators of collaboration, in a range of complex decision-making contexts including scientific inquiry, environmental and urban planning, resources management, and education [9]. It has also been suggested that visualisation is a powerful cognitive tool [10]. The term visualisation is used here in its familiar sense and fundamentally meaning "to form and manipulate a mental image." In this context, visual-interactive artefacts constitute physical counterparts to mental images. In everyday life, visual-interaction is essential to problem solving and decision-making, as it enables people to use concrete means to grapple with abstract information. Visual-interaction may simply entail the formation and manipulation of images, with paper and pencil, or any other technological tools, to investigate, discover, understand and explain concepts, facts and ideas. In spite of this potential, we do not find many research projects addressing group decision making from a visual-interactive perspective, in particular considering the meeting context.

2. Meeting Scenarios

Next we will mention the different meeting scenarios addressed by our research. A more detailed description can be found in [11].

Deliberate meeting: The deliberate meeting is mostly related to group problem solving and decision-making. The fundamental purpose of the deliberate meeting is to apply structured and rational procedures to systematically reduce the distance to set goals. The role of the leader/facilitator is central in deliberate meetings to focus the group on the decision process. Information management in deliberate meetings fundamentally concerns shared data.

Meeting ecosystem: The meeting ecosystem is associated to an ill-defined or unexpected reality. The most significant difference to the deliberate meeting is that advance planning is compromised. The fundamental purpose of the meeting ecosystem is thus to mobilize a group towards the identification of the best strategy to achieve the intended goals (which may also be compromised [12]). The meeting ecosystem may be regarded as an aggregate of sub-meetings with different goals. From the outset, it resembles an organized chaos, where participants flexibly move across different sub-meetings while contributing with their expertise to resolve a wide variety of problems. This type of behavior has been observed in collaboratories [13]. The critical information management role in the meeting ecosystem is situation awareness. The participants rely on shared data to deal with this organized chaos: setting up sub-groups, defining tasks, sub-tasks and to-do lists, and exchanging information between different shared contexts. Another important role to consider is integrating information produced by the sub-groups.

Creative/design meeting: This type of meeting is associated to the collaborative generation of ideas and plans. The most common structure supporting creativity and design relies on the several principles attributed to the brainstorming technique [14]: free-wheeling is welcomed, quantity is wanted, criticism is avoided and combination and improvement are sought. Considering this fairly simple structure, the most important roles associated to information management are visualization and conceptualization. Sketching affords the visual symbols and spatial relationships necessary to express ideas in a rapid and efficient way during design activities [15]. Parallel work should not only be possible but encouraged, to increase the group productivity.

Ad-hoc meeting: There is one major intention behind ad-hoc meetings: information sharing. Most meetings in organizations are ad-hoc: unscheduled, spontaneous, lacking an agenda, and with an opportunistic selection of participants [16]. In spite of an apparent informality, we identify two different motivations based on the participants' work relationships: the need to share important information between coworkers, which is related with a horizontal type of relationship; and the need to exert management control, which is associated to a vertical type of relationship. During an ad-hoc meeting, the participants are focused on information sharing, which may be centrally moderated. Social protocols are necessary to moderate information sharing. Information synchronization may be beneficial to offer the group an overall perception of the work carried out in the meeting.

Learning meeting: This type of meeting is focused on the group exploration and structuring of knowledge with the support and guidance from a knowledgeable person. Learning meetings emphasize the role of technology supporting the teachers' goals and strategies. In this respect, information management tools help focusing the students on the information conveyed by the teacher, while facilitating the set up and conduction of parallel activities. According to [17], the degree of anonymity supported by information technology in this scenario helps reducing evaluation apprehension by allowing group members to execute their activities without having to expose themselves in front of the group; and parallelism aids reducing domination, since more persons may express their ideas at the same time.

3. Decision-Making Elements

Several taxonomies identifying decision-making elements relevant to our discussion have been proposed in the research literature. One of the earliest and mostly cited ones is the task-process taxonomy [7, 18], which differentiates between task structure, focused on the specific group conditions in focal situations such as brainstorming or voting [19]; and process structure, addressing the more general conditions under which the group accomplishes the set goals, such as anonymity and proximity. Other available taxonomies highlight the distinctions between hardware, software and people [20], coordination modes [21], collaborative services [22], facilitation support [23] and other more specific conditions. In our work we adopted the general purpose of the task-process taxonomy, however separating the task dimension in two categories:

- Task dimension

    o   Macro level – Regards the task from the perspective of the group, i.e. the actions taken by the group as a whole.

    o   Micro level – Regards the task from the perspective of the individual participants in the group task, addressing the conditions under which the participants communicate, coordinate and collaborate with the others to accomplish their goals.

- Process dimension
  - o Adopts a broad perspective over the decision-making process, including the assumption that a collection of tasks may have to be managed to improve the group's performance.

Based on this taxonomy, we analyzed our meeting scenarios to come up with a collection of relevant decision-making elements. In Table 1 we present the several elements that were captured this way.

Scenario	Process	Macro	Micro
Deliberate	Lead participants Focus participants	Agenda, Discussion Wrap-up	Updating information
Ecosystem	Move between sub-meetings	Goals, Strategy, Solution Tasks/subtasks	Information exchange Information integration
Creative / Design	Free-welling Brainstorming Brainsketching	Ideas, Designs, Plans	Writing, Sketching Spatial relationships Visual symbols
Ad-hoc	Coworker Management control Moderate information sharing	Outcomes, Agreements Schedules, To-do list Deadlines	Private and public information Information sharing and synchronization
Learning	Setting activities Guidance	Structured activities, Problem solving, Ideas generation Organization of ideas Assessment	Structure knowledge Share knowledge

Table 1. Decision making elements

The next step in our approach consisted in aggregating the decision-making elements that were perceived as having similar behavior.

4. Feature Sets for Visual Decision Making

We grouped the decision-making elements shown in Table 1 according to their behavior similarity. For instance, both the agenda and wrap-up elements are usually very similar because the participants generate the same artifact: a list with topics. The functionality necessary for the group to interact with this common artifact is of course very similar and constitutes what we designate the "feature set" of these decision making elements. The several feature sets obtained this way are described below in a tabular form. Each one of these tables has three columns describing respectively the name associated to the feature set, the main behavior associated to the feature set, and additional information, restrictions or variations associated to the main behavior.

4.1. Process features

Our first feature set aims at helping the leader/facilitator setting group tasks and focusing the participants' attention in the selected tasks. In our approach this is accomplished with the notions of "pages" and "groups." Pages are associated to groups of participants by the leader/facilitator.

5.1a – Setting working groups and assigning activities to them. The leader/facilitator assigns participants to working sessions by dragging participant's icons into groups.	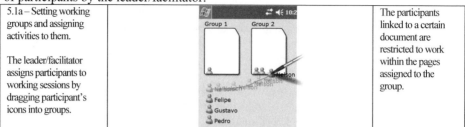	The participants linked to a certain document are restricted to work within the pages assigned to the group.

The second feature set aims at helping the leader/facilitator governing the users' focus of attention and managing shared information.

5.1b – Governing the focus of attention. The leader/facilitator organizes the users' focus of attention through the selection of pages.	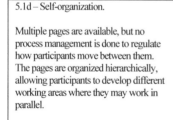	The participants work collaboratively in the selected page.

The following two features address the situations where no process management is needed, thus yielding to self-organization. These features assume respectively the collaboration restricted to one single page, thus supporting brainstorming, brainsketching and co-working situations; and collaboration supported by several pages, required e.g. by meeting ecosystems.

5.1c – Restricted self-organization. No process management is done. All participants interact freely with the system. Only one page is available.		There is one single focus of attention, which serves to coordinate the group's work.

5.1d – Self-organization. Multiple pages are available, but no process management is done to regulate how participants move between them. The pages are organized hierarchically, allowing participants to develop different working areas where they may work in parallel.	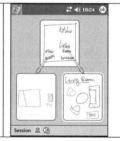	Participants may freely switch between pages (double-clicking and other methods are available for switching between pages).

4.2. Task-Macro features

The first feature set considered in this category supports a varied collection of meeting activities which fundamental purpose is to generate a list of items. This includes activities such as agenda building, brainstorming, producing a list of meeting outcomes, a to-do list, meeting wrap-up, and defining goals and solutions. The adopted approach organizes these items in one single page. More complex uses of list items can be supported with additional sketches (discussed in 5.3b). For instance, in the example below we illustrate how a SWAT analysis page was defined by combining writing with several lines forming the typical SWAT 2x2 matrix.

| 5.2a – Generate list items.

Organized lists allow several group-oriented tasks (such as voting and prioritizing). | 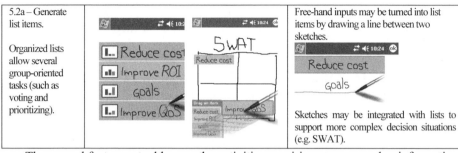 | Free-hand inputs may be turned into list items by drawing a line between two sketches.

Sketches may be integrated with lists to support more complex decision situations (e.g. SWAT). |

The second feature set addresses the activities requiring more complex information structures than the simple list defined above. Examples include planning activities, organizing ideas and problem solving situations. In our approach this functionality is supported with hierarchical pages. An overview page is also supplied, allowing the participants to take a glance at the whole information structure and navigate to a specific page. Note that SWAT analysis may also be implemented this way.

| 5.2b – Manage hierarchical items.

 Hierarchical structure of pages. There is an overview page showing all pages and their structural relations. | 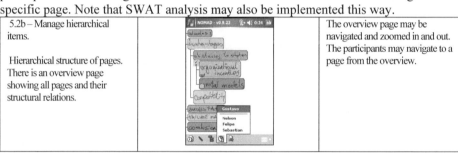 | The overview page may be navigated and zoomed in and out. The participants may navigate to a page from the overview. |

4.3. Task-Micro features

The first feature set considered in this category supports the production of writing and sketching using freehand input. Keyboard input is also considered as an alternative for writing. Common functionality such as selecting and moving elements is supported.

| 5.3a – Managing text and sketches with pen-based gestures.

Collaborative or individual contents may be created based on freehand and keyboard inputs. Sketches may be done over backdrops or recently taken photographs in camera-enabled devices. | 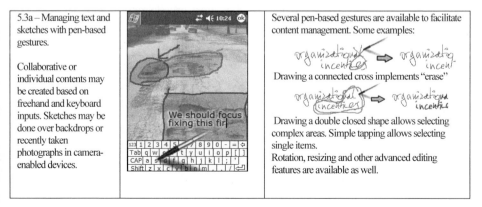 | Several pen-based gestures are available to facilitate content management. Some examples:

Drawing a connected cross implements "erase"

Drawing a double closed shape allows selecting complex areas. Simple tapping allows selecting single items.
Rotation, resizing and other advanced editing features are available as well. |

Sketching affords establishing spatial, visual and conceptual relationships between visual elements, a type of functionality considered in the following feature set.

5.3b – Conceptual relationships. Sketches allow organizing concepts on implicit-meaning distribution.	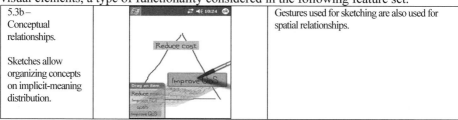	Gestures used for sketching are also used for spatial relationships.

The following two feature sets concern additional ways to structure knowledge. The first one concerns managing list items, while the second one addresses managing links to pages. In the later case links are visually represented as icons and may be followed by double-clicking.

5.3c – Structuring knowledge with list items. List item may be moved and merged to afford organizing concepts (e.g. combining ideas).	Example illustrating the selection and merging of two list items by dragging and dropping one list item over another. 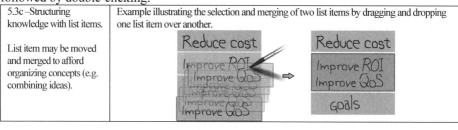

5.3d – Structuring knowledge with links. Managing links affords structural knowledge.	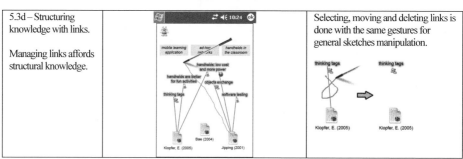	Selecting, moving and deleting links is done with the same gestures for general sketches manipulation.

In the context of the micro perspective, many participants' activities require managing private and public information. In our approach, private information is created and managed in special private pages, which may be created by a participant whenever it is necessary. Also, in many situations the participants may have to transfer information between private pages and between private and public spaces. The following category concerns the functionality necessary to transfer information between pages using an "offer area."

5.3e – Managing private and public information. The participants may create and work individually on private or public pages.	

5.3f – Governing information exchange. Moving items between two participants' private spaces and between private and public spaces.	One participant drags a visual element to an offer area. The other participant drags the offered element from the offer area into his/her private page. 

5. Application

The whole collection of feature sets described in the previous section has been implemented in a mobile application designated NOMAD. This application runs on Personal Digital Assistants utilizing the Windows Mobile operating system. The technical details about the implementation of low-level functionality, including ad-hoc networking, information exchange between multiple devices, synchronization, and in particular the implementation of the special interactions required by the features sets are described in detail in another paper [24]. In this paper we will instead focus on demonstrating how the combination of the visual-interactive features built into the application could effectively support group decision-making in the adopted meeting scenarios. To recap, the implemented visual-interactive features include:

- Setting work groups and assigning activities
- Governing the focus of attention
- Setting self-organization
- Structuring knowledge with list items and hierarchical items
- Managing text and sketches with pen-based gestures
- Creating conceptual relationships
- Managing private and public information
- Governing information exchange between private and public spaces

Screen dumps showing the implementation of these visual-interactive features have been given above. In particular, figures shown along with feature sets 5.2a, 5.2b 5.3d and 5.3f provide a good view of the application. These visual-interactive features have been utilized to accomplish many traditional decision-making tasks. For instance, the typical brainstorming activity has been supported by one single page with list items using the 5.2a feature set. The planning activity has been supported with hierarchical pages (5.1d for creation and 5.2b for navigation). Two well-known meeting artifacts, the agenda and meeting report, have also been implemented with pages and list items described in 5.2a. Besides these simple decision-making cases, more complex meeting situations have also been implemented with NOMAD:

- Supporting creative design meetings in the field, where participants have to generate ideas, discuss them, refine them, and select a subset of ideas to be further refined in the office. The feature set 5.3a has been used to sketch design ideas over a photograph of the subject being discussed taken on site.

These design ideas were then recursively refined on new pages, linked to the previous one using the feature set 5.1d. The feature set 5.1a was used to differentiate between the group of people working in the field and in the office. The feature set 5.3f was used to exchange private information among the field participants, as well as to distribute work among the office participants, so they could offline work on the design ideas.

- Meeting ecosystems and ad-hoc meetings have also been well supported by NOMAD. The mobile nature of the application makes it possible to start a meeting anytime and anyplace. For a certain meeting participant, to move among sub-meeting has been as easy as moving among different shared pages hierarchically organized. This was achieved with feature set 5.1d, allowing different working spaces to be shared, and with 5.2b, allowing a swift and easy change between the working areas. The feature set 5.1a has been used whenever more formal working groups were needed, restricting the users' access to particular working areas. The flexible nature of meeting ecosystems and ad-hoc meetings was well in line with the developed functionality, since there is no workflow modeling activities and restricting users' participation. Members could decide which specific features they would like to adopt, ranging from totally free-willing to chauffeured and guided situations.

- More structured meetings, especially those oriented to take decisions according to the classical decision-making steps of setting and agenda, brainstorming, groan, voting, selecting and follow-up have also been experimented with NOMAD. Feature sets 5.1c, 5.2a and 5.3c were used to define the agenda, brainstorm, merge several ideas after the brainstorming session, and finally vote. In order to keep flexibility, NOMAD does not guide or impose the meeting members to go through the different stages of a structured meeting. Instead, NOMAD supports different configurations adapted to the different stages in decision-making. We think members take benefits from a structured meeting only if they beforehand understand the necessity of a particular set of stages and agree to follow them. Having such an agreement, the participants may then adopt the NOMAD configuration that best fits their choice.

- In structured as well as non-structured meetings it is important to generate information about the outcomes, for instance to implement a follow-up. For this, we realized that a concise information structure is of paramount importance. Feature set 5.3b and 5.3b have been used to support this, since they can relate different pieces of information in a simple yet meaningful way.

Collaborative decision-making using NOMAD typically starts with the creation of the first page of a new project. The subsequent activities (such as creating groups, linking pages, etc.) as well as the order they are performed depend on what the users may need or want to do. Overall, we have observed very significant flexibility implementing most meeting arrangements falling within the limits of the scenarios described in section 2. We have also observed very significant flexibility relative to the presence or absences of the leader/facilitator. NOMAD is not highly dependent on the leader/facilitator to prepare and conduct the technology, as only feature sets 5.1a and 5.1b require one.

Although NOMAD has been used in multiple situations, it has not yet been subject to a "formal" evaluation process. We have several reasons for currently avoiding such an evaluation. The fundamental one is founded on the observations by Gray and

Mandiwalla [8] that experimental research with this type of technology is tied to the particular characteristics of individual prototype systems, which can be insightful but is difficult to generalize and predict. Experimental research requires a relatively stable context that we do not find in our prototype neither in the currently available mobile technology. Furthermore, the research literature on experiments with this types of technology has shown very inconclusive and sometimes conflicting results [7]. We believe that in the current context performing laboratory experiments with our prototype would contribute with more inconclusive results. From our point of view, research with this technology is still in a state where design ideas must be evaluated in a qualitative insightful way.

6. Discussion

Our decision-making approach is organized in twelve feature sets, where four sets were classified as process, two as task-macro and six as task-micro. The most commonly used visual-interactive artifact is the "page", that serves multiple purposes and is supported with very rich functionality, such as setting groups and sub-groups, focusing the groups' attention, allowing the participants to move between different tasks, supporting private and public activities, and organizing more complex information with multiple pages and links.

Another important visual-interactive artifact is the list item. Apparently, many different decision-making activities evolve around creating and modifying information organized as lists, which gives this simple information structure a powerful role in visual decision making. Rich functionality is also associated to list items, allowing the participants to create items by sketching, to move, drag and collapse items using the pencil, and to turn them private or public.

The smallest visual-interactive artifacts considered in our approach are the written text, sketches and sketches expressing conceptual relationships. Again, very rich functionality is available to facilitate interaction between the meeting participants, including the selection of multiple artifacts using specific movements with the pencil.

One interesting characteristic of our approach is that it clearly parts away from the traditional group decision support approach. We will discuss why in some detail. Although many different group decision support tools have already been developed, they seem to fall into one of the two following categories: the technology-driven and the model-driven [25]. The former shows strong concerns for the role and impact of the technology on the group decision process [7]. A central focus is the development of various tools supporting specific group tasks (e.g. brainstorming, categorizing and voting [26]) and their orchestration, mostly often conducted by a human facilitator [23]. Antunes et al. [27] point out the general-purpose nature of technology-driven tools generates a major organizational problem, since decision making is always performed in specific organizational contexts that are well known to participants but ignored by the technology.

The model-driven approach regards decision modeling as the fundamental requirement to support group participants articulating and structuring complex problems [25]. The emphasis is thus on utilizing decision models and methodologies capable to help eliciting and reconciling the participants' doubts, concerns and different views over the problem at hand. Morton et al. [25] point out the model-driven approach essentially works as a problem consultation tool, basically supporting strategy consultants performing their work with organizations and thus highly dependent on them. Therefore the target population for this type of tools is very narrow.

We share the view of Gray and Mandiwalla [8], who advocate a rethinking of decision-making technology, moving away from tools like brainstorming and voting, which are hardly used in organizations, and also less dependent on champions such as facilitators or strategy consultants. We believe our approach falls neither in the technology-driven nor the model-driven approaches. We may classify our approach as visually-driven: essentially focused on managing information artifacts that we commonly observe in meetings: pages with various types of information, lists with topics, and multiple pages when necessary. Our approach provides the basic visual elements necessary to make decisions, including complex strategic decisions such as SWAT, but does not make any assumptions about the specific tasks at hand.

Also, our approach does not make any assumptions about decision models and methodologies. The developed feature sets are sufficiently generic to be independent from such decision models and methodologies. The process features are also sufficiently generic to avoid any preconceptions about decision processes, be they more rational or more convoluted. In summary and in our view, the proposed visually-driven approach supports group decision-making using less assumptions about what decision-making should be, and how it should be organized from the information systems and process perspectives.

Acknowledgments.

This paper was funded by Fondecyt 1085010 and the Portuguese Foundation for Science and Technology, Projects PTDC/EIA/67589/2006 and PTDC/EIA/67589/2006.

References

[1]   Nyerges, T., Montejano, R., Oshiro, C., Dadswell, M.: Group-Based Geographic Information Systems for Transportation Site Selection. Transportation Research C 5 (1997) 349-369
[2]   Bell, M., Hobbs, B., Ellis, H.: The Use of Multi-Criteria Decision-Making Methods in the Integrated Assessment of Climate Change: Implications for Ia Practitioners. Socio-Economic Planning Sciences 37 (2003) 289–316289–316316
[3]   Charters, S., Knight, C., Thomas, N., Munro, M.: Visualisation for Informed Decision Making; from Code to Components. Proceedings of the 14th international Conference on Software Engineering and Knowledge Engineering. ACM Press, Ischia, Italy (2002) 765-772
[4]   Monzani, J., Bendahan, S., Pigneur, Y.: Decision and Visualization for Negotiation. Proceedings of the 37th Annual Hawaii International Conference on System Sciences, 2004 (2004)
[5]   Gutwin, C., Greenberg, S.: The Effects of Workspace Awareness Support on the Usability of Real-Time Distributed Groupware. ACM Transactions on Computer-Human Interaction 6 (1999) 243-281
[6]   Shim, J., Warkentin, M., Courtney, J., Power, D., Sharda, R., Carlsson, C.: Past, Present, and Future of Decision Support Technology. Decision Support Systems 3 (2002) 111-126
[7]   Fjermestad, J., Hiltz, S.: An Assessment of Group Support Systems Experimental Research: Methodology and Results. Journal of Management Information Systems 15 (1999) 7-149
[8]   Gray, P., Mandiwalla, M.: New Directions for GDSS. Group Decision and Negotiation 8 (1999) 77-83
[9]   Brown, J.R., van Dam, A., Earnshaw, R., Encarnação, J., Guedf, R., Preece, J., Schneiderman, B., Vince, J.: Human-Centered Computing, Online Communities and Virtual Environments, Special Report on the First Join European Commission/National Science Foundation Advanced Research Workshop. Computer Graphics 33 (1999) 42–62
[10] Rieber, L.: A Historical Review of Visualisation in Human Cognition. Educational Technology, Research and Development 43 (1995) 1042-1629

[11] Zurita, G., Antunes, P., Baloian, N., Carriço, L., Baytelman, F.: Using PDAs in Meetings: Patterns, Architecture and Components. Journal of Universal Computer Science 14 (2008)

[12] Rosenhead, J. (ed.): Rational Analysis for a Problematic World. Jonh Wiley & Sons, Chichester, England (1989)

[13] Mark, G.: Extreme Collaboration. Communications of the ACM 45 (2002) 89-93

[14] Osborn, A.: Applied Imagination. Charles Scribner's Sons, New York (1963)

[15] Forbus, K., Ferguson, R., Usher, J.: Towards a Computational Model of Sketching. IUI '01: Proceedings of the 6th international conference on Intelligent user interfaces, Santa Fe, New Mexico (2001) 77-83

[16] Romano, N., Nunamaker, J.: Meeting Analysis: Findings from Research and Practice. Proceedings of the 34th Hawaii International Conference on Systems Science, Hawaii (2001)

[17] Tyran, G., Sherpherd, M.: Collaborative Technology in the Classrom: A Review of the GSS Research and a Researh Framework. Information Technology and Management 2 (2001) 395-418

[18] Nunamaker, J., Dennis, A., Valacich, J., Vogel, D., George, J.: Electronic Meeting Systems to Support Group Work: Theory and Practice at Arizona. Communications of the ACM 34 (1991) 40-61

[19] McGrath, J.: Groups: Interaction and Performance. Prentice-Hall, Englewood Cliffs, NJ (1984)

[20] Kraemer, K., King, J.: Computer-Based Systems for Cooperative Work and Group Decision Making. ACM Computing Surveys 20 (1988) 115-146

[21] Malone, T., Crowston, K.: The Interdisciplinary Study of Coordination. ACM Computing Surveys 26 (1994) 87-119

[22] Bafoutsou, G., Mentzas, G.: Review and Functional Classification of Collaborative Systems. International Journal of Information Management 22 (2002) 281-305

[23] Antunes, P., Ho, T.: The Design of a GDSS Meeting Preparation Tool. Group Decision and Negotiation 10 (2001) 5-25

[24] Baloian, N., Zurita, G., Antunes , P., Baytelman, F.: A Flexible, Lightweight Middleware Supporting the Development of Distributed Applications across Platforms. The 11th International Conference on CSCW in Design, Melbourne, Australia (2007)

[25] Morton, A., Ackermann, F., Belton, V.: Technology-Driven and Model-Driven Approaches to Group Decision Support: Focus, Research Philosophy, and Key Concepts. European Journal of Information Systems 12 (2003) 110-126

[26] Nunamaker, J., Briggs, R., Mittleman, D., Vogel, D., Balthazard, P.: Lessons from a Dozen Years of Group Support Systems Research: A Discussion of Lab and Field Findings. Journal of Management Information Systems 13 (1997) 163-207

[27] Antunes, P., Costa, C., Pino, J.: The Use of Genre Analysis in the Design of Electronic Meeting Systems. Information Research 11 (2006)

Collaborative Decision Making: Perspectives and Challenges
P. Zaraté et al. (Eds.)
IOS Press, 2008

Mobile Shared Workspaces to Support Construction Inspection Activities

Sergio F. OCHOA[a], José A. PINO[a], Gabriel BRAVO[a], Nicolás DUJOVNE[a],
Andrés NEYEM[a]
[a]*Department of Computer Science, University of Chile, Chile*
{sochoa, jpino, gabravo, ndujovne, aneyem}@dcc.uchile.cl

Abstract. Typically, mobile shared workspaces are not used in the construction industry. However, they could play an important role to increase communication among workers, organize work more efficiently, reduce the coordination cost, and keep an updated overview of the project. This paper presents a MSW designed to support inspection processes in construction projects. This application allows mobile workers several functionalities, including doing annotations on digital maps, creating tasks linked to the annotations, synchronizing information of a project, collaborating on-demand and exchanging information among collaborators.

Keywords. Mobile Collaboration, Construction Industry, Support of Directional Communication, Mobile Shared Wokrkspaces, Loosely-Coupled Work.

Introduction

Several technological trends are affecting the future of mobility and mobile working [4]. Moore's law, stating that the computing power available for a given price doubles every 18 months, is expected to hold at least for the next years. At the same time, limitations such as battery life are expected to decrease at a rapid pace. Low cost telecommunication services will be available in the next few years, such as WiMax and WiMax Mobility [4]. This will promote the inclusion of mobile application in many scenarios, such as education, health, productive processes, security and business [20].

A kind of mobile groupware application that is being studied is the mobile shared workspaces (MSW), mainly because of the impact they could have in productive scenarios [20; 3]. These systems allow mobile workers to collaborate with other people or systems in an ad-hoc way (like a plug & play mechanism), adapting themselves depending on the context information [21]. Several researchers indicate that a mobile version of the traditional shared workspaces could produce an important positive impact on the productivity of mobile workers and on the quality of their work [16; 20; 3; 4]. Each mobile shared workspace represents a portion of the office (information and services) that is available to a mobile worker's computing device. Therefore, MSW may allow these people to work almost any-time and any-place.

The list of mobile workers that could benefit from the use of MSW includes several types of engineers, physicians, salesman, police officers, firefighters and persons conducting inspection processes (Figure 1) [17; 6; 20; 19; 21]. All of them carry out activities that fall in the category of "loosely coupled work" [18]. In this type of work, mobile workers carry out individual tasks most of the time, and they collaborate on-demand. Therefore, they require MSW embedding functionalities to support discretionary collaboration (e.g., data sharing, data synchronization, user/session management and automatic communication mechanisms) and awareness mechanisms that help them to decide when it is a good time to communicate (e.g., users' connection, users' proximity and users' availability).

Figure 1. MSW Supporting Loosely Coupled Work

This paper presents a mobile shared workspace able to support inspection activities in construction scenarios. These collaborative work scenarios involve much shared information, which need to be known by several professionals (and companies) participating in the building process. Therefore, they have to keep their shared information updated and synchronized. Currently this information is managed mainly through blueprints, turning the management process expensive, slow, inflexible and error-prone.

The MSW presented in this paper has been designed to deal with these limitations. Next section describes the collaboration scenario for construction inspection activities. Section 2 presents the related work. Section 3 describes the proposed mobile shared workspace. Section 4 presents the results of the preliminary evaluation and section 5 mentions the main conclusions and further work.

1. Collaboration Scenario

In the building and construction industry, mobile shared workspaces could play an important role to increase communication among workers, organize work more efficiently and reduce coordination cost. This industry is characterized by: (a) dispersed teams that jointly work on the development of a new site, (b) usually these teams do not belong to the same company, (c) they cannot use fixed communication infrastructure, (d) they need to be on the move to carry out the assigned work and (e) their supporting information is hard copied in a blue print or similar documents. The main contractor usually sub-contract and coordinate the activities of several specialized companies, which are in charge of building the main structure, electrical facilities, water systems, etc.

(a)   (b)

Figure 2. (a) Current situation in construction inspections, (b) future situation based on MSW usage.

For example, electrical engineers belonging to the company "A" need to be on the move in order to inspect and record the state of the electrical facilities that are being developed by company employees deployed on several construction sites. Twice a week, three electrical engineers visit each construction site with the goal to get an updated state of the work (Fig. 2a). They inspect various parts of the physical infrastructure and record the advances on a blue print. Such annotations are difficult to share with others, even with the partners, because they are based on physical marks on a paper. Therefore, the integration of the annotations is always a difficult, slow and error-prone task. Similarly, the process of reporting the advances to the main contractor is frequently late and unreliable.

This paper presents a MSW not only to support the work of inspectors, but also to keep informed the main contractor. It could also be useful to generate tasks based on the annotations and to assign resources to them. Now, the set of blue prints will be replaced by digital maps usable through MSW running on a Tablet PC (Fig. 2b). This solution will allow to share and synchronize the information available in the MSW among several users. In the case of the presented example, after each inspection, the engineers could synchronize the used workspaces in order to get a whole view of the work state for such site (or project). Then they could inform the main contractor about the work state, also by synchronizing a common workspace. They can also interact remotely with their company main office (with the server) in order to deliver the annotations (synchronize data) and download the information of the next construction site to visit.

2. Related Work

Several collaborative solutions have been proposed to support mobile workers in specific settings [1; 8; 13; 14; 22]. Although these proposals have shown to be useful to support specific collaborative activities, they were not designed as general solutions, therefore they are not reusable. In addition, these collaborative solutions are not applicable to the above scenario because they are not able to deal with the ad-hoc collaboration and loosely-coupled work [17].

On the other hand, there are several interesting initiatives in the middleware area, which propose reusable functions to support collaboration in peer-to-peer networks. LaCOLLA [12] and iClouds [10] are two of them. Although these frameworks offer spontaneous mobile user interaction and file exchange support in mobile ad-hoc networks, they do not provide support to exchange shared objects, synchronize files or work without connecting to a server.

There are also frameworks providing specific functionalities to support mobile collaboration through an API, such as YCab [5] and JXTA [11]. Here, every device and software component is a peer and can easily cooperate with other peers. Although these frameworks have shown to be useful to support collaboration in peer-to-peer networks, they also require a wired or fixed wireless network. Therefore, they are not well suited for an ad-hoc mobile work setting.

Finally, there are several proposals to share information in P2P networks, even considering mobile computing devices [9; 15]. Typical examples are tuple-based distributed systems derived from LINDA [7], such as: FT-LINDA, JINI, PLinda, T-spaces, Lime, JavaSpaces and GRACE. Despite the fact these implementations work in P2P networks, they use centralized components that provide the binding among components of the distributed system. Summarizing, there are no MSW designed to be used specifically for construction inspections; and the current frameworks are limited when supporting mobile collaboration and loosely-coupled work.

3. The Mobile Shared Workspace

Several Projects can be managed simultaneously in the MSW. Each of them can include several maps that can store one or more annotations. In turn, each annotation will generate one or more tasks that will be assigned to a sub-contracted company or a particular worker. The functionality that allows mobile users manage this information is available through the workspace main user interface (Fig. 3). Typically, each annotation is related to a specific location on the blueprint, and a task is related to a particular annotation.

This user interface separates the functionality in multiple panels: (1) Main Menu, (2) Navigation/Visualization Menu, (3) Blueprints Manager, (4) Annotations Manager, and (5) Shared Panel. Next, a brief explanation of the panels is presented.

1. Main Menu. The application must provide the basic functionality for handling several projects. Each project is represented by an XML file storing all related information. The associated manipulation menu provides facilities for creating, opening, storing, saving, re-naming, importing/exporting and synchronizing projects. Creation of a new project triggers the creation of the corresponding XML file. Then, the various blueprints intended for inspections (e.g., the electrical one) get embedded in that project. Typically, more than one blueprint is used for any floor of the construction to be inspected. Inspectors are able to open a project and make as many annotations as they need. Afterwards, they can save or rename it,

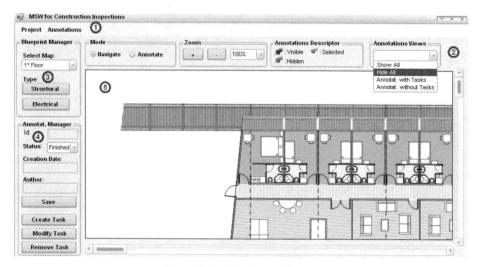

Figure 3. MSW main user interface

which produces an update of the XML file associated to the inspected project. The functionality related to importing/exporting projects are file transfers, where the files format is validated in order to determine whether it adheres or not to a project format. Since a complete project is represented with an XML file, the projects can be synchronized through a functionality provided by the Service-Oriented Mobile Unit (SOMU) platform [17]. This process spends from some seconds to a few minutes depending on the information to be synchronized and the bandwidth of the communication channel between sender and receiver.

On the other hand, the main menu also allows showing or hiding all the annotations available in the map shown on the shared panel (panel 5). It allows inspectors to easily access the points to be reviewed.

2. Navigation/Visualization Menu. This panel implements the functionality required to navigate the information shown on the shared panel (panel 5) and also do annotations on that information. The navigation *mode* indicates the functionalities the inspector will have available with the user interface. A "Navigate" mode means the mobile workers will be able to scroll and zoom-in/zoom-out maps shown on the shared panel. In addition, they will be able to manage the visualization of these annotations (e.g., show, hide, select) but they cannot add or remove them. Adding or removing annotations can be done just if the mode is set as "Annotate". The text related to an annotation cannot be modified in order to avoid inconsistencies between the one the inspector writes and the annotation read by the worker in charge of handling it. If the annotation needs to be changed, it should be removed and then re-created indicating whatever the inspector wants. Fig. 4 shows two annotations; each one is related to the place where the pin is located. Provided the *Annotations View* is set to "*Annotations with Tasks*", just the annotations having tasks related to them are shown on the map.

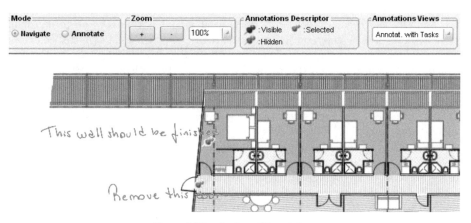

Figure 4. Visualization of Annotations

3. Blueprints Managers. This panel is available once the inspector has selected a project to work on. A particular floor of the building can be selected to be inspected using the blueprints manager, and then a particular map can be loaded on the shared panel. It allows the inspector to start the inspection process. The inspector reviews annotations on that map or adds/removes some of them based on what he/she observes during the physical inspection.

4. Annotations Manager. This panel allows handling all information related to an annotation. It shows all the data related to the annotation being selected on the shared panel, e.g., author of the annotation, current state and date it was done. The panel also allows changing the state of an annotation, and therefore the state of all the tasks related to it. The tasks related to an annotation can be added, modified or removed using this panel. Each task has a single assignment and a resource in charge of handling it (i.e., a sub-contracted company or a specific worker).

5. Shared panel. This is the main portion of the MSW user interface. There, the shared information is input, reviewed and modified by the inspectors. Typically, visualizations and annotations are the main functions that mobile workers use on this panel.

3.1. Performing Collaborative Work with the MSW

A construction site inspector follows five steps when reviewing a project without technology support: (1) get the blueprints required to support the inspection, (2) carry out the inspection, (3) take the updated blueprints to the company main office (this typically occurs when the inspections round is finished), (4) assign resources to handle pending issues, and (5) notify updates (if applicable) and assignments to the involved persons. Then, these assigned persons must retrieve relevant information from a copy of the blueprint marked by the inspector and try to address each annotation. Finally, a similar process is carried out when they report the results of the work done.

The functionality provided by this MSW allows changing the process to flexible, fast, accurate and reliable one. Now, the inspector does not need to go to the main office to get/leave a copy of the project because the MSW allows inspectors to retrieve/submit a project and its updates through Wi-Fi or telephone networks. The cost of data synchronization and the flexibility to carry out such process is remarkably better now. Data synchronization requires little time, it can be done almost everywhere and the error rate due to annotation replication problems is close to zero.

An inspector can now share their annotations (if applicable) with fellows or collaborators (even from other companies) before leaving the construction site being inspected. The process is simple, fast and error free. A similar process can be conducted by persons in charge of handling the inspector's comments, when they (using the MSW) have to report back to the main constructor the results of the work done. Thus, the effort to keep these persons coordinated is notably reduced.

3.2. Interaction with MS Project

According to the feedback received from civil engineers that carry out a preliminary evaluation of the MSW, one of the best features of the tool is its association with the MS Project 2007 software product. This feature links annotations with the MS Project tasks related to them. All tasks are stored in a file (inside the XML Project file) with MS Project format. Therefore it can be exported to be viewed and modified using this product, which is well used in construction management.

The process of task creation and follow-up in MS Project is associated to the authorization function of the tool. Various types of users are recognized by the tool and assigned different task access levels, namely:

- *Full Access:* The user may create, modify state and delete tasks.
- *Admin:* The user may create and modify state, but the user may not delete tasks.
- *Normal:* The user may only read existing tasks involving the user himself/herself as a resource.
- *No access:* The user is not allowed to access any task related data.

A new task in the Gantt chart associated to the Project is created by selecting the annotation, and then, clicking on the Create Task button (panel 4), which will display a dialog window. The initial task parameters should be entered: name, initial date, duration, previous tasks, resources, etc. (Fig. 5). The result will be a new task with those parameters stored in the Gantt chart.

Modification of a task is done as follows. The user must select an annotation associated to the task. Then, the user must click on the "Modify Task" button (panel 4). The system will display a dialog window. The information related to task duration, state and responsible person can be updated (Fig. 5). On the other hand, the process to delete a task requires selecting the annotation associated to the task to be deleted and clicking the "Remove Task" button (panel 4). In this latter case, the user should enter

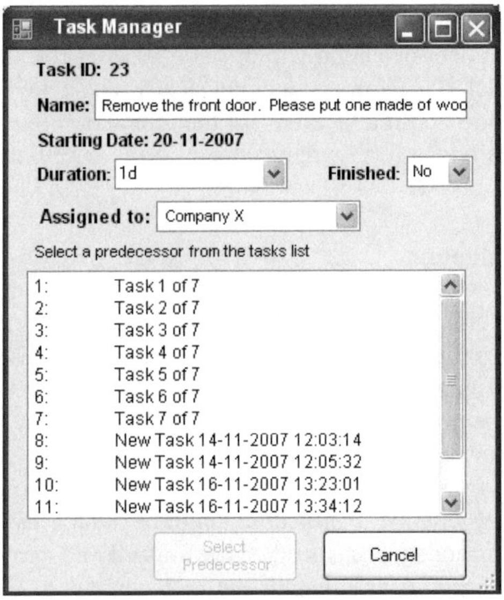

Figure 5. MSW Task Manager

an explanation for deleting the task. The project data will now include date and time of deletion, the user name and the explanation.

These task maintenance activities are made easy if the user selects a convenient way to display annotations. The user is allowed to see only those annotations without associated tasks, only those having associated tasks, or another criterion (there are a few other filters available). The user can choose the filtering option in the upper part of the user interface window.

3.3. Implementation Issues

The presented Mobile Shared Workspace was implemented in C# using the .Net Framework. The application follows a traditional groupware system architecture with three layers. These layers provide functionality required for communication, coordination and collaboration [17]. The functionality of the two lower layers (communication and coordination) is provided by the SOMU platform [17], on which this application runs. The supporting platform is stable and robust. The communication among collaborators is supported mainly by Mobile Ad-hoc Networks (MANETs) [2].

The implementation of this MSW involves just standard technologies in order to ease the interoperability among MSWs belonging to different companies participating in the construction process. The project data is stored in XML, the interactions among collaborators are supported by Web Services and the communication support is mainly provided through MANETs that adhere to the IEEE 802.11b/g norm. The MSW also includes communication support via traditional telephone networks.

Although the MSW is completely functional, there are some useful functions from SOMU that are currently being embedded in the MSW user interface. For example, automatic peer detection. Typically, mobile workers doing loosely-coupled work collaborate on-demand; therefore, they need to know when a partner is close and available. Automatic peer detection will provide an inspector the awareness required to know when potential collaborators are physically close to him/her. Thus, s/he can determine the appropriate time to carry out the interaction (e.g., data synchronization). We believe this feature can further reduce the effort to coordinate collaborators.

4. Preliminary Evaluation

Typically, loosely coupled work carried out by construction inspectors requires: autonomy, interoperability, shared information availability, discretionary collaboration, information synchronization, low coordination cost and awareness of users' reachability [17]. The proposed MSW deals with most of these requirements.

A preliminary evaluation of the application was done by two civil engineers that used to be involved in construction inspection processes. They ran the application on a TabletPC. Once they opened a project example provided by the authors, they made annotations, created/modify tasks and synchronized the project among them. They found the performance and usability of the tool was good. Besides, they highlighted three features that could provide an important contribution to the work in this area: on-demand data synchronization, on-demand data exchange (files transfer) and the possibility to create MS Project tasks linked to an annotation.

These engineers think the time and cost of the coordination processes can be reduced to really low values when the MSW is used. However, the users must feel comfortable using the application and they must trust it. Otherwise, the possible benefits will not be obtained. Two additional aspects they highlighted were related to the use of TabletPCs. They thought a battery providing more use time was needed. They also disliked the need to charge these devices during the inspection processes.

Summarizing, we can say the first evaluation shows the proposed MSW is attractive and useful for construction inspectors. Furthermore, it can provide important benefits to reduce the effort required to coordinate the persons involved in inspections processes. However, the users should trust in the services the application provides them and they have to be able to use a TabletPC.

5. Conclusions and Future Work

Typically, mobile shared workspaces are not used in the construction industry, however they could play an important role in order to increase communication among workers, organize work more efficiently, reduce the coordination cost, and keep an updated overview of the project. This paper presents a MSW designed to support inspection processes in construction projects. This application allows mobile workers several functionalities, such as doing annotations on digital maps, creating tasks linked to the annotations, synchronizing information of a project, collaborating on-demand and exchanging information among collaborators.

The tool was evaluated by two civil engineers experienced in construction inspection. They found the application to be useful and usable. In addition, they highlighted the coordination time and cost involved in inspection processes can be reduced to low values when the MSW is used. Therefore the use of this type of application could represent an interesting contribution for the construction industry.

Currently additional features are being added to the MSW (e.g., users location awareness and automatic peers detection), particularly the capabilities to do audio annotations on the map. In addition, a test experience is being designed to be applied in a real construction project.

Acknowledgement

This work was partially supported by Fondecyt (Chile), grants N°: 11060467 and 1080352 and LACCIR grant No. R0308LAC004. The work of Andrés Neyem was partially supported by the Scholarship for Thesis Completion from Conicyt (Chile) and NIC Chile Scholarship.

References

[1]   André, P., Antunes, P.: "SaGISC: A Geo-Collaborative System". Proc. of CRIWG 2004. LNCS 3198, 175-191. San Jose, Costa Rica, Sept. 2004.
[2]   Aldunate, R., Ochoa, S., Pena-Mora, F., Nussbaum, M.: "Robust Mobile Ad-hoc Space for Collaboration to Support Disaster Relief Efforts Involving Critical Physical Infrastructure". ASCE Journal of Computing in Civil Engineering 20(1). 13-27.
[3]   Andriessen, J. H. E., Vartiainen, M. (eds.): "Mobile Virtual Work: A New Paradigm?". Springer, 2006.
[4]   Brugnoli, M.C., Davide, F. Slagter, R.: "The Future of Mobility and of Mobile Services". In: P. Cunningham and M. Cunningham (eds.), Innovation and the Knowledge Economy: Issues, Applications, Case Studies, IOS Press. 2005, 1043-1055.
[5]   Buszko, D., Lee, W., Helal, A.: "Decentralized Ad-Hoc Groupware API and Framework for Mobile Collaboration". ACM GROUP, ACM Press, 5-14.
[6]   Favela, J, Tentori, M. Castro, L., González V. Moran, E., Martinez-Garcia, A.: "Activity Recognition for Context-aware Hospital Applications: Issues and Opportunities for the Deployment of Pervasive Networks". MONET 12(2-3). 2007, 155-171.
[7]   Gelernter, D.: "Generative Communication in Linda"; ACM Transactions on Programming Languages and Systems, 7(1). 80-112.
[8]   Guerrero, L., Pino, J., Collazos, C., Inostroza, A., Ochoa, S.: "Mobile Support for Collaborative Work". Proc. of CRIWG'04, LNCS 3198, 363-375. San Jose, Costa Rica, Sept. 2004.
[9]   Hauswirth, M., Podnar, I., Decaer, S.: "On P2P Collaboration Infrastructures"; WETICE'05, IEEE CS Press, 66-71. Linköping, Sweden, June 13-15, 2005.
[10] Heinemann, A., Kangasharju, J., Lyardet, F., Mühlhäuser, M.: "iClouds: Peer-to-Peer Information Sharing in Mobile Environments". Euro-Par'03, LNCS 2790, 1038-1045. Klagenfurt, Austria, August 26 - 29, 2003.
[11] JXTA Project, 2008. URL; http://www.jxta.org. Last visit: January 2008.
[12] Marques, J., Navarro, L.: "LaCOLLA: A Middleware to Support Self-sufficient Collaborative Groups"; Computing and Informatics, 25(6). 2006, 571-595.
[13] Menchaca-Mendez, R., Gutierrez-Arias, E., Favela, J.: "Opportunistic Interaction in P2P Ubiquitous Environments"; Proc. of CRIWG'04, LNCS 3198, 349-362. San Jose, Costa Rica, Sept. 2004.
[14] Muñoz, M.A., Rodriguez, M., Favela, J., Martinez-Garcia, A.I., Gonzalez, V.M.: "Context-Aware Mobile Communication in Hospitals". IEEE Computer 36 (9), 38-46.
[15] Neyem, A., Ochoa, S., Guerrero, L., Pino, J.: "Sharing Information Resources in Mobile Ad-hoc Networks". Proc. of CRIWG 2005, LNCS 3706, 351-358. Porto de Galinhas, Brazil. Sept. 2005.
[16] Neyem, A., Ochoa, S.F., Pino, J.A. Designing Mobile Shared Workspaces for Loosely Coupled Workgroups. Proc. of CRIWG 2007. LNCS 4715. 173-190. Bariloche, Argentina. Sept. 2007.
[17] Neyem, A., Ochoa, S.F., Pino, J.A.: "Integrating Service-Oriented Mobile Units to Support Collaboration in Ad-hoc Scenarios". Journal of Universal Computer Science 14(1), pp. 88-122.

[18] Pinelle, D., Gutwin, C.: "A Groupware Design Framework for Loosely Coupled Workgroups". European Conference on Computer-Supported Cooperative Work. 2005, 119-139.

[19] Spinelli, G. and Brodie, J.: "Towards an Understanding of Common Information Spaces in Distributed and Mobile Work". Proc. of HCI'03, Crete, Greece. 2003, 22-27.

[20] Schaffers, H., Brodt, T., Pallot, M., Prinz, W. (eds).: "The Future Workplace - Perspectives on Mobile and Collaborative Working". Telematica Instituut, The Netherlands. 2006.

[21] Tarasewich, P.: "Designing Mobile Commerce Applications". Communications of the ACM, 46(12). 2003, pp. 57-60.

[22] Zurita, G., Baloian, N.: "Handheld Electronic Meeting Support". Proc. of CRIWG 2005, LNCS 3706. 341-350. Porto de Galinhas, Brazil. Sept. 2005.

Collaborative Decision Making in ERP

Collaborative Decision Making: Perspectives and Challenges
P. Zaraté et al. (Eds.)
IOS Press, 2008

Why a collaborative approach is needed in innovation adoption: the case of ERP

David Sammon[a] — Frederic Adam[a]
[a]*Business Information Systems*
University College Cork
Cork, Ireland
dsammon@afis.ucc.ie, fadam@afis.ucc.ie

Abstract. There is an abundant literature on IS adoption, aimed at both the individual and organizational levels of analysis. This literature highlights the complexity of the process of IT adoption and implementation and the importance of carrying out relevant and applicable research in this area. The area of ERP adoption has been particularly rich in the last 15 years, as increasing numbers of companies acquired ERP with comparatively low success rates. In this paper, we hypothesise that the high failure rate of ERP implementations is related to the failure to adopt a truly collaborative approach in the ERP project. In order to verify our ideas, we carried out four case studies of firms having implemented ERP, seeking to confirm if there was a relation between the level of collaboration they had achieved and their level of success with the application. Our findings confirm the importance and core value of the *People* factor in the success of an ERP project – the *Best Personnel Factor*, as we labeled it, and of all the sub-factors connected to it, upstream and downstream, We conclude that, when these aspects of the collaborative process followed by organizations coherently fall into place, the probability of success with ERP is higher.

Keywords: Collaborative approach, ERP project, team work, people factor

1. Introduction

Whilst the area of adoption and diffusion of IT innovation is one of the main areas of attention in the IS field [1, 2], there has been evidence that organisations have sometimes substituted a hasty and incomplete approach to their adoption decisions, preferring to "jump on the bandwagon' as their managers try to conform to the latest fad or fashion [3]. Abrahamson [3, 4] has identified a number of target-market socio-psychological influences that impact upon the evolution of fads and managerial fashions. He stated that the vulnerabilities of managers in being swayed to pursue these fads are leveraged by such fashion setters as consulting firms, management gurus, business publishers and business schools that are dedicated to the pursuit of progress.

Swanson and Ramiller [2] have described the area of ERP as one of those areas where the very strong discourse of vendors and consultants have pushed managers and organisations in large numbers towards adoption of ERP applications, but not always for the right reasons. Ideally, the process of ERP adoption and implementation should begin with a vendor/consultant-independent, methodology-independent and 'pre-planning' or 'intelligence phase' thought process which considers whether to undertake an enterprise-wide ERP project, and why and how to implement it. However, the research literature offers very little evidence that this is taking place. Perhaps as a result, the decision making processes of managers in the ERP market are often characterised by weak rationales [5, 2], limited understanding of key concepts defining an ERP system [6, 7, 2, 8], and a high implementation failure rate [7], perhaps as low as 50 % [9, 10]. In fact, an estimated 60 to 90 % of ERP projects fail to fulfill the promise of significant return, identified in the project initiation phase.

In this paper, we argue that the failure to consider ERP adoption and implementation projects as ventures that require a collaborative, cross disciplinary approach is responsible for this failure to capitalise on ERP investments. In order to confirm the validity of this claim, we carried out four longitudinal case studies of ERP projects to establish whether there is a correlation between the success of the venture and the adoption of a collaborative, people-oriented approach to the organisation and management of the project. The next section reflects on the evolution of managerial fads and fashions and seeks to characterise ERP projects in terms of the difficulties that must be addressed if an organisation is to follow a *mindful* approach to adoption [2]. We then operationalise the concept of a collaborative approach to ERP in terms of the actions an organisation can be expected to take in order to promote such an approach. We then present our research protocol and the case studies before presenting the findings and conclusions of our study.

2. Fads, Fashions and the ERP Bandwagon

The techniques that intermittently emerge from within the fashion setting community are transient in nature, however, some gain legitimacy and become ingrained in management culture [11]. The approach that is typically used to engineer self-replicating demand for a new fad of fashion is the identification of performance benefits offered by the new method, and a corresponding performance gap suffered by those that have not adopted it [4]. This results in the "bandwagon effect', which has been observed by researchers in many areas, including that of ERP applications [12, 13, 14, 2]. The ERP area is an excellent example of legitimisation of a technological improvement in that it is characterised by a strong vendor and consultant push whereby organisations appear to have little choice with regard to the selection and implementation of an ERP package.

According to Abrahamson [4], fashion setters are constantly creating new techniques or methods, which are selected for introduction into the 'fashion cycle'. Therefore, effective processing expands the technique into a *rhetoric* or business philosophy and the proliferation of the new dictum is then supported by dissemination agents [4]. If and when a bandwagon develops around an IT innovation, the *mindless* organisations may join in, get caught up in the momentum generated by prior adopters, and impressed by 'success stories' that appear to validate the innovation as a good, maybe even an irresistible, idea [15, 16, 2]. To justify adoption the organisation may be content with the rationale that 'everyone is doing it' or the justification that 'its time to catch up'. As a result, the *mindless* organisation places its faith in what the broader community appears to know – in common competences – rather than its own distinctive competence [16, 2]. The very interesting side effect which this approach has is that *mindless* implementation of a new concept will lead to negative experiences which gives a fresh opportunity to push a new release or new implementation approach to those who did not manage to derive benefits the first time around. Figure 1 presents an adaptation of the illustration presented in a consultancy company's brochure that seeks to leverage the low success rate of ERP projects.

Figure 1: Myth and Reality of ERP Benefit Realisation

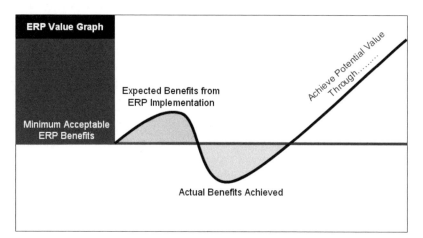

Gill and Whittle [17] have identified a personality type within western corporate types that borders on neurosis or psychosis and thrives on 'boldness and risk taking', with a fascination for new techniques. They explained that this has contributed to a quick-fix approach to organisational change and the ready adoption of systems with a lack of preparation. For example, methodologies such as Management by Objective (MBO), Organisational Development (OD), Total Quality Management (TQM), Quality Circles and now ERP are promoted as a packaged 'cure-all' solution to any difficulties and are based on aspects of social/technical disciplines.

The downside of this trend is that the level of managerial understanding of technological innovations is generally low, and managers need to understand what is critical for a successful project implementation. For instance, an organisation committing to the implementation of an enterprise-wide system needs to be empowered and made aware of the complexities of the enterprise systems market, and needs to internally assess, if not their readiness for an enterprise-wide ERP system, their ability to manage the fashion setters (the consultants and the vendors) within the enterprise systems market. This requires pooling some key resources within the organisation while adding and integrating key external resources to these internal resources in a complex collaborative process.

Swanson and Ramiller [2] have presented an adaptation of the concept of *mindlessness* to characterise organisations and their flawed approaches to pursuing IT innovations. While the article presented is a true reflection of the ERP market today, it is exploratory and theoretical in nature, and gives no real direction as to how to operationalise the concept. Their theoretically motivated discussion provides quite practical implications, in that *"deficient understanding – handmaiden to mindlessness – has been identified as a prime cause of firms' widespread failures with IT investments"* [2, p.577]. However, more needs to be done to understand what organisations must do in their pursuits of complex innovating IT projects. In this paper, we investigate the notion that there is a need for collaborative approaches to understanding and adopting IT innovations.

3. Why a collaborative approach is needed for ERP projects

In understanding what process is required for a *mindful* approach to IT innovations, it is important to characterise ERP projects so a good fit can be found. As McGrath [18, p.53] stated *"If we want to learn about groups as vehicles for performing tasks, we must either (a) assume that all tasks are alike, in regard to how groups of various kinds can and do perform them; or (b) take into account differences in group performance as they arise from differences in tasks"*. Previous attempts to provide such a classification of group tasks revealed great contradictions in the findings of studies of task performance [18]. The dichotomy between intellectual tasks (more efficiently performed by individuals) and motor tasks (more efficiently performed by groups) was originally used to account for these contradictions before Carter *et al.* [19] went beyond this simple dichotomy to propose a classification of group tasks involving seven types: (1) clerical, (2) discussion, (3) intellectual, (4) construction, (5) mechanical assembly, (6) motor co-ordination and (7) reasoning. As noted by McGrath[18], this classification is not totally satisfactory as it fails to take into account the nature of the products or outcomes of the tasks studied and, more importantly, the nature of the relations between members of the group (e.g.: to what extent they are required to work co-operatively). The first systematic attempt to uncover the different characteristics of group tasks came from Shaw's survey of small group research [20] where he isolated six properties or of group task, namely: Intellective versus Manipulative, task Difficulty, Intrinsic Interest, Population Familiarity, Solution Multiplicity versus Specificity, Cooperation Requirements. These dimensions indicate the different factors that must be taken into account in order to completely define a specific task in which a group is involved. These dimensions include properties of the task itself as well as properties of the group and of the setting in which the group tackles the task rather than just a classification of group tasks.

This on-going debate points to the complexities inherent in tasks related to IT innovation adoption and implementation, in that ERP projects for instance, gather most of the different types of group tasks previously identified and rates high in terms of difficulty when it comes to the need for collaboration. One of the key issues in terms of the performance of the organisation engaged in an ERP project is understanding how well the inputs of group members are integrated to produce an outcome. ERP project are clearly not *Eureka* types of problems, whereby if one person knows the answer, the group is bound to recognise that it is the right answer [18]. ERP projects require that the inputs of the members are somehow aggregated in the problem solving process[18]. Based on Steiner's [21] classification, an ERP project is akin to a *conjunctive task* (where all members of the group must succeed), with also properties of *additive tasks* (tasks where the contributions of the members are added to yield a meaningful, aggregated outcome) whilst at the same time being essentially a *divisible task* where some members of the group attempt to achieve one aim while the rest of the group must achieve another, related goal [21]. McGrath [18, p.58] reached a conclusion, very fitting to the description of ERP projects that the most complex group tasks require *"not so much a summing of members' outputs as a complicated co-ordination of their efforts"*.

To us, this translates into the need to understand the importance of the *people* factor in IT innovation adoption. As a result, we identified references to this key factor in previous ERP literature as presented in Tables 1 and 2 (a&b). In Table 1, a quick literature review of proposed tasks in setting up the ERP project indicates that people related factors are listed in 12 out of 30 listed activities, far ahead of any other definitive area of activity. In particular, *Nah et al.* [22] focus 5 of their required actions on staffing the ERP project.

Table 1: ERP Planning Phase Activities

References	ERP Planning Activities
Bancroft *et al.* [23]	Set-up of the steering committees Selection and structuring of the project team Development of the projects guiding principles Creation of a project plan
Markus and Tanis [6]	Development of the business case for the ERP Package selection Identification of the project manager Budget and schedule approval
Parr and Shanks [7]	Selection of an ERP Assembly of a steering committee Determination of high level project scope and broad implementation approach Selection of a project team manager Resource determination
Shakir [24]	Choose consultant Form selection committee Definition of key business processes (KBP) Inviting vendors to bid Vendor short-listing
Nah *et al.* [22]	ERP Teamwork & Composition Top Management Support Business Plan & Vision Effective Communication Project Management Project Champion Appropriate Business & IT Legacy Systems
Chen [25]	Needs assessment and choosing the right ERP system Matching business process with the ERP system Understanding new organisational requirements Economic and strategic justification of ERP projects

In Table 2 (a&b), a summary of the Critical Success Factor (CSF) literature on ERP shows the importance of what we term the *Actors Critical Factor Area*, i.e. of those CSFs that focus on ensuring that the ERP project is the 'number one' priority of top managers and as a result, the best internal staff are allocated to the project full-time. Furthermore, adequate resources need to be allocated to the education and training effort of personnel throughout the project.

Table 2 (a): The *Actors Critical Factor Area* for ERP Project Implementation

Critical Success Factors	Importance of Critical Factor Area	References
Project Team Composition Top Management Commitment and Support External Expertise (ERP Consultants and Vendors) Education and Training	Organisations need to assemble a team capable of making and executing the changes required. Clearly understand the issues and ensure that cross-functional coordination exists The 'people element' and training aspect of an ERP implementation have historically received the least amount of attention	[23, 10, 26, 6, 27, 9, 7, 22, 28, 8, 29]

Table 2 (b) also provides an insight into what has been reported in the literature as constituting a success or failure in ERP implementation with regard to the CSFs comprising our *Actors Critical Factor Area*.

Table 2 (b): Explaining the *Actors Critical Factor Area*

Characteristic of the Actors Critical Factor Area	The Actors Critical Factor Area is considered a Success when….	It is considered a Failure when….
Management of in-house and external human resources in a coordinated process	A cross-functional project team exists, consisting of the most knowledgeable organisational personnel	Project team fails to ensure that the technical goals, along with the 'people' element and business changes are addressed
Cross-functional coordination enabled by project management structures, such as a steering committee, ensuring appropriate involvement of all stakeholders	The project team is dedicated solely to the project, with no other responsibilities in the organisation for the duration of the project	Top management commitment and support are poor
	High-level executives have a strong commitment to the project	A lack of coordination leads to delays in implementation and organisational conflicts, while piecemeal approach neglects the very purpose of an integrated package
Creation of a team environment that can lead to a 'cross-pollination' effect, resulting in a more collaborative and self-sufficient mix of talent and responsibilities	The reinforcement of a team environment exists	
	Team members are encouraged to support each other and work to common goals	Resource training is undertaken with little commitment and financial support
	Employees are trained in using the system on a day-to-day basis	Training effort, is a poor fit to the need of the project

4. The *Actors Critical Factor Area* for ERP Project Implementation

The need for top management commitment and support for an enterprise-wide ERP project has been found to be a critical factor in creating an environment for implementation success [30, 10, 31, 28, 32]. Sarker and Lee [32] also found that an open and honest communication, and a balanced and empowered implementation team are necessary 'conditions/precursors' for successful enterprise-wide ERP implementations. Gargeya and Brady [28] also stated that the attitude of senior managers *"will affect not only the flow of funds and information to the project, but also the subordinates' view of the project, its future impact upon the company as a whole, and its impact upon the employees as valued and capable individuals"* (p.510). Therefore, a successful project is more likely where senior management is committed and support the project throughout the process [10, 22].

Furthermore, organisational decision-makers should take the exercise of selecting internal resources seriously [10], as too often organisations do not realise the impact of choosing the staff with the right skill set [10]. Staff should not only be experts in the firm's processes but also be aware of the best business practices in the industry [10]. Staff on an ERP project should exhibit the ability to understand the overall needs of the organisation and should play an important role in guiding the project efforts in the right direction [10].

Gargeya and Brady [28, p.511] commented that *"the 'people element' and training aspect of an ERP implementation have historically received the least amount of attention"* and inadequate resources made available to the training efforts have been reported as the root cause of failed implementations. Staehr *et al.* [33] also observed that the relevance of the training effort was questioned within the organisation and the training system did not use 'real' data, making it impossible for users to understand how the SAP system would really function post 'go-live'. Furthermore, users were also expected to supplement the basic training sessions provided by finding time to spend in the training environment during their normal working hours. Therefore, the criticality attributed to education and training and the material resources provided for change management, training, and support, had an impact on the outcomes of the project and the benefits gained from the use of the SAP system [33].

Thus, we can characterise the ERP project team as ideally a cross-functional team [22] consisting of a mix of consultants, vendors and the 'best' staff of the organisation [34, 10, 35, 22]. Bingi *et al.* [10, p.14] remarked on the importance of having the best staff on the project team, stating that *"selecting the right employees to participate in the implementation process and motivating them is critical for the implementation's success"*. Team members need to be dedicated [10] and assigned full time to the project [22]. The team should be familiar with the business functions and products so that they understand what needs to be done to support major business processes [35, 22]. As a result, both business and technical knowledge are essential for successful implementation [10, 22]. Therefore, finding the right consultant and retaining them through the implementation is vital [10]. In fact, Bingi *et al.* [10] commented that hiring a consultant is just the 'tip of the iceberg', while managing these consultants is even more challenging as it may determine the success or failure of a project.

This discussion firmly characterises the decision to adopt an IT innovation, for instance an ERP application, as a collective, collaborative process, reliant on the right mix of participants, with the right distribution of roles and the right level of understanding of the concepts involved in the adoption and implementation process.

5. Research Objective and Research Methods

In order to confirm the extent to which the use of a collaborative approach to ERP projects is correlated with the success of the project, we investigated ERP projects in four different organisations. The selection of cases is an important aspect of any type of research approach, especially for multiple case study research. Furthermore, a theoretical sampling plan, or a purposeful strategy [36], should be followed where cases are chosen for theoretical not statistical reasons [37]. As with hypothesis-testing research, the concept of an appropriate population is critical as it controls extraneous variation and helps define the limits for generalising the findings.

This research study followed a deliberate theoretical sampling plan. In an effort to guide the case selection, the insights of Stake [38] have been drawn upon, where an *instrumental* study extended to several cases is to be undertaken. A single *intrinsic* case would not in itself fulfil the objective of this research study, however, jointly studying a number of *instrumental* cases would better facilitate investigating the enterprise-wide ERP phenomenon, where the diverse organisational stories of those 'living the case' could be teased out [38]. In the context of this study, for an organisation to be considered suitable it had to have undertaken an ERP project, and at the time of the study, be in the post-implementation phase for all or part of the project, depending on the implementation approach followed by the organisation.

Over a two month period, over 20 organisations were contacted to establish whether they were interested in participating in the research study. Interviews were conducted in 7 sites where more information was obtained about the ERP projects. This somewhat *opportunistic* [36] approach to purposeful sampling of research sites concluded with the selection of four organisations, namely: SerCom Solutions, Banta Global Turnkey (BGT), the Irish Health Services (now the Health Service Executive -

HSE), and An Post. The advantage of this approach was that during this initial selection phase, a greater understanding of the characteristics of each organisation, its operations and complexities, the competitive forces at play, etc. was gained. More importantly, an initial perception of the enterprise-wide ERP project and its outcomes was built up, as in Table 3.

Table 3: Initial Perceptions of Cases Selected for the Research Study

Factor	SerCom	BGT	HSE	An Post
Sector	Private	Private	Public	Public
Package	SAP R/3	JDE World	SAP R/3	JDE OneWorld
ERP Footprint	Core Operations (Manufacturing and Logistics)	Core Operations (Supply Chain Manufacturing and Finance)	HR / Payroll	Finance
ERP System Type	Value Chain Operations	Value Chain Operations	Support Operations	Support Operations
Project Type	Business Change	IT	IT	Business Change
Enterprise-Wide View	Yes	No	No	Yes
Start date	2000	1995	1997	1997
Outcome	Very Successful	Near Failure	Failure (suspended)	Partly Successful
Point-of-Contact Comment	*The project required n huge effort from all involved but it was a great success*	*I could tell you all the things not to do. We have not done well with our ERP project*	*This project is going badly. It will face huge issues in-use as it is being rolled-out nationally*	*We have learned some hard lessons but that's the nature of these projects*

Over a 2 year period, data from these four 4 was collected by way of 35 interviews totaling 84 hours and documentation analysis, consisting of minutes of meetings and other project documentation made available to the researchers. These figures indicate the depth of understanding which the access obtained by the researchers yielded in each of the four case studies and adds confidence to the validity of our observations.

6. Analysing the *People* Factor in the Four ERP Projects

The evidence from the four cases studied focused on what we termed the ***Best Business Personnel Principle*** of project management, where it can be established that the best, most committed staff were available to the project on a full-time basis. Our observations indicate that there is a fundamental paradox in selecting team members for such projects, namely that the personnel that can least spared by the business are the ones that can most comprehensively contribute to the project. In practice, all areas of the business that are impacted by the introduction of the ERP package need to commit in advance to release these personnel as their full-time representatives on the project team. Therefore, we sought to establish whether organisational decision-makers took the exercise of selecting internal resources seriously and did allocate their best staff.

Our cross case analysis leads to the conclusion that the factors connected to the *Actors Critical Factor Area* (Table 2 a&b) were the most impotant ones that could be observed in all four cases. Others aspects of project management which we measured in our study were found in one or two out of the four cases, the absence of what we have termed the ***Best Business Personnel Principle*** caused problems to all our organisations. Irrespective of the efforts made at the outset of the project by some of the organisations (SerCom and An Post), issues relating to skill levels of staff on the project team, and their release from their business roles, and full-time allocation to the project, were a cause of major problems. Thus, all of the organisations experienced implementation problems as a result of this *Best Business Personnel Principle* not being *mindfully* addressed as the outset of their enterprise-wide ERP projects.

The IT Director in SerCom summed up their experiences with this aspect of project management, commenting retrospectively that *"it is all about getting things done quickly and having the correct people to be able to deliver the required functionality. Ultimately, there is nothing worse than mediocrity when you are trying to implement an ERP system for a fast-changing business"*. The IT Director, whom so many claimed was the key to SAP functioning so smoothly in support of the SerCom business, believed that possessing internal skill sets is crucial to having flexibility in the system (best staff involvement in the project implementation process), and the ability to manage that flexibility post 'go-live' (knowledgeable staff supporting the business in-use). As a result, within SerCom, where a relatively small project team existed during implementation, the retention of these knowledgeable business and IT personnel comprising that team, and the relocation of these personnel back into their functional business areas post-implementation, was one of the organisation's biggest positives. This relocation of key project resources has afforded SerCom the opportunity to sustain the business and grow for the future with the certainty that knowledge of the SAP infrastructure remains within the organisation.

Even in SerCom, the most positive case of our sample, two functional areas did not provide their best internal business resources to the project, as evidenced by the fact that the skill set of these representatives was questioned by our informants. As a consequence, these functional areas did not receive the same immediate benefits from the implementation of the SAP infrastructure as other functional areas, and aspects of the ERP system had to be retrofitted in support of these functional areas post 'go-live'. In the other three cases evidence also supports the fact that managers were reluctant to give up their best human resources full-time to the project initiatives. For example, within BGT, the Health Services and An Post, a reluctance to provide the best internal business resources to their respective projects, which it is argued was as a direct result of a lack of 'top management commitment and support' to the project from the outset, led to an immature understanding of existing business processes and new business process transactions, in the new technological environment, and further delivered a less than desirable project outcome in terms of ERP functionality. Indeed to further compound this impact, as observed in An Post, BGT and to a lesser extent in SerCom, 'super-users' did not always know the business and the system and in some instances did not deliver quality training to the end-users. Evidence suggests that this can conclusively be linked to the fact that relatively inexperienced internal business resources became 'super-users' for their functional areas and delivered inadequate training in their respective areas. Within these cases it was reported that this inadequate quality of training delivered to the functional areas, that these 'super-users' represented, led to time delays in the appropriate system functionality knowledge being transferred to end-users in those areas, and user groups found straightforward but 'newly enhanced' business processes difficult.

The An Post case study reveals another aspect of the *Best Business Personnel Principle*: in comparison with SerCom, An Post had a much larger project team, which was largely made up of external consultants (presumably very knowledgeable about ERP). As a result, very few resources with a real working knowledge of the JD

Edwards system remained in the firm post-implementation to maintain the ERP infrastructure in support of the business. Even when project team members were internal An Post staff, some of them were contract staff and in some instances recent graduate recruits with a low level of understanding of the organisation's business processes. One business area in An Post, when selecting its project team members, took the decision to employ a contract accountant, not readily familiar with existing business processes, which in turn made it very difficult to evaluate 'best practice' when introducing the ERP to support the specific business processes of this area. One of the roles performed by this project team member was an analysis of the business requirements documents in Phase 1 of the project. In retrospect this was a mistake, as a lot of valuable knowledge departed from the organisation, when this person departed. Also, the team member for this business area lacked support at a sufficiently knowledgeable level within An Post, meaning that for most issues requiring attention, clearance was obtained at a higher level, before any decisions were made. This resulted in unnecessary delays during the implementation phase, with constant meetings being arranged to resolve standard issues. Furthermore, the original project team except for one team member, all left An Post before the project was completed, leaving one resident *expert* within the organisation post 'go-live'. According to the Business Support Manager *"the 'brain-drain' affected the Business Units' ability to further develop their business processes and support the live users"*. As a result, the opportunity to tailor the ERP to the needs of certain areas was lost and no one was left to answer the question as to *'why the system did what it did in this way?'* or *'how could the systems do what it does to better serve the business needs?'*

The evidence in these cases confirms that a lack of adequate business resources, in a post-implementation environment, leads to confusion within an organisation as to the fit between the system infrastructure and the enhancement potential, in support of the changing business requirements. A similar problem was identified in BGT where constant reference was made to the fact that attracting and retaining resources of a high calibre was extremely difficult and a time consuming process. The critical element of success from the BGT perspective was to have an appreciation between business and IT resources of the skill sets they possessed and forge a tight working relationship between these resources. However, the reality within BGT has centred on trying to hire, as opposed to retain, resources with an exceptionally high appreciation of business and IT, and the functionality of the BGT business.

Thus, the case data shows that it is *mindless* for an organisation to undertake an enterprise-wide ERP project and not commit to allocating the best internal business resources to the project team on a full-time basis. On the other hand if organisations are *mindful* of this **Best Business Personnel Principle**, we can conclude that the severity of emerging implementation problems will be reduced, and the ability of the organisation to address these problems in a timely fashion will be increased. It is interesting to note that the SerCom case indicates that being aware of the risk associated with the **Best Business Personnel Principle** early on in the lifecycle of the project is not sufficient to avoid its pitfall. Although SerCom rates very highly in terms of assigning proper resources to the project, the fact that key business resources did not always adequately support their business areas as 'super-users' led to similar problems, as the lack of a coherent approach led to, in the other organisations. Therefore, we can establish that the **Best Business Personnel Principle** impacts more that just the implementation phase of a project lifecycle, it also impacts on an organisation's ability, at go-live, to have end-user ownership and usability of the system. This may seem like a rather simplistic observation, but it has a damaging impact on an organisation's abilities with the implemented system in-use, post go-live.

7. Conclusion

The **Best Business Personnel Principle** which we have discussed has many downstream and upstream aspects. In terms of upstream impacts, the support of top management to the project team and the perception of functional managers as to the importance of the project are obviously critical in getting the CSFs inherent in the *Actors Critical Factor Area* right. Associated to the **Best Business Personnel Principle** is the presence of good communication about the project, which allows the project team to keep organisational actors abreast of the conduct and progress of the project and the need for certain changes.

Downstream from the **Best Business Personnel Principle**, the impact of incorrect decisions will be felt in terms of organisational buy-in, resistance to change and the effectiveness of the organisation to exploit the new technologies. This places the **Best Business Personnel Principle** at the centre of a web of interrelated factors, which altogether constrain or promote the degree to which organisations will be able to realise the benefits from the innovations they decide to adopt.

8. Bibliography

[1]   Davis, F. (1989) "Perceived Usefulness, Perceived Ease of Use, and User Acceptance of Information Technology", *MIS Quarterly*, 13(3), 318-340.
[2]   Swanson, E.B. and Ramiller, N.C. (2004) "Innovating mindfully with information technology", *MIS Quarterly*, 28(4), 553-583.
[3]   Abrahamson, E. (1991) "Managerial fads and fashions: the diffusion and rejection of innovations", *Academy of Management Review,* 16(3), 586-612.
[4]   Abrahamson, E. (1996) "Management fashion", *Academy of Management Review,* 21(1), 254-285.
[5]   Caldas, M. and Wood, T. (1998) "How consultants can help organizations survive the ERP frenzy". Accessed 28th March 2000 at: http://www.gv.br/prof_alunos/thomaz/ingles/paper6.htm.
[6]   Markus, M.L. and Tanis, C. The enterprise systems experience--From adoption to success. In R. W. Zmud, Ed, Framing the Domains of IT Research: Glimpsing the Future Through the Past. Cincinnati, OH: Pinnaflex Educational Resources, Inc.
[7]   Parr, A. and Shanks, G. (2000) "A model of ERP project implementation", *Journal of Information Technology*, 15, 289-303.
[8]   Kim, Y., Lee, Z. and Gosain, S. (2005) "Impediments to successful ERP implementation process", *Business Process Management Journal*, 11(2), 158-170.
[9]   Stefanou, C. (2000) "The selection process of ERP systems", *Proceedings of the 6th Americas Conference on Information Systems (AMCIS)*, August 10-13, Long Beach California, 988-991.
[10] Bingi, P., Sharma, M. and Godla, J. (1999) "Critical issues affecting an ERP implementation", *Information Systems Management*, 16(3), 7-14.
[11] Ponzi, L. and Koenig, M. (2002) "Knowledge management: Another management fad?" *Information Research*, 8(1). Accessed: 6th January 2005 from: http://InformationR.net/ir/8-1/paper145.html.
[12] Hossain, L. and Shakir, M. (2001) "Stakeholder involvement framework for understanding the decision making process of ERP selection in New Zealand", *Journal of Decision Systems*, 10(1) 11-27.
[13] Wood, T. and Caldas, M. (2001) "Reductionism and complex thinking during ERP implementations", *Business Process Management Journal*, 7(5), 387-393.
[14] Sammon, D. and Adam, F. (2002) "Decision making in the ERP community", *Proceedings of the 10th European Conference on Information Systems*, June 2002, Gdansk, Poland.
[15] Strang, D. and Macy, M.W. (2001) "In search of excellence: Fads, success stories, and adaptive emulation", *American Journal of Sociology*, 107(1), 147-182.

[16] Adam, F and Sammon, D. (2004) "ERP software selection - widening the debate", in Adam, F. and Sammon, D., *The Enterprise Resource Planning Decade: Lessons Learned And Issues For The Future*, Idea Publishing Group, Hershey, PS.

[17] Gill, J. and Whittle, S. (1992) "Management by panacea: Accounting for transience", *Journal of Management Studies,* 30(2), 282-295.

[18] McGrath, J. E (1984) *Groups - Interaction and Performance*, Prentice-Hall, Englewood Cliffs, N.J.

[19] Carter, L.F., Haythorn, W.W. and Howell, M.A. (1950) "A further investigation of the criteria of leadership", *Journal of Abnormal and Social Psychology*, 46, 350-358.

[20] Shaw, M.E. (1973) "Scaling group tasks: a method for dimensional analysis", *JSAS Catalogue of Selected Documents in Psychology*, 3, p. 8.

[21] Steiner, I. D. (1972) *Group Processes and Productivity*, Academic Press, New York.

[22] Nah, F.F.H., Lau, J.L.S., and Kuang, J. (2001) "Critical factors for successful implementation of enterprise systems", *Business Process Management Journal*, 7(3), 285-296.

[23] Bancroft, N., Seip, H. and Sprengel, A. (1998) *Implementing SAP R/3: How to Introduce a Large System into a Large Organisation*, 2nd Edition, Manning Publications, Greenwich.

[24] Shakir, M. (2000) "Decision making in the evaluation, selection and implementation of ERP systems", *Proceedings of the 6th Americas Conference on Information Systems (AMCIS)*, August 10-13 2000, Long Beach California, 1033-1038.

[25] Chen, I.J. (2001) "Planning for ERP systems: analysis and future trend", *Business Process Management Journal*, 7(5), 374-386.

[26] Slater, D. (1998) "The hidden costs of enterprise software", *CIO Magazine*, January p. .22.

[27] Sumner, M. (2000) "Risk factors in enterprise-wide/ERP projects", *Journal of Information Technology*, 15, 317-327.

[28] Gargeya, V.B. and Brady, C. (2005) "Success and failure factors of adopting SAP in ERP system implementation", *Business Process Management Journal*, 11(5), 501-516.

[29] Finney, S. and Corbett, M. (2007) "ERP implementation: a compilation and analysis of critical success factors", *Business Process Management Journal*, 13(3), 329-347.

[30] Zerega, B. (1997) "Management support a must for big bang", *InfoWorld*, 8 September, p. 100.

[31] Davenport, T. (2000) *Mission Critical – Realizing the Promise of Enterprise Systems*, Harvard Business School Publishing, Boston, MA, .

[32] Sarker, S. and Lee, A. (2000) "Using a case study to test the role of three key social enablers in ERP implementation", in *Proceedings of the 21st International Conference on Information Systems*, 414-425.

[33] Staehr, L., Shanks, G. and Seddon, P. (2004) "Understanding the business Consequences of ERP systems", in Adam, F. and Sammon, D., *The Enterprise Resource Planning Decade: Lessons Learned And Issues For The Future*, Idea Publishing Group, Hershey, PS, 72-91.

[34] Buckhout, S., Frey, E., and Nemec, J (1999) "Making ERP succeed: Turning fear into promise", *IEEE Engineering Management Review*, 116-123.

[35] Rosario, J.G. (2000) *On The Leading Edge: Critical Success Factors In ERP Implementation Projects,* BusinessWorld, The Philippines.

[36] Patton, M. Q. (1990) *Qualitative Evaluation and Research Methods,* Sage Publications, Thousand Oaks, California.

[37] Eisenhardt, K. (1989) Building theories from case study research. *Academy of Management Review*, 14(4), 532-550.

[38] Stake, R.E. (2000) "Case studies", in Denzin and Lincoln (Eds) *Handbook of Qualitative Research,* Sage Publications, London.

Studying the impact of ERP on collaborative decision making – a case study

Fergal Carton[a] — Frederic Adam[a]
[a]Business Information Systems
University College Cork,
Cork Ireland
fcarton@afis.ucc.ie, fadam@afis.ucc.ie

Abstract: ERP applications have been proposed as solution to many current operational problems. For instance, ERP support decision makers by making key data visible in a timely fashion. The price of this visibility is extensive standardisation of business processes. Multinationals in particular need to impose a common way of working throughout their different sites in order to better control performance. ERP systems provide a common language, using a shared data store and integrated business processes. At the same time, organisations are subject to constant evolution, where shareholder expectations, customer demands or organic growth may result in standard processes no longer "fitting" with reality. This paper reports on a mature ERP implementation, focusing on an element of operational decision making that is becoming increasingly collaborative: sales order fulfilment. Growing complexity in the products on offer have resulted in a fragmented supply chain, including the use of "cross docks" to combine third party products with in-house elements on the same sales order. Commit date decisions for customer shipments, increasingly involve a high degree of collaboration between managers from the different plants. The study indicates that collaborative processes supported by highly integrated information systems do not always lead to more collaborative behaviour because the loss of flexibility imposed by the standardised processes constrains what organisational actors can or cannot do.

Keywords: ERP, decision making, collaboration, sales orders, globalisation

Introduction

The ERP concept, with its total system approach, seems a powerful tool to allow firms to plan for, execute and control complex operations involving multiple business partners and manufacturing and distribution sites. The existence of a common platform to share data and execute shared processes seems a good match for today's managers facing increasingly globalised operations and transactions. With a centralised repository of all revenue and expenditure corporate data, and based on a common user interface, ERP systems democratise access to performance information and provide means to execute transactions and support decisions on resource commitment.

However, highly detailed visibility of the steps in a shared business process comes at a price. ERP applications impose a coherent but uncompromising logic on all collaborating actors. This logic is based on a general case scenario that is extremely efficient in dealing with standard transactions, but makes dealing with changes to plans or other unexpected circumstance, precisely the task of decision makers, very difficult and cumbersome. ERP users experience severe constraints in adjusting the evolving reality of business activities to "what the system wants" and the flexibility that is required in collaborating with other users outside the strict framework of what is allowed by the configured software may be lacking.

The potential of highly integrated enterprise systems for supporting collaborative decisions must therefore be investigated in the light of certain factors; namely that, when selecting and implementing an ERP system, companies are looking at a good fit with basic operations, not with the need to allow actors to collaborate in their decision processes; that managers rely on many tacit processes for key decisions in the execution of business processes that are not necessarily analysed in detail [1], nor widely communicated; that the data model of ERP applications is inventory centric, and therefore lacks the scope to be able to support managers in decisions that involve trading off the costs related to different resources administered by different constituencies within the firm, as would be required for a truly collaborative approach. In addition, an ERP implementation implies many assumptions about the company and how it operates at a specific point in time [2]. These assumptions may change over time, due to the organisation changes what it does or reacts to new opportunities or threats, leading to radical changes in its business model. The extension of the product set, or the adoption of new distribution channels, are examples of "structural" process changes that have a clear impact on back office execution activities.

In this paper, we present a case study of a firm in the high tech manufacturing sector which has carried out a global implementation of a single instance ERP system 3 years previously. It is focused on a key aspect of customer-facing operational decision making: sales order fulfillment. This activity involves the matching of individual sales orders with product supply, i.e. available finished goods. Complexity has arisen in this process due to the rapidly evolving product set on offer, and to the globalisation of the supply network. The paper begins by considering the need for collaboration in the execution of business processes and the consequent collaborative requirements for the systems that support managers in these tasks. It then briefly presents our methodology before studying the difficulties faced by managers in enacting collaborative decision processes and the inadequacy of the ERP application in support of this task.

1. Collaboration, Decisions, and ERPS

Although, computer-based systems can help with decision making and information dissemination, managers also spend considerable effort in their role of "go-between", allocating work to subordinates and networking with internal and external peers [3, 4]. How computer systems can be used for these activities still is largely unknown. Envisioning the impact of ERP on all levels of decision making processes of the firm is therefore extremely ambitious. Post-ERP, the decision process may have changed insofar as there are new or modified sources of information and / or different steps in the process. Key decisions may change as the system now incorporates some of the conditions and exception traps which were previously dealt with manually. The methods used for collaborating across processes and across stages in these processes may be altered such that actors may gain more visibility on what is happening operationally in their organisation, but may have lost the capability to make decisions towards more flexibility in meeting customer (internal and external) demands [5].

Organisational actors will find out, post-implementation, if all the parameters they need for decision making have been taken into account in setting up the ERP. Else, they will have to live with reduced flexibility or workarounds until the ERP is updated. Post go-live, the impetus and resources required to change the ERP evaporate, and the workarounds become the rule until the next ERP upgrade. This is particularly critical in relation to the softer aspect of business processes, notably the conversations which managers are used to holding face to face and which can be the part of the process where most value is being added [6, 7]. These softer aspects, because they are not amenable to coding in the shape of business rules, are likely to be overlooked. As a result, managers may find themselves post-implementation in situations where complex discussions are simplified to the extent that they could be understood by the software specialists who coded the template, but are no longer serving their decision making purposes [1]. This has been observed in the centralisation of purchasing activity in multinationals, where local buyers have lost their ability to negotiate with preferred local suppliers, instead merely placing orders through a centralised system, leaving them with no human operator to deal with. This may be very efficient in the general case, but leaves firms exposed in situations where volumes change at short notice or a configuration must be changed for a special order. In these cases, the collaborative aspects of the process have been sacrificed to the principle of standardization [5].

Thus, implementing an ERP system may actually complicate decision making for managers. Although managers may be privy to the reasoning behind the configuration options embodied in the business template as implemented by the firm, they will be dissuaded from proposing any changes to these decisions pre or post-implementation. The tight timescales for the implementation of ERP systems don't allow an adequate margin for questioning the corporate template being rolled out. Managers are thus expected to take on different process models, with parameters they had little influence on, and with little room to manoeuvre on a day to day basis.

In ERP projects, organisations rather than individuals seek to adopt integrating mechanisms which increase their information processing capabilities [8] but don't consider the actions of managers. ERP systems are integration mechanisms in Galbraith's parlance, allowing routine and predictable tasks to be automated. As such, they may take the organisation towards a more routinised decision making. Winter [9] however suggests that there should be a conscious choice in the selection of which matters to treat routinely, and which to treat with some deliberation. It is debatable whether such selection occurs in an ERP project in that the choices inherent in implementing and configuring ERP processes amount to minimising the choices to be made by users regarding the day to day routine work. For example, if Sales Orders (SO's) are parameterised within an ERP such that fulfilment locations (distribution centers) are a direct function of customer address, and the items on that sales order are all available from that location, then these SO's can be "processed" automatically, and the decision making has been simplified and the efficiency of the fulfillment process improved by allowing faster SO turnaround times. On the other hand, as the complexity of the items on the sales order grows, expanding to include not only products but also services, the ability of the system to adapt to the new requirement is reduced.

Thus, the implementation of ERP should, in theory, facilitate collaborative decision making by virtue of the standardised operational processes throughout the firm, and the subsequent visibility of transactional data to managers. However, the assumptions made regarding how the business works at the time of implementation rarely remain unchanged, and new models for doing business may have unpredictable effects on the reliability and relevance of the business process encoded in the ERP. In an effort to understand how the collaborative potential of ERP systems becomes thwarted by business reality, we carried out a case study in a firm with a mature ERP application to study in detail the decision making routines in the area of distribution. The case conclusions represent an initial step towards understanding how ERPs can be adapted to help managers collaborate in a fast changing world.

2. Research objective, questions and methods

In this research, an in-depth case study of a successful multinational company (MNC) was used to explore the role of ERP in supporting managerial decision making. One of the challenges of research into the impact of integrated applications such as ERP is the scope of their impact in the different functions of the organisation. Interlinking modules cover all aspects of business activity from procurement to production and from sales orders to invoicing. In this case, the focus of the research was narrowed down to one process where demand meets supply, namely, the sales order fulfilment process. We selected this business process because it is one of the most critical processes from the perspective of customer satisfaction, and because distribution is highly labour intensive in terms of management time and effort. It is also very data dependent, and is therefore an area where most organisations seek the highest degree of automation. Indeed one of the underlying principles of the ERP business model is that sales orders will consume finished goods in an automated fashion. Based on the observations we presented in section 1, this may lead to severe tensions, as managers seek to offer high levels of responsiveness to customer demands, using a technology that is so standardised that it prevents them from collaborating effectively, leading to attempts to optimise performance within each stage of the process, to the detriment of the overall effectiveness of the firm. Thus the research lens is narrowed to one aspect of how businesses operate, but how the requirement for collaboration between managers is met in this area is crucial to the success of the business.

This research is part of a larger project where we investigated the complete landscape of business processes affected by the ERP in the firm. This approach allowed us to determine which areas where the most interesting from the point of view of our research goal – that of understanding the impact of ERP applications on managerial decision making. The Distribution function is at the crossroads between supply and demand, and represents "where the rubber meets the road", and hence our interest in this area. Planning and manufacturing will ultimately be tested by their ability to make enough raw materials and finished goods available to meet customer demand. Finance, riding shotgun between sales and production, will require not only that orders are fulfilled, but that the credit for the customers concerned is good, and that the margins are acceptable. The efficient flow of information between the actors involved and the integrity of that data is vital to both customer satisfaction and company performance.

The importance of distribution activities is also borne out in the overall case data, where "Deliver" and "Quote to cash" processes were mentioned most frequently (48%) across the range of decision domains covered in our analysis and across the range of managers interviewed. This means that the Deliver process is by far the most frequently mentioned by all managers in the firm as one critical to operations. The fact that, as already stated in the introduction, the distribution process is getting increasingly collaborative in the case study firm justifies the aims of this paper.

Qualitative data can help researchers understand the dynamics underlying complex relationships, that is, the "why" of what is happening [10]. The approach adopted in this research was to triangulate views of key decision maker from the different areas involved. It was felt that this qualitative approach represented a non-judgmental, exploratory way for managers, who have themselves internalized the logic of the "way things are done", to elucidate their own decision patterns and biases. Extreme pressure on the sales order fulfilment cycle at quarter end is an observable management headache. However, it is difficult (for all concerned) to identify the causality between the variables involved, or to delineate definitively between the effects of transaction volume, administration inefficiency or information system shortcoming.

Single case studies pose an additional challenge of extricating the findings from their specific organisational context towards generalisable principles. This risk of bias was attenuated by a number of factors. Firstly, ERP packages are based on a common view of the underlying business model. The gaps between this model and the way companies operate may vary from case to case, but the latency impact on decision making is comparable. Secondly, publicly quoted MNC's operate under the scrutiny of the Stock Exchange, and the top-down pressure on keeping inventory and costs low, while maintaining profit margins and customer satisfaction, is universal. Finally, managers are faced with the same daily challenges in any business, ensuring that resources are being used efficiently and effectively in the execution of corporate goals.

The research objective was operationalised into 3 separate research questions which yielded a complete picture of the "footprint" of ERP in different aspects of the managers' responsibilities. **Research Question 1** was concerned with discovering the goals pursued by distribution managers at different sites and from a headquarters perspective. The crucial point was to understand how these goals were evolving based on the changing business model. **Research Question 2** was concerned with a more granular view of decisions relating to demand capture, sales order allocation and shipment of finished goods on a day to day basis, and the perceptions of managers of what the critical issues were. **Research Question 3** drew on the output from Question 2 and explored the footprint of ERP in this decisional domain.

These questions were investigated during an in-depth field study of SIT Ltd (not the company's real name), a large multinational manufacturing organisation. From April to August 2005, 46 interviews were carried out with middle and senior managers in manufacturing operations and finance in Ireland and the US. SIT went live on their ERP system in October 2001, so these interviews reflected the views of managers using a relatively mature system, which is why this firm was selected.

The next section outlines the background to SIT as a company and the context of the ERP implementation.

3. Case study background

SIT see themselves as the market leader in data management solutions, specialising in helping customers to derive more value from their corporate data. The company is following an aggressive growth, with 17% growth in consolidated revenue in 2005. Revenues have since then continued to grow, topping $11.2 billion in 2006. SIT Ltd employs over 26,500 people in 52 operations worldwide. Manufacturing is concentrated in three sites, one of which is Cork.

Over time, SIT has evolved from a hardware firm to a "solutions" company, delivering information "lifecycle" tools and consulting services. A key complexity of this trend towards full service offerings is the management of the information flows related to executing a single customer order, which increasingly is constituted of hardware, software and services. Many of these revenue lines are executed by multiple locations, over different time horizons, yet the customer will require a single sales order, single invoice and single goods shipment.

SIT implemented a single instance global ERP system in 2001. This big bang implementation addressed user requirements for transaction processing in all back office activities relating to sales order processing, manufacturing, materials planning, distribution and finance. The Oracle based system supports 4,500 users in 52 countries worldwide, 3 of which involve manufacturing operations.

Sales demand is focused through the ERP based quotation and sales order processing system. Although a "build to plan" operation, SIT suffers from the hockey stick effect on sales, whereby the majority of sales is only confirmed in the final 2 weeks of the quarter, which places huge pressures on managers, operators and systems. This pressure is principally felt in the execution cycle: the processing of orders from approval through to shipment. One of the key questions underlying this research is whether the ERP, through which all transactional data flows, helps the actors involved to collaborate in these decisions, or hinders the decision process by introducing latency.

4. Findings of the case study

4.1. Research Question 1: Organisational goals

In SIT, top management communicate high level goals in terms of revenues and product mix at quarterly shareholder briefings. This communication draws a line in the sand both for the sales organisation and the three manufacturing operations and their respective supply chains. Goals and budgets are disseminated downwards through each functional organisation and geography. Manufacturing are driven by product availability plans, sales are driven by revenue targets, and Finance are driven by external shareholder expectations of revenue and profitability. Distribution are balanced between the two goals of revenue and unit shipments, but above all conscious of the dollar value represented by what they call "backlog", i.e., pending approved orders, which mean unfulfilled demand. Distribution aim to finish the quarter with nothing in backlog, therefore not being seen to leave potential revenue "on the shelf".

At a global level, the goals are subject to frequent change, depending upon the messages that company officers wish to transmit to the stock market regarding SIT's performance, or according to unpredicted trends in demand. At an operational level, these changes directly influence managerial decisions. Changes to goals permeate right down to the execution level, where distribution and customer operations are making decisions on what backlog orders to ship based on sales targets. These targets are viewed simultaneously in terms of revenue, margin, product and geographic region.

A key issue in achieving corporate goals is that revenue targets use *average* prices which capture neither the complexity of the products or the seasonality of sales activities. SIT's data storage solutions are required to fit the customer's specific technical infrastructure, thus the products are highly configurable, and consequently the sales procedure for higher end solutions can be long. Hockey stick pressure on sales reps to close their deals in the current quarter implies that the actual price on any given customer order can vary considerably as the bargaining power of customers increases.

Finance is moving to global shared service models in both revenue and expenditure. Sales activity is by definition local, but sales order processing is being centralised. The notion of a single point of entry for a sales order, and therefore single invoice and payment from the customer, is the holy grail for an organisation with a supply chain that is fragmenting, and a product set that is getting more complex.

The customer requirement for a single invoice is well understood by Distribution and Finance. SIT products are complex, and are installed at the heart of the customers' IT infrastructure. Taking corporate servers off-line in order to commission the new storage solution requires advance planning and close co-ordination between the IT department and its business users. The gathering of all SIT components for a given customer order into one physical shipment is critical so that the disruption to normal services is minimised. This is explained clearly by a Distribution manager in Cork:

> It's like if you were ordering a home entertainment system, you don't want the VCR coming today and the TV tomorrow, and the DVD coming the next day. You want it all at once

The critical point in this process is the multiple actors involved from Finance, Sales, Production, quality control and Distribution, all with different objectives stated in different units (dollars of revenue, number of units of product, number of complete shipments, …) and with exclusive access to certain parts of an essentially shared process. The requirement for collaboration is high, with sales being highly dependent on the timely availability of products (there is practically no buffer stocks) of the right configuration. In certain cases, products may be taken from a de-expedited order to fulfil a higher value or higher margin order. As pressure increases towards quarter end, the potential for conflict between the managers administering the different aspects of the sales order processing / product allocation / shipping process becomes quite high and the need for collaboration increases as a result.

Thus, the SIT case illustrates the trend in multinationals towards a culture based on a "load and chase" philosophy. High level goals are set at the beginning of the period and communicated broadly, being thereafter treated as set in stone. Variations in demand, on the other hand, cause uneven patterns of operational activity and place huge strain on the execution organisation. Reacting to actual versus plan updates becomes an onerous part of execution activity requiring high level of co-operation, as distinct from simply dealing with execution issues. Exactly how this decentralisation of responsibility impacts the collaborative behaviour of managers is explored next.

4.2. Research Question 2: Management decisions

SIT has built a reputation for customer service and flexibility, offering products that adapt to customers IT infrastructure regardless of their operating systems, connectivity requirements and data management needs. The fact that these infrastructures may not evolve as quickly as SIT's products is an ongoing thorn in the side of the execution organisation, as a Distribution manager in Cork described:

> one of the things we do is allow customers order anything, of any configuration, of anything they want. So, you know, the lunatic stuff that gets ordered, like, 7 generations old stuff, is still in your backlog, it's still there, there's still some customers looking for it.

The goal of maintaining single shipments for all the elements on the sales order was mentioned in section 4.1 above. Local distribution managers are focused on delivering customers everything ordered within the commit dates, no matter how late in the quarter orders are received. The headache is that the lead times on the different elements of an order may be very different. This is exacerbated at quarter end when available stock in finished goods is rapidly diminishing. The decisions for Distribution managers involve a trade-off between the customer benefit of a single shipment and the SIT benefit of recognising the revenue for at least some of the ordered items. A Distribution manager in Boston commented on this dilemma:

> you're going to run out of stock on a quarter-end so you've got a choice, do I give him half of what he wants, and it's not so much "can I give him half of what he wants", and it's more can I take half the revenue, by giving him half of what he wants". And the answer to that is always yes, give him half of what he wants and take half the revenue, because the number one goal is to get the revenue in.

Finance, on the other hand, are focused on achieving complete shipments so that the revenue related to the original sales order can be fully recognised, and so that the invoice can be issued and cash collected as early as possible. Any mismatch between a sales order and an invoice can mean a delay in cash collection, which hurts cash flow. From the customer viewpoint, obtaining approval for a single large purchase order is also usually more efficient than several smaller ones. This creates tension as distribution managers attempt to ship anything that can be shipped, whether complete orders or not.

Traditionally the three SIT manufacturing organisations dealt with the shipment demands of their own customers (defined by their geographic location). The two US plants delivered all customers based in the Americas, and the Cork plant looked after all other shipments (EMEA and Asia Pacific regions). However, since the implementation of the ERP, SIT has moved to "globalise the whole allocate-to-fulfil process". This new requirement has evolved as the complexity of what is being included in the single shipment has increased, including many third party products. The price book now contains 1400 products. This is a mindset change for distribution, who are used to physically handling everything that goes out the door, and also a process challenge, as a corporate Distribution director explained:

> What you want to be able to do, and that's where this group is here, now, when demand comes in from the field, you want to very quickly be able to say, I don't care about the orgs, I just want to be able to use the factories as source of supply, very quickly, very accurately, and you

know what, after they all supply their pieces, have the ability to bring it all back together again down here, in one consolidated delivery to the customer

What was initially a local decision process is now elevated to a global level. Commit dates would be allocated according to the same criteria of plant capacity and material availability, but with the added sophistication of being able to compare these variables across different plants. Visibility of information centrally is key in making such collaborative decision making possible. SIT did not have an automated answer to this issue, and were at the stage of realising the limitations in their ERP based processes.

Meanwhile sales operations, a sales support group working alongside their colleagues in Distribution, but reporting to the Finance organization, are concentrated on trying to get the "highest dollars out". This implies not simply reducing backlog, but reducing it in an order of priority which optimizes the chances of hitting revenue targets for the different lines of the business and reduces the risk of the corporation being penalised on the stock market. Decisions are therefore based on a view of backlog orders that reflects their dollar value. Distribution operate a difficult balancing act between the sales operations focus on revenue, and the execution focus on physically preparing and shipping the products that are allocated to orders, all within a shrinking window of time as quarter end approaches. This gives rise to a type of decision making that can only be characterised as "decision by walkabout", as distribution technicians go down to the factory floor and begin "babysitting orders out the door" (in their own words), trying to gain commitment from manufacturing that a particular bundle of products is going to be readied for shipment before the due date has elapsed. The walkabout element of the process seems a throwback to the old days of logistics, but it is in fact necessitated by the fact that work orders, capable of making the link between work in progress and sales orders, were not implemented in the ERP system. Operators are therefore unable to automatically assign items of finished goods to orders in backlog. In this instance, face to face communication is the only reliable way to ensure the smooth and accurate execution of the transactions, despite the large investment in ERP technology.

In the next section we will look at the data concerning the value of the ERP system in decision making concerning the Deliver process.

4.3. Research Question 3: ERP value in managerial decision making

At a local distribution level, it is highly debatable whether the ERP investment can be considered beneficial. Managers were asked about the value of ERP to their decision making in the Deliver process, and Table 1 gives a summary of the quantitative analysis of the interview transcripts. In this table, "-" denotes negative opinions, "+" denotes positive opinions and "=" denotes neutral opinions. Opinions were classified into themes (mentioned in Section 2 above) that group together concerns of a common nature. For example, comments made by managers on the flexibility of the ERP application to adapt to the changing way of working were grouped under "Flexibility". The table shows the dominance of negative opinions on the impact of ERP (84%) and the polarisation around negative or positive opinions (only 6% of references to the value of ERP in terms of the Deliver process were neutral). The high proportion of negative opinions concerning the impact of ERP on the Deliver process, (84%), is highly significant given that this is the key business activity strongly related to customers' perception of the firm.

Table 1. Value of ERP in the Deliver process by theme (n=123 coded observations)

Theme	Negative		Positive		Neutral		Total
Flexibility	26	905	2	7%	1	3%	29
Latency	24	92	2	8			26
Manual	14	100					14
Granularity	8	73	2	18	1	9	11
Correlation	6	75	2	25			8
Gap virtual / physical	7	88			1	12	8
KPI	4	57	1	14	2	29	7
Accuracy / consistency	5	71	2	29			7
Automation	3	50	2	33	1	17	6
Centralisation	3	75			1	25	4
Aggregation	3	100					3
Total	**103**	**84**	**13**	**11**	**7**	**8**	**123**

Table 1 shows that the most frequently mentioned themes were Flexibility, Latency, Manual (decision processes), and Granularity (of information). These themes, collectively making up 65% of the coded observations, are discussed below in relation to their impact on collaborative decision making.

The negative impact in terms of flexibility is felt at two levels. One, in terms of the poor fit between current ways of working and the application software, there is dissatisfaction that the template ERP processes do not support a more collaborative model for distribution decisions. Although control of these processes has now been centralised and standardised, this has not resulted in an improvement in decision making performance when it comes to collective decisions on the sourcing of components for a given order. One senior Director for worldwide distribution explains the constraints imposed by the implementation choice of managing inventory by plant:

> so you could have an order that could be coming from 7 or 8 different places, so the ability to manage that order is becoming much more difficult, because the way we structured ERP was really by factory. So what's happened is that the factory is no longer the primary source of material, it's one of the many sources.

Another functionality limitation relates to the increasing use of a "cross dock" model where a new type of inventory location, managed potentially by a third party, is used to compile and expedite the elements of a sales order from different sources. This requires an ability to confirm the shipment of elements of the order individually, such that the status of the order could be updated at a later time as new components are delivered to the cross dock. The ERP system does not allow this, however, forcing the user to re-enter the order in its entirety when one element is being updated.

At a second level, flexibility is concerned with the ability to have changes made to the template processes, and frustration is evident with the organisational response to such requests. Particularly with reference to a more global approach to distribution, it is acknowledged that the ERP system is "hindering change". At the time of the case study, SIT were adding new suppliers on a weekly basis. It was recognised that the ERP design was not intended to support collaborative decision processes across different plants. One corporate Director for Distribution described the challenge:

the way that we are constructed is vertically integrated, and it was never intended that this org wants to source from this org, it wasn't how Oracle was set up. Not good. And I'm sure it's a challenge that companies are facing that have multi-plants like we do

Thus, the closer association with other actors at sister plants involved in the distribution decision has not been taken into account in the design of the application and neither is it evident how the template processes could be updated to facilitate communicating with these new groupings, both inside and outside the firm. The distribution activity is therefore one which has evolved beyond the boundaries of the ERP system under pressure from external business factors. Decision making in this area has to bridge the gap between the reality of the discussions required by the new types of transactions and the possibilities of the ERP.

Latency is another by-product of the centralisation of transaction processing onto one technical platform, and this has impacted the shipment of products at the very moment that high performance levels are required. Transactional latency impacts distribution, when the visibility of up to date shipments is impaired by the slow processing time that afflicts the single instance ERP system when the volumes reach quarter end peaks. This means that management cannot see the orders moving off backlog, as they are shipped, and therefore lose visibility of performance to target. The situation is described by a corporate distribution manager:

Because we're going on our merry way, making decisions, and we don't realise that the information we are looking at is 2, 3 hours old. And it just causes havoc because people then physically go to do something and they're like, what drives? The drives, they're showing on the system, they should be right there! I tell you, I just went out there, there's nothing there!

Furthermore, the information required by managers to make decisions is contained in a number of systems, including the ERP, associated data warehouses and manual tools such as spreadsheets. The more systems are involved, the greater the information latency. Equally, the multiplication of systems introduces data integrity issues. The effect on decision making is dramatic, as described by a corporate Finance controller:

Performance issues, are 2 things, process and reporting, and they are correlated, as part of the [decision] process relies on data coming back out of Oracle. Processing time, that starts to lengthen, then reporting is impacted, then visibility …

It is accepted by managers that the performance issues are caused to a large extent by the extremely manual allocation process. A more automated approach will be required in future, which would tie in better with the ERP model of inventory consumption. This, in turn, would have to involve greater standardisation on product configurations, reducing the complexity of the customer offer in order to facilitate execution. The Cork based Distribution director put it thus:

I think somewhere along the line we'll have to automate the allocation side, I think we'll have to standardize configurations

Though this may solve the communication problems we highlighted earlier in this section, it is unpredictable what effect this will have on managers' attempts to meet customer demands and satisfy the revenue optimisation objectives.

To conclude this section, ERP systems provide a platform for collaborative work by linking the work of dispersed organisational actors in real time via a transaction based workflow system. In this case study, however, the collaboration benefits of ERP are compromised by the performance of the technical solution in terms of its processing power, and in terms of its adaptability to changes in the business, notably the network of actors involved in the decision who must communicate amongst each other the sometimes conflicting requirements they must satisfy in executing transactions.

5. Lessons from the case study

This research indicates that ERPs have a significant effect on the collaborative aspects of managerial decision making in large multi-site firms, such as multinational corporations. Of course, the aim of our paper was never to consider whether ERPs are groupware tools, as indeed, they are not designed as such. Nevertheless, given the shared data, common technical architecture and shared processes in an ERP, we expected to find some evidence that managers involved in complex collaborative processes in firms equipped with ERP systems would be able to leverage the workflow automation aspects of the software to develop interactive and collaborative approaches to their decision making in a critical customer facing business process.

Although the context of the case clearly shows an increasing requirement for collaboration and discussion amongst managers in the achievement of the goals of maximising customer satisfaction whilst at the same time maximising revenues from sales, we found that the implementation of ERP did not support an increasingly collaborative process. Because the application is highly inflexible in the way it imposes a way of doing things, and which users are allowed to participate, managers are constrained in what they can do, and this impedes their communication. Even when managers understand what could be done to facilitate the work of other actors, the ERP may forbid attempts to show flexibility towards customers or towards other internal actors. For instance, the latency present in the application when the volume of transactions increases means that the communication between sales managers and operational managers is complicated as the former attempt to initiate shipments which the latter cannot execute because the goods have already been taken out of the stocks by transactions not yet processed in the application. Furthermore, when there are opportunities to provide products featuring configurations that are advantageous to customers and can also yield higher margins for the firm, the application may tell operators that the proposed configuration is not valid, requiring additional steps until the shipment can finally take place. Yet, the collaborative model imposed by the new style of transaction will become the norm in the medium term and the communication overhead of executing these new transactions will increase drastically unless the ERP application is updated to reflect the new realities of the business.

In the final analysis, this case study indicates that the notions of centralisation and collaboration should not be confused. When a process is centralised and all actors can see it and share data about it, there is certainly the opportunity to improve the outcome of the decision making processes. However, when this centralisation is achieved at the expense of flexibility by exclusive reliance on a rigidly applied standardised solution, then, there is no real possibility for actors to leverage the application to develop their collaboration. Given the work that is invested by managers in modelling business processes in their ERP projects, this appears to be a missed opportunity.

Further research in the areas of ERP and collaboration should focus on trying to determine how the standard features of ERPs can be fine tuned for supporting groups in a way that is not only good for increased control, but that also facilitates collaboration. Comparing the architecture of ERPs and those proposed in the literature on Group Support Systems [eg: 11, 12] may be a starting point for such a research endeavour.

References

[1]   Lee, Z. and Lee, J. (2000) "An ERP implementation case study from a knowledge transfer perspective", *Journal of Information Technology*, 15, 281-288.
[2]   Davenport, T. (1998) Putting the Enterprise into the Enterprise System, *Harvard Business Review*, July-August, 131-131.
[3]   Mintzberg, H. (1973) The Nature of Managerial Work, Harper and Row, New York.
[4]   Kotter, J. (1984), What effective managers really do, *Harvard Business Review*, November/December, 156-167.
[5]   Carton, F. and Adam, F (2007) L'impact des ERP sur la prise de décision managériale, in Penz and Vinck (Eds) *L'équipement de l'organisation: Les ERP à l'usage*, Hermes, Paris.
[6]   Daft R. L. and Lengel R. H. (1986) Organisational information requirements media richness and structural design, Management Science, 32(5), 554-571.
[7]   Daft R. Lengel R. and Trevino L. (1987) Message equivocality media selection and manager performance: implications for information systems, MIS Quarterly, 11, 355-366.
[8]   Galbraith J. (1974) Organisation design: an information processing view, *Interfaces*, 4(3), 28-37.
[9]   Winter, S. G. (1985) The case for 'mechanistic' decision making, Chapter four in Pennings *et al.* (Eds), *Organisational Strategy and Change*, Jossey-Bass Publishers, London, 99-113
[10] Eisenhardt, K.M. (1989), Building Theories from Case Study Research, Academy of Management Review, 14(4), 532-550.
[11] DeSanctis, G and Gallupe, B (1987) A Foundation for the Study of GDSS, Management Science, 33(5), 589-609.
[12] Zaraté, P and Adla, A. (2006) Group DSS: A Proposed Architecture, EURO XXI, Reykjavik, Iceland, July 2-5, 2006.

Collaborative Decision Making: Perspectives and Challenges
P. Zaraté et al. (Eds.)
IOS Press, 2008

Building a Common Understanding of Critical Success Factors for an ERP Project Implementation

David SAMMON[a] and Frederic ADAM[a]

[a]*Business Information Systems, University College Cork, Ireland*

Abstract. This paper reports on a novel approach to Enterprise Resource Planning (ERP) project implementation and introduces the use of a sense-making workshop to facilitate an improved shared understanding of the Critical Success Factors (CSFs) for the implementation of such an IT innovation. The sense-making workshop strives to overcome hindering knowledge barriers by raising stakeholder awareness through the development of a logically minimal Boolean expression (truth function) which promotes discussion and a shared understanding as to the project preparations required for the successful implementation of an ERP package in an organisational context. The design of the sense-making workshop requires participants to use a set of CSFs for ERP project implementation and a simple scenario in order to retrospectively make sense of the actions taken during the ERP project (represented in the scenario) and therefore represent their individual understanding as a truth function. A process of Boolean minimisation is then used (facilitated through the construction of a truth table and a prime implicant chart) to achieve logically maximum parsimony in the form of a logically minimal Boolean expression (truth function) which is representative of the workshop participants' shared understanding of the CSFs at play in the scenario.

Keywords. Enterprise Resource Planning, Implementation, Critical Success Factors (CSFs), Comparative Method, Sense-Making Workshop

Introduction

Over the past decade Enterprise Resource Planning (ERP) packages have become a major part of the organisational landscape and form the cornerstone of IS architectures for an ever increasing percentage of organisations. Despite the strong push toward implementing ERP packages in the wider organisational community and the experience accumulated over 20 years of large scale integrated systems implementations, there is, in relation to ERP deployment, a lack of understanding to counter the difficulties that can arise when organisations fail to ensure that all the required factors of success are present in their projects. In this respect it is extremely important that organisational decision-makers are conscious of their organisations understanding of Critical Success Factors (CSFs) at the outset of an ERP project; as problems not addressed, or factors not considered at the initial stages of a project, can have serious consequences at later stages, and impact the overall outcome of the project.

In this paper we contend that the level of managerial understanding of technological innovations (e.g. ERP project implementations) is generally low, and managers need to be made aware of the factors that are critical for the successful implementation of such an innovation. Therefore, specific tools and methods must be proposed to provide managers with a means of assessing their organisation's level of understanding before they embark on complex innovating pursuits (like ERP) and, from this self-assessment, to offer the means to improve the starting point.

The remainder of this paper is structured as follows. In the next section the theoretical foundation for the research is presented. This is followed by a brief discussion on sense-making. Our proposed method is then illustrated with a specific focus on the steps involved in undertaking a sense-making workshop. In an effort to illustrate these steps we describe the Boolean minimisation process that should be undertaken in the workshop, where we use a sample set of data from a sense-making workshop conducted with 26 managers currently studying on an executive education programme (MBA). Finally, we conclude with an examination of the sense-making workshop outputs and the need to promote discussion amongst workshop participants to raise their awareness and achieve a greater shared understanding of the CSFs for ERP project implementation.

1. Theoretical Foundation

1.1. A Shared Understanding of CSFs

Research on CSFs for ERP project implementation has reached significant importance within the IS community [1]. Despite research reports being published throughout the past fifteen years documenting various CSFs for ERP project implementations [2], there has been a notable lack of research attention on the complex relationships between the factors that combine to drastically affect the implementation of an ERP project. In fact, Finney and Corbett comment that *"there is limited research that has attempted to produce an expansive collection of CSFs"* [2, p.341]. Therefore, the volume of literature relating to the factors critical to ERP project implementations falls short of providing organisational decision-makers with the necessary tools and methodologies to identify and understand the key issues facing them at the outset of the project. Therefore, this is a sufficient condition to move beyond the current research output which has provided *"only a partial aid to the practitioner struggling to understand the implications of their actions"* as *"the vast majority of the literature [CSFs for ERP project implementations] focuses on 'static' CSFs, often for the development stage of the life-cycle, and generally not explicitly linked to outcomes"* [3, pp.59 & 67]. As a result, the impact of managerial understanding of these CSFs on achieving desired ERP project outcomes needs to be identified in order to propose research results *"valuable for making sense out of problems where there are many potential factors influencing the outcome, and where the researcher hopes to make a set of practical recommendations based on the most influential factors"* [4, p.176].

The CSF concept has resulted from nearly 40 years of cumulative research about decision-making, planning, and IS [5]. While, Rockart's original CSF methodology [6] focused on individual managers and on each manager's current information needs, some criticisms have been documented regarding the use of the CSF approach because of this reliance on managers' responses [7,8]. Peffers *et al.* extended the CSF method to effectively incorporate economical participation by many in and around the organisation and refer to this method as Critical Success Chains (CSC), arguing that *"broad participation is important because knowledge of potentially important opportunities is widespread in the organisation and methods that restrict participation in the planning process effectively waste this knowledge, an important firm asset. Also, broad participation in IS planning may help lead to user buy-in, important for successful implementation of IS plans"* [5, p.53]. However, in some organisations participants may assume that everything that the organisation needs is already known or that 'there are strategic planners, upper level managers', who are the only people with sufficient breath of knowledge to think about what is good for the organisation [9,5]. This can result in suboptimal implementation and use of IT resources because knowledge from around the organisation about what is important is potentially ignored [10,5]. In addition, an exclusive focus on senior manager knowledge may miss other potentially important opportunities for adopting IT innovations [5].

In effect, extending the CSF method requires studying the views of personnel at various levels in the organisation, in addition to those at the executive level, for example [11,5]. It has been argued that widespread user participation may contribute to the successful implementation of IT innovations, as users 'buy-in' to the need for systems [12,13,14,5]. Therefore, while extensive user involvement in identifying CSFs for ERP project implementation could be expensive [5], the method proposed in this paper (sense-making workshop) will increase the level of understanding of the CSFs at an individual participant level and will further promote a shared common understanding amongst all organisational personnel involved. As a result, a motivation to extend the usefulness of CSFs comes from this need for 'information richness' [15,5] in ERP project implementations. Implicitly, the sense-making workshop can highlight 'latent structure' in the needs of the organisation by linking project outcomes (as represented in the scenario) to the *presence* or *absence* of specific CSFs. Therefore, by extending the role of CSFs in ERP project implementations and by providing an economical method we can make explicit the relationships implicitly discovered and express them in a rich and useful manner, using aspects of the comparative method proposed by Ragin [16]. Furthermore, we can take advantage of the strengths of CSF analysis, while making a contribution to an organisation's ability to prepare and implement an ERP project, where project outcomes are closer to initial expectations, ensuring a greater degree of success.

1.2. Components of a Sense-Making Process

There are many differing perspectives on the definition and true meaning of the sense-making process, however, a range of descriptions have been used to describe the concept; for example, 'placing of stimuli into a mental framework used to direct interpretations'; 'recurring process of forming anticipations and assumptions and the subsequent interpretation of experiences that deviate from these anticipations and assumptions'; and the 'reciprocal interaction of information seeking, meaning ascription, and action'. Therefore, these descriptions of the sense-making process are used as a metaphor for 'understanding' and 'meaning making', and describe a broad and all-encompassing, subjective, mental activity whereby individuals make sense of themselves, others, and events. Indeed, embracing the arguments of Weick [17] it can be appreciated that sense-making is not decision-making, as it encompasses more than how cues (information) are interpreted, and as a result is concerned with how the cues are internalised in the first instance and how individuals decide to focus on specific cues. Therefore, sense-making is about such things as placement of items into frameworks, comprehending, constructing meaning, and interacting in pursuit of mutual understanding and patterning [17].

Seligman [18] argues that the sense-making perspective provides a 'look under the hood' of the adopter's mental engine. "It is meant to complement, not replace those other perspectives on adoption, just as an understanding of how an automobile engine works is complementary to an understanding of how to drive" [18, p.110]. However, in spite of its originality, the impact of sense-making theory on the Information Systems (IS) community has been modest [19,18]. In fact, as with other theoretical notions, one reason for this modest impact is that there are few practical proposals on how to implement the theory, and empirical studies on the impact of using a sense-making theory-based approach are lacking [19]. As a result, it is important for us to appreciate the value of studying sense-making in the adoption of IT innovations and, in the context of this paper that of ERP project implementations. Seligman [18] argued that examining a series of sense-making cycles may facilitate a better understanding of an adoption process as opposed to focusing on what could be considered the making of a single decision. Indeed, as highlighted by Boland, the impact of a sense-making exercise "on the managers' cognitive and emotional experience and their commitment to use the method in other decisions suggest that sense-making can enhance the group process of inquiry during the initial stages [of planning]" [20, p.868].

2. Building a Common Understanding of CSFs for ERP Implementation

There are three important aspects of the sense-making process, namely: 'action', 'meaning ascription' and 'information seeking'. Therefore, the sense-making cycle can be defined as the process of taking action, extracting information from stimuli resulting from that action, and incorporating information and stimuli resulting from that action into the mental frameworks that guide further action [21,18]. Indeed, this definition embraces the notion that action precedes cognition (thinking) and focuses cognition [22,21,18]. In fact, Ashmos and Nathan [23] commented that action is a precondition to sense-making. Therefore, if understanding is facilitated by action, managers have to take some action and see what happens [22]. Indeed, Weick commented that there is a *"delicate tradeoff between dangerous action which produces understanding and safe inaction which produces confusion"* [22, p.503]. It is argued that this 'taking of action' will determine the *appropriate action* based on a review of the outcomes of the action taken [22]. However, here in lies the problem with regard to the practicality of using sense-making.

There is a need for a method to facilitate 'dangerous action producing understanding' [22] which is similar to the 'doing first' model of decision-making proposed by Mintzberg and Westley [24]. In fact, Mintzberg and Westley commented that doing first requires *"doing various things, finding out which among them works, making sense of that and repeating the successful behaviours while discarding the rest"* [24, p.91]. Therefore, 'doing first' requires action and the necessary thinking can happen after the action, based on trying something and then learning from it. However, given the complexity of an ERP project implementation and given the prohibitive cost of incorrect action, or indeed safe inaction producing incorrect outcomes, organisations cannot afford to get it wrong. Therefore, what is required is an inexpensive environment for the experimentation that 'doing first' requires, but where the outcomes of actions can be reflected on and therefore can inform future decisions to act. This illustrates the real value-added of our proposed method (sense-making workshop). To summarise, while action is important and produces learning, in the context of the proposed sense-making workshop and the method of organisational self-assessment, the action is being undertaken in an environment which may present managerial decision makers with opportunities for improvisations around the CSFs for ERP project implementation. Therefore, decision makers may be able to use the benefit of *foresight* as opposed to *hindsight* in their approach to ERP project implementation. As an example, we propose that the sense-making workshop should be used in situations where an organisation: is about to undertake an ERP project implementation; is interested in assessing their project progress at a critical juncture along the project lifecycle (during a phased implementation approach); wants to retrospectively assess their approach to acting on the CSFs for ERP project implementation in a recently completed project.

2.1. The Design of the Sense-Making Workshop

The design of the sense-making workshop embraces the work carried out by Boland [20] on retrospective sense-making, the notation and rules of Ragin's [16] work on comparative method, and the dialectical method, as described by Mason and Mitroff [25]. Ultimately, by its design the sense-making workshop suggests that *theses* and *antitheses* will be proposed by workshop participants around their understanding of [1] their individual truth function of CSFs following an examination of the scenario, and [2] the logically minimal Boolean expression (truth function) of CSFs generated by the workshop facilitator to represent the groups overall interpretation of the scenario. Therefore, the output of the sense-making workshop results in synthesis/consensus amongst participants through creative conflict. To achieve this workshop outcome the steps of the novel method proposed in this paper are outlined in the following sections. These sections illustrate the means by which a shared understanding of CSFs for ERP project implementation can be achieved from a group of individuals' perceptions of the CSFs at play in an ERP project implementation scenario.

2.1.1. Making Sense of the ERP Project Implementation Scenario

A scenario of an ERP project implementation is presented to workshop participants, as illustrated in Table 1. Participants make sense of the scenario based on their individual understanding of the actions that have been taken during the ERP project implementation; therefore, they imagine themselves as having been part of the project. Therefore, participants undertake a sense-making process of internalising and attributing meaning to what they understand is at play in the project scenario.

Table 1. Example of an ERP Project Implementation Scenario

In Case A, the vision and primary goal of the project was never clearly articulated, communicated, understood, and agreed throughout the sites of the company. Where the primary goal of the ERP project may have been to transform the HRM (Human Resource Management) function in the company, it was simply perceived as the computerisation of employee records and the replacement of existing site-specific HR/Payroll systems. Furthermore, at the outset, involvement in the project was not compulsory across the sites of the company, while those sites involved were given total autonomy in how they approached the project. Therefore, the ERP package was implemented on a site by site basis, embracing 'as-is' site specific business processes. Very little attempt was made to analyse existing business processes in an effort to prioritise requirements and introduce process improvements wherever possible across the entire company. Furthermore, there was a reluctance to provide the best business personnel to the project.

To formalise their individual understanding each participant classifies the scenario against the *presence* or *absence* of CSFs for ERP project implementations extracted from the available academic literature (see for example [2]). Therefore, for the purposes of the sense-making workshop we provide participants with twelve CSFs for ERP project implementation and a brief description, as illustrated in Table 2. However, it has to be clarified that the CSF list is only used to capture and classify each participant's individual understanding of the CSFs that are at play in the scenario and whether they perceive them as having a *presence* or *absence* for ERP project implementations; therefore, the CSF list is simply an organising tool and does not need to be an absolute truth.

Having completed the sense-making process of the scenario each participant can formalise their interpretation and generate their own individual truth function for the scenario. Table 3 illustrates this output from our sense-making workshop conducted with 26 managers currently studying on an executive education programme (MBA). If a participant identified the *presence* of a CSF they represented its existence with the number 1, however, if they identified the *absence* of a CSF they represented it with 0. Furthermore, participants left a CSF uncategorised (blank) if they believed it not to be at play based on their interpretation of the scenario.

Table 2. Critical Success Factors

Critical Success Factor (CSF)	Legend	Description
Existence of Actual Strategic Business Need	ASBN	articulating a business vision and a justification for the project
Specific Project Goals and Objectives	PGO	identifying clear goals and objectives for the project
Top Management Commitment and Support	TMCS	need to have committed leadership at the top management level
Prioritised Business Requirements	PBR	consideration of the current systems in place and the processes they support used as an indicator of the nature and scale of business problems that need to be solved
Allocation of Best Internal Business Resources	BIBR	an implementation team that is comprised of the organisation's best and brightest individuals allocated to the project full-time
Effective Communication	EC	ensure that open communication occurs within the entire organisation
Definitive Project Scope	PS	to appreciate the footprint of the ERP implementation and ensure that required business problems are solved
Required Organisational Buy-In	OBI	need to keep all organisational personnel impacted by the project informed about the project to avoid misconceptions
Required System Functionality	SF	a complete description of how the business will operate and be supported by the ERP package in-use
Accurate Project Time-Frame	PT	produce a timeline for project implementation and ensure ongoing management of the implementation plan
Accurate Project Costing	PC	to know up-front exactly what the implementation costs
Ownership of the Project	OP	secure the support of opinion leaders throughout the organisation and build user acceptance of the project and a positive employee attitude

2.1.2. From Individual Truth Functions to the Group's Truth Function

Following this input stage of the sense-making workshop a process of Boolean minimisation (embracing the work of Ragin [16]) is used by the workshop facilitator to generate a logically minimal Boolean expression, representing logically maximum parsimony. The outcome of this minimisation process generates a truth function representative of the entire groups' shared meaning (understanding) of the *presence* or *absence* of the CSFs at play in the scenario of the ERP project implementation they examined. For the purposes of this study any CSF with a frequency above 50% is included in the Boolean minimisation process. Using 50% in not suggesting an absolute truth but it does suggest that where at least half of the participants identify a CSF as being at play in the scenario, it is worthy of inclusion in the construction of the truth table. Therefore, the truth table presented in Table 4 contains 9 CSFs (input variables) which were identified as causally relevant features (presented by the workshop participants) of the scenario. Also, in Table 4 the frequency column represents the number of times a combination appears (the workshop participants' interpretations of the combination *absence/presence* dichotomy of CSFs). Therefore, in the construction of the truth table there were 512 possible combinations (2^9) and only 7 valid combinations were identified from the 26 workshop participant's individual truth functions. For a participant's truth function to be considered valid an entry (1 or 0) must be provided for each of the 9 CSFs. As an example, participants 5 and 7 from Table 3 share the same interpretation of the combination of CSFs. So this *absence/presence* combination of CSFs has a frequency value of 2 (as represented in the first row of Table 4).

Table 3. Workshop Participants Interpretation of the Future Scenario

Participant #	ASBN	PGO	TMCS	PBR	BIBR	EC	PS	OBI	SF	PT	PC	OP
1	1	0	0		0	0	0	0				0
2	0		0		0		0		1	0	0	0
3	1	0	0		0	0	0	0		0		0
4	1	0	0	0	0	0	0	0		0		0
5	1	1	0	0	0	0	0	0	0	0	0	0
6	0	1	0	0	0	0	0	0		0	0	0
7	1	1	0	0	0	0	0	0	0		0	0
8	1	0		1	0	0	0	0				0
9		1	0	0	0	0		0	0			0
10		1		0	0	0		0				0
11	0	0		0	0							
12	1	0	0	0	0	0	1			0	0	0
13	1	1		0	0			0				
14	1	1		0	0	0		0	0			0
15	0	0	0	0	0	0		0				0
16	0	0	0	0	0	0	0	0	0	0	0	0
17	0	0	0	0	0	0		0		0		
18	1	0	0		0	0	0	0				0
19	0	1	0	1	0	0	0	0	1			0
20	0	0	0	0	0	0		0				
21	0	0	0	0	0	0	0					
22	0	0	0	0	0	0	0	0	0			0
23		1		0	0	0	0	0				0
24		1	1	0	0	0	0		0			0
25	0	1	0		0	0		0				
26		0		0	0		0	0	0			0
frequency %	81	96	73	81	96	88	61.5	85	38	30.8	23.1	80.8

Table 4. Truth Table for the ERP Project Implementation Scenario

ASBN	PGO	TMCS	PBR	BIBR	EC	PS	OBI	OP	frequency
1	1	0	0	0	0	0	0	0	2
1	0	0	0	0	0	0	0	0	1
0	1	0	1	0	0	0	0	0	1
0	1	0	0	0	0	0	0	0	1
0	0	0	0	0	0	0	0	0	2

According the Ragin "the restrictive character of combinatorial logic seems to indicate that the Boolean approach simply compounds complexity on top of complexity" [16, p.93]. As a result, there is a need to simplify this complexity, namely undertake Boolean minimisation. Therefore, a number of steps are adhered to following the construction of a truth table (Table 4) in an effort to unravel complexity. In our case there were five primitive expressions identified in the truth table (Table 4) and these form the columns of Table 5. These primitive expressions are the combination of the 9 CSFs that have a frequency of >=1. To further reduce complexity, prime implicants were determined from these primitive expressions. These prime implicants form the rows of Table 5. The goal of this phase of the minimisation process is to 'cover' as many of the primitive expressions as possible with a logically minimal number of prime implicants [16]. In our search for maximum parsimony there were three essential prime implicants identified that covered all five primitive expressions, as illustrated in Table 5. Again, this is not an absolute truth regarding the relevant prime implicants that cover all primitive expressions. However, the prime implicants presented in Table 5 capture a combination of CSFs representing the common CSFs identified by each workshop participant as part of their sense-making exercise.

Table 5. Prime Implicant Chart

primitive expressions

prime implicants	ASBN*PGO*tmcs*pbr*bibr*ec*ps*obi*op	ASBN*pgo*tmcs*pbr*bibr*ec*ps*obi*op	asbn*PGO*tmcs*PBR*bibr*ec*ps*obi*op	asbn*PGO*tmcs*pbr*bibr*ec*ps*obi*op	asbn*pgo*tmcs*pbr*bibr*ec*ps*obi*op
ASBN*tmcs*pbr*bibr*ec*ps*obi*op	X	X			
PGO*tmcs*bibr*ec*ps*obi*op	X		X	X	
asbn*pgo*tmcs*pbr*bibr*ec*ps*obi*op					X

The value of this Boolean minimisation process is to take a vast array of conjunctural causations between CSFs expressed by workshop participants and facilitate the generation of an explicit statement of multiple conjunctural causation, which is a logically minimal equation achieving maximum logical parsimony. As a result, *"the equation that results from use of the prime implicant chart is a logically minimal Boolean expression"* [16, p.98]. Our equation is as follows:

$$Y = (ASBN*tmcs*pbr*bibr*ec*ps*obi*op) + (PGO*tmcs*bibr*ec*ps*obi*op) + (asbn*pgo*tmcs*pbr*bibr*ec*ps*obi*op)$$

In this equation, Y represents the project outcome with respect to the scenario. The '+' symbol represents a logical OR and the '*' symbol represents a logical AND. The *absence/presence* of the relevant variables (CSFs) is represented through lowercase and uppercase lettering respectively.

3. Discussion

One of the main concerns of this sense-making exercise centres on the need for workshop participants to develop a shared understanding of the CSFs for ERP project implementation; therefore moving from individual interpretations of criticality to a synthesis using a common vocabulary. Therefore, Tables 3, 4 and 5 highlight this progression from complexity to simplicity representing the workshop participants' synthesised understanding of the combined *absence/presence* of CSFs in the scenario. Both the individual truth functions and the truth function of the group are then used to promote discussion amongst the workshop participants (facilitated by the workshop facilitator). This discussion is aimed at highlighting and resolving the differences in interpretation around the CSFs, as illustrated in Table 6.

Table 6. A Tabular Representation of the Logically Minimal Boolean Expression

prime implicant 1	ASBN	tmcs	pbr	ec	ps	obi	op		
prime implicant 2		tmcs		ec	ps	obi	op	PGO	bibr
prime implicant 3	asbn	tmcs	pbr	ec	ps	obi	op	pgo	bibr
soft consensus exists		X	X	X	X	X	X		X
discussion needed	X							X	

While our equation illustrates that there are three combinations of CSFs that capture the individual workshop participants' interpretation of the scenario, presented in Table 1, there are obvious contradictions inherent in these combinations as illustrated in Table 6 (following the completion of the Boolean minimisation process). Therefore, the sense-making workshop embraces the dialectical approach ([25]) and introduces creative conflict to help identify and challenge assumptions to create new perceptions. The dialectical method avoids adversarial decision processes, where for example, one workshop participant deems themselves to win, while another workshop participant is deemed to lose with regard to deciding on the preferred course of action to take in addressing a CSF for an ERP project implementation. The logically minimal Boolean expression ensures that this form of adversarial decision-making is avoided. However, the sense-making workshop does not simply want to satisfy all workshop participants through 'soft' consensus by identifying and recording agreements that already exist, while they may not have been previously recognised. For example, as illustrated in Table 6, if 'tmcs' or 'obi' are seen as absent in the scenario and the prime implicants do not suggest otherwise, this would highlight that a soft consensus exists around these factors. In fact, the merit of the workshop is that in embracing the dialectical processes, where the focus of workshop participants is on disagreements which are turned into agreements, or indeed there is a transformation in the dialogue in that direction. Therefore, creative conflict through discussion will produce a greater overall understanding, amongst workshop participants, of the actions and decisions that should be taken to better prepare for an ERP project implementation. For example in this sense-making workshop the *absence/presence* of the 'ASBN' and 'PGO' CSFs needs to be better understood through discussion by the workshop participants because there is no agreement as to their *absence/presence* in the scenario. Therefore, workshop participants will raise their collective awareness and resolve disagreements through discussion around ERP project implementation within their organisational context. As a result, from this dialectic between opposing views a greater understanding of the CSFs for ERP project implementation can emerge with a pooling of information in pursuit of better decision-making. Therefore, these discussions amongst workshop participants will produce statements of conjunctual combinations of CSFs that are deemed *necessary* for their ERP project implementation.

4. Concluding Remarks

We accept that the outputs of the sense-making exercise are subjective and the researchers have been very much involved in the interpretation and construction of the logically minimal Boolean expression; however, we also argue that we would never otherwise be aware of, or indeed discuss, these CSF *absence/presence* relationships. This illustrates the usefulness of the sense-making workshop exercise in an effort to appreciate the importance of the CSFs that are *necessary* for ERP project implementation. While the scenario used in our workshop was relatively simplistic, it generated a variety of interpretations and complexities. Therefore, if the scenario was scaled up to represent a more comprehensive organisational environment, or a number of mini-scenarios were used, the outputs of the approach would become even more enhanced, with further variables and expressions to examine and debate.

It is proposed that a workshop environment, promoting the enacted sense-making of outcomes, in light of the level of participant's awareness of the CSFs for ERP project implementation (before any decisions or actions are taken), will promote the establishment of a *mindful* [26] approach to ERP project implementation. In fact, the sense-making workshop proposed in this paper can be viewed as one operationalisation of the concept of *mindfulness* discussed by Swanson and Ramiller [26].

References

[1] Remus, U. (2007) "Critical success factors for implementing enterprise portals. A comparison with ERP implementations", Business Process Management Journal, 13(4), pp.538-552.
[2] Finney, S. and Corbett, M. (2007) "ERP implementation: a compilation and analysis of critical success factors", *Business Process Management Journal*, 13(3), pp.329-347.
[3] King, S.F. and Burgess, T.F. (2006) "Beyond critical success factors: a dynamic model of enterprise system innovation", *International Journal of Information Management*, 26(1), pp.59-69.
[4] Lam, W. (2005) "Investigating success factors in enterprise application integration: a case-drive analysis", *European Journal of Information Systems*, 14(2), pp.175-187.

[5] Peffers, K., Gengler, C.E. and Tuunanen. T. (2003) "Extending Critical Success Factors Methodology to Facilitate Broadly Participative Information Systems Planning", *Journal of Management Information Systems*, 20(1), pp.51-85.

[6] Rockart, J. (1979) "Chief executives define their own data needs", *Harvard Business Review*, 57(2), pp.81-93.

[7] Davis, G. (1979) "Comments on the critical success factors method for obtaining management information requirements in article by John F. Rockart: Chief Executives define their own data needs", *MIS Quarterly*, 3(3), pp.57-58.

[8] Boynton, A. and Zmud, A. (1984) "An assessment of critical success factors", *Sloan Management Review*, 25(4), pp.17-27.

[9] Tillquist, J. (2000) "Institutional bridging: How conceptions of IT-enabled change shape the planning process", *Journal of Management Information Systems*, 17(2), pp.115-152.

[10] Lee, B. and Menon, N.M. (2000) "Information technology value through different normative lenses", *Journal of Management Information Systems*, 16(4), pp.99-119.

[11] Rockart, J. (1982) "The changing role of the information systems executive: A critical success factors perspective", *Sloan Management Review*, 24(1), pp.3-13.

[12] Earl. M.J. (1993) "Experiences in strategic information systems planning", *MIS Quarterly*, 7(1), pp.1-24.

[13] Gottschalk. P. (1999) "Strategic information systems planning: The IT strategy implementation matrix", *European Journal of Information Systems*, 8(2), pp.107-118.

[14] Hackney, R., Kawalek. J. and Dhillon, G. (1999) "Strategic information systems planning: Perspectives on the role of 'end-user' revisited", *Journal of End User Computing*, 11(2), pp.3-12.

[15] Sambamurthy, V., Venkataraman, S. and DeSanctis, G. (1993) "The design of information technology planning systems for varying organizational contexts", *European Journal of Information Systems*, 2(1), pp.23-35.

[16] Ragin, C. (1987) *The Comparative Method: Moving Beyond Qualitative and Quantitative Strategies*, University of California Press, Berkeley/Los Angeles/London.

[17] Weick, K.E. (1995) *Sensemaking in Organizations*, Sage, Thousand Oaks, CA.

[18] Seligman, L. (2006) "Sensemaking throughout adoption and the innovation-decision process", *European Journal of Innovation Management*, 9(1), pp.108-120.

[19] Lyytinen, K. (1987) "Different perspectives on information systems: Problems and solutions", *ACM Computing Surveys*, 19(1), pp.5-46.

[20] Boland, R.J. (1984) "Sense-making of accounting data as a technique of organisational diagnosis", *Management Science*, 30(7), pp.868-882.

[21] Thomas, J., Clark, S. and Gioia, D. (1993) "Strategic sensemaking and organizational performance: linkages among scanning, interpretation, and outcomes", *Academy of Management Journal*, 36(2), pp.239-270.

[22] Weick, K.E. (1988) "Enacted sensemaking in a crisis situation", *Journal of Management Studies*, 25, pp.305-317.

[23] Ashmos, D.P. and Nathan, M.L. (2002) "Team sense-making: a mental model for navigating unchartered territories", *Journal of Managerial Issues*, 14(2), pp.198-217.

[24] Mintzberg, H. and Westley, F. (2001) "Decision making: It's not what you think", *Sloan Management Review*, Spring, pp.89-93.

[25] Mason, R.O. and Mitroff, I.I. (1981) *Challenging strategic planning assumptions*, Wiley, New York.

[26] Swanson, E.B. and Ramiller, N.C. (2004) "Innovating mindfully with information technology", *MIS Quarterly*, 28(4), pp.553-583.

Knowledge Management
for Collaborative Decision Making

Collaborative Decision Making: Perspectives and Challenges
P. Zaraté et al. (Eds.)
IOS Press, 2008

Knowledge Acquisition for the Creation of Assistance Tools to the Management of Air Traffic Control

David ANNEBICQUE[1], Igor CREVITS, Thierry POULAIN, Serge DEBERNARD
LAMIH UMR CNRS 8530, France

Abstract. This paper presents an approach which has for objective to model new tools allowing to help the controllers to assume the incessant increase of the air traffic (actual version of the platform AMANDA V2), as well as help them in the negotiation phase and cooperation with their counterparts of adjacent sector (objectives of the new version of AMANDA). Help them in furnishing some tools able to quickly share information, and to maintain good common situation awareness. An approach is proposed, it is divided in three main phases. A first phase which consists of understand and to model the decision-making process of controllers. The second phase introduces a multiple criteria decision-making methodology. This Methodology has for objective to understand in more details the activities of controllers and the cases of cooperation with adjacent sectors. Finally, the last phase is the operational level of the approach, and consists of an application of repertory grid methodology in order to guide the interviews with the different participants of the study. This will allow realizing the knowledge acquisition, keeping in mind objective to develop new tools. To conclude this paper, the last part presents an example of application of this approach and the first results.

Keywords. Multiple Criteria Decision Making (MCDM), Repertory Grid, Human-Machine Cooperation, Situation Awareness, Air Traffic Control.

Introduction

The DGAC (French acronym for General Direction of Civil Aviation) foresees that in the next 10 to 20 years the air traffic will double or even triple. This increase of traffic will be impossible to assume with the current control methods. Indeed in a mental point of view, the number of aircraft and information to manage will be considerable and operators risk to be overloaded at certain times of the day, to the detriment of safety. It therefore becomes necessary to assist controllers in their work, offering them new tools and new ways of working that will allow them to assume this increase.

The LAMIH works with the DGAC since many years in this optical. The laboratory has developed several platform with a common philosophy which is to keep the operator at the centre of the loop, and thus to develop cooperative systems. The

---

[1] Corresponding Author : David ANNEBICQUE, LAMIH UMR CNRS 8530, University of Valenciennes, Le Mont Houy, F 59313 Valenciennes CEDEX 9, France; E-mail: david.annebicque@univ-valenciennes.fr.

objectives are to extend the principles developed in the last platform, and for this it is necessary to understand how the planning controllers (PC) work.

To understand and analyse the activities of the PC, a multiple criteria analysis is proposed. This methodology will serve as support for the modelling of new space of cooperation between controllers of different sectors. A repertory grid methodology will be applied in order to guide the knowledge acquisition. This methodology is the operational part for the multiple criteria analysis.

This paper begins with a presentation of Air Traffic Control (ATC), with its problematic of traffic increase. The second part presents the project AMANDA (Automated machine MAN Delegation of Action), in its current version as well as the objectives of the new version. A third part presents the approach which is put in place, it is divided into three parts: the decision-making process modelling, application of a methodology multiple criteria decision making (MCDM) to support the collection of information and then the repertory grid as operational aspect of the knowledge acquisition. Finally a final section presents a first decision model based on the expertise of a "decision engineer".

1. Management of en-route air traffic

1.1. Organisation of Air Traffic Control

The ATC is organized in 3 layers: « Airport control », « Approach and terminal control » and « en-route control ». This latter layer manages flights passing through in the airspace between departure airport and the approach control of the destination airport. The Objective of en-route ATC is to guarantee the safety of aircraft and theirs passengers. To do this the controllers must take care that aircraft remain separate by a minimum separation distance (in vertical and horizontal level), while ensuring that they also respect the economic constraints of time and fuel consumption.

To simplify the management and the supervision of traffic, airspace is divided in geographical sector and in level of 1.000 feet. A sector is permanently supervised by two controllers, composed of a Planning Controller (PC) and an Executive Controller (EC). The PC coordinates the movement of aircraft between his sector and the adjacent sectors. This coordination consists in a negotiation of entrance levels and exit levels. The PC takes care too, to regulate the workload of EC. For his/her part, EC is in charge of sector supervision, that's mean to supervise that the aircraft respect the flight plans, and to maintain the safety distances. If the EC detects a possibility of crossing under this safety distance, he/she must do all is possible to restore the separation distances and avoid the conflict. Generally it is necessary to reroute one of the aircraft, and then to take back this aircraft in is original trajectory when the separation is guarantee. This action is called conflict resolution.

1.2. Motivation of the study

Some statistics can quickly demonstrate the problem of air traffic control. In 25 years (1977 to 2002) the traffic transiting in the French airspace has increased of 250% [1]. The Air traffic is today higher than 2.500.000 aircraft per year that gives on average 7.000 aircraft per day. In a sector like Bordeaux for instance, the controllers must manage 20 to 25 aircraft per hour, this is the reasonable limit for the controllers. The

DGAC foresee that in 10 to 20 years these statistics go double even triple. The controllers risk thus to have some difficulties to manage this increase with actual tools (radar view, strip, telephone, radio) and risk to be overloaded to certain moment of the day, and this to the detriment of the security. Reduce sectors is now impossible, because the conflicts resolutions need a minimal geographical area.

A total automation of the ATC is impossible too, outside psychological consequence that this would induce to the passengers, the techniques to realise this automation, imply an entirely instrumentation of aircraft, that is not economically conceivable. Currently to avoid these overload of controllers, who could not maintain an optimal security level, different solutions are adopted, like the planning of flights and the regulation to the departure of airports, or the coordination between sectors that allows reducing the complexity of air conflict even to avoid that these conflicts had really happen.

2. Project AMANDA

The question is approached in terms of assistance to the controllers. Tools which help to improve the regulation of the workload of controllers are proposed. It is imperative that these tools come within perfectly the control tasks and the work of controllers (as a pair, as individually), to produce a beneficial effect. It is in this perspective that the project AMANDA [2, 3, 4], as well as others project developed in the laboratory since fifteen years [5, 6, 7], takes its place. These projects have always a same philosophy, which is to keep Human, operator, in the control loop. These projects do not research to fully automate the management of ATC, which would result in loss of competences forf the operators, as well as a loss of situation awareness (SA) [8, 9], which would prevent operators to be able to react event of default by a system.

2.1. AMANDA V2

AMANDA V2 assists controllers (PC and EC) of one sector, in giving some tools which be able to allow a delegation of task [3], but also some tools which permit to share rapidly a same representation of airspace, and conflicts, and thus to maintain a common SA.

2.1.1. STAR

AMANDA integrates a tool of trajectory calculation and of assistance to the resolution of air conflict, called STAR. STAR works in cooperation with the controller. The controller detects a conflict; he/she has the possibility to use STAR to help his/her to resolve the conflict. To do this the controller indicates the strategy (called directive) that he/she desires apply to resolve the conflict. A directive or strategy is like, for example, « AFR1542 PASS_BEHIND KLM1080 ». STAR takes into account this directive in order to propose a solution. To do this STAR calculates the whole of trajectories which response to the directive, without, of course, create new conflict. STAR proposes then ONE trajectory to the controller (after a choice in function of some criteria like number of deviation, consumption of kerosene…). The controller can examine the solution proposed by STAR. If the solution is satisfactory, the controller can delegate the effectuation, that's mean the sending of instructions to aircraft. In this case STAR has in charge to communicate instructions (change of heading, FL…) directly to the aircraft. Thus the controller is discharged of the effectuation and communication with pilots.

2.1.2. Common Work Space (CWS)

The CWS [10, 11, 12] is an essential notion introduced with AMANDA. This space allows a sharing of information between all agents (human, like controllers and artificial like STAR). Each agent can introduce new information in this CWS according to its competencies (know-how), and in accordance to its role (authority) in the process. All the agents can take this information into account in order to carry out their tasks, or to control and check those of the other agents.

This CWS allows mainly to maintain a common situation awareness between the two controllers, to share their representation of the problems (here in sense of air conflict or loss of separation) to supervise and/or to resolve. The controllers have the responsibility to maintain up to date this space, in order to, on the one hand to preserve a coherent "picture" of the situation and airspace, and on the other hand to inform the platform, and mainly STAR, with the conflicts that they detect.

2.2. Experimental results

The principles presented were tested experimentally with the help of qualified controllers regularly practising their functions. For that three scenarios of traffic were designed to test three experimental situations differentiated by the level of assistance provided [3]. The scenarios simulate a realistic traffic (traffic configurations usually encountered on a real sector) but twice more loaded than into reality.

From a general point of view, the general principle of providing assistance allowing a regulation of workload has been recognized relevant by controllers. In the situation where STAR and CWS assisted controllers, 93% of clusters expected were created. For 75% of these clusters a directive or a differed order was selected and 63% of those directives or differed orders have been delegated to STAR. In terms of workload, the tools available allowed to controllers to manage without any difficulty the traffic load.

The experimentations have emphasized that the tools have favoured the anticipation of controllers. However this anticipation has been increase by the absence of simulation of adjacent sectors. Indeed, the PC was liberate of the management of coordinations with the adjacent sectors, and has an entirely liberty to change the level of entry or exit of aircraft. This excess of anticipation has allowed to the PC to act on traffic and aircraft in order to reduce the number of conflicts. The workload of EC has been artificially reduced.

The module STAR has proved unsuited to the practice of the EC. Indeed, the calculation methods used provide a trajectory avoiding the aircraft at the meadows of the standard separation and returning to the original trajectory in the shortest. The controllers were then disconcerted by the efficiency of STAR. In addition, taking into account the unstable aircraft (changing flight level) by STAR was not optimal, as is the concept of "interfering" aircraft (aircraft that the system considers necessary to take into account to solve the conflict, and in many cases an unstable aircraft). The controllers do not seem to have this notion of interference, for them an aircraft is in the conflict or it is not.

2.3. AMANDA V3

The objectives of this new study are [4]: the integration of adjacent sectors and improvement of trajectory calculation, STAR. This integration of adjacent sectors consists of an extension of CWS principles to the cooperation between Planning Controllers of adjacent sectors. This new CWS will:

- Facilitate the negotiations between sectors; in allowing to quickly visualizing the flight concerned by negotiations (the workload, the time necessary, and the risk of ambiguity will be reduce).
- Allow to share between sectors: changes in the trajectory of aircraft, this should help to reduce uncertainty about the positions and conditions of entry for flights in a sector.

Concerning the module of calculation STAR, it is too much "efficacious" compared to the methods and habits of controllers. Indeed, the calculation methods use mathematical methods to provide the new trajectory allowing resolving the conflict. That gives "perfect" trajectories, avoiding the conflict aircraft at the meadows of the minimal separation distance (5 NM) and returning to the shortest to the original trajectory. This tool does not include additional factors introduced by controllers such as a safety margin above the minimal separation distance (15NM), a deviation rate (heading) comfortable (<30 °), an anticipation of unstable aircraft. The controllers were then surprised by the trajectories provided by STAR.

By adding the notion of adjacent sector, the decision evolves; it came out of the sector. It is therefore necessary to analyze and integrate in a coherent manner the decisions inside the sector and those outsides. To do this, a decision making model is required; it is the object of the following point.

2.4. Approach

The study is divided into three phases. The first phase focuses on the analysis and the structuring of the decision-making process. Several questions come up here. First of all, an analysis of the decisions of PC in phases of coordination with the adjacent sectors is required. But these decisions must be put in coherence with the decisions of the PC in the intern management of his/her sector. They must be also put in coherence with the intern management of the sector by the EC. This phase will conduct in a description of a coherent control decision process. This point is developed in more details in section 3.1.

The second phase is methodological. It aims to structure each decision of decision-making process. A general methodological framework must be researched to promote the coherence of each decision considering their links with the decision-making process. Several participants contribute to the decision; each one according to his/her owns value system. The methodological framework must also allow structuring the exchanges between the different participants in the decision. It should also help to identify, to represent and to manipulate the different value systems of the participants. This phase is described in section 3.2

The third phase is classic in the field of decision-support, it is the modelling phase. This phase aims to identify and to structure the elements allowing designing some tools to aid the decision makers. It is therefore necessary to collect the decisions elements handled by the controllers. It is important to note that the controllers are not the only holders of these elements. Staffs of Air Navigation in charge of the training of controllers have a favourable position in this phase. It is the same with "decision engineer", designers of tools present in AMANDA. However air traffic controllers are the only ones who can make validation judgments of model (through the results they produce). This phase is developed in section 3.3.

3. Structuring of problem

3.1. Decision-making process

The decisions of control are in line with a continuum. At the most complete level, they consist of to change the trajectory of the aircraft by applying adjustments to flights parameters of aircraft in order to resolve, operationally, a conflicting situation. The EC has in charge this operational level, and he/she can cooperate with STAR. It is the axis 3 on the figure 1, below.

Previously, these operational decisions have been prepared by the PC who has information before EC. The PC may already identify a conflict situation and inform the EC at the good time. This latter will integrate this new situation in the management of his/her traffic. He/she will specify the preparation, and the "pre detection" of PC to be able to operationalize later. The EC occupies a central position in the tactical level (axis 2 on figure 1) in collaboration with the PC. The CWS constitutes a cooperation help between the two controllers. The EC also has the possibility of cooperating with STAR in this tactical management.

Finally, at the sector level (axis 1 on figure 1), the PC is the first to have available the information about flights which preparing to pass in the sector. The PC gets a strategic vision of potential conflicting situations. The CWS enables him/her to explain this vision and to share it in order to the EC exploit these information to manage the sector. In the context of this strategic management, PC may come into contact with adjacent sectors with in order to change flights levels of entry or exit of aircraft to avoid a conflict in his/her s0ector and thus reduce preventively the workload of EC. The CWS is therefore quite naturally an area of strategic management between PC, coherent with the tactical management by the synthetic vision which it presents.

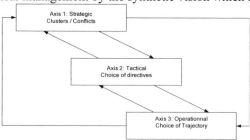

Figure 1. Synthesis diagram of three axes of the study, and the links between them.

These three axes are studied as independently as possible with the aim of obtain refined results and focused results on a specific problem, and therefore provide the opportunity to deepen each level. But the axes are interconnected; indeed choice a trajectory without having problems is somewhat surprising. It is thus quite logically, that appeared influence between axis 1 and 2 and between axis 2 and 3. The existence of operational decisions quickly appears plausible in the current state of our thinking.

These quickly decisions correspond on a direct link between the axis 1 and the axis 3. This possibility will be studied.

3.2. Multiple criteria methodology

The job of an air traffic controller is characterized by the research for a compromise between different value systems. This is typically the concept of managing flows aircraft. Thereby, the controllers act on the traffic by ensuring optimal security, while trying to reduce delays and the consumption of fuel. ATC is by nature multiple criteria. It is quite unrealistic to summarize the actions taken by the controllers in a single goal, which would be safety, the cost or time. In addition, the actions of the controllers constitute the terminal part of the management of control situations. They are therefore the result of decisions taken previously by controllers. Consequently, it seems appropriate to address the design of aid with the point of view of the methodology of Multiple Criteria Decision Making (MCDM).

The MCDM methodology [14] replaces the concept of decision as resulting from the wider concept of the decision-making process wherein several participants can play a role in their own interests. For that reason, the study of decision-making problem is itself accentuated.

The MCDM methodology proceeds in four levels (figure 2). The first level is to clearly define the potential actions. The potential actions are all possibilities (real or fictitious) on the basis of which the decision is made. The criteria (level 2) are the factors (witness of the decision) which characterize the potential actions for decide. Preferences (level 3) are a set of rules by which the potential actions are put in relation across criteria. Finally, the level 4 is the establishment of a recommendation. This is the operational level of the methodology, the implementation.

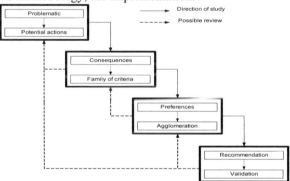

Figure 2. Synthesis diagram of the Multiple criteria Decision Making methodology (MCDM).

The study of three axes independently will therefore lead to conduct three MCDM, and thus to define three problematic; obtain three families of criteria… But the recommendation (level 4) will be most certainly more overall. For example during cooperation between PC, the strategic level, the PC can be lead to justify his/her requests, the operational level. In any case, it will result of these three studies only one cooperative system, a single platform. This platform will be composed of different decisions, tools different responding and corresponding to each of the recommendations and axes, but they will be grouped within a single environment, CWS.

Human Machine Cooperation aspect is the unifying thread of the study. This aspect takes place essentially in the level 4, the recommendation. The main objective is to understand the steps and the use that the controllers do of adjacent sectors, their manner of cooperate… Human Machine Cooperation aspect can thus be considered as a synthesis of MCDM.

3.3. Repertory grid

Repertory grid is a methodology developed by an American psychologist, Georges Kelly (1955) [15], in order to study the psychological construct in pathological case (schizophrenia…).This method will allow compare « elements » (different event, actions, states or entities). To do that, the method will « force » the patient to ask him/her and thus establish a list of « constructs », as exhaustive as possible. The constructs are divided in two groups: the similarities and contrasts. Each construct (similarities or contrasts) will be then evaluated or weighted in function of the different elements of the grid. The elements, the constructs, and the weighting will represent the « construct map » of the patient.

The standard representation of a repertory grid is a matrix, with in column, the elements, and in rows, the constructs. The constructs are divided in two poles, and generally the similarities, obtained in first, are on the left of the matrix, and the contrasts are on the right (see table 1). At the intersection of each pair element-construct there is a weighting given by the subject and which represents how the subject applies or evaluates a construct in relation to an element.

Table 1. Standard representation of repertory grid

	ELEMENTS	
Constructs: **Similarities**	Weight	Constructs: **Contrasts**

To establish the list of constructs, it is several methods; one of the most common is the "triad methods" which consist in taking 3 elements and to ask itself what two elements have in common that the third has not. The list of similarities and contrasts is thus obtained in comparing each element with this method, or until the subject has no new construct to propose. The second step is to complete the grid with weightings. It is possible to use 5 weightings (1, 2, 3, 4 and 5) or 9. The most frequently use is a weighting of 5, avoiding thus a too important dispersion. The principle is the following: the subject uses a 1 if the element is near of the notion of similarities of the construct, and 5 if it is rather the contrast side. A 2 (similarity) or 4 (contrast) will be used if the notion, evoked by the construct, is less evident that previously. And finally a weighting 3 exists, if the subject can not, or be not able to evaluate the element, the subject has no preference.

The overall problem detection / resolution of conflict is divided in three axes. These axes will be studied independently. Three MCDM will be therefore applied, and hence at least a repertory grid for each MCDM [16]. The grids will be built with the results of the AMANDA V2 experiments.

During the AMANDA V2 experiments, all data have been recorded, that means that it is possible to replay what the controllers have made (creation of clusters, choice of directives and deviation of aircraft, use of interfaces…). Data will be used in order to identify interesting cases, and to use them for interviews with the different participants (controllers, instructors, but also "decision engineer", in this case, the designers of experimental situations). Interesting case means for example, if the reactions of controllers were different: the creation of cluster, or in the choice of a directive or a trajectory to be applied. This analysis of the results will provide a number of cases which will be then submitted in a first time to the "decision engineers", which will try to understand and to explain the actions of controllers and this with another point of view.

4. A first decision model

From the results of AMANDA V2 experiments, a collection of grid was built, and presents to the participants a variety of elements (in sense of Kelly) that they will be analyze. These elements are the potential actions relative to the studied axis. In axis 1 (conflict detection, clusters), it is the typical conflicting situation in the sector, or conflicts which have aroused among controllers varied and different responses. The first grid (for which the elements submitted to the participants are presented in the table 2) is based on both a conflict fairly typical for the sector (here Bordeaux), and for which the responses of controllers are all different.

Table 2. Repertory grid proposed to the subject

BAL632	BAL632	BAL632	BAL632	BAL632
KLM1884	KLM1884	KLM1884	KLM1884	KLM1884
BCS1080	AFR1657	AFR1657	AFR1657	
	BCS1080	AEL2789		

The table 2 corresponds to the elements which are in the repertory grid, presented to the controllers. This table is composed by the different clusters proposed by controllers[2] during AMANDA V2 experiments. The first row corresponds to the real conflict. That means that the BAL632 and the KLM1884 pass on the beacon "VELIN" with less of one minute. These two aircraft are not separated by the minimal distance of separation (5NM). The second row corresponds to the additional aircraft that the controllers of Bordeaux have choice to take into account to resolve the conflict. These aircraft are called "interfering aircraft", that means that they are not directly in conflict with the BAL632 or with the KLM1884, but it is necessary to take these aircraft into account to resolve the conflict. For example if the controller reroute the BAL632 it is necessary to take care to the AFR1657 which is just behind the KLM1884. These interfering or contextual aircraft are thus constraint in the phase of resolution.

This first grid is proposed to a « decision engineer », who is one of the designers of the platform, and who has created the experimental situation. He known relatively well the sector and its configuration, and have a good expertise of the job of controllers.

The first key point is the variety of responses from different pairs of controllers during the experiments. All controllers have detected the conflicts and included the BAL632 and the KLM1884 in the cluster, but what would have mean if these two aircraft are not in the cluster? The likely answer is that in this case the aircraft had been reroute upstream (previous sector), and thus the conflict did not exist. This manoeuvre involves coordination between the two sectors.

---

[2] A radar view is proposed in figure 3 to better understand the situation

The second construct proposed by the subject concerns the presence of the AFR1657. The AFR1657 is not engaged directly in the conflict, but to take into account for a resolution. For the subject, the AFR1657 is therefore essential in the conflict because it constrains strongly the BAL632 trajectory. For him the fact that it is not here in some clusters does not mean that controllers do not taken into account of this aircraft, but they exclude certain resolutions which can be problematic. It appears that controllers have an idea of how they will resolve the conflict, before the creation of the cluster.

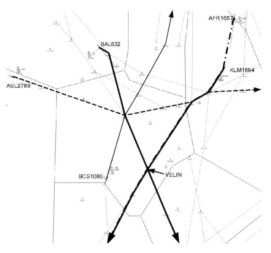

Figure 3. Radar view of the conflict

The third constructs proposed, is the case of BCS1080, which is an unstable aircraft (changing Flight Level). In other words, it will necessarily come to cross flight level 350, where the conflict is situated. The controllers do not control well the climb ratio (or down) of aircraft. In the same way that AFR1657, BCS1080 will therefore constrain the future trajectory of BAL632. Half of the pairs have added this aircraft, and have decided to climb very early so that it does not interfere with the trajectory of BAL632 (with the exception that the pilot acts rapidly). This requires anticipation for instruction on BCS1080, maybe even upstream of the sector, and therefore coordination. The other pairs felt that the aircraft was not a problem, because it has enough time to climb, and not interfere with the trajectory of BAL632.

Finally the fourth construct proposed by the subject is the case of AEL2789. The AEL2789 only included in a single cluster. It is true that its involvement in the conflict is not obvious because it is relatively far from the aircraft (BAL632 and KLM1884). However, it must be taken into account if the controller chose to reroute the AFR1657 to put behind the BAL632. In this case the AFR1657 will be closer to the AEL2789 and it is necessary to supervise the distance between this two aircraft. For other pairs, for which a deviation on the AFR1657 was not envisaged, the AEL2789 was no problem, and had no reason to be included in the cluster.

The first point which appear, and which is important is the fact that controllers already have a fairly accurate idea of how they will resolve a conflict even before creating the cluster. This "knowledge" of the solution is very decisive for the choice of aircraft to be taken into account. Depending on the strategy already established, the controllers therefore choose only the aircraft that will be a problem in the application of their strategy for resolving the conflict. This is therefore clearly a link between the axis 2 and the axis 1 of the decision-making process (Figure 1).

From this first grid, it is already possible to extract criteria, which are subject to confirmation with other grids and validated by controllers. The first criterion is that to be in a cluster, an aircraft must really be a problem and have an involvement towards the resolution strategy that the controller has imagined. It is the case of the AFR1657.

The second issue concerns the unstable aircraft (here the BCS1080). The controllers do not control well these aircraft, and their trajectories. So an important criterion will be the anticipation. Anticipating an unstable aircraft can make possible that this aircraft will be on its new level before it crosses the initial problem (2 pairs of controllers do it and they consider that the BCS1080 is not embarrassing). But this anticipation takes time, and a reasonable workload, and involves coordination in most cases. This can become difficult with the increase of traffic.

Table 3. Result of first repertory grid

Similarities	BAL632 KLM1884 BCS1080	BAL632 KLM1884 AFR1657 BCS1080	BAL632 KLM1884 AFR1657 AEL2789	BAL632 KLM1884 AFR1657	BAL632 KLM1884	Contrast
BAL-KLM Basis conflict	1	1	1	1	1	Absence of BAL-KLM
AFR constraint BAL632	5	1	1	1	5	AFR take into account, not included
BCS constraint BAL Anticipation	1	1	5	5	5	BCS1080 is another conflict.
AEL in conflict if action on AFR	5	5	1	5	5	AEL no problem

5. Conclusion

This paper begins with an introduction of Air Traffic Control and presents the problematic, which is the increase in air traffic. The second part presents the platform AMANDA developed in the laboratory, which has for objectives to help controllers in their tasks, only on one controlling position for the moment.

The platform is composed of two main tools: A module for trajectories calculating, as well as delegation of tasks (STAR), and a space of cooperation between the controllers and the tools, called Common Work Space (CWS). Thanks to these tools, the controllers can cooperate more efficiently, and to discharge a portion of the activity (the calculation and application of trajectories) to manage new aircraft. These tools have been tested with professional controllers and have obtained encouraging results. These results lead to the new version, AMANDA V3 which is the centre of this article. The objectives of this new version are presented at the end of the second part, and they concerned particularly the introduction of adjacent sectors.

The third part concerns the establishment of an approach to model the new tools of AMANDA V3. This approach is divided into three main points; the first is to model the decision-making process of controllers. The second point is a presentation of the MCDM methodology. This MCDM will guide the study. And the last point concerns the repertory grid methodology, which will serve of operational support to the MCDM, and will support the interviews and the knowledge acquisition. Finally a last section presents an initial decision model, and an application of the approach to one axis of our decision-making process.

The continuation of this study will be to achieve other grid on three axes, in order to obtain as much information as possible, and to determine a set of criteria and a model of preferences. This work will be done largely with decision engineers, who are also the designers of the platform. Then it will be necessary to validate all the criteria and preferences with operational controllers.

Acknowledgments

We want to thank the DGAC/SDER/DTI for their financial support. We also thank all the personnel of the ATC, which by its availability and its collaboration made it possible to develop, and to evaluate the various platforms. This work is supported in part by the Nord Pas-de-Calais region and FEDER (European Funds for Regional Development) through the project AUTORIS T31.

References

[1]   DGAC, Direction générale de l'aviation civile, contrôle des routes du ciel. http://www.aviation-civile.gouv.fr/html/actu_gd/routciel.htm
[2]   S. Debernard, S. Cathelain, I. Crévits, T. Poulain, AMANDA Project: Delegation of tasks in the air-traffic control domain, *Cooperative Systems design, IOS PRES*, (2002), 173-190.
[3]   B. Guiost, S. Debernard, T. Poulain, P. Millot, Supporting Air-Traffic Controllers by Delegating Tasks, In *IEEE-SMC* (2004), 164-169.
[4]   D. Annebicque, S. Debernard, T. Poulain, I. Crévits, *AMANDA V3: Toward a Common Work Space between air Traffic Controllers*, In ACHI 08, Sainte Luce, Martinique, February, 2008.
[5]   F. Vanderhaegen, I. Crévits, S. Debernard, P. Millot, Human-machine cooperation: Toward activity regulation assistance for different air traffic control levels, *International Journal on Human-Computer Interaction*, **6** (1994), 65-104.
[6]   M-P. Lemoine, S. Debernard, I. Crévits, P. Millot, Cooperation between Humans and Machines: First results of an Experiment with a Multi-Level Cooperative Organisation in Air Traffic Control, *Computer Supported Cooperative Work: The Journal of Collaborative Computing*, **5** (1996), 299-321.
[7]   I. Crévits, S. Debernard, F. Vanderhaegen, P. Millot, *Multi level cooperation in air traffic control*. 4th International Conference on Human-Machine Interaction and Artificial Intelligence in Aerospace, France, 1993.
[8]   M.R. Endsley, D.B. Kaber, Level of automation, effects on performance, situation awareness and workload in a dynamic control task, *Ergonomics*, **42** (1999), 462-492.
[9]   M.R. Endsley, Automation and situation awareness, *Automation and human performance: Theory and application*, (1996), 163-181.
[10]   M.-P. Pacaux-Lemoine, S. Debernard, A common work space to support the Air Traffic Control, *Control Engineering Practice, A journal of IFAC*, **10** (2002), 571-576.
[11]   B. Guiost, S. Debernard, Common Work Space or How to Support Cooperative Activities between Human Operators and Machine: Application to Air Traffic Control, *12ᵗʰ International Conference on Human-Computer Interaction*, Springer, **13** (2007).
[12]   R. Bentley, T. Rodden, P. Sawyer, I. Sommerville, An architecture for tailoring cooperative cooperative multi-user displays, *4th Computer – supported cooperative work*, (1992) 187-194.
[13]   B. Guiost, S. Debernard, T. Poulain, P. Millot, *Task Allocation in Air Traffic Control Involving a Common Workspace and a Cooperative Support System*, IFAC ASBHS, Nancy, France, 2006.
[14]   B. Roy, *Multicriteria Methodology for Decision Aiding*. Kluwer. London, 1996
[15]   GA. Kelly, *The psychology of personal constructs*, New York: Norton, 1955.
[16]   R. Scheubrein, S. Zionts, A problem structuring front end for a multiple criteria decision support system. *Computers & Operations Research*, **33** (2004), 18-31.

Collaborative Decision Making: Perspectives and Challenges
P. Zaraté et al. (Eds.)
IOS Press, 2008

Manual Collaboration Systems: Decision Support or Support for Situated Choices

Reeva LEDERMAN[a] and Robert B. JOHNSTON[b]
[a] *University of Melbourne*
[b] *University College Dublin*

Abstract. This paper challenges the idea of calling the activity that occurs in many collaborative systems "decision making". It suggests that the term decision-making implies a level of deliberation which does not appear to reflect the reality of how activity takes place in these systems. To examine this, the paper selects a type of system discussed previously in the CSCW literature, a whiteboard based scheduling system in an intensive care ward. It finds in fact that much of the activity that occurs in this system is reactive and routine. It shows why the design of this system reduces the need for actors to evaluate choices (when choosing is the hallmark of decision making) and instead allows activity to take place routinely through situated choices.

Keywords. Decision making, deliberative theory, situated action, collaborative systems

1. Introduction

This paper will examine the use of manual collaborative information systems involving coordinative mechanisms. These mechanisms are used for collaborative activities in dynamic environments and have been discussed in the literature at length. They include whiteboards for hospital scheduling [1–3], manual air traffic control (ATC) systems involving paper flight strips [4–7] and emergency ambulance dispatch systems that use paper cards organized in a physical allocation box [8–11].

Much research into collaborative systems has taken the view that it is valid to study such systems by evaluating the decision making approaches taken by users. Studies of interesting collaborative systems in the literature mentioned above such as ambulance control systems, air traffic control systems and hospital whiteboard systems have all been approached from the view that action in these systems occurs as a result of a highly cognitive decision making process. Many authors examining such systems do so in the context of decision making theory [9,12,13]. These authors are interested in the intentionality of individuals and processes of decision making, such as Naturalistic Decision Making [9,12,13].

However an examination of many of the collaborative systems discussed in the literature suggests that some forms of activity are not guided by the evaluation of choices and may involve triggers to activity unrelated to what is commonly referred to as decision making. In ATC research actors are recorded using artefacts to "highlight, remind and reinforce [7 p. 5]" the actions of users and of "glancing" at artefacts and "quickly picking out" cues for action [6 p. 11]. In emergency ambulance research actors are recorded relying on the "non-verbal cues" of other actors [14] or other environmental stimuli [15] in working out how to act.

Understanding how activity takes place in these systems is important because the study of activity in systems leads to new and better uses of methodologies for design and development. So, while these systems have been observed to work effectively as manual information systems, the failure to develop suitable designs and methodologies to computerize comes at a high cost, preventing the scaling up of such systems [7,16]. In both France and the US air traffic control systems are considered safe, yet the current manual aspects of the systems that have been retained are seen to constrain the level of air traffic possible [6,17]. While manual air traffic control systems have been replaced in many parts of the world, where they have not been replaced it is because controllers have not been given tools equally suitable "for managing large amounts of information in short periods of time" [17 p. 3]. Further, while many effective manual systems are found in hospitals they are problematic because they "leave no permanent trace.... thus cannot provide management information about unit processes and activities [18 p. 10], a significant impediment in the modern hospital system. Consequently, it is worthwhile studying such systems to work out whether the activity that takes place in such systems is in fact decision making or whether it is of a form that may be better categorized differently and regarded differently for the purposes of future design.

This paper will first discuss two prevalent approaches to activity, a deliberative, decision making approach and an alternative situated action approach. It will then present one commonly discussed manual information system, a whiteboard based collaborative hospital scheduling system. Finally, the paper will make conclusions about how activity occurs by analysing the ways in which actors use this system.

2. Support for Decision Making Versus Situated Choice

All information systems are purposeful and designed to achieve certain goals and to carry out certain activities relevant to these goals. This is the case also with collaborative information systems, where actors share goals. Therefore it is important to understand the nature of the activities in collaborative systems to determine how such systems can be made more effective and thus achieve goals. There are two main theories which address the nature of purposeful activity, the first is the deliberative approach which asserts that people use an abstract model of the world to deduce actions that will achieve a goal [19] and the second approach is a situated theory of action which "posits that, by and large, human action is a direct, unmediated response to situations encountered in the course of routine activity [20 p. 53]".

Actors following a deliberative approach apply deductive processes, or decision making, to the task of determining what to do. Under the deliberative model, the world is represented as symbols and objects which actors use to formulate a plan of action. Using this plan the actor develops a series of actions as part of the decision making process, which will transform the current state of the world into some preferred state. When deliberating, actors "maintain a mental representation of the world which they use to reason out what to do next [20 p. 2]".

There is a large body of theory which examines how individuals make decisions [21,22] going back to Jeremy Bentham (1748–1832) which takes a deliberative approach. These works describe decision making as involving knowing what choices of action are possible, what the outcome of such choices are and a level of rationality in deliberating over these choices to evaluate or maximize outcomes [23].

Many of the artefacts used in collaborative systems have been previously studied from a deliberative viewpoint and referred to in the literature as decision making supports and the work carried out with them as decision making work [24] using planning [25] and cognitive based models [26]. Kaempf et al., for example, examine a collaborative navel command and control environment where many activities described are clearly reactive [13]. However, while these authors claim that in 95% of cases actions are routine, they still suggest that in managing routine, actors make decisions and adopt a "Recognitional- Primed Decision model" [13].

The second approach, a situated approach, is a possible alternative model for behaviour in such systems. This approach suggests that it is possible to act with "minimum or no representation of future desired states [20 p. 4]" if the environment of action is sufficiently conducive [27]. In this mode of acting, actors use rule-like responses to aspects of the environment, such as physical artefacts or social structures, which are perceived with their senses or through familiarity in order to act routinely.

In the situations within many manual collaborative systems described in this literature actors appear to have access to an environment where not a lot of information is explicitly represented but where structure in the environment is used to support action [1,28,29]. So for example, an air traffic controller knows how to act in controlling a particular flight by looking at the arrangement of a number of paper flight strips laid out on table, even though the information for this particular flight is transitive and is not recorded anywhere else in writing or in any formalised way. Many of the collaborative manual information systems in the literature seem to be comprised of forms of activity, where participants in these systems use their tacit knowledge of work practices and various cues perceived directly from the work environment to perform manual tasks. Consequently, it seems valuable to consider this aspect of these systems, and to explore whether an alternative approach to activity within these systems other than what is traditionally known as decision making, may be useful.

The following case study will be used to analyze activity within a common manual collaborative system.

3. ICU Bed Management System (ICU)

This case study takes place in a large, busy environment, the intensive care unit of a 360–390-bed acute tertiary referral hospital. Fifty interviews were conducted with staff as they viewed and used the whiteboard. Each interview was about 10-15 minutes duration. The collaborative aspects of work for which the RMIS provides information support include staff members selecting patients for discharge and staff members accepting new patients into the ward.

The intensive care unit has 24 beds, including 20 Intensive Care beds and four High Dependency beds. It provides a full range of adult intensive care services, catering for patients from within the hospital and also via the Emergency Department and transfers from other hospitals. The unit handles more than 2000 admissions annually. Typical patient conditions include neurological trauma, general trauma, complex respiratory management, sepsis, oncology, cardiac surgery, renal failure, post operative management, infectious diseases and multiple organ failure.

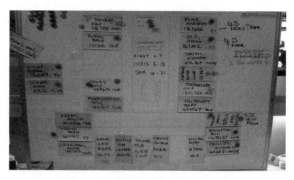

Figure 1. Whiteboard in the ICU ward.

The information system under examination is a bed allocation system within the ICU which monitors the movement in and out of the ward of ICU patients and supports ancillary activities associated with this movement such as visits to discharging patients from physiotherapists or chaplains. The goal of the system is to record the current status of bed usage and manage movement in and out of beds in the short term. The utilization of beds is recorded on a central information artefact, the system whiteboard (Fig. 1) which operates in the highly dynamic environment with a constantly functioning admissions procedure presenting patients to the system.

3.1. Organisational Components

Staff: The staff employed in the ICU ward include a head nurse, other ICU nurses, medical resident doctors, medical specialists, physiotherapists, chaplains, ward clerks as well as cleaning staff and technical staff who set up beds and equipment.

Work Area: The work area is a large space about 400 × 400 metres. Around the edge of the work area are 24 intensive care beds. In the centre is a nurses station which has two ward clerks sitting at one end closest to the door of the ward so they can see patients and visitors coming in and out, and a whiteboard running along the left hand side of the station, in front of which it is possible to stand and view the ward.

Bed Cubicles: The 24 bed cubicles are arranged around the outer perimeter of the ward and surround the nurses station which sits in the middle. Each bed cubicle contains a bed and a surround of about 6 × 6 metres for medical equipment, a sink and a chair for visitors. All cubicles can be viewed, by facing or turning around, from a standing position next to the whiteboard in the nurses' station.

Whiteboard: The board sits in a prominent position in the nurses' station. It is designed with a large rectangle in the middle representing the nurses' station with blank rectangles drawn around it corresponding to the actual physical position of each bed relative to the nurses' station. There are 24 positions on the board each representing one cubicle and space in the centre of the board for additional nursing information and space around the sides for additional patient information.

The board is located in a central position in full view of the beds that it depicts. It is positioned in such a way that it can be viewed simultaneously by a number of staff. These are many kinds of staff (doctors, nurses, chaplains, physiotherapists) and they come up to the board all day. Additionally, the board is positioned at right angles to two ward clerks who maintain further written information about patients on two computers. The information on these computers is largely for auditing purposes and does not specifically relate to the bed allocation task.

There are a number of items on the board: writing produced by eraseable and non-erasable coloured board markers, magnetised name labels and coloured magnets. Aside from the information on the magnetised name labels (described below) there is a large volume of information placed around the labels which is written up by staff over the course of the day. This information describes relevant activity such as a surgery taking place at a particular time or the possibility of a bed being available in another ward for a patient to be discharged into. The mere placement of this information next to a patient label gives staff a feel for the bed management situation. Just seeing lots of writing around the labels tells staff that there is considerable movement afoot – the writing does not need to be read to proceed with many routine tasks, such as proceeding to select a patient for discharge. That is, once it is obvious that there is a need to free up beds certain activities proceed. It is only when specific information about a particular incoming patient is required that information on the board may actually be read and addressed in non-routine ways.

Name Labels: The whiteboard is used with a set of magnetic name labels which adhere the board and have patient names written on them. These name labels are eras-able and re-useable but bed numbers drawn on the squares on the board are not eras-able. In this way users can rely on the constancy of certain information even though the labels are used in multiple ways on the board. The name written on a magnetic card placed on rectangle 21, for example, always corresponds to the patient in bed 21, al-though the same label may indicate different things if moved to a different part of the board.

Patient names are written on the name labels with coloured markers. A name writ-ten in blue marker is a cardiac patient and a name written in black marker can be any other non-cardiac patient.

Coloured magnets: In addition to the name labels there are coloured plastic mag-nets in groups at the top of the board. These can be taken and placed on particular bed cubicles on the whiteboard on top of the name labels or next to them. An orange mag-net means possible discharge from ICU, a green magnet definite discharge, a red mag-net means incoming patient, a blue means that the patient requires isolating for infec-tion control and yellow means the patient is palliating and will receive no further treatment. Patients with red magnets may not have yet been allocated a bed but may be placed as "pending" set to the left side of the board. These colours and placements al-low staff to perceive at a glance what the bed allocation situation is without having to actually read any patient information.

3.2. Procedures

The system for managing bed occupancy takes place around the whiteboard continually during the day as patients move in and out of beds. The head nurse starts her 7.30 shift by standing in front of the board and reviewing any movement overnight. There is a chronic bed shortage and a patient can only be moved out of ICU if a bed is available in another ward. Similarly managing nurses from other wards often need to procure ICU beds for urgent cases that need to be transferred out of general wards. Conse-quently, the daily procedure for the managing nurse involves a constant fielding of questions about bed availability that need to be dealt with quickly over the telephone through just a glance at the board.

The hospital staff and ward clerks interact with each other around the board continually throughout the day, providing mutually valuable patient information. Sometimes this information is gauged from the board, sometimes it is just overheard and absorbed as a result of physical proximity, sometimes it is actively elicited.

There is a constant shortage of ICU beds and when there is a risk of an ICU bed not being available post surgery, surgery is often postponed. As a result of this, action relating to bed allocation need to be taken efficiently with all significant information ready to hand for the staff involved in the activity. Users of the system can tell instantly whether or not admissions or discharges can proceed. They do this, not just by looking at the board and perceiving whether or not bed spaces are available, but also by being able to simultaneously grasp the full picture from the ward: the information on the right and left sides of the board lets staff know about the status of possible discharges and admissions and the information available from viewing and sensing the ward itself supplements this knowledge. For example, a cardiac patient, patient one, might be marked for possible discharge. They cannot leave however, without a cardio-thoracic physiotherapist seeing them. If the nurse planning the discharge can see by looking out at the ward that the physio is occupied with another patient they know that patient one will not be leaving immediately. Thus, the situating of the board within the ward system itself is essential for the execution of the bed management task.

The work practices and specific tacit rules of the workplace, which include the use of the board, trigger certain routine responses in staff imbued with a familiarity with these rules, many of which have evolved gradually through input from the current batch of staff. For example, a cardiac surgeon knows that blue patients are cardiac patients. As a result of this, when s/he views the board s/he need pay no attention to half of it. Similarly, chaplains are keen to tend to palliating patients and might only look for yellow magnets. These physical features allow the selection of patients to be routinised once the significance of particular colours, for example, is known to the staff member. Other "local" knowledge is also important to bed management. For example, staff know that a "2pm heart" patient listed on the right of the board (see Fig. 1) for possible admission will not arrive before 5pm. All of this knowledge allows tasks to be performed in a tacit and routinised manner.

The name labels and magnets can be picked up and transferred from one position on the board and fitted easily into another position. Staff are often seen picking up and putting down the labels as they discuss placement decisions together. The tangiblness of the physical label, as well as the actual handling of it, seems to be important in conceptualising the patient movements.

The board layout facilitates the addition of extra information proximate to the actual patient to which the information refers. This information is often transitory and may relate to a situation that has not yet been "firmed up". On Figure 1 above for example, the possibility of the patient in bed 1, Herbert Black, being transferred to 4S is raised by a notation to the right "4S HDU (High Dependency Unit)?". There is space next to each numbered position for writing about possible patient destinations which allows decisions about other admissions or discharges to be made in the context of this possibility.

Referring to Fig. 1 there are many things that staff can observe at a glance. For example, "Kirst" who is designated beds 1–7, needs only to attend to the first 7 beds on the right (which make up her patient list) when she comes up to look at the board; an AM heart patient listed on the right, (Johnston), has now been crossed off so no longer needs to be considered for admission; three patients on the left are expecting to come in but are not yet in beds (one of these is not firmed up and so put askew), and while there is a bit of uncertainty as a result of the number of orange stickers there are also two empty beds, so the situation is not as difficult to manage as on some other days. A doctor standing in front of the board can perceive all of this while also observing the busyness of the ward itself, listening to the ward clerks converse on the phone to operating theatres about expected admissions and in view of the ward entrance where patients are being wheeled in. Thus a full body of information relating to admission and discharge is immediately available without any reading or recourse to patient records.

4. Analysis

In this section the findings of the case study are evaluated under a number of emergent headings. This analysis produces a number of significant findings which suggest that most of the activity in these systems conforms better to a situated action approach than to standard definitions of decision making.

4.1. Much of the Work Activity Is Routine and Results from a Limiting of Action Choices

Previous authors include the idea of repeated patterns or recurrence as a central characteristic of routine (Becker, 2004). Common definitions include the view of routine as: "an activity that occurs more then once and becomes second nature to participants through repetition" [30–32]. The issue of a routine activity becoming "second nature" is crucial to this analysis. Not only is it important to identify routine activity but also to consider what aspects of these systems make it possible for actors to behave as though an activity is second nature and to act without apparent decision making. Thinking back to the discussion of decision making given earlier, the crucial issue is the idea of evaluating choices. How these systems seem to operate and make routinisation possible, is in reducing the need to evaluate by constraining choices.

In this system, actors use aspects of the physical layout to limit and simplify action choices. The physical layout of the whiteboard, designed to represent the physical layout of the ward, provides the first indicator to staff of how they need to act. A staff member perusing the board and wanting to perform an activity relating to the next empty bed, (for example, allocating it to a future patient) only has to glance at the board, see the green magnet on the label with Emily Collins, bed 20, and know instantly where the bed is in the ward and that it is going to be vacated. The layout of the board makes it possible to do a second check of actually looking over at the bed itself. In this way, the choices of a bed for the next patient are fully constrained and made obvious by physical structures in the system, and no evaluation of choices is necessary.

Similarly, the use of different colours on the board, not just for the magnets, also constrains choice. A cardio-thoracic physiotherapist for example only needs to see cardiac patients who are all written in blue on the board and are also generally placed on the left hand side of the board and correspondingly, on the left hand side of the ward. When the physiotherapist goes to the ward s/he needs to see patients who are being discharged. Again, the ability to select out Emily Collins in bed 20 is easily routinised and requires no decision making of any kind. This is because a series of physical layers comprised of the board layout, the placement on the board of the bed label in a particular bed slot, the placement on a particular side of the board, and designating the patient with a green magnet, all contribute to indicating the same action choice: that Emily Collins is the patient that needs to be seen. Additionally, the fact that the physical layout of the board corresponds to the physical layout of the ward directs the physiotherapist right to her side without deliberation.

4.2. Environmental Structures Rather Than Mental Models Inform Activity

Decision making as stated earlier, presumes that actors have a mental representation of the world which they use in deciding what to do next. This case study suggests, however, that instead of deliberating on a mental model, actors respond reactively to stimuli in the environment, including both physical and social structures. Through familiarity with the system, structures take on a meaning for action which does not have to be thought about by practised users.

In these systems physical structures such as a name label can be placed on corresponding bed slots on the board. While it is possible in theory to place two labels on the same slot, it would not really be possible to do so in an unambiguous way and see both labels. Similarly, the board is set up for 24 beds and the borders of the beds are drawn with a non-eraseable marker. These constraints make it difficult to put two patients in the same bed or put more patients in the ward than there are beds. In this way, the board mirrors the physical constraints of the ward where it is only possible in the ward to have 24 patients and one patient in each bed. These constraints are evident in the physical structure and able to be directly perceived by actors without reference to mental models.

Social structure has been defined as "a set of social units..(sharing)..certain rules and procedures in the use of resources, (and) entrusted to occupants (agents) who act on the rules and procedures" [33 p. 33]. Social structures, as evident in this system, such as writing a name label in blue, do not physically prevent an activity in the way that a physical structure such as a full bed prevents a patient being put in it. However, social structures still regulate action. If a patient label is written in blue, actors know to place it on the left of the board with the other heart patients for example. A nurse's perception of the actions that can be performed with regard to the coloured magnets and the colouring of labels are learnt through constant reinforcing of a socially determined structure which associates the magnets with particular workplace conventions. Once reinforced, the presence of such structures can be acted on routinely, without having to evaluate choices.

4.3. The Need to Take Part in "Decision Making" Is Reduced by Lightweight Systems

The system documented here is a lightweight system. Lighter weight systems suggest systems that are more agile, have low levels of documentation and contain limited formalised representation. This compares to heavy weight systems where these is complex, detailed planning and development involved, following established development methods, and data and procedures are collected and codified in a formal manner. This system is lightweight principally because it has not so much been designed, but has evolved through use by users adopting the mechanisms which make it easy to use without significant deliberation. It is able to be lightweight because the various token and artefacts used in the system are multi purpose and have flexible meanings.

The data in this system often seems to be repeated multiple times. For example to convey that a patient is a heart patient their name label can be written in red, a red heart can be drawn next to their name and the label can be placed on a particular side of the board. However, because the media can be written on, coloured and positioned in multiple ways and thus afford multiple representational possibilities, data can be repeated while keeping the system light weight and without any other artefacts or components needing to be added to the system.

The repetition of data facilitates routine and reduces the need for "decision making" because it reinforces single courses of action when the repeated data all points to the same action choice. Data in this system is repeated but can still be seen at a glance and the information conveyed multiple times without it needing to be read or processed. This duplicate information, which is reinforcing and valuable, adds no more weight to the system than if the information was, for example, written in a colour which was not informational or placed in a way where the type of patient was not easily perceivable. Thus the ability to perceive the action opportunities through the structure of the representational materials makes the redundancy possible without reducing the effectiveness of the systems in managing routine, where otherwise it would make the systems cumbersome to use.

If formalised data, which had to be read or deliberated upon, was presented multiple times, it would interfere with routine by making it difficult to determine possible action and create a need for choosing between options, or decision making. However, the structure of the representational materials in these systems (for example the way data is able to be coloured or placed) enables opportunities for action without any need for cognitive processing. Consequently, the use of the this type of representational material makes it possible to reinforce routinisation, when it might be expected that redundancy would make systems heavier weight and interfere with routinisation. Despite the same data being represented many times, the systems are not heavy weight or unwieldy. Because of the nature of these representational materials, the impact is counterintuitive: the redundant data contributes rather than detracts from the effectiveness of routinisation in these systems.

5. Conclusion

This paper concludes that the processes performed using these artifact based systems are not largely decision making at all in the sense that decision making implies deliberation and cognitive processing of information. Rather this paper claims that much of the activity involving these co-odinative mechanisms is routinised and reactive and occurs in response to stimuli in the environment or situation which are directly perceived and acted upon non-deliberatively. To call such responses "decision making" clouds our understanding of how actors use such artifact based systems and leads to flawed methodologies for their design and use.

This paper has shown how such systems use physical and social structures to constrain action choices and make it possible for action to occur through the detection of environmental structure as opposed to actors referring to mental models and "deciding", by evaluating action choices. The reliance on such structures for providing information for action allows the systems to be lightweight, which further supports routine as actors do not have to work through or evaluate large volumes of formalised representations which require reading or other forms of deliberation. Rather, actors directly perceive action opportunities in the environment and react to them. Consideration of these issues may lead to new information engineering methodologies to better deal with fluid, routinised, real-time action in collaborative systems such as the one presented in this research. This may provide opportunities for more effective computerization of such systems through the use of methodologies based on a situated approach.

References

[1]   Schmidt, K. and C. Simone, *Coordination Mechanisms: Towards a Conceptual Foundation of CSCW Systems Design.* The Journal of Collaborative Computing, 1996. **5**: p. 155-200.
[2]   Favela, J., et al., *Integrating context-aware public displays into a mobile hospital information system.* Informaiton Technology in Biomedicine, 2004. **8**(3): p. 279-286.
[3]   Bardram, J. and C. Bossen. *A web of co-ordinating artifacts:collaborative work at a hospital ward.* in *2005 International ACM SIGGROUP conference on supportign Group work.* 2005. Florida, USA: ACM.
[4]   Hopkin, D. *Automated Flight Strip Usage: Lessons From the Function of Paper Strips.* in *Proceedings on AIAA/NASA/FAA/HFS symposium on challenges in aviation human factors.* 1991.
[5]   Hughes, J., et al., *The Automation of Air Traffic Control*, in *Lancaster Sociotechnics Group.* 1988, University of Lancaster: Lancaster.
[6]   Mackay, W., *Is Paper Safer? The Role of Paper Flight Strips in Air Traffic Control.* ACM Transactions on Computer- Human Interaction, 1999. **6**(4): p. 311-340.
[7]   Mackay, W., et al. *Reinventing the Familiar: Exploring an Augmented Reality Design Space for Air Traffic Control.* In *CHI'98.* 1998. Los Angeles,CA.
[8]   Fitzgerald, G. and N. Russo, *The turnaround of the London Ambulance Service Computer-Aided Despatch System (LASCAD).* European Journal Of Information Systems, 2005. **14**: p. 244-257.
[9]   Wong, W., *The Integrated Decision Model in Emergency Dispatch Mangement and Its Implications for Design.* Australian Journal of Information Systems, 2000. **2**(7): p. 95-101.
[10] Blandford, A. and W. Wong, *Situation awareness in emergency medical dispatch.* International Journal of Human Computer Studies, 2004. **61**(4): p. 421-452.
[11] Blandford, A., et al. *Multiple Viewpoints On Computer Supported Team Work: A Case Study On Ambulance Dispatch.* In *People and Computers XVII, HCI 2002.* 2002. London: British Computer Society.
[12] Endsley, M., *Towards a Theory of Situation Awareness in Dynamic Systems.* Human Factors, 1995. **37**(1): p. 32-64.
[13] Kaempf, G., et al., *Decision Making in Complex Navel Command and Control Environemts.* Human Factors, 1996. **38**(2): p. 220-231.
[14] Wong, W. and A. Blandford. *Field Research in HCI: A Case Study.* in *CHINZ03.* 2003. Aukland: SIDCHI.
[15] McCarthy, J., et al. *Locating the Scene: The Particular and the General in Contexts for Ambulance Control.* In *Group 97.* 1999. Phoenix Arizona: ACM.
[16] Dowell, J., *Formulating the Cognitive Design Problem of Air Traffic Management.* International Journal of Human Computer Studies, 1998. **49**: p. 743-766.
[17] Poole, R., *The Urgent Need to reform the FAA's Traffic Control System.* Report of the Heritage Foundation, 2007. **Backgrounder 2007**.
[18] Wears, R., et al., *Emergency Department Status Boards: user-evolved artefacts for inter-and intragroup co-ordination.* Cognition, Technology and Work, 2006(December, 2006).
[19] Vera, A. and H. Simon, *Situated Action: Reply to Reviewers.* Cognotive Science, 1993. **17**: p. 77-86.
[20] Johnston, R., V. Waller, and S. Milton, *Situated Information Systems: supporting routine activity in systems.* Journal of Business Information Systems, 2005. **1**(1/2): p. 53-82.
[21] Edwards, W., *The Theory of Decision Making.* Psychological Bulletin, 1954. **51**(4): p. 380-416.
[22] Simon, H., *Theories in Decision Making in Economics and Behavioural Science*, in *Readings in Applied Microeconomic Theory*, R. Kuenne, Editor. 2000, Blackwell Publishing. p. 17-43.
[23] Stanovich, K. and R. West, *Individual Differences in Reasoning: Implications for the Rationlaity Debate?* Behavioural and Brain Sciences, 2000. **23**: p. 645-665.
[24] Bodker, S. and E. Christiansen. *Lost and Found in Flexibility.* In *IRIS.* 2002. Dansk.
[25] Plasters, C. and J. Seagull. *Co-ordination Challenges in Operating Room Management: An Indepth Field Study.* In *AMIA Annual Symposium.* 2003: AMIA.
[26] Cohen, T., et al., *A Cognitive Blueprint of collaboration in context: Distributed Cognition.* Artificial Intelligence in Medicine, 2006. **37**: p. 73-83.
[27] Agre, P. and I. Horswill, *Lifeworld Analysis.* Journal of Artificial Intelligence Research, 1997. **6**: p. 111-145.

[28] Schoggen, P., *Behavior Settings*. 1989: Stanford University Press.

[29] Hutchins, E., *Cognition in the Wild*. 1995, Massachusetts: MIT Press.

[30] Becker, M., *Organizational Routines: a review of the literature*. Industrial and Corporate Change, 2004. **13**(4): p. 643-677.

[31] Cohen, M.D., *Individual Learning and Organisational Routine: Emerging Connections*. Organisation Science, 1991. **2**: p. 135-139.

[32] Pentland, B.T. and H. Reuter, *Organisational Routines as Grammers of Action*. Administrative Sciences Quarterly, 1994. **39**: p. 484-510.

[33] Lim, N., *Social Capital: A Theory of Social Structure and Action*. 2001, Cambridge, Mass.: Cambridge University Press.

Collaborative Decision Making: Perspectives and Challenges
P. Zaraté et al. (Eds.)
IOS Press, 2008

Knowledge distribution in e-maintenance activities

Anne GARCIA [a,*], Daniel NOYES [a], Philippe CLERMONT [a]

[a] *Laboratoire Génie de Production – École Nationale d'Ingénieurs de Tarbes*
47, avenue d'Azereix B.P. 1629, 65016 Tarbes cedex, France

Abstract. This communication deals with the implication of the intangible resources required to maintenance operations (knowledge and skill) and, more particularly, for their localization relative to the implementation site. The performance of the maintenance function is directly indexed with the availability of knowledge-related resources which are required. We study the performance effects of the local and external (via the e-service) knowledge distribution. A formulation of the problem is elaborated to evaluate the e-maintenance impact at these situations, preceding a step of optimization. A simulation tool is suggested in order to model e-maintenance situations and to evaluate the knowledge availability required to maintenance operations. We present the principle of the simulator with the implication of one actor of maintenance and with the combined implication of two actors.

Keywords. Collaborative decision making, maintenance, ICTs (Information and Communication Technologies), performance evaluation, knowledge management.

Introduction

The Information and Communication Technologies (ICTs) involve many changes in the companies functioning. Maintenance function is also disrupted by the ICTs integration. The working methods of the maintainers evolve with the access to distributed knowledge, the intervention of remote actors (not on the action site)…

The ICTs effects on the maintainers are the improvement of his working frame by a reinforcement of the intangible resources like skill and knowledge. These resources can be distributed and accessible by the e-service, to keep only locally their "optimal" proportion. In all the cases, the availability of knowledge-related resources via ICTs tools or e-service like network, emails, videoconferences tools, groupware… will influence the collaboration forms. The ICTs induce or improve the collaborative work, even in maintenance cases.

We focus our study on the performance of the collaborative decision making in e-maintenance situations. The availability of the intangible resources will be directly linked with the performance of the decision making. The decision will be correct only if knowledge required to the definition of the problem and to the search of solutions is sufficient. We are thus interested to assess the availability of the required knowledge in a context of maintenance activities. For all that, we develop a simulation tool in order

---

* Corresponding author: Laboratoire Génie de Production – École Nationale d'Ingénieurs de Tarbes - 47, avenue d'Azereix B.P. 1629, 65016 Tarbes cedex, France. E-mail: anne.garcia@enit.fr.

to evaluate the collaborative decision and the intangible knowledge availability which are required to obtain a reliable decision.

This communication is organized in three parts.

First, we present the general working frame from the description of collaborative decision making process within the e-maintenance context. After, we propose a formulation of the knowledge distribution problem and the e-service reliability. Then, we give the general principles of the simulation tool. Finally, we present some results established.

1. Study context

1.1. Collaborative decision

The decision generally corresponds to a complex activity, made of several mechanisms, which can be carried out by one or several actors.

For Simon [1], the decision making process is organised into four stages:
— "intelligence", phase of data gathering the problem to solve and its context,
— "design", phase of development of potential solutions to answer the problem,
— "choice", phase of choice and implementation of the best solution to the problem according to the selected evaluation criteria,
— "review", phase of supervision, which takes place after the application of the decision taken.

For a collaborative decision making process, the realization by several actors of these stages involves issues and constraints which differ from a mono-actor decision.

In Figure 1 a description of the collaborative decision making process is adapted from the definition of Simon and the work of Soubie and Zaraté [2].

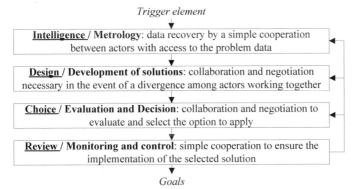

Figure 1. Collaborative decision making process adapted of Simon and Soubie

The collaboration forms among the actors involved in the collaborative decision making process differ according to the considered stage. We will detail the collaboration forms for the four stages of the collaboration decision making process.

The search for problem information (stage 1) generally implies only a simple actor's cooperation. It is most often a collect of data and information required to the problem definition.

The development, evaluation and choice of solutions (stages 2 and 3) generally imply a true collaboration (stronger than cooperation) [3]. These activities correspond to the achievement of a common objective [4] [5]. They can need negotiation methods in order to find agreements or compromise satisfying the various actors and can induce actions of joint decision [6].

The control of applied decision (stage 4) implies generally only cooperation among the actors concerned. These actors carry out their own mission without sharing the objectives of the collaborative decision.

Let us note that, in all the cases, the coordination mechanisms can be implicated [7] which aims at synchronizing the work of the various actors [8].

The actors' collaboration forms can be affected by the spatial and temporal context of realization. Four situations are possible: located or distributed asynchronous collaboration, co-localised or distributed synchronous collaboration [9] [10]. We are mainly here interested in the distributed aspect of the collaborative situations. Our study is centred on the distributed synchronous collaboration which appears most interesting to study in the e-maintenance context because of the possible advantages of interactivity and reactivity of the collaborative actions.

1.2. Collaborative decision in e-maintenance

Several situations are possible for a local operator (present near the equipment) to solve a problem via the e-service, during a maintenance operation on an equipment.

By the e-service, the operator can collect external knowledge coming from data bases, remote expert… (Figure 2a) and use external supports improving his knowledge and means of decision.

Three collaborative decision cases can be distinguished (Figure 2b):
- local decision: the operator keeps its decisional power,
- external decision: the decision is not taken by the operator but by another remote actor, distant of the action site,
- multi-actor decision: several actors (operator, maintainer, remote expert…) collaborate, sharing their skill to make a joint decision.

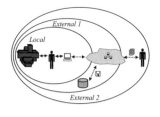

Decision type	What about the choice? Who make the decision? Actor Local ◄┄┄► Actor External	
Local	*Choice*	
External		*Choice*
Multi-actor	*Choice*	*Choice*

2a. Maintenance environment   **2b.** Detail of collaborative situations according to the decision type

Figure 2. Collaborative situations in maintenance

After this presentation of the study context and its issues about the collaborative decision making and the maintenance with remote resources, we formulate the availability of knowledge required to maintenance activities distinguishing local and remote knowledge.

2. Problem formulation

2.1. Evaluation of the collaborative decision in e-maintenance

The Figure 3 is a model of a maintenance activity. On this figure, the input / output of the maintenance activity are:
- input: request for a preventive or curative operation on equipment,
- output: result of the maintenance activity with four operation quality levels: failure, degraded, conformed or improved working.

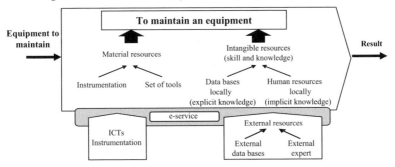

Figure 3. Modelling of a maintenance activity

The maintenance activities require material resources like tools, equipment, spare parts… and intangible resources like information, knowledge and skill.

The e-service can extend the activity field of these intangible resources [11] [12] and contribute to the management of material resources while making accessible and remote actionable [13]. Also it allows to access to the external knowledge availability (by data bases access, expert consultations) that the maintainer needs.

Lot of work deals with the availability, the allocation and the monitoring of the material resources [14] [15], so, these problems aren't considered in this work. However, we will focus on the remote intangible resources available from the e-service, on the distribution problem between local and external knowledge required to maintenance operations and on the induced performance.

We consider that the maintenance activity performance is directly indexed with the availability of the required intangible resources (knowledge and skill), which are accessible locally and/or via the e-service [16]. The knowledge distribution can evolve between two extreme cases illustrated in Figure 4: all local (physically available near the equipment) or all external (only available via e-service).

We state that the rate of knowledge distribution corresponds to "a %" of external knowledge via e-service (K_E) and therefore (1-a) % of local knowledge available (K_L).

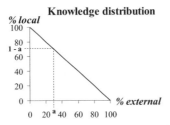

Figure 4. Problem of knowledge distribution

Maintenance activities can be classified by complexity levels. The standard AFNOR X60-000 [17] identifies five distinct levels from the simple operation by the operator to the work of rebuilding inducing a return in central repair shop.

The total knowledge K_T required for maintenance activities corresponds to the full knowledge of the five AFNOR levels of maintenance:

$$K_T = K_{1T} + K_{2T} + K_{3T} + K_{4T} + K_{5T} \quad \text{so:} \quad K_T = \sum_{i=1}^{5} K_{iT} \tag{1}$$

If we designate by "a_i" the rate of external knowledge at the level i:

$$K_{TL} = \sum_{i=1}^{5} (1 - a_i) * K_{iT} \quad \text{and} \quad K_{TE} = \sum_{i=1}^{5} a_i * K_{iT} \tag{2}$$

And the total knowledge (K_T) can be defined like:

$$K_T = \Sigma K_{TL} + \Sigma K_{TE} \tag{3}$$

2.2. Formulation of the knowledge distribution

Several factors can influence the availability of knowledge required:
- the nature and the number of actors: operator, maintainer of level 1, maintainer of level 2, expert,... as well as their location compared with the action site,
- the rate of distribution between local and external modes,
- the level of the operation complexity (according to the five AFNOR levels),
- the involvement of the actors in the maintenance operation.

The goal is to find the best balance between two extreme cases: all the local knowledge (K_{TL}) and all the external knowledge (K_{TE}), accessible by the e-service functionalities. This choice of the best knowledge distribution can be treated as an optimization problem with classical tools for linear programming. It is sufficient to express this problem in a system form composed by an objective function to optimize and constraints to respect.

The definition of duration criterion distinguishing the duration of local operations (d_L) and external operations (d_E) allows to set up the total duration of the operations (D_T) carried out with the total knowledge K_T:

$$D_T = d_L * K_{TL} + d_E * K_{TE} \tag{4}$$

A cost criterion can be related to the knowledge, in the same way as the duration. We only consider cost and duration relating to knowledge and their accessibility for the maintainer. We don't take into account all the maintenance costs. We distinguish the cost of local (c_L) and external (c_E) knowledge that enable us to determine the total cost of a maintenance department (C_T) associated with the knowledge K_T:

$$C_T = c_L * K_{TL} + c_E * K_{TE} \tag{5}$$

We can express Eqs. (4) and (5) with the five AFNOR levels:

$$D_T = \sum_{i=1}^{5} K_{iT} * \left[d_{iL} * (1 - a_i) + d_{iE} * a_i \right] \tag{6}$$

$$C_T = \sum_{i=1}^{5} K_{iT} * \left[c_{iL} * (1 - a_i) + c_{iE} * a_i \right] \tag{7}$$

with: $1 \leq i \leq 5$, according to five levels of maintenance,
  c_{iL}: cost of local available knowledge K_{iT},
  c_{iE}: cost of external available knowledge K_{iT},
  d_{iL}: time of local available knowledge K_{iT},
  d_{iE}: time of external available knowledge K_{iT},
  K_{iT}: total knowledge for the level i,
  a_i: rate of external knowledge K_{iT}.

Note. According to the studied case, the difference of cost Δc_i ($\Delta c_i = c_{iL} - c_{iE}$) between local and external cost could be positive or negative.

The typical problem consists in optimizing a functional system depending on the solution of knowledge distribution under limit conditions. Then, it is necessary to optimize some variables by acting on the rate of knowledge distribution (a_i). The constraints involved in the problem formalization can be divided into two categories:
  – general constraints,
  – specific constraints depending on the maintenance strategy chosen.
The general constraints concern the costs and the durations with a possible indicator limitation, according to the allocated budget and temporal constraints' of operations:

$$D_T \leq D_{max} \quad \text{and} \quad C_T \leq C_{max} \tag{8}$$

with: D_T et C_T defined respectively by Eqs. (6) and (7) and D_{max} and C_{max} corresponding limits.
The constraints depending on the chosen maintenance strategy will be related to the knowledge distribution between local and external modes and to the knowledge implementation. Several formulations of problem are possible and the most current are:
  – for a given knowledge, minimize the involved cost with a given duration,
  – for a given cost, maximize the knowledge available (either at the level of department or for a nominal operation).

2.3. Evolution in case of e-service fault

If we consider the evolution of the maintenance system performance, the operation quality is directly related to the e-service functionalities and can be affected by the occurrence of network problems (loss of network, accessibility). Let us designate "x" the probability of loss of the e-service functionalities. We express the effectively available knowledge (K_{eff}) by:

$$K_{eff} = K_{TL} + (1 - x) * K_{TE}$$

$$K_{eff} = (1-a)*K_T + (1-x)*a*K_T, \text{ so: } K_{eff} = K_T*(1-a*x) \tag{9}$$

After these formulations of the performance and of the knowledge distribution between local and external modes, we can tackle the development of a simulation tool with the aim to implement these formulations. This tool has to model maintenance situations, like is described in next part.

3. Definition of MKBS tool: simulator of e-maintenance situations

3.1. Objectives of the simulator

The aim of the developed tool is to propose a mean to evaluate performance of e-maintenance scenarios. This tool is used to model and assess these scenarios and thus establishes an adjustable knowledge distribution. Even if the use of dedicated tools for simulation can be considered, we chose to develop a specific simulator offering better flexibility.

With MKBS tool (Maintenance Knowledge-Based Simulation), we can describe and simulate several maintenance situations by allowing various settings (detailed further). It was programmed into C++ language.

The simulator working is started by an operation occurrence on equipment (preventive or corrective maintenance). The realization of this operation requires the implication of resources, in particular, maintenance actors and knowledge use:
– implicit knowledge (held by actors) or explicit knowledge (formalized),
– knowledge of variable complexity, depending on the maintenance level,
– local knowledge near the equipment (local mode) or remotely (external mode).

The simulation tool makes us possible to configure and evaluate the knowledge distribution between local and external modes. The knowledge implication to solve a maintenance operation is the result of interactions and exchanges between maintenance actors. So, we find collaboration situations presented in paragraph 1.2, with the elements described in Figure 2.

We explained the simulation principles in two stages:
– the implication of the single operator (describing the basic working),
– the combined implication of the single operator and an expert.

3.2. Single operator

This first analysis level is described in Figure 5.

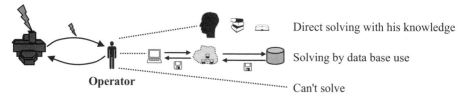

Figure 5. Failure processing by a single operator

When the failure occurs, if the operator is available, three scenarios are possible:

- (A) the operator has the required knowledge and can directly solve the failure: he has the skill or the good information is in the operating handbook,
- (B) the operator does not have all the required knowledge but he can recover it by data bases consultation available via e-service tools,
- (C) the operator may not have the knowledge required and can't solve the failure.

In this situation involving a single operator, the distribution between local and external modes is quite simple: the direct solving (A) corresponds to the local mode and the processing with the data base (B) is the external mode. The algorithm representing this first principle is presented in Figure 6.

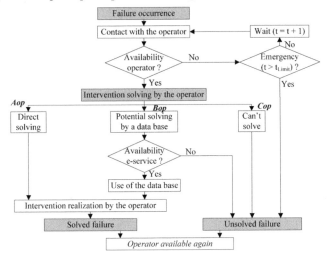

Figure 6. Algorithm of the failure processing by the single operator

3.3. Operator and expert

After describing the elementary mechanisms of the simulator, we present the second stage with two maintenance actors: the operator and the expert.

3.3.1. Principle

The second stage is the continuation of the first just described; when the operator can not solve the failure (case C), he calls an expert to help him. The expert has a higher level of knowledge and can help the operator to solve the failure. The processing by the expert is the same mechanism as the operator's processing.

The algorithm describing this functioning is exposed on Figure 7 and includes:

- the call of an expert if the operator cannot solve the failure or if he is not available for this urgent operation[*],
- a degraded mode of processing if there is e-service failure,
- the operator's work with the expert,
- the expert situation: local (after his coming to the equipment) or external (communicating with the e-service).

---

[*] This "urgent" nature was modelled to correspond to a realistic maintenance situation where the unavailability of the operator leads to expert's request.

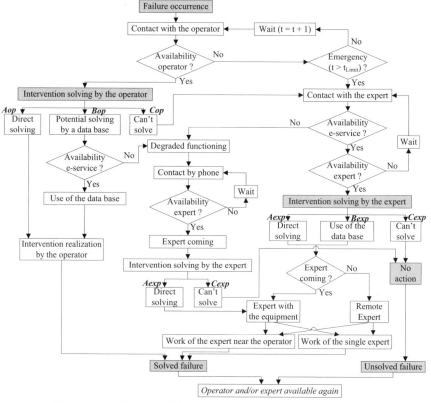

Figure 7. Algorithm of the failure processing by the operator helped by the expert

This algorithm allows a precise setting of the described situations. To analyse the knowledge distribution between local and external modes, we have chosen:

- only one test of the e-service functioning, during all the solving operations,
- the mono-operation processing (no parallel solving of several failures).

3.3.2. Validation tests and simulation results

Before tackle the simulator results, the simulator validity was checked by a convergence study of results. We have led several simulation sets, with the same parameters, in different situations. We have evaluated the rate of e-service use for each operation simulated. Then, we have determined the maximum difference between the results of the different sets. For example, we have get a variation of 1.4 % in nominal value of the rate of e-service use (with a 50/50 knowledge distribution: 50% local and 50% external, for a total e-service functioning), with 10,000 operations simulated. This variation is fairly low. The indicator has enabled to scale the number of operations to simulate.

The simulator programming allows the extraction of some synthetic results about maintenance scenarios. This evaluation results are: number of treated operations, durations and average cost of operations. The characterization of the average operation requires several simulations to test the various scenarios discussed in part 3.2 and 3.3.1 We also simulated various knowledge distributions between local and external modes, with various rates of e-service failure (x) leading to the results of the Figure 8.

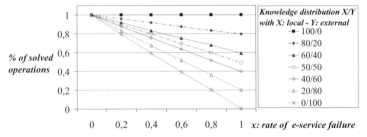

Figure 8. Operations solving evolution, depending on the rate of e-service failure

Among the curves of the Figure 8, the situation with x=1 (total e-service failure) corresponds to a local processing where the external knowledge is not available. This explained the decrease observed in all the curves excepted in the 100/0 (corresponding to the cases in local mode). For example, with 60/40 distribution of knowledge and for x=1, only 60 % of operations are solved.

This result allows to globally size the knowledge repartition in a maintenance department. In order to guarantee a fixed repair rate, for a rate x given, we can determine the global knowledge repartition between local and external modes. For example, to guarantee 80 % of processed operations and with a rate of e-service failure about 40 %, we can externalize about 50% of knowledge, but no more. Beyond, we can't guarantee the 80 % of operation solved.

The distribution of several processing situations can also be deduced from simulations. We made a state of these situations in the case of a 20/80 knowledge distribution which is presented in Figure 9. We chose a distribution with a large external knowledge to highlight the gaps between the different scenarios.

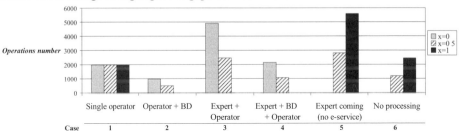

Figure 9. Histogram of various cases, depending on the rate of e-service failure, for a 20/80 distribution

This histogram summarizes the various processing options, with / without e-service, for an operation requiring / not requiring the expert knowledge, with / without an operator. The "single operator" (case 1) represents the local processing. The cases 2, 3 et 4 represent the use of external knowledge. The cases 3 and 4 correspond to a remote work between the local operator and the remote expert. The "expert coming" is a degraded scenario because of the e-service failure. As we can see, an important external contribution of knowledge (80%) induced a processing highly dependent on the failure rate of the e-service (x).

In the collaboration field, we find again the three typical situations (paragraph 1.2):
 − local decision: operator or expert collaborating with a data base (cases 2 and 5),
 − external decision: the operator can't solved and ask the expert's help (3 and 4),
 − multi-actor decision: local operator and remote expert working together (3 and 4).

We have studied the setting duration according to three different strategies:
- D1: shorter durations locally: shorter solving duration for the single operator than via the e-service,
- D2: same durations whatever the knowledge location: same solving duration for all the cases, with or without e-service,
- D3: shorter durations in external mode: shorter solving duration with data base or remote expert than with single operator.

For the first strategy (D1), the Table 1 presents durations and costs for various cases with operator and expert. The "Single Operator" case is the reference for duration and cost. The "Expert + Operator" case represents a same duration (ratio 1) and a cost increased by 3 (the hourly cost of the expert is twice as big as the operator cost). We evaluated these values from the analysis of real cases.

Table 1. Duration and cost settings for various cases with operator and expert

Processing \ Case	Single Operator	Operator + BD	Expert + Operator	Expert + BD + Operator	Expert coming (no e-service)
Relative duration	1	2	1	2	4
Relative cost	1	1.1	3	3.3	4

With this cost and duration setting, we studied the evolution of the average cost of an operation, depending on the rate of e-service failure and for various configurations of knowledge distribution (Figure 10).

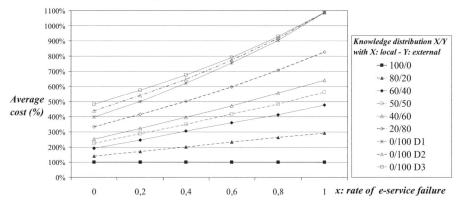

Figure 10. Average cost evolution of an operation, based on the reference of the single operator case

The evolution of the average cost of operation depends on the reference cost of a basic processing realized with only local knowledge (reference cost). The costs setting done shows a higher cost in external solving. Similarly, an increase in the rate of e-service failure means an increase in the operation cost.

We have focused on the 0/100 knowledge distribution (all external knowledge) applying the three duration strategies (D1, D2 & D3). For these three curves, we can see that the locally mode has a lower cost than the same durations, even, the same duration has a lower cost than the external mode.

It is also important to observe that the operation cost almost reaches ten times as the only local processing.

Conclusion

In this communication, we present a study of the knowledge distribution problem between local and external modes that is a key element to define the best maintenance organisation. We established a formulation of this problem with adaptable settings of the main factors influencing the knowledge distribution and the quality and performance of maintenance operations. With this theoretical formulation, we set up a maintenance simulator tool, the MKBS (Maintenance Knowledge-Based Simulation). The first results given by the simulator made it possible to validate this formulation. Then, it enabled to evaluate the performance (cost and duration) of various knowledge distribution strategies for a mono-operation solving and a reliability rate of e-service.

The main perspective of our works is to extend the representativeness of the simulated models, in order to identify the best knowledge distribution for a reparation rate given, with two actions.
Firstly, we want to make other simulations while considering more complex maintenance scenarios with parallel solving of several failures. So, we will have to integrate new constraints like the availability control or the definition of assignment strategies. Then, we will improve the knowledge evaluation in order to quantify and characterize the explicit and implicit knowledge required in maintenance activities.

References

[1] H. A. Simon, *The new science of management decision*, Prentice-Hall, New Jersey, 1977.
[2] J.-L. Soubie, P. Zaraté, Distributed Decision Making: A Proposal of Support Through Cooperative Systems, *Group Decision and Negotiation* **14** (2005), 147–158.
[3] P. H. Lubich, *Towards a CSCW framework for scientific cooperation in Europe*, Springer Verlag, 1995.
[4] S. George, Apprentissage collectif à distance. SPLACH : un environnement informatique support d'une pédagogie de projet, Thèse de doctorat, Université du Maine, France, 2001.
[5] P. Girard, V. Robin, Analysis of collaboration for project design management, *Computers in Industry* **57** (2006), 817–826.
[6] S. Sankaran, T. Bui, An organizational model for transitional negotiations: concepts, design and applications, *Group Decision and Negotiation* **17** (2008), 157–173.
[7] J.-P. Neuville, La tentation opportuniste : figures et dynamique de la coopération interindividuelle dans le partenariat industriel, *Revue Française de Sociologie* **39** (1998), 71–103.
[8] X. Li, Q. Wang, Coordination mechanisms of supply chain systems, *European Journal of Operational Research* **179** (2007), 1–16.
[9] T. Rodden, A Survey of CSCW Systems, *Interacting with Computers* **3** (1991), 319–353.
[10] P. Renevier, Systèmes Mixtes Collaboratifs sur Supports Mobiles : Conception et Réalisation, Thèse de doctorat, Université Joseph-Fourier - Grenoble I, 2004.
[11] S. A. Carlsson, Enhancing Knowledge Acquisition through the use of ICT, *IFIP TC8/WG8.3 International Conference on Decision Support in an Uncertain and Complex World*, 2004.
[12] H. Kaffel, S. D'Amours, D. Ait-Kadi, Les critères techniques pour le choix des acteurs dans un système de maintenance distribuée, *Colloque international francophone PENTOM'03*, France, 2003.
[13] H. Fiori de Castro, K. Lucchesi Cavalca, Maintenance resources optimisation applied to a manufacturing system, *Reliability Engineering and System Safety* **91** (2006), 413–420.
[14] E. K. Bish, K. Y. Lin, S.-J. Hong, Production, Manufacturing and Logistics: Allocation of flexible and indivisible resources with decision postponement and demand learning, *European Journal of Operational Research* **187** (2008), 429–441.
[15] C. Elegbede, K. Adjallah, Availability allocation to repairable systems with genetic algorithms: a multi-objective formulation, *Reliability Engineering and System Safety* **82** (2003), 319–330.
[16] D. Noyes, A. Garcia, P. Clermont, Influence des ressources immatérielles liées à la e-maintenance dans l'allocation de maintenabilité, *Colloque international francophone PENTOM'07*, Belgique, 2007.
[17] Norme AFNOR X 60-000, *Maintenance industrielle – Fonction maintenance*, Ed. AFNOR, 2002.

Collaborative Decision Making: Perspectives and Challenges
P. Zaraté et al. (Eds.)
IOS Press, 2008

Analysis and Intuition in Strategic Decision Making:
The Case of California

Zita ZOLTAY PAPRIKA[a]

[a]*Corvinus University of Budapest, Hungary*

Abstract. This paper reports the results of a study that attempts to assess the effects of decision making circumstances focusing mainly on the approaches applied and the managerial skills and capabilities the decision makers built on during concrete strategic decision making procedures. The study was conducted in California between September 2005 and June 2006 and it was sponsored by a Fulbright Research Scholarship Grant. The continuation of the research is sponsored by the OTKA 68799 Research Grant.

Keywords. strategic decision making, rationality, intuition

Introduction

Many management scholars believe that the *process* used to make strategic decisions affects the quality of those decisions. However several authors have observed not enough research on the strategic decision making process. Empirical tests of factors that have been hypothesized to affect the way strategic decisions are made notably are absent. [1]

Strategic decisions are those that affect the direction of the firm. These major decisions concern areas such as new products and markets, product or service development, acquisitions and mergers, subsidiaries and affiliates, joint ventures, strategic alliances, finding a site for a new investment, reorganisation, and other important matters. Strategic decision making is usually conducted by the firm's top management, led by the CEO or President of the company. That is why in this research twenty top level managers were targeted: twelve were CEOs, Presidents, Vice Presidents or Chief Financial Officers (I will call them Executives), while eight were founders and majority owners of their own enterprises (they will be called Entrepreneurs). Sixteen respondents were male, four were female. The average respondent has been working for 28.7 years in general, for 13.8 years for the actual company and for 8.4 years in the current position. 60 percent of the respondents have a graduate business degree, 60 % have an undergraduate degree, seven of them have an MBA or a PhD and two out of these seven have both an MBA and a PhD. One respondent was working on his PhD.

The interviews took two and a half hours on the average, varying from two hours up to five hours. During the interviews a preliminary structured list of questions was followed. With each respondent I investigated the circumstances of four different strategic decision cases from their practice. They could choose the cases on their own. Using this technique a database of 80 strategic decisions could be built up.

1. Background

Kathleen M. Eisenhardt, professor of strategy and organization at Stanford University found that top managers at more effective firms were able to make quick and high quality decisions that were highly supported throughout the firm. Her studies identified four areas in which effective decision makers outperformed counterparts at less effective firms [2]:

1. building collective *intuition*
2. stimulating conflict
3. maintaining a pace or schedule for decision making
4. defusing political behaviour.

In my research I focused on the role of *intuition* in strategic decision making. As Ashley F. Fields stated intuition is one of the more mysterious concepts associated with the study of human capital [3]. Classical theoreticians, from Carl Jung [4] through Chester Barnard [5] and Abraham Maslow [6] have commented on the existence and value of intuition in organisational settings. Carl Jung said: "intuition does not denote something contrary to reason, but something outside of the province of reason." It is real and it is not in our heads and our head can not control it. Harold Leavitt [7] viewed intuition as a valuable weapon to be used against the heavily analytical practices, which gave rise to his derisive term "analysis paralysis". Fascination with the subject of intuition remains alive and well in recent years too.

Intuition is usually defined as knowing or sensing something without the use of rational processes. Alternatively, it has been described as a perception of reality not known to consciousness, in which the intuition knows, but does not know *how* it knows. Westcott redefined intuition as a rational process, stating that it is a process in which an individual reaches a conclusion on the basis of less explicit information than is ordinarily required to reach that decision [8]. Weston Agor argued that intuition is a built-in capacity that some of us have and some do not [9]. In my research I basically relied on the definition given by Martha Sinclair and Neal Ashkanasy. According to these authors intuition is a non-sequential information processing mode, which comprises both cognitive and affective elements and results in direct knowing without any use of conscious reasoning [10]. Practically it is an unconscious process of making decisions on the basis of experience and accumulated judgment.

Isenberg, who studied managers in Fortune 500 firms, found that they combine both rational and intuitive methods in decision making [11]. Parikh studied more than 1300 managers and found that intuition is cross-national [12]. Catford's study of 57 business professionals demonstrated that intuition was used commonly as a business tool [13]. These and many other researchers have demonstrated that intuition is used regularly in the conduct of business [3].

Interestingly more than half of today's intuition books are authored by females. Psychologists debate whether the intuition gap is truly intrinsic to gender. Whatever the reason, Western tradition has historically viewed rational thinking as masculine and intuition as feminine. Women's way of thinking gives greater latitude to subjective knowledge. Some personality tests show that nearly six in ten men score as "thinkers" (claiming to make decisions objectively, using logic) while three in four women score as "feelers" (claiming to make decisions subjectively, based on what they feel right) [14].

In recent years instinct appears ascendant. Decision makers have good reasons to prefer instinct. In a study executives said they use their intuition as much as their analytical skills, but credited 80% of their success to instinct [15]. Henry Mintzberg explains that strategic thinking calls for creativity and synthesis and this is better served by intuition than to analysis [16]. Buchanan and O'Connell cited some famous statements related to intuition [15]:

> "Pragmatists act on evidence, Heroes act on guts."
> "Intuition is one of the X-factors separating the men from the boys."

One feature common to all the authors cited above is an inability to articulate a coherent, consistent, and verifiable theory of what underlines the intuitive phenomenon. These researchers unanimously declare that "something" really exists, but they can not agree on just "what" exists or "why" it works as it does [3]. Recent advances in cognitive science and artificial intelligence suggest that there is nothing mystical or magical about intuitive processes and that they are not paranormal or irrational. Rather, intuitive processes evolve from long experience and learning and consist of the mass of facts, patterns, concepts, abstractions, and generally what we call formal knowledge or beliefs, which are impressed in our minds [11], [17] . Intuition is not the opposite of rationality, nor is it a random process of guessing, as we very often think. It is a sophisticated form of reasoning based on chunking that an expert hones over years of job specific experience. Consequently intuition does not come easily, it requires years of experience in problem solving and is founded upon a solid and complete grasp of the details of the business. However, in some cases it compresses experience and learning into seconds – as it was shown in some cases during my interviews.

2. Rational/Intuitive Orientation

The lack of field studies in strategic decision making processes called for a research study to examine concrete real life cases and to analyse:
1. How top level managers really make strategic decisions,
2. How Entrepreneurs and Executives differ, if at all, in their approach to strategic decision making processes when they combine rational thinking with their intuition,
3. Similarities and differences, if any, in management skills between Entrepreneurs and Executives.

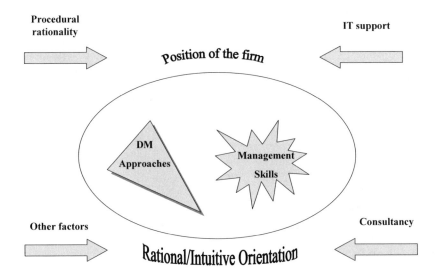

Figure 1. The logic of the research model

Rational/Intuitive Orientation is a concept which has yet to make a significant impact on mainstream decision making research. Consequently, no well-established indicators of Rational/Intuitive Orientation exist. Based on understanding the concept, however two optional indicators (decision making approaches and management skills) were identified in this study.

In the literature of decision theory, several models of organisational decision making can be found. These differ from each other in the sense that they use other prerequisites of decision makers and also refer to the organisational connections of decision makers. On the basis of the above dimensions two different models and decision making mechanisms were identified (analytical and intuitive). Eleven management skills were investigated and rated as to whether they support analytical or intuitive thinking. In this chapter we will focus on the core of the above mentioned research model namely on Rational/Intuitive Orientation.

The main hypotheses of the research can be summarized as follows:

H1: Intuition plays a key role in strategic decision making since strategic problems are ill-structured and hence can not be programmed. Decision makers at the top level combine analytical and intuitive approaches, but more heavily rely on their intuition.

H2: Intuitive decision making is more favoured by independent decision makers (Entrepreneurs) who have extended control over their firms and are more often in the final decision maker's position. When they put the dot on the "i" they are almost always intuitive.

H3: The level of management skills is high. The creative/intuitive skills are even more developed in the sample.

Herbert Simon was the first to distinguish between the two extreme types of decisions. He called recurring, routine-like or ready-made ones *programmed decisions*, while those being unique and unstructured with long-term impacts were called *non-programmed decisions* [18]. Programmed and non-programmed decisions naturally set the two extreme poles of one continuum and the appearance of interim cases is much more probable. In the course of company operations it happens very rarely that a decision situation clearly corresponds to the terminology of the programmed or non-programmed decisions. On the other hand, most managers develop some kind of practice for the handling of non-programmed decision situations that can be successfully applied, if a ready-made solution can be fitted to an actual situation. Certain non-programmed decisions may become programmed in the course of time in a company's practice.

A central part of this survey consisted of the examination of 20 plus 60 real strategic decisions. At the beginning of the interview every respondent could mention a "big case" which was mainly non-programmed. When I asked the respondents to quote three more decision cases, they mainly mentioned *semi-programmed* problems which could be positioned somewhere between the programmed and non-programmed extremes. These cases were not as "big" as the previous 20 decision situations, but they still had long term consequences and strategic importance. Practically each participant could mention four cases, one "big case" and three semi-structured cases. This is how the database of the survey was built up based on the cases of the twenty contributors.

In the interest of comparability, the semi-structured decision cases were classified into categories that are borrowed from the *„Bradford Studies"* [19]. According to this, I distinguished

- investment

- reorganization

- acquisition

- fund-raising

- marketing

- service or product development

- production

- finding a site for investment

- human resource management

- quality management

- other decisions.

Service or product development (10), investment (9), reorganization (9), marketing (8), finding a site for investment (7) decisions were the most frequently mentioned cases. But I also found at least a single case for each other category.

The respondents mixed the analytical and intuitive problem solving approaches when they made these decisions. As they argued they found it very difficult to use only the rational approach for these semi-programmed decisions, therefore intuitive decision making was very often valuable and also applied. But it was also typical that decision makers made their decisions and later developed rational sounding reasons for the decision after the fact. It seemed that for some reasons they like to be seen rational. However, some of them were very proud of relying on their instinct in solving particular cases. Demonstrating the concept of bounded rationality the respondents recognized that at least in part their decisions were based on intuition, gut feeling, "seat of the pants". This was most typical in marketing cases, where they needed more experience and judgment than sequential logic or explicit reasons to make those decisions. As they explained it, they made these decisions based upon what they believed to be right, rather than upon what they could document with hard data. But in the other categories, especially in cases of service or product development, investment, acquisition and finding a site decisions they did not find it appropriate to apply this kind of logic.

When the respondents were given an extra opportunity to rethink their earlier answers concerning the analytical and intuitive approaches in their cases, they changed their mind only slightly. If they could repeat the same decisions, which will of course never happen, they would rely more on analysis in marketing decisions too, but in service product development cases interestingly would give more room for intuition.

Clearly, there were major perceived differences between Entrepreneurs' and Executives' answers in term of how their decisions were made. One of the main differences is that Executives tend to exhibit more characteristics of analytical decision making than Entrepreneurs do. Executives more heavily rely on the analytical approach. However, it is interesting to note that Entrepreneurs are more careful in cases of investment decisions, where they insist on preliminary analytical investigation. A logical explanation could be that they risk their own money when investing and are therefore more careful about it.

3. Management skills

The quality of the decision making activity and the company's success is considerably influenced by the fact of who makes the decisions, what skills and capabilities they have, what their managerial style is, and also what techniques and methods they use in the course of decision making. Consequently, it is not only the applied decision making approach and the managerial style that leave their mark on decision making, but it is equally important, what level of professional abilities, education and experience the managers have.

What characteristics or individual skills must a management have to be successful? The survey embraced the general abilities of management. What is more, in the in-depth interviews I encouraged respondents to make some self-evaluations. I asked them to define their strengths and weaknesses according to the investigated characteristics and skills by evaluating themselves on a five point Likert scale. However, the first task was to rank the skills according to their importance. Considering the opinions of all respondents (N=20), the "image of the ideal manager" fulfilling all expectations of management was appeared as shown in decreasing order:
1. excellent communication skills
2. sense for business
3. problem solving skills
4. practice minded behaviour

5. ability to represent ideas
6. risk taking nature
7. expertise
8. organising skills
9. executive skills
10. analytical skills
11. use of PC and computers

Some interesting features are revealed from this ranking. Naturally, the top and the bottom of the list are worth attention, since the skills there outline a manager-image frequently mentioned during the interviews. The major task of a manager is to communicate inside and outside of the company (as they stated they do most of the marketing) while the use of computers at top level is not a must since they can get all necessary IT support whenever they need. The other skills could be divided into two subgroups in the order. As one of the respondents stated those skills are more important - and happen to be in the upper part of the list - which you can not buy, and those which are available through different channels i.e. consultancy like organising skills, analytical skills or IT knowledge are in the second half of the list.

If we compare these results to the actual self-assessments we can see an interesting evidence of cognitive dissonance. The respondents ranked less important their weaknesses and more important their strengths. They were far beyond the average performers (if we define this category on a five point scale with the middle position indicated by 3) on all criteria except one, the use of computers, but as we saw earlier they did not feel that fact as a disadvantage. They are very good communicators which I can confirm based on my personal experiences. They quite heavily rely on their accumulated knowledge and experiences and expertise and equipped with the necessary problem solving skills. They named as a real strength their sense for business. We can not forget that two-fifth of them are founder and majority owner of his or her enterprise in the sample. Two of them started a totally new business when recognized a new business opportunity. They left behind their emerging and safe career and chose an unknown challenging new field. Both of them are very successful in their new businesses.

We know that some skills and capabilities support more the intuitive way of problem solving than the others. My research method also involved interviewing a dozen university professors in an effort to link the management skills involved in this research with the analytical or intuitive way of problem solving. A quick survey was designed and the professors were asked to evaluate the above mentioned skills by indicating whether these skills supported analytical or intuitive thinking strongly. They could mark only one answer for each skill. All of the respondents had strong management background since they were teaching either in the field of Organizational Behavior or Decision Sciences.

The skills were split into two groups depending on their role supporting intuitive or analytical problem solving. According to the opinion of the university professors with a management background, intuitive thinking and problem solving are best supported by the following skills: willingness to take risks, sense for business, ability to represent ideas, practice minded behaviour and excellent communication skills. On the other hand different skills take precedence when problems require analytical solutions. The skills that most support this approach were determined to be: analytical skills, computer skills, organising skills, professional expertise and problem solving skills. Not surprisingly executive skills are somewhere between these two groups of skills since effective leadership requires a combination of analytical and intuitive approaches.

Subsequently I revised this distinction at two points. Most of the authors [10], [20], [21] agree, that intuition is nothing else than experience put into practice. This demystified definition of intuition shows how one can become expert in one's profession through one's cumulative experience or knowledge. Klein argues that intuition is a developed sense helping to put experience into recognizable patterns for future use (Klein, 2004). As it is well-known good communication skills often go with good analytical skills, since both are the functions of the left hemisphere [22].

Putting this split into practice the chart of the managers shows a rather balanced picture of their analytical and intuitive skills. *Problem solving skills* lead the rank of the analytical skills while *business sense* is the most important strength among the intuitive skills. Among the 80 analyzed decision cases I found much that confirms the importance of the business sense as the path towards the success. The weaknesses are compensated by the high level of strengths. Lack of the *computer knowledge* or *organising skills* do not seem to be a big problem because top level managers can easily find someone to do these jobs.

The largest gap could be recognized in case of the ability to represent ideas. Entrepreneurs do not have to "sell" their decisions, because they are typically the final decision makers, consequently for them this skill is not a must. Their priorities are instead: risk taking nature, problem solving skills, sense for business and communication skills. Executives consider the ability to represent ideas far more important than the Entrepreneurs. Analytical and organizing skills are ranked a little bit higher by them too.

Differences between groups that exceed 10 percent are considered to be very significant in survey research. There were relatively large differences in this research between the two responding groups according to the capabilities and skills based on their self assessments (Figure 2). Entrepreneurs have better business sense and they are ready to take far more risks. They evaluated their problem solving skills slightly higher than the Executives. Executives' strengths are in ability to represent ideas, analytical skills and executive skills. The more balanced picture emerged when we compare practice minded behavior, communication skills and expertise.

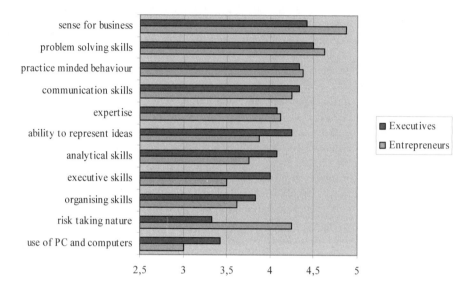

Figure 2. Differences in management skills of Executives and Entrepreneurs

4. Future Trends

When analyzing these findings it must be remembered that these results were based on self-assessments. Rarely are self assessments and independent (objective) assessments congruent. However, we do not have any techniques to measure the level of the different management skills and capabilities or decision making approaches objectively yet. Even though we feel that it might be a lack of agreement between the self assessments and an imaginative objective assessment of these parameters. We call this gap "the coefficient of self delusion". This coefficient can be positive (when the objective rating is higher than the self assessment) or it can be negative (when the objective ratings are lower than the self assessments). The positive coefficient of self delusion occurs with people who either are genuinely humble or may be trying to avoid over-inflating their self-ratings for a variety of reasons e.g. because of their cultural background. The negative coefficient of self delusion usually occurs with people who are not conscious of the impact of their behaviors on others or they have an inflated sense of self. In either case, it is important to investigate why the assessment gap exists and reflect upon ways that it can be narrowed, perhaps even closed, which is a big research challenge.

There is a big debate at the present time whether the analytical or the intuitive way of thinking is more powerful in the business arena. Thomas Davenport argued that some companies have built their very businesses on their ability to collect, analyze and act on data. Every company can learn from what these firms do. [23]. The popular "head versus formula" controversy that is based mostly on laboratory studies in the past, established the superiority of the rational-analytical approach over the soft judgmental or intuitive approach. The extension of this approach to strategic decision making is problematic, however. This is because strategic decisions are characterized by incomplete knowledge. Consequently, it may be impossible to identify quantitative equations among variables and find numeric values for parameters and initial states. That is why people still use their heads instead of formulas in strategic cases [24]. As a conclusion of the very intensive debate by now there is an agreement that intuition is not an irrational process. It is based on a deep understanding of the situation. It is a complex phenomenon that draws from the store of knowledge in our subconscious and is rooted in past experience. It is quick, but not necessarily biased as presumed in previous research on rational decision making [24].

5. Conclusion

In everyday language we tend to use the word "intuitive" with some connotation of "irrational". This is probably due to Bergson [25] who attached great importance to intuition but interpreted it as a mystic force which by definition could not be subject of rational means of inquiry [26]. However, almost a hundred years of research in various fields of science now leads to a reversal of this interpretation. In the management literature of our days we can read that intuition is not arbitrary or irrational because it is based on years of practice and hands on experience. Managers started to accept that new interpretation and they believe that their intuition is part of their business knowledge. Decision support systems might help to strengthen this perception by providing user-friendly tools to obtain and sort the necessary knowledge for successful decisions. It will probably take time until this view is widely recognized.

There was an other interesting finding when I compared the decision making practice of the Executives and the Entrepreneurs. Both groups relied quite heavily on the analysis in the preparation phase of the decision making process, which gave big room for decision support applications. However, Executives were ready to follow the decision support systems' recommendations in the moment of choce while Entrepreneurs preferred to follow their intuition. As a conclusion we can state that Entrepreneurs' support must focus mainly on the preparation phase of decisions and should let them to decide.

This study showed that Executives in a corporate setting tend to view decision making differently than Entrepreneurs. Since they are typically given a fixed amount of budgeted resources to work with, they tend to define a problem in terms of *what can be done* with the resources in hand. Entrepreneurs, on the other hand, will likely pose the problem in terms of an *objective*. "This is what I want to get done", they usually state and then start to worry about finding the resources to accomplish that objective. As a result entrepreneurial decision makers feel less constrained by the lack of resources. They are famous for making "seat-of-the-pants" decisions, which means they make quick decisions based on a good feeling or intuition. This kind of challenge required different skills from the Entrepreneurs than from the Executives.

There was an other interesting finding when I compared the decision making practice of the Executives and the Entrepreneurs. Both groups relied quite heavily on the analysis in the preparation phase of the decision making process, which gave big room for decision support applications. However, Executives were ready to follow the decision support systems' recommendations in the moment of choce while Entrepreneurs preferred to follow their intuition. As a conclusion we can state that Entrepreneurs' support must focus mainly on the preparation phase of decisions and should let them to decide.

References

[1]   Frederickson, J. W., Effects of decision motive and organizational performance level on strategic decision processes. *Academy of Management Journal*, Vol. 28. No. 4., (1985), 821-843.
[2]   Eisenhardt, K. M., Strategy as Strategic Decision making. *Sloan Management Review*, (1998), Spring 65.
[3]   Fields, A. F., Intuition engineering. Organizational Engineering Institute, (2000)
[4]   Jung, C. G, Modern man in search of a soul. New York: Harcourt Brace, (1934)

[5]   Barnard, C., Functions of the executive. Cambridge: Harvard University Press, (1938)

[6]   Maslow, A., Motivation and Personality. New York, Harper & Row, (1954)

[7]   Leavitt, H. J., Beyond the analytic manager. Part II California Management Review, 17 (4) (1975). p. 11-21.

[8]   Westcott, M., Toward a contemporary psychology of intuition. A historical and empirical inquiry. New York: Holt Rinehart & Winston, Inc., (1968)

[9]   Agor, W., The measurement, use, and development of intellectual capital to increase public sector productivity. Public Personnel Management, Summer (1997), 175-186.

[10]   Sinclair, M., & Ashkanasy, N. M., Intuition. *Management Learning*, Vol. 36.No. 3, (2005), 353-370.

[11]   Isenberg, D., How senior managers think. Harvard Business Review, (1984), November-December, 81-90.

[12]   Parikh, J., Intuition: the new frontier of management. Blackwell Business, Oxford, UK, (1994)

[13]   Catford, L. Creative problem solving in business, Doctoral dissertation, Stanford University. UMI Dissertation Services, (1987)

[14]   Meyers, D. G., The powers & perils of intuition. *Psychology Today*, (2002), November-December

[15]   Buchanan, L., & O'Connell, A., A Brief History of Decision making. Harvard Business Review, January (2006), p. 32-42.

[16]   Mintzberg, H., & Westley, F., Decision Making: It's Not What You Think. MIT Sloan Management Review, Vol. 42, No. 3, (2001), 89-93

[17]   Simon, H. A., Making management decisions: The role of intuition and emotion. Academy of Management EXECUTIVE, February, (1987), 57-64.

[18]   Simon, H. A., Korlátozott racionalitás. Válogatott tanulmányok. KJK Budapest, (1982)

[19]   Hickson, D., & Butler, R., & Cray, D., & Mallory, G., & Wilson, D., Top Decisions: Strategic Decision Making in Organizations. Basil Blackwell, (1986)

[20]   Csikszentmihalyi, M., Creativity. Flow and the Psychology of Discovery and Invention. Harper Collins Publishers, (1996)

[21]   Klein, G., The Power of Intuition. How to Use Your Gut Feelings to Make Better Decisions at Work. Random House, (2004)

[22]   Browning, G., Emergenetics: Tap into the New Science of Success. Harper Collins, (2005)

[23]   Davenport, T. H., Competing on analytics. *Harvard Business Review*, January, (2006), 99-107.

[24]   Khatri, N., & Alvin, H. N., The role of intuition in strategic decision making, Human Relations, Volume 53. 57-86, The Travistock Institute, SAGE Publications, (2000)

[25]   Bergson, H., Introduction to Methaphysics. English Translation, New York, (1911)

[26]   Wierzbicki, A.J. On the Role of Intuition in Decision Making and Some Ways of Multicriteria Aid of Intuition. Journal of Multi-Criteria Decision Analysis, Vol. 6, (1997), 65-76

Collaborative Decision Making Applications

Collaborative Decision Making: Perspectives and Challenges
P. Zaraté et al. (Eds.)
IOS Press, 2008

Decision Support for Mainport Strategic Planning

Roland A.A. WIJNEN[a1], Roy T.H. CHIN[a], Warren E. WALKER[a], and
Jan H. KWAKKEL[a]

[a]*Faculty of Technology, Policy and Management, Delft University
of Technology, the Netherlands.*

Abstract. A mainport is a large transport hub (airport or seaport) with multi-modal
connections. Mainport strategic planning develops long-term plans for matching
capacity and demand while staying within environmental constraints and achieving
financial success. Mainport planning is difficult, since it involves many
stakeholders, multiple (often conflicting) criteria, uncertainty about the future, and
many potential strategic plans. Many mainport strategic plans have resulted in
costly failures, due in part to the processes and tools the planners use. They often
consider only a single forecast for the future, consider few alternative strategies,
and exclude stakeholders, resulting in plans that quickly become obsolete and may
be opposed by stakeholders. Avoiding such failures requires an integrated
approach to decision support that enables *collaboration* among stakeholders. Such
an approach requires an effective way to deal with many inputs and outputs
enabling the extraction of relevant information for decisionmaking and its
presentation in transparent and understandable ways. We propose a Decision
Support System (DSS) that provides a way for decisionmakers and stakeholders to
quickly and easily generate alternative strategic plans and evaluate them with
respect to a large number of outcomes of interest for a wide range of plausible
scenarios. This paper describes an architecture for such a DSS.

Keywords: mainport planning, multi-actor systems, DSS, software architecture,
uncertainty

1. Introduction

A mainport is a major seaport or airport with multi-modal connections that serves as a
gateway to the hinterland. The term mainport has its origins in the Netherlands and
reveals the focus of the Dutch government on transport and infrastructure as an
important economic driver [1]. Due to this focus, rapid growth of Dutch ports,
particularly Amsterdam Airport Schiphol and the seaports of Amsterdam and
Rotterdam, has been facilitated. The growth of these mainports has been accompanied
by controversy as well, because of land use issues and environmental impacts. Strategic
planning for mainports is, therefore, a complex multi-stakeholder problem, in the face
of uncertainty about the future. It is a difficult and lengthy process that often produces
plans that are either outdated, difficult to implement, or both. This is because of three
major problems: (1) an inefficient problem-solving process for mainport planning

---

[1] Corresponding Author. Research Associate, Delft University of Technology, P.O. Box 5015, 2600 GA,
Delft, The Netherlands; Email: r.a.a.wijnen@tudelft.nl.

problems; (2) inadequate consideration of the uncertain future; and (3) a lack of stakeholder involvement.

Current approaches to mainport strategic planning make it difficult, if not impossible, to rapidly produce flexible plans for the short-, middle-, and long-term that are acceptable to all mainport stakeholders and adaptable to the constantly changing external environment. What is needed is an approach to planning that enables rapid estimation of the impacts of alternative strategic plans and continuous collaboration among all stakeholders. Such an approach can be facilitated by a Decision Support System (DSS). We use Turban's definition of a DSS as 'an interactive, flexible, and adaptable computer-based information system, developed for supporting the solution of a non-structured management problem for improved decision making' [2].

This paper describes an architecture for such a DSS. It is structured as follows. Section 2 describes mainport planning in general, discusses its problems, and identifies the need for a DSS. Section 3 identifies the DSS users, and presents a software architecture for a DSS for mainport strategic planning. Section 4 discusses the services designed on top of this architecture and how they address the current problems with mainport planning. Section 5 presents some final remarks.

2. Mainport Strategic Planning

Basically, the planning problem is to find an appropriate match between capacity and demand, given a number of constraints (e.g. environmental and/or financial). Both airports and seaports have to be managed such that demand for services matches the capacity of the infrastructure. At the same time, the mainport operator has to manage the environmental impacts of the future mainport operation. Part of the business process of mainport operators is, therefore, to formulate and implement plans that make sure that mainport capacity matches demand and societal needs as the future unfolds.

The traditional approach for the planning of seaports and airports aims at producing individual plans for the short- middle-, and long term. These plans are generally at a high level of aggregation and are produced using a 'predict-and-act' approach. That is, a single prediction of future demand is made through forecasting, and a plan is developed to accommodate that demand. The plans are mainly developed from inside the organization, although occasionally a limited group of stakeholders is consulted. Such a planning approach does not work well anymore because of two reasons: (1) the world is changing fast, resulting in constant changes in demand for transport services [3, 4], which requires constant changes to the plans; and (2) proposed changes to a mainport's infrastructure or operation are difficult to implement if they do not satisfy the objectives of the mainport's stakeholders [5]. As a result, there is growing opposition to the expansion plans of mainports around the world [6, 7].

In light of these new developments, the traditional planning approach of merely trying to keep pace with the growing demand is not enough anymore. Mainport operators have to think strategically about the accommodation of growing demand, while at the same time considering ways to mitigate the adverse effects of this growth. Ideally, this should result in a strategic plan that not only satisfies the mainport operator's business objectives, but also satisfies the objectives of its stakeholders (communities, customers, suppliers, regulators, governments, etc.). Additionally, these plans have to be developed within limited time and budget. In modern day mainport planning, current and future societal conditions (i.e. developments in technology, demography, regulations, and demand), the potential impact of a plan on the mainport's capacity, and its economic, environmental, and land use effects need to be considered *simultaneously*. Strategic planning, therefore, is essential for the long-term success of the mainport operator's organization.

2.1. Problems with Current Mainport Strategic Planning

Traditional mainport strategic planning has three major problems: (1) an inefficient problem-solving process; (2) an inadequate approach for modeling the future; and (3) a lack of involvement of the mainport stakeholders.

1. Strategic planning for mainports requires evaluating each of the different strategic plans that could potentially be implemented. Often, different people (from different organizations or departments) work on different questions, each using different models/tools, assumptions, and data. Currently the different aspects are generally analyzed separately. So, it is difficult to produce a consistent, integrated set of results that can be used to analyze the effects of a specific strategic plan. Even if the separate analyses used consistent assumptions and data, an integral view of the mainport's performance could be produced only by manually collecting, combining, and post-processing the individual results, which is very time-consuming;
2. Planners consider only a limited number of plausible futures (usually only one). As stated by Ascher and repeated by many others: 'the forecast is always wrong' [8, 9]. Therefore the traditional 'predict-and-act' approach to mainport planning is likely to produce a plan that performs poorly. The future that is considered is usually a single trend extrapolation of demand. Besides demand, other external factors, such as technology, regulations, and demographics should be seriously considered when modeling the future, because they also have impacts on demand and the entire mainport system;
3. Stakeholders are usually not directly involved in the mainport strategic planning process. If some stakeholders feel that the plan for a mainport's development does not satisfy their objectives, the implementation of the plan can be delayed or hampered significantly [1, 10].

2.2. Solving the Problems with a Decision Support System

By conducting a thorough analysis of the practice of mainport planning, we found that the major fundamental cause of the problems mentioned above is the dispersion of knowledge, data and information, and tools within the organization of the mainport operator and those of its stakeholders [11, 12]. Many resources are involved, both inside as well as outside the organization; a large amount of data are involved, requiring a significant number of people, possibly using analytic tools, to turn the data into information relevant for decisionmaking. In addition, as the planning process progresses, the world keeps changing and management needs to make decisions in a shifting environment. For example, a planning project at the Port of Rotterdam (PoR) can take up to ten months. In the end the decisionmakers are informed by a report, but this provides them with a static image of a future situation, which may even at this time be outdated due to new developments. Airports like Amsterdam Airport Schiphol or Boston Logan Airport have included new runways in their strategic plans, but because of stakeholder opposition, they have taken more than 30 years to become operational.

Currently, it is difficult for resources to be integrated, consolidated, and focused on producing an effective strategic plan for developing the mainport. People, data and information, and tools cannot quickly be deployed for analysis and subsequent synthesis so that the relevant information for decisionmaking becomes quickly available. Inherently, this leads to an inefficient strategic planning process that is not able to support the creation of a transparent strategic plan that is acceptable to all stakeholders.

The problems discussed in Section 2.1 can, however, be addressed by a DSS that supports a multi-stakeholder approach for addressing the wide range of planning problems and efficiently integrates the analytical and human resources within the mainport's organization. Zachary [13] identifies six generic needs that a DSS needs to fulfill: (1) projecting into the future despite uncertainty; (2) making trade-offs among competing goals, which implies that different alternatives can be evaluated and compared; (3) managing large amounts of information simultaneously; (4) analyzing complex situations within constraints on time and resources; (5) visualizing and manipulating those visualizations; and (6) making heuristic judgments, even if they are only qualitative. The next section presents the software architecture for a DSS that addresses these needs and that solves the aforementioned problems with mainport strategic planning.

3. Architecture for a DSS for Mainport Strategic Planning

The software development process used to successfully develop a DSS should be iterative, evolutionary, and adaptive [14]. It is very important that the DSS development is driven by user requirements, which starts with identifying the users themselves. This seems obvious, but does not appear to be common practice in DSS development projects [15]. In the next section, we identify the users and briefly discuss their interaction with the DSS. Section 3.2 presents the software architecture that realizes these interactions.

3.1. Identifying the DSS Users

The first step in the DSS development process is to analyze the business activities, in order to identify the scope and users for the software system. The result of this activity is a conceptual model that describes the DSS users (or actors) in terms of their roles in the strategic planning effort, as shown in Figure 1. There are three major roles in the mainport strategic planning effort, which are performed by one or more persons, depending on the size of the mainport operator's organization. These roles will be played by the three types of users of the DSS. The roles and their main goals are:

- **Decisionmakers:** The persons that have the decision power to develop and implement a strategic plan for the mainport's development, operation, and management. They *define* the *decisionmaking context*, and disseminate and share information related to decisionmaking.

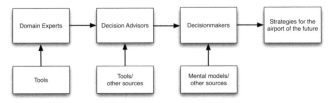

Figure 1: The DSS users, based on their roles in a mainport strategic planning effort.

Decisionmakers from the mainport operator and its stakeholders *compare* the strategic plan for business as usual with other *strategic plans* that have been evaluated so that they can determine which strategic plan is collectively preferred for implementation;

- **Decision advisors:** The persons that advise the people that make the actual decisions. They *develop scenarios* describing different plausible futures, *identify strategic plans* that potentially solve the problem or seize an opportunity, and *evaluate* the *strategic plans* in terms of the mainport's performance within each of the scenarios;

- **Domain experts:** The persons that have specific knowledge of the mainport system (e.g. of the infrastructure, environmental impacts, land use, etc.) and its operation. They *support* the decision advisors in the preparation, execution, and evaluation of *quantitative analyses* of the mainport's performance in terms of e.g. infrastructure capacity, delay, noise, emissions, and financial results, using a variety of analytical tools.

Role Theory has been identified to have considerable potential in aiding the design of adequate methods for decision support [16]. Based on the literature, however, we can conclude that most DSS projects have not seriously used it [15].

3.2. The Architecture

The architecture of the proposed DSS is presented in Figure 2, which shows the structure of the DSS, its users, and the interface between the DSS and existing resources. The DSS has a layered design based on the Layers pattern [17], with each layer partitioned into modules, each of which has a clear responsibility. Within the modules there is a further partitioning into submodules and classes, so that the design is truly modular, making the DSS easy to maintain, extend, and customize for specific mainport operators. Three layers have been designed: (1) the User Interface and Application Layer; (2) the Domain Layer; and (3) the Technical Services Layer, each of which is discussed below.

User Interface and Application Control Layer: The User Interface (UI) is the interface between the DSS and its users. The DSS users are related to the roles defined in the conceptual model (see Figure 1). So, decisionmakers, decision advisors, and domain experts are the users of the DSS.

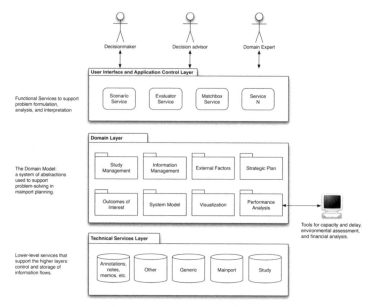

Figure 2: The architecture of the DSS.

The persons adopting these roles can be from the mainport operator's organization or its stakeholders (and different roles may be played by the same person). Their activities related to a strategic planning effort are supported by the DSS through a number of services. For a more detailed discussion of the UI and its most relevant services, see Section 4.

Domain Layer: The Domain Layer provides the domain and business related functionality of the DSS. The Domain Layer features an object-oriented model (i.e. a so-called Domain Model [18]) of the mainport planning domain. On the one hand, the design of the Domain Model is driven by a policy analysis approach [19]. The DSS is thus based on a well-defined and systematic methodology for problem-solving, which is an important requirement for software that is to support strategic planning at the management level [20]. On the other hand, the design is driven by Visualization Theory, in order to provide efficient ways of presenting information to decisionmakers, their advisors, and the experts [12].

The definition of the modules is not made from the developer's point of view (possibly resulting in a structure that nobody else can understand) but from the users' point of view – the point of view of the domain and business activity [18, 21]. In order to identify modules, the concepts from the domain needed to be discovered and defined consistently. Eight modules have been defined that organize a mainport strategic planning study such that a DSS user is able to efficiently solve a broad class of mainport planning problems. These eight modules and their responsibilities are:

- **Study module:** Responsible for capturing the context (i.e. the stakeholders and their objectives) of a planning problem, and keeping track of the different scenarios and strategic plans that have been developed.
- **Information Management module:** Responsible for capturing general information that is used during the planning effort. This module supports sharing of all kinds of documentation (minutes of project meetings, reports, annotations, guidelines, etc.) throughout the project.

- **External Factors module:** Responsible for capturing the external factors describing economic, technological, demographic, and regulatory developments that make up the scenarios.
- **Strategic Plan module:** Responsible for holding information related to alternative strategic plans, which change the mainport's infrastructure, operations, and management.
- **Outcomes of Interest module:** Responsible for organizing collections of outcome indicators for different aspects of the mainport's performance, e.g. capacity, delay, noise, emissions, and financial results.
- **System Model module:** Responsible for providing a representation of the mainport system based on the terminology and language of the DSS users.
- **Visualization module:** Responsible for providing structures to present different types of information to the various users in a clear, usable, and understandable way.
- **Performance Analysis module:** Responsible for quantifying the mainport's performance (including pre- and post-processing) in terms of specific outcome indicators, using third-party tools available inside the organization or provided by outside consultants.

In terms of the *workflow* with respect to the DSS users, the functionality of the modules is used as follows:

1. A decision advisor creates a new study for investigating a planning problem, based on input from the decisionmakers (**Study module**);
4. The decision advisors and experts develop multiple scenarios, describing different plausible futures (**External Factors module**);
5. Experts specify the characteristics of the mainport (**System Model module**);
6. Different strategic plans are defined (**Strategic Plan module**) by the decision advisors;
7. Each of the strategic plans is evaluated against each of the scenarios by the decision advisor for specific periods of interest within the planning period (e.g. 2010, 2015, 2020). For each period of interest:
    a. The effect of the external factors (captured by the scenario representing forces outside the control of decisionmakers) on the System Model is determined (by the DSS);
    b. The effect of the strategic plan (which is under the control of the decisionmakers) on the System Model is determined (by the DSS);
    c. The experts and decision advisors evaluate the mainport's performance in terms of the outcomes of interest (**Outcomes of Interest and Performance Analysis module**);
8. Decision advisors present the results of the strategic plans that have been evaluated to the decisionmakers, so that they can compare and discuss each of the strategic plans (**Visualization module**);
9. The decisionmakers come to an agreement about the strategic plan that is preferred for implementation. If there is no agreement, (part of) the workflow is started again.

The **Information Management** module provides generic functionality for sharing information and can therefore be used at any time and as many times as needed during each of the steps of this workflow.

The various users are associated with the mainport operator or any of its stakeholders. The DSS itself does not enforce nor imply a particular process for collaboration among the mainport operator and stakeholders (our motivation for this design choice is discussed in Section 5). The Domain Layer is the heart of the DSS and provides the foundation for building the services described in Section 4. More information about the principles used to design this layer can be found in [11]. Detailed information about the design and implementation of the Visualization and Information Management modules is provided by [12].

Technical Services Layer: The Technical Services Layer incorporates lower-level, more generic services used by the higher-level layers, mainly providing functionality for disclosing data needed for setting up a study or permanently storing the user-generated information within a study. For this purpose, a Database Management System is used that manages the various databases. As such it helps (at the data level) to meet Zachary's third need: managing large amounts of information simultaneously. This layer is not discussed any further.

4. The Core Services of the DSS

This section presents the most architecturally significant services, namely those that are essential for addressing each of the problems with mainport strategic planning identified in Section 2.1. First, the **Scenario Service** is described, which provides planners with functionality to better take into account an uncertain future. Secondly, the **Evaluator Service** is described, which provides decision advisors and experts a means to efficiently evaluate different strategic plans. Finally, the **Matchbox Service** is described, facilitating comparison and discussion of all the potential strategic plans by the decisionmakers and mainport stakeholders. Together, the services meet Zachary's fourth need: analyzing complex situations within constraints on time and resources.

4.1. Scenario Service for Developing Scenarios

The Scenario Service deals with the second problem identified in Section 2.1 – the lack of a method to model the uncertain future. As such, it directly meets Zachary's first need, i.e. the need to project into the future despite uncertainty. A scenario is defined as a description of the assumed development of external factors that form the context for the decisionmaking problem, not including the strategic planning decisions made by managers.

Mainport planning needs to analyze all the relevant future developments quantitatively. Different developments need to be combined into multiple scenarios that consistently describe plausible futures. For a mainport, this means obtaining information about (1) economic developments that drive demand; (2) technological developments affecting ways in which demand can be accommodated; (3) demographic developments, specifying the density and distribution of people living in the vicinity of the mainport; and (4) regulatory developments, putting constraints on some aspects of a mainport's activities. The DSS captures information about these factors that can be used by decision advisors and domain experts to create multiple scenarios.

Figure 3 shows an illustration of the Scenario Service. On the left hand side of the window, a tree is presented. The tree covers the planning period (here, for the years 2006 -2016) and has nodes for a number of distinct years. On the right hand side, a notebook with a number of pages is provided. The information shown on the pages of the notebook depends on the period of interest that the user selects in the tree on the left. The notebook contains five pages: Overview, Economic, Technological, Regulations, and Demographic. The Overview page shows the name of the scenario, a short description of the scenario, and the editing history. The Economy page provides options for specifying economic developments as far as they influence demand. The Technology page can be used to specify technological developments. For example, in the case of airport planning this page will provide options for specifying developments in aircraft size, engines, and Air Traffic Management. The Regulations page gives the user options to specify regulatory developments, for example about noise impact, or local air quality.

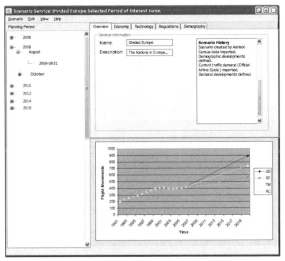

Figure 3: The Scenario Service.

The Demography page allows the user to specify developments in the density and distribution of people living in the vicinity of the mainport. The display part at the bottom left corner of the window allows for visual inspection of the data that are entered.

4.2. Evaluator Service for Evaluating Strategic Plans

The Evaluator Service solves the first problem identified in Section 2.1 – the inefficiency of the problem-solving process – by providing the means for the integral evaluation of the effects of strategic plans for a particular period of interest. As such, it also supports the first part of Zachary's second need: it provides functionality to evaluate different alternatives (the second part of the Zachary' second need – comparing alternatives and making trade-offs among competing goals – is supported by the Matchbox Service, discussed in Section 4.3).

The Evaluator Service, shown in Figure 4, provides functionality for evaluating the effects of a strategic plan on mainport performance for a given scenario. Just as the Scenario Service, the Evaluator Service has a tree for visualizing the planning period (on the left); a notebook is used to present the outcomes of interest (on the right). For each year, a user is able to specify days to conduct performance analysis on a daily basis (if required).

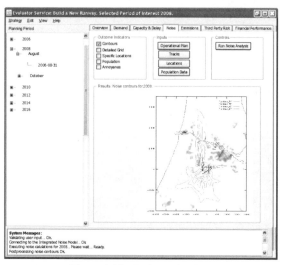

Figure 4: The Evaluator Service.

There is a drop-down box for selecting the scenarios against which the strategy is to be evaluated. The notebook features an Overview page, where the user can specify particular outcome indicators (e.g. noise contours, emission contours, and population counts). Next, the Demand page for analyzing the traffic demand that is to be allocated is provided; the demand itself is derived from the selected scenario. The other pages are dedicated to each of the Outcomes of Interest. The computations with the specific tools are started from the page related to a specific Outcome of Interest. The results from the computations are presented in the lower half of the page (e.g. the noise analysis results, shown in Figure 4). The Evaluator relies heavily on the visualization functionality in the Domain Layer, as can be seen in Figure 4. As such, it fulfills Zachary's fifth need: visualizing and manipulating those visualizations.

4.3. Matchbox Service for Comparing Strategic Plans

The Matchbox Service is designed to solve the third problem identified in Section 2.1 – a lack of involvement of all the stakeholders – by providing a means to present different strategic plans to the mainport operator and its stakeholders. Using information about specific strategic plans, a constructive discussion about which strategic plan is collectively preferred for implementation, can take place. As such, this service meets Zachary's second need – making trade offs among competing goals. It also supports the sixth need – making heuristic judgments, even if they are only qualitative.

The DSS provides scorecards that present the effects of each of the strategic plans for each of the scenarios as a means for discussion among stakeholders. The rows of a scorecard are related to the strategic plans, including the business as usual plan. As shown in Figure 5, the Matchbox Service provides a scorecard that can be used for the comparison of alternative strategic plans. Each of the strategic plans can be assessed in terms of their performance and compared among each other and the business as usual plan.

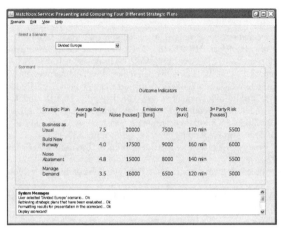

Figure 5: The Matchbox Service.

5. Final Remarks

Mainport strategic planning is a difficult activity, because of the complexity of the mainport system and the many stakeholders that are involved. Currently, the people involved in the planning effort need to process an overwhelming amount of information in order to come up with the relevant information for the decisionmakers. Most of the times, they are not able to do that in a timely manner; the number of alternative plans is also limited, raising opposition against the plans by the mainport's stakeholders.

We have described a Decision Support System that can solve these problems. The DSS would explicitly support the involvement of all the stakeholders, so that the mainport operator and its stakeholders would be able to collaborate in defining, evaluating, and comparing a range of strategic plans. As such, a collaborative setting would be created that would facilitate the selection of a strategic plan that adequately satisfies all the parties affected by a mainport's development. We have presented the overall architecture of such a DSS, showing how it meets the needs of the people involved in mainport strategic planning. Concrete examples of the services provided by the DSS that directly address the current problems of mainport strategic planning were discussed in detail.

In Section 3.2 we mentioned that the DSS does not enforce a specific way of collaboration among the mainport operator and the stakeholders. This design choice was motivated by the fact that a specific collaboration process will differ from problem to problem and from one multi-stakeholder context to another. Obviously, it is important to consider how to set up the actual interactive and participatory use of decision support systems [22]. However, a necessary precondition is DSS functionality that explicitly supports information gathering, processing, and sharing in a multi-stakeholder context, which was realized through the DSS architecture and services described before. The focus of our future work will shift from content-support (this paper) to process-support, building upon the existing body of knowledge in this field.

References

[1]   Kolk, A. van der Veen, M. (2002). 'Dilemmas of Balancing Organizational and Public Interests: How Environment Affects Strategy in Dutch Main Ports'. European Management Journal, Vol. 20, No.1, pp. 45-54.

[2]   Turban, E. (1995). Decision support and expert systems: management support systems. Prentice Hall.

[3]   M.B. Charles, Barnes, P., Ryan, N., Clayton, J. (2007). 'Airport futures: Towards a critique of the aerotropolis model', Journal of Futures (2007), Vol. 39, Issue 9, pp. 1009-1028.

[4]   Mason, K.J., Alamdari, F. (2007). 'EU network carriers, low cost carriers and consumer behaviour: A Delphi study of future trends'. Journal of Air Transport Management, Vol. 13, Issue 5, pp. 299-310.

[5]   Soneryd, L. (2004). 'Public involvement in the planning process: EIA and lessons from the Örebro airport extension, Sweden'. Environmental Science & Policy, Vol. 7, Issue 1, pp. 59-68.

[6]   May, M., Hill, S.B. (2006). 'Questioning airport expansion—A case study of Canberra International Airport'. Journal of Transport Geography, Vol. 14, Issue 6, pp. 437-450.

[7]   Baird, A. (1999). 'Analysis of private seaport development: the port of Felixstowe'. Transport Policy. Vol. 6, pp. 109-122.

[8]   W. Ascher (1978) Forecasting: an Appraisal for Policy-makers and Planners, Johns Hopkins University Press, Baltimore.

[9]   de Neufville, R., Odoni, A. (2003). Airport Systems: Planning, Design, and Management. McGraw-Hill Professional, New York.

[10]   Goetz, A.R., Szyliowicz, J.S. (1997). 'Revisiting transportation planning and decision making theory: The case of Denver International Airport'. Transportation Research Part A, Vol.31, pp. 263-280.

[11]   Wijnen, R.A.A., Walker, W.E., Kwakkel, J.H. (2008). 'Decision Support for Airport Strategic Planning', Transportation Planning and Technology (Special Issue on Approaches for Developing the Airport of the Future), Volume 31, Issue 1, pp. 1-34.

[12]   Chin, R.T.H. (2007). Mainport Planning Suite: software services to support mainport planning. Doctoral Dissertation, Delft University of Technology, The Netherlands.

[13]   Zachary, W., (1998) 'Decision Support Systems: Designing to Extend the Cognitive Limits', in Martin G. Helander (ed.), Handbook of Human-Computer Interaction. Elsevier Science Publishers, Amsterdam.

[14]   Carter, Grace M., Michael P. Murray, Robert G. Walker, and Warren E. Walker, Building Organizational Decision Support Systems, Academic Press, Inc., Cambridge, Massachusetts, 1992.

[15]   G. Dodson, D. Arnott, G. Pervan (2006). 'The Client and User in Decision Support Systems: Review and Research Agenda'. In F. Adam, P. Brezillon, S. Carlsson and P. Humphreys (eds.), Creativity and Innovation in Decision Making and Decision Support, Volume I. Decision Support Press, London, UK.

[16]   Vari, A., Vecsenyi, J. (1984). 'Designing decision support methods in organizations'. Acta Psychologica, Vol. 56, Issues 1-3, pp. 141-151.

[17]   Larman, C. (2005). Applying UML and Patterns: an introduction to object-oriented analysis and design and iterative development. Prentice Hall, Upper Saddle River, United States.

[18]   Evans, E. (2004). Domain-Driven Design. Addison Wesley, Upper Saddle River, N.J., United States.

[19]   Walker, Warren E. (2000). 'Policy Analysis: A Systematic Approach to Supporting Policymaking in the Public Sector', Journal of Multicriteria Decision Analysis, Volume 9, No. 1-3, pp. 11-27.

[20]   Wagner, C. (2004). 'Enterprise strategy management systems: current and next generation'. Journal of Strategic Information Systems, Vol. 13, pp. 105-128.

[21]   Medvidovic, N., Dashofy, E.M., and Taylor, R.N. (2007). 'Moving architectural description from under the technology lamppost'. Information and Software Technology, Vol. 49, pp. 12-31.

[22]   Goosen, H., Janssen R., Vermaat J.E. (2007). 'Decision support for participatory wetland decision-making'. Ecological Engineering, Vol. 30, pp. 187-199.

A Multi-Criteria Decision Aiding System to Support Monitoring in a Public Administration

Maria Franca NORESE[a,1] and Simona BORRELLI[b]

[a]*Dep. Sistemi di produzione ed economia dell'azienda, Politecnico di Torino, Italy*
[b]*Finpiemonte S.p.A., Torino, Italy*

Abstract. The Piedmont Region Financial Institute has had to construct a procedure and a system to monitor projects that a regional law has financed. In this context, the integration of a new data reading approach in a monitoring procedure has been proposed and a multi-criteria decision aiding method, ELECTRE TRI, has been applied to the problem, first to explain a possible use of the acquired information and then to be integrated in the information system. The Model base of the prototype system was used, as a shared space and a common framework, to better understand the aims and information needs of the monitoring process and therefore to read data and orient information acquisition. The application of ELECTRE TRI to the models analytically synthesizes the information elements, to face the difficulties of the monitoring process in its different phases and to support decisions, in terms of modifications and integrations of activities for future law applications.

Keywords. ELECTRE TRI, public administration, monitoring process, collaborative problem formulation and decision-making

Introduction

An administrative process, to stimulate and finance "integrated planning" actions in the tourism sector, was activated in Piedmont, a Region in the north west of Italy, through Regional Law n° 4 of 24 January 2000 (R.L. N. 4/2000). The law has the aim of involving local agencies in the territory, to promote the development of new areas with tourist possibilities, revitalize declining tourist areas or qualitatively improve important tourist areas, according to the sustainable tourism principle.

R.L. N. 4/2000 explicitly activated (and financed) a monitoring process to acquire knowledge not only on the courses of action and the results of the financed agencies, but also on the long and complicated law implementation process, in order to improve future activities in relation to the same law and to the design of new financing processes.

---

[1] Corresponding Author: Maria Franca Norese, DISPEA-Politecnico di Torino, Corso Duca degli Abbruzzi 24, 10129 Torino, Italy; E-mail: mariafranca.norese@polito.it.

Finpiemonte, the Piedmont Region Financial Institute, is often required to administer the procedure of financing the accepted projects and to control the project realizations, in relation to different regional laws. In this case, it was also involved in constructing a procedure to monitor the law implementation process and a system to synthesize all the acquired information elements.

Multi-criteria models and methods were proposed in the monitoring process as a common framework and vocabulary for the involved actors, technicians and experts, to understand the situation and acquire a shared vision of the problem, to support the definition of some monitoring procedures and orient the information acquisition, and as an operational tool, to read and synthesize all the elements of the monitoring information system.

The different activities of this monitoring process in the first law implementation are described in the next section and then related to the proposal of using a "multi-criteria approach to the problem of data acquisition" and its tools (models and methods), to support the decision makers when the monitoring results have to be used. The third section deals with the integration of a multi-criteria decision aiding method, ELECTRE TRI, with the monitoring process and the monitoring information system, above all to describe and anticipate how the acquired information can be synthesized and oriented towards specific monitoring goals and then to use all the acquired information elements and propose modifications and integrations of the law implementation activities. The last section discusses the integration of ELECTRE TRI in a system that has to be perceived and used as a useful tool for the organization, not only at the end of the monitoring, but in all the phases of the process.

1. The Monitoring Process and Procedures

The monitoring process, in relation to R.L. N. 4/2000, is complex because of the simultaneous presence of several critical elements. The multi-organizational nature of the decisional and operational context was the first element of complexity. The Piedmont Region was involved in four sectors and Finpiemonte in two sectors, the Contribution Management (financing and control activities) and the Back Office, which was created to define and activate the monitoring procedures.

Public organizations, which operate at a central level, often require data about the different law implementation procedures that are activated at local levels (States, Regions, Districts or local Agencies), to monitor a situation. However, at the local level, it is not always clear how and why the monitoring process is activated and above all what feedback can be obtained during and by this monitoring process. This situation is different and new, because the monitoring process is activated autonomously, for internal reasons. Therefore, when the law was activated, monitoring was a new (and then complex) analysis context for the two involved organizations that required the acquisition of new competencies.

Another element of complexity was the not always easy or immediate communication between the involved sectors. Each passage from one sector to another required a great deal of time and time (to understand the not completely structured operational situation, to develop the matter and implement each activity, to wait for the documents and to complete the data that have to be introduced in the database) was unavoidably another element of complexity.

The law was activated in 2000 and the first application was very long. The evaluation and selection activities of the feasibility studies were carried out during the year 2001. The projects were presented during the year 2002 and were then evaluated, but very few of them were actually started the same year. The development of the projects often required more than three years (the maximum acceptable extension for the law), sometimes even five years. Only at the end of 2007 were all the projects considered completed (or they abandoned).

The cognitive needs were not completely clear during the first monitoring phase and the first documents on the financed projects were produced more than six months after monitoring had been started. Therefore, the first activities and above all the structure of the monitoring database were defined without any knowledge of the projects and the documents the proponents had elaborated.

The realization of all the financed projects was controlled during their global development, until the last months in 2007. The results, in terms of "development of new tourist areas and revitalizing and improving of the old areas, according to the sustainable tourism principle", will only be evaluated in the future, after a period of time whose length is connected to the content of each specific intervention and the nature of its territory. Other possible results, such as acquired competences in integrated planning and coordination capability or transferability of the adopted approach, were observed during the monitoring through interviews and questionnaires.

The main activities in 2002 were the structuring of a database with the description of all the financed projects and the definition of the monitoring form, the Back Office team used each year from 2003 to 2005 to verify the progress of each project (the beginning of each project; the percentage of the work that is made each year; interruption requests and motivations; project variant requests and motivations; motivations of the delays in relation to the project planning; renunciations and motivations). The administrative data concerning the financing of the projects (the percentage of the project that is financed each year; official interruptions; output costs) were easily introduced into the database with the support of the Finpiemonte Contribution Management sector. The interviews with some leaders of the Integrated Plans (IPs)[2] and a questionnaire for all the other leaders were implemented in 2003 and 2004. A research group, involving the process actors and some technicians, was constituted in 2003 to analyse the first monitoring activities and to orient the next phases towards the development and correct use of the monitoring system. A "table of experts" was constituted at the end of 2004 to propose some improvements to the law and its implementation process, and some actions to activate the last phase of monitoring. These experts analysed the nature of this complex law, from different points of view, the monitoring procedures and fifteen IPs, as a sample of all the financed plans.

Uncertainties on the final purposes of the monitoring process were present when the process was started. The proposal of using multi-criteria (MC) models and methods

---

[2] An integrated plan can include several intervention projects and involve different beneficiary subjects and has to be promoted and coordinated by a public Agency.

as a general language to read and orient the action of information acquisition was elaborated in the first months of the monitoring process to aid the decision, not only at the end of the process, but also in the first phases, above all to support the problem formulation, in terms of better understanding and definition of the aims and informative needs of the monitoring process. A "fictitious" MC model was elaborated to illustrate how administrative and technical data, but also points of view from interviews and questionnaires, can be synthesized in models, for example to distinguish situations of adequate project development, from others that require control actions and/or a deeper analysis to avoid similar criticalities in the future.

The same MC language was again used during the monitoring process to propose possible uses of the acquired information to the involved actors and to the experts and to illustrate an analytical approach, in which the quantitative and qualitative data are synthesized to answer specific monitoring questions and to obtain some useful results. Some simple MC models were developed as examples to introduce the main concepts of multi-criteria decision aiding and to describe different MC comparison situations. The ELECTRE TRI method was used, with the first available data, to propose an analytical approach to the need of using the monitoring information system in a context of decision aiding and to propose the structure of a possible Decision Support System.

In the next section, the possible use of an analytical tool, ELECTRE TRI, is analysed in relation to some specific goals of the process and to some results of the monitoring process.

2. A Multi-Criteria Approach to Use the Data of the Monitoring Process

Only 90 of the 177 feasibility studies were accepted, in relation of the first application of R.L. N. 4/2000, and 333 projects, from the original 1705 project hypotheses, were financed. The monitoring process was activated to acquire information on the projects during their realization (i.e. to observe them in order to act if there were significant differences between the observed behaviour and the expected behaviour) and to examine the implementation process itself and its main phases, in order to improve future process design, project selection and project development support activities.

A multi-criteria method, ELECTRE TRI, was initially proposed, in relation to these aims, to anticipate how the acquired monitoring information could be synthesized and oriented to specific monitoring goals. It was introduced above all as a description of how the monitoring results could be synthesized and used to distinguish different levels of implementation validity and connect them to actions (and decisions) of process control and/or improvement of future law applications.

ELECTRE TRI [1,2] is a sorting method which allows an *action* to be evaluated according to multiple criteria and, in relation to its absolute merit, be assigned to one of the k pre-specified ordered categories: C^1 (the worst),..., C^k (the best). Each C^j category is limited by two reference actions (profiles), its upper and lower limits. Each evaluated action is compared to all the ordered profiles and assigned to one category in relation to the results of these comparisons.

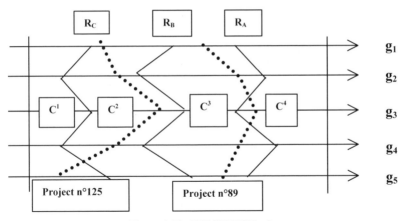

Figure 1. The ELECTRE TRI scheme.

A very simple scheme (see Fig. 1) was chosen to visually represent and propose the logic of the ELECTRE TRI method. The actions in the scheme are two projects and three profiles are present as a reference pattern that can be used to distinguish situations at different criticality levels. The profiles identify good behaviour (reference R_A), realistically acceptable conduct, with some "physiological" differences from the ideal one (reference R_B) and a critical situation (reference R_C). The model that the scheme synthesizes distinguishes the categories of *ideal conditions* (C^4), *acceptable conditions* (C^3), *presence of marginal criticalities* which can be analysed to understand the causes and, in some cases, to solve them (C^2) and *presence of widespread criticalities* whose causes have to be identified to avoid developing similar situations in the future (C^1).

Each project (or IP, as a set of projects) is compared to all the reference profiles and assigned to one category. A critical situation can be faced if it is identified early on (first potentiality of a monitoring system). The frequency of similar critical situations can suggest specific process improvement actions (second aim of the system).

The scheme was used to anticipate and "analytically guarantee" a possible use of the monitoring data, focalising attention less on the method and more on the real problem: the definition of models that are consistent with specific process improving or control actions.

Several MC models and ELECTRE TRI applications can be developed using data and knowledge elements that are included in the database the Back Office team produced. Each model has to be oriented to a specific decision context and only the context knowledge can produce significant and consistent model elements.

The formal definition of a consistent family of criteria is the first and most arduous task in MC modelling but, in this case, an incremental approach is made possible throughout the passage from the simplest problems and models to the more complicated monitoring aims and can reduce the modelling difficulties.

The performances of each action (in this case, a single project or an IP that can include several projects or a specific kind of integrated plan) have to be defined for each criterion, in relation to the information elements the monitoring activities have acquired or to the data that are not yet available but the future monitoring of the project results can obtain.

All the parameters of an MC model for ELECTRE TRI (the reference profiles, the thresholds that characterize pseudo-criteria, the importance and veto power of each criterion and the cut threshold) have to be defined, but the constructive learning which is proposed in [3–5] can support a step-by-step definition of the parameters and a consolidation of knowledge elements for the model base of a future DSS.

The simplest model we proposed to introduce the main concepts is related to the behaviour of the 333 projects during their realization. Some of these had not been started, some others had been started late but had recuperated the lost time, some projects had not recuperated the time they lost at the start or lost time during their development, some projects had been started on time and the work had been completed on time. The scheme of figure 1 can be used to analyse the *Progress of the project development*. Two projects are evaluated, as the reference profiles R_A, R_B and R_C, in relation to the criteria: delay at the start (g_1), delay at the end of the first phase (mid point of the project development) (g_2), delay at the end (g_3), nature of the delay (g_4), presence of different criticalities (g_5). The ELECTRE TRI scheme makes this reading evident: if 'number 89' was initially judged as a potentially risky project and/or 'number 125' as a good project, the evaluation and selection model and its use have to be critically analysed before any future applications. The possible reasons for this result have to be examined, above all if several projects are assigned to categories C^1 and C^2 and only very few to the other categories. When very few projects of categories C^3 and C^4 are included in the IP that the experts qualified as the least consistent to the objectives of the law, the analysis of the reasons can become easier. Qualitative information, above all from the interviews to the IP leaders, can be inserted in an MC model. Sometimes it becomes essential to distinguish the causes and suggest possible improvements.

The same scheme shown in Fig. 1 can be used to introduce a totally different cognitive and decisional problem. When the data arrive from the activities of monitoring the results of each project will be evaluated, for example, to recognize a gap between the monitored realization and the ex ante perceived project validity. In this case, a model can evaluate the project realization, in terms of costs (g_1), global time (g_2), direct employment (g_3) and indirect employment (g_4) generated during the project development and tourist development of the area (g_5).

The models have to be developed in relation to the cognitive and decisional requirements, but sometimes these requirements are not clear and can be deduced starting from the available data and knowledge elements, their validity and real meaning. The application of ELECTRE TRI can support this problem formulation which activates the data acquisition and, in a subsequent phase, the decision in relation to the monitoring results.

3. ELECTRE TRI and the Monitoring System

An application of the method was conducted in relation to the most formal (and numerical) part of the monitoring system. In this case, the *Progress of the project development* model is quite simple, but includes a more complicated element: the analysed actions are not the projects, but all the IPs that include more than one project. Two reference profiles distinguish categories C^3 (surely adequate IPs, in terms of project design and management and capacity of involving proponents and possible partners in the planning and development activities), C^2, of the IPs that present marginal criticalities or a general poor adequacy, and C^1, of the total inadequacy in terms of development process.

The IPs are evaluated in relation to the "Design weakness" aspect, by two criteria (*Scheduling skill* (g_1), which evaluates the global delay of each Plan in relation to the prevision, and *Anomalies in the project developments* (g_2), with the percent of projects that present interruptions of the work and/or long delays at the start) and to the "Limits in the involvement of the proponents" aspect by three criteria (*Presence of unrealised projects* (g_3), due to renunciation or financing revocation, *Anomalies in the financing requests* (g_4), due to missing or delayed requests, and *Monitoring refusal* (g_5), in terms of lack of communication between the project proponents and the monitoring actors).

The model parameters (the evaluations of the reference profiles, the thresholds of indifference and preference, the veto power and the importance of the criteria) were defined using the ELECTRE TRI Assistant procedure of SW ELECTRE TRI 2.0 [6], with the acquired indications on the nature of some monitored IPs, and their inclusions in specific categories, and in relation to two weight scenarios (the first considers the two aspects, "Design weakness" and "Limits in the involvement of the proponents", as being equally important and the second which sees the first aspect as less important than the second, because the involvement of the proponents is an explicit aim of the law).

The ELECTRE TRI method was applied to 46 IPs, in relations to the two weight scenarios and some parameters were modified (the cutting level and some weights and veto thresholds, each alone and in combination with the others, in the two scenarios), to analyse the sensitivity of the result to these changes. Only five IPs resulted to be stably assigned to the best category (C^3), twenty-two to the intermediary category (C^2) and only one, AL – 20, to the last (C^1). The other IPs were assigned to different categories (C^3 and C^2 or C^2 and C^1) by the two assignment procedures, the pessimistic (or conjunctive) and the optimistic (or disjunctive), for one or more of the tested parameter sets.

In order to also represent these assignments, that are more sensitive to the parameter choice, two new categories, $C^{3/2}$ and $C^{1/2}$, which are indicated in Table 1, were introduced to include the eighteen less robust assignments. This result can be compared with the ranking of the 46 IPs that resulted from the ex-ante selection model. The number in brackets indicates the position of each Plan in the original ranking in Table 1.

The result of a very limited MC model, which only includes the simplest and "quantitative" data of the monitoring, allowed some analyses to be conducted. A comparison with the ex-ante evaluation underlined a quite evident difference. AL – 20 is the only Plan in the worst category C^1 and it was in position 21 in the original ranking of 46 IPs. VC – 5 is in category $C^{1/2}$, but it was in the sixth position. At the same time, nine IPs that ELECTRE TRI assigned to the best categories (C^3 and $C^{3/2}$) were in the last positions in the original ranking. Some of these nine IPs were also analysed by the "table of experts" and qualified as not satisfying the aims of the law: integration, innovation and territorial sustainability. All these IPs include a very limited number of projects in relation to the other Plans.

Table 1. Assignment of the IPs to the categories

C^1	$C^{1/2}$	C^2	$C^{3/2}$	C^3
AL – 20 (21)	VC – 5 (6)	AT – 14 (1)	CN – 20 (7)	VB – 2 (26)
	AL – 7 (11)	TO – 33 (2)	TO 12/4/00 (27)	CN – 4 (29)
	AL – 5 (13)	VB – 7 (3)	TO 17/4/00 (35)	TO – 39 (31)
	TO – 38 (14)	VB – 4 (4)	CN – 6 (38)	CN – 22 (37)
	TO – 15 (15)	VC – 8 (5)		CN – 8 (40)
	CN – 23 (19)	BI – 1 (8)		
	CN – 21 (28)	TO – 40 (9)		
	TO – 25 (30)	VB – 3 (10)		
	TO – 4 (32)	CN – 12 (12)		
	TO – 29 (41)	AL – 6 (16)		
	AL 9/4/00 (42)	VC – 6 (18)		
	CN 3/4/00 (43)	VB – 8 (17)		
	TO – 41 (45)	CN – 24 (20)		
	AT – 10 (46)	TO – 2 (22)		
		AT – 11 (23)		
		AT – 13 (24)		
		TO – 3 (25)		
		BI – 2 (33)		
		CN – 14 (44)		
		AT – 2 (36)		
		BI – 9 (39)		
		CN – 14 (44)		

Some questions sprang to mind in relation to these elements. Can the Plans that satisfy the aims of the law be so complex that their implementation becomes inconsistent with its planning? Can the higher number of projects in a Plan and above all their rich integration and then interconnection be the main cause of the long delay of these IPs in relation to the previsions? Can the proponents in the design and then in the implementation phase of the process be supported, and how?

The critical situation of almost all the 46 IPs in relation to criterion g_1, the global delay of each Plan in relation to the prevision, is the most evident element of the evaluation model and possibly the main reason for some sensitive results. How can this criticality be deeply analysed and eliminated or at least limited in future applications?

In a new analysis, the IPs could be distinguished in categories that include only homogenous Plans (in terms of adequacy to the law aims and complexity). Analysing the elements of each category and elaborating new models, with more oriented information, may be the answer to these questions.

Only one Plan, CN-20, is in the "high" category $C^{3/2}$ and in a good position (the 7th) of the selection model ranking. This Plan can constitute an "exemplary case" that has to be studied, in order to understand the reasons for this positive anomaly and it can be used as a reference, both in the redesigning of the law implementation and in the guidelines the Back Office team has to produce at the end of the monitoring activities. In the same way, some elements of categories C^1 and $C^{1/2}$ should be studied in terms of risks that have to be avoided.

Global models will only be possible when the effects of the interventions become visible, but now, at the end of the IP development monitoring, the related data could be deeply analysed and sometimes 'interpreted'. The IPs can be classified in homogeneous categories (for example in terms of consistency with the law) and at least one model can be proposed for each category, to synthesize the significant information.

The result analysis of each model can produce new questions and activate an enrichment of the model. It can also identify specific typologies, in positive or negative terms, which can be proposed as references to be used in the guidelines.

The comparison of the monitoring results with the starting conditions of each Plan (in terms of ex-ante evaluation, financed percent of the request, changes from the feasibility study to the IP, ...), that are included in the information system, is also useful to deduce motivations of the critical situations and to suggest possible improvement actions.

These combined analyses require the complete integration of ELECTRE TRI in a system that includes all the acquired elements (the structured ones, but also the knowledge elements that were acquired from interviews and questionnaires) in its database. This system should use the ELECTRE TRI results (analysis of the assignment to the categories and consequent new questions or information requirements) to update or develop the database and to generate new elements for the Model base (see Fig. 2). The Model base includes the set of models that were used in the first monitoring phases to illustrate the (possible) use of the data in different decision contexts and the new models that are now being developed to classify the IPs in homogenous classes and recognize the critical ones and the best, in relation to the different intervention contexts.

The integration of an MC method in the monitoring system is at present only a prototype and a proposal for the actors, but the authors feel that in the future the ELECTRE TRI approach to the problem, which was perceived as very clear and well structured, could help define better working hypotheses and link them to public administration decision processes.

4. Conclusive Remarks

Acquiring data is important in order to know the evolution of a process in a public administration and to improve its results. The problem of how to monitor the global process should be analysed in relation to the specific cognitive and operational aims of the decision makers (DMs). The problem becomes more difficult if the monitoring is a new requirement for the organization and there are uncertainties concerning the need of competencies, the effectiveness of the procedures and the potentiality of the new technologies. On the other hand, organizing monitoring activities is difficult when the process that has to be monitored is new and complex, and has not yet produced documented elements that can be used to make previsions on the complexity of the new activities. The global problem has to be formulated incrementally and collectively, when the first data are acquired and each involved actor (decisional or technical) can analyse the situation and face and control the uncertainty.

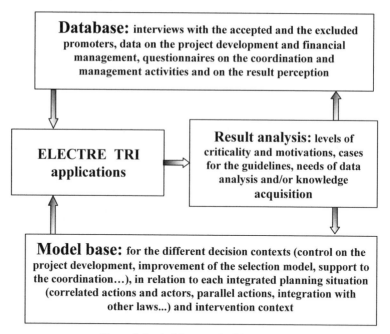

Figure 2. Logical framework of the system.

Formal MC models and methods support this incremental and cooperative problem formulation process. The disaggregating of the problem into its different dimensions [7] and the idea that all the different monitoring results can be synthesized in consistent models facilitates the design of the monitoring activities and the acquisition of useful knowledge elements.

Each result, in this kind of process, however, requires time, and much more than in other similar processes. Now, after six years, the last phase of the work has started. Finpiemonte has to design the most complicated and time consuming activities of monitoring the results of the implemented law on the territory and, at the same time, of using data and information that have just been acquired. The concept that an integrated system can produce important suggestions for the decision has to be translated into an operational approach that involves technical and decisional roles.

The MC approach to the problem has become normal practice in this decisional and technical group and the ELECTRE TRI structure has been considered clear and has been well accepted. The challenge now becomes that of involving all the actors in the operational definition of a system that could be perceived and used as a useful tool for the organization and not as a control system.

References

[1] Yu, W. (1992), ELECTRE TRI : Aspects mèthodologiques et manuel d'utilization, *Document du LAM-SADE n°74*, Université Paris-Dauphine.
[2] Roy, B. and Bouyssou, D. (1993), *Aide multicritère à la décision: mèthodes et cas*, Economica, Collection Gestion, Paris.
[3] Dias L., Mousseau V., Figuera J., Clìmaco J. (2000), An aggregation/disaggregation approach to obtain robust conclusions with ELECTRE TRI, *Cahier du LAMSADE n°174*, Université Paris-Dauphine.

[4] Dias L. and Climaco J., (1999), On computing ELECTRE's credibility indices under partial information, *Journal of Multi-Criteria Decision Analysis*, 8, 74-92.

[5] Dias L. and Climaco J. (2000), ELECTRE TRI for groups with imprecise information on parameter values, *Group Decision and Negotiation*, 9 (5), 355-377.

[6] Mousseau, V., Slowinski R., Zielniewicz P. (1999), ELECTRE TRI 2.0, a methodological guide and user's manual, *Document du LAMSADE n°111*, Université Paris-Dauphine.

[7] Norese, M.F. (1995), MACRAME: a problem formulation and model-structuring assistant in multiactorial contexts, *European Journal of Operational Research*, 84, 25-34.

Collaborative Decision Making: Perspectives and Challenges
P. Zaraté et al. (Eds.)
IOS Press, 2008

An integrated decision support environment for organisational decision making

Shaofeng LIU[1], Alex HB DUFFY, Robert Ian WHITFIELD and Iain M BOYLE
Computer Aided Design Centre, DMEM Department, University of Strathclyde
Glasgow

Abstract. Traditional decision support systems are based on the paradigm of a single decision maker working at a stand-alone computer or terminal who has a specific decision to make with a specific goal in mind. Organisational decision support systems aim to support decision makers at all levels of an organisation (from executive, middle management managers to operators), who have a variety of decisions to make, with different priorities, often in a distributed environment. Such systems are designed and developed with extra functionality to meet the challenge. This paper proposes an Integrated Decision Support Environment (IDSE) for organisational decision making. The IDSE is designed and developed based on distributed client/server networking, with a combination of tight and loose integration approaches for information exchange and communication. The prototype of the IDSE demonstrates a good balance between flexibility and reliability.

Keywords. Hybrid integration approach, decision support environment, organisational decision making, flexibility and reliability

Introduction

Over last several decades decision support systems (DSS) have experienced a paradigm shift from a stand-alone system that supports a single decision maker to make a specific decision through group decision support systems (GDSS) to organisational decision support systems (ODSS), through which distributed decision makers interact with one another and their decisions are co-ordinated towards mutually defined goals, i.e. the goals of organisations. Organisational decision making is a demanding task because the decisions that need to be made involve all aspects of an organisation including their products, technologies and personnel management. When considering the impact from the whole supply chain and global market such as end customers, material providers and product retailers, organisational decision making is further complicated. Due to the nature of organisational decision making in terms of its complexity, dynamics, multiple goals and often opaqueness, various types of decisions need to be made at different

---

[1] Corresponding Author: Shaofeng Liu, Computer Aided Design Centre, Department of Design Manufacture and Engineering Management, University of Strathclyde, G1 1XJ, UK; E-mail: Shaofeng.liu@strath.ac.uk

times and in different organisational units. Further they can be well–structured, semi-structured, ill-structured or unstructured [1]. These decisions can be also made at different levels of organisation such as strategic, tactical or operational. Therefore, decision support for organisational decision making is a big challenge, which has motivated broad interest in research on ODSS in recent years [2]. This paper proposes a novel framework of an Integrated Decision Support Environment (IDSE) aiming to meet the new challenges of organisational decision making, in dynamic situations, through a hybrid integration approach. The paper is organised as follows: Section 1 gives an overview of related work. The concept of the IDSE is proposed in Section 2, followed by Section 3 focussing on the integration strategies that enable IDSE functionality. Section 4 discusses further issues and draws conclusions.

1. Related work

A decision support environment distinguishes itself from a decision support system, and other information systems, by the feature of functionality reconfiguration. IDSE is a decision support environment that can provide flexible functions according to the changes of decision settings for varied applications. Most traditional decision support systems provide fixed functions despite their success in many application areas [3-5]. Other information systems such as EDP (Electronic Data Processing), MS/OP (Management Science and Operations Research) and MIS (Management Information Systems) have made contributions to decision support from the perspectives of data/information provision and management, but they also do not address the changing nature of decision making and provide corresponding solutions [6]. One stream of research attempted to address this issue was the proposal of DSS generators [7-8]. The DSS generators can assemble necessary capabilities from a set of DSS tools (new technology, new languages, new hardware and software) to configure specific DSS faster and easier to develop models, data and user interfaces that are customised to the application's requirements. The IDSE however goes one step further, which can integrate capabilities from a set of systems to configure a computer environment for varied decisions under varied situations, including decision making on ill-structured and non-structured decision problems.

　　IDSE is designed and developed based on the ODSS concept and therefore differs from a GDSS (Group Decision Support Systems) and EIS (Executive Information Systems). GDSS and EIS (now called Enterprise Information Systems) were both developed as complementary to but more powerful support tools than traditional DSS, in the sense that GDSS can provide brainstorming, idea evaluation and communication facilities to support team problem solving [9-11], and EIS extended the scope of DSS from personal or small group use to the corporate level and can provide a wide variety of information such as critical success metrics, key information indicators, reports with the ability to drilldown to underlying detail, budget information, plans and objectives, competitive information, news and more [12-14]. ODSS were developed based on the advances in GDSS and EIS, but had its focus on organisational decision making. It provides a mechanism for a large, geographically dispersed, decentralised organisation to allow individual managers to make decisions within their own domains while maintaining consistency with the decisions made by other managers and organisational goals. In short, it provides distributed decision support to distributed decision making on varied applications. Carter et al [2] summarised the difference of an ODSS from a traditional DSS in five aspects including purposes, politics, approach to building, focus on functions and components. This paper will focus on its technical side and discuss IDSE from system integration viewpoint (i.e. the components and relationships between components) and explore how the system integration approach will provide new strengths to ODSS.

The characteristics of the IDSE lie in two dimensions, as summarised in Figure 1: firstly its flexibility of functionality, and secondly its capability to support organisational rather than individual or team (group) decision making.

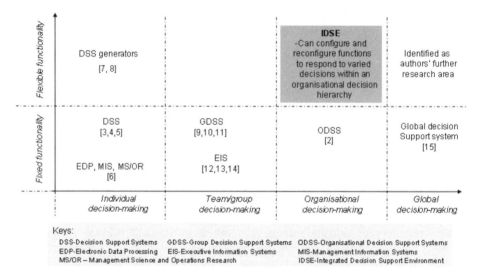

Figure 1. IDSE position relative to DSS and other information systems

2. Framework of the Integrated Decision Support Environment

The basic paradigm for a traditional DSS is that it consists of three major components: a model base management system (MBMS) with a model base, a database management system (DBMS) with a database, and a user interface (UI) dialog system that manages the interaction between the user, and the model base and the database. Due to the limitation of the functions provided by the three components and the "hardwiring" between the components, a DSS is destined to support specific applications with specific decisions under specific settings for specific users (decision makers), as illustrated in Figure 2(a). In an ODSS, these three basic components are still often the same as those of a traditional DSS, although there may be differences on how the components are designed and used.

To support organisational decision making, with varied applications that deal with varied decisions under varied settings for varied users (decision makers), an ODSS requires additional elements and functions. For example, network for communication. More importantly, it requires flexible but reliable mechanisms that allow agile configuration of the system components to provide support to the varied applications. This is realised through a hybrid integration approach within IDSE, as shown in the Figure 2(b). The three components (i.e. the UI, the DBMS and the MBMS) comprise the basic components of the IDSE. The three basic components provide constant and fundamental support to applications (represented by a straight through symbol ⬚↑ in the Figure 2(b)). IDSE has four additional components: a DM (decision management) component, an RR (resource reasoning) component, a CPM (change prediction and management) component, and a CW (collaborative working) component. Their support to applications is flexible based on the configuration of the components (represented by a switch symbol ⊠ in the Figure 2(b)). This section will discuss the key additional components of IDSE and their relationships, and Section 3 will discuss the integration issue in detail.

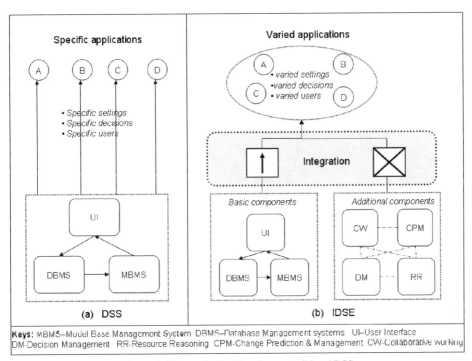

Figure 2. How an IDSE differs from a traditional DSS

2.1. The relationships between the three basic components

Figure 3 shows how the three subsystems (the MBMS, the DBMS and the UI) identified as basic components of IDSE work together to support decision makers (users). Decision makers initiate the communication with the IDSE and provide necessary inputs. The UI subsystem then talks to the MBMS to answer user queries, performs relevant sensitivity (what-if) and other analytical tasks. In the meantime, it talks to the DBMS to access data as required. The DBMS also provides direct data and information support to the MBMS. The solid arrows in the Figure 3 show that direct data and information access and sharing occur between the components. The direction of the arrows represents information flow. The close relationship between the three basic components implies that a tight integration approach would be appropriate in this case (to be discussed in Section 3 in detail).

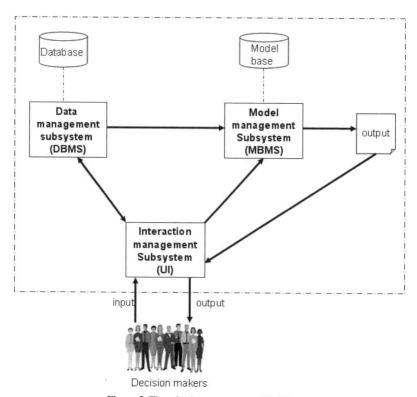

Figure 3. Three basic components of IDSE

2.2. IDSE additional components and their relationships

Efficient and effective organisational decision making depends not only on the decision maker making good judgement on resources that are required for the decision tasks, but also on good management of decision hierarchy where decision makers position in, and decision maker's interaction and collaboration with fellow decision makers. Especially when decision makers try to make changes of the decisions, how the consequences will propagate along the decision hierarchy. Based on the above considerations, four key additional components have been identified for the IDSE: a decision management (DM) component, a resource reasoning (RR) component, a change prediction and management (CPM) component and a collaborative working (CW) component. The DM component is designed to manage decision hierarchies and dependencies in an organisation as well as COA (Course of Action) planning. The RR component provides IDSE with the capability to search for the right resources including facilities and human resources across organisation units for decision tasks. This is developed from state-of-the-art ontology mapping techniques and a well-developed resource knowledge repository. The major function of the CPM component is to provide the IDSE with the capability of assessing any changes of decisions and their consequence propagation along hierarchies and organisational units before a change is carried out. Finally, the CW component provides interactive and collaborative capability to team decision making in an organisation when mutual decision goals (i.e. the organisational goals) are defined but decision preferences vary for different decision makers at different organisational levels. While these four components have their distinguished functions, the specification of the dependencies between the components allows them to communicate and to interact with each other, and to invoke and call services from each other when necessary. Figure 4 illustrates the relationships between the four components represented with SysML [16]. In the component diagram, the directions of the arrows show the information flow from one component to another, and the labels attached to the arrows show the nature of the messages that are communicated between the components.

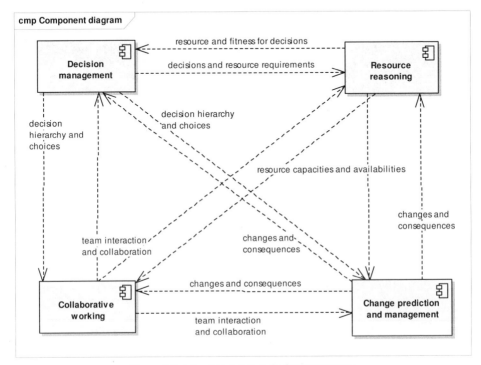

Figure 4. Relationships between the four components

2.3. IDSE communication mechanisms

This section discusses three communication mechanisms that enable distributed decision making across dispersed organisation units and determine IDSE performance: communication standard XML and remote procedure call XML-RPC, Java Networking Model and port mapping, and secure communication mechanisms.

2.3.1. Communication standard XML and XML-RPC

Communication standards are necessary because they provide a mutual "language" for IDSE components to "understand" each other's request and response. XML (eXtensible Mark-up Language) [17] has been used as a standard for IDSE communication because of its purity (pure data without side factors), popularity and user-friendliness. When IDSE components communicate over network using HTTP, XML-RPC (Remote Procedure Call) is used as the remote call protocol. An XML-RPC message is an

HTTP-POST request. The body of the request is in XML. A procedure executes on the server and the value it returns is also formatted in XML.

The basic construct of an XML-RPC protocol for IDSE is shown in Figure 5, viewed with XMLSpy. Four elements as the first level children of *<IDSEMethodCall>* are important to communication: a *<sender>*, a *<receiver>*, a *<methodName>* and a number of *<param>*. The definition of the *<sender>* and *<receiver>* ensures that the message is communicated between the right components (from the right source to the right target). *<functionName>* element indicates the nature of the function (the reason to call a method), e.g. to report an error when something goes wrong. The details of the error then are described in *<params>*.

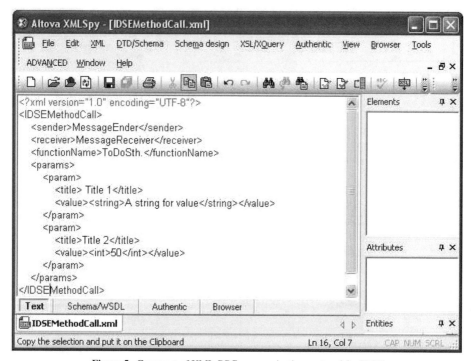

Figure 5. Construct of XML-RPC communication protocol for IDSE

2.3.2. Java Networking Model and port mapping

The IDSE employs a client/ server architecture on network, communication between different components will need the identification of the IP address and the port number. The following figure 6 illustrates the Java Networking Model. The server assigns a port number. When a client requests a connection, the server opens the socket connection with an *accept()* method. The client then is able to establish a connection with the host on the assigned port. Thus, a communication channel is created with both server and client knowing where the communication is from and where to go for a particular purpose. To avoid communication chaos and maintain consistency, specific port numbers are assigned to all defined components of the IDSE.

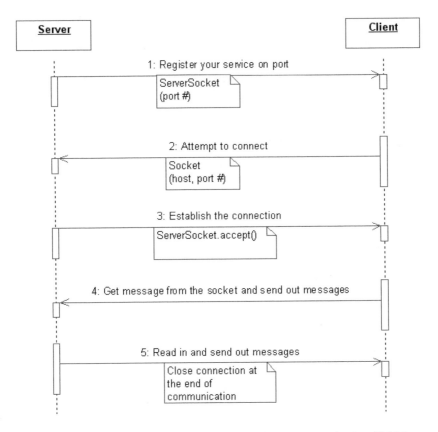

Figure 6. J a v a   N e t w o r k i n g   M o d e l   w i t h   U M L

2.3.3. Secure network communication mechanisms

Any information not transmitted through a secure channel on a network is subject to unseen eavesdropping. If security of information is an issue, then it is essential precautions be taken to provide secure communication between IDSE components. Java Secure Socket Extension (JSSE) has been identified and implemented for IDSE first prototype to meet the above requirements (Other methods could be incorporated as required). There are three key steps in secure data and information transmission from a Sender to a Receiver, as shown in Figure 7. These are encryption, decryption and authentication.

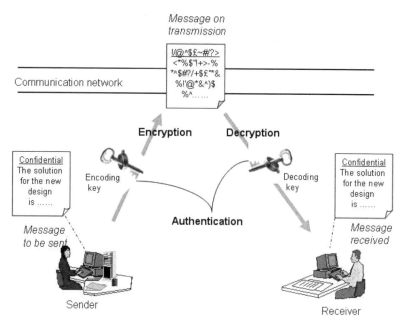

Figure 7. JSSE secure communication for IDSE

Encryption is the process of encoding messages before they enter the network, then decoding them at the receiving end of the transfer, so that receivers can interpret them [18]. The process works because if you scramble messages before you send them, eavesdroppers who might intercept them cannot decipher them without the decoding key. Some authentication mechanisms and software tools have been available for the key management such as self-signed certification and third-party certification. If you encrypt a message using your private key, you have "signed" it. A receiver can verify that the message came from you by using your public key to decode it. Third-party authority certificate is able to handle the issue with more sophisticated solutions. Secure Socket Layer (SSL), developed by Netscape, is currently a popular public-key encryption method used on the Internet and is implemented within IDSE.

3. A hybrid integration approach for the IDSE

Section 2 has discussed the basic components, additional components and the communication mechanisms for IDSE. This section will discuss a hybrid integration approach that binds all the components to the communication network to form the IDSE, which works as a coherent software environment to provide reliable and flexible support to organisational decision making. This is an evolution of the authors' previous research on a hybrid integration approach for distributed design co-ordination [19].

The hybrid integration approach taken to develop the IDSE is a combination of tight integration (through integration standards) and loose integration (through integration middleware). Specifically, the integration of the three basic components is undertaken through a tight approach, and the integration of additional components is undertaken through the loose integration approach. The difference between the tight integration (also called coupling) and loose integration (also called cohesion) within the

IDSE is that tight integration binds components (such as DBMS and MBMS) together in such a way that they are dependent on each other, sharing data, methods and interfaces. In contrast to tight integration, loose integration is the "act or state of sticking together" or "the logical agreement" [20]. Cohesively integrated components (such as DM, RR, CPM and CW) are independent from one another. Changes to any source and target components should not affect the others directly. In this case, information is still shared between components but without worrying about changes to the components, leveraging some type of middleware layer to move information between components, and make adjustments for differences in component semantics. The tradeoffs have been considered in the IDSE through a combination use of integration middleware for cohesion and integration standards for tight coupling, as shown in Figure 8.

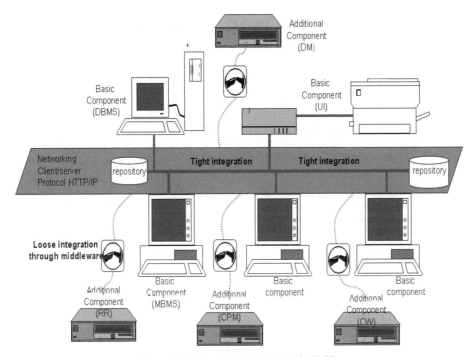

Figure 8. Tight and loose integration for IDSE

The advantage of having a combination of tight and loose integration within the IDSE is that the balance between reliability and flexibility is maintained. Through the loose integration with middleware, components such as DM, RR, CPM and CW can be added to, changed or removed from IDSE without typically requiring changes to any of the other components according to the varied application requirements in the organisational decision making domain. Integration middleware (a special piece of software in the case of IDSE) thus provides the technology infrastructure of most-cohesive integration solution. It is able to account for the differences between components, accommodating differences in application semantics within a middle-tier process. Despite the flexibility provided by the integration middleware, common decision making processes are to be reused within IDSE, therefore tight integration through standards such as XML and XML-RPC provides high speed and method sharing with great reliability. The disadvantage of having the hybrid integration approach is its complexity of implementation. In the future, IDSE will look into exploration of Web Service as an integration standard, and Java EE (Java Enterprise Edition platform) will be investigated as the new integration broker for IDSE.

4. Discussion and conclusions

This paper has proposed an Integration Decision Support Environment based on a study of DSS evolution and challenges of decision making in modern organisations. The key features of the IDSE which distinguishes itself from a traditional DSS can be summarised as:
(1) IDSE can support varied applications, i.e. varied decisions under varied situations for varied decision makers. Traditional DSS normally support specific applications with specific decisions under specific situations for a single decision maker working on a stand-alone computer.
(2) IDSE consists of more functional components than a traditional DSS. In addition to the basic components of a database management system, a model base management system and a user interaction system, the IDSE also has a decision management component, a resource reasoning component, a change prediction and management component, and a collaborative working component. These components empower IDSE with extra functionality that can manage decision hierarchy, reason the right resources for decisions based on ontology mapping, predict changes and propagation path, as well as team interaction and collaboration.
(3) The combined use of a tight integration and loose integration approach within IDSE provides good balance between the integration reliability and flexibility.

Further work will be research on new additional components to expand IDSE functionality to support global decision making [15, 21]. In the meantime, exploration on new integration mechanisms including Web Service and Java EE technology will be undertaken to enable global communication.

Acknowledgement

The research reported in this paper was undertaken at the Computer Aided Design Centre in University of Strathclyde. It was funded by both BAE Systems and UK Engineering and Physical Science Research Council (EPSRC) under grant number EP/D505461/1 for project "Network Enabled Capability Through Innovative Systems Engineering (NECTISE)".

References

[1]   D. Lee, P. Newman, R. Price: *Decision Making in Organisations*. Financial Times Management, 1999.
[2]   G.M. Carter, M.P. Murray, R.G. Walker, W.E. Walker: *Building Organisational Decision Support Systems*. Academic Press Inc. Boston, 1992.
[3]   J.P. Shim, M. Warkentin, J.F. Courtney, D.J. Power, R. Sharda, C. Carlsson: Past, present, and future of decision support technology. *Decision Support Systems* 33 (2002), 111-126.

[4]   C. Carlsson, E. Turban: DSS: directions for the next decade. *Decision Support Systems* 33 (2002), 105-110.
[5]   S.B. Eom: Decision support systems research: current state and trends. *Industrial Management and Data Systems* 99(1999), 213-220.
[6]   G.W. Hopple: *The state of the art in decision support systems.* QED Information Sciences Inc, 1988.
[7]   R.H. Sprague, H.J. Watson: *Decision Support Systems: Putting Theory into Practice.* Prentice-Hall International Editions, 1986.
[8]   K. Hemant, S. Sridhar, C. Herrick: Beyond spreadsheets: tools for building decision support systems. *Computer*, March 1999.
[9]   G. DeSanctis, R.B. Gallupe: A foundation for the study of group decision support systems. *Management Science* 33(1987), 589-609.
[10] R. Anson, R.P. Bostrom, B.E. Wynne.: An experiment assessing group system and facilitator effects on meeting outcomes. *Management Science* 41(1995), 189-208.
[11] M. Limayem, P. Banerjee, L. Ma: Impact of GDSS: opening the black box. *Decision Support Systems* 42 (2006), 945-957.
[12] J.J. Elam, D.G. Leidner: EIS adoption, use and impact: the executive perspective. *Decision Support Systems* 14(1995), 89-103.
[13] T. Kosaka: *The first investigation of executive information systems practices in Japanese firms.* Proceedings of the TIMS/ORMA Conference, Boston, 1994.
[14] D.J. Power: A brief history of decision support systems. DSS Resource.COM, 2003. available at http://DSSResources.COM/history/dsshistory.html
[15] S. Liu, R.I.M. Young: Utilising information and knowledge models to support global manufacturing co-ordination decisions. *International Journal of Computer Integrated Manufacturing* 17(2004), 479-492.
[16] SysML: System Modelling Language, available online at: http://www.omgsysml.org/
[17] XML: eXtensible Mark-up Language from W3C, available at: http://www.w3.org/xml
[18] L Jessup, J. Valacich: *Information Systems Today: Why Information System Matters?* Pearson Prentice Hall, New Jersey. Second edition, 2006.
[19] R.I. Whitfield, A.H.B. Duffy, G. Coates, W. Hills: Distributed design co-ordination. *Research in Engineering Design* 13(2002), 243-252.
[20] D.S. Linthicum: *Next Generation Application Integration: from Simple Information to Web Services.* Addison-Wesley, Boston, 2004.
[21] S. Liu, R.I.M. Young: An exploration of key information models and their relationships in global manufacturing decision support. *Proceedings of the Institution of Mechanical Engineers, Part B: Journal of Engineering Manufacture* 221(2007), 711-724.

Collaborative Decision Making: Perspectives and Challenges
P. Zaraté et al. (Eds.)
IOS Press, 2008

Supporting decisions about the introduction of genetically modified crops

Marko BOHANEC[1,a,b] and Martin ŽNIDARŠIČ[a]

[a]*Jožef Stefan Institute, Ljubljana, Slovenia*
[b]*University of Nova Gorica, Nova Gorica, Slovenia*

Abstract. Genetically modified (GM) crops have become a real option in modern agriculture. They offer advantages for agricultural production, but they also raise concerns about their ecological and economic impacts. Decisions about GM crops are complex and call for decision support. This paper presents an application of qualitative multi-attribute modeling methodology DEX to the development of model-based decision support systems in two European research projects, ECOGEN and SIGMEA. Three main multi-attribute models were developed for the assessment of GM-crop impacts in terms of (1) economy and ecology, (2) soil quality, and (3) co-existence. All these models were developed in collaboration of domain experts and decision analysts using the software tool DEXi. In the paper, we describe the applied methodology and outline the three models, their implementation and some results of their application. In particular, we discuss our lessons learned and highlight the strong and weak points of this approach.

Keywords. model-based decision support systems, qualitative multi-attribute models, expert collaboration, application in agronomy, genetically modified crops

Introduction

Decision problems that arose with the introduction of genetically modified (GM) crops in agriculture are very diverse in their topics, scales and complexities. However, most of them have one thing in common: they are interdisciplinary and thus require collaboration of experts from various disciplines. The interdisciplinary nature of these problems demands considerable efforts for the purpose of mutual understanding, communication and collaboration.

It is not surprising that the use of decision models is beneficial in the analysis of complex problems. However, in interdisciplinary settings, such as the one described above, decision models can serve also for a common knowledge representation and an efficient form of communication. Communicating knowledge through decision models helps keeping a common focus and a common level of representational detail. Already during the model construction process, we can sometimes indicate which parts of the problem domain are lacking knowledge and need further research. Later on, the model's prototypes inspire discussions and promote sharing of expert opinions.

This paper presents three models and corresponding software that were developed for the purpose of decision analysis in the European projects ECOGEN and SIGMEA.

---

[1] Corresponding author: Marko Bohanec, Jožef Stefan Institute, Department of Knowledge Technologies, Jamova cesta 39, SI-1000, Ljubljana, Slovenia, E-mail: marko.bohanec@ijs.si

They cover different problems that are associated with the introduction of GM crops in agriculture. The use of decision models in these settings proved to be beneficial, not only for decision analysis, but also for the purpose of communication and common knowledge representation.

1. Background

GM crops represent a recent innovation in agriculture. On the one hand, GM crops have genetic characteristics, such as resistance to pests and tolerance to herbicides, which are beneficial for agricultural production. On the other hand, the use of GM crops raises concerns about their potential ecological and economic consequences [1]. Decision-making about GM crops is extremely difficult as it involves many factors that are difficult to assess and control, but may have significant long-term or irreversible consequences to the environment and food production [2].

The authors of this paper were engaged as decision analysts in two projects funded by the European Commission: ECOGEN [3] and SIGMEA [4]. These projects investigated the impacts of using GM crops in European agriculture. ECOGEN was more specific of the two: it addressed ecological and economic impacts of using GM maize at the farm level and was particularly focused on soil biology. SIGMEA extended this focus to other types of GM crops, to the regional-level context and to the co-existence of GM and non-GM crop production.

2. Methodology

An important goal of both ECOGEN and SIGMEA was to develop computer-based decision support systems [5,6] for the assessment of impacts of using GM crops. Methodologically, we have addressed this goal with the construction of model-based decision support systems, taking the approach of qualitative multi-attribute modeling and using the method DEX [7,8]. Following this methodology, one develops a hierarchical model, consisting of qualitative attributes and decision rules. This model is used to evaluate and analyze decision alternatives. A qualitative DEX model is characterized by the following:

- Each model consists of a number of hierarchically structured variables called *attributes*. Terminal nodes of the hierarchy represent *input attributes*. These are aggregated through several levels of *aggregate attributes* into the overall assessment, which is represented by one or more *root attributes*.
- All the attributes in the model are *qualitative*: they can take only discrete symbolic values.
- The aggregation of values in the model is defined by *decision rules*.

The principal software tool that implements the DEX methodology is called DEXi [9]. DEXi is easy to use and allows very fast and convenient model construction. It facilitates the development of attribute trees, definition of decision rules, evaluation of options, "what-if" analysis and graphical output. DEXi is freely available at http://kt.ijs.si/MarkoBohanec/dexi.html.

Usually, DEX models are developed in collaboration between decision analysts and experts in the given field. Typically, experts suggest attributes and decision rules, while decision analysts conduct the process and define components of the model. The model is gradually "hand-crafted" through the four steps [8]: (1) identifying attributes, (2) structuring attributes, (3) defining attribute scales, and (4) defining decision rules. The steps can be iterated if necessary.

There were three major DEX models developed in ECOGEN and SIGMEA, called "Grignon Model", ESQI and SMAC. The "Grignon Model" is a large and complex model aimed at the assessment of ecological and economic impacts of maize cropping systems at a farm level. ESQI (ECOGEN Soil Quality Index) is a specific model for the assessment of the impact of cropping systems on soil quality. SMAC (SIGMEA MAize Coexistence) assesses the co-existence of GM and non-GM maize at the field level. These models are outlined in the following three sections, respectively.

3. The "Grignon Model"

The "Grignon Model" [10] is a qualitative multi-attribute DEX model aimed at economic and ecological assessment of cropping systems that involve GM and non-GM maize. Cropping systems are described by four groups of features: (1) crop sub-type, (2) regional and farm-level context, (3) crop protection and crop management strategies, and (4) expected characteristics of the harvest. The cropping systems evaluation is based on four groups of ecological and two groups of economic indicators: biodiversity, water quality, greenhouse gasses, soil biodiversity, above-ground biodiversity, production value and variable costs.

Overall, the model consists of 22 basic and 63 aggregate attributes. The two topmost levels of its structure are shown in Figure 1. There are two root aggregate attributes, ECOLOGY and ECONOMY, each of which is further decomposed into the corresponding ecological and economic indicators. The attributes below the top two levels are decomposed further, giving an elaborate and complex hierarchical structure. It is beyond the scope of this paper to describe the structure in detail; the reader is referred to [10]. Nevertheless, we wish to highlight the complexity of the model. This is illustrated by Figure 2, which shows the complete hierarchical decomposition of two (out of four) ecological indicators: *soil biodiversity* and above-ground *biodiversity*. Notice that the parent attributes are gradually decomposed into more and more detail. The decomposition ends at input attributes that describe basic features of cropping systems, which are represented by the attributes shown at the very bottom of Figure 2. The structure is a true hierarchy (i.e., directed acyclic graph): it contains attributes, such as *pest control*, which influence more than a single parent attribute.

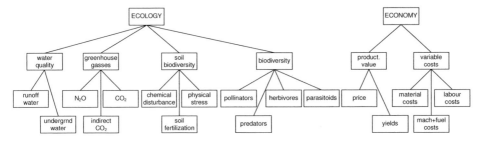

Figure 1. The two topmost levels of the "Grignon Model".

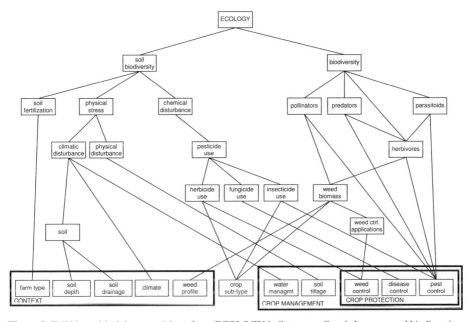

Figure 2. Full hierarchical decomposition of two ECOLOGY indicators: soil and above-ground biodiversity.

Table 1 illustrates another important aspect of DEX modeling: decision rules. Decision rules specify a bottom-up aggregation of values in the model; each aggregate (internal) attribute has an associated set of rules. Table 1 shows specific rules defined by a soil expert that specify the aggregation of *physical stress*, *soil fertilization* and *chemical disturbance* into the aggregate attribute *soil biodiversity*. Each numbered row in the table represents a rule that maps qualitative *low-medium-high* values of the former three attributes into the increasing five-valued ordinal scale of the latter attribute. The notation '*' represents any value, and the symbols '<=' and '>=' denote comparison operators. The second row in the table presents average weights of the contributing attributes, which are estimated by linear regression from the defined rules (see [11] for further information on this method and on the relation between weights and rules in DEX).

Table 1. Expert-defined decision rules for *soil biodiversity*.

	physical_stress	soil_fertilization	chem_disturbance	soil_biodiversity
	60%	25%	15%	
1	high	low	*	1
2	high	<=medium	high	1
3	high	medium	>=medium	2
4	high	>=medium	medium	2
5	high	*high*	<=medium	2
6	medium	low	high	2
7	high	*high*	*low*	3
8	medium	<=medium	>=medium	3
9	medium	*	medium	3
10	medium	medium	*	3
11	medium	>=medium	<=medium	3
12	*low*	low	high	3
13	medium	*high*	*low*	4
14	*low*	low	>=medium	4
15	*low*	<=medium	medium	4
16	*low*	medium	<=medium	4
17	*low*	>=medium	*low*	5
18	*low*	*high*	*	5

The "Grignon Model" has been developed in collaboration of six experts drawn from agronomy, ecology and economics, and two decision analysts. The foundation for the model was developed during a series of meetings that took place in 2005 at INRA, Grignon, France (hence the name of the model). The model has been then refined through an extensive e-mail communication and four face-to-face meetings.

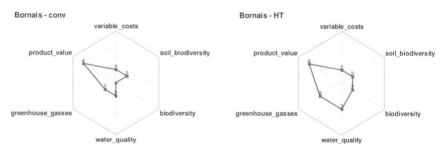

Figure 3. Evaluation of two cropping systems in Bornais, France.

To date, this model has been applied and evaluated in three applications. The first one involved six hypothetical (but typical) cropping systems and was conducted mainly to verify the model and explore its potential. The remaining two applications addressed real cropping systems and locations. In one case, we analyzed eight cropping systems that were studied within the ECOGEN project, and in the other case we studied 14 cropping systems applied on four field locations in France. A typical application result is shown in Figure 3, which presents the evaluation of two maize cropping systems used in Bornais, France. The first one involves conventional (non-GM) maize, and the second one involves HT (herbicide-tolerant) GM maize. Overall, using the five-valued ordinal scale, these cropping systems were evaluated as 2 and 3, respectively. Figure 3 presents the decomposition of the overall evaluation into partial evaluations corresponding to the six attributes that occur at the second level of the attribute hierarchy. These evaluations indicate some possible advantages of the HT maize with respect to *greenhouse gasses*, *water quality* and *biodiversity*.

4. Soil Quality Index

ECOGEN Soil Quality Index (ESQI for short) is a specific DEXi model to assess soil quality from the observed biological parameters. The main aim was to produce a soil quality score based on soil biodiversity and soil functioning, using the field measurement data obtained during the ECOGEN project [13]. In the model, this is reflected in the hierarchy of attributes, which is split into two main parts (Figure 4): the smaller sub-tree on the left assesses soil diversity using indicators of species richness, whereas the larger sub-hierarchy on the right assesses soil functioning using indicators which mostly depend on the biomass of soil organisms. The elements of the model are described in detail in [12]. The techniques for the sampling, extraction, enumeration and identification of soil organisms are further detailed in [13,14,15].

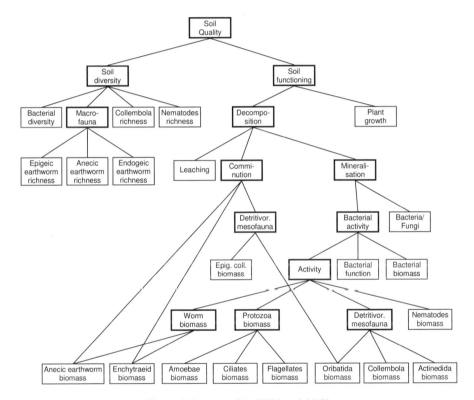

Figure 4. Structure of the ESQI model [12].

In total, the ESQI model consists of 21 basic and 13 aggregate attributes. This model was developed similarly as the "Grignon Model", with six contributing experts, five of which were soil biologists, and two decision analysts. The development took three one-day face-to-face meetings, followed by some minor e-mail correspondence.

The results of this development were twofold. First, using ECOGEN data collected in 2003, we thoroughly analyzed eight cropping systems on three locations: Foulum in Denmark, and Varois and Narbons in France (for site details see [13]). The results are primarily interesting for soil biologists. At this point, however, we wish to emphasize that this analysis revealed relevant scientific and technical findings, such as [12]:

> The use of *Bt*-maize in Foulum positively affects *Soil functioning* (with ploughing) and *Soil diversity* (when using minimum tillage). Minimum tillage positively affects *Nematode richness*, *Detritivorous mesofauna* and *Protozoa biomass*, leading to better *Activity*.

The second result is a publicly available implementation of the ESQI model at http://kt.ijs.si/MarkoBohanec/ESQI/ESQI.php. This web page provides a basic user interface for data entry and evaluation of a single crop-management option. On the data-entry page (Figure 5, left), the user can enter the input by simply clicking appropriate attribute values. After evaluation, the web page presents results in a tree-like form similar to DEXi (Figure 5, right). In the case of missing data, the tree can be pruned at any internal aggregate attribute. Notice that in Figure 5, the model is pruned at *Macrofauna diversity* and *Detritivorous mesofauna (M)*.

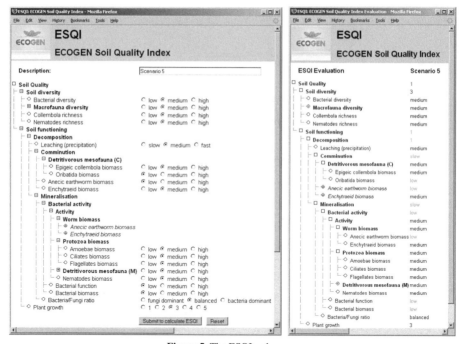

Figure 5. The ESQI web page.

5. Maize Co-Existence

The third model, called SMAC (SIGMEA MAize Co-Existence), is aimed at the assessment of coexistence between GM and conventional maize at a field level [16]. Input attributes of the model describe fields on which maize is grown (see the bottom part of Figure 6). We assess the situation where there is one GM field surrounded by several non-GM fields. The question is whether these fields can co-exist, that is, if the level of genetic interference (which in maize occurs mainly by cross-pollination) is lower than some prescribed threshold. The interference is expressed in terms of *adventitious presence* (AP), which refers to the unintentional and incidental commingling of trace amounts of one type of seed, grain or food product with another. According to EU regulations, the threshold for co-existence is usually set to 0.9 %. In the SMAC model (Figure 6), the AP is determined according to the properties of the GM field and its surrounding environment (*organic* and *GM* production in the *neighborhood*, used *seeds*, *regional GM pressure*), and its relation with each other non-GM field (*distance* between the fields, *relative size* of the fields, prevailing *wind direction*, etc.).

The SMAC model has 13 basic and 8 aggregate attributes. It was developed by two experts and two decision analysts during two face-to-face meetings. It is interesting to note that decision rules for *cross pollination* and below, which represent the essential and most difficult part of the model, were not formulated by the experts themselves, as elsewhere in the model, but were derived from simulations obtained previously by the system called MAPOD® [17]. MAPOD simulates the biological behavior of maize plants and assesses the amount of exchanged pollen under various conditions.

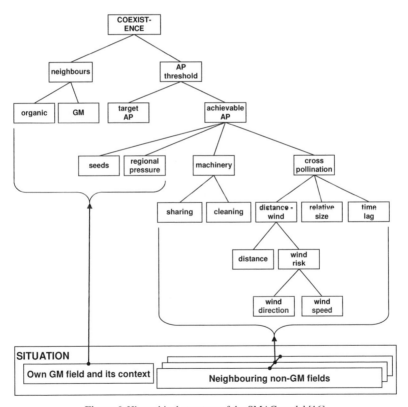

Figure 6. Hierarchical structure of the SMAC model [16].

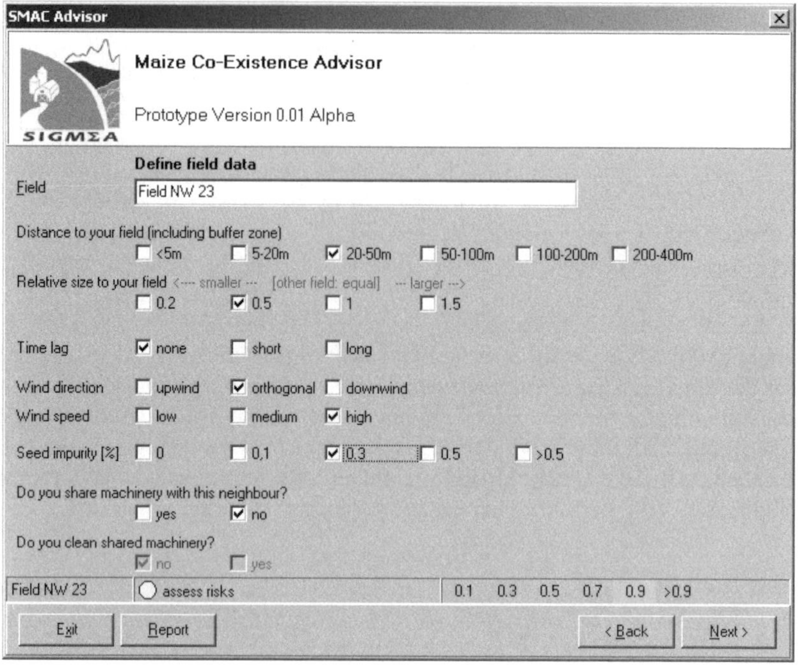

Figure 7. SMAC Advisor user interface: gathering data about a non-GM field.

We implemented the SMAC model in a decision-support tool called *SMAC Advisor* [16]. SMAC Advisor provides a friendly wizard-type user interface (Figure 7) in which it guides the user (farmer, administrative worker or policy maker in agronomy) through the steps of the decision process: gathering data about the involved fields, assessing the achievable adventitious presence and giving one of the four recommendations: GM farming is (1) allowed, (2) disallowed, (3) possibly allowed, but continue assessing risks, or (4) possibly disallowed, but continue considering other measures of AP prevention.

6. Discussion

The three models described in this paper present three working applications of qualitative multi-attribute modeling methodology DEX and the software tool DEXi in agronomy. They are aimed at providing decision-support in the complex area of using genetically modified crops. The main contributions of this work are:

- developed three DEXi models for assessing various aspects of GM cropping systems: ecological and economic impacts (the "Grignon Model"), impacts on soil quality (ESQI) and the co-existence of GM and non-GM crops (SMAC);
- analyzed a number of specific cropping systems in France and Denmark;
- implemented the publicly available Web-based implementation of ESQI;
- implemented the "wizard-type" decision-support tool SMAC Advisor.

During this development, we have learned a number of lessons, both positive and negative. The good news is that the DEX methodology turned out to be particularly suitable for modeling this type of decision problems in agronomy, which are complex, which integrate a number of disciplines, such as agronomy, biology, ecology and economics, and which do not have an established formal methodology for the assessment of cropping systems. DEX's qualitative approach, which uses symbolic attributes and decision rules, seemed the right choice and was also very well accepted by the experts.

The developed models represent a practical means of encapsulating complex systems and provide a general overview to the assessment of cropping systems. The models contain a considerable amount of knowledge collected in the underlying disciplines. This knowledge is explicitly and clearly articulated in the form of attributes and their relationships, formally represented by a hierarchical structure and decision rules. This formal representation can be easily communicated among experts, discussed and possibly adapted using available computer tools.

All the models are operational, either through DEXi or in the form of special-purpose software. In addition to the evaluation and comparison of cropping systems, the tools facilitate explanation, which is obtained by "drilling-down" into lower levels of the models, looking at the evaluations obtained there and finding out how these contributed to the final assessment. Furthermore, the models can be (and have been) used to answer "what-if" questions [12] and even to propose new cropping systems. Inherent to the DEX methodology is also the ability of models to deal with missing or imprecise data of assessed cropping systems.

On a less positive side, however, we should point out that these models address the decision problems at a very general level: they integrate many different disciplines, but cannot capture specific details of any of these disciplines. The models use discrete descriptive attributes, which are granular and qualitative, and all numeric variables must be discretized. This inevitably requires a generalization and simplification of the modeled concepts. The models' operation is governed by "if-then" rules, which are "shallow" in the sense that they only define direct relationships between conditions and consequences, but do not model any "deeper" properties (e.g., biological, physical, chemical, economical) of the underlying systems. Clearly, there is a need to integrate both qualitative and quantitative information in such models. This can be possibly addressed either by an extension of DEX itself or supplementing it with one or more existing quantitative multi-attribute methods.

As it turned out during the model development process, "hand-crafting" of such models is difficult and requires a lot of effort. The development requires communication and understanding between decision analysts and experts from various disciplines. In our case, face-to-face meetings were indispensable: they boosted the development process, which was then continued through e-mail communication. However, the communication by e-mail has been found much less satisfactory and tended to fade away after just a few weeks. This aspect of the process needs improvement, possibly by using better communication channels, such as web meetings, and also by providing and using appropriate web-based group-support software tools.

In spite of all the experience gained in previous applications of DEXi in other problem domains, agronomy appeared particularly hard and challenging for the existing methodology and software. Previously, DEXi was able to work only with tree-structured models, but could not deal with general hierarchies (i.e., directed acyclic graphs), which were required for this problem. Consequently, we had to extend DEXi with this feature. But even this was not enough. Eventually, this problem motivated us to start developing a new software tool called proDEX [18]. In comparison with DEXi, this program extends the modeling capabilities using general hierarchical concept structures, probabilistic utility functions, and numerical values of basic attributes.

Further work will be taken in three main directions. First, in the application area of agronomy and GM crops, the developed models will be further validated and applied in specific cropping-system assessment problems. There are plans to extend the models in many ways: to other GM crops than maize, such as oil-seed rape, to the regional rather than field level, to more than one agricultural season, etc. Currently, this work continues in the framework of the EU project Co-Extra [19], which investigates the co-existence and traceability of GM products in food and feed supply chains. Second, from the methodological viewpoint, we see the challenge in combining qualitative DEX models with other types of models, such as quantitative or mechanistic, that are used in decision analysis, agronomy, ecology and economy. This includes the comparison of DEX with established quantitative multi-criteria methods, such as AHP and ELECTRE. This also includes the development of new software tools such as proDEX. Third, as the development of such models requires an intensive expert collaboration, we need to investigate the use of video-conferencing and other web-based collaboration-support tools specifically for the development of DEX models.

Acknowledgements

ECOGEN and SIGMEA were funded by the contracts QLK5-CT-2002-01666 and FP6-SSP1-2002-502981, respectively, from the European Commission. The work of Jožef Stefan Institute is supported by the Slovenian Research Agency programme *Knowledge Technologies* (2004-2008). The authors thank the contributing experts: Frédérique Angevin, Sandra Caul, Jérôme Cortet, Marko Debeljak, Sašo Džeroski, Bryan Griffiths, Paul H. Krogh, Antoine Messéan, Sara Scatasta, Jacqueline Thompson and Justus Wesseler.

References

[1]   Uzogara, S. G., 2000. The impact of genetic modification of human foods in the 21st century: A review. *Biotechnology Advances* 18(3), 179–206.
[2]   Hails, R., 2002. Assessing the risks associated with new agricultural practices. *Nature* 418, 685–688.
[3]   ECOGEN, 2002. *Soil ecological and economic evaluation of genetically modified crops.* Project, funded by the Fifth European Community Framework Programme, contract QLK5-CT-2002-01666. http://www.ecogen.dk
[4]   SIGMEA, 2003. *Sustainable introduction of genetically modified crops into European agriculture.* Specific targeted research project, funded by the Sixth European Community Framework Programme, contract SSP1-2002-502981. http://sigmea.dyndns.org/
[5]   Mallach, E.G., 2000. *Decision support and data warehouse systems.* McGraw-Hill.
[6]   Turban, E., Aronson, J.E., Liang, T.P., 2004. *Decision support systems and intelligent systems* (7th Edition). Prentice Hall.
[7]   Bohanec, M., Rajkovič, V., 1990. DEX: An expert system shell for decision support, *Sistemica* 1(1), 145-157.
[8]   Bohanec, M., 2003. Decision support. In: D. Mladenić, N. Lavrač, M. Bohanec, S. Moyle (Editors), *Data mining and decision support: Integration and collaboration.* Kluwer Academic Publishers, 23–35.

[9] Bohanec, M, 2007: *DEXi: Program for multi-attribute decision making, User's manual, Version 2.00.* IJS Report DP-9596, Jožef Stefan Institute, Ljubljana. http://kt.ijs.si/MarkoBohanec/pub/DEXiManual20p.pdf

[10] Bohanec, M., Messéan, A., Scatasta, S., Džeroski, S., Žnidaršič, M., 2005. A qualitative multi-attribute model for economic and ecological evaluation of genetically modified crops. In: *EnviroInfo Brno 2005*, Masaryk University in Brno, 661–668.

[11] Bohanec, M., Zupan, B., 2004. A function-decomposition method for development of hierarchical multi-attribute decision models, *Decision Support Systems* 36, 215-233.

[12] Bohanec, M., Cortet, J., Griffiths, B., Žnidaršič, M., Debeljak, M., Caul, S., Thompson, J., Krogh, P.H., 2007. A qualitative multi-attribute model for assessing the impact of cropping systems on soil quality. *Pedobiologia* 51(3), 207–218.

[13] Andersen, M.N., Sausse, C., Lacroix, B., Caul, S., Messéan, A., 2007. Agricultural studies of GM maize and field experimental infrastructure of ECOGEN. *Pedobiologia* 51(3), 175–184.

[14] Cortet, J., Griffiths, B.S., Bohanec, M., Demšar, D., Andersen, M.N., Caul, S., Birch, A.N.E., Pernin, C., Tabone, E., de Vaufleury, A., Ke, X., Krogh, P.H., 2007. Evaluation of effects of transgenic Bt maize on microarthropods in a European multi-site experiment. *Pedobiologia* 51(3), 207–218.

[15] Griffiths, B., Caul, S., Thompson, J., Birch, A.N.E., Cortet, J., Andersen, M.N., Krogh, P.H., 2007. Microbial and microfaunal community structure in cropping systems with genetically modified plants. *Pedobiologia* 51(3), 195–206.

[16] Bohanec, M., Messéan, A., Angevin, F., Žnidaršič, M., 2006. SMAC Advisor: A decision-support tool on coexistence of genetically-modified and conventional maize. In: *Proc. Information Society IS 2006*, Ljubljana, 9–12.

[17] Messéan, A., Angevin F, Gómez-Barbero, M., Menrad, K., Rodríguez-Cerezo, E., 2006: *New case studies on the coexistence of GM and non-GM crops in European agriculture.* European Commission, Technical Report EUR 22102 EN.

[18] Žnidaršič, M., Bohanec, M., Zupan, B., 2006. proDEX – A DSS tool for environmental decision-making. *Environmental Modelling & Software* 21, 1514–1516.

[19] Co-Extra, 2005. *GM and non-GM supply chains: Their co-existence and traceability.* Project, funded by the Sixth European Community Framework Programme, contract FP6-FOOD-2005-7158: http://www.coextra.eu/

Part II

Short Papers

Tools for Collaborative Decision Making

Collaborative Decision Making: Perspectives and Challenges
P. Zaraté et al. (Eds.)
IOS Press, 2008

A Distributed Facilitation Framework

Abdelkader ADLA[1,2], Pascale ZARATE[1,3], Jean-Luc SOUBIE[1]
1: IRIT – Paul Sabatier University, Toulouse, France
2: Computer Science Department, University of Oran, Algeria
3: GI, ENSIACET, INPT, Toulouse, France
{adla, zarate, soubie}@irit.fr

Abstract. Most meetings are perceived to be extremely unproductive in terms of efficiently utilizing the participants' time and effectively achieving the meeting objectives. Indeed, meetings consume a great deal of time and effort in organizations. These problems occur frequently because effective guidelines or procedures are not used. To overcome these problems, we propose in this paper a framework for distributed facilitation incorporating a model of the decision making processes. In this framework many group facilitation tasks are automated, at least partially to increase the ability of the facilitator to monitor and control the meeting process.

Key words. GDSS, Distributed facilitation, Distributed Decision Making

Introduction

In the virtual organization, GDSS seem extremely adequate to improve strategic decisions made at the upper levels of the organizational structures, through better information acquisition, perception of different perspectives and options, and consensus formation. This thread leads to an increasing presence of GDSS in organization, and facilitation activities must accompany such movement, augmenting the interest of the facilitator.

A few studies have focused on the method used to interact with the GDSS, with emphasis on the use of facilitators [1, 2, 3]. Indeed, Research on facilitation in that field is still sparse, and relatively little attention has been given to support for group facilitation [4, 5]. An integration of good computer tools with effective human facilitation can lead to a more effective meeting than either by itself. A significant question is how to effectively plan, coordinate, and direct – to "facilitate" – the work of group members who are using a GDSS.

With the recent advances in GDSS, many group facilitation tasks can be automated, at least partially to increase the bandwidth of group communication and the ability of the facilitator to monitor and control the meeting process. Hence an automated process to aid even the most inexperienced facilitator must include tools to monitor group and individual behaviours, indicators to know when to offer or integrate information, as well as know when to employ particular techniques to move the group towards congruence.

To this end, we consider the support to inexperienced facilitators by incorporating a model of the decision making process. The selected model provides a detailed view of decision making process. Having a model of the decision making process built into the system should enable intelligent decisional guidance. It enables the facilitator to appropriately choose and use the framework's tools and techniques in the group decision-making processes, to monitor group's behaviour, and to provide cues and customized explanations accordingly.

The remaining part of the paper is organized as follows. First, we present the distributed facilitation concept, followed by an overview of facilitation systems used in group decision making. Next, we present our framework for distributed facilitation. Finally, we present an example of scenario.

1. Distributed facilitation

Group facilitation is a process in which a person who is acceptable to all members of the group intervenes to help improving the way it identifies and solves problems, and makes decision [6]. Facilitation, on the other hand, is a dynamic process that involves managing relationships between people, tasks, and technology, as well as structuring tasks and contributing to the effective accomplishment of the meeting's outcomes.

Ackermann [7] found facilitation helped groups to contribute freely to the discussion, to concentrate on the task, to sustain interest and motivation to solve the problem, to review progress and to address complicated issues rather than ignore them. Human facilitation has been identified as a group of activities that the facilitator carries out before, during, and after a meeting in order to help a group during the decision making process [8]. Previous studies found that group performance is improved when individuals participate in the facilitated discussion and receive cognitive feedback [9]. From a virtual organization perspective, the facilitator is in a critical position monitoring efficiency, quality and commitment to solutions, and reporting results to the organization. In this sense, he is considered as the most crucial element of a GDSS [10]

Automated facilitation is the enrichment of a GDSS with cues that guide decision makers towards successful structuring and execution of the decision making process [11]. Like human facilitation, automated facilitation consists of providing the group with decisional guidance in order to help them achieve their own outcomes. However, the tasks that have been automated generally represent the more routine, repeatable tasks that do not necessarily impact or indicate behaviours, and do not support means to develop the skills of inexperienced facilitators.

2. Facilitating group decision making

Distributed meetings are frequently attended by participants who are physically separate and rely on networked computers to interact with one another and with a facilitator. Facilitating distributed group enables to improve the quality of outputs [4, 12, 13]. There have been numerous studies in the literature about distributed facilitation during the past decade:

SAMM [3] provides an agenda with the possibility of defining sub-agendas, entering, viewing, modifying and deleting topics where topics and tasks can be organized in a list. The meeting chauffeur is responsible for matching agenda tasks with the problem-solving methods supported by the system.

The ESP system (Expert System Planer) [5], uses an expert system approach to help facilitators preparing an agenda and selecting GDSS tools. ESP addresses three main concerns: determining the appropriate participants for the meeting, scheduling a calendar for the meeting, and identifying which GDSS tools may be most adequate to tackle the problem. ESP does not recommend any decision process, which classifies this functionality as technology facilitation. One negative characteristic of ESP is that it produces opaque recommendations, which do not allow facilitators to interpret the decisions made by the system.

The SISCO system [14] provides a good example of content facilitation. This system is not intended to substitute meetings but to provide a pre-meeting discussion environment where no decisions are made.

COPE [7] is a system that supports content and strategy formulation by multiple groups along time. Furthermore, the system uses various computational techniques to cluster concepts into manageable parts and identify most central concepts, which supports development facilitation.

Antunes and Ho [14] present a view of meeting facilitation that blends together the different classifications. The view is strictly focussed on the pre-meeting phase.

Unfortunately, there are not many examples of more advanced systems. The above systems do not support means to develop the skills of inexperienced facilitators. They are mostly beneficial for expert facilitators and none of them support the notion of decision process model. [4] report that facilitators are most likely to either adapt a generic process or select one from a toolkit. Both the generic and toolkit approaches require prior experience with a large range of problems and thus are not applicable in the context of an experienced facilitator. The above observations raise another question, of how can inexperienced facilitators start using GDSS, at least with a reasonable probability of success. Several authors [4, 15] suggested an expert system approach capable to develop facilitation skills. These expert systems would include the recognition and interpretation of patterns of activity and possible facilitator's interventions.

3. A Framework for distributed facilitation

The goal of the framework is to develop skills necessary to design and conduct an effective and productive facilitated distributed meeting. The framework tools are integrated as embedded facilitation, illuminating the effect of the intelligent management tools reducing, but not eliminating intervention from the facilitator. To reach this goal, we explore how to model the group facilitation process and to manage the monitoring and control activities among human and software tools. Our approach to the development of facilitation skills considers the support to inexperienced facilitators by incorporating a model of the decision making processes. The first step of our design consists then in the selection of a model describing the group decision process. Although many rational models that we have seen related to GDSS could have been used, we adopted an approach for supporting the facilitation in GDSS stemmed from our analysis and observations of the previous models [14, 15, 8]. According to our approach, the facilitator involvement in group meeting is conceptually divided into a three phase process, see Table 1: Pre-meeting, During meeting and Post meeting:

Pre-meeting	During meeting	Post-meeting
. Instructing the group on the use of a decision model; . Planning the session and definition of an agenda of the topics and activities to be undertaken; . Selection of participants, definition of the roles of the participants and negotiating a contract; . Identifying and formulating the problem; . Defining the ground rules for the process; . Clarifying and getting agreement on outcomes to be addressed; . Reviewing previous meetings; . Defining time limits.	. Manage group process and promote effective tasks behaviours; . Keep the participants focused on the agenda; . Skilfully and unobtrusively steer the group toward the desired outcomes; . Help the group adapting and executing the agenda to accomplish the task outcomes; . Defining a list of criteria the group wanted to use; . Clarifying the meaning of criteria, eliminating any duplicates; . Weighting the criteria in order of importance; . Reaching agreement on the criteria weights listed by the group; . Selecting the alternatives for evaluation; . Evaluating the alternatives against the criteria; . Calculating scoring based on the criteria weights and ratings; . Examining the ranges in the alternative ratings; . Ranking the alternatives and providing comparisons data; . Explaining the scoring process; . Determining the agreement conditions; . Identifying and selecting group decision;	. Summarizing the meeting, detailing each point that requires future action; . Immediate dissemination of results to reinforce the agreements made; . Evaluating the meting and suggesting changes for meetings; . Generating post-meeting reports.

Table 1. The three phase decision making process

To support the selected decision process model, we propose the distributed software architecture depicted in Figure 1 [16]. The architecture is, in essence, decentralized in terms of databases, model bases and knowledge engines, should make the best use of the available knowledge to offer optimally cooperation capabilities for the participants, and is designed to facilitate collaboration and communication among decision making group through mediated man-man cooperation allowing the group of decision makers and the facilitator to make collective decision. This kind of cooperation uses a machine as an intermediate communication medium.

The software architecture is composed of the following modules:

Dialogue Manager: The dialogue manager allow the facilitator and the participants to interact across a like type client-server network which may be web-based to allow distant decision makers to participate.

Group Memory: A group memory is used to implement the meeting repository storing all the meeting related information including meeting setup information, the trace of previous sessions, and intermediate results. It is essential to be able to capitalize knowledge of the decision-makers implicated in the distributed decision processes so that each can refer to it if necessary. Moreover, the decision-makers implicated in distributed and decision processes are supported by this tool by reusing existent resolutions for instance or simply parties of already established resolutions.

Session Planning: A session planning is made at facilitator disposal to set up and manage a meeting. The facilitator defines all the details related to planning decision-making processes. These include naming and describing agenda topics, scheduling, creation of participant lists, notification through e-mail, and definition of issues, expected outcomes. This function is the most important activity supported, since it specifies the sequence of tasks to be conducted during the actual meeting.

Group Toolkit: A set of tools to support group activities that can be classified into three major categories: (1) Idea generation: each decision maker tries to generate alternatives using his CI-DSS that integrate a local expert knowledge. An electronic brainstorming tool may also be used; (2) Idea organization: the facilitator uses tools to organize the ideas transmitted by participants (e.g. remove redundant alternatives); (3) Idea evaluation tools: a set of tools are made at the group disposal to rate, rank, multi-criteria evaluate the alternatives before choosing a solution. Each group tool has two versions: (a) participation version as private screen; it is used by a meeting participant engaging in a meeting activity; (b) Facilitation version as public screen; it is used by a meeting facilitator to set up parameters or data items associated with a meeting activity.

The Cooperative Intelligent DSS (CI-DSS): In the proposed system each networked decision maker is supported by a cooperative intelligent DSS (CI-DSS) [17]. An intelligent reasoning process is performed by the system to generate alternatives. Decision-makers review their overall viability and make suggestions.

The Group facilitation Support System: The selected decision process model provides a detailed view of decision making processes. It enables the facilitator to appropriately choose and use the system's functional capabilities.

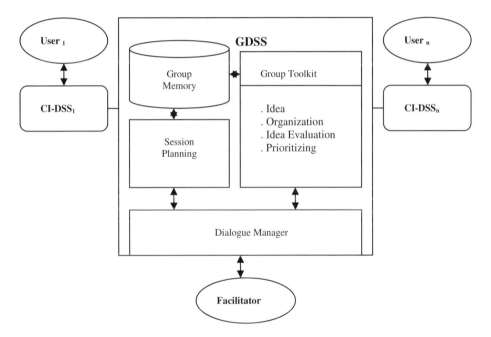

Figure 1. Distributed GDSS Architecture

The particular facilitation techniques the facilitator focuses on at various times depend on the particular stage of the meeting process, see Table2:

Stage	Tools and Techniques
Generating alternatives	. Electronic Brainstorming: NGT, Delphi . CI-DSS
Organizing alternatives	. Categorizer . Conceptual sort . Clustering
Evaluating alternatives	. Rating . Ranking . Voting . Multi-criteria analysis . Preference aggregation
Choosing a solution	. Selection

Table 2. Using tools and techniques during meeting phase

4. Example of application

Gas Liquefying Zone (GLZ) is a plant specialised in liquefying gas. It is one of several plants (a dozen on a national scale) which compose a parent oil company. The management system of the boiler combustion is one of the most critical systems for the good functioning of the plant. The exploiting staff is often confronted with situations that impose a quick reaction of decision-making.

In a contingency situation (i.e. breakdown of a boiler) it is the duty of the process administrator at a local site to identify and diagnose the breakdown. The handling of a boiler breakdown consists of three main steps: discerning defects while the boiler is functioning, diagnosing defects, and proposing one or several appropriate actions of repair. There are two types of breakdown that may occur: 1) automatically signposted to the operator by means of a triggered-off alarm, the flag is pointed out on the board (control room). It acquaints with a particular alarm. 2) Intercepted by the operator (case of defectiveness of the sensor where no alarm is triggered off but the boiler does not work), the operator explores a large research space of potential defects.

For the process administrator, there is two ways to solve the problem. In the former, he uses his specific CI-DSS to diagnose the problem and to carry out the actions of repair. In the latter, he performs a set of tests on the site. If no solution can be found locally, the operator informs the process administrator who makes contact with other process administrators and/or operators of the parent company and even calls on the technical services of the boilers manufacturer located abroad.

An on-line "meeting" is used to represent a group decision making for the specific problem at hand. We will show how our distributed facilitation framework may provide answers to this challenge. The decision making process consists of the following two phases:

4.1. Pre-meeting

In this phase, the facilitator achieves two activities:

- Using the contract-net protocol, the facilitator selects the participants (the process administrators and/or operators of the other plants of the parent company and technical services of the boiler manufacturer), and defines the ground rules for the process. A list of potential participants (a participant roster) is made at the facilitator disposal.
- The facilitator plans the decision making process, defines an agenda of the tasks and activities to be undertaken, establishes deadlines for each of them, introduces the participants, provides meeting goals/purpose, and presents the problem.

4.2. During meeting

The problem resolution is achieved at two levels: the decision maker level (alternative generation) and the group level (alternative organization and evaluation, and solution choice):

- Generating alternatives:

To create the solution alternatives to the problem at hand, each participant uses his CI-DSS (figure 2). Different methods are envisaged to achieve a task. The system chooses a method dynamically to achieve it. In order to do that, given the name of the task to be solve (wording of problem), the system constructs an action plan to be carried out (a sub-graph of tasks-methods hierarchy). The issued alternatives are then put in the private space. Each participant can select some of his private alternatives to be exposed to the group. Participants have a delay for private creation of alternatives. Afterwards, the facilitator makes public the alternative proposals on the shared (public) space to the group.

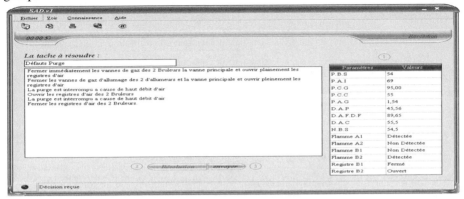

Figure 2. Problem solving by a participant

- Organizing alternatives:

The similar or duplicated alternatives are eliminated or merged. The alternatives containing the same keywords are retrieved for the facilitator to review, and then they are merged or deleted. Idea organization in a distributed environment is mainly the facilitator's responsibility.

- Evaluating alternatives

Participants submit their evaluations or votes (figure 3). They also view group results that include group averages and standard deviations (figure 4). A large standard deviation may indicate a lack of consensus on an alternative or issue. The facilitator brings issues with large standard deviations to participant's attention for further discussion. The participants recast their votes to see whether the team can come to a consensus. Four evaluation tools are developed: Rating, Ranking, selection, and multi-criteria evaluation tools.

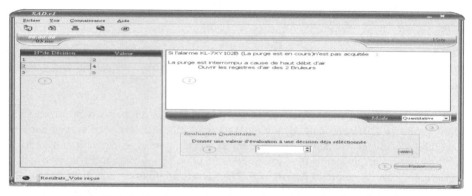

Figure 3. Evaluating the alternatives by a participant according the voting tool

Figure 4. Group evaluation by the facilitator

Then the system will go to the next step: the decision step. At this stage one alternative is chosen according to the evaluation tool used. This decision constitutes the collective decision made by the group. We will then have the post meeting step. At the time of the closure of a meeting, a number of questions, options and arguments have been generated. Participants are supposed to be aware of the contents of the meeting, but a remainder mechanism is necessary, particularly when the number of items is high. To help participants to access the elements during the meeting, summary and cross-reference reports are made available by the system.

5. Conclusion

We considered in this paper the support to inexperienced facilitators by incorporating a model of the decision making process. The selected model provides a detailed view of decision making process. Having a model of the decision making process built into the system should enable intelligent decisional guidance. It enables the facilitator to appropriately choose and use the system's functional capabilities in the group decision-making processes, to monitor group's behaviour, and to provide cues and customized explanations accordingly. Thus, the facilitator uses this framework to help select appropriate GDSS tools or techniques to be used in the meeting. The particular facilitation techniques the facilitator focuses on at various times depend on the particular stage of the meeting process. One of our basic assumptions is that the facilitator shapes and guides the meeting process and the use of the GDSS, rather than the GDSS driving the group to accomplish meeting outcomes.

References

[1] B.C. Wheeler, J.S. Valacich, Facilitation, GSS, and training as sources of process restrictiveness and guidance for structured group decision making: an empirical assessment, *Information Systems Research*, **7/4**, 1996, 429-450.

[2] M. Khalifa, R. Davidson, R.C.W. Kwork, The effects of process and content facilitation restrictiveness on GSS-mediated collaborative learning. *Group decision and negotiations*, **11/5**, 2002, 345-361.

[3] G. Dickson, S. Poole, A.R. DeSanctis, An overview of the GDSS research project and the SAMM system. Computer Augmented Teamwork: A guided tour, *Van Nostrand Reinold*, 1992.

[4] F. Niederman, R.J. Volkema, The effects of facilitator characteristics on meeting preparation, set-up, and implementation, *Small Group Research*, **30/3**, 1999, 330-360.

[5] Z. Wong, M. Aiken, Automated facilitation of electronic meetings, *Information & Management*, 41/ 2, 2003, 125-134.

[6] R. Schwarz, The skilled facilitator, *Jossey-Bass Publishers*, 1994.

[7] F. Ackermann, C. Eden, Issues in computer and non-computer supported GDSSs, *Decision Support Systems*, **12**, 1994, 381-390.

[8] R.P Bostrom, R. Anson, V.K. Clawson, Group facilitation and group support systems. In L. Jessup and J. Valacich (eds.), group support systems: new perspectives. *NewYyork: Macmillan*, 1993, 146-168.

[9] P. Reagan-Cirincione, Improving the accuracy of group facilitation social judgement analysis and information technology, organizational behaviour and human decision processes, 58/ 2, 1994, 246-270.

[10] J. Nunamaker, R. Briggs, D. Mittleman, D. Vogel, P. Balthazard, Lessons from a dozen years of group support systems research: a discussion of lab and field findings, *Journal of Management Information Systems*, **13/3**, 1997, 163-207.

[11] M. Liamayem, A.R. DeSanctis, Providing decisional guidance for multi-criteria decision making in groups, information systems research, **11/4**, 2000, 386-401.

[12] M.J. McQaid, R.O. Briggs, D. Gillman, R. Hauck, Tools for distributed facilitation, *Proceedings of the 33rd HICSS*, 4-7 January 2000.

[13] R.O. Briggs, C.J. De Vreede, N.F. Nunamaker, D.H. Tobey, ThinkLets: achieving predictable, repeatable patterns of group interaction with group support systems (GSS), *Proceedings of the 34th HICSS*, 2001.

[14] P. Antunes, T. Ho, Facilitation tool – A tool to assist facilitators managing group decision support systems, *Proceedings of the 9th Annual Worshop on Information technologies and systems, Charlotte, NC, USA*, **11-12**, 1999, 87-92.

[15] M. Aiken, M. Vanjani, An automated GDSS facilitator, *28th Annual Conf. of the Southwest Decision Sciences Institute*, Dallas, Texas, March 1998.

[16] A. Adla, , J.L. Soubie, P. Zaraté, A cooperative Intelligent Decision Support System for Boilers Combustion Management based on a Distributed Architecture, *Journal of Decision Systems (JDS)*, **16/2**, 2007, 241-263, Hermes Lavoisier.

[17] A. Adla, P. Zaraté, A Cooperative Intelligent Decision Support System, *IEEE International Conference on Service Systems and Service Management (ICSSSSM'06)*, October 25-27, 2006, Troyes (France).

Collaborative Decision Making: Perspectives and Challenges
P. Zaraté et al. (Eds.)
IOS Press, 2008

Developing Effective Corporate Performance Management Systems: A Design-Science Investigation

Rattanan Nantiyakul[a] and Rob Meredith[a]
[a]Centre for Decision Support and Enterprise Systems Research
Monash University, Australia

Abstract: Corporate Performance Management (CPM) has been recognised as having an important role to play in the effective management of organisations. However, a number of researchers have identified that developing IT support for CPM systems can be difficult. Developers need methods and tools to guide CPM system development. Using a design-science approach, this paper describes the use of a CPM systems development method, RED-CPM, and a CPM systems development environment, Performatica, at a large manufacturing company.

Keywords: corporate performance management, data quality, data warehousing, evolutionary development, design science

Introduction

Although, the CPM concept has been widely adopted and extended across a large number of industries and organisation types [1], researchers have identified that developing a CPM system can be difficult, with a low success rate [2-4]. A review of the literature on the development of CPM systems highlights four issues. The first issue is the poor data quality of CPM system data sources. This problem may have a negative effect on the overall organisation performance and may even lead to CPM system failure [3, 4]. The second is that a dispersed IT infrastructure providing data to a CPM system can result in a number of problems, such as difficulties in providing a enterprise-wide view, and problematic data schemas that poorly support management reporting [2, 4]. The third issue is the evolutionary nature of CPM systems. We propose that a CPM system is a special kind of decision support system (DSS) [5] that requires the ability to continuously define and redefine suitable performance measures and system functionalities [3]. The fourth issue is that the complexity of the CPM system design task, which not only involves the selection and definition of an appropriate set of measures, but also the integration with the rest of the organisation and the market place [2]. This requires a large number of people with experience and knowledge collaborating and guiding the organisation through the CPM process.

This paper describes a design-science research project to provide guidance to developers of CPM systems. The method adopted follows that proposed by Arnott [6], and incorporates a participatory case study at a Thai manufacturing firm that demonstrates the utility of a suggested CPM system development method and development environment. These tools will help practitioners to increase development reliability by providing principles that limit the range of system features and development activities to a more manageable set. The success of the project was evaluated using DeLone and McLean's [7] model of information systems (IS) success.

1. Design-Science

Hevner et al [8] define the purpose of design research is to "create and evaluate IT artefacts intended to solve identified organisational problems." Based on the primary purpose of the research, which focuses on improving the performance and feasibility of CPM systems development by designing the two artefacts described above, a design-science approach has been adopted for this project. Arnott [6] provides a general design-science research method, which consists of the following phases:

Problem Recognition: Realisation by the researchers of a specific design problem for which an artefact may be required. In this case, the problem is that of designing and implementing a CPM system in an organisation as addressed in the introduction.

Suggestion: Theories and concepts that might inform the development of one or more artefacts are drawn upon. For this project, literature focusing on data quality, data warehouse design and evolutionary systems development have been used to inform artefact construction.

Artefact Development: the two artefacts developed are a development methodology, called RED-CPM, and a tool called Performatica that provides a supportive development environment.

Evaluation: A participatory case study is used to evaluate the two artefacts in terms of their feasibility and effectiveness, drawing on DeLone and McLean's model.

Reflection: The results and knowledge obtained from artefact development should be consolidated and made explicit, and fed back into revision of the artefacts' designs.

2. The Suggestions and Artefact Development

Existing theories focusing on data quality [9], data warehouse design [10], and evolutionary development [5, 6] have been drawn upon to design the two artefacts as part of the suggestion process of the design-science research method. Moody and Shanks' [9] framework for data quality has been used to deal with the problem of what is often poor quality data in source systems. The framework is comprised of several components: quality factors, stakeholders, quality metrics, and improvement strategies. A lack of an appropriate method for evaluating and improving data quality increases the degree of data quality problem in CPM system data sources. Multi-dimensional modelling proposed by Kimball & Ross [10] is a well-known technique used in data warehouse design, which enables an organisation to consolidate an enterprise-wide view from disparate data sources [11]. This helps to address the issue of a diverse IT infrastructure that provides the data to the CPM system. Keen [5] originally argued that evolutionary systems development with a high level of user involvement is a necessary aspect of the development of any system designed to support decision makers. Given that CPM systems are designed to support strategic business decision making, users may gain an understanding of appropriate sets of performance measures as well as changing their information needs for making decisions related to those measures. This requires the ability for the CPM system to be adaptable and to evolve for managing the complexity of the development process.

Based on the problems and suggestions outlined above, two artefacts were designed and constructed in this project. The primary artefact is a CPM systems development method, called Rapid Evolutionary Development for CPM (RED-CPM). The secondary artefact is a software tool called Performatica that can be used to help in the rapid development of a CPM system. As presented in Figure 1, the RED-CPM methodology consists of major cycles indicated by the shaded ellipses and development activities indicated by unshaded ellipses. Each cycle consists of overlapping activities that can be triggered at anytime, back and forth during the cycle.

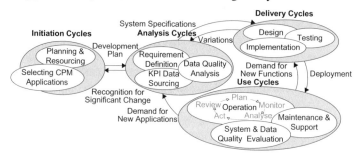

Figure 1: The RED-CPM Systems Development Method

Initiation cycles occur when the client recognises either a need for a new CPM application, or a need for significant change in an existing application. The planning & resourcing activity involves establishing an appropriate CPM development team, and finding an executive champion. Desired CPM applications can then be selected. An initial development plan can be put together mapping out the remainder of the project, although this may be subject to change later on. Analysis cycles are triggered either by the plan from Initiation, or are triggered as a result of emerging demand from system usage (see Use below). Analysis cycles involve three iterative activities – requirements definition, a data quality review based on the data quality management framework [9], and KPI data sourcing. The output of the analysis cycle is a high-level specification that is understandable to both users and system developers. As with the development plan, changes may be made to the system specification as new knowledge and requirements emerge. Delivery cycles are triggered by the system specification or by demand for new functions as requested from Use cycles. In these cycles, there are three activities involved: design, implementation, and testing. The CPM system development tool can also be used in these cycles in order to allow the developers to perform rapid development. The design and implementation activities are iterative. Each development iteration normally emphasises on a single business area and the creation of multi-dimensional models along with the concept of bus architecture [10]. Before deployment, the system should be tested repeatedly using a test plan until satisfactory results achieved. Use cycles consist of three major activities: operation, which the CPM system is used to plan, monitor, analyse, act, and review the corporate performance. Maintenance and support can be provided along with system operation. System and data quality evaluation can be conducted to ensure the performance and quality of the system. As the decision makers change their understanding the basic principle of the CPM decision task, the CPM system should be refined and new versions or applications should be implemented [5]. The action of a use cycle often leads to a new analysis cycle, and occasionally a new initiation cycle.

Based on the concept of data warehousing along with multi-dimensional modelling [9], Performatica is a web-based CPM tool, which comprises a series of interactive data warehouse reports. Each report is then linked to one or more key performance indicators (KPIs), which are displayed using graphical views such as gauges and charts. The overall process of sourcing data through to delivery of CPM information to the end user is governed by the data quality framework [9]. In conjunction with RED-CPM, Performatica enables an evolutionary development approach by managing system components in a modular fashion, reducing complexity for developers as they receive user feedback and undergo another development cycle.

3. Proof of Concept: A Case Study

This section describes a case study at a Thai manufacturing company using the two artefacts described above to develop a CPM system. It serves as the evaluation step in the design-science process, and assesses the two artefacts' feasibility and effectiveness. The project was conducted over a period of three months at the end of 2006. Selection of the research site was opportunistic and the project consisted of two major phases – CPM system development and project evaluation. The first phase involved the use of Performatica to develop a CPM system using the RED-CPM method. The author was both the systems analyst and the developer for the project. Experiences were recorded in reflective diaries. The second phase involved conducting confidential interviews to investigate the success of the resulting CPM system around the end of the project. DeLone and McLean's model of IS success [8] was used as a framework for the interview questions. There was a total of nine participants involved in the development and use of the system. The client organisation and participants' identities have been masked.

PETROCHEM (Thailand) is a large manufacturer, which provides petrochemical products to customers in both domestic and international markets. The concept of CPM was not new to PETROCHEM: it had been carried out using a paper-based system since the organisation was established in the mid 1990's. At the end of each year, a list of KPIs and associated targets were created, and then revised based on market conditions at the beginning of the second quarter each year. The paper-based CPM system was time consuming and needed the intensive cooperation of several key people from each department. PETROCHEM was also struggling with the ability to respond to corporate performance questions from the head office in Japan. The RED-CPM method was used at PETROCHEM as follows:

First Initiation Cycle: Once the need for a new CPM system was realised, the Planning & Resourcing activity of RED-CPM was started. An initial meeting was organised by the PETROCHEM vice president. In this meeting, there were two senior managers involved in KPI reporting: the IT manager and the vice president who subsequently joined the system development team. The vice president was invited to be an executive champion for the project. A potential set of CPM applications was also discussed and selected. A development plan used to guide the direction of the development process was created. This brief plan included scheduling a time frame of the project, identifying potential users, and defining hardware and software requirements for the system.

First Analysis Cycle: The first pass through the analysis cycle began with a requirements definition process. Based on the suggestions of the system development team, marketing, logistics production and HR were selected for inclusion in the system and were prioritised based on the physical location of the business units. The marketing and logistics areas were selected as the first two areas, followed by production and HR. A number of interviews were later conducted in order to gather detailed requirements from each user in the first two areas. During these interviews, the data quality framework was outlined and a data quality review was conducted. Detailed specifications of the CPM system, which bridge the gap between the analysis and delivery cycles in RED-CPM, were developed. The specification served as a foundation for the design of the user interface, system logic, data structures, and network requirements for the system.

First Delivery Cycle: This cycle produced the first version of the CPM system. The design and implementation activities were iterative and consisted of a number of development iterations. Each iteration emphasises a single business area and the creation of a single 'star schema'-based data mart [10]. After system testing was completed, the system was then deployed to the users.

First Use Cycle: The system was first used by the marketing manager to monitor sales volumes for PETROCHEM's major products. The logistics manager also used the system to analyse the cost of transportation to various destinations per various freight agencies for both domestic and export shipments. While the vice president used the system, he spotted significant variances between sales ordered, invoiced and shipped quantities. After an intensive investigation, problems with the existing business processes were identified as a result of the use of the system. This led to a change in process, which can be seen as a significant impact of the new CPM system on the organisation. During this use cycle, a system evaluation was carried out focusing on the quality of the data presented and performance of the system through feedback obtained from the users. While using the system, managers frequently asked for adjustments to reports, which is indicative of demand for new functionality as a result of use, typically seen with other kinds of DSS [5]. The subsequent system modifications are described by the interaction between use and delivery cycles in the RED-CPM methodology. During use, managers also recommended the system to the warehouse manger and other staff. They were interested and asked the developers to accommodate their KPIs as well as developing new analysis reports, which significantly increased the amount of information contained in the system. This new demand for system application triggered the second analysis cycle.

Second Analysis Cycle: The developer gathered and analysed requirements from the warehouse manager and other staff. There were a number of data items required for these new demands, which were only available on an employee's computer and stored in the spreadsheet format. This became a major roadblock for the developer to proceed, because the spreadsheets containing the data had various layouts which changed over time. This issue was reported to the vice president, acting as the project champion. His decision resulted in triggering a second initiation cycle.

Second Initiation Cycle: The vice president made a decision to allocate new resources and change the logic and structure of the system. Two employees from major business areas were assigned to gather and transform the data in the spreadsheets into more reliable format. The logic of Performatica was also changed to enable this process. As the number of users and volume of data contained within the system increased, there were a number of complaints from the users regarding speed and performance. This was reported to the IT manager, who later decided to modify the hardware and software specifications of the system by upgrading the operating system and the capacity of the server. Based on these new resources, the project plan was revised. This resulted in a new evolutionary development loop that triggered the following cycles.

Third Analysis Cycle and Third Delivery Cycle: The template that could be uploaded into the system data warehouse was designed based on existing reports that were currently used. This was to minimise any extra workload for the data provider staff as much as possible. The upload function was then developed. The new operating system and the new server hardware were also installed. In these cycles, the requirements for the HR and production business areas were also gathered, analysed and incorporated in to the system using the same requirements definition procedures as presented in the first analysis cycle. This also included conducting data quality reviews for the two new areas. This process allowed for the "bus architecture" [10], which allows separate data warehouses implemented by different groups, even at different times to fit together. System testing was then completed prior to deployment to users.

Final Use Cycle: In this final use cycle (for this case study – the system is still in use today), the staff responsible for data preparation were trained in relation to gathering and transforming data using the templates referred to above. As a result of the training, the data in spreadsheets was available in a reliable fashion to the organisation. In this cycle, there were still new requirements coming from users for functions and applications of the system, which may trigger new delivery or analysis cycles at a later time. Most users indicated that the CPM system was good enough at that stage for serving their CPM task requirements.

3.1. Project Evaluation

A number of well-accepted theories can be used as a framework to evaluate the effectiveness and feasibility of the CPM system developed for PETROCHEM. Such theories include the Technology Acceptance Model (TAM) [12], the Technology Transition Model (TTM) [13], and DeLone and McLean's model for IS success [7]. Based on individual user's perceptions, TAM and TTM consists of a set of factors that influence IS use. However, focusing only on individual's use of the system may not be sufficient to evaluate the project. System usage is an inadequate proxy indicator of the impact that a CPM system has on the economic, financial, and behavioural [14] aspects of an organisation. Even low usage of such systems can deliver significant benefits, DeLone and McLean's model [7] is better able to capture these kinds of outcomes than either TAM or TTM.

Users' opinions were canvassed in regards to each of DeLone and McLean's evaluation factors:

System Quality: Users of the CPM system generally felt that the system provides the flexibility to change in response to new demands. One respondent supported this by stating "It is quite flexible, especially when I upload the data using Excel spreadsheets into the system, I am able to modify the reports and adjust the screen layout based on what I wanted". The users also believed that the system was easy to use. One of the respondents commented that "I have experiences in using a number of software for the CPM. I think those are complex. But [the system] is not difficult to use it. I don't have any problem". Although most users indicated that the system is quick and responsive, some users found that large reports and the increasing number of users can slow down the system. One user's frustration was evident from the comment, "When I drill down on a large report, it is very slow. And sometime the page is shifted".

Information Quality: Users believed that the CPM system gives them information they could not get access to before in the source systems. One user mentioned that "[The CPM system] gave me ideas about how to improve the current ERP and what data that should be collected from our business process". The users also perceived that information provided by the system is understandable and meets their requirements. This was supported by a user who stated that "I can understand the information provided by the system. It can mostly answer my questions".

Use: The frequency of use of the CPM system may vary by the functions that a particular user requires. It ranged from two times a day to as little as once a month. An executive stated that "I use the system in monthly executive meetings, because it is summarised and helps in generating reports which involve in management reviews and management decisions". In contrast, the logistics manager who seemed to make the most use of the system claimed that "we currently have three staff and they use the system every time before booking product transportation. I also use it to monitor the shipments, comparing between each quarter and see the trend". However, some users provided negative feedback on system usage. One of the users mentioned that "the system has a limitation that some data is not yet integrated into the system, so I make only a little use of it".

User satisfaction: Most users indicated positive satisfaction with the system. One of the users stated that "I am very satisfied. The presentation is beautiful, responsive, and easy to use". A large number of users believed that they will continue to use the system and will recommend it to others. An executive claimed that "it will be a policy of the company that we will encourage the employees to input the data and receive the results from the system. It will be used as a standard for presentation tool and will be integrated it as a part of our intranet system".

Individual Impact: Users generally felt that the system positively impacted their individual performance. One respondent believed that the system helped him to accomplish tasks in his job. He claimed that "It helps me to accomplish my task easier and quicker to make decisions. In the past we didn't have real time data. We needed to pull the data from the past or forecast data to perform analysis. But now we can have real time data, which I think it is better". Moreover, some users believed that using the system improved their performance and productivity in their job. One respondent suggested that "It can shorten time to do my work. It can also help to cross check with my spreadsheets".

Organisational Impact: As mentioned previously, there was a quantity variances issue observed in the first use cycle, which leaded to an improvement in the business process. This can be viewed as a significantly positive organisational impact as a result of the development of the CPM system.

Although there were some negative issues identified, the users generally provided positive perceptions of the CPM system in every measure of the IS success model. By this assessment, the CPM system project itself can be considered a success. While this is neither sufficient nor necessary in describing the level of success of the two artefacts themselves, it shows that Performatica and RED-CPM together are capable of assisting in the development of such a successful system.

4. Reflection and Conclusion

This case study can be viewed as an example of evolutionary development as described by Keen [5]. The case exhibited two major adaptive loops triggered by system use, with corresponding changes in organisational processes. Two levels of adaptation were observed, with small level functional changes, as well as higher level changes in application. This process is significantly different to more linear, traditional development processes such as the classical 'waterfall' model. The findings from the development process show that RED-CPM and Performatica were both effective and feasible at PETROCHEM.

Two main limitations apply to this research. The first is that this is a single case, and only demonstrates the two artefacts as feasible tools for the development of CPM systems. Further cases and corresponding refinement of the artefacts is necessary to show how effective they actually are. The second is that while the study employed a number of methods to obtain data, the study still depended heavily on the participants to respond openly. Given the participatory nature of the study, there is the potential that respondents may have, in part, been responding the researcher as a developer, rather than solely to attributes and properties of the system and its impact.

CPM is a key organisational issue, but one that has had mixed results for the IT industry. The development of RED-CPM to guide CPM systems development to help solving the issues of data quality, data warehouse design, and evolutionary development, and Performatica to facilitate that evolution as well as reducing the technical complexity of the task will hopefully improve the IT industry's track record in CPM systems development.

References

[1] Malmi, T., *Balanced Scorecards in* Finnish *companies: A research note*. Management Accounting Research, 2001. **12**(2): p. 207-220.
[2] Lohman, C., L. Fortuin, and M. Wouters, *Designing a performance measurement system: A case study*. European Journal of Operational Research, 2004. **156**(2): p. 267-286.
[3] Neely, A., et al., *Performance measurement system design: Should process based approaches be adopted?* International Journal of Production Economics, 1996. **46-47**: p. 423-431.
[4] Wagner, S.M. and L. Kaufmann, *Overcoming the main barriers in initiating and using purchasing-BSCs*. Journal of Purchasing and Supply Management, 2004. **10**(6): p. 269-281.
[5] Keen, P.G., *Adaptive design for decision support systems*. Data Base, 1980. **12**(1/2): p. 15–25.
[6] Arnott, D., *Cognitive biases and decision support systems development: A design science approach*. Information Systems Journal, 2006. **16**: p. 55-78.
[7] DeLone, W.H. and E.R. McLean, *Information systems success: The quest for the dependent variable*. Information Systems Research, 1992. **3**(1): p. 60-95.
[8] Hevner, A.R., S.T. March, and J. Park, *Design science in information system research*. MIS Quarterly, 2004. **28**(1): p. 75-105.
[9] Moody, D.L. and G.G. Shanks, *Improving the quality of data models: Empirical validation of a quality management framework*. Information Systems Journal, 2003. **28**: p. 619-650.
[10] Kimball, R.L. and M. Ross, *The data warehouse toolkit: The complete guide to dimensional modelling*. 2002, US: John Wiley & Sons.
[11] Inmon, W.H., *Building the data warehouse*. 1996, New York: John Wiley & Sons, Inc.
[12] Davis, F.D., *Perceived Usefulness, Perceived Ease of Use, and User Acceptance of Information Technology*. MIS Quarterly, 1989. **13**(3): p. 319-340.
[13] Briggs, R.O., et al., *A technology transition model derived from field investigation of GSS use aboard the U.S.S. CORONADO*. Journal of Management Information Systems, 1998. **15**(3): p. 151 - 195.
[14] Molla, A. and P. Licker, *E-Commerce systems success: An attempt to extend and respecify the DeLone and McLean model of IS success*. Journal of Electronic Commerce Research, 2001. **2**(4): p. 132-141.

Collaborative Decision Making: Perspectives and Challenges
P. Zaraté et al. (Eds.)
IOS Press, 2008

Decision Support Systems Research: Current State, Problems, and Future Directions

Sean EOM[1],a

aDepartment of Accounting and MIS
Southeast Missouri State University
Cape Girardeau, MO, USA

Abstract. As the progress in the DSS area continues, periodic evaluations of DSS research are often necessary to examine critical issues in DSS area. This paper examines current state, problems, opportunities, and future   research directions of DSS research, and. Using author co-citation analysis approach, this research provides the answers to the several key questions posed by Keen and Kuhn. Kuhn believes that in order for any scientific communities to transit from the pre- to post paradigm period, we need to know who we are as the members of scientific community and what we share between the member of the DSS area and what academics and practitioners in DSS share. Keen addressed three main needs of MIS research to be a coherent field. They are clarification of reference disciplines, defining the dependent variables, and building a cumulative tradition. This research aims to answer those five questions. We suggest that DSS researchers need to look at possible changes of research directions from empirical research emphasis to broaden its scope to take a new approach: the design science paradigm.

Keywords. Theory, Practice, Reference Disciplines, Dependent Variables, Cumulative Research Tradition.

Introduction

Since the term "decision support systems" was coined in the early 1970s, the decision support systems area has become a coherent and substantive field in terms of three main needs of information systems research suggested by Keen [1]. Reference disciplines of decision support systems (DSS) are clarified [2] ; the dependent variables of DSS research have been defined [3, 4]; and a cumulative research tradition has been established [2]. As the progress in the DSS area continues, periodical assessment of the current state of the DSS area is necessary to see what has been done, where we are heading, what are critical issues, and where should we go from here.

Using author co-citation analysis approach, this research aims to provide the answers to the several key questions posed by Keen and Kuhn. Kuhn believes that in

---

[1] Corresponding Author: Sean Eom, Department of Accounting and MIS, Southeast Missouri State University, Cape Girardeau, MO 63701, USA; E-mail: sbeom@semo.edu

order for any scientific communities to transit from the pre- to post paradigm period, the following two questions must be answered.
- Who are the members of a Scientific Community?
- What Do Its Members Share?

Keen addressed three main needs of MIS research to be a coherent field.
- What are the reference disciplines?
- What are the dependent variables?
- Are we building a cumulative research tradition?

The purpose of this research is to review critically the current state of our field, problems, opportunity, and future directions. The following section describes the current state of DSS area, followed by the problem area, opportunities, and future directions.

1. Current State of the DSS area

1.1 Who Are The Members Of A Scientific Community?

According to Kuhn [5], a very broad and abstract definition of a paradigm is "what the members of a scientific community share, *and*, conversely a scientific community consists of men who share a paradigm." The members of a scientific community are those who are uniquely responsible for the pursuit of a set of shared goals and those who have a subject matter of their own. One objective approach to finding the member of DSS communities is to discover the linkages among citations [6]. Communities of this sort are the units that produce and validate scientific knowledge [5]. Any study of paradigm-directed or paradigm-shattering research must begin by locating the responsible group or groups. This research identified a group of 119 influential and responsible DSS researchers and 66 researchers in various reference disciplines [7]. They represent major forces that have charted and perhaps will chart the future directions for DSS research and redirect DSS research efforts toward a common paradigm.

In three and a half decades of DSS research efforts to advance decision support systems as a coherent discipline, the DSS community has achieved several of the important prerequisite conditions defined by Kuhn.

1.2 What Do Its Members Share?

What do its members share that accounts for the relative unanimity of their professional judgments (paradigm as the constellation of group commitment)? They share "a paradigm or sets of paradigms" or "a theory or sets of theories." Paradigms are defined by Kuhn as "universally recognized scientific achievements that for a time provide model problems and solutions to a community of practitioners," but the term "'disciplinary matrix" was suggested by Kuhn later. He explained this term in this way: 'disciplinary' because it refers to the common possession of the practitioners of a particular discipline; 'matrix' because it is composed of ordered elements of various sorts, each requiring further specification. The various sorts include: (1) symbolic generalization such as Newton's Second Law of Motion, written as f = *ma* or statements like 'action equals reaction'; (2) shared commitments to beliefs such as: heat is kinetic energy of the constituent parts of bodies; (3) shared values; and (4) exemplars that can be used as the concrete problem - solution example that students encounter from the start of their education.

The term paradigms were defined in many ways. Paradigms are the achievement that was "sufficiently unprecedented to attract an enduring group of adherents away from competing modes of scientific activities." Furthermore, the achievement is "sufficiently open-ended to leave all sorts of problems for the redefined groups of practitioners to resolve"(Kuhn 1970b, p.73). Others, such as Burrell and Morgan (1979, p.23), used this term loosely as a "commonality of perspective which binds the work of a group of theorists together."

Applying the stringent definition of Kuhn's paradigm, DSS communities may have not yielded such "universally recognized scientific achievements that for a time provide model problems and solutions to a community of practitioners." Cocitation analysis is a valuable tool for inferring the structure of paradigms [8].   Applying the paradigm definition of Burrell and Morgan [9], the factors identified over the thirty five year period reflect the commonality of perspective inferred from the work of researchers in DSS and related areas in many reference disciplines [7].

- Group support systems
- Model management
- Foundations
- Evaluation
- User interface
- Multiple criteria decision support systems/negotiation support systems
- Two unnamed factors

1.2.1 What Do Academics and Practitioners Share?

A critical issue to be examined is whether DSS theories are useful for practicing managers in guiding the integrated process of designing, developing, implementing, and evaluating the decision support system. When comparing the result of the factor analysis based on two different bibliographic databases (one for implemented specific DSS applications and the other for entire DSS research publication database), we reach two conclusions. First, several DSS research subspecialties identified in the previous studies did not appear in this study. They include design, model management, user interface, implementation, and evaluation. This result tells DSS researchers that the current accumulated knowledge in these areas are not robust enough to be used in the process of designing, implementing, and evaluating decision support systems, which is the backbone of the DSS research framework by Keen and Scott Morton. For more discussions on the relationships between theory and practice, see [10].

1.3 What Are the Reference Disciplines for Decision Support Systems?

The question of reference disciplines raised by Keen has now been fully answered. This is another prerequisite condition for any academic discipline to progress toward a coherent discipline. There have been a number of assumed reference disciplines in the DSS/information systems areas, such as cognitive science/psychology, computer science, macro economics, management accounting, management science, information economics, organizational science, political science, etc. This study has provided clear evidence of the influence of

- Cognitive psychology
- Social psychology
- Computer-supported cooperative work (CSCW)
- Management science
- Multiple criteria decision making
- Organizational communication
- Managerial communication
- Information processing psychology
- Cognitive science

Kaplan[11] wrote: "And it is a measure of its success in these inquiries that it is asked in turn to give its riches to other disciplines. ...... The autonomy of inquiry is in no way incompatible with the mature dependency of the several sciences on one another." DSS researchers have taken research models, concepts, theories, and assumptions from the various reference disciplines over the past three decades. Now we are beginning to see the diffusion of DSS ideas and DSS applications in many other fields. For example, Ebsco host online databases show that DSS articles are now being published in a plethora of diverse journals. These journals were not the publication outlets for publishing DSS application articles when the first survey of published DSS articles were conducted [12].

1.4 What are the dependent variables?

This research did not aim to answer the question of the dependent variable for DSS research. Fortunately, the issue of the dependent variable has been examined by DeLone and McLean (1992), based on the review of 180 empirical studies that have attempted to measure some aspects of "MIS success." Their study presents a more integrated view of the concept of information systems (I/S) success and formulated a more comprehensive model of information systems success.

Seddon [4] presented and justified a respecified and slightly extended version of the DeLone and McLean model because the inclusion of both variance and process interpretations in their model can be confusing. Seddon demonstrated that the term, IS use" in the D&M model can be interpreted in three different ways—as a variable that proxies for the benefits from use, as the dependent variable, and as an event in a process leading to individual or organizational impact. The extended model clarified the meaning of IS use and introduced four new variables (expectations, consequences, perceived usefulness, and net benefits to society) and reassembled the links among the variables.

What does this re-specified model of IS success really imply to the DSS researchers? We need to redesign the empirical research models that take these dependent variables explicitly into consideration for the next round of empirical research. Implemented DSS that appeared in *Interfaces* are the systems that significantly increased the net benefits to individual, groups, organizations in terms of financial and non-financial benefits. These benefits include increasing profits, decreasing costs, efficiency, and shortening cycle-time, etc. The decision support systems that only satisfy their users without regard to the financial implications may not be implemented. Even so, they will be short-lived. Therefore, any empirical research based on the model with only user-satisfaction as the dependent variables are less/no valuable to real world organizations.

2. Problems and opportunities: Where Should the DSS Community Go from Here?

ACA analysis of the bibliometric data over the past three and a half decades (1970-2004) leads us to conclude that over the past three and a half decades, a consensus has been reached among a group of DSS researchers as to the existence of a body of phenomena that is worthy of scientific study, as shown in the factors appearing in [7]. Further, numerous empirical studies have been conducted to establish a particular fact or a generalization to articulate theories of decision support.

I have attempted to chronicle the main events in the DSS area, successive increments of concept, idea, facts, frameworks, etc. As stated earlier, building a cumulative research tradition is an on-going process. Several areas of DSS research subspecialties that emerged in this study provide us with concrete evidence as to the existence of a cumulative DSS research tradition.

2.1. Empirical Studies in Trouble?

Despite the cumulative research tradition, we have accumulated conflicting and/or inconsistent results from numerous empirical studies in the areas of GDSS, user interface, and implementation. Results from some research streams (cognitive styles research) are invalidated and are deleted to the "field of memory"[13, p.58]. In GSS/EMS areas, GSS researchers enumerated important sources of group processes and losses and therefore designed integrated GSS research model to evaluate the potential EMS effects on the outcomes of GSS supported meetings. The earlier GDSS/GSS research treated the GDSS/GSS process as a black-box that is too complex to comprehend. We accumulated knowledge on each factor/construct that is responsible for process gains or losses. There seems to be an agreement on the effects of each process variable on process gains or losses. However, GSS researchers concluded that while most studies have found EMS use to improve effectiveness, efficiency, and satisfaction, they also found different effects in different situations. The effects depend on interactions among more than three dozens of constructs in the meeting process. Isolating the individual effects of EMS components and three sets of characteristics has proven to be difficult. Consequently, very few GSS empirical studies have been conducted since 1992. Those studies such as Reining and Shin [14] corroborated the conclusion of Nunamaker et al.[15] in regard to the effects of contextual factors on the GSS outcomes. They could not pinpoint which specific contextual factor was responsible for the outcome produced.

2.2. Altering the Prevailing Paradigm: The Design Science Paradigm

Renewed debates on the identity and legitimacy of the information systems (IS) were ignited by Benbasat and Zmud [16]. They used the concept of "IT artifact" to define the intellectual core of information systems.

In response to Benbasat and Zmud's proposal, Alter criticized the concept of IT artifact and proposed "the systems in organizations" as the intellectual core of IS. Reactions to these proposals varied. Some suggest a possible convergence of the two constructs [17]. Some believe that it is too early to define the core of IS and the attempt to narrow the field to a core is misguided, at least at this point in time [18]. One particular interesting argument attracted my attention was raised by Livari [19].

Livari suggests that IS should define the identity of the IS discipline in terms of its distinctive mission as an applied discipline to support IS expert in practice, instead of the prevailing approach of the North American IS research community. He believes this approach failed to a great extent. It focuses on building descriptive-explanatory theories with an implicit assumption that they will lead to practical implications for practicing managers. He further argues that due to the nature of the prevailing research topics emphasizing rigor more than practical relevance, practitioners are not interested in the major IS journals.

We should emphasize more the nature of information systems as an applied, engineering like discipline that develops various "meta-artifacts" to support the development of IS artifacts. Building such meta-artifacts is a complementary approach to the "theory-with-practical-implications" type of research. Primacy assigned to theory and research method has effectively excluded constructive research of building meta-artifacts from the major IS journals (p.2).

2.3. The Design Science Paradigm

Defining the cores of DSS as a science of meta-artifacts will be a promising approach. Recently, the information systems community finally realized that both the design science paradigm and the behavioral science paradigm are foundational to the IS discipline [20]. The two approaches are complementary and distinct paradigms to manage and develop information systems in organization to improve effectiveness and efficiency of an organization. [21].

Conclusions

The research reported here provides hard evidence that decision support systems have made meaningful progress over the past three decades. As a field of study, DSS is in the process of solidifying its domain and demarcating its reference disciplines. The study traced the complete and dynamic dimensions of the intellectual history of the DSS field to identify emerging, stagnant, continuously growing, and dying areas. This research provides strong evidence of the formation of the consensus building stage among a group of scientists about the existence of a body of phenomena that is worthy of scientific study[5]. The prerequisites for moving toward the second stage of empirical study for generalizations appear to have been met. Nevertheless, the DSS community failed to produce "universally recognized scientific achievements that for a time provide model problems and solutions to a community of practitioners."

The serious problem of the DSS community is that the practitioners and theoreticians are living in two different isolated worlds. Practice and theory are two different sides of the same coin. Unfortunately, each does not feel the need and benefits of the other's presence. Newer implementation of improved DSS is built from the new technological development in hardware and software, not from the results of the empirical research in GSS, user-interface, implementation, and design. DSS practice and theory must maintain symbiotical relationships. In doing so, we propose the future DSS research should be redirected to define the cores of DSS as a science of meta-artifacts. This is to say that we need both the design science paradigm and the behavioral science paradigm in the DSS area.

References

[1]   P. G. W. Keen, MIS Research: Reference Disciplines and a Cumulative Tradition, in *Proceedings of The First International Conference on Information Systems*, E. R. McLean, Ed. Philadelphia, PA, (1980), 9-18.

[2]   S. B. Eom, Decision Support Systems Research (1970-1999): A Cumulative Tradition and Reference Disciplines. Lewiston, New York: Edwin Mellen Press, 2002.

[3]   W. H. DeLone and E. R. McLean, Information System Success: The Quest for The Dependent Variable, *Information Systems Research* **3** (1992), 60-95.

[4]   P. B. Seddon, A respecification and Extension of The DeLone and McLean Model of Is Success, *Information Systems Research* **8** (1997), 240-253.

[5]   T. S. Kuhn, *The Structure of Scientific revolutions*, 2nd ed. Chicago: The University of Chicago Press, 1970.

[6]   E. Garfield, *The use of Citation data in Writing The History of Science*. Philadelphia, PA: Institute of Scientific Information, 1964.

[7]   S. B. Eom, *The Development of Decision Support Systems Research: A Bibliometrical Approach*. Lewiston, NY: The Edwin Mellen Press, 2007.

[8]   H. Small, Co-Citation context analysis and The Structure of paradigms, *Journal of Documentation* **36** (1980), 183-196.

[9]   G. Burrell and G. Morgan, *Sociological paradigms and organizational Analysis: elements of the sociology of corporate life*. London: Heinemann Books, 1979.

[10] S. B. Eom, The theory-practice divide in decision support systems research, in *The 2006 IFIP International Conference on Creativity and Innovation in Decision Making and Decision Support (CIDMDS 2006), An IFIP TC8/WG8.3 Open Conference*. London, England, (2006).

[11] A. Kaplan, *The conduct of Inquiry: Methodology for behavioral Science*. New Brunswick, NJ: Transaction Publishers, 1998.

[12] H. B. Eom and S. M. Lee, A Survey of Decision Support System Applications (1971-April 1988), *Interfaces* **20** (1990), 65-79.

[13] M. Foucault, *The Archaeology of Knowledge and the Discourse on Language*. New York: Pantheon, 1972.

[14] B. A. Reinig and B. Shin, The dynamic effects of group support systems on group meetings, *Journal of Management Information Systems* **19** (2002), 303-325.

[15] J. F. Nunamaker, Jr., A. R. Dennis, J. S. Valacich, D. R. Vogel, and J. F. George, Electronic Meeting Systems to Support Group Work, *Communications of The ACM* **34** (1991), 40-61.

[16] I. Benbasat and R. W. Zmud, The Identity Crisis within the IS Discipline: Defining and Communicating the Discipline's Core Properties, *MIS Quarterly* **27** (2003), 183-194.

[17] Y. A. Wu and C. Saunders, The IS Core - VI: Further Along the Road to the IT Artifact, *Communications of AIS* **12** (2003), 1-11.

[18] M. D. Myers, The IS Core - VIII Defining the Core Properties of the IS Disciplines: Not Yet, Not Now, *Communications of the AIS* **12** (2003), 1-12.

[19] J. Livari, The IS Core -VII Towards Information Systems as a Science of Meta-Artifacts, *Communications of AIS* **12** (2003), 1-25.

[20] A. R. Hevner, S. T. March, J. Park, and S. Ram, Design science in information systems research, *MIS Quarterly* **28** (2004), 75-105.

[21] S. T. March and G. Smith, Design and Natural Science Research on Information Technology, *Decision Support Systems* **15** (1995), 251-266.

Collaborative Decision Making:
Cases Studies

Collaborative Decision Making: Perspectives and Challenges
P. Zaraté et al. (Eds.)
IOS Press, 2008

A Ubiquitous DSS in Training Corporate Executive Staff

Stanisław STANEK[a], Henryk SROKA[a], Sebastian KOSTRUBAŁA[a],
Zbigniew TWARDOWSKI[a]

[a]*Information Science Department, Katowice University of Economics, Poland*

Abstract. The paper presents the results of the authors' continued research on effective computer support for the decision making process. The recent evolution of the corporate world has made it necessary to offer computer support to mobile decision makers. As the contemporary organization's operations have gained unprecedented momentum and its structures are becoming networked or virtual, managers increasingly often make decisions from remote locations and within different time frames. This awareness has encouraged the authors to direct experiments with their research vehicle, the Intelligent Compute Strategy Game, toward a ubiquitous decision support system (ubiDSS), with a view to developing the Game into a fully-fledged management training tool. The paper describes the rationale as well as the technicalities and, in addition, delivers a description of a sample game session.

Keywords. context-aware, decision support, ubiquitous computing, user context, user interface

Introduction

The idea of spreading computers ubiquitously but invisibly throughout the environment is attributed to Mark Weiser and his colleagues from the Electronics and Imaging Laboratory of the Xerox Palo Alto Research Center (PARC). Indeed, it can be said that ubiquitous computing originated at PARC in the late 1980s. Soon that vision developed into a new field of computer science which "speculated on a physical world richly and invisibly interwoven with sensors, actuators, displays, and computational elements, embedded seamlessly in the everyday objects of our lives and connected through a continuous network" [1].

At the turn of the century, Abowd and Mynatt acknowledged that "the proliferation of computing into the physical world promises more than ubiquitous availability of computing infrastructure; it suggests new paradigms of interaction inspired by the constant access to information and computational capabilities" [2]. They took special interest in three interaction themes: natural interfaces, context-aware applications, and automated capture and access.

Today, the ongoing progress in computer networks and the rapid development of mobile telecommunications are shifting the design context of many computer support solutions that have so far had an established presence in the information technology industry. One of the opportunities that arise is that of extending computer support to mobile decision makers.

A few years ago similar considerations set us on a research path leading toward what is epitomized by the term *ubiquity*. In computer science, researcher will often use the term to insist that the user be provided with access to required information regardless of time and place and irrespective of the action being performed. A ubiquitous decision support system (ubiDSS) is thus capable of discretely delivering personalized computer support, and it minimizes the skill level required of the user by employing multi-agent and Web-based technologies which can automatically recognize the context and make decisions on the user's behalf [3].

This paper addresses some emerging opportunities and limitations in computer support for the decision making process. It aims as well to present the authors' experiences with building a ubiDSS for the Intelligent Computer Strategy Game in the Internet (ICSGi), their long-standing research vehicle. Its consistent evolution has reached a point where mobile players can increase their knowledge and skills through making strategic decisions at any time and place of their choice, and using a variety of terminal devices. In developing the Game's hybrid platform, we chiefly relied on SAS technology and Consorg's proprietary Optima Controlling software.

1. The Research Model

At previous IFIP conferences, the authors presented a hybrid Analyzer-Simulator-Communicator architecture that allowed the integration of heterogeneous information technologies [4]. In the following years, the architecture was further developed and enhanced to incorporate transaction systems as data sources [5], to better accommodate and support the user's creativity [6], and to increase its applicability [7].

Our further studies and implementations aiming at improved cooperation among decision makers are associated with the notion of ubiDSS, which has been highlighted in the introductory chapter. The way it has been incorporated into the prior Analyzer-Simulator-Communicator architecture is shown in Figure 1.

Focus has been centered on the organization and its environment, with clearly distinguished individual decision makers. The Communicator layer contains sensors that feed information into a context-aware support system. Both theoretical research and practical studies indicate the need to diversify user interfaces (e.g. by introducing direct manipulation, including anthropomorphic element and extending the autonomy of interface agents) to suit each specific user's requirements. Data as well as metadata (rules) offered by the Communicator are integrated with models, data bases, data warehouses and knowledge bases at higher layers. Remote decision makers taking non-simultaneous actions can make use of the outcomes of simulations and of expert opinions provided by the Analyzer and the Simulator layers.

For concepts that fuelled our efforts and for approaches that we found useful we are indebted to many other researchers including: Y. Rogers et al. [8] - for the idea of ubiquitous learning; M. Funabashi et al. [9] – for their contribution to the development of middleware for ubiquitous computing; J. San Pedro at al. [10], E. De Lara et al. [11] – for their comments on collaboration and multimedia authoring on mobile devices; D.M. Hilbert and J. Trevor [12] – for their research on personalized shared ubiquitous services; N.F. Noy [13] – for her survey of ontology-based approaches; and M. Dertouzos [14] – for his insights into human-centered systems.

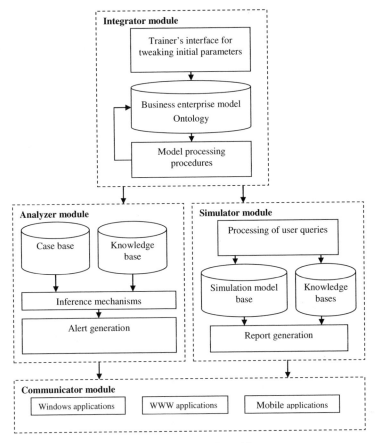

Figure 1. The research model.

The Intelligent Computer Strategy Game in the Internet (http://ae2000.ki.ae.katowice.pl) which is described in the subsequent chapters was created in the 1990s and has since been developed in line with the above considerations for use in university education and in management training as well as for use as a consulting tool in financial decision making. In particular, the following chapters will show how the Game has evolved toward a ubiDSS, illustrating its current functionality with a sample decision making session.

2. The Building Blocks of a Dedicated ubiDSS

2.1. Scheme of Operation

The environment is dedicated to the training of groups of managers in the area of controlling and is made up of integrated modules providing support for the learning process as well as for group work and for the decision making process. The trainees are not tied directly to their computers, to their workplace, or to any other specific location. When and where the decision is made is left to each user's sole discretion, while the system is supposed to adjust to each situation and support the user in a way that is most appropriate at a particular moment. It should be noted that decision making support is understood to comprise self-driven analysis by the control system and the broadcast of alerts to users in the event a threat is detected in relevant areas of the enterprise's operations.

The system's scheme of operation could be divided into several stages, some of which follow one another while others depend on the occurrence of certain events within the training environment. Training scenarios are elaborated by the trainer and implemented as a game which the trainees play on a simulation platform mimicking the operations of a business enterprise and called the Intelligent Computer Strategy Game in the Internet (it is based on the model described in the preceding chapter). As the first step in each game session, the trainer inputs the initial parameters of the model. In the next step, the model is cyclically processed, simulating the subsequent periods in the life of a virtual enterprise. For each scenario, there is a set of conditions which determine (e.g. the number of stages, or "game turns", over which the enterprise must be kept going, that is, it may not go bankrupt) whether the players successfully completed the task. Through the initial parameters, the model can be configured to bring up a problem which the trainees must solve. It is possible to set up the parameters in such a way that they will not lead to an immediate threat to the enterprise's operations, yet they will generate dangers later on as the game proceeds (i.e. the trainer programs for dormant problems to arise). Since a ubiDSS is deployed in the training process, there is no strictly defined moment in time at which the users are expected to make a decision, e.g. immediately on startup. Furthermore, in order to avoid the need to continuously monitor the enterprise, the system offers a support module which looks out for threats and produces an alert on detecting one. The users, however, should realize that it cannot detect every single problem and always do it early enough, therefore they are advised to also make use of the Simulator module available within the system.

At the core of the system, there are the model definition and the model processing algorithms, making up the module designated as the Integrator. All of the Integrator module has been implemented on the SAS system server which is, in general, responsible for the processing and storage of all numerical data utilized throughout the game; this means that the SAS system also, outside the Integrator, executes operations for the Simulator module. Qualitative information used by the Analyzer and the Simulator modules is processed via MEXES expert system. To communicate with the user, the environment utilizes traditional Windows applications interfaces and WWW pages, as well as mobile device interfaces.

2.2. The Analyzer Module

During the game, the Analyzer examines the enterprise's condition at each step and searches the case base to identify, using the information collected, circumstances which have been defined as threats. If a particular case is not found in the case base, the module accesses the knowledge base which uses a mechanism of inference under uncertainty. The expert system returns hypotheses indicative of threats along with probability ratios assigned to them. If the probability of any of the hypotheses is above a pre-defined threshold level, the system generates an alert.

The alert must always be conveyed to the user. The user may refuse to react to it; insofar as the Analyzer module is concerned, all that matters is the fact that the information has been delivered to the user. If the user is working with a traditional

Windows application, the alert is transmitted in the form of a message from the active application. Otherwise the information is sent as an SMS message.

2.3. The Simulator Module

On receipt of an alert, and whenever a condition likely to affect the enterprise's standing calls for their attention, users will access the most important component of the system – the Simulator module. The module has evolved from the Intelligent Computer Strategy Game in the Internet and allows users to perform a wide range of analyses on the enterprise including the classical ratio analyses alongside advanced analyses conducted by the expert system. In addition, each user can conduct a number of customizable simulations that are saved to a private area inaccessible to other users. There is, however, a possibility to publish individual users' simulations for the benefit of other trainees by placing them in specially designed discussion forums. In order to facilitate popular access to information, which is stressed as an essential ubiDSS feature, the Simulator module can be run on traditional desktop computers as well as via Internet applications and on mobile devices such as palmtops or cellular phones. The module communicates with terminal applications via XML packets, which provides for extensibility of the environment. In the case of Internet applications, data presentation is handled by the Internet module of the SAS system (IntrNET), which captures incoming information and uses it to generate Web pages. With mobile devices, this is slightly more complex, due to the small size of their displays and lower data transfer rates. The latter limitation has made it necessary to send out crude information stripped of any graphical elements, while the graphical interface is later contributed by the application running on the mobile device. The solution has been developed using Java technology, which accounts for its easy adaptability to a variety of mobile devices.

3. Examples of Decision Training Sessions with the Use of a ubiDSS

3.1. Decision Scenarios

The system's existing base of decision scenarios includes e.g.: (1) working capital management under high levels of debt, (2) managing a portfolio of investment projects with varied periods of return, (3) budget negotiations within a complex organizational structure – a holding company, a capital group, etc., (4) capital structure optimization. Each scenario has been based on the developers' (paper authors') prior experience relating to the implementation of decisions support systems in business organizations [6]. During a game session, three aspects of the decision process are considered within each scenario:

- The decision problem aspect where, by way of introduction to the area of computerized decision support, are discussed diverse circumstances in which similar problems occur, as well as their consequences and solutions applied in different business organizations.
- The group work aspect, where emphasis is placed on the techniques of creative problem solving and the issues of interpersonal communication along with their significance for the process of complex problem solving.

- The technology aspect, where a number of possibilities are investigated (a) for extensive use of computer models in describing a problem, and (b) for deploying modern data processing technology to generate solution proposals.

3.2. Practical Example Based on Elements of a Selected Decision Scenario

3.2.1. Introduction to the Problem Area – the Decision Problem Aspect

The enterprise intends to increase its market share through a dynamic growth in sales revenues (S) – cf. Figure 2. Among the key factors affecting the competitive structure of the market are the price and the distribution network. The price elasticity of demand is so high that, in order to achieve its objectives, the enterprise is going to, at the initial phase of product launch, reduce its costs through e.g. a very aggressive working capital (WC) management policy. The projected working capital requirement (OC) far exceeds the enterprise's available financial resources (OCF), therefore the plan assumes that the increase in sales will be financed from revolving loans and, to a lesser extent, by trade creditors (i.e. by suppliers). The management board believes that the projected revenue from sales (CFP) will gradually permit the company to repay the debts and increase the proportion of its own funds in working capital, which will secure the performance of further development objectives. The shortage of cash to finance the sales growth entails a significantly increased risk of collapse in revenues, which would result in a failure to achieve the target in terms of market position.

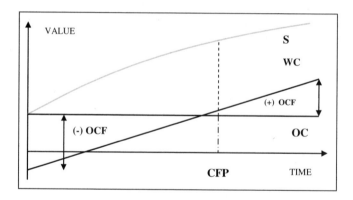

Figure 2. The key factors affecting the competitive structure of the market.

In the last quarter of the budget year, the company aimed to substantially strengthen the stability of sales financing, in an attempt to gradually increase the engagement of the company's own funds until the level deemed safe is reached (i.e. position C1/B1, cf. Figure 3 - Current Plan). The pace at which the parameters affecting financial liquidity are growing is, however, considerably lower than projected. Hence, a hypothesis is put forth, based on expert system conclusions, that the perceived deviation may have an impact on the ultimate performance of the objective.

In the scenario being considered, then, it is the financial controller's task to monitor and analyze the level of operating risk that is directly linked to the enterprise's financial liquidity and to warn, as early as possible, of any deviations that could hinder the performance of the objectives adopted. The monitoring task involves coordination of incoming information originating in different areas of the enterprise's operation (logistics and procurement, production, sales, finance) as well as in its environment (suppliers, customers, competition, demand-supply-prices). Analyses are carried out across two aspects: (1) no deviations have occurred yet and the perceived signals from the environment and/or from within the enterprise suggest a possibility that a deviation will soon occur, (2) a deviation has already occurred and it is necessary to assess its likely effects.

Financial Liquidity Risk	
Budget	Moderate level of financial liquidity risk (position B1/A)
Current plan	Moderate level of financial liquidity risk (position C1/B1)
Current performance	Increased level of financial liquidity risk (position C1)

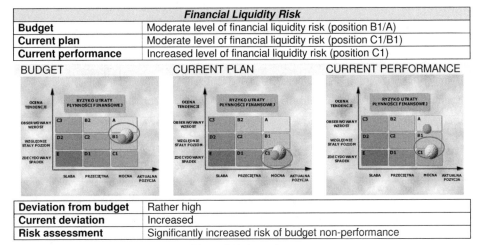

Deviation from budget	Rather high
Current deviation	Increased
Risk assessment	Significantly increased risk of budget non-performance

Figure 3. Risk matrices.

3.2.2. Identification of Risk Factors – the Group Work Aspect

The key factors (parameters) we want to monitor are those affecting the level of financial liquidity risk. A list of such factors is elaborated during a "meeting of experts". The factors are at the same time ranked according to their impact on financial liquidity risk, and defined in terms of their mutual interactions and their relations with other parameters influencing the performance of the scenario being examined. Both the investigation and the definitions are accomplished with the use of computer-aided creative problem solving

All the factors identified are ultimately broken down into four categories: active, critical, passive and marginal (or boundary) factors. Precedence is given to critical factors, whose fluctuations may be grounds for broadcasting an alert to advise of looming threats to goal performance. Parameters are monitored in a synthetic arrangement – in the form of 9-field risk matrices where the targets are presented in the form of, respectively, (a) operating budget at the end of the budget period, (b) current period plan, and (c) current plan performance (see Figure 3). Within the scenario being considered, an assumption has been made that financial liquidity will be stabilized at the end of the budget period, showing a trend toward further improvement of the position (position B1/A in the risk matrix).

3.2.3. Assessing the Significance of Deviations – the Technology Aspect

• *Initial diagnosis*

As a result of the initial investigation, the following actions will be taken: (1) the symptom (deviation) will be ignored as insignificant, (2) the symptom is subject to close observation, without a prior verification of its significance, in order to ascertain the likelihood of threats emerging in the future, (3) the signals/deviations identified will be examined for significance. As a first step, an analysis of strengths and weaknesses in budget performance is conducted with a view to possible deviations from target parameters. Next, a report is created and customized for transmission to mobile devices or desktop devices. Within the scenario being considered, the analysis will concentrate on factors bearing directly on the enterprise's financial liquidity.

Evaluation of Strengths and Weaknesses, Opportunities and Threats			
	PLAN	PERFORMANCE	EVALUATION
Return on sales (RoS)	20%	17%	Possibly a strength
Sales dynamics	Very high	Stable	*Threat*
Working capital level [days](WC)	45	40	Possibly a strength
Working capital dynamics	Stable	Decrease	*Threat*
Working capital requirements	20	70	Weakness
Working capital requirements dynamics	Decrease	**Rapid growth**	*Possible threat*
Net cash balance	25	-30	Weakness
Net cash balance dynamics	Increase	Decrease	*Possible threat*
Liabilities due	30%	40%	Neutral
Liabilities due dynamics	Stable	Stable	Opportunity
Percentage of overdue debt	0	0	Strength
Percentage of overdue debt dynamics	Stable	Stable	Opportunity

Figure 4. An opportunities and threats report available on mobile devices.

The initial examination of the opportunities and threats clearly indicates that the projected sales dynamics may collapse due to the lack of sufficient financing for operating activities. Although the return on sales (RoS) remains high, the working capital is not growing fast enough to allow the enterprise to reach a point where the growth of sales becomes self-financing. On the contrary, it can be perceived that the requirement for working capital is rapidly increasing and the net cash is plunging into the negative. The deviation may therefore be significant and it is necessary to investigate the causes of the increased demand for funding. An analysis of the tentatively significant deviations will result in: (1) reassurance that the identified symptoms do not pose a threat to the achievement of the objectives, (2) identifying the effects of the existing or predictable deviations and proposing measures to ensure plan performance, (3) identifying the effects of the existing or predictable deviations that are significant enough to make it likely that alternative scenarios of plan performance will be followed or that corrections to plan will be made. In this case, there will be a need to hold a meeting of experts to assess the consequences of the deviations identified.

- *In-depth multidimensional analysis of deviations by experts*

At this stage, the first step is to diagnose the problem along the plan-performance-deviation axis in an effort to identify how weaknesses can be reduced by enhancing opportunities, and how strengths could be used to eliminate threats. This stage of the process is supported by the capability of mining in multidimensional data bases and knowledge bases in search of relevant correlations: weaknesses – opportunities, strengths – threats. Within the proposed approach, the so called knowledge base browser OLESAP (On Line Expert Systems Analytical Processing) is employed alongside a classical OLAP cube viewer. The tool has been consistently developed; within the environment being discussed, it can handle seven dimensions of analysis: time, organizational unit, data variant, knowledge bases, expert, case, and metrics.

	EXPERT 1		EXPERT 2		EXPERT 3	
	Performance	Deviation	Performance	Deviation	Performance	Deviation
January	D1/E/D2/C2	opportunity	D1/E/D2/C2	opportunity	D1/E/D2/C2	opportunity
February	D1/E/D2/C2	opportunity	D1/E/D2/C2	opportunity	D1/E/D2/C2	opportunity
March	D1/E/D2/C2	opportunity	D1/E/D2/C2	opportunity	D1/E/D2/C2	opportunity
April	D1/C2	opportunity	D1/C2	opportunity	D1/E/D2/C2	no evaluation
May	D1/C2	opportunity	D1/C2	opportunity	D1/E/D2/C2	no evaluation
June	C1/D1/C2/B1	opportunity	D1/C2	opportunity	D1/C2	no evaluation
July	C1/D1/C2/B1	opportunity	C1/D1/C2/B1	no evaluation	D1/C2	threat
August	C1/D1/C2/B1	opportunity	C1	threat	D1/C2	threat
September	C1	threat	C1	threat	D1	threat

Figure 5. OLESAP browser report – an analysis and evaluation of deviations month by month delivered by three independent experts.

The plan assumes there will be two critical points. The first one is expected to occur between April and May, when the financial condition is supposed to stabilize, and the other at the turn of the third quarter, where strong growth dynamics should lead to achieving the projected target at the end of the budget period. The evaluation of deviations delivered by three independent experts clearly indicates threats to the performance of the budget at the end of the third quarter (cf. Figure 5). The threats result not so much from the position at the end of September (B1/C1) as from the predicted trend. At the same time, it should be observed that the threats had been perceived since July by expert no. 3 and since August by expert no. 2. In addition, both these experts differed from expert no. 1 in their assessment of current budget performance. This repeated alert should make it possible to react to the deviations early enough and take effective remedying measures in response to emerging dangers.

Each of the evaluations (conclusions from the expert system) is underpinned with a detailed report clarifying the expert's outlook on the problem.

4. Conclusions

The concept of decision scenario building on the basis of real problems and the simultaneous focus on the decision problem, group work and computerized data processing technology allow a realistic simulation of decision making contexts in management training. As a result, the trainees are inspired to freely generate multi-variant scenarios for viable solutions to the problem and to assess the risk of a crisis actually happening.

Launching computer support at isolated decision making processes may not contribute to effectively using the opportunities arising in an organization's environment. The ubiDSS concept neatly corresponds with the need to encourage close cooperation among major organizational actors and to support the coordination of activities within a decision making process. Large quantities of information entering the system from a number of sensors make it possible to address support at an essentially broader decision context.

The ongoing progress in technology has built up incredible potential and is opening up new prospects for decision support. The contemporary network technologies and services (including e.g. the WML and Java languages), combined with advanced telecommunications, have taken us to a point where we can easily develop the functionality of Internet applications toward mobile and ubiquitous systems.

References

[1]   Weiser M., Gold R., Brown J.S. (1999). The Origins of Ubiquitous Computing Research at PARC in the Late 1980s. *IBM Systems Journal*, Vol. 38, No. 4.
[2]   Abowd G., Mynatt D. (2000). Charting Past, Present, and Future Research in Ubiquitous Computing. *ACM Transactions on Computer-Human Interaction*, Vol. 7, No. 1, pp. 29-58.
[3]   Kwon O., Yoo K., Suh Y. (2005). UbiDSS: A Proactive Intelligent Decision Support System as an Expert System Deploying Ubiquitous Computing Technologies. *Expert Systems with Applications*, 28(2005), pp. 149–161.
[4]   Stanek S., Sroka H., Twardowski Z. (2003). Decision Support Systems and New Information Technologies at the Beginning of the Internet Age. In T. Bui, H.Sroka, S. Stanek, J. Gołuchowski (Eds), DSS in the Uncertainty of the Internet Age, Proceedings of the 2003 IFIP International Conference. Publisher of the Karol Adamiecki University of Economics, Katowice.
[5]   Stanek S., Sroka H., Twardowski Z. (2004). Directions for an ERP based DSS. In R. Meredith, G. Shanks, D. Arnott, S. Carlsson (Eds), Proceedings of the 2004 IFIP International Conference on Decision Support Systems (DSS 2004) "Decision Support in an Uncertain and Complex World". Monash University.
[6]   Stanek S., Sroka H., Twardowski Z. (2006). A Financial Consulting Support System based on the Data-Dialog-Modeling-Communication-Creativity Paradigm. In F. Adam, P. Brézillon, S. Carlsson, P. Humphreys (Eds), Creativity and Innovation in Decision Making and Decision Support, Proceedings of the IFIP WG8.3 International Conference on Creativity and Innvoation in Decision Making and Decision Support. London.
[7]   Stanek S., Sroka H., Twardowski Z. (2007). "A Decision Support System in Diagnosing the Financial Condition of an Organization". Journal of Decision Systems, Vol.16 – No. 2/2007, pp. 173-196.
[8]   Rogers Y., Price S., Randel C., Frases D.S., Weal M. and Fitzpatrick G. (2005). Ubi-learning Integrates Indoor and Outdoor Experiences. *Communications of the ACM*, 18(1), pp. 55-59.
[9]   Funabashi M., Kawano K., Sameshima S., Kato H. (2002). Middleware Technology for Ubiquitous Computing. In Proceedings of IEEE International Conference on Systems, Man and Cybernetics, volume 2, pp. 623–628.
[10]   San Pedro J., Burstein F., Cao P., Churilov L., Zaslavsky A., Wassertheil J. (2004). Mobile Decision Support for Triage in Emergency Departments. In R. Meredith, G. Shanks, D. Arnott, S. Carlsson (Eds), Proceedings of the 2004 IFIP International Conference on Decision Support Systems "Decision Support in an Uncertain and Complex World". Monash University.
[11]   De Lara E., Kumar R., Wallach D.S., Zwaenepoel W. (2003). Collaboration and multimedia authoring on mobile devices. In Proceedings of MobiSys 2003, San Francisco, USA.
[12]   Hilbert D.M., Trevor J. (2004). Personalizing Shared Ubiquitous Devices. *Interactions*, 11(3), pp. 34–43.
[13]   Noy N.F. (2004).Semantic Integration: A Survey of Ontology-Based Approaches. SIGMOD Rec., 33(4), pp. 65–70.
[14]   Dertouzos M.L. (2002). Human-centered systems. In "The invisible future: the seamless integration of technology into everyday life", pp. 181–191. McGraw-Hill, Inc., New York, NY, USA.

459

Decision Deck's VIP Analysis to Support Online Collaborative Decision-Making

João N. CLÍMACO[a,b], João A. COSTA[a], Luis C. DIAS[a,b,1], Paulo MELO[a,b]

[a] *INESC Coimbra*
[b] *Faculty of Economics, University of Coimbra*

Abstract: We present the VIP Analysis plug-in of Decision Deck 1.1, a platform that hosts different evaluation methods to assist decision makers in the collaborative evaluation of alternatives in a multi-criteria and multi-experts setting. VIP Analysis is a tool for aggregation of multicriteria performances by means of an additive value function under imprecise information. It allows conducting a multicriteria analysis for selecting an alternative when the decision makers are not able to (or do not wish to) fix precise values for the importance parameters. These parameters are seen as variables that may take several values subject to constraints. VIP Analysis incorporates different methods to support the progressive reduction of the number of alternatives, introducing a concept of tolerance that lets decision makers use some of the methods in a more flexible manner. The original VIP Analysis was programmed in the late 1990s using Borland Delphi, whereas the Decision Deck version was programmed in Java and accesses data stored as a (possibly remote) MySQL database. Its main innovation is to allow several users working on the same problem under different roles: coordinator, evaluator, and decision-maker.

1. Introduction

VIP Analysis[1] is a multi-criteria decision support tool to evaluate a discrete set of alternatives in choice problems. Its main characteristic is that it does not require a Decision Maker (DM) to indicate precise values for the trade-offs between different criteria. Rather, it can accept imprecise information (namely intervals and linear constraints) on these values. VIP Analysis may be used to discover robust conclusions, i.e. those that hold for every admissible combination of the parameters, and to identify which results are more affected by the imprecision in the parameter values, i.e. the variability of the results.

In its original form, VIP Analysis can be a useful tool for a single user, which can be a single DM, or someone using the tool to support the discussion of a group gathered at the same location, as in a decision conference[2]. In this work, we introduce a new version that allows a group of actors engaged in a decision process to collaborate over the internet, hence not needing to meet at the same location, nor at the same time. We used the Decision Deck (D^2) platform, a free program offering a generic multi-criteria evaluation structure where new methods can be plugged-in. The platform allows a workflow-like organization of the decision process, where multiple users can intervene in coordinating roles, specialist evaluation roles, or as decision analysts

---

[1] Corresponding Author: Luís C. Dias, INESC Coimbra, Rua Antero de Quental, 199, 3000-033 Coimbra, PORTUGAL; E-mail: ldias@inescc.pt

dealing with the more political aspects of the problem (e.g., defining the importance of the evaluation criteria).

A new version of VIP Analysis was built as a Decision Deck plug-in. It was built from scratch, since Decision Deck is programmed in Java and is platform-independent, whereas the original version had been programmed in Pascal using Borland Delphi, targeted for Microsoft Windows systems only. Moreover, the access to data had to be completely changed from text files based storage to database storage. This was seen as an opportunity to change some of the features of VIP Analysis, abandoning some of the less used ones and introducing some new capabilities.

This paper describes the result of this migration process. The basic decision-aiding concepts of VIP Analysis are described in Section 2. The target platform, Decision Deck, is briefly presented in Section 3. Section 4 describes D^2VIP-A, the VIP Analysis plug-in developed for Decision Deck. Section 5 concludes the paper, discussing the advantages and shortcomings of D^2VIP-A, as well as indicating plans for future developments.

2. Basic VIP Analysis Concepts

This section overviews the VIP Analysis methodology[1]. The purpose of VIP Analysis is the support of the evaluation of a discrete set of alternatives, in order to choose the most preferred one, according to a multiattribute additive value function[3]. The global value of an alternative a_i is a sum of its values for the n criteria $(v_1(a_i),...,v_n(a_i))$, weighted by n scaling weights $w=(w_1,...,w_n)$ that indirectly reflect the importance of the criteria:

$$V(a_i,w) = \sum_{j=1}^{n} w_j v_j(a_i), \text{ with } \sum_{j=1}^{n} w_j = 1 \text{ and } w_j \geq 0. \tag{1}$$

One of the most difficult steps of the decision aid process is setting the values of the scaling weights, since these parameters will reflect the DM's values and trade-offs (e.g., how much would you be willing to lose in attribute "cost" to gain one unit in attribute "safety"?). Indeed, not only DMs may find it hard to provide precise figures about their preferences, taking into account how these figures match their intuitive notion of importance, but also these preferences may change as the decision aid process evolves. Moreover, the questioning techniques that can be used to elicit the values of the importance parameters may require more time and patience than the DMs can spare and, in group decision situations, the opinions and preferences of the DMs diverge frequently.

To overcome these difficulties, VIP Analysis proposes to advance in the decision process with **V**ariable **I**nterdependent **P**arameters. This means that instead of requiring precise values for the scaling weights, it can accept intervals or any other linear constraints on these values. For instance a group of DMs may be doubtful about setting $w_1=0.2$ and $w_2=0.1$ (these precise values) but may find it easy to agree that $w_1>w_2$. This kind of information is often designated as poor, imprecise, incomplete, or partial information (e.g., see [1, 4]). The constraints usually stem from imprecise answers from the DM (e.g. providing an interval for the trade-off rate between two criteria) or from holistic judgments about alternatives that the DM is able to compare (e.g. a_1 is preferred to a_2).

Let W denote the set of all combinations (vectors) of parameter values $(w_1,...,w_n)$ that satisfy all the established constraints. Once W is defined, VIP Analysis may be used to discover robust conclusions (those that hold for every combination in W) and to identify which results are more affected by the imprecision in the parameter values (the results that vary more). VIP Analysis can be seen as a toolbox offering complementary approaches to analyze a decision situation with imprecise information. The results produced by VIP Analysis from a set W of acceptable combinations of values for the importance parameters and a set $A=\{a_1,...,a_m\}$ of alternatives include the following:

a) Computation of a range of value for each alternative $a_i \in A$: the minimum value of a_i given W can be computed by solving a linear program (LP) with the scaling weights $w=(w_1,...,w_n)$ as variables

$$\min\{V(a_i,w): w \in W\}, \tag{2}$$

and similarly the maximum value of a_i given W can be computed by solving another LP

$$\max\{V(a_i,w): w \in W\}. \tag{3}$$

If the maximum value for an alternative a_x is less than the minimum value for an alternative a_y, then the first alternative could be discarded as the second one is clearly superior. The minimum value may be used as a ranking rule – the "maximin" rule (e.g., [5]).

b) Computation of the highest difference of value for each ordered pair of alternatives: given an ordered pair of alternatives $(a_i,a_j) \in A^2$ and W, an LP may be solved to find the maximum possible advantage of the first alternative over the second one

$$m_{ij} = \max\{V(a_i,w)-V(a_j,w): w \in W\}. \tag{4}$$

If the maximum difference is negative or null then $V(a_j,w) \geq V(a_i,w) \ \forall w \in W$, which we denote as $a_j \Delta a_i$ (a_j "dominates" a_i). If the maximum difference does not exceed a tolerance parameter ε, then $V(a_j,w) \geq V(a_i,w)-\varepsilon \ \forall w \in W$, and we denote this as $a_j \Delta_\varepsilon a_i$ (a_j "quasi-dominates" a_i with tolerance ε).

c) Computation of the "maximum regret" associated with choosing each alternative: given an alternative $a_i \in A$, the set $A\setminus\{a_i\}$, and W, this amounts to find the maximum difference of value by which a_i can lose to another alternative in $A\setminus\{a_i\}$. The scaling weights $w=(w_1,...,w_n)$ are considered as variables (rather than being fixed) to allow the regret to be as high as possible given A and W

$$Regret_{\max}(a_i) = \max_{w \in W}\left\{ \max_{j=1,...,m;\, j \neq i} \{V(a_j,w)\} - V(a_i,w) \right\}. \tag{5}$$

Rather than directly computing Eq. (5), after finding the maximal differences of value from Eq. (4) for all pairs of alternatives, the maximum regret associated with choosing each one can be found by noting that (see [1]):

$$Regret_{\max}(a_i) = \max_{j=1,...,m;\, j \neq i} \{m_{ji}\} \tag{6}$$

If $Regret_{max}(a_i) \leq 0$ then we can say that a_i is "optimal"; if $Regret_{max}(a_i) \leq \varepsilon$ we can say that a_i is "quasi-optimal" with tolerance ε. The "minimax regret" rule can also be used to rank alternatives (e.g., [5]).

The outputs of VIP Analysis may allow the decision process to progress, as DMs learn about the model and the problem, postponing the elicitation questions they find difficult to answer, or prone to generate conflict. For instance, they may not agree on precise values for the scaling weights, but may agree on a ranking of those weights. Or they may merely agree on a partial ranking (e.g. $w_1 \geq w_2$; $w_1 \geq w_3$ and $w_3 \geq w_4$). In any case, VIP Analysis provides results that may allow to eliminate some alternatives or to highlight the most promising ones. Furthermore, the results can be used to direct the elicitation of further information with the purpose of progressively reducing the imprecision (e.g. "can alternative a_x really attain such a high value?", "can all DMs agree that a_x is worse than a_y?"). Very often, only a few constraints, for instance a ranking of the scaling weights suffice to clearly indicating one or two alternatives as being potentially the best ones [1, 5].

A first implementation of VIP Analysis has been programmed in Pascal language (Borland Delphi). It has been offered as a freeware executable file to everyone who has requested it from its authors. The list of requests is now over 150 users long (not counting students from the authors' university), mostly academics but also from industry and government institutions, from dozens of different countries.

3. The Decision Deck Platform

The Decision Deck (D^2) project in its own words "aims at developing a generic decision aid platform composed of modular and interconnected software components" [6]. These software components implement the common functionalities of a large range of multiple criteria decision aid (MCDA) methods which makes it possible to easily integrate as plug-in additional methods.

The platform, an evolution of the EVAL project (a previous project, funded by the Wallonia Region in Belgium), intends to support alternatives evaluation in a multi-criteria and multi-user (multi-expert) context[7]. In practice, it is based on the concept of a heavy client, communicating (mostly asynchronously and securely) with a database server (MySQL), where the data of the models and users are stored. The client is written in Java, and as such is mostly system independent (running both in Windows and Linux). The whole project is open-source, being available under the terms of the GNU General Public License[8].

Since there are a great number of MCDA methods which could be used to provide alternative evaluation support, the platform itself is MCDA method agnostic, providing just common functionalities (users management, input of criteria, alternatives and evaluations, data presentation and edition). Some common functionalities, although considered are not yet available (like workflow management and session structuring).

To use the platform, each user must have an account. Associated to each account there are one or more roles[7], which describe functions and capabilities of users, which can include: *Administrator* - manages the software and database, including the creation of users and assignment of roles; *Alternatives designer* - proposes some alternatives; *Criteria designer* - defines criteria to evaluate alternatives; *Evaluator* - provides evaluation for the alternatives on the prescribed criteria; *Decision Maker* -

expresses preferences on alternatives and criteria; *Observer* - "silent" stakeholder who gets informed of the other stakeholders' activity. The concept of Alternative, Criteria, Evaluation and Preference must be adequate to the MCDA method used. Some further roles can also be considered in this design, e.g., *Facilitator* - manages the interaction between the stakeholders of the decision process; *Preferences merger* - meta-decision maker who aggregates preferences, from several Decision Makers. Each account / stakeholder may possess several of the roles at the same time, but must explicitly choose which one to use on each session.

The actual MCDA method support is provided by plug-in code (MCDA method specific). This code is integrated in the client, and in each D^2 version several plug-ins can be active at the same time. As the code is distributed under an open-source license, developers are encouraged to provide new MCDA method plug-ins to improve the platform. This implementation via plug-ins allows for the decomposition of MCDA methods in common functional components and component re-use. For previously implemented MCDA this approach requires the developer to become familiar with the previous source code, and rewrite the code, conforming to good coding practice to facilitate collaborative development. Although a plug-in creation tool is provided in the current version of D^2 to help create a "MCDA method skeleton" to be filled in, this approach requires a non-trivial amount of work. In fact, to minimize work in getting existing applications to interact with D^2, a web-component, named D3 is being developed to facilitate such a task using web-services [9], but it was not yet ready to be used in this project.

4. The VIP Analysis Plug-in

D^2VIP-A, the VIP Analysis plug-in developed for Decision Deck, considers three types of roles for its users: Coordinator (encompasses the roles of Administrator, Alternatives designer, and Criteria designer; more than one coordinator may be present in a decision process), Evaluator, and Decision-Maker (DM). This distinction did not exist in the original VIP Analysis software, which assumed a single user. We will present the plug-in by indicating what possibilities are offered to each of the three roles.

Acting as a Coordinator, the user can create a new problem. The coordinator is the only type of user who can set the problem's name, the names of the alternatives, and of the criteria, and define the other users that can work on the problem and their roles. Optionally, a Coordinator can define the shape of value functions (see Figure 1 as an example) that nonlinearly translate the performances of the alternatives on the criteria into a value scale reflecting subjective attractiveness of the performance levels (e.g. an increase in performance from 0 to 5 on a given criterion can correspond to a value increase is greater than the one resulting from an increase in performance from 5 to 10). In contrast, the original version of VIP Analysis assumed that the performances of the alternatives had already been converted into value or utility units. If a Coordinator allows it, each DM can set his or her own value functions; otherwise, all the DMs must use the functions defined by the Coordinator.

Acting as an Evaluator, the user can indicate only the performance of the each alternative on different criteria, according to his or her expertise. Since evaluators are not supposed to be experts for all the evaluation criteria, each one can leave the evaluations of the alternatives void on some criteria. A Coordinator can indicate a weight for each one of the evaluators, reflecting different degrees of confidence in the

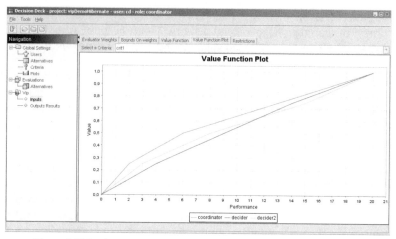

Figure 1. Value functions of a Coordinator and two DMs for a given criterion.

evaluations. This originates a virtual evaluator, whose evaluations for each criterion correspond to the weighted averages of the evaluators that filled in performance values for that criterion.

In the role of a DM, the user can specify value functions and can also specify weights for the evaluators (if the Coordinator allows either action). This means that a Coordinator can allow each DM to be free to set value functions and to weigh evaluators, or can ensure that all DMs work with the same value scales and performances. The DM is the only role that can specify the method's preference-related parameters, i.e. the scaling weights $(w_1,...,w_n)$. In VIP Analysis, the DMs are allowed (or in fact encouraged) to avoid indicating precise numerical bounds for the weights. Rather, they can indicate absolute bounds (e.g., $w_j{\geq}0.05$), trade-off bounds (e.g., $w_j{\leq}2w_k$), and/or any kind of linear constraint. One of the innovations with respect to the interface of the original VIP Analysis is the possibility of using a table to easily introduce minimum and maximum trade-off ratios among pairs of criteria.

After introducing the inputs, the DM can compute the minimum and maximum value for each alternative, and the pair-wise confrontation values m_{ij} (Figure 2) leading to the maximum regret values. Playing with a tolerance value the DM can relax the definitions of dominance and optimality by considering quasi-dominance and quasi-optimality [1], as shown in Figure 2. The results are presented not only in tabular form, but also graphically (Figure 3). The Coordinator also has access to these results for each individual DM who has filled in all the inputs.

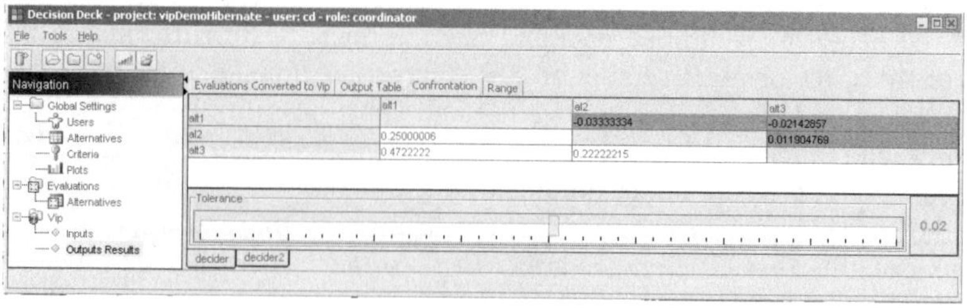

Figure 2. Maximum differences of value (quasi-dominance situations highlighted for a chosen tolerance 0.02).

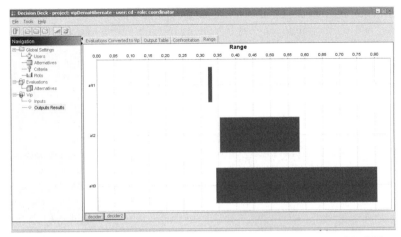

Figure 3. Graphical display of value range for different alternatives, for one of the DMs.

The domain visualization of optimality regions present in the original VIP Analysis was not implemented in this new version: it worked only for problems with 2 or 3 degrees of freedom and had been implemented mainly for pedagogical purposes. Another feature of the original software that was not deemed worth implementing was the criteria-based (de)activation of alternatives: all alternatives are considered as active unless deleted. Another important difference between the original VIP Analysis and D²VIP-A concerns the way data is stored. The former uses text files stored at the user's computer, which could be created and read using a word processor (or even a spreadsheet). D²VIP-A uses a MySQL database, which can be accessed concurrently by many users if located on a network server (possibly connected to the Internet). However, this increased flexibility in distributed access comes at the cost of not being easy to interact with common office applications. Furthermore, the need to install a MySQL database server makes D²VIP-A unwieldy for individual use on a single PC.

5. Concluding Remarks

This paper presented the VIP Analysis plug-in of D². This new implementation maintains the methodology of the original version unchanged, but benefits from the integration in the Decision Deck environment. In this environment, D²VIP-A is included side by side with other multi-criteria evaluation methods, offering the potential users an integrated and uniform interface. The plug-in strategy of D² also allowed reusing already programmed modules. Another noteworthy benefit of the platform is the independence towards any operative system (whereas the original VIP Analysis only runs on Microsoft Windows). We can also mention the possibility of having multiple users collaborating over a network on different roles attributed by the coordinator. Although explicit support for workflow is not included in the present version, it may be included in the future.

Regardless of the improvements, we cannot consider that the old version of VIP Analysis has become obsolete and should cease to be distributed. Some users may prefer the previous version due to the differences in implemented features, but these are small; we expect most users who will choose the older version in the future will do so for its simpler data management (no need to install an SQL server) in single-user situations, and the possibility to easily edit inputs and outputs on a spreadsheet or a word processor.

We can identify some current limitations of D^2VIP-A for multi-user collaboration. Firstly, it is poor as a communication channel, requiring other programs (e-mail, irc, or other) for an effective coordination and for informal exchange of information. Secondly, mechanisms provided to support mutual awareness [10], such as knowing who is logged in at a given moment, what are those users doing, or what has changed during an user's absence, are insufficient or non-existing. Some of the feedback mechanisms proposed in [11] have not been implemented due to these limitations.

Future work is underway to overcome these limitations concerning communication and awareness, allowing to fully implementing a Group Decision Support System. Other aspects such as offering workflow support with tools such as timelines and agendas, or facilitation importation / exportation of inputs and outputs from / to other applications are also planned. The future implementation will be based on web-services to allow its integration in D3, as well as to allow simpler browser-based interfaces.

Acknowledgements

The D^2VIP-A plug-in conception and implementation was supported by FCT / FEDER project POCI/EGE/58371/2004. The technical support and advice from Gilles Dodinet and Michel Zam, from Karmic Software is gratefully acknowledged.

References

[1]   L. C. Dias, and J. C. N. Clímaco, "Additive Aggregation with Variable Interdependent Parameters: the VIP Analysis Software," *Journal of the Operational Research Society,* vol. 51, pp. 1070-1082, 2000.

[2]   L. Phillips, and M. C. Phillips, "Facilitated Work Groups: Theory and Practice," *Journal of Operational Research Society,* vol. 44, pp. 533-549, 1993.

[3]   R. L. Keeney, and H. Raiffa, *Decisions with Multiple Objectives: Preferences and Value Tradeoff,* New York: Wiley, 1976.

[4]   M. Weber, "Decision Making with Incomplete Information," *European Journal of Operational Research,* vol. 28, pp. 44-57, 1987.

[5]   A. A. Salo, and R. P. Hämäläinen, "Preference Ratios in Multiattribute Evaluation (PRIME) - Elicitation and Decision Procedures Under Incomplete Information," *IEEE Transactions on Systems, Man, and Cybernetics - Part A: Systems and Humans,* vol. 31, pp. 533-545, 2001.

[6]   Decision Deck. "Decision Deck Introduction," Dec, 2007; http://decision-deck.sourceforge.net/index.html.

[7]   R. Bisdorff, V. Mousseau, and M. Pirlot, "Decision Deck : An MCDA software platform," in 65th meeting of the MCDA Euro Working Group, Poznan, 2007.

[8]   Free Software Foundation. "GNU General Public License," Nov, 2007; http://www.fsf.org/copyleft/gpl.html.

[9]   Decision Deck. "Decision Deck D3 Overview," Mar, 2008; http://decision-deck.sourceforge.net/d3/index.html.

[10] C. Gutwin, and S. Greenberg, "A Descriptive Framework of Workspace Awareness for Real-Time Groupware," *Computer Supported Cooperative Work (CSCW),* vol. 11, no. 3-4, pp. 411-446, 2002.

[11] L. C. Dias, and J. C. N. Clímaco, "Dealing with Imprecise Information in Group Multicriteria Decisions: A Methodology and a GDSS Architecture," *European Journal of Operational Research* vol. 160, no. 2, pp. 291-307, 2005.

Collaborative Decision Making: Perspectives and Challenges
P. Zaraté et al. (Eds.)
IOS Press, 2008

Redesigning Decision Processes as a Response to Regulatory Change: a Case Study in Inter-departmental Collaboration

Csaba CSÁKI[a]

[a]*Dept. of Accounting, Finance and Business Information Systems,
University College Cork, Cork, Ireland*

Abstract. Changes in the regulatory environment require the reengineering of existing business processes – and decision making processes are no exception. Decision related to procurement and supplier relationships have far-reaching effects. When Hungary has joined the EU in 2004 the accession brought on changes for the energy market as all players became subject to the Act on Public Procurement. This paper reports on how a Hungarian firm coped with the challenge of moving from commercial procurement to accommodate the requirements of Public Procurement rules. As research results indicate, the key to their success was strong leadership and the development of a decision process based on collaboration.

Keywords. public procurement, regulatory environment, tender evaluation methodology, award criteria, decision theory, decision support

Introduction

Modern day organizations operate in an increasingly regulated environment. Changes in the regulatory environment force strategic decisions but the courses of action that may be taken could become fairly limited. Successful implementation of any strategic decision may require changes in organizational structure and culture [1], [2].

A major regulatory change took place in Hungary when the country joined the European Union May 1, 2004. Several European Council Directives have affected the countries that joined the EU at that time. Most importantly for Hungary, the Act on Public Procurement [3] needed to be lined up with EU rules bringing on considerable changes and uncertainties. Interestingly enough, the biggest change affected not public entities, rather commercial enterprises operating in the water, energy, transport, and telecommunications sector [4], [3]. Furthermore, their suppliers who wished to respond to purchase calls under Public Procurement also had to make sure that their proposals adhere to related requirements of the new law. It was hard to predict their response to the changes.

These events presented an opportunity to investigate various aspect of how corporations react to a new environment brought on by regulatory changes. Procurement as strategic area involves decisions of considerable consequences and the reorganization of related decision processes to line up with outside expectations and rules appeared to be a major challenge. Evaluating suppliers and their offers is key to selecting reliable partners. The law, however, places serious limitations on how information may be collected and what actions may or may not be taken.

The research-in-progress presented in this paper examines how organizations reorganize their decision making processes to satisfy outside constraints without compromising their strategic interest. The preliminary results suggest that the motivational factors involved point towards the utilization of outside consulting help, but resistance could still hinder the acceptance of new decision support techniques.

1. Public Procurement as an Organizational Decision Making Problem

1.1. Procurement and Public Procurement

Procurement is the process of acquiring goods, works and services. Organizations are under growing pressure to increase quality while cutting costs. Committing to the right supplier could lead to competitive advantage, while delay in delivery, issues with quality, or disputes over fulfilment of a contract could have devastating effect on the operation of an enterprise. It is recognized that success of organizations does not depend on their own operations only, but they work as part of a value chain connecting together a network of suppliers and customers [5].

Procurement is not only an organizational function and strategic vehicle, it is also a project and managerial task. Procurement as a process spans from identification of needs through to the end of a services contract or even to the end of the useful life of an asset. It includes the design and delivery of those works, products or services, the assessment of their quality, and the evaluations and reviews that will lead to further procurement [6]. It is inherently a multidisciplinary activity. It would typically require the participation or opinion of future users of the goods or services in question. It needs domain experts to collect and organize requirements as well as financial experts to estimate costs and allocate the budget. Since supplier relations are typically expressed in the form of supply contracts legal people need to be involved as well. Therefore, procurement specialists not only have to map the market, communicate and negotiate with suppliers, and run the procurement exercise as a project, they have to deal with the often contradicting expectations of the various internal stakeholders as well.

Public Procurement (PP) as a function of government is utilized not only to secure goods and services required by public sector organizations for their missions and to support services provided to taxpayers, but it is also used as a strategic tool [7] to implement national policies and to achieve social and other objectives [8].

Scientific discussions of PP concern strategic issues of governing such as relationships of the regulatory environment [9], the possible support of high-level policy goals [10], emerging practices involving private financing [11], questions surrounding the development of long-term supplier relationships, or investigation of the effect of strategic procurement decisions on particular sector markets [12]. These strategic challenges seemed to overshadow the problems of everyday procurement activities, the issues public officers and private procurement professionals face as decision makers when trying to cope with the requirements placed upon them by the environment [13], [14]. There seem to be limited research reported on the methodological aspects of developing contract award criteria [15].

1.2. Public Procurement Decision Making and the Hungarian PP Law

Procurement procedures are decision processes: the procuring authority has to compare the proposals (submitted in response to a contract notice) against pre-set criteria and needs to choose one of them or reject all of them. Procurement procedures are also group decision processes as various organizational leaders (managers, officials etc.) meet and their interests and preferences clash during the process. Making the proper decision usually calls for a wide range of expertise to be harnessed. The outcome has different implications for each respective unit involved. Negotiation among the stakeholders is an essential part of completing the task. In more complex cases, resolving negotiations and other issues among the stakeholders as well as among the experts is not a straightforward exercise and may require professional help.

Admittedly, the main goal of special EU PP regulations is to promote transparency and competition across member states [4] whilst ensuring the possibility of obtaining the best value for money for contracts. As pointed out by Erridge et al. [16], above goals create requirements that point towards a "rational" model of decision making. Purchasers should go through a rigorous process of collecting information and the resulting specification should be available to all potential suppliers along with clearly defined selection criteria. This logic leads to the use of competitive tendering which is still the main vehicle in the EU Directives although they allow for a range of supplier selection methods. The Hungarian Act further limits the use of certain procedures types. The law is centred on open (competitive tendering) procedures and there are strict conditions on the application of all other solutions, such as negotiations or competitive dialogue. Public service providers – who may be private enterprises – have less limited access to negotiated solutions.

There are strict timelines to observe. This means that there is a minimum length of time any procedure of a certain type might take. There are rules on how to modify preset deadlines or to revoke a tender. The law determines the steps of the process in considerable details. It also standardizes and restricts the means how to collect information and the methods to be used for selection of tenderers. It limits the means of evaluating the ability and past performance of potential suppliers. Disqualification may only be based upon certain type of documentation and references and the decision could only lead to a yes or no outcome. Criteria related to the supplier itself may not be used as part of the awarding. Once a purchasing project is initiated, the law sets a specific course leading up to the CFP or RFP. The procuring entity has less control over who will reply to its invitations. Legal challenges could lead to potential delay.

Most decisions mean searching for alternatives and iteratively modifying them along with the goals, objectives, and value-relations according to options available. However, public procurement decision making is methodologically restricted by the law [17]. For open procedures the law creates a normative decision making environment. Procurement experts need to fix the rules in advance how the winner is selected, without direct influence on the alternatives by the decision maker.

A PP procedure is neither an interactive nor an iterative decision making process. The contracting authority (CA) may not make a mistake: if the contract notice or the technical documentation is faulty or contains errors those may not be corrected. The last resort may be to recall the procedure, but not without legal consequences. Assembling the selection and contract award criteria in harmony with the goals and the technical documentation is crucial and experienced PP consultants have sophisticated solutions how to achieve the objectives utilizing the limited means available.

2. Research Questions and Methods

In a larger scope the research was concerned with the nature of organizational reaction to regulatory changes (in comparison to changes in the market or technology). In this paper only findings related to two research questions are reported. First, the research wanted to investigate how a major change in the regulatory environment would be reflected in the organizational decision making process. In addition, it inquired how various factors such as mode of collaboration or use of decision support inform the response and determine successful adaptation to the new environment.

The research followed a qualitative methodology based on in-depth case studies. Data collection comprised of three parts to ensure triangulation: interviews served as the main research instrument which was augmented by collection of relevant documents. In *the case presented in this paper*, there were nine one-on-one interviews and a group interview with company employees who participated in the transition: almost every people involved were reached with at least one from each functional area involved. In addition, there were 4 expert interviews conducted: two from the consultant firm selected to guide the transition, one PP expert, and one academic involved in research of Hungarian management practices. Documents analysed included corporate web pages, minutes of transition planning meetings, work-products of transition task forces, description of the official corporate procedure developed, and documents related to individual PP procedures conducted.

3. Description of the Case

3.1. The Company

The company in question is a large coal-based electricity producer. The plant generator blocks are lignite-fired and the company owns and operates its own coal mines using strip-mining solution. The company has gone through considerable changes during the last two decades – reflecting the changes in Hungarian economy and society. Up to the late 80s the company was state-owned but in 1995 the plant was taken over by foreign ownership. The company is now a wholly owned subsidiary of an international electricity giant. Group management identifies regulations as the biggest risk threatening their positions and growth in the electricity transmission and distribution market. Furthermore, one third of the Group's revenues come from regulated business.

3.2. Corporate Procurement Processes before EU

Large-scale procurement of goods and services includes conveyor belts, up-keep and renovation of mining equipment, maintenance and servicing of generators, and major renovation and retrofit of whole generator blocks. The company typically procures from supplier-dominated markets. For example, there are only a few reliable players in the heavy-duty conveyor belt business. Since the useful life of most of the machinery spans several decades, proactive maintenance and purchasing replacement parts dominates the daily routine. Purchasing new equipment or executing a major retrofit project is a huge exercise that requires careful planning and draws in enormous costs. Furthermore, maintenance and retrofit projects typically require bringing a large portion of the operations to a halt. This kind of stoppage is costly and does not leave much room for errors or delays. As these projects involve a lot of service and assembly work, the ability of the supplier to carry out such a huge and complex project is essential.

Before the changes in 2004 there were guidelines what each supply contract needs to contain. In addition, there were sample contracts prepared. Planning of major purchases was done twice a year and in half a year in advance. To acquire quotes a Request For Quotes (letter of interest) was sent to potential selected suppliers. After privatization procurement was brought under the influence of the parent company in an attempt to capitalize on a lowered number of technological variations and decreased number of strategic suppliers. Procurement projects were organized around authorization procedures. Various departments got involved at given stages as the project unfolded. Requests were raised by the operational or maintenance engineers. Costs estimates were prepared by the finance department and the proposal was reviewed by executive management. If it received a "green light" it became a project with full budgeting done again by financial people. Even if constructions, such as expansion type developments were raised by upper management, the bulk of the project was run by the operation and maintenance departments. Procurement people were only involved once the technical plan started to take shape. They usually sent out RFIs to test the market for potential suppliers and solutions. Some less formal discussion could be initiated with regular contractors and construction firms in the industry. With technical and financial details more or less finalized the project was ready for executive approval. After negotiations and selection of a supplier the legal department ironed out the details of the contract. The final sign off belonged to the President. As the parent company inserted more control, technical specifications were also reviewed by engineers at Group Headquarters, while any sample material had to be sent to the central lab. This approach led to a sequential review and authorization process taking considerable time.

3.3. The Transition Process and the Resulting Organizational Structure and Roles

When the company had learned late 2003 that they would be affected by the EU PP regulations after the upcoming accession of Hungary to the EU in 2004, the President appointed the Director of Strategic Development to be accountable for creating an acceptable and compliant solution. They also hired outside consultant to aid the organizational restructuring process. The goal of the exercise was clear and well communicated. It was not just about meeting legal obligations at a minimal level and with minimum effort: it was a conscious decision on the part of (national) executives to make the best out of the situation.

Purchases related to electricity used by the public would fall under PP rules: this meant appr. 75% of electricity produced. It was established that for the purpose of PP the value of all purchases have to be aggregated. The existing signing procedures needed to be lined up with new requirements of the PP procedure. Further issues concerned development of the corporate policy, stages of individual purchasing projects and related intermediate options, understanding the consequences of choices made, resolving the collision of technical, financial and legal issues and concerns. All professions and departments affected by Public Procurement were represented: lawyers from the Department of Legal Affairs, maintenance people and operation engineers from both the mining and the power plant side, purchasing professionals, as well as the leader of the Department of Finance.

One new organizational unit was created called Public Procurement Office directly reporting to the Director of Operations. To avoid administrative dominance, a Corporate Public Procurement Council (CPPC) was also established representing all departments. For individual purchasing procedures Project Teams would be formed along with an Evaluation Committee.

The corporate PP regulations named the President as the decision maker in all affairs. The PP Office would mainly deal with planning activities, administration, and interfacing the PP function to the outside world such as the PP Council, the PP Lectorat, the EU administration, or the economic operators as well as the outside consultant if necessary. All planned projects need to be reported to the PP office well in advance so it can assess the aggregate value of various product and service groups subject to the law. It is the responsibility of the Corporate PP Council to oversee all individual PP projects, review proposals and contract decisions for the President, and review and update corporate PP policies time to time. Individual PP project teams are set up on demand to create PP documentation. They also prepare recommendations regarding evaluation criteria for proposals. However, actual evaluation of proposals received is done by a separate Evaluation Committee appointed by the CPPC. The PP Office is under the Director of Operations, the CPPC is directly linked to the Board of Directors, while the activities of individual projects are all monitored by the CPPC.

Both within the CPPC and individual PP project teams all parties concerned are represented or at least informed and kept in the loop. Project owners, who initiated the procurement, are leading the individual project teams thereby ensuring the right content for invitation documents. This ensures that neither of the functions could dominate and overpower the decision making discourse on the one hand (as is used to be the case in the past), nor any of the potential stakeholders are left out on the other. The solution was integrated with the commercial branch of purchasing without interrupting it.

The consulting firm has also arranged for all related training needs to be met. Not only PP legal and administrative training was offered, but the package included understanding of potential problems, use of evaluation and simulation techniques and tools, as well as decision making and project management skills development: an overall integrated view of the whole process. People from various parts of the organization all became aware what it takes to run PP procedures and what the dangers might be. Special training was arranged for engineers on how to build criteria system that fits the law yet allows for control of supplier response.

3.4. The Public Procurement Practice Now

During the last four years since moved under PP, the company had run around a dozen large scale PP projects a year on average. The first ten projects (in 2004 and early 2005) were executed under the supervision of the consulting company who not only provided PP legal knowledge but used a Decision Support System as well. The software was based on multi-attribute evaluation model augmented with specific rules to meet the requirements as set by the Hungarian PP Act.

The outside expertise was mainly used to get a head start and to gain experience. By late 2005 the role of the consultant was reduced to a 'per-need' basis. In lieu of consultants, procurement projects regularly stay away from open procedures and rely on negotiations instead: in 2004 half of the procedures were of the type "open", in 2005 the ratio reduced to a quarter, while in 2006 there was only one non-negotiated procedure run. There seemed to be no need identified to use sophisticated evaluation methods. Engineers involved in PP projects preferred to determine specific requirements leaving no room for rewarding extra performance. Technical specifications were set narrow leaving no room for differences in offers to be evaluated. Most of the evaluations were based on either lowest price or price with a few financial or delivery conditions. With the selection process and awarding criteria so simplified engineers and public procurement officials did not feel the use for the DSS anymore.

The company's supplier base had been affected as well. A few major market players decided not to put in the effort to learn the new legal rules, while small suppliers did not have the bandwidth and depth of legal expertise to cope with the administrative challenge (or had no resources to learn). On the other hand, new players showed up who had considerable experience how to "play the rules" but probably would have not been considered by the company otherwise.

4. Reflections on the Case Study

Leadership and governance played a crucial role in the success of the transformation of the organization. The company's President made it his own mission to make the transfer not only a success, but also a way to establish a (new) standard for purchasing. The appointment of the Strategic Director to lead the transformation clearly indicates the importance of the mission. The uncompromising leadership and direction setting enabled a constructive solution and also provided empowerment for all those involved: anyone, who was affected, could raise their voice. Procurement function was not only considered strategic but the related issues are raised to the executive level and people involved in procurement activities are respected and recognised. People involved were allowed to take charge. They managed to shape the framework and gradually learnt the "tricks of the trade".

The fear of schedule slips did not seem justified: what was lost by longer PP legal procedures were made up by the efficiency gained by reorganizing the old, lengthy authorization process with a new team approach with all major stakeholders involved.

The complexity of the law, the importance of experience, and knowledge of peculiar solutions alongside familiarity with the arbitration process were strong motivators to pull in outside expertise, as subtleties of the law were hard to learn. Once consultant participation was reduced, practitioners did not have the confidence of controlling the selection criteria and the outcome of evaluation. Over time the overall forces pointed towards the selection of restricted negotiated procedures typically resulting in a lowest price selection criterion. This did not leave much manoeuvring room for strategic goals to fit in especially with the departing of important former suppliers. The normative, rational expectations of the law at the evaluation process and methodology level thus led to a different, satisficing set of criteria at a higher level: acceptance by all stakeholders.

Technical people appeared to be suspicious of the software used and offered by the consultant. Although they use computers on the job daily, they prefer to have full understanding and control of the tools they use. They believe that any evaluation or simulation needed could be achieved by using Excel tables. There appeared to be a lack of trust towards the Decision Support System used by the consultant. There seems to be a higher need to fulfil administrative and documentation requirements than to use sophisticated evaluation techniques.

References

[1]   Bourgeois, L. J. III. & Brodwin, D. R., Strategic Implementation: Five approaches to an allusive phenomenon, *Strategic Management Journal* **5** (1984), 241-264.

[2]   Skivington, J. E., & Daft, R. L., A study of organizational 'framework' and 'process' modalities for the implementation of business-level strategic decisions. *Journal of Management Studies* **28** (1991), 45-68.

[3]   Hungarian Act on Public Procurement, Act CXXIX of 2003 on Public Procurement, [On-line] Available at http://www.kozbeszerzes.hu/index.php?akt_menu=86&details=70, [Last retrieved: May 7, 2006] and Act CLXXII of 2005 (December 19, 2005) on the amendment of Act CXXIX of 2003 on Public   Procurement.   [On-line]   Available   at http://www.kozbeszerzes.hu/index.php?akt_menu=86&details=90. [Last retrieved January 7, 2008].

[4]   European Commission, Directive 2004/17/EC of the European Parliament and of the Council of 31 March 2004 coordinating the procurement procedures of entities operating in the water, energy, transport and postal services sectors, *Official Journal* **L 134** 30/04/2004, 1-113.

[5]   Porter, M. E., & Millar, V. E., How Information Gives You Competitive Advantage, *Harvard Business Review* July–August 1985.

[6]   Hughes, M., *Evaluation of the Local Government Procurement Agenda - Baseline Survey Report*. The Office of the Deputy Prime Minister, London, 2005. [On-line]. Available at www.odpm.gov.uk. [Last retrieved April 20, 2006].

[7]   Harland, C. M., Bakker, E. F., Caldwell, N. D., Phillips, W. E. & Walker, H. L., *The Changing Role of Public Procurement - Executive Report of the Second Workshop, International Research Study on Public Procurement*, Bath, UK: Centre for Research in Strategic Purchasing and Supply, University of Bath School of Management, 2005.

[8]   Thai, K. V., Challenges in Public Procurement: An International Perspective—Symposium Introduction, *Journal of Public Procurement* **4** (2004), 312-318.

[9]   Krüger, K., Ban-on-Negotiations in Tender Procedures: Undermining Best Value for Money? *Journal of Public Procurement* **4** (2004), 397-436.

[10] Erridge, A., UK Public Procurement Policy and the Delivery of Public Value, in Thai, K. V., et al. (Eds.), *Challenges in Public Procurement: An International Perspective,* PrAcademics Press, Boca Raton, Florida, USA, 2005, 335-354.

[11] Lawther, W. C., & Martin, L. L., Public Procurement Partnerships, in Thai, K. V., et al. (Eds.), *Challenges in Public Procurement: An International Perspective,* PrAcademics Press, Boca Raton, Florida, USA, 2005, 151-177.

[12] Caldwell, N. D., Walker, H., Harland, C., Knight, L., & Zheng, J., Promoting Competitive Markets: The Role of Public Procurement, in Thai, K. V., et al. (Eds.), *Challenges in Public Procurement: An International Perspective*, PrAcademics Press, Boca Raton, Florida, USA, 2005, 315-334.

[13] Thai, K. V., Public Procurement Re-examined, *Journal of Public Procurement* **1** (2001), 9-50.

[14] Harland, C., Gibbs, J., & Sutton, R., Supply Strategy for the Public Sector: Framing the Issues, *Proceedings of the International Purchasing and Supply Research and Education Association (IPSERA) Annual Conference*, London, Western Ontario, 2000.

[15] Soudry, O., Promoting Economy: Electronic Reverse Auctions Under the EC Directives on Public Procurement, *Journal of Public Procurement* **4** (2004), 340-374.

[16] Erridge, A., Fee, R., & McIlroy, J., An Assessment of Competitive Tendering using Transaction Cost Analysis, *Public Money & Management* **July-September** (1999), 37-42.

[17] Gelléri, P., & Csáki, Cs., Conditions and Benefits of Applying Decision Technological Solutions as a Tool to Curb Corruption within the Procurement Process: The Case of Hungary, *European Journal of Purchasing and Supply Management - Special Issue on Public Procurement* **11** (2006), 252-259.

Organisational Collaborative
Decision Making

Collaborative Decision Making: Perspectives and Challenges
P. Zarate et al. (Eds.)
IOS Press, 2008

Initial Steps in Designing and Delivering Training to Enable Managers to Use the SL Environment to Support Organizational Decision-Making

M. Susan WURTZ, Ph.D., SPHR and Dan POWER, Ph.D.
University of Northern Iowa, College of Business Administration

Abstract. Using virtual worlds such as the Second Life environment for Decision Support activities will require large investments in training. This paper argues that following the processes described by Robert F. Mager for basing the design of instructional strategies and materials on thorough preliminary analyses (Goal Analysis, Performance Problem Analysis, Skills Hierarchy Analysis and Participant Assessment), will ensure that the training is effective and efficient and that several common pitfalls will be avoided. These analyses are themselves a decision support system in that the analyses will suggest that certain training expectations and processes will be effective but the analyses do not dictate every aspect of the design of instructional strategies and materials. Designing effective training in this area will include beta testing and/or control group experimentation. Several questions for testing and/or experimentation are posed.

Keywords. Second Life, Virtual Worlds, Training

Introduction

It has been suggested that Second Life, a multi-user visual simulation, may be a valuable tool for enhancing collaboration in using Decision Support Systems. This paper will begin with a brief description of Second Life, focusing specifically on the aspects of Second Life that make it attractive for use in interactive business processes and pointing out issues of user acceptance and user ability that could render Second Life applications problematic.

We will address those issues from a training perspective, employing the analyses suggested by Robert Mager [1]. The process starts with Goal Analysis and proceeds through Performance Problem Analysis, Task Analysis, and Skills Hierarchy Analysis. Assessment of the intended participants is conducted parallel with these four processes.

We will describe each of these processes as they would be applied to developing training for participating in DSS activities in the SL environment, pointing out the value gained from, and the pitfalls avoided by the training processes. The paper concludes by identifying the subsequent steps in designing the training program and exploring a few of the instructional design questions that arise.

These analyses are themselves a decision support system in that the analyses will suggest that certain training expectations and processes will be effective but the analyses do not dictate every aspect of the design of instructional strategies and materials. Carrying out these analyses requires significant collaboration between and among the

HR/Trainers, IT specialists, those who are subject-matter-experts in SL and managers in the organization who are responsible for seeing that organizational activities support the organization's strategic needs.

1. Interactive Business Process in Second Life

Second Life, owned by Linden Lab, is a virtual world. A core element of such a world is graphics that generate a three dimensional environment enabling it to be an immersive experience for the users [2]. But Second Life goes beyond that in that the world in which people are immersed is the world they built and shaped. Participation takes place through avatars. As a side note, the term avatar is used in Hindu philosophy to mean the physical manifestation of a divine entity; in the context of virtual worlds it means the virtual manifestation of a physical (human) being. We will leave it to others to draw any conclusions from comparing the two meanings.

The appearance and actions of an avatar are controlled by the individual participant. In Second Life they are called Residents. Residents interact with each other in that virtual world, they create and shape the elements of that world, and, as they build and shape the virtual world, they have an impact on each other. It is the combination of interactivity and creativity in Second Life that opens it for use in real life business applications. The Second Life web materials [3] list examples of organizations using Second Life for collaboration, research and conceptualization, simulation and prototyping, events, brand promotion, philanthropy and fundraising, political organizations, education and training and communication IBM, Dell, Cisco and Sun Microsystems are among the real life organizations making extensive use of Second Life. Reuters maintains a Second Life presence and provides news-wire services concerning Second Life. One of the trends reported in several Reuters releases is organizations that are closing down their Second Life presence. But the organizations are not giving up on virtual worlds – they are moving to others. A recent study by Virtual-Worlds Consortium listed Qwag Forums, Forterra, ProtonMedia, Wonderland, Multiverse and Activeworlds as alternatives to Second Life [4]. The study concluded that "Second Life will remain the leading VW platform for collaborative work in academia, but the case is less so in government and industry." However, whether it is Second Life or another platform, interest in using virtual worlds for real world business activities is strong.

There are motivational barriers to acceptance of learning to use virtual worlds for real world business. Three principles laid out by Carl R. Rogers are particularly relevant here:

1. A person learns significantly only those things which he perceives as being involved in the maintenance of, or enhancement of, the structure of self.
2. Experience which, if assimilated, would involve a change in the organization of self tends to be resisted through denial or distortion of symbolization.
3. The structure and organization of self appear to become more rigid under threat; to relax its boundaries when completely free from threat. Experience which is perceived as inconsistent with the self can only be assimilated if the current organization of self is relaxed and expanded to include it [5].

These elements are interrelated when it comes to managers learning how to use a virtual world. One barrier is the game connotation often associated with virtual worlds. It can be difficult for managers to see why learning about what they see as a game is important. Further, there is often a "slacker" stigma associated with those who play such games. Without previous experience with using avatars, the learning curve is steep. First attempts to control an avatar often include undignified moments, something that managers may not tolerate well.

Given the importance of the structure of self, and the fact that an avatar is an alternate self, the psychology of avatar use becomes an issue. For example, people using taller and more attractive avatars displayed more self-confidence and were higher in degree of intimacy as they directed the movement and interaction of those avatars [6]. But in real life, not everyone can be taller and not everyone can be more attractive. Ethical questions of veracity enter the picture when a virtual world is used for real world business.

2. Training Needs for Participating in DSS Activities in the SL Environment:

In his white paper, "What are the advantages and disadvantages of using Second Life for decision support?" Dan Power [7] wrote:

> Based upon what I have experienced, I am promoting the need for Second Life "train the trainer workshops" in organizations that want to use SL for decision support. The workshops should include a mix of HR, IT and junior executives and the purpose should be skill building and exploring decision support using Second Life.

In his article, Power cites Tom Samson:

> The first hurdle is to make it easier to get started in SL. Based on my experiences the best way to get a new executive into SL is to mentor them through the learning process based on their individual learning styles. ... I don't believe that IT/HR people are the best to help an executive get into SL. The most effective teacher will be a peer who has developed the skills and then helps their counterpart learn.

These comments highlight the need to apply some of the standard analyses used in designing training programs. In particular, Samson's preference to rely on mentoring rather than IT or HR could be problematic. Qualified HR/Trainers know how to design and deliver training that takes advantage of individual differences without running into some of the pitfalls that go un-noticed by those not trained in training. Those pitfalls will become apparent as we go through each of the analyses. The solution is to blend the two – use peer mentors but make sure the peer mentors have been provided with training materials and strategies that accommodate and capitalize on individual learning style and avoid common pitfalls.

2.1. Goal Analysis

Goal Analysis begins with stating the goal as an organizational outcome. Mager advises phrasing the goal as an outcome you want to achieve rather than as a process you want people to use. That distinction helps avoid getting too quickly to thinking about how you are going to achieve that outcome. It is common for non-trainers to jump too quickly to *how* they will teach something without enough thought concerning *what* they will be teaching. As a result, they may end up teaching very well on a subject that is the wrong subject. Here the goal could be: We make effective decisions due to DSS activities in the SL environment.

With the goal stated as an organizational outcome, we can assess how important that outcome is to the organization, thinking in terms of dealing with barriers to effec-

Table 1.

Potential DSS Benefits from SL Environment
1. Having all participants in the same place at the same time experiencing the same events brings a degree of immediacy and focus to the activity.
2. Spontaneous organic formation of sub-groups can be essential for successful decisions.
3. SL offers the ability to structure and restructure space and materials (shop floors and conference rooms alike) virtually instantaneously and with minimal (or no) cost.
4. Major jet lag can be replaced with relatively minor sleep-shortages, and travel costs may be foregone altogether.

tive DSS. For organizations with multiple locations, especially those with global operations, bringing a widely dispersed group of experts together to engage in face-to-face decision-making is prohibitively expensive and time consuming. Use of the internet and company intranets for real-time video conferencing helps, but such techniques cannot escape being too linear and too much a series of talking heads. Further, effective decision making often requires the ability to spontaneously and organically form and reform into sub groups. Again, use of the internet and company intranets for real-time video conferencing helps but such use cannot achieve spontaneity to the degree desirable. If these are the barriers to effective Decision Support, we need to ask if using the SL environment for decision support will help us overcome these barriers. Table 1 lists four ways in which use of SL may lead to better DSS. Undoubtedly there are additional general factors that support the importance of this goal, and there would be situation-specific factors as well. But these four establish a reasonably compelling case that the goal is worth pursuing.

Given a goal stated as an outcome, the next step is to define that goal in terms of human behavior. With this step we are coming to an understanding of exactly what we mean by the goal by stating it as performances. Table 2 illustrates the performance statements we might use for this training program. Most of the time we will be thinking in terms of performances that will be happening, though there are times when it is useful to state performances that will NOT be happening. In this case, we could phrase item 6 from Table 2 as, "Managers do not engage in pranks or griefing."

The benefit from Goal Analysis is that we have a clear and specific picture of what we want to achieve. Having that picture in the form of human behavior adds to the clarity of the picture and helps us when it comes to designing aspects of the training later on. We are not likely to find out later that some people did not understand the purpose and expected value of the program.

2.2. Performance Problem Analysis

With Performance Problem Analysis (Table 3) it may seem we are trying to talk ourselves out of doing any training, and in fact, that is exactly what we are doing. Applying training when no training is need or applying training when it will do no good because other organizational factors are out of alignment is a pathway to high costs and negative returns. The actions that can result from Performance Problem Analysis are shown in bold print. It would be rare to end up with only one action. In most cases, you can count on ending up with a set of actions that includes both administrative actions and training.

Table 2.

Performance Statements for DSS in the SL environment
 	
Goal: We make effective decisions due to DSS activities in the SL environment
 	
We will be able to say we have achieved this goal when:
 	
1) Managers participate in the various decision-making activities through their SL avatars.
    a) They communicate with other individuals and with the group using voice connection through headphones and microphones.
    b) During a conference session, they form and re-form subgroups as needed based on how the decision-making process unfolds.
    c) They meet separately with sub-groups as needed.
2) Managers build rapport with each other by participating in (and perhaps creating) social activities through their SL avatars.
3) Managers shape and adjust SL space to create effective conference facilities.
4) Managers shape and adjust SL space to create realistic virtual tests of models, processes and interactions.
5) Managers maintain records (in various forms) of the group's SL interactions and outcomes.
6) Managers follow norms of interaction with other SL participants that reflect well on the organization.
7) If and when organizational colleagues engage in inappropriate interactions with the SL environment and/or with other SL participants (both organizational members and non-members), managers notice the inappropriate interactions and take steps to curtail them.
8) When managers encounter inappropriate behavior on the part of non-organizational SL participants, the managers take appropriate action to:
    a) protect themselves and their colleagues,
    b) protect the organization's public relations,
    c) bring the inappropriate behavior to the attention of Linden Labs.

Pitfall Alert: This analysis may seem unnecessarily lengthy and cumbersome. However, no qualified trainer would skip any aspect of Performance Problem Analysis. Not only do people tend to resent being trained on something they already know (or at least once knew), but arranging for practice sessions and arranging for coaching and feedback is far less expensive than training. Further, even if the mangers truly do not have the knowledge and skills, the training sessions are worthless if any of the other factors that contribute to performance gaps exist. A complete Performance Problem Analysis is necessary to know when training is required and when it is not, and to know what else is required in addition to training.

In order to answer some of these questions, we have to know the managers' current levels of interest, knowledge and skills. The best way to find out about that is to talk with them. When we do that, we are conducting Participant Assessment. As it happens we are so early in this field, it is probably safe to assume that the gap between desired and actual performance is due to lack of knowledge and skills. But that assumption will rapidly become untenable and very soon it will become foolish to undertake any training initiatives in this area without doing a complete Performance Problem Analysis.

2.3. Task Analysis

Each performance statement for which the Performance Problem Analysis indicated there is a need for training must be expanded and detailed through Task Analysis. Task Analysis involves observing experts as they carry out the performances to discover exactly what they do and, when it matters, the order in which they do things. This is

Table 3.

Steps in Performance Problem Analysis

1) Specify the performance that is actually happening
2) Compare the actual performance to the desired performance (the performance statement)
3) Specify the differences between the actual performance and the desired performance. For each gap, assess the degree to which the gap is due to :
     a) managers not knowing what is expected of them
        i) in that case, **clarify expectations as needed**
     b) a lack of required time, materials and/or tools
        i) in that case, **provide time, materials and/or tools as needed**
     c) managers being rewarded for NOT performing as desired
        i) in that case, **remove the dysfunctional rewards**
     d) managers NOT being rewarded for performing as desired
        i) in that case, **add rewards as needed**
     e) managers not having the necessary knowledge/skills
4) Where the performance gap is due to managers not having the necessary knowledge and skills, consider:
     a) Did the managers *ever* have and use the necessary knowledge and skills?
        i) If not, consider:
           (1) Is each manager willing and able to learn the necessary knowledge and skills?
              (a) If so, **prepare and deliver training to develop the necessary knowledge and skills.**
              (b) If not, **re-define the job expectations and/or replace the mangers.**
        ii) If the managers did once have the necessary knowledge and skills but cannot perform as desired now, consider:
           (1) Has it been a relatively long time since the manager applied the knowledge and skills?
              (a) If so, **arrange for practice sessions to refresh their knowledge and skills.**
              (b) If not (the managers have been applying the knowledge and skills relatively regularly and frequently but not effectively), **arrange for coaching and feedback to refresh their knowledge and skills.**

probably the most complex part of developing training. In some ways it is good if the person developing the training materials has absolutely no expertise in the subject matter. Experts often have so internalized some aspects of the work that they are not aware of carrying out those tasks or how they are doing so. (This is one reason that it is not unusual to find that those who do the task very well are very bad at training others to do the task.) The naive observer is not likely to make the error of skipping over crucial task elements on the assumption that "everyone knows _____."

Pitfall Alert: Again it may seem unduly burdensome, but task analysis assures that the training (the very expensive training) does not cover unnecessary topics, nor miss any necessary ones. In some cases, when the trainees can understand and follow the task flow chart with little or no explanations from the trainer, the flow chart itself turns out to be the only training necessary. Such instances are rare, but they do happen. In almost any case, the task flow chart gets continued use after the training as a job aid for on-the-job reference, for practice sessions and for coaching and feedback sessions.

2.4. Skills Hierarchy Analysis

Each action and decision revealed in the Task Analysis requires a specific set of knowledge and skill. The next task of the trainer is to develop a list of the knowledge and skills that are necessary to carry out the task.

This is a major element in creating eager trainees. One of the inescapable facts when it comes to training adults (and perhaps especially training very busy managers) is that they will resist taking the time for training unless they know exactly why they are learning what they are learning. Generally that means they want to know when and how they will apply the training and why they cannot perform without the training. Being able to point specifically to steps in the task to justify the knowledge and skill being taught legitimizes the trainer and the trainer's expectations in the eyes of the trainees. Here again, as we assess the Trainees' level of enthusiasm (or lack of enthusiasm) for the topic, we are working on Participant Assessment.

In compiling a list of the knowledge and skills used in carrying out a performance, it will become evident that there are some interdependencies. A person could not learn some of the elements without having already learned other elements. Such interdependencies dictate the order in which the trainer must teach the material.

Pitfall Alert: This aspect of training can be particularly problematic in that the order in which knowledge and skills are USED in carrying out the task and the order in which the knowledge and skills must BE LEARNED, are often very different. The first impulse of non-trainer trainers is to teach a performance in the order in which it occurs. That often simply cannot work, even though it is the natural impulse. Here again, being able to point specifically to the interdependencies of the knowledge and skills to be taught goes a long way to legitimizing the amount of time and effort the trainer is asking the trainees to invest.

Another practical value of skills hierarchy analysis is that a trainer may discover that even though the trainees really could not carry out the performance, the gap was not entirely due to lack of knowledge and skill. Analysis at this level may show that the trainees already do have some of the knowledge and skills and only need to be reminded to use them. Or it may be a matter of needing nothing more than practice or coaching and feedback. For example, trainees who have played certain games already know about moving an avatar around a virtual environment, seeing others' avatars move around, and interacting with those others. Unnecessary training wastes resources and annoys the trainees.

A skills hierarchy also allows us to set prerequisites for the training program. It may be that there are certain skills and knowledge that trainees must have before they will be able to benefit from this training program. Knowing that will save both the trainees and the trainers from embarking on a training initiative that is doomed for failure from the very start.

2.5. Subsequent Processes in Designing the Training

It is only when these preliminary analyses have been done that we are in a position to generate instructional strategies and materials that will meet the needs. The next steps involve designing instruments and methods for determining how effective the instruction was (how much the trainees learned – and yes, plans for measuring the effectiveness of instruction should be developed before designing the instructional activities), writing instructional objectives, planning instructional activities that specify what the trainees will do, when and with what materials and equipment and what the trainers will do, when and with what materials and equipment.

Most often, non-trainers begin with step 3 above – planning instructional activities. Readers should now be able to see how skipping the preliminary analyses and going directly to planning instructional activities lowers the probability that the training will be effective and increases the probability that the training efforts will generate problems instead of solving problems.

3. Where Next?

The largest and perhaps hardest task ahead is to create a clear and complete picture of the behaviors we want the managers to be able to use and the knowledge and skills that are required for those behaviors (Task Analysis and Skills Hierarchy Analysis). However, with our focus on SL, it could also be a fun part given that SL incorporates many elements of gaming and anyone working in this area probably finds the technology and its applications intrinsically motivating. Also, people who choose to work as trainers often do it in part because they are knowledge junkies who enjoy learning about pretty much anything and everything.

Even without completing the Task Analyses, Skill Hierarchy Analyses and Participant Assessments, we can anticipate some generic issues concerning the design of instructional strategies and materials that will require either beta testing and/or control group experimentation.

1. Is it better to have the trainees first connect to SL using SL's Orientation Island or to have the trainees start out in the company's virtual training facility?
2. Is it better to have trainees start by customizing their avatar or to have the avatars already generated and waiting in the training facility when the trainees connect?
3. Is it better to have trainees work immediately with an avatar that reflects the trainees' real world appearances (to generate personal investment in the process) or to start with pre-generated "everyman" avatars (to protect self-image from initial clumsiness)?

Undoubtedly other questions will emerge as we go along. We anticipate an exciting adventure.

References

[1] Mager, Robert R. and Peter Pipe, *Analyzing Performance Problems*, 3rd Ed., (The Center for Effective Performance, Inc., 1983); *Goal analysis*, 3rd. Ed., (The Center for Effective Performance, Inc., 1983); *Making Instruction Work*, 2nd Ed., (The Center for Effective Performance, Inc., 1988).
[2] Karlsson, Jonas, "Taking care of Xerox Business – Virtually," *Research Technology Management*, Vol. 51, Iss. 1, p. 15, January 2008.
[3] "Second Life Grid: How Organizations Use The Platform," URL http://secondlifegrid.net/how.
[4] Trondsen, Elif, "Virtual Worlds and Collaborative Work: Survey Results." Virtual-Worlds Consortium, March 2008, URL http://www.sric-bi.com/news/VWCcollabwksurvey2008-03.pdf
[5] Knowles, Malcolm S., *The Adult Learner: A Neglected Species*, 3rd. Ed., Gulf Publishing Co., Houston, 1984.
[6] Bailenson, J. N., Yee, N., Merget, D. and Schroeder, R. (2006). The effect of behavioral realism and form realism of real-time avatar faces on verbal disclosure, nonverbal disclosure, emotion recognition, and copresence in dyadic interaction. *PRESENCE: Teleoperators and Virtual Environments*, 15, 359-372.
[7] Power, D., "What are the advantages and disadvantages of using Second Life for decision support?" *DSS News*, Vol. 8, No. 15, July 29, 2007, URL http://dssresources.com/newsletters/195.php.

Regional Policy DSS:
Result Indicators Definition Problems

Maryse SALLES[1]
IRIT/Université Toulouse 1, France

Abstract. This paper addresses the issue of public decision support in regional economic development, being more particularly concerned with result indicators definition. The decisions taken within such a framework necessarily are cooperative in nature and involve various players, even though the culture of decision-making and cooperation is almost nonexistent in the regional governments. In this context, the definition of result indicators requires the reformulation of generally vague and non-quantified objectives. The conception of decision support systems therefore calls for prior considerable work on the decision system itself. The first part of this paper gives a general survey of regional economic policy definition. The second part focuses on the knowledge that may be identified in the texts of the Midi-Pyrenees Regional Council. The analysis is carried out on the basis of a three-level grid (representations, models, norms). The third and last part proposes an ontology co-building approach on regional development, illustrated by examples from the CAVALA project. The ontologies presented respect the heterogeneity of the various players' views of the world. They facilitate the players' awareness of the different views of the world at stake and help explain the concepts they use.

Keywords. Public decision support systems, group decision-making, result indicators, ontologies, polydoxies

Introduction

This paper deals with the means of supporting economic development-related territorial public decision-making at the French Regional Authorities level, with special emphasis placed on results evaluation.

The complexity of the subject as well as of decision-making situations (owing especially to their strong cooperative nature) requires us to clarify the general issue of decision-making facilitation in this context. We shall then be in a position to define decision support systems (DSS). The purpose of this paper is to expound the elements of this issue through examples from a multidisciplinary research project (the CAVALA project) that is being conducted in partnership with the Midi-Pyrenees Regional Authority.

The team's previous works [13,14] have contributed to identifying more precisely the aims of research through an analysis of regional economic policies. The field of regional economic development is indeed under elaboration, its concepts and terminology not having been stabilised yet. Moreover, besides competing schools of thought,

---
[1] Corresponding Author: IRIT/UT1, UFR Informatique, 2, rue Doyen Gabriel Marty, 31042 Toulouse Cedex 9, France; E-mail: Maryse.Salles@univ-tlse1.fr.

there also are non-homogeneous and non-explained opinions and beliefs which are likely to influence decisions strongly. Regional economic development strategies are therefore expressed within a world of vague and implicit knowledge. Furthermore, the culture of decision-making still remains almost nonexistent in the regional governments, even though their missions have considerably increased within a short time. It appears obvious that, in this context, neither the organisation of the global decision system (breakdown and quantification of objectives, choice of action means, definition of evaluation indicators, *etc.*) nor the decision-making process are an easy task to undertake.

The conception of decision support systems should consequently be preceded by substantial work on the decision system itself. As concerns the evaluation of action results, such a work should first be aimed at defining appropriate indicators to assess the achievement of objectives. The indicators and objectives being closely linked, the "quality" of the latter should be evaluated as well (clarity, precision, feasibility, measurability, horizontal and vertical coherence, *etc.*). A more global analysis of policies ought to be conducted on the basis of policy texts, with the aim of identifying the knowledge at work.

The first part of this paper will look at already existing elements on the definition of indicators. Illustration will be provided through the example of the Regional Plan for Economic Development[2] (RPED) in the Midi-Pyrenees Region. The RPED-related challenge and the implication of multiple players throughout the elaboration process will induce us to wonder about the shared knowledge used to draw up this document. The second part will then be devoted to the knowledge that can be identified or reconstructed on the basis of the texts issued by the regional government. The level of clarity, coherence, and effectiveness of such knowledge will be scrutinised through a three-level grid (representations, models, and norms). The conclusions of this analysis will lead us to propose, in a third and last part, an approach to co-building a common language, which could be shared by all of the players involved, with examples from the CAVALA project. Such a work is, in our opinion, a first unavoidable step towards supporting the definition of evaluation indicators and, more broadly, the implementation of strategic objectives.

1. An Overview of Existing Elements in Terms of Policy Definition and Action Evaluation (French Regions)

In accordance with the law dated 13th August 2004, and for the first time in their history, most French Regional Councils have elaborated a Regional Plan for Economic Development, which lays down their policy for the next years to come. The French Regional Authorities, which already apply these policies, are presently working on their specification, with special emphasis on the definition of monitoring and evaluation indicators.

The Midi-Pyrenees Regional Council held a very wide range of consultations prior to issuing its RPED in 2006. The RPED [10] remains expressed at a relatively general level, which makes it difficult for the parties concerned to implement it (for instance, the objectives set in it generally are imprecise and non-quantified, with no indicator defined). A second document [11] has been drawn up, which has not been released yet

---

[2] In French: Schéma Régional de Développement Economique (SRDE).

and is still evolving. It consists of "action description sheets" expounding each action's objectives, content, targets, partners, expected results, and associated indicators (the last two points being very scarcely and poorly provided). So most part of evaluation indicators remain to be produced.

The global lack of monitoring and evaluation tools at the regional level [5] is regularly pointed up. Several studies further deplore the poor clarity of such indicators, when these do exist, as well as the fact that they are "disconnected" from the objectives set. A study undertaken in the Rhone-Alpes Region indicates that "some preliminary serious thinking on the structure of programme objectives has been conducted as part of the mission", along with the "*a posteriori* reconstruction or reformulation of these objectives". The elaboration of evaluation indicators – the last phase of the policy definition process – is actually related to all of the previous upstream phases, inasmuch as such indicators weigh up the precision and coherence of the objectives whose achievement they are to assess.

To conclude this section, we must underline that the RPED's collective elaboration has not resulted in capitalisation of knowledge, even poorly formalised. The RPED text does not include any explanation on paradigmatic choices. It does not either define the concepts or methods used to produce them. The absence of such elements and the complexity of the decisions at stake render policy implementation difficult. Likewise, the conception of any decision support system seems quite premature at this stage. Our paper's approach is based on the revelation (or building) of a clear language shared by all of the parties involved in the decision-making process. In the following section, we mean to analyse RPED texts so as to identify the knowledge at work, as well as assess its degree of clarity and coherence.

2. Structure of Identifiable Knowledge in RPED Texts

The work presented in this section takes the analysis of the two RPED volumes as its starting point. A first "manual" analysis (based on text reading) was followed by a second analysis carried out with the help of both the SYNTEX syntax analyser [2] and TERMINAE ontology building platform [1].[3] The analysis was conducted with the support of a grid which distinguishes three levels in the expression of knowledge (as described in detail in [12,13]): the level of representations (views of the world, schools of thought, opinions, *etc.*); the level of models (methods, action logics, class definition principles, *etc.*); the level of norms (procedures, nomenclatures, reference systems).

2.1. The Level of Representations (Views of the World, Doxas)

The information expressed in the RPED, like any information, is not regarded here as a simple "image" of reality, but as the expression of views of the world. Representations may, depending on the circumstances, be equated with relatively homogeneous and coherent schools of thought, or with partly confuse and poorly structured opinions. On this account, representations take us back to the broader notion of doxa.[4]

---

[3] I am thankful to Didier Bourigault who kindly made SYNTEX available for the purposes of this study, as well as the TERMINAE designers (including Nathalie Aussenac-Gilles) who permitted use of the platform.

[4] From the Greek δόξα (opinion): a more or less homogeneous set of shared beliefs.

The doxas found in the RPED partly are those of players from the Regional Council and those "imported" from other organisations. These "exogenous" views of the world, however, have mostly been formed for other purposes than territorial development policy support. Their utilisation in the elaboration of policies is probably not neutral. In the case of the Midi-Pyrenees Region, several meaningful representations may be identified in the RPED. These opinions are underlying and very rarely expressed directly in the text. There can be several successive conflicting representations in one and the same document (this is particularly true for the representations of the territory). These have a major influence on both the level of models and of norms insofar as, each time, they determine specific and sometimes irreconcilable "universes of discourse" (in the sense of information systems).

The territory thus is the subject of two contradictory views (not explained as such): it is either regarded as a space receiving potential pre-existing and mobile external resources, or as a place of coordination unveiled on the occasion of a project's implementation. The first view relates to *spaces with fixed borders*, which are mainly expressed in the RPED's diagnosis part through administrative territorial divisions (region, departments, communes), or INSEE zonings.[5] The second view corresponds to *territories with changing borders* (such as the "Pays" or "metropolitan communities"). In the latter case, territories are revealed as "collective cognitive systems". Their geometry depends on the players' coordination process. These territories are sometimes expressed in the RPED through new notions like "emerging territory" or "changing territory", which generally are not defined.

The contradictory views of the territory can intuitively be understood as complicating the interpretation of strategic axes, the precision and quantification of the objectives, and, in the end, the definition of indicators.

2.2. The Level of Models or Methods

Representations are general views that are not formalised enough to provide concrete guidance of action. To prepare for policy implementation, representations need to be transposed into *i)* information describing the axes and objectives formalised, *ii)* action logics, *iii)* methods to define typologies, *iv)* principles to determine sets of indicators, *etc.* This transposition is carried out on the basis of so-called *models and methods*, which are sometimes partly detailed in RPED texts, but are more generally to be rebuilt. For example, the type of activity aggregation used in the RPED's diagnosis part has been borrowed from the INSEE (sectors mainly). It is to be noted that the logic of such aggregations meets the requirements of Government Accounting [4], but not those of a Region's decision-makers. Furthermore, aggregations refer to global conceptions of economy, which are not always consistent with those of the Regional Council [13]. On the other hand, the actions proposed in the RPED's second part are based on notions which relate to other types of aggregation and correspond more closely to the feelings or analyses of the parties involved in the field. Unfortunately, the method to define a "strategic sector" or "changing activity" is not given. In addition, the terms "field" and "sector" are not very stable in the document, referring to variable levels of aggregation from one word occurrence to the other. As for operational decisions, they should be able to utilise directly usable information. So we shall now proceed to examine one last level of expression.

---

[5] French national institute of economic and statistical information.

2.3. The Level of Norms

The level of norms constitutes the most operational stage of information. It is produced through application of the previous level's models and methods. Any member of the Regional Council services who processes an enterprise's financial support application should, for instance, have at his disposal an activities reference system, a list of priority sectors or territories, a set of eligibility criteria, *etc*. It is at the level of norms that evaluation indicators are – or should be – found. In the RPED's two volumes, this level is little present though. The norm definition process is still under way and is all the more complex since the upper levels of representations and models have not yet been sufficiently explained or formalised.

2.4. Consequences in Terms of Evaluation Indicators Definition

In this context, two types of risks would be entailed in defining evaluation indicators that would not consider the underlying views of the world. It would first be risky to embed in norms (indicators) a set of policies that are partially or totally inconsistent due to conflicting views of the world and/or a lack of formalisation at the level of models. The second risk would be that the indicators chosen reflect only one of these representations, which would thus come to be regarded as the sole reality. This could jeopardise the various players' necessary agreement and impede the emergence of innovative views. Evaluation indicators definition support, which, as has been underlined above, can involve some preliminary serious thinking on or even an *a posteriori* reformulation of the objectives set, should therefore come within the scope of a knowledge formalising approach.

The third and last section presents the work conducted along these lines, with illustration from the CAVALA project.

3. Elements for an Approach to Evaluation Indicators Co-Building

The CAVALA project[6] has a double objective. Its first aim is to produce a set of evaluation indicators on the Regional Council's economic policy, with special emphasis placed on some specific action. But the project goes even further through its ambition to conceive an approach which could later be applicable to other RPED actions. Such an approach favours the collaborative work of the various parties involved, enabling them to co-build a common language (in the form of *ontologies*). CAVALA brings together researchers from the IRIT and LEREPS[7] and is presently under way.

3.1. Points of View, Doxas and Polydoxies

In Section 2, we have underlined the major repercussions some or other view of the world (or doxa) may have on policy definition. In the CAVALA project, the ontology building process focuses first on this level of representations, which exhibits a range of specific and complex problems. Doxa is a rather broad concept which encompasses the

---

[6] CAVALA: economic development regional policy monitoring and evaluation cooperative method.
[7] IRIT: Institut de Recherche en Informatique de Toulouse; LEREPS: Laboratoire d'Études et de Recherche sur l'Économie, les Politiques et les Systèmes sociaux.

notions of "common sense", opinion, social representation, and even ideology. The notion of doxa thus seems quite remote from that of "point of view" as used in databases, knowledge engineering, or decision support systems (DSS). In the literature of such domains indeed, multiple points of view generally are points of view on *one entity*, which is supposed to have its own proper existence independently of the various points of view [3]. In the field of DSS, the type of point of view that is most often dealt with is that understood as a partial view of a given entity, with each point of view pertaining to a "family of characteristics" of such entity. A doxa constitutes a set of knowledge that is much broader than a point of view. It expresses itself at various precision levels. It can include incoherent or contradictory subsets, and may partially or totally be very difficult to clarify. Rastier [9] points out that "a doxa's simplest materialisation remains a lexicon". So it appears possible to identify doxa "markers" within texts and to propose a lexicon (in the form of light ontologies) in order to – partially – uncover a doxa.

The analysis in Section 2 has revealed the existence of several doxas in RPED texts. The Regional Council thus seems to carry several different doxas, which sometimes appear in the text in close succession. The Region may be regarded here as a *polydoxical organisation* (in the sense of Monteil *et al.* [8]). It, in fact, mobilises, in the RPED document, "a set of multiple beliefs concerning one object, which coexist in a latent state and may be externalised individually (…)".

3.2. A Polydoxical Ontologies-Based "Maieutic" Support

It is not our place to judge the value of the different doxas, be it in terms of their coherence, their effectiveness, and *a fortiori* their capacity to denote the "real". Our position as DSS developers is mainly maieutic here. Our goal is to raise the regional players' awareness of the doxas in which the concepts they use are embedded. Such a task must be followed by the understanding of the *models*, *methods*, and *norms*, which any doxa entails "naturally". It is therefore necessary to reveal and clarify concepts that are often highly abstract. It is essential as well to determine the sometimes complex relations (or at least some of them) existing amongst such concepts. This kind of work pertains to the ontology building process. The need which this construction meets is markedly different from the first need commonly associated with ontologies, namely that which consists in facilitating communication through a consensus on the meaning of terms [6]. It may somewhat provocatively be claimed that, in the end, the CAVALA project is aimed at reaching a consensus on the existence of *irreducible divergences* amongst the different views of the world at stake. In the first place, there will not be any attempt to reach a consensus on a single meaning for each concept, nor will the global coherence of the ontologies built be sought. A high level of formalisation does not seem necessary at this stage of the project. Instead, the focus is on a conceptualisation concerned with "is-a" and "is-a-part-of" relations, which should give rise to light ontologies.

We shall qualify these ontologies as *polydoxical ontologies* in that they respect the plural nature of the players' representations and are not meant to be aligned in their totality.

Several ontologies are being elaborated on the basis of various sources: texts issued by the Regional Council, regional economic development-related research papers, documents and conceptual models from the INSEE databases, *etc.* Presented below is a simplified extract on the notion of territory. The two following figures bring out different concept hierarchies obtained according to the views at stake (only "is-a" relations are considered).

1. <u>Territory as a geographical area, or space</u>, which involves spaces with fixed borders. The breakdown logic is administrative or conventional (INSEE):

2. <u>Territory as a collective cognitive system (CCS)</u>. The breakdown logic is based on the type and object of the coordination (understood as a process):

It appears that the different views are not easily reconcilable even when the ontology is integrated into a high-level ontology (like the DOLCE "foundational ontology"). At the highest level indeed, DOLCE makes a distinction between *endurants* and *perdurants* [7]: the first view of the territory is an endurant, whereas the latter is a perdurant.

The consequences on the objectives or indicators are different depending on which view of the territory is adopted. A critical case arises when an objective is defined according to a specific view of the territory and the indicators are set in accordance with another. An economic development objective may very well refer to the notion of territory viewed as a collective cognitive system. If, as is very often the case, the indicators only are localised indicators (*e.g.* the number of jobs created or maintained, the firms' volume of business in a given administrative zone), there is no information available in order to assess the process of territorial construction.

4. Conclusion

This paper has addressed the issue of result indicators definition support within the framework of the regional governments' economic development policy. Special emphasis has been laid on the complex, non-formalised, and partially contradictory nature of the knowledge used and expressed in policy texts. In this context, the definition of indicators requires the clarification of objectives and, more broadly, of the knowledge used. Such knowledge expresses doxas (views of the world) of which the parties involved are not always conscious. We thus consider that indicators definition support should first and foremost be regarded as facilitating the players' awareness of their own doxas. This process must take the form of a cooperative work and be backed through access to ontologies that formalise the main doxas found in the field. In conclusion, we wish to point out that the regional economic development research domain offers huge potentialities. The growing number of Regional Council missions, the financial stakes involved, and the national or European regulation constraints, lead the Regional Authorities to attain a high-level culture of decision-making within a very short time. We hope that the CAVALA project will help support the Midi-Pyrenees Regional Council in this effort.

References

[1] BIEBOW B., SZULMAN S., TERMINAE, A Linguistic-Based Tool for the Building of a Domain Ontology, *11th European Workshop, Knowledge Acquisition, Modelling and Management*, Dagstuhl, Germany, 1999.

[2] BOURIGAULT D., FABRE C., Approche linguistique pour l'analyse syntaxique de corpus, *Cahiers de Grammaire*, Université Toulouse-Le Mirail, **25**, 2000, 131-151.

[3] CAHIER J.-P., ZAHER L.H., LEBOEUF J.P., PÉTARD X., GUITTARD C., Une expérience de co-construction de "carte de thèmes" dans le domaine des logiciels libres, *Colloque En route vers Lisbonne*, Luxembourg, October 12-13, 2004.

[4] DESROSIÈRES, Alain, Du réalisme des objets de la comptabilité nationale, *Congrès de l'Association Française de Sciences Économiques*, Paris, Sept. 2003.

[5] ERNST & YOUNG, *Étude portant sur l'évaluation des Contrats de Plan Etat Région 2000-2006*, Vol. 1, 2007.

[6] GUARINO, Nicola, *Foundational Ontologies for the Semantic Web*, 2002.

[7] MASOLO C., BORGO S., GANGEMI A., GUARINO N., OLTRAMARI A., SCHNEIDER L., *The WonderWeb Library of Foundational Ontologies and the DOLCE ontology*, WonderWeb D18, 2003.

[8] MONTEIL J.-M., BAVENT L., LACASSAGNE M.-F., Attribution et mobilisation d'une appartenance idéologique: un effet polydoxique, *Psychologie française*, **31**, 1986, 115-121.

[9] RASTIER, François, Doxa et lexique en corpus – pour une sémantique des ideologies, *Texto !*, December 2004.

[10] RÉGION MIDI-PYRÉNÉES, *Schéma Régional de Développement Économique*, 2006.

[11] RÉGION MIDI-PYRÉNÉES, *Schéma Régional de Développement Économique, Tome 2, Fiches-Actions*, 2006.

[12] SALLES, Maryse, Présentation du dossier Représentations, modèles et normes pour l'entreprise, *Revue Droit et Société*, **65**, 2007, 21-26.

[13] SALLES, Maryse, COLLETIS, Gabriel, Représentations de l'entreprise dans les systèmes d'information statistique et décision dans les collectivités territoriales, *Revue Droit et Société*, **65**, 2007, 53-74.

[14] SALLES, Maryse, Éléments pour une méthode d'audit des politiques d'aides aux entreprises des regions, *Veille Stratégique Scientifique et Technologique (VSST 2007)*, Marrakech, Morocco, October 21-25, 2007.

Mins.

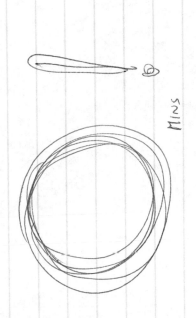

Mins

Press

STOP

TIME: LEFT

Collaborative Decision Making: Perspectives and Challenges
P. Zaraté et al. (Eds.)
IOS Press, 2008

How to Improve Collaborative Decision Making in the Context of Knowledge Management

Inès SAAD[a,1], Michel GRUNDTSEIN[b] and Camille ROSENTHAL-SABROUX[b]

[a] *MIS-UPJV, Amiens School of Management, Amiens, France*
[b] *LAMSADE, University of Paris Dauphine, Paris, France*

Abstract. In this paper we present a Multi-criteria Classification Methodology for identifying and evaluating crucial knowledge. We aim to identify, on the one hand, the explicit and tacit crucial knowledge to be preserved in the organizational memory, and on the other hand the tacit knowledge that is hard to formalize.

Keywords. Multi-criteria Decision Aid, Dominance-based Rough Set Approach, Decision Rules, Knowledge Management

Introduction

Crucial knowledge refers to knowledge that contribute to the organization processes and that involve an overhead when lost. Determining crucial knowledge is an important step in capitalizing on the company's knowledge [1]. It aims to choose relevant knowledge for improving efficiency of knowledge management. This step deals with the location of crucial knowledge. It consists, in particular, in identifying crucial knowledge, making cartographies of them, estimating their economic value and classifying them.

It is indeed difficult to capitalize knowledge, i.e. to elicit, acquire, model, manage and exploit knowledge. It involves heavy investment in order to locate heterogeneous knowledge available in different forms and locations, to elicit, if possible, the know-how [16] into explicit knowledge and to capitalize both types of knowledge. Thus, determining crucial Knowledge is an important challenge given that organisation resources are limited and huge quantity of knowledge is complex to exploit by end users.

In this paper, we propose a multi-criteria methodology to identify and qualify Crucial Knowledge, in order to justify the need of capitalizing knowledge. In other words, we aim to identify, on the one hand, the explicit and tacit crucial knowledge to be preserved in the organizational memory, and on the other hand the tacit knowledge that is hard to formalize. The objective of this methodology is to response to the following question: (i) How to identify the knowledge that should be evaluated? (ii) How to use adequate criteria for knowledge evaluation? (iii) How to aggregate different point of view of decision makers?

This paper is organized as follows. In the next section, we report some related research works. We then introduce our proposed multicriteria methodology in Section 2.

---

[1] Corresponding Author: Inès Saad, Groupe Sup de Co Amiens Picardie, 18 place Saint Michel – 80038 Amiens France; E-mail: ines.saad@u-picardie.fr.

In Section 2.1, we describe the construction of the reference crucial knowledge. The preference model to identify crucial knowledge is presented in Section 2.2 and Section 2.3 presents the classification of potential crucial knowledge. In Section 3, we present a case study. Finally, conclusions are presented in Section 4.

1. Research Studies

The need for pertinent and crucial knowledge in any knowledge capitalizing operation has been proved by several authors (e.g. [1–3,8,10,17]). Only few theoretical and empirical works are available in literature. We may distinguish two classes of methods: methods based on knowledge domains and methods based on processes. The main distinctive feature of these methods is related to the approaches used (i) to collect knowledge to be evaluated and (ii) to construct criteria and evaluate knowledge in respect to these criteria.

Concerning knowledge collection, we think that the method proposed by [8] enables to study the area and to clarify the needs in knowledge required to deal with pertinent problems through the modelling and analysis of sensitive processes in the company. This approach involves all the actors participating in the area of the study. In similar way, [3] bases on identifying the process to identify the sources of information. Finally, the method proposed by [2] is evenly based on both a series of interviews with the leaders, and the study of strategic documents. These two last approaches suppose that the leaders are able to identify the knowledge to evaluate.

Our analysis of these approaches at the level of criteria construction and knowledge evaluation permits us to remark that the methods proposed by [2,7] construct criteria intuitively. In turn, Tseng and Huang propose to compute the average score of each attribute of the knowledge as a function of the evaluations provided by each analyst. Then, the analyst evaluates the importance of knowledge in respect to each problem. Finally, the average global is computed for each analyst. One limitation of this method is that the scales used are quantitative. However, due to the imprecise nature of the knowledge, qualitative scales are preferred.

2. Methodoly

The methodology for crucial knowledge identification and evaluation is composed of three phases.

2.1. Phase 1: Determining "Reference Crucial Knowledge"

The first phase is relative to constructive learning devoted to infer the preference model of the decision makers. Constructive learning, as opposite to descriptive learning, suppose that the preference model is not pre-existing but is interactively constructed by explicitly implying the decision maker. Practically, it consists in inferring, through the DRSA (Dominance-based Rough Set Approach) [4,5] method which is an extension of rough set theory [11] and which is devoted to multi-criteria sorting problems of a set of decision rules from some holistic information in terms of assignment examples provided by the decision makers. This set of rules may be used in the same project or in other similar or new projects. However, for similar or new projects an adaptation of the set of decision rules to the project under consideration often required. This phase includes also the identification, using GAMETH®, of a set of reference crucial knowledge.

We have adapted the GAMETH® Framework [15] to construct reference crucial knowledge that is, identifying sensitive process, and critical activities, and clarifying the need of knowledge to solve problems linked with critical activities.

The approach used contains three steps. First, we identify the sensitive processes with the leaders. These Processes will be the object of an in-depth analysis. In fact, we believe that the analysis of the processes is not attainable in the short period. The second stage consists, on the one hand, in modelling sensitive processes identified and on the other hand, in analyzing critical activities associated to each sensitive process. The third stage consists of identifying two types of knowledge: unmastered and mastered knowledge; which is crucial for the activity.

2.2. Phase 2: Constructing Preference Model

The second phase includes the construction of preference model and the evaluation of knowledge with the respect to a convenient set of criteria. Three sub-families of criteria were constructed: (i) knowledge vulnerability family that are devoted to measure the risk of knowledge lost and the cost of its (re)creation; (ii) knowledge role family that are used to measure the contribution of the knowledge in the project objectives. Each criterion of this family corresponds to an objective; and (iii) use duration family that is devoted to measure the use duration of the knowledge basing on the company average and long term objectives. The criteria used to evaluate the reference crucial knowledge were constructed through a combination of the top-down and bottom-up approaches. The top-down approach was used to identify the indicators from which the criteria $g_1,..., g_{15}$ are constructed. These indicators were defined basing on the theoretical research in knowledge engineering, strategic management and artificial intelligence domains and on the empirical studies. To evaluate each knowledge K_i in respect to each objective O_j, we have developed the computing model [15]. The evaluation of knowledge in respecter to criteria of families (i) and (iii) are normally provided by the decision maker. However, in practice the decision makers may show some difficulty in directly evaluating knowledge in respect to some complex criteria. To overcome this problem, complex criteria are decomposed into several more simple indicators. The decision makers can easily evaluate these indictors.

Once all knowledge items are evaluated with respect to all criteria, the next step is an iterative procedure permitting to conjointly infer the decision rules. Two decision classes have been defined $Cl1$: "non crucial knowledge" and $Cl2$: "crucial knowledge". This procedure is based on Dominance-based Rough set approach (DRSA) [4–6]. This procedure is composed of four substeps:

- The first substep consists in determining, with the help of each decision-maker, assignments of a set of knowledge items reference crucial knowledge in the following decision classes: Cl1 "non crucial knowledge" and Cl2 "crucial knowledge" (Table 1). The decision table contains, in addition to the columns relative to vulnerability and those relative to contribution degree and use duration criteria, as many columns as decision makers. Once the decision table is generated, it will be used as the input of the second substep.

Table 1. Decision table for one decision maker

Knowledge of reference	Criteria			Decision
K_1	g_1	...	g_m	Cl1/Cl2
...	$g_1(k_1)$	...	$g_m(k_1)$	...
K_n	$g_1(k_n)$	...	$g_m(k_m)$	Cl1/Cl2

Table 2. Performance table

Potential crucial knowledge	Criteria		
K_1	g_1	...	g_m
...	$g_1(k_1)$	...	$g_m(k_1)$
K_n	$g_1(k_n)$	...	$g_m(k_m)$

- The second substep consists in inferring decision rules for each assignment sample determined in the preceding stage. To do so, we use the DRSA.
- The third substep consists in modifying sample assignments or evaluations with the concerned decision-maker, when inconsistencies are detected in the decision rules base.
- The last substep consists in determining decision rules that are collectively accepted.

2.3. Phase 3: Classifying "Potential Crucial Knowledge"

In the third phase, the decision maker use the preference models of the different stakeholders defined in the second phase to assign the new knowledge which is called potential crucial knowledge, to the classes Cl1 or Cl2. The results are stored in a performance table. The structure of the performance table is shown in Table 2.

More specifically, a multi-criteria classification of potential crucial knowledge is performed on the basis of the decision rules that have been collectively identified by the decision maker(s) in the second phase. The term of potential crucial knowledge should be mapped to the concept of "potential action" as defined in the multi-criteria decision-aid theory, that is, "real or virtual actions considered by at least one stakeholder as a temporally realistic one" [13]. The term "stakeholder", as defined by [13], refers to "individuals or groups of individuals who, because of their value system, directly or indirectly influence the decisions, either at first degree because of their intervention or at second degree by the manner in which they use the action of other individuals". Thus, potential crucial knowledge is the knowledge that has been temporary, identified as crucial by at least one stakeholder. The generated potential crucial knowledge are analyzed and then evaluated against the criteria identified in the second phase. Then, they are assigned in one of two decision classes Cl1 or Cl2. This phase composed of four steps. The second and third steps are similar to those of the second phase. In the first step the decision makers identify the set of potential crucial knowledge to be evaluated. In practice, it is often difficult to evaluate all the knowledge. Several methods may be used to support the decision maker in this step as DELPHI [17] and GA-METH®.

In the last step, the rules base is used to classify potential crucial knowledge, into one of the decision classes Cl_1 and Cl_2. In fact, one potential crucial knowledge is regarded as effectively crucial if there exists at least one decision rule within the rules base, whose premises are paired with the evaluation of this knowledge on the set of criteria. The general form of a decision rule is:

If $gj(k) \geq rgj$; $\forall j \in \{1,...,m\}$ then $k \in Cl2$ where

$g1,..., gm$ is a family of m criteria,
$gj(k)$ is the performance of the knowledge k on criterion gj,
$(rg_1,..., rg_m) \in Vg1 \times \cdots \times Vgm$ is the minimum performance of a knowledge k on the set of criteria.

3. Case Study

The proposed methodology was conceived and validated in the automobile Company. More specifically, we have focalized on the depollution system. The objective of the car Company is to transfer the knowledge developed in the depollution system for use:

- with other types of vehicles,
- with projects concerned with definition of the new systems.

3.1. Phase 1: Determining "Reference Crucial Knowledge"

To identify the reference crucial knowledge, we have applied GAMETH® framework. This framework is composed of three steps [16].

3.2. Phase 2: Constructing Preference Model

3.2.1. Step 1. In-Depth Analysis of "Knowledge of Reference"

The second phase of our methodology concerns the in depth analysis of knowledge. Since our objective is to identify crucial knowledge, we have analyzed and characterized those knowledge that are mobilized in the different critical activities related to each sensitive process.

3.2.2. Step 2. Construction of Criteria and Evaluation of Reference Crucial Knowledge

The criteria used in our application are: (i) *knowledge vulnerability family* including the eight criteria $g_1,..., g_8$ that are devoted to measure the risk of knowledge lost and the cost of its (re)creation; (ii) *knowledge role family* including the criteria $g_9,..., g_{14}$ that are used to measure the contribution of the knowledge in the project objectives. The criteria $g_9,..., g_{14}$ are specific to the depollution system project and should be replaced by other ones for other projects and (iii) *it use duration family* including the criterion g_{15} that is devoted to measure the use duration of the knowledge basing on the company average and long term objectives. Once criteria family is constructed, we need to evaluate each knowledge of reference in respect to all criteria.

3.2.3. Step 3. Inference of Decision Rules

To infer rules, we have constructed four decision tables containing the evaluations of 34 reference crucial knowledge in respect to 15 criteria and to the assignment examples provided by four decision makers.

The rule 2 is traduced as follows:

IF K_i. Substitutable-Level is "at least weak"
   and
      K_i. Rarety-Level is "at least rare"
   and
      K_i. Competitivity is "at least high"
   and
      K_i. Use-duration is at least "average"
THEN K_i is in *Cl2*

This rule means that a piece of knowledge K_i is considered crucial (i.e. K_i belongs to the class of crucial *Cl2*), if it is difficult to replace it, it is scares, have an important impact on commercial position of the company and also has convenient use duration.

3.3. Phase 3: Classifying Potential Crucial Knowledge

In this phase, the system use decision rules defined in the second phase to assign potential crucial knowledge to either *Cl1* or *Cl2*. Those assigned to Cl2 are the crucial ones that need to be capitalized on.

3.3.1. Step 1: Definition of a "Potential Crucial Knowledge" Set

First, we have identified, with the help of the stakeholder, the decision makers implied in this third phase. There are 6 implied decision makers. With all these decision makers, we have first retained all the knowledge that are supposed potentially crucial and than we have combined some ones (that they find very detailed) and removed/added some another ones. The final list is obtained after individuals' discussion with the different decision makers and validated with all of them. The choice of the set is facilitated by the analysis of process and activities performed during the definition of reference crucial knowledge process.

3.3.2. Step 2: In-Depth Analysis of Potential Crucial Knowledge

We have applied for each "potential crucial knowledge" the same process as applied in step 1 of phase 2.

3.3.3. Step 3: Evaluation of Potential Crucial Knowledge

We have evaluated all potential crucial knowledge in respect to all criteria constructed in step 2 of phase 2. The obtained performance table contains the evaluation of each "potential crucial knowledge" in respect to criteria related to:

- The vulnerability of knowledge (i.e. g_1, g_2, g_3, g_4, g_5, g_6, g_7, g_8);
- The role of knowledge for each objective (i.e. g_9, g_{10}, g_{11}, g_{12}, g_{13}, g_{14}); and
- Use duration (i.e. g_{15}).

3.3.4. Step 4: Application of Decision Rules

We have used the performance table containing the evaluation of different reference crucial knowledge as input in this phase. Thus, it will be required only one rule (that characterize knowledge required a capitalizing operation) is verified to conclude that the knowledge is crucial.

4. Conclusion

In this paper we have presented a novel methodology based on multicriteria Frameworke to identify crucial knowledge. This methodology consists of three phases. In the first phase, we have adapted and demonstrated the use of GAMETH$^{®}$ to identify the set of Reference Crucial Knowledge. During the second phase, a preference model, which is a set of "if ... then ..." decision rules, is inferred from exemplary assignment of some reference crucial knowledge to two decision classes: Cl1 "not Crucial Knowledge" and Cl2 "Crucial knowledge". In the third phase, a multi-criteria classification of Potential Crucial Knowledge is performed on the basis of the decision rules that have been collectively identified by the decision makers.

References

[1] Dieng, R., Corby, O., Giboin, A. and Rybière, M. Methods and tools for corporate knowledge management. Technical report, INRIA, ACACIA project, 1999.
[2] Ermine, J.L., Boughzala, I. and Tounkara, T. Critical knowledge map as a decision tool for knowledge transfer actions. *The Electronic journal of Knowledge Management*, 4(2), 2006, 129-140.
[3] Golebiowska, J. *Exploitation des ontologies pour la mémoire d'un projet véhicule : méthode et outil SAMOVAR*. PhD thesis, University of Nice-Sophia Antipolis, France, 2002.
[4] Greco, S., Matarazzo, B. and Slowinski, R. Rough sets theory for multicriteria decision analysis. *European Journal of Operational Research*, 12(9), 2001, 1-47.
[5] Greco, S., Matarazzo, B., Slowinski, R. and Stefanowski, J. An algorithm for induction of decision rules consistent with dominance principle. In W. Ziarko and Y. Yao, editors, Proc. 2nd Int. Conference on Rough Sets and Current Trends in Computing, Banff, 2000, 266-275.
[6] Grzymala-Busse, J. A new version of the rule induction system LERS. *Fundamental Informaticae*, 1997, 27-39.
[7] Grundstein, M., Rosenthal-Sabroux, C. and Pachulski, A. Reinforcing Decision Aid by Capitalizing on Company's Knowledge. *European Journal of Operational Research*, 14(5), 2006, 256-272.
[8] Grundstein, M. From capitalizing on Company Knowledge to Knowledge Management. In: *Knowledge Management, Classic and Contemporary Works* (Morey, D., M. Maybury and B. Thuraisingham, Ed.), Chap. 12. The MIT Press, Massachusetts, 2000, 261-287.
[9] Noh, J.B., Lee, K.C. and Kim, J.K. A cased-based reasoning approach to cognitive map-driven tacit knowledge management. *Expert Systems with application*, 19, 2000, 249-259.
[10] Nonaka, I. and Takeuchi, H. The knowledge *creating company: How Japanese companies create the dynamics of innovation*. Oxford University Press, New York, 1995.
[11] Pawlak, Z. Rough sets. *International Journal of Information & Computer Sciences*. 11, 1982, 341-356.
[12] Polanyi, M. *The tacit dimension*. Routledge & Kegan Paul Ltd. London, 1966.
[13] Roy, B. A missing link in OR-DA: robustness analysis. Foundations of Computing and Decision Sciences. 1998.

[14] Saad, I., Rosenthal-Sabroux, C. and Chakhar, S. K-DSS: A decision support system for identifying and evaluating crucial knowledge. In Proceedings of The 11th International Conference on Information Processing and Management of Uncertainty (IPMU 2006), volume I, Paris, France, July 2-7, 2006, 331–338.

[15] Saad, I., Rosenthal-Sabroux, C. and Grundstein, M. Improving the Decision Making Process in The Design project by Capitalizing on Company's Crucial Knowledge. *Group Decision and Negotiation*, 14, 2005, 131-145.

[16] Saad, I., Grundstein, M. and Rosenthal-Saboux, M. Locating the Company's Crucial knowledge to Specify Corporate Memory: A Case Study in Automotive Company. In: *Knowledge management and organisational workshop proceedings, IJCAI, Acapulco*, 2003, 75-84.

[17] Tseng, B. and Huang, C. Capitalizing on Knowledge: A Novel Approach to Crucial Knowledge Determination. *IEEE Transactions on Systems, Man, and Cybernetics Part A: Systems and Humans.* 35, 2005, 919-931.

Subject Index

Author Index

1ᵗ Keynote (Robert (Bob) Winter, St Gullen)

– what is "information logistics", after 20 yrs of data warehousing & business
ᶜ planning, implementation & control of cross-unit data flow intelligence